THE
ANNUAL REGISTER,
OR A VIEW OF THE
HISTORY, POLITICKS,
AND
LITERATURE,
Of the YEAR 1758.

FIRST EDITED IN 1758 BY EDMUND BURKE

New Introduction by
Paul Langford
Professor of Modern History, Oxford University
and Rector of Lincoln College, Oxford

ProQuest, USA & UK
ISBN 978-1-60030-829-1

The 1758 Annual Register , Special Collector's Edition
(Original title: *The Annual Register, or a View of the History, Politics, and Literature for the Year 175*
First edited by Edmund Burke in 1758. New Introduction by Paul Langford.

Published by
ProQuest
7200 Wisconsin Ave.
United States of America and
The Quorum
P.O. Box 1346
Barnswell Road
Cambridge UK CB5 8SW

ISBN 978-1-60030-829-1

Cover art by John C. Moss
Printed in the USA by
The Sheridan Books, Chelsea, MI USA

INTRODUCTION

e Publishers

e launching of the *Annual Register* on 12 May 1759 was the work of the well-tablished publisher Robert Dodsley (1703-64) and his brother James (1724-). Dodsley's role was by no means minor. In his youth he had been footman successive families of quality. As a poet he made a mark and by 1735 he was le to establish his own publishing business. Alexander Pope's literary and litical circles gave him an entrée to the fashionable world not often commanded by booksellers and publishers. By the early 1750s his successes cluded Thomas Gray's *Elegy in a Country Church Yard*, Voltaire's *Age of uis XIV* in English, Joseph Warton's *Works of Virgil*, and Edward Young's *etical Works*.

Dodsley had never been shy of the periodical market but it took him time to netrate it. His *Publick Register* of 1741 offered news, essays, poetry, and litary criticism. It failed within five months thanks to a fierce campaign waged its rival, Edward Cave's (1691-1754) *Gentleman's Magazine*. A further fort was made in March 1746 when *The Museum, or Literary and Historical gister,* was launched. It was intended to put to shame other periodicals. espite its distinguished editor Mark Akenside, and its employment of well own authors, it lasted only eighteen months. Challenging the monthlies was idently more difficult than Dodsley supposed.

A third attempt was much more successful. *The World* ran from January 1753 r three full years. It was well regarded and profitable. It closed only to permit odsley and a new partner, William Strahan (1715-85), to launch a new periodal, which unlike the earlier publications was essentially a newspaper. The *ndon Chronicle*, first published on New Year's Day in 1757, was one of the te eighteenth century's most successful thrice weekly journals. In modern rms it would be considered a quality newspaper dedicated to high standards of s news as well as much of the commentary that it printed. Despite the success the *London Chronicle* Dodsley withdrew from his share in its management ery soon, mainly because he thought its high-minded mission was contamiated by low political abuse imported from other journals. But he had in mind other enterprise, one which still flourishes today, the *Annual Register*.

urke the Compiler

he stable from whence the *Annual Register* came in the late 1750s included ajor works by major authors—Samuel Johnson, John Dyer, Soame Jenyns, avid Hume, and Oliver Goldsmith. Alongside them was the novice Edmund urke (1729-97), whose *Philosophical Enquiry into the Origin of our Ideas of e Sublime and Beautiful* (1757) rocketed him to fame both at home and over-eas. He was entitled to consider himself a rising star of polite and instructive letters. Burke's contract with the Dodsleys was agreed in April 1758. It spe fied £100 per annum and allowed three months notice of withdrawal on eith side. The document, not revealed until the twentieth century, is the earli undeniable evidence of Burke's role. What is much more surprising is that the is so little additional evidence. Burke very rarely referred to himself in this co text. There are a few references in his correspondence to the *Annual Regist* In public he was even more restrained.

Whatever restricted Burke it was not any doubt about the relationship with t Dodsley brothers. Burke's major publications over five decades were to be pu lished by them. Only James's illness in the years before his death in 1797 ma Burke move his later writings to the Rivington brothers, Charles (1754-183 and Francis (1745-1822). The *Annual Register* evidently passed to the Rivin tons at the same time, though Burke himself had by that time abandoned h interest in it. It was, nonetheless, close associates of his who were presumab responsible for moving its publication along with Burke's own works. Thom English (c. 1725-98), French Laurence (1757-1809), the Rev. Richard Lauren (1760-1838), and the Rev. Walker King (1751-1827) had all been involved in i composition over many years.

Burke's authorship was rarely a matter of personal self-esteem, at any ra beyond his earliest writings. But his silence on the subject of his influence the *Annual Register* is startling. It has also led to much confusion. In the yea following his death in 1797 numerous claims were made that he had played large part in the management of the *Annual Register* almost into the last pha of his life. Well into the twentieth century this continued to be thought a pla sible assertion. Only in the last half century has it been established that he mu have largely abandoned his editorial responsibilities in the mid-1760s when l launched himself on a political career associated with Lord Rockingham, lead of the Whig party and Prime Minister in 1765-66. His election to Parliament January 1766 occupied him still further.

Even so there remains uncertainty about the point at which he gave up h journalism completely. Also debatable is the extent to which those portions the early volumes were wholly his own work. Some assumptions, nonetheles seem likely. The simplest is Burke's letter to Dodsley, dated 9 February 176 which notes that 'our Work is in the press, and advances prosperously'. Th would at least suggest that Burke had been doing what his contract specifie 'writing, collecting and compiling' from 1758 to 1764. There is also gener agreement that by 1767 Burke ceased to write or edit later volumes, though h may well have continued to have some degree of supervision and perhaps ma have made occasional contributions of his own. The three years between 176 and 1767 have given rise to much scholarly dispute. At some point in th period his assistant Thomas English must have largely taken over the work c writing and editing. In short, in all of Burke's immense canon of works th *Annual Register* is something of a scholarly quagmire, unlikely to reveal mor than occasional outcrops of solid ground, most of them associated with th early volumes.

If Burke made no attempt to reveal himself as author of those things which he rote between 1758 and 1764 he probably considered the post that of a jour- yman, rather than that of a gentlemanly author. Addison, Steele, Fielding and hnson had all gained fame in editing and writing periodical works. But the *nnual Register* was more in the nature of a compilation, however much Burke ught to ensure its quality. In any case he had other irons in the fire. He had ready published his *Vindication of Natural Society*, with the Dodsleys, in 756. If it did not impress as much as its successor, the *Sublime and Beautiful*, satirical treatment of Bolingbroke's ideas aroused interest. In 1757 Burke d his kinsman William Burke (1728-98) also published with the Dodsleys *An ccount of the European Settlements in America*. It was not only a searching say on overseas exploration and colonisation, but well chosen against the ckground of the first global war involving all the imperial powers of the day.

This was not all. Two months before the appearance of *An Account* and the *ublime and Beautiful* Burke had already signed a contract with the Dodsleys r £300 to write *An Essay towards an Abridgment of the English History*, a ngle volume work from Caesar to the reign of Queen Anne. He undertook to omplete this commitment in December 1758, a considerable burden. None of was published during his lifetime, nor did he get beyond the reign of King ohn. It seems likely that Burke's work on the *Annual Register* would have seri- usly interrupted his historical writing. In any event he seems not to have sumed any laurels for taking on the new periodical. Was this a favour for his ublishers? Or was money the prime inducement?

redecessors

wo kinds of originality might have nonetheless had some appeal to Burke. ne was editorial selection to achieve a degree of amusement and instruction, om very diverse sources. One of the clauses of the contract was that the editor ould have access to all the necessary printed materials from which to choose. he other was the writing of 'The History of the Present War' or the 'Historical rticle' as it later became. It was not a new idea. In one form or another his- orical narratives had figured in the great expansion of earlier eighteenth-century eriodicals, whether in monthly or annual form.

There is little doubt that the emphasis had been on the great wars of the turn f the seventeenth and eighteenth centuries, along with the domestic political nstability that went with them. The coming of relative peace after the Hanover- an Accession did not immediately kill off these earlier annual compilations. By e mid-1720s, however, almost the only example that lingered on was the *His- orical Register, Containing an Impartial Relation of All Transactions*. It ran om 1717 (for the year 1716) to 1738 in twenty-three volumes. During its early ears it reckoned to be a contemporary survey of most of the countries of urope. Later it was more concerned with the politics and history of Britain self. Even this, however, was largely in the nature of a compilation, bringing ogether state papers and parliamentary affairs mostly gathered from the news- apers. It was capable of connecting varied material. Whether it achieved a high level of commentary and analysis was another matter. In any case it was more in the nature of a monthly collected into a complete volume, resembling the *Gentleman's Magazine* and the *London Magazine*.

Between the 1720s and the 1750s the only annual magazine attempted was *The Annals of Europe*, spanning the years 1739 to 1743 in six volumes between 1740 and 1745, published initially by George Hawkins and later in partnership with Thomas Astley. The editor and compiler was one George Gordon. He included much of the conventional material but he was also an authentic author. He seems to have been primarily a writer on scientific and mathematical matters, but his part in *The Annals of Europe* took him into the realm of government and politics. The War of Jenkins' Ear and the succeeding War of the Austrian Succession created a major market for a public excited by the first major war involving Britain since 1713. Gordon tended to divide his narrative into sections, country by country. Nonetheless, he succeeded in establishing an effective historical account, though it was not always easy to follow its chronology. He did however seek to separate out public documents that often confused the commentaries in which they were embedded. For reasons which are unclear the series stopped in 1745, despite the remaining years of a war that ended only in 1748. The Jacobite Rebellion of 1745, the revival of French supremacy in the Low Countries, and Britain's engagement in overseas warfare were all of surpassing interest to a public fascinated by military, naval and diplomatic activities.

Burke's Innovation

Dodsley's restless search for a both polite and profitable annual journal turned out to be a major advance on his earlier attempts. From an early stage the *Annual Register* was a considerable success. Its publisher conducted a substantial advertising campaign in 1758 and subsequent years. Four newspapers—the *Public Advertiser*, the *London Chronicle*, the *Whitehall Evening Post* and the *London Evening Post*—regularly announced forthcoming volumes and equally regularly publicised them once they were available in the bookshops. Sales are hard to estimate but contemporary opinion was plainly impressed. At six shillings in bound volumes it was well positioned for a solidly respectable market. It was published in Dublin as well as London.

There is little doubt, however, that it was the Seven Years War that provided the Dodsleys such success. The scope as published was 'history, politicks and literature'. Burke's innovation was undoubtedly centred on the first two. He paid particular attention to the necessity for grounding them in the context of the mid-1750s. As he explained in his preface, 'We have not in our first article confined ourselves to the history of the year. We have taken the war from its commencement. It is a subject which requires all the pains which we could bestow upon it, and deserves much more skilful workmen. None was ever more formed to interest curiosity; from the importance of the events, the dignity of the persons concerned, the greatness of the actions performed, and the amazing revolutions of fortune.'[1]

Setting the scene was crucial. The conflicts of 1739-48 had gradually evolved to what eventually constituted a global war embracing most of Europe, the nericas and, in some measure, Asia. The breakdown of peace in 1756 was uch more spectacular. In the space of a few months numerous theatres of war ploded in flames. In the spring of 1756 war was declared between France and itain, commencing almost at once with the capture of Minorca by the French .vy, the worst maritime disaster for Britain since the Dutch war of 1665-7 ider Charles II. At the same time Frederick II invaded Saxony, without the ghtest justification for an attack on a neighbour that had no aggressive intenons. By the summer of 1757 the grand alliance of Austria, France, Russia and veden had invaded Germany from every direction. This was war with a ngeance. The number and diversity of its battlefields exceeded those of the ar of the Spanish Succession and looked forward to the Napoleonic Wars.

The sheer catalogue of belligerent activity gave Burke the ideal opportunity describe and analyse a war of dramatic dimensions. He relished the challnge, rather boastfully. 'The reader will find the events of this war, which has en carried on in the four quarters of the world, and which he has hitherto seen a scattered manner, united into one connected narrative, and continued to the d of the campaign of seventeen hundred and fifty-eight. To effect this from e broken and unconnected materials, has been a work of more labour than may first appear; and if we have performed what we intended in any sort to the ader's satisfaction, we may lay claim to some merit.'[2] There is more than a nt here that he had found the task distinctly onerous.

How did Burke sustain this 'one connected narrative'? A key strategic decion was to divide the materials, which in previous such compilations had been sembled from diverse sources. The historical section as a whole accounted r 234 pages in a volume of 503 pages. It included a separate 'Chronicle' of 5 pages for 1758, comprehending numerous kinds of news, some of which d to do with the war. In particular it listed minor engagements, on land and sea. In the *Annals of Europe* such encounters had been mixed up with the rger conflicts, in the process making it much harder to present the strategic gnificance of the latter. Burke, by contrast, was able to concentrate on the verall picture of a complex war. He also separated out a section for 'State apers' 'to illustrate and confirm the facts advanced in the historical part'.[3] his section ran to 91 pages, considerably more than the amount devoted to the rrative itself. In this way the author was being given room to develop a genne narrative shorn of the significant documentation, which in the context of s argument and analysis was unnecessary. In total, 'The History of the Prest War' filled 77 pages.

he History of the Present War

urke's 'History' could not have been successful without the author himself nding the war particularly fascinating. It was a contemporary history, the outome of which was yet unknown. The *Abridgment* that he was presumably writg at this time is highly accessible but can hardly convey the excitement and drama that lights up Burke's prose in the 'History'. He seeks accuracy but mi imises unnecessary detail, for fear of getting in the way of the flow of narrati Only those figures that are essential to Burke's priorities are identified and pe sonalised. Chapters concentrate on key regions—central Europe, weste Europe, and Britain's maritime warfare on either side of the Atlantic. But t chapters are short and they pick up the threads of others with ease.

The opening chapters cover the background. The first deals with the drift war in 1755 and 1756. The second briefly analyses the political stability that fo lowed the death of the Prime Minister, Henry Pelham, in 1754. Burke avoids a naming of the politicians. He also ignores party labels—Whigs, Tories, Jac bites, and so on. It was not difficult to identify them, nonetheless. The 'o Whigs' of the Walpole and Pelham years were currently led by the Duke of Ne castle. The second grouping was associated with Henry Fox, a follower of Wa pole and supposedly the most cynical of politicians. The third had another Wh leader, William Pitt, whose appeal was as much to Tory country gentlemen as 'patriot' Whigs. Burke approved of the coalition of the first and the third as t most feasible and practical arrangement, one which he called the 'healing mea ure'. As for the war, four chapters dealt with 1757, the remaining nine with 175 Future volumes would concentrate solely on the year in question.

Particularly interesting was Burke's prioritisation of subjects. It might ha been supposed that he would treat Britain as the centrepiece of the narrative, a Europe as its sideshow. In fact Britain's amphibious raids on the coast France, its troops in western Germany under Prince Ferdinand of Brunswic and its military activities in India and North America seemed more like t sideshow. Instead the spotlight was on continental Europe and more specifical on Frederick II of Prussia, whether victim or victor. This was not of cour intended to relegate Britain to insignificance. On the contrary, with Prussia a new-found ally of Britain, Frederick II was a kind of adopted British hero. this stage Burke seems to have made the King of Prussia his beau ideal, give take one or two cautious remarks by way of rendering him human.

Burke's dramatis personae were not numerous but they were sufficient to pr vide a satisfying supporting cast, mostly generals, such as Austria's Marsh Daun, France's Duc de Richelieu, Prince Ferdinand of Brunswick, and so o All are provided with enough characterisation to fit their roles, though Burk provided only a minimum in cases where players were briefly on stage– notably Clive, Wolfe, and others. Only one British participant was given notab praise. The third Duke of Marlborough died of fever at Munster in Octob 1758. 'Never did the nation lose in one man, a temper more candid and bene olent, manners more amiable and open, a more primitive integrity, a mo exalted generosity, a more warm and feeling heart.'[4] It is strange that Cliv whose victory at Plassey in June 1757 was described by Burke in Chapter VI was given far less by way of panegyric than Marlborough, whose exploits we not remarkable. What is quite extraordinary is the complete absence of th Prime Minister, William Pitt. He figures only as Mr. P., the leader of the coal tion, in the first volume of the *Annual Register*. The two subsequent volume so ignore him, despite the 'annus mirabilis' of Britain's unprecedented victo-es in 1759. Only in the 1761 volume was Pitt eventually permitted a role, and en merely on account of his resignation from office. Burke eventually knowledged his leadership in war, while regretting his political inflexibility. he King of Prussia, on the other hand, was rarely allowed to leave the scene ithout praise.

ederick the Great

is understandable that the King of Prussia should be the key figure. His rep-ation in France was that of a supposedly enlightened despot. From the begin-ng of his reign and the start of the War of Austrian Succession he had trans-rmed the status of his country and wrenched the prosperous province of Sile-a from Austria. When war clouds gathered again in 1756 he had ignited the ar in Europe. His generalship in 1757 and 1758 was central to Burke's narra-ve. Frederick's virtues shone in defeat as in victory, according to Burke. hen Marshal Daun's defeat of Frederick's army at Kolin in June 1757 forced im to withdraw from Bohemia, Burke remarked that 'The smile of fortune akes conquerors; it is her malice which discovers heroes.'[5]

It was a preparation, of course, for the two great battles in the last weeks of 757. At Rossbach, in Saxony, French and Imperial forces were overwhelmed, anks to the King's alleged address to his troops, which apparently inspired hat Burke called 'a sort of heroic phrenzy.'[6] A few weeks later at Leuthen, in ilesia, the Austrians were also heavily defeated. Burke's conclusion was that e story of 1757 was 'not the history of a country, but of a single campaign.'[7] he story of 1758 was not dissimilar: a sequence of Prussian marches in ohemia, Silesia and Saxony, diverting Austria's forces from Silesia itself and e Brandenburg homeland. More threatening to the latter was the Russian inva-on. The carnage inflicted on Brandenburg from the east was appalling. Fred-rick had little choice in the midst of his tireless activity beyond his own bound-ries but to repel the Russians. The climax occurred at Zorndorf in August 758. Burke considered it a clear victory for Prussia. It was hardly that. It flicted fearful losses upon a population which was by no means limitless, left e Russians at large, and forced the King once more to turn to the south to lieve his brother.

Reporting war was about propaganda as well as carnage. Unsurprisingly the ritish press gave all the advantages to Frederick II. Not only was he the princi-al belligerent ally that Britain had, he was the only Protestant prince command-g a major power against the Catholic states of southern Europe. Burke did not nce refer to his nominal Protestantism nor did he consider that the war could be garded as a religious conflict. On the other hand he undoubtedly gave the ben-fit of the doubt to Prussia, and against the alliance of France, Austria and Russia.

This tendency is striking where he writes of the horrors of war, a preoccupa-on which surfaced from time to time throughout his career, extending eventu-lly to the horrors of revolution. In 'The History of the Present War' his cata-gue included the harshness of Richelieu in Hanover, the torture of East India

Company servants in the Black Hole of Calcutta, the savagery of American Ind ans in the war between France and Britain, and the barbarity of Russians i Brandenburg. In the case of Europe, Burke was plainly bent on transferring th alleged guilt of the Anglo-Prussian alliance to its enemies.

One of the worst atrocities of the Seven Years War was the burning of th wealthiest and finest parts of Dresden, the capital of the Elector of Saxony, o 10 November 1758. Ten pages of Burke's 'State Papers' were devoted to th subject. The destruction was the work of the Prussian Governor, Cou Schmettau and his troops, when the Austrian general Marshal Daun set abo besieging the city. The Saxon appeal to the Diet at Ratisbon included the ba oneting of citizens escaping from their homes, a shoemaker running away wit his infant on a pillow, only to see it thrown into the flames by a militia ma and the destruction in one inn alone—the Golden Hart—of ninety men an women within. The advancing Austrian and Croat hussars were said to hav given their own bread to the sufferers and risked their lives to rescue victim from the holocaust. The remainder of the papers published by Burke prove that the Prussian action had been grossly exaggerated by 'the gazettes of th Austrian faction'. In his narrative Burke concluded 'A calamity so dreadfu needs no high colouring. However, as little mischief attended such a combus tion, as the nature of the thing could admit. Very few lost their lives; but man their whole substance.'[8]

Nonetheless, though Burke repeatedly praised Frederick II, at one point h expressed a clear reservation. The King's return to Saxony, following Daun' inability to retake Dresden, was accompanied by a regime of exactions inflicte on the population at large. It stemmed from a royal declaration to the effect th he had now subdued Saxony twice, in 1757 and 1758. Burke seems to have bee genuinely shocked by Frederick II's brutal treatment of the country's resident 'If the King of Prussia had a right, as perhaps he had, to consider Saxony as lawful conquest, he certainly seemed not to consider the people as subjects, whe he continued to exact the most severe contributions; and in a manner too ver little becoming a lawful sovereign.' A city reduced to extreme exhaustion an suffering had 'a claim to be governed in such a manner as becomes a just Prince Nor was it remotely right that the cruelties visited by Russians on the King' people in his own country should be punished by retaliation against a provinc that had no intentional part in Russia's involvement in the war. 'We heartily wis we could praise the King of Prussia as much for his temperate use of his con quest, as for those wonderful and heroic qualities by which he obtained it.'[9]

Diverse Matters

The 'History of the Present War', the 'Chronicle' and 'State Papers' occupie slightly less than half the volume. The rest had to do with essentially literar concerns, though in practice they are hardly worth classifying too definitivel They overlapped in numerous ways. In the first volume of the *Annual Registe* Burke designed five categories: 'Characters', 'Extraordinary Adventures', 'Lit erary and Miscellaneous Essays', 'Poetry' and an 'Account of Remarkabl ooks'. These were modified the following year, abandoning the 'Extraordi-ary Adventures', adding 'Useful Projects' and 'Antiquities'. The most striking ature of the first volume made it clear how enterprising Burke could be. There as little about his choice of matter that suggested the more traditional hack-ork of previous such volumes. In none of the categories identified did he pre-nd to be offering completeness or even representativeness. Without apology is own judgement determined what he published.

Most of these categories nonetheless figured in numerous other periodicals—e monthlies, the reviews and various literary compilations of current writings. he most distinctive was the category of 'Characters'. Appropriately in the light f Burke's earlier narrative, his first choice was Montesquieu's essay on the King f Prussia. It was wise of him to note that it might be considered 'somewhat wards panegyric'. Montesquieu described the King as 'modest and magnani-ous after victory; he becomes the generous protector of his subdued, and cap-ve enemies.'[10] This was exactly the one doubt that Burke apparently entertained bout Frederick II's humanity. Voltaire and Montesquieu followed successively mong the 'Characters'. Again Europe seemed to loom large.

Perhaps more interesting was his selection of several characters delineated by is countryman Jonathan Swift, not least because he offered a brief commentary f his own on them. The characters were all enemies of Swift's Tory friends in e last years of Queen Anne, ranging from the Duke of Marlborough to Robert Valpole. Swift had intended to publish them in his own lifetime but it was only 1758 that they were released on the public. Burke remarked that they 'may erve as a striking example of the melancholy effects of prejudice, and party eal; a zeal, which whilst it corrupts the heart, vitiates the understanding itself, nd could mislead a writer of so penetrating a genius as Doctor Swift, to imag-ne that posterity would accept satire in the place of history.'[11]

In the second half of the volume Burke only sought items which simultane-usly struck the reader as extraordinary and also taught him or her to learn from . Like many of his age Burke was an auto-didact, not in point of naivety but n search for what was both novel and useful. Every category was apparently apable of collapsing into another. His interests were extraordinarily unpre-ictable. Typical was his fascination with distant or past cultures. They cropped p in diverse categories. Under 'Characters' the Laplander Ulan Smolenzco zernznigorff figured himself as a resident of the Arctic circle and also a trav-ller in European cities. 'Extraordinary Adventures' included a narrative of Robert Eastburn in captivity among the Indians in North America. 'Literary and Miscellaneous Essays' involved an account of the Jesuits in Paraguay (as it hap-ened relating to the Burkes' *Account of European Settlements*). 'Poetry' rep-esented 'the Indian philosopher', and an 'Account of Remarkable Books' urned to the Life of Philip of Macedon. But much the same was true of antiq-ities, natural history, strange phenomena, useful discoveries, and so on. Burke's gift for selecting the empirical and exemplary runs through the volume. What is missing? Not much. Theology, mathematics, medicine figure less markedly in the first volume, however, than in subsequent ones.

The Survival of the Annual Register

It is remarkable that an annual review born of a single, seven year war shoul have survived where so many others failed. It has to be said that while Burk provided the perfect contents with which to launch it, it was the Dodsleys emphasis on quality and commitment that ensured its success for so long. I his own lifetime Burke would have been aware that some ten editions of th 1758 volume were reissued. Even so, Burke would surely have been startle that the series would continue for at least 250 years. The worst crisis was i the 1790s. When Burke died in 1797 the then editors had yet to get beyon 1792. Nonetheless, the storm was weathered as the *Annual Register* entere the nineteenth century.

Burke evidently rather underestimated even his own early endeavours. H was at some pains to distance them from what he hoped would be his mor scholarly historical work. From the outset he warned of the limitations of hi 'History of the Present War' at the very end of the final chapter in the 175 volume. 'In the mass of materials of a dubious authority, it is equally hard t know what ought to be chosen.' Yet a reader may understand 'a connected serie of those very remarkable and interesting events which this war has produced and which he has hitherto no where seen but in a loose detached manner. If w can do this, we are satisfied; for we do not pretend to give the name of histor to what we have written.'[12]

This was an awkward dilemma, emphasising the utility of the history of th war while admitting that a contemporary history could be never be authoritative When the volume for 1760 was published in 1761 his preface noted, 'Thes Annual Histories, imperfect and inaccurate as they evidently must be, are yet o considerable use; ... in short, they supply, for a time, the place of a solid and regular history, which is not to be expected in many years after the events.' Whe the war finished, he became still more nervous. The volume for 1762, publishe in 1763, went out of its way to admit that the war was virtually over but tha other matter would be provided, not least in relation to European and domesti affairs. The volume for 1763, published in 1764, reminded readers that 'on th close of our last volume, we became apprehensive of a deficiency of material towards furnishing an history of the succeeding years.' What had formerly bee called the 'History of the Present War', was now to be called the 'History o Europe'. This was particularly odd since there was almost nothing in continental Europe that featured. Most of the section was about the last stages o Britain's war overseas and its internal domestic politics. Burke must have bee well aware that the articles between 1758 and 1763 were already being published in various editions as a separate work for the war as whole. It wa unlikely that peacetime matters would provide the coherent narrative that wa naturally provided. Before long Burke himself was to leave the historical article to others. If nothing else, however, his own historical narrative had place the *Annual Register* upon a remarkably firm foundation.

ajor Sources

ıe most recent full biography of Edmund Burke is F.P. Lock, *Edmund Burke*, vols., Oxford, 1998, 2006. His letters are *The Correspondence of Edmund urke*, ed. ThomasW. Copeland and others, 10 vols., Cambridge, 1958-78. The ost recent edition of his works are *Writings and Speeches of Edmund Burke*, l. Paul Langford and others, vols. I-III, V-IX to date, Oxford, 1981-.

otnotes

nnual Register (1758)

p. v-vi.

). vi.

). vi.

). 62.

). 18.

). 22.

). 27.

). 61.

). 64.

p. 235.

pp. 256-62.

p. 77.

aul Langford
rofessor of Modern History, Oxford University
ector of Lincoln College, Oxford.

PREFACE.

SOME of the Learned have been very ſevere upon ſuch works as we now lay before the Public. Their ſeverity would have been juſt, if ſuch works had been recommended or uſed to the excluſion of more important ſtudies. Thoſe who aſpire to a ſolid erudition, muſt undoubtedly take other methods to acquire it. They have their labour and their merit. But there are readers of another order, who muſt not be left wholly unprovided: For ſuch readers, it is our province to collect matters of a lighter nature; but pleaſing even by their levity; by their variety; and their aptitude to enter into common converſation. Things of this ſort often gradually and imperceptibly inſinuate a taſte for knowledge, and in ſome meaſure gratify that taſte. They ſteal ſome moments from the round of diſſipation and pleaſure. They relieve the minds of men of buſineſs, who cannot paſs from ſevere labour to ſevere ſtudy, with an elegant relaxation. They preſerve the ſtrenuous idleneſs of many from a worſe employment.

These

Theſe pretenſions we have in common with all the other periodical compilers; and the ſame apology ſerves us all. But it will be expected, that in offering a new performance to the Public, we ſhould mention ſome new and peculiar advantage which we pretend to have over our fellow-labourers. Some ſuch advantages we *flatter ourſelves we poſſeſs*, partly ariſing from our ſcheme of an annual rather than a monthly publication; partly from our own attention and induſtry.

Not confined *to a monthly publication*, we have an opportunity of examining with care the products of the year, and of ſelecting what many appear moſt particularly deſerving *of notice. We have from the ſame* cauſe the advantage of order; we are better able to rank the ſeveral kinds under their proper heads; at leaſt with as much exactneſs as *the nature of a miſcellany will admit.*

But, beſides this advantage derived from our general ſcheme, we derive ſomething from our own labour. We have not in our *firſt article confined ourſelves to the hiſtory of* the year. We have taken the war from its commencement. It is a ſubject which requires all the pains which we could beſtow upon

upon it; and deserves much more skilful workmen. None was ever more formed to interest curiosity; from the importance of the events, the dignity of the persons concerned, the greatness of the actions performed, and the amazing revolutions of fortune. The reader will find the events of this war, which has been carried on in the four quarters of the world, and which he has hitherto seen in a scattered manner, united into one connected narrative, and continued to the end of the campaign of seventeen hundred and fifty-eight. To effect this from the broken and unconnected materials, has been a work of more labour than may at first appear; and if we have performed what we intended in any sort to the reader's satisfaction, we may lay claim to some merit.

We have made an article of State Papers. They serve to illustrate and confirm the facts advanced in the historical part; and our readers will not be displeased to see so many curious and important pieces together.

Endeavouring to be as extensively useful as possible, we aimed at uniting the plan of the Magazines with that of the Reviews. We have

have given abſtracts of ſome of the beſt books publiſhed within the year, with remarks upon them. We have obſerved upon none which we could not praiſe; not that we pretend to have obſerved on all that are praiſeworthy. Thoſe that do not deſerve to be well ſpoken of, do not deſerve to be ſpoken of at all.

Though we think our plan tolerably well calculated for a literary amuſement, we do not pretend that the Public will not have ſomething to excuſe, as well as to applaud. Our acquaintance with their ſentiments in that reſpect will increaſe our employment for the enſuing year, and excite us to amend the faults which we may have committed in this.

THE

ANNUAL REGISTER,

For the YEAR 1758.

THE

HISTORY

OF THE

PRESENT WAR.

CHAP. I.

Origin of the troubles in North America. Admiral Boſcawen and General Braddock ſent thither. Operations intended. Two French Men of War taken. Braddock defeated. General Johnſon repulſes the French. French threaten an invaſion. Fort St. Philip beſieged and taken. Treaty with Ruſſia, the ſpirit of it. Alliance with the King of Pruſſia. Ground of the quarrel between her Imperial Majeſty and that monarch. Treaty of Petersbourg. Treaty of Verſailles. King of Pruſſia enters Saxony and Bohemia. Battle of Lowoſitz. Saxon army ſurrenders.

THE original plan of this work propoſed no more than that each volume ſhould contain a narrative of thoſe events which diſtinguiſh its own year. But, becauſe we have entered upon our undertaking in the heat of an almoſt general and very important war, I thought it would not be unneceſſary or diſagreeable to look a little farther back. It would be difficult, perfectly to underſtand the operations of the ſeveral powers at war, during the laſt year, without reviewing the tranſactions of the preceding years; nor would it be eaſy to enter into the ſpirit of theſe without examining the cauſes which

 more

more nearly or remotely operated to produce these troubles that have involved so many parts of the world in one common distraction.

The war into which all parties and interests seem now to be so perfectly blended, arose from causes which originally had not the least connection: the uncertain limits of the English and French territories in America; and the mutual claims of the houses of Austria and Brandenbourg on the dutchy of Silesia. It is no wonder that the two former powers seizing on a country in which they considered the right of the natural inhabitants as nothing, should find it a very difficult matter to settle their own. For a long time neither of these powers were sufficiently acquainted with the geography of America, to enable them to ascertain the limits of their several pretensions with any tolerable exactness; nor, indeed, were these matters deemed of sufficient moment to call for a very laborious discussion. At the treaty of Utrecht, whilst so many more important interests, or what then seemed more important, were discussed, the limits of Nova Scotia, then called Acadia, were expressed only in general terms, and left to be put on a more certain footing by subsequent negotiations. These negotiations pursued with no vigour, and drawn out into an excessive length, seemed only to increase the former confusion. After the accession of the present royal family, a French connection, perhaps necessary from the circumstances of the time, and afterwards a certain negligence of all affairs but those of our domestic polity, suffered this important point to vanish almost wholly out of our consideration. During this interval, our colonies on the continent of North America, extended themselves on every side. Whilst agriculture and the maritime commerce flourished on their coasts, the Indian trade drew several of our wandering dealers far into the inland country, and beyond the great mountains. Here they found themselves in a delightful climate, in a soil abundantly fruitful, and watered with many fair and navigable rivers. These advantages, joined to those of the Indian trade, appeared to compensate for its remoteness from the sea. It was judged that as the first settlers on the coast, we had a good right to the inland country; and, if so, to the navigation of the Misisippi, which opened another door to the ocean. With these views, a company of merchants and planters, obtained a charter for a considerable tract of land near the river Ohio, on the western side of the Allegeney mountains, but within the province of Virginia; and the adventurers began to settle pursuant to the terms of their patent.

Now began to shoot forth the seeds of another dispute, which had long lain unobserved, but which proved altogether as thorny and intricate as that concerning the limits of Acadia. The French pretending to have first discovered the mouths of the Misisippi, claimed the whole adjacent country, towards New Mexico on the East, quite to the Apalachian or Allegeney moutains on the West. They drove off the new settlers, and built a strong fort called du Quesne, on the forks of the river Monongahela; a situation which commanded the entrance into all the country on the Ohio and Misisippi.

The reader will observe, that I do not pretend to decide concerning the right of either nation in in this conteſt. It is evident enough, that the conſideration of the right had much leſs influence on both parties than the conſideration of conveniency. Should the French be able to unite Canada to their colonies at the mouth of Miſiſippi by a poſſeſſion of all that vaſt country which lies between them, the Engliſh colonies muſt loſe all ſhare in the Indian trade in time of peace; and in time of war be expoſed to continual dangers, or to the ruinouſly chargeable defence of a frontier more than 1500 miles in length. If on the contrary, the French ſhould fail to make good theſe claims on the Ohio, and thoſe on Nova Scotia, their two colonies entirely diſunited, and the entrance into one ſhut up for the winter ſeaſon by froſt, and the entrance into the other difficult in all ſeaſons by the banks at the mouth of the Miſiſippi, muſt certainly loſe all their value to France, and in their fall involve much of the fortune of their great ſettlements in the Weſt-Indies.

Both nations being fully perſuaded of this, no longer looked on the affair of the Ohio as a matter of indifference. They prepared to cut the gordian knot of the long and intricate negotiation by the ſword. Ships were fitted ont, and ſome troops ſilently ſent off from Breſt. General Braddock ſailed to Virginia with about 1500 regular troops; 24 men of war under the Admirals Boſcawen and Moſtyn were ordered to America, to intercept the French ſupplies. Orders were ſent to our colonies to arm; and three operations were actually undertaken, one againſt Fort du Queſne under Braddock; the other two againſt the French forts in Nova Scotia, and the fort of Crown Point on the frontiers of New York.

1755.

The two courts in the mean time breathed nothing but peace, and exchanged reciprocal profeſſions of friendſhip and good will, which deceived neither party.

They who are of opinion that the paſſions and characters of the ruling men influence all public concerns as much as the public intereſts themſelves, thought they ſaw other cauſes operating to haſten this breach. On the death of a great miniſter which happened ſome time before, the adminiſtration was new moulded. Some perſons then taken in, were conſidered as belonging to a party not perfectly united with the remains of the old adminiſtration. It was thought that the leading man of this party propoſed to work out the old ſervants of the crown, in order to make way for a more uniform ſyſtem. As long as peace ſubſiſts government is ſupported by itſelf; and any change is difficult. But the conduct of a war is a thing critical to a miniſtry. The leader of this party therefore, conſcious of his own talents, which all men acknowledged to be conſpicuous, and of his connections which were conſiderable, warmly puſhed on a war, ſeconded by the fairneſs of the public motives, and the general voice of the people. In this war his friends relied that things muſt neceſſarily be ſo embarraſſed, that the old party would find themſelves obliged to retire, and to leave the ſtage clear for them to ſerve their country according to their own plans, and on their own terms. This deſign was believed to be puſhed forward by another great man of that party, who had played a game nearly of the ſame kind before, and in whom an advanced age had not abated any thing of his natural fire and love of violent councils.

Things came to a crisis by the taking of two French men of war by the admirals Boscawen and Mostyn. June 10. The operations by land were carried on with vigour; but whether conducted with equal judgment we stand too near the time to decide. June 16. However, the French fort at Beausejour was taken, and soon after those on St. John's river were abandoned; by which we remained masters of all Nova Scotia. The principal expedition was that against Fort du Quesne, under General Braddock. That General abounding too much in his own sense for the degree of military knowledge he possessed, commanding in a country where he did not know, and carrying on a species of war in which he had no experience, suffered himself when he had advanced within ten miles of Fort du Quesne, to be surprised by an ambuscade of French and Indians. July 9. His army was seized with a pannic from the unusual appearance, and horrid cries of the savages; they fled in confusion; they were totally defeated with a considerable slaughter, especially of their officers. The General himself, after having had five horses killed under him, was mortally wounded; wiping away all the errors of his conduct by an honourable death for his country.

The nation was something consoled for this loss in the signal advantage gained by General Johnson Sep. 7. who commanded the expedition designed against Crown Point. He was attacked in his retrenchments by the French General Dieskau; but the assailants wanting cannon, and firing from too great a distance, were totally defeated, and Dieskau himself was made prisoner. This victory, tho' very honourable for Mr. Johnson and the provincial troops under his command, yet, as it was gained late in the season, and as the army was in no very good condition, it had no consequences. On the whole, we seemed, after allowing for this victory, and for the dislodgement of the French from Nova Scotia, to have had the worst part in the campaign; considering the sanguine expectations which had been formed, and the great superiority of strength which we exerted, or were able to have exerted, in that part of the world.

During this summer our court took a resolution not to wait the precarious operations of our arms in America for redress of the grievances complained of, but to strike such a blow as would at once put a security into our hands, for the evacuating the places the enemy had fortified in our territories, and disable them in the two most material points, the resources of their trade and their seamen. Their merchant ships were every where attacked, as if war had been actually declared, and vast numbers brought into our ports. The French made all Europe resound with complaints of what they called a proceeding so unjust, and a violation of the law of nations so flagrant and unprecedented. But, whether it was that they were really in no condition to act, or that they intended to influence the other courts in their favour, by a shew of extraordinary moderation, they contented themselves with this, and neither declared war nor made any sort of reprisal for several months after. 1756. At length they began to act; several bodies of troops moved to the coasts of Picardy, Normandy and Brittany; and all things threatned an invasion on some part of this kingdom. Under the shadow

ſhadow of this ſtratagem, they got ready in the harbour of Toulon a fleet of twelve men of war of the April 18. line with the utmoſt expedition, which convoyed an army of about 11,000 men, under command of the Duke de Richlieu, to the iſland of Minorca. April 25. In a few days they opened trenches before St. Philip's fort.

This was done whilſt the nation trembled under a ſhameful pannic, too public to be concealed, too fatal in its conſequences to be ever forgotten. The real invaſion did not leſſen our fears of the imaginary one; it threw us into a confuſion that ſuffered us to be ſenſible of nothing but our own weakneſs. We did not look upon ourſelves ſufficiently ſecured by the arrival of the Hanoverian and Heſſian troops, which the ſame weakneſs had induced us to call to our aſſiſtance. The miniſtry ſeemed to have been infected with the common terror; for, though they had very early notice of the French deſigns, ſuch was the apprehenſion of the invaſion, or ſuch the ill-contrived diſpoſition of our navy, that Admiral Byng was not diſpatched to the Mediterranean before the 5th of April, and then with a ſquadron of no more than ten ſhips of the line.

The engagement with the French May 12. fleet under M. Galiſſoniere; the retreat of Byng by which the garriſon of fort St. Philip was cut off from all hopes of June 29. relief; the ſurrender of that garriſon after nine weeks open trenches; the ſentiments of the court and the public, on the different merits of the governor and the admiral; the oppoſition of ſome, who thought the one too highly honoured, and the other too ſeverely cenſured, and the meaſures which rather indignation at our loſſes and diſgraces, than a cool ſenſe of things, obliged us to take, are known to all the world. Our affairs were in ſuch a condition that we were driven to the expedient of a court martial to revive the Britiſh ſpirit, and to the unfortunate neceſſity of ſhedding the blood of an admiral, a perſon of a Feb. 14. 1757. noble family, as a ſacrifice to the diſcipline of our navy.

From this melancholy picture, let us turn our eyes another way, and review the ſteps by which this war came to involve the reſt of the contending powers. The French, amongſt the other plans they formed for diſtreſſing our affairs, made no ſecret of their deſign of attacking his Majeſty's German dominions. Theſe countries evidently had no ſort of connection with the matters which gave riſe to the war. But being under a Sovereign ſo remarkably affectionate to his native country; they judged he might be terrified into a relaxation of his rights in America, to preſerve Hanover from the calamities with which it was threatened. Their politics, however, in this inſtance proved as unſucceſsful as they were unjuſt. No motion was made toward an abatement in our claims with regard to America: his Majeſty took other methods for the preſervation of the peace of Germany. His Britiſh ſubjects by their repreſentatives, not more generouſly than reaſonably, reſolved to defend the Hanoverians if attacked in their quarrel. To anſwer this purpoſe, the miniſtry entered into a ſubſidy treaty with the Empreſs of Ruſſia, in virtue of which ſhe was to hold 55,000 men in readineſs to be ſent on a requiſition wherever the Britiſh ſervice required.

The alliance with Ruffia was chofen for reafons which were then fufficiently plaufible ; though it is to be hoped they never can fubfift again. The long ill underftanding between the King of Pruffia and our court, and his clofe connection with that of Verfailles, raifed no ill-grounded apprehenfions that he might be induced to act a dangerous part on this occafion. Ruffia was therefore a proper ally, who had both a political and perfonal enmity to this monarch, and who would be fure to employ a great power with great vigour in fuch a caufe. But this fyftem was in a fhort time totally reverfed. The King of Pruffia had been too well apprifed of the clofe conjunction of the courts of Peterfbourg and Vienna, and of the real motive to that conjunction, to have the leaft defign of embroiling himfelf with England. Matters were therefore very foon explained, and the treaty between his Pruffian majefty and this court, to keep all foreigners out of the Empire, was figned at London in January 1756. Thefe treaties were cenfured as inconfiftent with each other ; but in reality they were confiftent enough, aiming precifely at the fame object, to oppofe the fcheme meditated by France for difturbing the affairs of Germany.

If reflecting on the fentiments of thefe courts, there was fomething unexpected in the alliance between Great Britain and Pruffia; it was foon followed by another alliance of a nature infinitely more furprifing. The Emprefs Queen of Hungary, finding England in no difpofition to co-operate in her defigns, had recourfe to other meafures The houfe of Auftria, which had formerly united Europe to preferve her from the power of France, now entered herfelf into the moft intimate union with that power. By this extraordinary revolution, the whole political fyftem of Europe affumed a new face ; it was indeed a revolution fo extraordinary, that we fhall be juftified if we interrupt the courfe of this narrative, to look back at the caufes which produced it.

The houfe of Brandenbourg, a little more than two centuries ago, was in a very humble condition. But by the part fhe took in the reformation, which put into her hands the eftates of the Teutonic order ; by a marriage from which fhe acquired the duchy of Cleves ; and by an uncommon fucceffion of able princes who carefully improved every turn in the affairs of Germany to their advantage, fhe raifed herfelf by degrees to a confiderable ftate, to an electorate, and at laft to a royalty, not only in name but in power. The late King of Pruffia, in order to ftrengthen this power, though he paft almoft his whole reign in the moft profound peace, gave his whole attention to his army ; frugal in all other refpects, in this alone he was expenfive ; it was his bufinefs, and, what was perhaps of greater moment, it was his only diverfion. Thus in a reign apparently inactive, there was always kept up an army of near 100,000 men, in as much exercife as they could have in peace, and formed with the moft perfect difcipline.

When his prefent majefty came to the throne, he immediately fhewed a difpofition of employing effectually that military force which his father had fpent his life only in forming and training. He managed his difpute with the bifhop of Liege by the fummary method of force : and feemed difpofed to carry all things with fo high a hand, as made him indeed much refpected, but much

much dreaded too by the Princes of the Empire, who ſaw that there was another power to be feared in Germany, beſides that of Auſtria. But theſe were ſmall matters, rather ſigns of the diſpoſition of this Prince, than exertions of it. He meditated much greater things; and only waited an opportunity to make good the ancient claims of his family on the moſt conſiderable part of the dutchy of Sileſia. The right to that dutchy had been a very intricate affair; but the houſe of Auſtria availing herſelf of the greatneſs of her power, and of a diſſenſion between the Elector Frederick II. and his ſon, prevailed with the Elector to give up that right for an equivalent; then ſhe perſuaded his ſon to confirm the treaty; and at the ſame time for a trivial conſideration to give up the equivalent itſelf. The King of Pruſſia, not thinking himſelf bound by theſe acts, though confirmed by a long poſſeſſion, took advantage of his own power and the embarraſſed circumſtances of the houſe of Auſtria, to reſume what their power and the embarraſſed circumſtances of his family had formerly deprived him of. Dec. 1740. For immediately on the death of Charles the 6th, when the Auſtrain greatneſs ſeemed irrecoverably loſt, he entered into Sileſia, and made himſelf maſter of the whole country with little oppoſition. Then uniting with the French and Bavarians, he ſecured his conqueſts by two deciſive victories, and by a June 11, 1742. treaty which yielded him the greateſt and beſt part of Sileſia and the whole county of Glatz. June 2, 1744. But the cauſe of the Emperor which the King of Pruſſia had embraced, ſoon cauſed a renewal of hoſtilities the Queen of Hungary ſaw herſelf defeated in three pitched battles; her new ally the King of Poland, driven from his German dominions, and the King of Pruſſia entering Dreſden in triumph, where he gave the law in a treaty, Dec. 1745. by which Sileſia was once more ſolemnly confirmed to him: in return to which he guarantied to the Queen of Hungary the reſt of her dominions.

The Queen of Hungary could not eaſily loſe the memory of the wound ſhe had received in the loſs of one of the fineſt and richeſt parts of all her dominions. Sileſia, which ſhe had juſt yielded, extends in length 200 miles along the courſe of the large and navigable river Oder. A country of the moſt exquiſite fertility and higheſt cultivation; abounding with men, abounding with valuable manufactures, and yielding a clear yearly revenue of 800,000 pounds ſterling. The peace was hardly concluded by which ſhe reſigned this valuable territory, than ſhe ſet on foot practices for recovering it. She entered into a treaty with the court of Peterſbourg, of an innocent and ſimply defenſive nature, May 22, 1746. ſo far as appeared to the public; but ſix ſecret and ſeparate articles were added to it; one of which provides, that in caſe his Pruſſian Majeſty ſhould attack her Majeſty the Empreſs Queen, or the Empreſs of Ruſſia, or even the republic of Poland, that this attack ſhould be conſidered as a breach of the treaty of Dreſden; that the right of the Empreſs Queen to Sileſia ceded by that treaty ſhould revive; and that the contracting powers ſhould mutually furniſh an army of 60,000 men to reinveſt the Empreſs Queen with that dutchy.

To this ſo extraordinary a treaty, the King of Poland was invited to accede; and he did fo far accede to it as to fhew he perfectly agreed in his fentiments with thefe courts But his fituation in the jaws of a formidable enemy, and the experience of paffed misfortunes, had rendered him fo wary, that he declined figning the treaty; but ftill, with the confent of the parties concerned, whom he fully convinced of his refolution to co-operate in all their meafures. He defired and they agreed, that in the fuccefs of their arms he fhould have a fhare in the fpoil, on the footing of a treaty for the eventual partition of the King of Pruffia's dominions made in the laft war. On thefe conditions the King of Poland without actually figning, was underftood, and received as a party to the treaty of Peterfbourg.

May 18, 1745.

In confequence of thefe meafures, all fort of means were employed to embroil the King of Pruffia's affairs in the North, and particularly to render him perfonally odious to the Czarina. When their machinations had taken full effect, and Ruffia was fixed in an unalterable enmity to that monarch, preparations of magazines and armies were made in Bohemia and Moravia; and the King of Poland, under pretence of a military amufement, drew together about 16,000 men, with which he occupied the ftrong and important poft of Pirna. The Queen of Hungary faw that fhe ftood in need of yet ftronger fupports than thefe in the arduous bufinefs fhe had undertaken. She found that Great Btitain, which had often done fo much for her diftrefs, would do little for her ambition: fhe therefore had recourfe to France, who joyfully accepting an alliance, that promifed to confound the whole Germanic body, concluded a treaty with the Emprefs at Verfailles the 1ft of May 1756, a remarkable æra in the political hiftory of Europe.

The fecret articles of the treaty of Peterfbourg, the fountain of the prefent troubles, and the fteps taken to put that treaty in execution, though formed and carried on with as much fecrecy as earneftnefs, could not efcape the vigilance of his Pruffian majefty, who watched all their motions, and had perfect intelligence of their moft hidden defigns. When therefore he perceived, that by the breach between England and France, the Emprefs Queen would take advantage of thefe troubles to avail herfelf of her alliances and her armaments; he ordered his minifter at Vienna to demand a clear explication, and proper affurances concerning the preparations he faw making: and receiving only a dry and equivocal anfwer, that the Emprefs had taken meafures for her own fecurity and that of her allies and friends, the King believed himfelf no longer bound to preferve any terms; a dangerous war was to be kept out of his own territories at any rate; and being always in perfect readinefs for action, he fell upon Saxony with a confiderable army.

Aug. 29.

At firft the King of Pruffia feemed only to demand a free paffage for his troops, and an obfervance of the neutrality profeffed by the King of Poland; but as he had very good reafons to diftruft fuch a neutrality, he demanded as a fecurity, that the Saxon troops fhould quit the ftrong poft they occupied, and difperfe themfelves immediately. This demand was refufed, and the King of Pruffia in confequence of that refufal, immediately formed a fort of blockade about the Saxon camp at Pirna, with a view to reduce it by famine, fince ſince its inacceſſible ſituation rendered an attack unadviſeable. There were in Bohemia two Auſtrian armies under M. Brown and M. Picolomini; to keep theſe in awe, M. Schwerin had entered Bohemia from the county of Glatz; and M. Keith had penetrated into that kingdom on the ſide of Miſnia. But the King of Pruſſia, not entirely confiding in theſe diſpoſitions; and ſtill apprehenſive that M. Brown might be able to convey ſome relief to the Saxons, reſolved to bring him to an action, to the ſucceſs of which he knew his own preſence would greatly contribute. He therefore left the blockade of the Saxon army, joined his forces under Keith, and engaged the Auſtrains at Lowoſitz.

Dec. 1.

Here he obtained a victory, which though it was not undiſputed with regard to the field of battle, yet with regard to the conſequence it was as deciſive as could be wiſhed. M. Brown found it impracticable to relieve the Saxons, notwithſtanding the judicious efforts he made for that purpoſe; and that army, after a vain attempt to retire from their difficult poſt, which had one fault, that it was as difficult to leave it as to force it, were obliged to ſurrender priſoners of war. The King of Poland quitted his German dominions; and the Pruſſians took up their winter quarters in Saxony, ſeized upon the revenues, levied exorbitant contributions, and obliged the country to furniſh recruits. This unhappy people ſaw their country exhauſted, and forced to bear the burthen of a war againſt itſelf. It was then, that the King of Pruſſia conſulting the rules of policy, more than thoſe of politeneſs, made himſelf maſter of the archives at Dreſden, in doing which ſome roughneſs was uſed towards the Queen; but he made himſelf amends for the clamour induſtriouſly raiſed on this pretence, by acquiring the originals of theſe pieces, which evinced to the world the reality of the deſign againſt him, and which therefore in a great meaſure juſtified the means he had taken to come at them, as well as the extraordinary ſeverities he uſed towards the unfortunate Saxons.

CHAP. II.

State of the Engliſh miniſtry. The characters and deſigns of the ſeveral factions. A coalition. Oſwego taken by the French. Calcutta taken by the Nabob. Angria reduced by Admiral Watſon.

WHILST the King of Pruſſia paſſed the winter in the moſt vigorous preparations for carrying on the war, his ally Great Britain preſented a very different face of things. The loſs of Minorca plunged the people into the utmoſt grief mixed with ſhame, for ſuch a blot on the national honour, and with indignation not only againſt thoſe who had acted weakly, but thoſe who had provided inſufficiently for the relief of that important poſſeſſion. The public reſentment, which at firſt ſeemed to have no other object than Byng, was ſoon turned againſt the miniſtry. The clamour in parliament was great; without doors it was exceſſive. Addreſſes praying a ſtrict enquiry into the cauſe of our misfortunes, were preſented from all parts of the kingdom. The miniſtry, notwithſtanding this general diſcontent, had a real

real ſtrength; and they might have ſtood, had they agreed amongſt themſelves. The commons could not be brought to any angry votes; and the reſult of the enquiry into the loſs of Minorca, was as favourable as they could have wiſhed. But Mr. F—— thought it not adviſeable to bear a large proportion of the odium cauſed by counſels, in which he had little ſhare. Perhaps, he thought this embarraſſment, a ſituation not unfavourable to the arrangement he had always aimed at; he therefore ſuddenly threw up an employment, which he hoped to reſume augmented with greater power.

On the removal of this principal prop, the whole ſtructure of the miniſtry fell to pieces. The D. of N. the Ld. Ch. the firſt lord of the admiralty reſigned; and the chiefs of the party by whoſe manœuvres they
Dec. 4. 1756. were diſplaced naturally ſucceeded to the management of affairs. They who had reſigned gave them no apparent oppoſition in parliament; but whether it was, that the new miniſtry were themſelves too freſh from oppoſition, and ſome of them too full of the popular manners that introduced them to court to be perfectly agreeable in the cloſet, or that they had made their bottom too narrow, after holding their employments for ſome months, to the great concern of the public, they in their turn were
April 5. 1757. obliged to quit their poſts. Thus was the helm of government a ſecond time abandoned. The caſe of the King and the nation was at that juncture truly deplorable. We were without any ally who could do us the leaſt ſervice, engaged in a war hitherto unſucceſsful, with the moſt formidable power in Europe; we almoſt deſpaired of our military virtue; public ſpirit appeared utterly extinguiſhed, whilſt the rage of faction burned with the utmoſt violence; our operations were totally ſuſpended; and having no miniſtry eſtabliſhed, we had no plan to follow.

Three factions divided the ruling men of the nation, for the groſs of the people ſeemed to have no further views than a redreſs of their grievances, by whatever means that could be brought about; the firſt of theſe factions was compoſed of thoſe who had grown to place and power, or had formed their connections under the old miniſtry. They were ſome of the moſt reſpectable perſons in the nation, and had undoubtedly the greateſt parliamentary intereſt. They had at the ſame time another intereſt hardly leſs conſiderable, that of the monied people; but in ſome points, and theſe material too, they were weak. They were not at all popular; a matter of great conſideration in a government like ours; and they were ſuppoſed by the groſs of the people, not to be under the direction of great political abilities.

The ſecond faction, though not ſuſpected of the want of ſufficient ability, was yet more unpopular than the former; they had not attempted to preſerve even the appearances eſſential to popularity; and to them the more eſſential, as their parliamentary ſtrength was, however reſpectable, much inferior to the firſt. If their influence at one court was able to ballance that of the old miniſtry, by means of a then powerful connection, that very connection made them far worſe at another court, and worſe with the generality of the people, who entertained, or pretended at leaſt to entertain, ſuſpicions of a nature the more dangerous, as they were only droped ed in hints and whiſpers, and never could come to a full and open explanation.

The third party had little parliamentary, and leſs court influence; but they had a prodigious popularity, which ſupplied every other defect. The abilities of their leader were of the moſt ſhining kind; his application equal to his abilities; his diſintereſtedneſs was confeſſed by his enemies; and though it would have ſhined in the days of heroiſm, was now the more valued, and ſet off to the greater advantage by the general ſelfiſhneſs which prevailed among the men of buſineſs The nation repoſed the moſt perfect confidence in his integrity and love to his country. This party, conſcious where its ſtrength lay, cultivated with great care the popularity which was the baſis of their power; even perhaps ſo as to impair on ſome occaſions the dignity of government.

Theſe three factions differed from each other extremely with regard to power, the grand object of all factions. But in the general ſcheme of their politics, the two firſt were pretty much agreed. Looking on France as the moſt conſtant and moſt dangerous enemy of Great Britain, they dreaded the increaſe of her power and influence among the neighbouring nations as the greateſt of all evils. To prevent ſo dangerous an aggrandiſement, they thought it abſolutely neceſſary to preſerve a conſtant attention to the balance of power, and to ſeek our particular ſafety and liberty in the general ſafety and liberty of Europe. A cloſe connection was therefore to be kept up with the powers of the continent, not only by continual negotiations, but by large ſubſidies, and even by aſſiſting them with our troops if the occaſion ſhould require ſuch aſſiſtance. For this purpoſe, as well as to ſecure the more effectually our preſent happy eſtabliſhment, a conſiderable regular land force ought to be conſtantly maintained. Our navy, they thought, ought by no means to be neglected; but it was only to be cultivated and employed ſubſerviently to the more comprehenſive continental ſyſtem. Theſe parties were far from being friends to arbitrary power, or in any ſort averſe to parliaments; they loved the conſtitution; but they were for preſerving the authority of government entire, and in its utmoſt lawful force. To make government more eaſy, knowing that many would diſturb it, from diſaffection, or diſguſt, or miſtaken notions of liberty, they thought it juſt to rule men by their intereſts, if they could not by their virtues, and they had long been in the practice of procuring a majority in parliament, by the diſtribution of the numerous lucrative places and employments which our conſtitution leaves in the diſpoſal of the crown. Several believed that no other method was practicable, conſidering the nature of mankind, and our particular form of government.

But the third and popular party, was influenced by different principles. They looked indeed on the power of France in the ſame light with the two former, and were of the ſame opinion concerning the neceſſity of ſetting bounds to it. In the means of attaining this end they differed. Our ſituation they thought dictated a narrower, but a more natural, a ſafer, and a leſs expenſive plan of politics, than that which had been adopted by the other party. We ought never to forget, ſaid they, that we are an iſland: and that this circumſtance ſo favourable both to our political and to our civil liberty, preſcribes fcribes to us a conduct very different from that of every other nation. Our natural ftrength is a maritime ftrength, as trade is our natural employment: thefe muft always go hand in hand, and they mutually fupport each other. But, if turning our back to our real interefts, and abandoning our natural element, we enter that inextricable labyrinth of continental politics; if we make ourfelves parties in every controverfy; if we exhauft our wealth in purchafing the ufelefs and precarious friendfhip of every petty prince or ftate; if we wafte the blood of our people in all the quarrels that may arife on the continent; fo far from going in the right way to reduce France, that we attack her on the ftrong fide, and only deftroy ourfelves by our ill-judged efforts againft the enemy. That we can have nothing to fear from the fuperiority of France on the continent, whilft we preferve our fuperiority at fea; that we can always cut the finews of the enemies ftrength by deftroying their traffic; that to fear an invafion from a power weak in its marine, is the idleft of all fears; that in cafe an invafion were poffible, a well-trained national militia, fupplying by their zeal the defects of their difcipline, would prove our beft protection; that a ftanding army is in whatever fhape dangerous to freedom; and that a government like ours, connected by its very effence with the liberty of the fubject, can never be in want of the fupports of defpotic power. As little is parliamentary influence neceffary. A government pleafing to the people, as every good government muft be, can never be generally oppofed; and men need no bribes to perfuade them to their duty.

Thefe notions fo oppofite in their extreams, might be reconciled in a medium, and ufed to temper each other. For as on one hand, it would be very abfurd to take no fort of advantage of our infular fituation, but to engage in all the bufinefs of the continent without referve, and to plunge ourfelves into real evils out of dread of poffible mifchiefs; fo on the other hand to think ourfelves wholly unconcerned in the fortunes of our neighbours on the continent, or to think of aiding them in any cafe, only by the way of diverfion with our fleets, would be a way of proceeding ftill more extravagant than the former. If fuch notions were reduced to practice, we might foon lofe all thefe advantages derived from a fituation which we abufed.

The reafonablenefs of fuch a temperament, could not be perceived during the ferment of that time, in which thefe topics were bandied to and fro with infinite heat. The refignation or rather deprivation of the popular miniftry, only increafed their popularity, and the general difcontent; the people could not believe that good meafures could be purfued when thofe, in whom alone they confided, were not employed; almoft all the corporations of the kingdom prefented the deprived minifters with their freedom, and addreffed them in the warmeft manner, teftifying the moft entire approbation of their conduct, and the fincereft concern to fee them out of employment.

This conflict between an old eftablifhed intereft, and the torrent of popularity, continued for a long time, and the nation was almoft ruined by it. It is not eafy nor perhaps quite proper to attempt to trace the fteps by which fo happy a coalition, as we have feen take place, was brought about But it was formed in fuch man-

manner, has held together with ſuch ſolidity, and produced ſuch excellent effects, as I believe the June 29. 1757. moſt ſanguine could not have hoped for at that time. Mr. P. was again reſtored to the office of ſecretary of ſtate, the D. of N. was placed at the head of the treaſury, Mr. F. was appointed paymaſter of the forces. This arrangement, which gave very general ſatisfaction, was however diſliked by thoſe whom their violent attachment to their party had inſpired with a narrow and excluſive ſpirit. It was the beſt meaſure, becauſe it was an healing meaſure; and it was little leſs than impoſſible for any particular party to carry on public buſineſs on its ſingle bottom.

It was high time that our domeſtic diſſenſions ſhould be compoſed at laſt. From every quarter of the world in which we had any concern, Aug 14 1756. we heard of nothing but loſſes and calamities. In America we loſt the fort of Oſwego. That fort ſituated at the mouth of the Onondaga river, commanded a commodious harbour on the lake Ontario. It was built by General Shirley, and deſigned to cover the country of the Five nations; to ſecure the Indian trade; to interrupt the communication between the French northern and ſouthern eſtabliſhments; and to open a way to our arms to attack the forts of Frontenac and Niagara. For theſe purpoſes, ſome frigates had been fitted out for cruiſing, and a number of boats prepared for the tranſportation of troops; but they all fell to the enemy with the fort, where 100 pieces of cannon were, and a conſiderable quantity of proviſion. 1600 men were made priſoners of war. The place made but a trifling reſiſtance, ſcarce holding out three days; the attempts to relieve it were too late. The French demoliſhed the fort.

Our loſſes were not confined to America. The Eaſt India company received a blow, which would have ſhaken an eſtabliſhment of leſs ſtrength to its foundations. The news of the war between France and England had not yet reached India, but a new and very formidable enemy was raiſed up in that quarter. The Nabob of Bengal (the Nabobs are a ſpecies of viceroys to the Grand Mogul, grown almoſt independent in their ſeveral provinces,) irritated at the protection given to one of his ſubjects in the Engliſh fort of Calcutta, and as it is ſaid, at the refuſal of ſome duties to which he claimed a right, levied a great army, and laid ſiege to that place. The governor, terrified by the numbers of the enemy, abandoned the fort with ſeveral of the principal perſons in the ſettlement, who ſaved themſelves with their moſt valuable effects on board the ſhips.

Thus deſerted, Mr. Hollwel the ſecond in command, bravely held the place to the laſt extremity, with a few gallant friends, and the remains of a feeble garriſon. A very noble defence was inſufficient to keep an untenable place, or to affect an ungenerous enemy. The fort was taken, and the garriſon being made priſoners, June 26. were thruſt into a narrow dungeon. Hollwel with a few others came out alive, to paint a ſcene of the moſt cruel diſtreſs which perhaps human nature ever ſuffered. The Eaſt India company loſt their principal ſettlement in Bengal, and a fort which ſecured to them the moſt valuable part of their trade.

In the ſpace of this unfortunate year we were ſtripped of Minorca and

and Oſwego; we apprehended an invaſion of Great Britain itſelf: our councils were torn to pieces by factions; and our military fame was every where in contempt. Amidſt Feb. 13. theſe loſſes, we conſidered as ſome advantage the reduction of the principal fort of Angria, a piratical prince, who had been many years troubleſome to the Engliſh trade in the Eaſt Indies. This ſervice was performed by Admiral Watſon in the beginning of the year.

CHAP. III.

State of the confederates againſt the King of Pruſſia. French paſs the Weſer. King of Pruſſia enters Bohemia. Battle of Prague. Prague inveſted. Count Daun takes the command of the Auſtrian army. Battle of Colin.

WHAT turn the Engliſh politics were like to take in the year 1757, ſeemed for ſome time uncertain. The new miniſtry did not ſeem well eſtabliſhed; nor was it well known whether they would purſue the plans and preſerve the connections of the old. Abroad every thing was prepared for opening the campaign with the utmoſt eclat. All Europe was in motion.

France, in order to demonſtrate to the Queen of Hungary the advantageous choice ſhe had made in connecting herſelf with the houſe of Bourbon, formed two great armies. The firſt was compoſed of near 80,000 men, the flower of the French troops, attended with a vaſt artillery, and commanded by M. de Etrees, a general of the beſt eſtabliſhed reputation ſhe had in her ſervice. Under him ſerved M. de Contades, M. Chevert, and the count de St. Germain, all officers of high character, and all fit to command in chief, if M. de Etrees had not been appointed to that eminence. This formidable army paſſed the Rhine, and marched by Weſtphalia, in order to invade the King of Pruſſia's dominions in quality of allies to the Empreſs Queen, and guardians of the liberties of the Empire, and to no other intent, as it was pretended; but in reality with a view to reduce Hanover alſo. They judged that their operations againſt the King of Pruſſia might be executed, and their ſcheme to drive the King of England into ſome conceſſions with regard to America, might be compleated by one and the ſame blow. The ſecond army was commanded by the Prince de Soubiſe; it conſiſted of about 25,000 men. This army was deſtined to ſtrengthen the Imperial army of execution; but before it had paſſed the Rhine it made itſelf maſter of Cleves, Meurs and Gueldres, whilſt a detachment from de Etrees's army ſeized upon the town of Embden, and whatever elſe belonged to Pruſſia in Eaſt Frieſland.

As ſoon as the King of Pruſſia had entered Saxony in the beginning of the preceding ſummer, proceſs was commenced againſt him in the Emperor's Aulic council, and before the diet of the Empire. It is not difficult to conceive how the affair muſt have been decided; when thoſe who feared the King of Pruſſia believed they had a fair opportunity to reduce him; and when thoſe who feared the houſe of Auſtria were by that very fear obliged to ſup-

support the power they dreaded: accustomed as they were to the influence of a family in which the Empire had so long been in a manner hereditary; and overawed by the appearances of a confederacy, the most formidable the world had ever yet seen. Accordingly the King of Prussia was condemned for contumacy; and the Fiscal had orders to notify to him that he was put under the ban of the Empire, and adjudged fallen from all the dignities and possessions which he held under it. The circles of the Empire were ordered to furnish their contingents of men and money to put this sentence in execution; but the contingents were collected slowly, the troops were badly composed, and probably this army had never been able to act if it had not been for the assistance afforded under the Prince de Soubise.

The Austrians who were principals in this quarrel, were not behind their auxiliaries in the greatness of their preparations; they made the most strenuous efforts, by which they assembled a body of upwards of 100,000 men in Bohemia, and committed the command to Prince Charles of Lorrain, assisted by M. Brown. In the North all things threatened the King of Prussia. The Czarina, true to her resentments and her engagements, had sent a body of 60,000 men commanded by M. Apraxin, who were in full march to invade the ducal Prussia, whilst a strong fleet was equipped in the Baltic, to co-operate with that army. Although the King of Sweden was allied in blood and inclinations to his Prussian majesty, yet the jealousy which the Senate entertained of their sovereign; the hope of recovering their ancient possessions in Pomerania by means of the present troubles, and in fine their old attachment to France newly cemented by intrigues and subsidies, made their ill inclinations to the cause of Prussia more than suspicious. Hitherto indeed nothing more than the tendency of their councils were fully known. The Duke of Mecklenbourg took the same party, and agreed to join the Swedish army when it should be assembled, with 6000 men; a proceeding which he has since had reason to repent bitterly. Thus were the forces of five mighty states *, each of which had in their turn been a terror to all Europe, united to reduce the heir of the Marquisses of Brandenbourg; and in such a point of danger and glory, had the great and formidable abilities of his Prussian majesty placed him, with little, in comparison, that could enable him to sustain the violence of so many shocks, except what those abilities supplied. But his astonishing œconomy, the incomparable order of his finances, the discipline of his armies beyond all praise, a sagacity that foresaw every thing, a vigilance that attended every thing, a constancy that no labour could subdue, a courage that no danger could dismay, an intuitive glance that catches the decisive moment, all these seemed to form a sort of balance to the vast weight against him, turned the wishes of his friends into hopes, and made them depend upon resources that are not within the power of calculation.

The only army that appeared in his favour was a body of between 30 and 40,000 Hanoverians and Hessians, who with some reinforcements of his own troops, formed an

* Austria, Russia, France, Sweden, the Empire.

army of obfervation, commanded by his Royal Highnefs the Duke of Cumberland; this army was pofted on the Wefer, to watch the motions of M. d'Etrees. The vaft and unwielded body of the French, encumbered as the French armies always are by an immenfe baggage and an innumerable multitude of mouths without hands, made a very flow progrefs through the rough and barren country that lies between the Rhine and the Wefer. All the abilities of the French general were employed in finding fubfiftence for his troops. His Royal Highnefs on the other hand, difplayed great abilities in throwing all poffible impediments in his way. But when thefe impediments were removed by the fuperiority of numbers, the Hanoverian army gradually gave way, yielding to that fuperiority, and the French troops paffed the Wefer without oppofition.

In the mean time, his Pruffian majefty being determined according to his maxim to lay the cloth as far from home as poffible; made his difpofitions for carrying the war into Bohemia as fpeedily as the feafon would admit. Three great bodies of his troops entered into that kingdom by three very different ways, but nearly at the fame time. M. Schwerin penetrated into it from Silefia. The Prince of Bevern entered with the corps under his command from Lufatia, and defeated as a preliminary to a more decifive victory, a body of 28,000 Auftrians who oppofed him. Ap. 21. The King himfelf prepared to enter Bohemia at a great diftance from the corps commanded by thefe generals; and as he feemed difpofed to march towards Egra, the enemy imagined he intended to execute fome defign diftinct from the object of his other armies. With this idea they detached a body of 20,000 men, to obferve his motions. The King of Pruffia finding that this feint had all its effect, made a fudden and mafterly movement to his left, by which he cut off all communication between that detachment and the main army of the Auftrians. Spirited with this advantage, he pufhed onwards with the utmoft rapidity to Prague, where he joined the corps under the Prince of Bevern and M. Schwerin, who had advanced with inconceivable diligence to meet him. Never were operations executed with more judgment, celerity and fuccefs.

The Auftrian army was little fhort of 100,000 men, May 6. and the fituation of their camp, fortified by every advantage of nature, and every contrivance of art, fuch as on common occafions might juftly be confidered as impregnable; but the Pruffians, being nearly as numerous as the enemy, infpired by a fociety of danger with their King, and filled with that noble enthufiafm, which, whilft it urges to daring enterprifes, almoft enfures their fuccefs, paffed moraffes, climbed precipices, faced batteries, and after a bloody and obftinate refiftance, totally defeated the Auftrians. They took their camp, military cheft, cannon, all the trophies of a complete victory. The lofs on the fide of the victor, as well as the vanquifhed, was very great; but both fides had yet a greater lofs in the death of two of the beft generals in Europe. M. Schwerin was killed at the age of eighty-two with the colonel's ftandard in his hand at the head of his regiment. M. Brown received a wound, which, from the chagrin he fuffered rather than from its own nature, proved mortal.

About

About 40,000 of the Auſtrian army took refuge in Prague. The reſt fled different ways. The King of Pruſſia loſt no time to inveſt the place, and to cut off all ſuccours. If on one hand ſuch an immenſe garriſon made an attack unadviſeable, on the other that formidable number itſelf ſeemed to make the reduction of the place by famine the more certain. The King of Pruſſia not relying ſolely on this, prepared to bombard the town. On the 29th of May, at midnight, after a moſt dreadful ſtorm of rain and thunder, as if it were to diſplay how much more ruinous the malice of men may be, than the greateſt terrors of nature, on the ſignal of a rocket, four batteries, which diſcharged every twenty-four hours two hundred and eighty-eight bombs, beſides a vaſt multitude of red hot balls, began to pour deſtruction on that unfortunate city, which was ſoon in flames in every part. The garriſon made a vigorous defence, and one well conducted and deſperate ſally: but they were repulſed with great loſs. The principal magiſtrates, burghers. and clergy, ſeeing their city on the point of being reduced to an heap of rubbiſh, made the moſt moving ſupplications to the commander to liſten to terms. The commander was deaf to their prayers. Twelve thouſand of the moſt uſeleſs mouths were driven out of the city. The Pruſſians forced them in again. The affairs of the Empreſs ſeemed verging to inevitable deſtruction; a whole army was upon the point of ſurrendering priſoners of war; the capital of Bohemia on the point of being taken, and with it all the reſt of that flouriſhing kingdom. The ſanguine friends of the King of Pruſſia began to compute the diſtance to Vienna.

In this deſperate ſituation of affairs, Leopold Count Daun entered on the ſtage, and began to turn the fortune of the war. This general never had commanded in chief before; but he was formed, by a long courſe of experience in various parts of Europe, under the greateſt generals and in the moſt illuſtrious ſcenes of action. Though of a very noble family, he had without the leaſt aſſiſtance from court favour, riſen inſenſibly by the ſlow gradation of mere merit, with much eſteem and without any noiſe. This general arrived within a few miles of Prague, the day after the great battle. He collected the fugitive parties of the Auſtrian army, and retired to a poſt of great ſtrength, from whence he fed the troops in Prague with hopes of relief. But as no man better underſtood the ſuperiority of the Pruſſian troops, and as he was ſenſible of the impreſſion which the late defeat had left upon his men, he carefully avoided to precipitate matters by an haſty action. He knew that the ſituation he had choſen would embarraſs the Pruſſians; that a large party of their army muſt be always employed to watch him; that this would weaken their efforts againſt the great body ſhut up in Prague, whilſt his own forces gained time to recover their ſpirits, and to increaſe in ſtrength by the daily ſuccours, which his court exerted all their powers to ſend him: with theſe ideas he waited in his entrenched camp at Colin, to act as events ſhould direct.

The King of Pruſſia was not leſs ſenſible than Count Daun of the effect of this conduct. He determined at all adventures to diſlodge him from the poſt he held; but whether it was that the King feared to weaken his army, which had actually an army to besiege, or whether he was blinded by a train of uniform success, which made him believe his arms irresistible under every disadvantage, or whatever were his motives or necessities, the whole army employed in this undertaking, including the Prince of Bevern's corps, did not exceed 32000 men, cavalry and infantry; and with these he was to attack 60,000 men, June 18. in one of the strongest situations which could be chosen, and defended by a vast train of artillery. Whatever the most impetuous and well regulated courage, whatever an order inspired by the remembrance of so many victories could do towards overcoming every kind of disadvantage, was done by the Prussians on this occasion. They returned to the attack seven times: in none of their victorious battles had their bravery been more conspicuous. Both the King's brothers were in the field; and they did every thing that could be expected from the King of Prussia's brothers. The King himself at the head of his cavalry, made one furious and concluding charge. Every thing was tried, and every thing was unsuccessful. The want of a sufficiently numerous infantry, in a ground where his cavalry could not support them, the want of an equal artillery, the advantageous situation of the enemy, their numbers, their bravery, their general, obliged the King of Prussia to quit the field. What his loss was is not so certain; it was undoubtedly great in the action, but still greater by desertions, and the innumerable ill consequences that follow a defeat.

Though the King of Prussia was defeated in this battle, and though he brought on his defeat, in a great measure, by some errors of his own, yet whatever small blemish his military skill might have suffered, his reputation was raised higher than ever, in the opinion of all judicious men, by the noble and candid manner in which he acknowledged his mistake, by the firmness with which he bore his misfortune, and by those astonishing strokes of genius and heroism, by which he retrieved his loss. The smiles of fortune makes conquerors; it is her malice which discovers heroes.

CHAP. IV.

Consequence of the battle of Colin. King of Prussia evacuates Bohemia. Battle of Hastenbeck. Convention of Closter-seven. Expedition to Rochfort. Russians enter Prussia. Austrians besiege Schweidnitz. French and Imperialists make incursions into Brandenburg. Swedes enter Pomerania. Battle of Norkitten. General Lehwald defeated. Bad condition of the King of Prussia.

NEVER was the old observation, *une bataille perdue a un mauvais cu*, more verified than in the consequences of the unfortunate battle of Colin. Though the King retired unpursued by his enemies, he was obliged to rejoin his own army before Prague without delay, and to raise the blockade of that place. The imprisoned Austrians with joy received Count Daun their deliverer, and their united forces became greatly superior to the Prussians. The King was in a short time obliged to evacuate Bohemia, and take refuge in Saxony. The Austrians

Auftrians harraffed him as much as poffible; but their armies, notwithftanding their great fuperiority, were not in a condition from their late fufferings to make any decifive attempt upon him, as the frontiers of Saxony abound with fituations eafily defended.

The King of Pruffia's misfortunes now poured in upon him at once, and from every quarter. The army commanded by the Duke of Cumberland, who continually retired before the French, after they had paffed the Wefer, came however to a refolution to make a ftand at Haftenbeck, within a few miles of Hammelen, where it was judged that the fuperior numbers of the enemy might be the leaft prejudicial; but notwithftanding the advantage of the fituation, the bravery of the Hanoverians, and the conduct of the D. the allied army was driven from the field of battle, and retreated towards Stade. July 25. By taking this route his Royal Highnefs was driven into a fort of *cul de fac*. Unable by his fituation to retire, or by his ftrength to advance, he was compelled to fign the remarkable capitulation of Clofterfeven, Sept. 8. by which 38000 Hanoverians laid down their arms, and were difperfed into different quarters of cantonment. The French army had a little before this changed its commander. Aug. 6. D'Etrees, the favourite of all the military men, was removed from the command, which was conferred on the Duke de Richlieu, who excelled him and all mankind in the profeffion of a courtier. The Hanoverians were now quite fubdued, and all the French force let loofe by this treaty, was ready to fall upon the King of Pruffia's dominions.

An enterprife was concerted in England againft the coaft of France, to make a diverfion in his favour, by drawing a part of the French army to the defence of their own country. England propofed to compafs another great defign, and which fhe had equally at heart, by the expedition, which was to give an effectual blow to the marine of France. The deftination of this armament was kept a profound fecret, and whilft it exercifed the penetration of all the politicians in Europe, it filled France with the moft ferious alarms. The Englifh fleet at laft appeared before Rochfort. Sept. 21 Some time was fpent before it could be refolved what plan was to be followed in the attack: at laft it was refolved to fecure the fmall ifle of Aix, from whence fome obftruction was apprehended to their landing. The ifland was foon reduced; but as a good deal of time was confumed in thefe deliberations and actions, the militia of the country had time to gather, and there was an appearance of two camps on the fhore. The commanders now took into confideration the badnefs of the coaft, the danger of landing, the time the enemy had to put the place in fuch a pofture of defence, as might make any fudden attempt, or *coup de main*, unfuccefsful: in confequence of thefe deliberations, they unanimoufly refolved to return without making Sept. 29 any attempt. The difappointment of the nation was equal to the fanguine hopes we had conceived; nothing could exceed the general difcontent. The military men blamed the plan of the expedition. The minifters, and with them the public voice, exclaimed at the execution. A *court of enquiry*, of officers of reputation, cenfured the commander; a *court martial*, of officers of reputation, ac-

acquitted him. The expedition ferved only in England to increafe and imbitter our diffenfions, and to turn our attention to vain difputes. It did nothing towards relieving the King of Pruffia.

The Ruffians, who had made for a long time a dilatory march, and feemed uncertain of their own refolutions, all at once haftened their motions. They entered the Ducal Pruffia under M. Apraxin and General Fermer, and marked their progrefs by a thoufand inhuman cruelties. A large body of Auftrians entered Silefia, and penetrated as far as Breflau. Then they made a turn backwards, and laid fiege to the important fortrefs of Schweidnitz, juftly confidered as the key of that duchy, which was the caufe of the war. Another body entered Lufatia, and made themfelves mafters of Zittau. Twenty-two thoufand Swedes pierced into the Pruffian Pomerania, took the towns of Anclam and Demmein, and laid the whole country under contribution. Richlieu, freed from all oppofition on the fide of Hanover, made his way into Halberftad, and the Old Marche of Brandenburg, firft exacting contributions, and then plundering the towns. The army of the Empire, reinforced by that of Prince de Soubife, after many delays, was at laft on full march to enter Saxony; this left the Auftrians at liberty to turn the greateft part of their forces to the reduction of Silefia. General Haddick pierced through Lufatia, paffed by the Pruffian armies, and fuddenly prefenting himfelf before the gates of Berlin, laid the King of Pruffia's capital under contribution; and though he retired on the approach of a body of Pruffians, yet he ftill kept poffeffion of his former poft, in order to interrupt the communication of the King with Silefia. The fate which feemed to have threatned the Emprefs fome months ago, was now looked upon as the certain lot of her antagonift. All his endeavours to retrieve his affairs had hitherto been equally brave and unfuccefsful. General Lehwald had orders at any hazard to engage the Ruffians: with thirty thoufand he attacked double that number ftrongly entrenched, at a place called Norkitten; but after feveral of thofe wonderful efforts, which the Pruffians alone know how to make, he was compelled to retire; but he retired in excellent order, without being purfued, having killed five times more of the enemy, than he had loft of his own men, and more formidable after his defeat, than the Ruffians after their victory. The King of Pruffia exerted himfelf upon every fide; his enemies almoft always fled before him; but whilft he purfued one body, another gained in fome other part upon him, and the winter came on faft, as his ftrength decayed, and his adverfaries multiplied from every quarter. The following letter, which appeared in the public papers about this time, paints the condition of that diftreffed monarch, in fo full a manner, that I fhall attempt no other defcription of it.

Aug. 30.

"Many perfons, who faw the King of Pruffia, when he paffed lately through Leipfic, cannot exprefs how much he is altered. They fay he is fo much worn away, that they fcarce knew him. This, indeed, is not to be wondered at; he hath not a body of iron, like Charles XII. and he endures as great fatigues as he did. He is as much on horfeback as Charles was, and often lies upon the ground. His inward ſufferings cannot be leſs than his outward. Let us caſt our eyes on a map of the Pruſſian dominions; and meaſure what he hath left of the many fair poſſeſſions he had in the month of April laſt, of which a ſpace of ſeven months hath ſtript him. Whence can he have men? he is ſhut out from the Empire; and from whence can he draw money? the duchy of Guelders, the duchy of Cleves, the principality of Moers, the county of Lingen, the county of Lipſtad, the principality of Minden, Eaſt-frieſland, Embden, and its infant company, part of the archbiſhoprick of Magdborgh, ſome other parts of the Marche, Ducal Pomerania, a great part of Sileſia, a great part of the kingdom of Pruſſia, Berlin itſelf, almoſt all his dominions, in ſhort, are either taken from him, or laid under contribution, and poſſeſſed by his enemies, who collect the public revenues, fatten on the contributions, and with the money which they draw from the electorate of Hanover, and other conqueſts, defray the expences of the war. This picture certainly differs greatly from that which the King of Pruſſia might have ſketched out, the day he took arms to enter Saxony. Add to this the Duke of Cumberland's convention, which deprived him of all his allies, and left him without any aſſiſtance whatever, excepting four or five hundred thouſand pounds ſterling, which the Britiſh parliament may give him. Add likewiſe ſome domeſtic uneaſineſſes."

CHAP. V.

Battle of Roſbach. Schweidnitz taken by the Auſtrians. Prince of Bevern attacked in his entrenchments. Breſlau taken by the Auſtrians. King of Pruſſia marches to Sileſia. The Battle of Liſſa. Breſlau retaken. Auſtrians driven out of Sileſia.

THIS was the King of Pruſſia's ſituation, when the will of Providence, and his own wonderful abilities, as wonderfully changed the ſcene. His majeſty deferred to bring on a deciſive action, diſtreſſed as his affairs were, until the approach of winter; had he marched to attack the Imperial army, whilſt it was at a conſiderable diſtance, he muſt either have left Saxony expoſed to the inſults of the Auſtrian parties, or have greatly weakened his own forces employed in the principal action. He therefore ſuffered the army of the Empire to advance to the frontiers of Miſnia, and even to threaten the ſiege of Leipſic, before he began to act againſt them: he however moved towards them, leaving an army in Luſatia to obſerve the Auſtrians. On his firſt motions, the enemy retired with precipitation. But when they had reinforced themſelves with numbers and courage ſufficient to perſuade them to advance, the King of Pruſſia in his turn retired. His reſolution ſeemed to have been to fight as near Miſnia as poſſible, and as deep in the winter as he conveniently might; for if he ſhould have the good fortune to ſucceed againſt the Imperial army, ſuch a blow at ſuch a ſeaſon, would effectually diſable them from acting any thing to his prejudice, for that year at leaſt; but if, on the contrary, he ſhould fail, Saxony was at hand, in which it would prove difficult for the enemy to make any impreſſion whilſt the winter continued. As for the time to be loſt by following this plan, and the advantage it would afford the Auſtrians in their deſigns on Sileſia, they were not to be compared with the advantages which the King received from it. He knew that Schweidnitz was ſtrong, and excellently provided; the Prince of Bevern was ſtrongly poſted near it to obſtruct the enemies operations; the winter would lean heavier on the beſiegers; and on the whole he had reaſon to truſt that his troops, animated by his own preſence and example, would prove far ſuperior to the enemy, in enduring all the hardſhips of a winter campaign.

After ſome time ſpent in various movements, between the allied army of the Imperialiſts and French on one ſide, and the Pruſſians on the other, the King reſolved to give battle to his enemies, who were now advanced to the confines of Miſnia. On the 24th of October, the King had taken his reſolution; at that time his army happened to be divided into ſeveral corps, ſome of them at a diſtance of no leſs than twenty leagues aſunder; yet ſuch were the ſpirit and excellent diſpoſition of the Pruſſians, that the junction of all theſe corps was fully effected on the 27th, and the King advanced towards the enemy. The enemy fell back at his approach, and repaſſed the Sala; they were followed cloſe. Nov. 5. The two armies met near the village of Roſbach.

The united army, commanded by the Prince of Saxe Hilburghauſen and the Prince of Soubiſe, was 50,000 men compleat. But the troops of the Circles were new raiſed, and many of them not well affected to the ſervice, nor to their French allies. The Pruſſians did not amount to 25,000; but then they were Pruſſians, and led on by the King of Pruſſia. As ſoon as the armies were formed, and the battle going to begin, which was to decide the fate of ſo many nations, and to determine between force and virtue, the King of Pruſſia addreſſed his troops nearly in the following words.

'My dear friends, the hour is 'come, in which all that is, and 'all that ought to be dear to us, 'depends upon the ſwords which 'are now drawn for the battle. 'Time permits me to ſay but little; nor is there occaſion to ſay 'much. You know that there is 'no labour, no hunger, no cold, 'no watching, no danger, that I 'have not ſhared with you hitherto; and you now ſee me ready 'to lay down my life with you 'and for you. All I aſk is the 'ſame pledge of fidelity and affection that I give. And let me 'add, not as an incitement to your 'courage, but as a teſtimony of 'my own gratitude, that from 'this hour, until you go into 'quarters, your pay ſhall be double. Acquit yourſelves like men, 'and put your confidence in 'God." The effect of this ſpeech was ſuch as cannot be deſcribed. The general emotion burſt in an univerſal ſhout, and the looks and demeanor of the men were animated to a ſort of heroic phrenſy. In this diſpoſition, which prognoſticated the ſucceſs, the engagement began.

In the beginning of the action the French cavalry came on with great ſpirit, but they were repulſed; ſome

ome regiments having gained an eminence defended themſelves bravely, but in the end they were totally routed. The infantry, both French and Imperialiſts, made but a faint reſiſtance. The King of Pruſſia in perſon expoſed to the hotteſt fire, led on his troops; the enemy gave way in every part; they were ſeized with a panic, and fled in the utmoſt diſorder. They left 3000 men dead on the field of battle; 63 pieces of cannon, many colours. Eight French generals, 250 officers of different ranks, and 6000 private men were taken. Night alone ſaved from total deſtruction the ſcattered remains of an army, that in the morning was ſo numerous and ſo formidable.

I have not undertaken on this, nor ſhall I undertake upon any other occaſion, in theſe preliminary chapters, to enter into the detail of all the various manœuvres of every battle; they are matters little underſtood by, and little intereſting to, the generality of readers. Beſides the accounts are ſometimes inaccurate, and ſeldom or never conſiſtent with each other.

The glorious ſucceſs of the battle of Rosbach, was ſuch as hardly wanted to be improved; the enemy was left totally incapable of action. The king was ſet free on that ſide; but it was a freedom which gave him no reſpite from his labours; it only gave him an opportunity of undergoing new labours in another part. The Auſtrians had a vaſt force, and had now began to make a proportionable progreſs in Sileſia. The dependence which the King had upon the fidelity of his generals there, ſeemed ſhaken by ſomething which then appeared, and ſtill ſeems ambiguous in their conduct. The Auſtrians after a ſiege from the 27th of October to the 11th of November, carried on under infinite difficulties and with a prodigious loſs, had reduced Schweidnitz, and obliged the Pruſſian garriſon of 4000 men to ſurrender priſoners of war. Soon after as they had intelligence of the victory of Rosbach, and knew that the King of Pruſſia was on full march to the relief of Sileſia, the Auſtrians reſolved to loſe no time to attack the Prince of Bevern in his ſtrong camp under the walls of Breſlau. A treble ſuperiority incited them to this attempt. They attacked the Prince's army with great reſolution, and their attack was ſuſtained with amazing intrepidity. Nov. 22 The ſlaughter of the Auſtrians was prodigious. A great part of their army had retired from the field of battle, and the reſt were preparing to retire; when all at once the Pruſſian generals unexpectedly took the ſame reſolution. A part of their army had ſuffered a great deal in the engagement. They became apprehenſive of a total defeat in caſe their intrenchments ſhould be forced in any part. With theſe ideas they retreated from the ſtrong poſt they occupied, and retired behind the Oder. The Auſtrians returning, with aſtoniſhment ſaw themſelves maſters of the field of battle, which they had but juſt been obliged to relinquiſh. What is remarkable, and what gave riſe to many conjectures, the Prince of Bevern going to reconnoitre without eſcort, and attended only by a groom, was taken two days after the battle by an advanced party of Croats, a ſmall body of whom had croſſed the Oder.

This advantage, though dearly bought, was immediately followed with many others. Breſlau Nov. 24 the capital of Sileſia immediately ſurrendered, where, as well as at Schweidnitz, they found vaſt ſtores of proviſion, ammuuition and money. All Sileſia was on the point of falling into their hands. Fortuns ſeems every where to have thrown the King of Pruſſia's affairs into diſtraction, in order to raiſe, and as it were to round his glory in eſtabliſhing them; and to have been even ſo jealous of his honour as not to permit his own excellent generals and incomparable troops to triumph any where but in his own preſence.

The King immediately after the battle of Rosbach, with thoſe troops which he had a few days before collected from places an hundred miles diſtant from each other, began a march of upwards of two hundred more, and led them from engaging one ſuperior army, to engage another ſtill more ſuperior; from danger to hardſhip, and from hardſhip to renewed danger. In a moſt rapid march he paſſed through Thuringia, through Miſnia, through Luſatia, in ſpite of the efforts of the generals Haddick and Marſhal, who were poſted in Luſatia to obſtruct him; and entering Sileſia arrived the 2d of December at Parchwitz upon the Oder. Here he was joined by the Prince of Bevern's corps who croſſed that river to meet him.

About this time an incident happened which was very remarkable; one of theſe agreeable adventures that relieve the mind amidſt the perpetual horror that attends a narrative of battles and bloodſhed. The garriſon of Schweidnitz had ſeen, with the greateſt reluctance, the capitulation which bound their hands from the ſervice of their King and country. Whilſt the Auſtrians were conducting them to priſon, on their route they chanced to hear of the victory their maſter had gained at Rosbach; animated with this news, they unanimouſly roſe upon the eſcort which conducted them, and which happened not to be very ſtrong, and entirely diſperſed it. Thus freed, they marched on not very certain of their way, in hope to rejoin ſome corps of the Pruſſian troops. The ſame fortune which freed them, led them directly to the army commanded by the King himſelf, which was haſtening to their relief. Great was the joy on both ſides at this unexpected meeting, for the priſoners had heard nothing of his majeſty's march. This little incident, whilſt it added a conſiderable ſtrength to the army, added likewiſe to its ſpirit, and ſeemed an happy omen of ſucceſs in the future engagement.

As his Pruſſian majeſty approached to Breſlau, the Auſtrians confiding in their ſuperiority, abandoned their ſtrong camp (the ſame which had been occupied by the Prince of Bevern) and reſolved to give the King battle. He was marching with the utmoſt diligence not to diſappoint them; and they met near the village of Leuthen. Dec. 5. The ground which the Auſtrians occupied was very advantageous, and every advantage of the ſituation was improved to the utmoſt, by the diligence and ſkill of Count Daun; who remembering that he was the only general who had ever carried the field from the King of Pruſſia, knew better than any body how difficult it was to obtain ſuch a victory. All the diſpoſitions were made accordingly; the ground they occupied was a plain, except that in ſome parts it had ſmall eminences; theſe they ſurrounded with artillery; the ground was alſo interſperſed with thickets, which

which they fought to turn to their advantage. On their right and left were hills on which they planted batteries of cannon. The ground in their front was interfected by many caufeways; and to make the whole more impracticable, the Auftrians had felled a vaft many trees, and fcattered them in the way. The King of Pruffia was not terrified with this fituation, nor with the confcioufnefs that above 70,000 excellent troops commanded by Count Daun were fo pofted. The Pruffians, who did not exceed as it is faid 36,000 men, attacked them with their ufual refolution. It was almoft impoffible at the beginning of the engagement for the Pruffian horfe to act, on account of the impediments we have juft mentioned, but a moft judicious difpofition of the king himfelf overcame that difadvantage; he had in his firft difpofitions placed four battalions behind the cavalry of his right wing, forefeeing that General Nadafti, who was placed with a corps de referve on the enemy's left, defigned to take him in flank. It happened as he had forefeen; that general's horfe attacked the King's right wing with great fury; but he was received with fo fevere a fire from the four battalions, that he was obliged to retire in diforder. Then the King's flank well covered and fupported was enabled to act with fuch order and vigour, that the enemy's right was obliged to give way. The Pruffian artillery which was incomparably ferved, and filenced that of the enemy, concurred to maintain the King's infantry, and to enable them to act in grounds where their horfe could give them but little affiftance. The Auftrians made a gallant refiftance during the whole battle. The panic of the enemy did not here, as at Rosbach, do half the bufinefs; every foot of ground was well difputed. The Auftrians rallied all their forces about Leuthen, which was defended upon all fides with intrenchments aud redoubts. After reiterated attacks made with the utmoft impetuofity, and fuftained with great firmnefs, the Pruffians maftered the poft; then the Auftrians fled on all parts; they were entirely routed. The King purfued them to Liffa. 6000 of the Auftrians were flain, 15,000 were made prifoners; and an immenfe artillery, upwards of 200 pieces of cannon were taken.

This great and decifive action was fought on the very fame day of the next month after the no lefs important and decifive battle of Rosbach. The confequences that followed the action of Leuthen, declared the entirenefs of the victory. Notwithftanding the rigour of the feafon, the fiege of Breflau was immediately undertaken, and profecuted with fuch fpirit, that by the 29th of December it furrendered; and with it furrendered the garrifon of 13000 men prifoners of war; the blockade of Schweidnitz was formed as clofely as the inclemency of the winter would permit; whilft the Pruffian parties not only repoffeffed thofe parts of Silefia which belonged to the King, but penetrating into the Auftrian divifion, reduced Jagerndorf, Troppau and Tetfchen, and left to the Emprefs Queen, except a forlorn garrifon in Schweidnitz, no fort of footing in that country, in which a few days before fhe reckoned her dominion perfectly eftablifhed.

CHAP. VI.

Ruffians and Swedes retire. Hanoverians refume their arms. Cruelty of the French. Condition of their army. Caftle of Harburg befieged. Recapitulation of the events of the year 1757.

AS the misfortunes of his Pruffian majefty after the battle of Colin, came on him all at once, fo his fucceffes after his victories at Rosbach and Liffa, flowed upon him all at once likewife, and in a full tide. The Ruffians, tho' they had repulfed General Lehwald, fuffered fo much in that action, and their barbarous method of making war had fo deftroyed the country, that they feemed to themfelves to have no way of fafety left but in retiring out of the Pruffia territories. This extraordinary retreat of fo great an army, and fo lately victorious, and ftill poffeffed of a good feaport in the country, could fcarcely be accounted for on thofe motives we have affigned, and aftonifhed all Europe, whilft it left General Lehwald at liberty to turns his arms into Pomerania againft the Swedes. The Swedes on this occafion did nothing worthy of their ancient military fame; but every where retiring, left the Pruffians an eafy conqueft, not only of the Pruffian but of every part of the Swedifh Pomerania, excepting the port of Stralfund; they left their allies of Mecklenbourg quite expofed to all the refentment of the King of Pruffia, who chaftifed them with the moft fevere contributions and levies. The French who had been ravaging the Old Marche of Brandenburg, evacuated that country immediately after the battle of Rofbach. But one of the greateft revolutions of fortune in the war, and one of the moft glorious and important confequences of that victory, was that the Hanoverian troops were enabled to refume their arms.

From the moment the capitulation of Clofter-feven was figned, the Duke de Richlieu, who came to the command only to reap the advantage, and fully the honour of another's conqueft, feemed to think of nothing but how to repair from the plunder of the unhappy Hanoverians, the fortune which he had fhattered by a thoufand vices. The moft exorbitant contributions were levied with the moft inflexible feverity; every exaction which was fubmitted to, only produced a new one ftill more extravagant; and all the orderly methods of plunder did not exempt them from the pillage, licentioufnefs and infolence of the French foldiery. However, in juftice to merit, we muft except from this general charge the conduct of the Duke de Randan, governor of Hanover for the French; who faved the capital of the electorate from utter ruin by the ftrictnefs of all his difcipline, by the prudence, the juftice and moderation of all his conduct; a conduct which does more real honour to his name than the moft fplendid victories.

The Duke de Richlieu's rapacioufnefs and oppreffion, whilft they leaned fo heavily on the conquered people, did the conquering army no kind of fervice. Intent only on plunder, which he did not confine to the enemy, he relaxed every part of military difcipline; and that numerous army which M. d'Etrees had

had sustained, and brought in health and spirits through the dismal desarts of Westphalia, under all the opposition of a skilful adversary, were now, in full peace, in the quiet possession of a conquered and plentiful country, reduced in their numbers, decayed in their health and their spirits, without cloaths, without subsistence, without order, without arms. In this condition they began at last to perceive that the Hanoverians, with the yoke of the capitulation about their necks, were still formidable. As they had broke almost every article of that treaty, they made no scruple to add another breach in order to secure them in all the rest. They attempted actually to take their arms from the Hanoverian and Hessian troops. These gallant troops, who had with a silent grief and indignation seen the distresses of their ruined country, were ravished to find that the victory at Rosbach encouraged their sovereign to resent at last this and all the other indignities they had suffered. They began to collect and to act, and under the command of the gallant Prince Ferdinand of Brunswick, reinforced with a body of Prussian troops, they broke from their confinement. They reduced the town of Harburg, and laid close siege to the castle, which it must be owned was defended very bravely. In all other respects the French did not seem in a condition to maintain their ground any where. Those troops, which a few months before had so submitted as to make it necessary to declare that they were *not prisoners of war* in order to explain their condition, were now on the point of pushing their adversaries to almost the same streights. Such was the force of French military discipline, and such the triumphs of Voltaire's hero.

The King of Prussia now saw the full effect of his counsels and his labours. His dominions were freed; his allies were enabled to assist him; and his enemies defeated, broken, and flying every where before him. In what light posterity will view these things is uncertain; we, under whose eyes, as we may say, they were atchieved, scarcely believed what we had seen. And perhaps in all the records of time, the compass of a single year, on the scene of a single country, never contained so many striking events, never displayed so many revolutions of fortune; revolutions not only beyond what might have been expected, but far beyond what the most sagacious foresight, reasoning from experience, and the nature of things, could possibly have imagined. The King of Prussia at first triumphant; the whole power of the Austrians totally defeated; their hopes utterly ruined: then their affairs suddenly re-established, their armies victorious, and the King of Prussia in his turn hurled down; defeated; abandoned by his allies; surrounded by his enemies; on the very edge of despair: then all at once raised beyond all hope, he sees the united Austrian, Imperial, and French power levelled with the ground. 40,000 Hanoverians, a whole army, submit to 80,000 French, and are only *not* prisoners of war. The French are peaceable masters of all the country between the Weser and the Elbe: anon, these subdued Hanoverians resume their arms; they recover their country, and the French in a little time think themselves not secure to the eastward of the Rhine. 400,000 men in action. Six pitched battles fought. Three great armies annihilated. The French army reduced and vanquished ed without fighting. The Russians victorious, and flying as if they had been vanquished. A confederacy, not of smaller potentates to humble one great power, but of five the greatest powers on earth to reduce one small potentate; all the force of these powers exerted and baffled. It happened as we have related; and it is not the history of a century, but of a single campaign.

CHAP. VII.

Preparations for an expedition to Louisbourg. Laid aside. Fort William-Henry taken. Exploits of Admiral Watson and Colonel Clive in India. Chandenagore a French fort taken. Victory over the Nabob. Nabob taken and beheaded. Revolution in Bengal. Treaty advantageous to the East-India company. Admiral Watson dies.

WITH regard to the part we had in the transactions of this year, though it was not so full of striking events, nor does it afford such a splendid subject for narrative, yet it is interesting to an English reader, and may perhaps prove more instructive; as it shews us in so strong a light, the miserable consequences of our political divisions, which produced a general unsteadiness in all our pursuits, and infused a languor and inactivity into all our military operations. For, whilst our commanders abroad knew not who were to reward their services or punish their neglects, and were not assured in what light even the best of their actions would be considered, (having reason to apprehend that they might not be judged of as they were in themselves, but as their appearances might answer the end of some ruling faction;) they naturally wanted that firmness and that enterprizing resolution, without which the best capacity, and intentions the most honest, can do nothing in war. The attachment of most men to their parties, weakened their affection to their country. It has been imagined that ministers did not always wish success even to their own schemes, lest obnoxious men should acquire credit by the execution of them; as it was suspected that officers even at the expence of their own reputation did not exert their faculties to the utmost, lest a disagreeable ministerial system should establish the credit of its counsels by the vigour of their operations. For my own part, I think that these refinements, in which there is often as much malice discovered as penetration, have carried the matter infinitely too far. But certain it is, that the spirit of personal parties and attachments, never carried to greater lengths than at that time, proved of very bad consequence, if it had no other effect than to raise and to give a colour to such suspicions as we have just mentioned. Whatever was the cause, it is most certain, that our success in America this year, no more answered to the greatness of our preparations and our hopes than it did in the two preceding.

The attack upon Crown Point, which had been a principal object of our attention in the beginning, seemed at this time to be laid aside; and an expedition to Louisbourg, undoubtedly a more considerable object in itself, supplied its place. Lord Loudon was to command the land

land forces in this expedition; Admiral Holborne the navy. The former left New York with a body of 6000 men, and
July 9.
failed to Halifax, where he was joined by the latter, who had failed from Corke on the 7th of May with a confiderable fleet, and much the fame number of land forces, which his lordfhip had brought from New York. When the united armies and fleets were on the point of departing for Louifbourg, news arrived at Halifax, that the Breft fleet, confifting of feventeen fhips of the line befides frigates, with great fupplies of military ftores, provifions, and men, were arrived at the harbour which they were preparing to attack. This news immediately fufpended their preparations. Councils of war were held one after another. The refult of the whole was, that as the place was fo well reinforced, the fleet of the French rather fuperior to our navy, and the feafon fo far advanced, it was the more prudent courfe to defer the enterprize to a more favourable opportunity. This refolution feems to have been the moft eligible in their circumftances, becaufe the council of war was almoft unanimous in it.

Lord Loudon returned to New York, and the admiral now freed from the care of the tranfports fet fail for Louifbourg, in hopes as it was faid, of drawing the French fleet to an engagement. But upon what grounds this hope was conceived, I confefs I cannot fee; as it could not be imagined, that the French fleet, having no fort of occafion to fight in order to protect Louifbourg, would chufe out of a bravado to bring on an unneceffary battle. However it was, the Englifh fquadron continued to cruife off that harbour until the 25th of September, when they were overtaken by a terrible ftorm, in which one of our fhips was loft, eleven difmafted, and the reft returned to England in a very fhattered condition. This was the end of the expedition to Louifbourg, from which fo much was expected. But it was not the worft confequence which attended it.

Since Ofwego had been taken, the French remained entirely mafters of all the lakes, and we could do nothing to obftruct their collecting the Indians from all parts, and obliging them to act in their favour. But our apprehenfions, (or what fhall they be called?) did more in favour of the French than their conquefts. Not fatisfied with the lofs of that important fortrefs, we ourfelves abandoned to the mercy of the enemy all the country of the Five nations, the only body of Indians who preferved even the appearance of friendfhip to us. The forts we had at the Great carrying Place were demolifhed; Wood Creek was induftrioufly ftopped up and filled with logs; by which it became evident to all thofe who knew that country, that our communication with our allied Indians was totally cut off; and what was worfe, our whole frontier left perfectly uncovered to the irruption of the enemies favages, who foon availed themfelves of our errors. For after the removal of thefe barriers, and the taking of Fort William-Henry, of which we fhall fpeak prefently, they deftroyed with fire and fword the fine fettlements which we poffeffed on the Mohawks river, and on thofe grounds called the German flats. Thus with a vaft increafe of our forces, and the cleareft fuperiority over the enemy, we only abandoned our allies, expofed our people, and relinquifhed a large and valuable tract of country. The

French

French ſoon made us feel effectually the want of what we had loſt, and what we had thrown away.

A conſiderable fort called Fort William-Henry, had been built on the ſouthern edge of the Lake George, in order to command that lake and to cover our frontiers; a garriſon of 2500 men defended it. General Webb with about 4000 men was poſted at no great diſtance. No ſooner had the French learned that my Lord Loudon with the body of the army was gone on the Louiſbourg expedition, than they prepared to take advantage of his abſence. They drew together all the forces which they had at Crown Point, Ticonderoga, and the adjacent poſts; they added a conſiderable body of Canadians, and a greater number of Indians than they had ever yet employed; the whole made near 8000 men. With theſe and a very good artillery, Monſieur Montcalm prepared to beſiege Fort William-Henry. It is ſaid that the advances of this commander were not made with ſo much ſecrecy as to prevent General Webb from having early intelligence of his motions; but unfortunately no credit being given to this intelligence, orders were not ſent to collect the militia in ſufficient time, which in conjunction with his own forces, and with thoſe in the fort, had either obliged the French to relinquiſh their attempt, or to have made it a very great hazard.

Aug. 3. But the ſiege being now regularly formed, and the beſiegers meeting but little oppoſition from within, and no diſturbance at all from without, the

9th. place was in ſix days ſurrendered by the advice of General Webb; whoſe intercepted letter M. Montcalm ſent into the fort.

The garriſon marched out with their arms, and engaged not to ſerve during eighteen months. The French ſavages paid no regard to the capitulation, but falling upon our men as they marched out, dragged away the little effects they had left, hawling the Indians and Blacks in our ſervice out of their ranks, ſcalping ſome, carrying off others, and committing a thouſand outrages and barbarities, from which the French commander endeavoured in vain to reſtrain them. All this was ſuffered by 2000 men with arms in their hands, from a diſorderly crew of ſavages. However the greateſt part of our men, though in a bad condition, got to Fort Edward, ſome by flight; ſome having ſurrendered themſelves to the French, were by them ſent home ſafe. The enemy demoliſhed the fort, carried off the proviſion, ammunition, artillery, and the veſſels which we had prepared on the lake, and departed without attempting any thing further. Neither was any thing further attempted on our ſide. And thus was finiſhed the third campaign in North America, where we had actually near 20,000 regular troops, a great number of provincial forces, and a great naval power of upwards of twenty ſhips of the line.

A war betwen the maritime powers is felt in all parts of the world. Not content with inflaming Europe and America, the diſſentions of the French and Engliſh purſued the tracks of their commerce, and the Ganges felt the fatal effects of a quarrel on the Ohio. But here the ſcene is changed greatly to the advantage of our nation; the bravery of Admiral Watſon and Colonel Clive, re-eſtabliſhed the military honour of the Engliſh, which was ſinking there as it had done in all other places. Admiral Watſon with

with no more than three ſhips of the line, ſailed from Madraſs, and after a tedious voyage arrived at the port
Dec. 5. of Balaſore in the kingdom of Bengal, where ſtrengthening his force with what recruits he could draw together, he entered the Ganges, and after a ſhort reſiſtance made himſelf maſter
Jan. 30. of Buſbudgiafort, which commanded that part of the river. This opened him a paſſage to the fort of Calcutta, the late principal ſettlement of the company in Bengal, and the ſcene of the deplorable ſufferings of ſo many of our unfortunate countrymen. Animated with revenge at the affecting ſight of this place, our ſhips and land forces attacked it with ſo much ſpirit, that the Indians ſurrendered it on the ſame day it was approached. A few days after Hugly, ſituated higher up on the Ganges, was reduced with as little difficulty.

The Nabob, who ſaw that the torrent of the Engliſh valour could not be reſiſted by ſuch feeble dams as forts defended by Indians, drew down a whole army conſiſting of 10,000 horſe, and 12,000 foot, to drive them from their conqueſts. Infinitely inferior as our troops were
Feb. 5. in number, they did not heſitate to attack the Nabob's army. Though our forces did not entirely rout the Indians, yet they made a great ſlaughter amongſt them; and they had ſo much the
9th. advantage of the field, that the Nabob was in a ſhort time glad to conclude a treaty of peace, by which the Engliſh Eaſt India company was re-eſtabliſhed in all its ancient privileges; an immunity from all taxes was granted, and a reſtitution promiſed for all that the trade had ſuffered in the taking of Calcutta.

When all obſtructions on the ſide of the Indians was removed, and the company's officers had taken poſſeſſion of their ancient eſtabliſhments, the admiral turned his arms againſt the French. He reſolved to attack Chandenagore, ſituated ſomewhat higher on the river than Calcutta; a place of conſiderable ſtrength, and the principal ſettlement of the French in that part in the Eaſt Indies. In this expedition Colonel Clive commanded 700 Europeans, and 1600 Black ſoldiers. The admirals Watſon and Pocock commanded the fleet, if it may be called a fleet, which conſiſted of no more than three ſhips of the line, the Kent, the Tyger, and the Saliſbury. The French prepared in the beſt manner they could to receive them, and ſunk ſeveral large veſſels both above and below their fort; but the admiral having by carefully ſounding, found a ſafe paſſage without being driven to the neceſſity of weighing up any of the ſhips, made ſo ſevere a fire upon the fort, in which he was ſeconded by Colonel Clive's batteries on the
Mar. 24. ſhore, that the place capitulated in leſs than three hours. 500 Europeans, and 700 Blacks ſurrendered priſoners of war; 183 pieces of cannon were found in the place, beſides a conſiderable value in goods and money. Four forts coſt our troops no more than four days to reduce them.

The judicious timeing of theſe ſeveral operations, as well as thoſe which followed, was not leſs laudable than the gallant ſpirit with which they were executed. Before the French were alarmed, care was taken to repoſſeſs all the poſts we formerly held; to humble the Nabob by ſome effectual blow; and by a treaty to tie up his hands from acting

ing againſt us. This Prince had ſhewed himſelf from the moment of *his ſigning that treaty, very little* inclined to abide by the ſtipulations he had made. He indeed promiſed abundantly, but always deferred the performance upon ſuch frivolous pretences, as evidently demonſtrated his ill intentions. The Engliſh commanders underſtood this proceeding perfectly well; but they reſolved to diſſemble their ſenſe of it, until they had broken the French power in this province, which they had greater reaſon to dread, ſmall as it was, than all the armies of the Nabob. When they had fully accompliſhed this by the taking of Chandenagore, they deliberated whether they ought not to recommence hoſtilities with the Indians. A reſolution in the affirmative had been attended with great difficulty and danger, if a moſt fortunate incident had not helped to enſure ſucceſs.

The Nabob Suraja Doula, the ſame who had the laſt year taken Calcutta, had ſhewn to his own ſubjects the ſame violent and perfidious ſpirit, which formerly and ſtill diſtreſſed the Engliſh. His generals were moſtly diſcontented, and ſome of them entered into a conſpiracy againſt him. Jaffier Ali Cawn one of his principal officers, a man of great power and intereſt, was at the head of this conſpiracy. As ſoon as their deſigns were ripened, they communicated them to the Engliſh government in Calcutta, praying their aſſiſtance. The chiefs there did not heſitate long what party they ſhould take; they entered into a treaty with Jaffier Ali Cawn and the conſpirators; and in conſequence of this treaty, our troops immediataly took the field under Colonel Clive. The admiral undertook to garriſon the fort of Chandenagore with his ſeamen, in order to leave the greater number of land forces for the ex*pedition. A detachment of fifty* ſeamen with their officers were added to ſerve as gunners. A 20 gun ſhip was ſtationed above Hugly, in order to preſerve a communication between Colonel Clive and the admiral.

Their preliminary meaſures being thus judiciouſly taken, they advanced up the river, and in a few days brought the Nabob's army of about 20,000 men, excluſive of thoſe who favoured the conſpirators, to an action, which was deciſive in favour of the Engliſh. Two conſiderable bodies commanded by Jaffier and Roy Dolub remained inactive in the engagement. The Nabob ſeeing himſelf ruined by the treachery of his officers, and the cowardice of his troops, fled with the few who continued faithful to him. June 22.

Jaffier Ali Cawn now declared himſelf openly; and entering Muxadavat the capital of the province with an army of his friends and victorious allies, he was placed by Colonel Clive in the ancient ſeat of the Nabobs, and received the homage of all ranks of people as Suba of Bengal, Bahar, and Orixa. The depoſed Nabob was ſoon after made priſoner, and put to death in his priſon by the conqueror. In about thirteen days this great revolution was accompliſhed; and with leſs force and trouble than often is required to take a petty village in Germany, was transferred the government of a vaſt kingdom, yielding in its dimenſions to few in Europe, but to none in the fertility of its ſoil, the number of its inhabitants, and the richneſs of its commerce. By the alliance with the new Nabob, and by the reduction of Chandenagore, the French were entirely driven out of 26.

of Bengal and all its dependencies. This was one of the articles of the treaty. By the other articles, a perpetual alliance offenſive and defenſive was made between the parties. The territories of the company were enlarged, and upwards of two millions ſterling was ſtipulated to be paid as an indemnification to the Eaſt-India company, and the ſufferers in the taking of Calcutta. The new Nabob full of gratitude to thoſe to whom he owed his dignity, gave beſides the above large ſums about 600,000 pounds, as a gratuity to the ſea ſquadron and the troops. However ſhort of expectation our enterpriſes in America fell this year, thoſe in the Eaſt-Indies greatly exceeded every thing we could hope from the forces which were employed. And it may be doubted whether all the great powers engaged in the preſent bloody wars in Europe, in which ſuch torrents of blood are ſpilled, and ſo many millions of treaſure are waſted, will in the concluſion reap amongſt them ſo much ſolid profit as the Engliſh Eaſt-India company did with an handful of men in a ſhort campaign. The joy of the nation at theſe ſignal ſucceſſes, was not a little damped by the death of Admiral Watſon, who loſt his life by the unwholeſomeneſs of the country, in which he had eſtabliſhed a great and laſting reputation. Colonel Clive ſtill lives to enjoy the fortune and honour he has acquired by his gallant actions. Aug. 16.

CHAP. VIII.

French retire out of Hanover. The taking of Hoya. Minden taken. Diſtreſs of the French. Generoſity of the Duke de Randan. The French retire beyond the Rhine. Recovery of Embden by Commodore Holmes.

1758. ALL the bloodſhed of the laſt campaign in Germany, and thoſe loſſes which both the victorious and vanquiſhed felt ſo very ſeverely, produced no overtures towards peace from any of the powers at war. And perhaps nothing ſo ſingular ever happened, as that ſo many ſtates, united, if not againſt their real intereſts, yet againſt all their former habits of connection, full of ſo many occaſions of jealouſy, abounding with matter of complaint againſt each other, and even involved in misfortunes which uſually deſtroy a mutual confidence, that not one of theſe powers either from fear, or hope, or wearineſs, or levity, deſiſted from their hoſtilities againſt the King of Pruſſia; nor did that monarch acquire one ally more by the admiration of his ſucceſſes, than he had formerly gained thro' compaſſion to his misfortunes. All the confederates preſerved the ſame attachment to each other, to him the ſame animoſity. It is equally a matter of great admiration: how the reſources even of theſe great ſtates, could keep pace with their ambition, and in a few months ſupply the place of great armies almoſt wholly deſtroyed. The King of Pruſſia by his victories had added to his natural reſources. The reſources were more conſiderable than is commonly imagined; and the poſſeſſion of Saxony which yielded him great ſupplies, ſaved his own revenue. He was indeed not quite ſo freſh as at the beginning of the war; but then the condition of the enemy was in many reſpects far worſe than his. His troops had beſides acquired a high reputation and a clear ſuperiority over all others. The conſideration, however, of an army greatly harraſſed, and a moſt ſevere winter, obliged him to reſtrain his ardor, and to attempt nothing againſt the Auſtrains in the months of January, February, and March. The ſame inaction, owing to much the ſame cauſes, prevailed amongſt the Hanoverians for a little time: but having been reinforced about the middle of February by a body of Pruſſian horſe, they put their whole army once more in motion.

The Duke de Richlieu had been recalled, and the Count of Clermont now commanded the French troops. This was their third commander in chief within the ſpace of a year; a circumſtance alone ſufficient to ſhew the unſteadineſs of their councils, and the irregularity of their operations. In effect, they every where retreated before the Hanoverians, whoſe main body marched on the right to the country of Bremen; whilſt a ſecond body under General Zaſtrow kept on the left towards Gifforn. They puſhed the French from poſt to poſt. They obliged them to evacuate Otterſberg, Bremen, and Werden. The caſtle of Rotterſberg was taken in ſix hours. A conſiderable detachment under Count Chabot was poſted at Hoya, a ſtrong fort upon the Weſer, and a place of ſuch conſequence that Prince Ferdinand reſolved to diſlodge the enemy from it. He appointed for that ſervice the hereditary Prince of Brunſwick, with four battalions of foot and ſome light horſe. This Prince, not twenty years of age, had already entered into the courſe of glory under the auſpices of his uncle, and full of ardor to ſignalize himſelf, with joy embraced the occaſion: and here he gave an earneſt of his fame, in one of the moſt lively and beſt conducted actions in the war. The firſt fruits of this young hero were ſuch as would have done honour to the maturity of the moſt experienced ſoldier.

The Prince had a broad and deep river to paſs. He had no means of tranſporting his men, but a ſingle float; ſo that a long time muſt be ſpent in getting them over; what was worſe, before half his troops were paſſed, a ſtrong wind aroſe, which rendered the float unſerviceable, and entirely cut off all communication between the Prince and the moſt conſiderable number of his party, whilſt the party he was going to attack was ſuperior to him, had his whole body been together. In this exigence the Prince came to a reſolution worthy of himſelf. He reſolved not to ſpend any time in attempts to bring over the reſt of his troops, much leſs to make any attempt to return to them; but to urge on boldly, in ſuch a manner as to poſſeſs the enemy with an opinion of his ſtrength, and to attack them briſkly before they could be undeceived. Therefore, between 4 and 5 o'clock in the morning, they marched with the utmoſt ſpeed directly to the town of Hoya When they were approached within a mile and an half of the place, another accident was on the point of defeating the whole enterpriſe. Their detachment fired by miſtake upon four of the enemies dragoons, who were patrolling; the firing was caught from one to another, and at laſt became general. This ſeemed more than enough to diſcover their motions and alarm the enemy. But the ſame ſpirit influenced the con-

Feb. 23.

duct

duct of every part of this affair; a bold countenance became neceſſary, and it was aſſumed; they marched with the utmoſt diligence to the town, and encountered the enemy at the bridge; a fierce fire, well ſupported on either ſide, enſued. The ground was ſuch, that the Prince could not bring up his whole detachment equally. Senſible of this diſadvantage, he formed a deſign to overcome it, as judicious as it was reſolute, which was to turn the enemy by attacking them in the rear; to execute this deſign, it was neceſſary to make a circuit about the town. Every thing ſucceeded: the attack on the enemies rear was made with bayonet fixed; a terrible ſlaughter enſued. The French abandoned the bridge, and fled in confuſion: the Prince having cleared the town of the enemy, joined the party he had left. The Count de Chabot threw himſelf with two battalions into the caſtle, with a reſolution to maintain himſelf there; but, in a little time, he capitulated, ſurrendering the place, his ſtores and magazines, his troops being permitted to march out. The Prince, who had no artillery, and who on account of the badneſs of the roads, deſpaired of bringing up heavy cannon, ſuffered them to depart. Six hundred and ſeventy men were made priſoners in the action, and a place of much importance, and which opened a paſſage over the Weſer, ſecured to the Hanoverians, with the loſs of leſs than 100 men killed and wounded. I have dwelt on this action, and deſcribed it as particularly as I could, though nothing deciſive in itſelf, becauſe it is not in pitched battles between great armies, where the moſt maſterly ſtrokes of conduct are always diſplayed; theſe leſſer affairs frequently call for as much or more of ſagacity, reſolution, and preſence of mind, in the commander; yet are they often ſlightly paſſed by, as matters of no conſequence, by the generality of people, who rather conſider the greatneſs of the event, than the ſpirit of the action.

Prince Ferdinand continued to advance, with his right on one ſide of the Weſer, and his left on the other; the French continued to retire, and ſucceſſively abandoned all the places they had occupied in the electorate, except Minden. A garriſon of 4000 men defended that place; but it was cloſely inveſted, and in nine days the whole garriſon ſurrendered priſoners of war. March 14. Several ſkirmiſhes happened between the advanced parties of the Hanoverian army and the French, always to the advantage of the former. The wretched condition of the French troops is hardly to be deſcribed or imagined: officers and ſoldiers involved in one common diſtreſs; the officers forgot their rank, and the ſoldiers their obedience; full hoſpitals and empty magazines; a rigorous ſeaſon, and bad covering; their baggage ſeized or abandoned, and the huſſars and hunters of the allied army continually harraſſing, pillaging, and cutting them off. It was no alleviation to their miſery, that the inhabitants of the country, which they abandoned, were reduced to the ſame extremities. The ſavage behaviour of ſome of their corps at their departure, took away all compaſſion from their ſufferings: but this was not univerſal. The Duke de Randan, who commanded in Hanover, quitted the place with the ſame virtue, that he had ſo long held it. Reſentment had no more power to perſuade him to act with rigour, in the adverse turn of the French affairs, than the pride of conquest had in their prosperity. When he had orders to evacuate the place, there were very considerable magazines of corn and forage, amassed for the use of the army; he had full time to burn them, and he had precedents enough to have justified the action, but he left the whole in the hands of the magistrates, to be gratuitously distributed to the poor: he employed all his vigilance to prevent the least disorder amongst his troops, and was himself the last man that marched out of the town. This behaviour, which did so much honour to his name and country, has made his memory for ever dear to the Hanoverians, drew tears of love and gratitude from his enemies, and acknowledgments from the generous Prince against whom he served.

The French through extreme difficulties, marched towards the Rhine in three columns. The several scattered bodies, which had united at Munster, formed the right. The body which came from Paderborn, and which was commanded by the Prince of Clermont in person, marched in the middle. The forces which had occupied Hesse, were on the left. In this order they reached the Rhine, which they all passed, except a body under Count Clermont, who still remained at Wesel, and resolved to maintain that post. The French army, which about four months before had passed the Rhine in numbers, and in a condition to make the most powerful enemies tremble, without any adverse stroke of war whatsoever, by a fate almost unparallelled, now repassed it like fugitives, in a condition the most deplorable, reduced to less than half their original number, and closely pursued by the enemy, which they had obliged to lay down their arms.

The same ill fortune, and the same despair of their affairs, followed them every where. On the arrival of a small English squadron, commanded by Commodore Holmes, before Embden, and their taking an advantageous situation, which cut off the communication between the town, and the mouth of the river Ems; the French garrison, consisting of near 4000 men, immediately evacuated the place. As soon as Mr. Holmes discovered their design, and that they were transporting their artillery and baggage up the river, he ordered out a few armed boats to pursue them. These took some of the enemies vessels, in which were the son of an officer of distinction, and a considerable sum of money. The Commodore without delay restored the son to his father, and offered to return the money, on receiving the officer's word of honour, that it was his private property. This affair is mentioned, not only to do justice to the judicious conduct by which a place of so much consideration was so easily carried, but also to that generosity of spirit, which so nobly distinguishes almost all those, who hold any rank in our service.

March 18.

19.

CHAP

CHAP. IX.

Alterations in the French ministry. The state of the English affairs in the year 1758. Subsidy treaty with the King of Prussia. Affairs of Sweden and Russia. Schweidnitz taken. King of Prussia enters Moravia and invests Olmutz. Conduct of Count Daun. Attacks the Prussian convoy. Siege of Olmutz raised. King of Prussia marches into Bohemia.

WHILST the French arms suffered such disgraces abroad, they endeavoured by an alteration of their councils at home, to restore their credit. Their ministers had been long the sport of female caprice; it was their power of pleasing a mistress, who governed their king, that alone qualified them to serve their country. Some of the most able men were turned out of their employments with disgrace; others retired from the public service with indignation; a certain low character had for a long time appeared in all the proceedings of France, both within and without. Even in their domestic disputes, and where something of a free and manly spirit appeared, this spirit evaporated, and spent itself upon unworthy and despicable objects. These contests, which involved the church, the law, and the crown, weakened them all; and the state felt all the ill effects of a disunion of its orders, without seeing an augmentation of power thrown into the scale of any. But now taught by their misfortunes and disgraces, they were obliged to an alteration in their conduct: they were obliged to call men to the public service upon public principles; at a time indeed, when in many respects things could only be altered, not mended; and wise and able ministers could do little more by their penetration and public spirit, than to see and lament the ruin, caused by the want of those virtues in their predecessors. The Duke de Belleisle, known to all Europe for his great abilities, and his great exploits, was at length placed at the head of the military department, as secretary at war. There appeared in the common prints a speech, said to be made by that nobleman in council; which if it be not authentic, contains at least such sentiments, as would come not unnaturally from a French patriot, and one who had served his king and country with honour during better times.

"I know, said he, the state of "our armies. It gives me great "grief, and no less indignation: "for besides the real evil of the "disorder in itself, the disgrace "and infamy which it reflects on "our government, and on the "whole nation, is still more to be "apprehended. The choice of "officers ought to be made with "mature deliberation. I know "but too well to what length the "want of discipline, pillaging "and robbing have been carried "on by the officers and common "men, after the example set them "by their generals. It mortifies "me to think I am a Frenchman; "my principles are known to be "very different from those which "are now followed. I had the "satisfaction to retain the esteem, "the friendship, and the consideration, of all the princes, noble-

 "men,

"men, and even of all the common people, in all parts of Germany where I commanded the King's forces. They lived there in the midst of abundance; every one was pleased; it fills my soul with anguish, to find that at present the French are held in execration; that every body is dispirited, and that many officers publickly say things that are criminal, and highly punishable. The evil is so great that it demands immediate redress. I can easily judge, by what passes in my own breast, of what our generals feel from the speeches they must daily hear in Germany, concerning our conduct; which indeed would lose much to be compared with that of our allies. I must particularly complain of the delays and irregularity of the posts; a service which is very ill provided for. I am likewise displeased with the negligence of our generals in returning answers; which is a manifest breach of their duty. Had I commanded the army, a thousand things, which are done, would not have been done; and others, which are neglected, would have been executed. I would have multiplied my communications; I would have had strong posts on the right, on the left, and in the center, lined with troops. I would have had magazines in every place. The quiet and satisfaction of the country should have been equal to their present dissatisfaction, at being harrassed and plundered; and we should have been as much beloved, as we are at present abhorred. The consequences are too apparent to need being mentioned. I must insist on these things, because late redress is better than the continuation of the evil."

M. de Belleisle being established in his office, turned all his attention to the cure of the evils, which he lamented; and exerted all the power that remained in the nation, to put their army in Germany once more upon a respectable footing. The expedition into Germany was originally a measure as contrary to the true interests of France, as it was to justice and equity; but having adopted that measure, the consequences which arose seemed to demand that it should be pursued with vigour. Therefore the connection with the Empress Queen was drawn closer than ever, and nothing was omitted to give a greater strength, and a better order to the army on the Rhine. But these endeavours, which strained all the sinews of France, already too much weakened by the almost total ruin of several essential branches of their trade, drew away all the resources necessary to support their navy. It was then in a sufficiently bad condition, from a want of seamen and stores; and there were no means found, or little attention used, to restore it: so that from a deficiency in the marine, it seemed to be equally impracticable to feed the war in America, or to preserve the coast of France itself from insults. Such was the condition of our enemies, at the opening of the campaign of 1758.

As to England, far from being exhausted by the war, or dispirited by our ill success, our hopes rose from our disappointments, and our resources seemed to be augmented by our expences; with such ease and alacrity were the necessary supplies

plies granted and raifed. Many errors and many abufes, which the war difcovered without making fatal, were corrected. The fpirit of our officers was revived by fear or by fhame. Our trade was well protected by the fuperiority, and prudent diftribution of our naval force. The revenue was frugally managed, and the whole ftate well cemented and bound together in all its parts, by the union of the adminiftration, by the patriotifm which animated it, and by the entire confidence which the people had in the prefiding abilities and intentions. As France perfifted in her attachment to the enemies of his Pruffian majefty, Great Britain entered into ftill clofer engagements with that monarch, the luftre of whofe virtues, fet off by his late wonderful fucceffes, quite turned our eyes from the objections which were raifed againft the confiftency of that alliance with our interefts. How far it is confiftent with them, is, I think, a much more difficult point to fettle, than the adherents to either party feem willing to allow. But it ought to be confidered, that the circumftances of affairs in the beginning of the war, hardly admited of any other choice; it had been the height of madnefs to have been on *ill terms with his Pruffian* majefty at that time; and it was impoffible to have keep good terms with him, without being on very bad ones with Vienna. Things were in an ill fituation; and the ballance of Germany was in danger of being overfet, what party foever fhould prevail. It was impoffible that England could have ftood neuter in this conteft: if fhe had, France would not have imitated her moderation; fhe would gladly have joined with the King of Pruffia to diftrefs Hanover, and reduce Auftria. Thefe two powers fo exerted, would doubtlefs compafs their end, unlefs we interpofed to prevent it; and we muft fooner or later have interpofed, unlefs we were refolved tamely to fee France and her allies giving laws to the continent. In a word, France would certainly have joined with one party or the other, and the party which fhe joined, would certainly by that union, prove dangerous to the common liberty, and muft therefore be oppofed by us; we muft have been in fpite of us engaged in the troubles of Germany, as we ever have been and ever fhall be as long as we are a people of confideration in Europe. The alliance with Pruffia was pointed out to us by the circumftances of his acting on the defenfive. The King of Pruffia meditated no conquefts. But her Imperial majefty indifputably aimed at the recovery of Silefia, which was to difturb the fettled order of things, and this defign was *the only caufe of the troubles in* that part of the world. I am fenfible, that this is, notwithftanding all that may be faid, a queftion of fome intricacy, and requires a confideration of many more particulars than the brevity of our defign will allow. But whether we chofe our party in this alliance judicioufly or not, we have, I imagine, very great reafon to be pleafed with a meafure, which has induced France to engage fo deeply in the affairs of Germany, at fo ruinous an expence of her blood and treafure. Our miniftry was at this time fully convinced of the prudence of the choice that had been made, and refolved to fupport his Pruffian majefty, and the army under Prince Ferdinand, in the moſt effectual manner; 100,000 l. was voted for the Hanoverian and Heſſian forces; and a convention Ap. 11. between the King of Pruſſia, and his Britannic majeſty, was ſigned at London, whereby the King of Great Britain engages to pay his Pruſſian majeſty, the ſum of 670,000 pounds ſterling; and each of the contracting powers engage to conclude no peace without the participation of the other.

The northern courts made no alteration in their ſyſtem. In Sweden, ſome real plots to diſturb the eſtabliſhed conſtitution ended in the ruin of their contrivers, ſome fictitious plots were ſet on foot to give a ſanction to meaſures againſt the crown party, which anſwered their ends; and, as the ruling power continued the ſame, and the internal diſſenſions the ſame, the hoſtilities againſt the King of Pruſſia were reſolved with the former animoſity, but promiſed to be purſued with the former langour. In Ruſſia, the Empreſs did not think her intentions well ſeconded by her miniſters. The great delays, and the unaccountable retreat in the laſt campaign, gave ground to ſuſpect, that ſhe had been betrayed by her miniſters, or her generals. M. Apraxin was removed from the command, and put under arreſt. He juſtified his conduct by expreſs orders from Count Beſtuchef. Beſtuchef was removed from his office, and put under arreſt alſo. Count Woronzoff ſucceeded Beſtuchef in his employment, and the generals Brown and Fermer took the command of the army in the place of Apraxin.

As ſoon as the ſeaſon permitted Apr. 3. the King of Pruſſia to recommence his operations, he laid ſiege to Schweidnitz, and puſhed it with ſo much vigour, that the place ſurrendered in thirteen days. 16. The garriſon reduced by ſickneſs during the blockade, and by their loſſes during the ſiege, from ſeven to little more than three thouſand men, yielded themſelves priſoners of war. By this ſtroke, the King of Pruſſia left his enemies no footing in any part of his dominions. His next conſideration was how to guard againſt their future attempts, and at the ſame time to make a vigorous attack upon ſome part of the Auſtrian territories. His forces were well ſtationed for both theſe purpoſes; for beſides the troops which Count Dohna commanded on the ſide of Pomerania, a conſiderable body were poſted between Wohlau and Glogau, in order to cover Sileſia from the fury of the Ruſſians, in caſe they ſhould make their inroad that way. An army, in a little time after, was formed in Saxony, commanded by his brother Prince Henry, which conſiſted of thirty battalions, and forty-five ſquadrons. It was deſtined to make head againſt the army of the Empire, which by amazing efforts made during the winter, and by the junction of a large body of Auſtrians, was now in a condition to act again. A ready communication was kept up between all the King of Pruſſia's armies, by a proper choice of poſts.

The King reſolved to make Moravia the theatre of the war this year. Moravia was freſh ground; a country as yet untouched by the ravages of war. If he ſhould ſucceed in his operations in this country, his ſucceſſes by opening to him the neareſt road to Vienna, muſt prove more deciſive than they could any where elſe. If he ſhould fail,

fail, the Auſtrians were at a diſtance from the center of his affairs, and would find it difficult to improve their advantages to his ruin. After the reduction of Schweidnitz, the King ordered two bodies of his troops to poſt themſelves in ſuch a manner, as to make it appear that he intended to carry the war into Bohemia. Whilſt he drew away the enemies attention from the real objects by theſe diſpoſitions, the main of his army, by a very rapid march, entered into Moravia in two columns, and made themſelves maſters, in a ſhort time and with little or no oppoſition, of all the poſts neceſſary to cover the troops to be employed in the ſiege of Olmutz. On the 27th of May the trenches were opened before that city.

May 3.

M. Daun was no ſooner appriſed of the King's march towards Moravia, than he took his route through Bohemia to that province. Notwithſtanding that the Empreſs Queen omitted no poſſible endeavours to aſſemble a juſt army againſt the King of Pruſſia; though ſhe had for that purpoſe exhauſted the Milaneſe and Tuſcany, and ſwept up the laſt recruits in her Danubian territories; M. Daun was not yet in a condition to give the King of Pruſſia battle: neither did his character lead him to truſt that to fortune, which he might enſure, though more ſlowly, by conduct. This wiſe general took his poſts from Gewics to Littau, in a mountainous country, in a ſituation where it was impoſſible to attack him. He had the fertile country of Bohemia, from whence he readily and certainly drew ſupplies, at his rear. He was from his poſition at the ſame time enabled to harraſs the Pruſſian army before Olmutz, and to intercept the convoys which were brought to them from Sileſia.

Olmutz, by the extent of its works, and other advantageous circumſtances, is a city which it is very difficult compleatly to inveſt. So that ſome of the King's poſts being neceſſarily weakened by occupying ſo great an extent of country, were attacked by Daun's detachments from time to time, with ſuch ſucceſs, that abundant ſuccours both of men and ammunition were thrown into the place. Theſe attacks were always made by night, and very few nights paſſed without ſome attack. The ſucceſs was various. But the operations of the ſiege were greatly diſturbed by theſe continual alarms. Beſides it is ſaid that the Auſtrians before the king's invaſion of this province, had deſtroyed all the forage in the neighbourhood of Olmutz. The horſe were obliged to forage at a great diſtance, which harraſſed them extremely. M. Daun took advantage of all theſe circumſtances. It was in vain that the King of Pruſſia endeavoured by all the arts of a great commander to provoke or entice him to an engagement. He profited of the advantages he had made, without being tempted by them to throw out of his hands the ſecure game he was playing.

The great object of M. Daun was the Pruſſian convoys. On receiving advice that a large and important one was to leave Troppau on the 25th of June, he took meaſures to intercept it. He ordered General Jahnus, who was at Muglitz on the left, to advance towards Bahrn, and a detachment which was at Prerau at a conſiderable diſtance to the right, to march to Stadt Leibe; ſo that theſe two corps ſhould on different

different sides attack the convoy at one and the same time. To further the execution of this project M. Daun himself approached the Prussian army, and directed all his motions as if he intended to give them battle. However, the King was too great a master in the game of generalship, which was now playing, to be deceived by this feint. He detached a considerable party under General Ziethen, to support his convoy, which was already about 7000 strong. Before this detachment could come up, the convoy was attacked, but the Austrians were repulsed. But M. Daun, who provided for every thing, quickly reinforced his parties, who renewed the engagement the next day. They first suffered the head of the convoy to go unmolested; but as the center was still embarrassed in a dangerous defile, they easily cut off the head from the rest, and then they attacked the center with the greatest fury. The Prussians made as good a resistance as the nature of the ground would suffer. General Ziethen did every thing which could be expected from an accomplished officer; but in the end they were entirely routed; all the waggons in that division were taken; the rear was pushed back towards Troppau; the head alone with great difficulty arrived at the Prussian camp.

This was a fatal stroke, because it came at a time when it was impossible to repair it. The siege of Olmutz had been all along attended with great difficulties; and now the news which every day arrived of the nearer and nearer approach of the Russians, called the King loudly to the defence of his own dominions. Already the Cossacks and Calmucks made incursions into Silesia, and by their ravages and cruelties, announced the approach of the great army. The siege must be raised; Moravia must be abandoned; Marshal Daun must have the honour of freeing his country, and driving away such an adversary as the King of Prussia, from a conquest deemed certain; all was performed without a battle, by a series of the most refined and vigorous manœuvres that ever were put in practice.

When the King of Prussia saw that the unprosperous situation of his affairs obliged him to retreat; he took a resolution, such as a victory inspires in others. He took advantage even of the excellent movement of M. Daun, by which that able general had advanced his quarters to Posnitz, and placed himself so as to support Olmutz in the most effectual manner; by this movement, however, he was obliged to uncover the frontiers of Bohemia. The King of Prussia, whom nothing could escape, was sensible of this advantage; and therefore, instead of falling back upon Silesia, which step would immediately have drawn the Austrian army into his dominions, he determined to retreat from one part of the enemies territories into another. The day before the siege was raised the firing of the Prussians continued as brisk as ever, and shewed no sort of sign of an intention to depart; but in the night the whole army took the road to Bohemia in two columns, and gained an entire march upon the Austrians. July 1. So that notwithstanding the utmost efforts which the enemy could make to overtake and harrass the King upon his march, he advanced into Bohemia with little molestation, seized upon a large magazine at Leutomissel, defeated some corps of Austrians who had attempted to disturb him in his progress, and arrived

arrived at Konigſgratz, one of the moſt important poſts in Bohemia, with all his ſick and wounded, with all his heavy baggage, all his heavy artillery, and military ſtores compleat. This place he poſſeſſed after driving from it a body of 7000 Auſtrians who were intrenched there. He immediately laid this city and ſeveral other diſtricts under contribution; but this plan not admitting any further operations on that ſide, he took no other advantage from this momentous poſt. He ſoon re-entered Sileſia, and marched with the moſt amazing diligence to encounter the Ruſſians, who had at this time united their divided corps under Brown and Fermer, and fixed the long fluctuating plan of their operations, by entering the New Marche of Brandenburg and laying ſiege to Cuſtrin. The reduction of this place could leave them but a few days march to Berlin; Count Dohna was not in a condition to oppoſe their progreſs, the King was ſtill at a great diſtance. But it is neceſſary to break our narrative of his affairs, however intereſting, to take a view of the operations of the armies on the Rhine. We leave the King of Pruſſia in full march, to give one body of his enemies battle, after executing a retreat from the other, in a manner that did his military genius the greateſt honour. So that on the whole, it is difficult to ſay, which gained the greateſt glory, the King of Pruſſia by his retreat, or M. Daun by the meaſures which obliged him to it.

CHAP. X.

Allies paſs the Rhine. Battle of Crevelt. Action at Sangerſhauſen. Action at Meer. Allies repaſs the Rhine.

PRINCE Ferdinand had it not in his power to cut off the retreat of the French over the Rhine; but he preſſed them cloſely, and prepared himſelf to croſs that river in purſuit of them. His deſign was to carry the war beyond the Maeſe, and thereby oblige the Prince de Soubiſe to abandon the enterpriſe he was preparing againſt Heſſe Caſſel. His highneſs executed the paſſage of the Rhine at Herven with the corps immediately under his command; then he ſent the bridge with which he ſerved himſelf ſo well up the river to Rees; the reſt of the troops paſſed there; the whole army were over before the 7th of June. The flattery of the laſt age ſaw with aſtoniſhment a paſſage of the Rhine by a French monarch, unoppoſed, at the head of a mighty army. We ſaw that river paſſed by the enemies of France, in the preſence of an army of 50,000 of that nation; it was an action which did not need the exaggerations of rhetoric.

June 1.

The French army retired as the Prince advanced, and took an advantageous camp which threatened to retard the operations of the allies. Their right was under Rhineberg; but the Prince by his well judged motions turned their left flank towards the convent of Campe, by which the French found themſelves obliged to quit their advantageous poſt, and to retire into Meurs. They ſtill kept towards the Rhine. The Prince advanced on the ſide of the Maeſe.

It

It was evident that whilft the French continued only to retire, it would prove impoffible for them to hinder the allies from executing the plan they propofed. They therefore thought it advifable to change their countenance. They had fallen back as far as Nuys; they now returned on their fteps, and advanced as far as Crevelt, within a few miles of Prince Ferdinand's camp. The Prince made the difpofitions for a battle, with his ufual vigour and prudence. He carefully reconnoitred the fituation of the enemy. He found that their right was at a village called Vifchelon; their left extended towards Anrath, where it was covered with a wood; Crevelt, which was in the front of their right, was occupied by a party of their troops. His highnefs refolved upon three attacks. The firft and real attack was on the flank of the enemies left wing; the other two were defigned to divert their attention, and prevent their fuccouring the object of his principal attack; for which purpofe he recommended to his generals to make the beft ufe of their heavy artillery, and not to advance too far unlefs they were perfectly affured of the fuccefs of the main operation.

Having made thefe wife difpofitions, and perfectly learned June 23. the beft routes by which the enemy might be approached, his highnefs put himfelf at the head of the grenadiers of his right wing, and advanced on the fide of Anrath in two columns. A cannonading violent and well fupported opened the action. The Hanoverian artillery was greatly fuperior to that of the French; but though the French loft many men, they loft no ground in this way, and their pofition in the wood made a clofe attack abfolutely neceffary. The hereditary Prince of Brunfwick put himfelf at the head of the firft line of foot, and with his ufual fpirit, advanced with the whole front directly to the wood. Here a furious fire of fmall arms commenced, which continued without the fmalleft intermiffion for two hours and a half. All the Hanoverian battalions threw themfelves into the wood. Two ditches well lined with infantry were oppofed to their fury. They were forced one after another. The enemies battalions were pufhed back, they were entirely broken, and fled out of the wood in a diforder which was irreparable. Their cavalry, who kept the beft countenance poffible, in fpite of the terrible fire of the Hanoverian artillery, and in fpite of the vigorous attempts of the Hanoverian horfe, who had by this time found means to gain the plain, covered the retreat of their fcattered infantry, and faved them from utter ruin. The right wing and the center, though they fuffered grievoufly by the cannonading, were no where broken, but retreated towards Nuys in the moft perfect order.

Seven thoufand of their beft troops were killed, wounded, and taken prifoners; but there was nothing in this battle fo grievous to France, and fo affecting even to the enemy, as the fate of the Count de Gifors. This young nobleman, the only fon of the Duke de Belleifle, not above twenty-five years of age, newly married to the heirefs of an illuftrious houfe, himfelf the laft hope of a moft noble family, was mortally wounded at the head of his regiment, which he brought up with the moft heroic courage, and infpired by his example to make

incre-

incredible efforts. He had been educated with all the care an excellent father could beftow on a fon of an uncommon genius, who was alone able to fupport the reputation of his family. To the pureft morals he had united the politeft manners; he had made a great proficiency in learning; he knew many branches of it, and loved all; he had feen every part of Europe, and read courts and nations with a difcerning eye; and wanting nothing to fulfil all hope, and to make him a perfect and lafting ornament and fupport to his country, but a knowledge in the military art, he entered that courfe of glory and danger, and fell in his firft campaign. The unhappy father and minifter faw his private misfortunes keep pace with the public calamities, and the tears of his family mingled with thofe of his country.

Prince Ferdinand gained a victory at Crevelt, which did the greateft honour to his military capacity and to the bravery of his troops. But it was a victory neither entire nor decifive. The French army on their own frontiers was quickly and ftrongly reinforced: fo that they were not only in a condition in fome fort to make head againft the allies, but was enabled to detach a confiderable reinforcement to the army of the Prince de Soubife on the other fide of the Rhine.

Although the Prince had reafon to imagine that he fhould not be able to keep his ground on this fide of the Rhine for any confiderable time, this did not hinder him from improving to the utmoft the advantage he had obtained. Whilft the French difabled by their late defeat, were in no condition to oppofe him, he paffed the Rhine with a large detachment, and appeared on the 28th of June before Duffeldorp, a city advantageoufly fituated on the river, and belonging to the Elector Palatine. A fevere bombardment obliged it to capitulate on the 7th of July. The garrifon, confifting of 2000 men, marched out with the honours of war. Prince Ferdinand placed here three battalions of Hanoverians, and threw a bridge of boats acrofs the river; by that means he multiplied his pofts aud communications on both fides of the Rhine; and threw a new and no fmall impediment in the way of the French, to retard their progrefs, in cafe he fhould find himfelf compelled to retire. After this, the army of the allies and that of France, fpent feveral days in making various marches and countermarches, as if they both propofed to bring on an action, to which however it does not appear that either party was very ftrongly inclined.

Prince Ferdinand ftill retained his hopes that the Prince of Yfenburg, who commanded the Heffian troops, would find the Prince of Soubife employment for fome time. He had originally laid his plan in fuch a manner, that by paffing the Maefe and transferring the feat of war into the enemies country he might draw the French from the Rhine, and perhaps oblige the Prince of Soubife to come to the affiftance of the main army under M. de Contades, who commanded in the room of Count Clermont, being now the fourth commander of the French troops fince they entered Germany. But whilft Prince Ferdinand pleafed himfelf with thofe hopes, and ftill continued to act as far as circumftances would admit in purfuance of this plan, he received

received an account which difconcerted all his meafures.

The Duke de Broglio fupported by the corps of the Prince de Soubife, with a much fuperior force, July 23. attacked and defeated the Heffian army of feven thoufand men near Sangerfhaufen. This opened to them the poffeffion of the Wefer. They might act in Weftphalia, on which fide foever they pleafed, and it was to be feared, that if they availed themfelves of the advantages they had, they might be able to intercept the Britifh troops. Thefe troops having been landed at Embden, were now on their march under the command of the Duke of Marlborough to reinforce the allied army. The Prince in this fituation of affairs, had no option left but an engagement with the French army, or a retreat over the Rhine. The former was not eafy to compafs, as the French induftrioufly declined a battle, and it became extremely dangerous to remain long in a pofition with the enemies army on his left, and the ftrong fortrefs of Gueldre on his right. In this fituation his fubfiftence became every day more difficult. To repafs the Rhine, had its difficulties too; the roads which led to that river were rendered almoft impaffable by the heavy rains; the river itfelf was fo fwelled with them that the bridge at Rees had been for fome time ufelefs.

Thefe difagreeable circumftances of the allied army did not efcape the penetration of Monfieur de Chevert, one of the ableft commanders among the French. He formed a plan upon them, which if it had fucceeded, muft have put the allies into the greateft perplexity. This general had fome time before paffed the Rhine, with an intention of making himfelf mafter of Duffeldorp, and he had prepared all things with great ability for that enterprife. The rains unufually heavy for that feafon, and fome other crofs accidents, had fruftrated his intentions. But perceiving that the fame accidents which defeated his defign, proved alfo unfavourable to the enemy, he refolved to turn his difappointment into an advantage, and from the ruins of his firft project to build another of yet greater importance. Baron Imhoff was pofted to the right of the Rhine in a ftrong fituation near Meer. He was to cover the bridge at Rees; to fecure a confiderable magazine; and to keep open communication between the Englifh reinforcements and the main army. The plan of Monfieur Chevert was to diflodge Imhoff, to burn the bridge at Rees, to make himfelf mafter of the magazine, and to render the junction of the Englifh troops with the Hanoverians impracticable. To execute this judicious fcheme, he united feveral detachments from the garrifon of Wefel, to a confiderable corps which he intended to have employed in the fiege of Duffeldorp. The whole made near 12,000 men. The troops under Imhoff were but fix battalions, aud four fquadrons, hardly 3000 in all.

When that general was apprifed of the defigns and motions of the French, he faw it was in vain to expect fuccours from the army of Prince Ferdinand. The fwell of the river had rendered all relief impoffible; all his hopes was therefore in his own genius and the bravery of his troops. He confidered that though the

pòft

poſt he occupied was ſufficiently ſtrong, the enemy might make themſelves maſters of Rees, by turning his camp, and thus execute one of the principal parts of their deſign; he conſidered the great difference between attacking and being attacked; he conſidered the effect of an attempt altogether unexpected by the enemy; he therefore took the reſolution of abandoning his poſt, and going out to meet them. Perceiving that the French were marching into difficult ground, he did not loſe a moment to begin the action.
Aug. 5. He ordered a ſmall party, which he had poſted in a little coppice, to fall upon the enemies left, which he obſerved to be uncovered; and appointed the fire of this party, as a ſignal for all the reſt to advance, and make the onſet with bayonets fixed. The French thus vigorouſly and unexpectedly attacked, fell into confuſion; their courage ill ſeconded the wiſdom of their general; they did not ſtand half an hour; they left the field of battle, eleven pieces of cannon, many priſoners, and much baggage to the Hanoverians, who drove them under the cannon of Weſel.

This ſignal advantage over ſuch a prodigious ſuperiority was not more gallantly obtained, than well purſued and improved. Imhoff ſaw that the rains had increaſed to ſuch a degree, as to leave no hopes for the allied army to paſs by the bridge at Rees. Having taken proper care of his magazines, he quitted his poſt at Meer, and being reinforced by ſome parties, who paſſed the river in boats, he marched with the utmoſt diligence towards the route of the Engliſh forces, and happily effected a junction, which had hitherto been attended with ſo many difficulties.

Prince Ferdinand in his retreat met with no obſtruction, but juſt what was ſufficient to diſplay more fully the gallantry of his officers, and the ſpirit of his troops. A town called Watchtendonck was on his left, as he retreated; this place, though not fortified, is a poſt of much importance, and being an iſland ſurrounded by the river Niers, is extremely difficult of acceſs. The French had thrown a body of troops into this place. The hereditary Prince, the firſt in every active ſervice, was employed to force it. The bridge on his approach had been drawn up. The Prince ſeeing that if he attempted to get down this bridge, the enemy would gain time to recollect themſelves, threw himſelf into the river; his grenadiers, animated by ſo gallant an example, plunged in after him, and furiouſly attacking the enemy with their bayonets, in a few minutes drove them from that poſt. This advantage, joined to that gained by General Imhoff, and the uncommon reſolution, which appeared in both theſe actions, awed the French. They found that their troops, raw, undiſciplined, and little fit for hard ſervice, were not to be relied upon; and they feared to bring on an action, which by being deciſive againſt them might draw on the moſt fatal conſequences. So that the Prince repaſſed the Rhine in a moſt excellent order, even with leſs trouble than he had at firſt paſſed it; and indeed with little moleſtation, but what he met with from the weather. Such exceſſive rains had fallen, that he in vain attempted a paſſage at Rhineberg

or

Aug. 9. and 10. or at his bridge of Rees; he effected it a little lower at a place called Griethuyſen.

Although Prince Ferdinand was obliged to paſs the Rhine, and to act more upon the defenſive for the future; yet his vigorous conduct in the beginning was very glorious to him, and very advantageous to the common cauſe. The French ſuffered greatly in their military reputation; the Hanoverians had gained a ſuperiority over them, and now ſo much of the campaign was waſted, that notwithſtanding the greatneſs of their numbers, it was not probable that they would find themſelves able to make any conſiderable progreſs in their deſigns againſt the King's electoral dominions for this year. The advantage gained by Broglio and Soubiſe was not attended with the conſequences, which might have been apprehended. Prince Yſenburg kept ſo good a countenance in a ſtrong poſt he had choſen, that the French did not chooſe to attack him again; and ſince Prince Ferdinand had repaſſed the Rhine, he might always be well ſupported.

CHAP. XI.

Retreat from Bohemia. Meaſures of Count Daun. Battle of Cuſtrin. King of Pruſſia marches into Saxony, and joins Prince Henry.

BY the retreat of the Pruſſians from Moravia, the war had aſſumed a new face. The generals who conducted it had changed hands. The King of Pruſſia was obliged to act upon the defenſive; M. Daun was now in a condition of diſplaying his talents in an offenſive war. The affairs of the King of Pruſſia were ſcarce ever in a more critical ſituation than at that time. The Ruſſians ſeemed at firſt diſpoſed to enter into Sileſia; but now they had united their ſeveral disjointed corps, penetrated into the New Marche of Brandenburg, and having commenced the ſiege of Cuſtrin, a place that threatened them with no great oppoſition, they were arrived within a few days march of Berlin. Count Dohna poſted with a greatly inferior force at Frankfort on the Oder, watched without being able to obſtruct their progreſs. In Pomerania, the generals Weedel and Manteufel oppoſed almoſt the ſame ineffectual efforts to the arms of Sweden. The army of the Empire and a conſiderable body of Auſtrians under General Haddick, advanced into Saxony, and poſſeſſing themſelves by degrees of thoſe ſtrong poſts, which compoſe the frontiers of Miſnia, they continually ſtreightened the quarters of Prince Henry. That Prince was ſtrongly encamped at Dippolſwalde, with about 20,000 men, in order to cover Dreſden, and command the courſe of the Elbe. Thus circumſtanced, the King could not find his account in remaining long in Bohemia, where it was impoſſible to effect any thing deciſive. Every thing depended upon his being able to drive the Ruſſians out of his territories, who with a mighty force ruined every place they arrived at, and ſeemed not only to make war againſt him, but againſt human nature itſelf.

M. Daun

M. Daun was soon apprised of the King of Prussia's intentions; but he considered that if he was to pursue the King into Silesia, he must encounter with difficulties almost insuperable; several strong places stood in his way, and it would prove easy for the Prussian troops left for the defence of that dutchy, to take an advantageous camp under one of those places, and thus oblige them to waste unprofitably the time, which might be employed in the execution of more judicious projects. Besides that in this manner of proceeding he could never act in concert, nor preserve any effectual communication with the several bodies of his allies. To push forward with his whole force directly to Berlin, could at best be regarded as a *coup de main*, which could prove nothing decisive in the campaign, even supposing the project should succeed; but it was rather probable that it would not succeed, as the King of Prussia might clear his hands of the Russians before the army of M. Daun could, for want of subsistence, arrive in the Lower Lusatia. Every consideration therefore pointed out the relief of Saxony as the great object of the Austrian operations. It was an object apparently to be compassed with greater ease, and if compassed, productive of more solid advantages than any other. The army of the Empire, already superior to that of Prince Henry, could co-operate in the design, and the recovery of Saxony once effected, the King of Prussia would see himself entirely divested of one of the principal resources he had to rely upon in the war, for money, provisions, and forage; whilst his hereditary dominions stripped of this strong barrier, defenceless in themselves, and assaulted on three sides by powerful armies, could scarce find them employment to the end of the campaign.

M. Daun having resolved upon his plan of operations, suffered the King of Prussia to continue his march towards the Russians, without any molestation: he contented himself with leaving a considerable body of troops, under the generals Harsch and de Ville, on the southern frontiers of Silesia, in order to form some enterprise upon that side, which might draw the attention and forces of the Prussians as far as possible from the great object of his operations. When he had made these dispositions he marched towards Saxony, through the country of Lusatia, by Zittau, Gorlitz, and Bautzen. His first project was bold. He proposed to cross the Elbe at Meissen; by which the communication between Dresden and Leipsic would be cut off at one stroke. Then he proposed to attack Prince Henry in his camp at Sedlitz, whilst the army of the Empire fell upon him in another quarter. Thus the Prince was to be put between two fires; and his retreat unto Dresden to be rendered impracticable; but upon more mature consideration, this project was laid aside. M. Daun reflected that the fortress of Sonnestein, of which he was not yet in possession, would prove no small impediment to his designs. Sept. 3. He considered that the position of Prince Henry opposite to the army of the Empire was too advantageous, to make an attack upon him adviseable: and unless the Prince could be induced to attack the Imperialists first, a point not to be expected in his circumstances, he might always find it easy to throw himself into Dresden, and by pro-

 per

per motions to preserve a free communication with the King. M. Daun was obliged to renounce his firſt deſign, but he was left at full liberty to form and to execute ſuch other plans for the relief of Saxony as his prudence could ſuggeſt.

About that time the Imperial court elated with their recent ſucceſs, began to ſhew with what moderation they were likely to behave if it continued and increaſed. They entirely threw off all the little appearances of reſpect they had hitherto retained for the King of Great Britain, and ſeveral other of the moſt reſpectable princes and perſons of the Empire. They made the abuſe of their authority go hand in hand with the ſucceſs of their arms. On the 21ſt of Auguſt a concluſum of the Aulic council was iſſued againſt the King of Great Britain, as Elector of Hanover, againſt the Landgrave of Heſſe-Caſſel, againſt Prince Ferdinand of Brunſwick, the Count of Lippe Buckebourg, and in general againſt all the adherents to the King of Pruſſia, threatening them with penalties in dignity, perſon and eſtate. In conſequence of this decree, letters avocatory were iſſued, notifying to the ſovereign princes, that if they did not within a limited time diſperſe their armies, break off their connection with the King of Pruſſia, pay their quota of Roman months, and ſend their contingents to the army of execution, they were put under the ban of the Empire. To all other perſons who held any dignity in the Empire, orders were given and penalties were threatened ſuitable to their condition. They in ſhort went all lengths but that of actually and formally putting them under the ban, which they would not have failed to do, if their ſucceſs had anſwered its beginnings. So little regard had the court of Vienna to former ſervices of the moſt intereſting nature; and ſo entirely did ſhe ſeem to forget that ſhe owed to the King of Great Britain, not only that power which ſhe now unjuſtly and ungratefully turned againſt him, but almoſt the very being of the houſe of Auſtria. So entirely did they forget that this monarch had expended his treaſures, employed his armies, and even expoſed his perſon in her cauſe, when it was not only abandoned, but attacked by almoſt all the reſt of Europe. However the violent proceedings of the Aulic council, drew no one ſtate or perſon from the Kings of Great Britain and Pruſſia; they rather had a contrary effect, in rouſing the whole Evangelic body to a ſenſe of their own danger. Much leſs were they able to ſtop the progreſs of the allied arms.

The King of Pruſſia conducted his retreat out of Bohemia in admirable order. The generals Jahnus and Laudon for ſeveral days hung upon his rear with two ſtrong bodies. They took advantageous poſts, ſometimes on one ſide, ſometimes on the other, ſometimes together, ſometimes ſeparately, and threw all poſſible impediments in his way. But the vigour of the Pruſſians drove them with loſs from every poſt. So that by the 6th of Auguſt, they were obliged entirely to deſiſt from their purſuit. The King of Pruſſia freed from this moleſtation marched with the utmoſt diligence by Wiſoca, Politz, Landſhut, and arrived on the 20th at Franckfort on the Oder. Here he joined the troops under Count Dohna. The army was

22d. was now in a condition to act, and they did not lose a moment's time to march against the enemy. All their vigour and expedition was not more than necessary. The Russians had besieged Custrin from the 15th. Though these people, scarcely emerged from barbarism, had not the most perfect skill in operations of this nature, they supplied that deficiency by a ferocity that scrupled nothing, by numbers whose lives they did not regard, and by a most formidable artillery, which rudely but furiously managed, only spread the more general and indiscriminate destruction. In effect, they threw such a multitude of bombs and red hot balls into that unfortunate city, that in a short time it was on fire in every quarter. Of the wretched inhabitants some were burned, some buried in the ruins, some killed by the balls that fell like hail in the streets: the surviving majority, safe neither within nor without their houses, abandoned their homes and their substance, and fled, many of them almost naked, out of the city on the side which was not invested. Never was beheld a more deplorable spectacle; nor was it easy to say which formed the more wretched appearance, those who perished, or those who escaped. Meanwhile, the governor, firm in his courage and fidelity, did every thing for the defence of the walls and ruins of the place; but the walls built in the old manner did not promise a successful defence; the enemy had posted themselves in the suburbs, and in the firing of the town, the principal magazine of the besieged was blown up.

The protector and avenger of his dominions, was now however at hand. On the 23d, the King of Prussia's whole army passed the Oder at Glustebiffel, about twenty English miles to the north-east of Custrin. The Russians on the first notice of his approach, broke up the siege of that place, and marched towards the villages of Zwicker and Zorndorff. It was the King's intention to wind round the left flank of their army, and to take them in the rear, by which he hoped to throw them into confusion. But in this he found himself disappointed. The Russian generals had foreseen his purpose, and made excellent dispositions. As the ground did not admit them to extend greatly in length, they threw themselves into a square body composed of four lines, forming a front almost equal on every side, and on every side surrounded by cannon and chevaux de frize. In this formidable disposition they waited the attack of the Prussians.

It was on the 25th of August that the King of Prussia, after a march of 56 days from the midst of Moravia, brought his army in presence of the Russians. The King had never been personally engaged with that enemy before. His troops had never obtained any advantage over them. The whole fortune of the war depended upon the event of this day. The Prussians were now in the closest sense to fight for their country, which was ready to fall under one of the severest scourges with which Providence has chastised a nation. Nothing was wanting which could inspire the soldier with revenge. Every where the marks of the

the enemies cruelty were before their eyes; the country desolated on every side, and the villages in flames all around the field of battle.

At nine o'clock in the morning the battle began by a fire of cannon and mortars, which rained on the right wing of the Russians without the least intermission for near two hours. Nothing could exceed the havock made by this terrible fire, nor the constancy with which the Muscovite foot, raw and unexperienced, sustained a slaughter that would have confounded and dispersed the compleatest veterans. They fell in their ranks; new regiments still pressed forward to fill their places, and to supply new slaughter. When the first line had fired away all their charges, they rushed forward on the Prussians. That firm body of the Prussian infantry which had often stood and often given so many terrible shocks, by one of those unaccountable movements of the human mind, that render every thing in war so precarious, gave way in the presence of their sovereign, and when they had in a manner secured the victory, retired in disorder before the half broken battalions of the Muscovites. Had the Russian officers known how to profit of this disorder; had they immediately thrown in their horse with vigour to compleat it, and entirely break that body; this had probably been the last day of the Prussian greatness. The King was not so negligent. For just in this anxious moment, whilst the battle was yet in suspence, by a very rapid and masterly motion, he brought all the cavalry of his right to the center, which with General Sedlitz at their head, bursting in upon the Russian foot, uncovered by their horse, and disordered even by their advantage, they pushed them back with a most miserable slaughter. The repulsed battalions of Prussia had time to recollect, and to form themselves; and now returning to the onset with a rage exasperated by their late disgrace, they entirely turned the ballance of the fight. The Russians were thrown into the most horrible confusion. The wind blew the dust and smoak full in their faces. They no longer distinguished friends or enemies. They fired upon each other. In this distraction they plundered their own baggage which stood between the lines, and intoxicated themselves with brandy. Orders were now no more heard or obeyed. The ranks fell in upon one another; and being crammed together in a narrow space, every shot discharged by the Prussians had its full effect; whilst the Russians kept up only a scattered fire without direction or effect, and quite over the heads of their enemies. It was now no longer battle, but a horrid and undistinguished carnage. Yet still (which is a wonderful circumstance) the Russians thus distracted and slaughtered, kept their ground. The action continued without intermission from nine in the morning until seven at night. At last the night itself, the fatigue of the Prussians, and a judicious attack on their right wing, which drew their attention on that side, gave the Russian army some respite to recover their order, and an opportunity of retiring a little from the scene of their disaster. On their side near 10,000 fell upon the

the ſpot; they had more than 10,000 wounded, moſt of them mortally; 939 officers, not including the inferior, were killed, wounded and taken priſoners; of two particular regiments conſiſting before the battle of 4595 effective men, only 1475 were left; their whole loſs on this bloody day was 21,529 men. That of the Pruſſians in every way did not amount to 2000.

The gazettes of both parties warmly diſputed the vain honour of the field of battle. On the moſt diligent enquiry, it appears that both parties ſpent the night on or very near the place of action. But this is an affair of little conſequence. The Pruſſians had all the fruits, and moſt of the proofs of a victory the moſt compleat and deciſive. A vaſt train of artillery taken, the military cheſt, a number of priſoners, many of them officers of high rank; the retreat of the Ruſſian army, the next and the following days; their general Fermor's requeſt for leave to bury the dead; their incapacity to advance or form any new enterpriſe; the King of Pruſſia's unmoleſted operations againſt his other enemies; all theſe form the moſt clear and certain demonſtration of a victory in all points, for which a victory is deſireable.

Nothing leſs indeed, than a very compleat victory could have done any eſſential ſervice to the King's affairs at that time, when four armies of his enemies were making their way to one common center, and threatened to unite in the heart of Brandenburg. The King renewed the attack on the Ruſſians the next morning. The event of the laſt day had ſhewed them, that there was no way of ſafety but in a retreat, and in effect they retreated before the Pruſſians as far as Landſperg on the frontiers of Poland. The King of Pruſſia was convinced that their late check muſt wholly diſable them from attempting any thing material againſt his dominions on that ſide; and he ſaw clearly that whatever he might hope to gain by improving his advantage againſt the Ruſſians, he muſt loſe far more by allowing his other enemies to make a progreſs on the ſide of Saxony. He ſatisfied himſelf therefore, with leaving a ſmall body of troops under Count Dohna, to obſerve the motions of the Muſcovite army; and marched with the greateſt part of his forces and the utmoſt expedition to the relief of Prince Henry.

M. Daun having laid aſide his firſt project for paſſing the Elbe at Meiſſen, enterpriſed nothing new on the ſide of Saxony for ſome days; he contented himſelf with taking a poſition at Stolpen to the eaſtward of the Elbe, by which, whilſt he preſerved to himſelf an eaſy communication with the army of the Empire, he interrupted the communication between Bautzen and Dreſden; he favoured the operations of General Laudon, who had advanced through the Lower Luſatia to the confines of Brandenburg; and by drawing the attention of the Pruſſian forces which were left in Sileſia to the northward of that dutchy, he facilitated the progreſs of the arms of the generals Harch and de Ville in the ſouthern parts. Admirable diſpoſitions without queſtion, if the time had not called for more vigorous meaſures, and if the reſcue of Saxony from the King of Pruſſia had not been the great object of the campaign! It is not impossible that the court of Vienna had still such an hankering after Silesia, as induced them to slacken their efforts on the side of Saxony, in hope, that if M. Daun could protect the operations there, so as to find full employment for the King of Prussia, their other forces might reduce Silesia with great facility; and thus perhaps by aiming at two such difficult objects at once, as it generally happens, they lost them both Upon any other supposition, it is not very easy to account for the seeming inactivity of M. Daun, while he had so fair a game in his hands. However advantageously Prince Henry might have chosen his post, or however strongly he might have secured it, yet, the prodigious superiority of the combined armies seems to have more than over-balanced that advantage, and to have justified, nay, to have demanded some bold and decisive attempt.

In fact, this appeared at length to be the marshal's own opinion. For when the strong fortress of Sonnestein most unaccountably surrendered, with a garrison of 1400 men, to the Austrian general Mac-

Sept. 5. Guire after the resistance of no more than a single day; M. Daun proposed that the Prince of Deux-Ponts should attack Prince Henry, whilst the grand army of the Austrians laying bridges between two fires, at a small distance from each other, should pass the Elbe, and falling at the same time on the

Sep. 10. Prussians, second the attack of the Imperialists, and cut off the retreat of their enemies towards Dresden. This was to bring matters to a speedy decision. But now the King of Prussia by the most rapid marches had reached the frontiers of Saxony. The whole design was disconcerted; and far from being able to dislodge Prince Henry, they found themselves utterly unable to prevent the King his brother from joining him, with the whole army. On Sep. 11.

his approach General Laudon abandoned his advantages in the Lower Lusatia, and fell back upon M. Daun; who himself retired from the neighbourhood of Dresden and fell back as far as Zittau. The army of the Empire possessed of the strong post of Pirna, which the Saxons had occupied in the beginning of the war, kept their ground; but did not undertake any thing. Thus in fifteen days the King of Prussia, by his unparalleled spirit, diligence and magnanimity, fought, and defeated a superior body of his enemies, in one extremity of his dominions, and baffled without fighting another superior body in the other extremity.

These advantages, glorious as they were, were not the only ones which followed the victory at Zorndorf. The Swedes, who directed their motions by those of their Russian allies, hastened their operations when that army had advanced into Brandenburg. General Wedel was detached from Saxony, to stop their progress; and the Prince of Bevern, now governor of Stetin, gave them some opposition. All this, however, had proved ineffectual, if the news of the defeat of the Russians had not alarmed the Swedes in such a manner, as to make them return with more expedition than they had advanced. Tho' the King of Prussia's affairs began to put on a better appearance by these efforts, the for-

fortune of the war ſtill hung in a very dubious ſcale. The enemy was ſtill ſuperior The Swedes and Ruſſians had ſtill ſome footing in his dominions. The Auſtrains and Imperialiſts were yet in Saxony; and if the King's armies had it in their power to take ſtrong ſituations; the enemy had the ſame advantages. The condition of things was extremely critical, and the leaſt error or misfortune threatened ſtill to plunge the King of Pruſſia into an abyſs of calamities.

CHAP. XII.

General Oberg defeated at Lanwerenhagen. King of Pruſſia ſurpriſed at Hohkirchen M. Keith and Prince Francis of Brunſwick killed. Affair at Gorlitz. King of Pruſſia marches into Sileſia. M. Daun inveſts Dreſden. The ſuburbs burned. King of Pruſſia raiſes the ſiege of Neiſs and Coſel. He returns into Saxony. The Auſtrians retire into Bohemia. Diſpoſitions for the winter.

THE operations of the armies in Weſtphalia, ſeemed for a long time to languiſh. The grand army of the French under M. de Contades, was wholly unable to drive Prince Ferdinand from the poſts which he had choſen ſo judiciouſly along the Lippe. The other diviſion of the French forces under the Prince de Soubiſe, had made no great progreſs on the ſide of Heſſe-Caſſel, againſt the Prince Iſenburg, who ſtill kept his ground in that principality, in order to protect the courſe of the Weſer, and to cover the electorate. The French were ſenſible that an attack on the principal army of the allies, would prove a very dangerous attempt, in which even if they ſhould have ſome ſucceſs, their progreſs into the King's electoral dominions muſt be very ſlow and difficult. But as the body of the allies employed in Heſſe-Caſſel was far the weakeſt, and as an advantage on that ſide promiſed them the command of the Weſer, and a better paſſage into the heart of the enemies country, they determined to make an attempt there. To further this deſign, a conſiderable detachment was made from the army of M. de Contades, which increaſed the Prince of Soubiſe's corps to at leaſt 30,000 men. Prince Ferdinand, who was ſufficiently aware of the enemies plan, had ſome time before ſent General Oberg with a ſtrong reinforcement to join the Prince Iſenburg; but notwithſtanding this reinforcement, the whole force of the allies in Heſſe did not exceed 15000. This body was attacked by the French at Lanwerenhagen, and their great ſuperiority, eſpecially in point of cavalry, obliged the allies to retire with the loſs of about 1500 men. The allies unable to keep the field, had however ſome woods in their rear which covered their retreat, and they preſerved ſo good a countenance as prevented their defeat from becoming total. Sept. 30.

Great conſequences might have been apprehended from this affair. But the vigilance of Prince Ferdinand, who had eſtabliſhed the moſt ready communications all along the Lippe, ſuffered the victorious army to reap but little advantage from their victory. That accompliſhed general advanced with the utmoſt expedition towards Rheda, and the Prince Iſenburg having fallen back upon him, they joined in ſuch a manner as perfectly to ſecure the Weſer, without loſing any thing on the ſide of the Rhine. And although theſe neceſſary motions, in ſome ſort uncovered the electorate, ſo as to lay it open to the incurſions of the enemies light troops, who penetrated even to the gates of Hanover; yet the French were not in a condition to eſtabliſh any conſiderable body, or to take any poſt of moment in that part.

During this time, the armies of the King of Pruſſia and M. Daun made no very remarkable movements. The marſhal kept his advantageous camp at Stolpen, by which he preſerved a communication with the army of the Empire. The army was ſecured by its inacceſſible ſituation, but it enterpriſed nothing of conſequence. The King of Pruſſia on the other hand, having taken poſſeſſion of the important poſt of Bautzen, which lies ſo opportunely for commanding at once both Miſnia and Luſatia, extended his right wing to Hohkirchen. By this poſition he preſerved a communication with the army of his brother Prince Henry, he protected Brandenburg from the incurſions of the Auſtrians, and at the ſame time that he ſecured theſe intereſting objects, he was better ſituated for throwing ſuccours into Sileſia, than he could be any where elſe conſiſtently with his general plan. The two armies kept the moſt watchful eye upon each other's motions. The principal aim of the King of Pruſſia, ſeemed to have been the preventing M. Daun from communicating with Bohemia. The great intention of M. Daun was to cut off the King from Sileſia. Things were ſo ballanced, that it did not ſeem poſſible by mere ſkill in marches and poſitions to anſwer theſe ends very fully: therefore a battle ſeemed inevitable. But it ſeemed too that conſidering the ſituations of both armies, a battle could not be attempted without extreme danger to the party who ſhould begin the attack.

M. Daun ſaw that if any more time was loſt without action, the very ſeaſon muſt oblige him to evacuate Saxony, and thus give up all the fruits of the campaign. He came to a reſolution of giving the King of Pruſſia battle. But even in the vigour of this reſolution, appeared the extreme caution which characteriſes that able general. Having communicated his deſign to the Prince of Deux-Ponts, and ſettled meaſures with him, he marched in the dead of a very dark night, in three columns, towards the right of the King of Pruſſia's camp. Notwithſtanding the darkneſs of the night, notwithſtanding the neceſſary di- Oct. 14. viſion of the Auſtrian army, the greatneſs of their numbers, and the length of way they had to march, yet ſuch was the wiſe conduct and great good fortune of this deſign, that they all arrived at the ſame time at the Pruſſian camp, none having loſt their way, without diſcovery, without confuſion, and began the attack with the utmoſt regularity and reſolution at five o'clock in the morning.

How

How the King's out-guards were kept ſo as to make ſuch a ſurpriſe practicable, is hard to ſay. It is hard to accuſe the vigilance of ſo able a commander, or the attention of ſo many finiſhed officers as ſerved under him. To ſpeak of treachery is a way of accounting for misfortunes, more common than reaſonable. However it was, the Pruſſians had not time to ſtrike their tents, when they found the enemy in the midſt of the camp, and an impetuous attack already begun. Scarce had the battle began, when a defeat ſeemed certain; not ſo much from the confuſion of the troops, as the irreparable loſs of two officers in the higheſt command, and of the greateſt merit. M. Keith received two muſquet balls, and fell dead upon the ſpot. Prince Francis of Brunſwick had his head ſhot off by a cannon ball as he mounted his horſe. The King of Pruſſia had then the whole of affairs to ſuſtain alone, at the time when he moſt wanted aſſiſtance. But his preſence of mind, his firmneſs, his activity, remedied in ſome meaſure the effects of this unforeſeen attack, and the loſſes and diſorders it had occaſioned; he was every where preſent, and inſpired his troops with an ardor like his own. The King ordered ſome detachments from his left, to reinforce his right wing; but in the moment the orders were received, the left itſelf was furiouſly attacked. General Retzow who commanded in that quarter, with difficulty repulſed the Auſtrians, and was not able to afford any conſiderable aſſiſtance to the right, which was alone obliged to ſupport the whole weight of the grand attack.

The Auſtrians in the beginning of the engagement had beaten them out of the village of Hohkirchen; as the fate of the day depended upon that poſt, the hotteſt of the diſpute was there. The Pruſſians made three bloody and unſucceſsful attacks on the village; on the fourth they carried it; but the Auſtrians pouring continually freſh troops upon that ſpot, drove them out at length after reiterated efforts, and a prodigious ſlaughter on all ſides. Then the King deſpairing of the fortune of that field, ordered a retreat; his troops which had been ſuddenly attacked in a dark night by ſuperior numbers, and had ran to arms ſome half naked, and all in the utmoſt confuſion, had notwithſtanding made a moſt vigorous reſiſtance, and maintained the fight for near five hours. They made their retreat in good order without being purſued, ſupported by the good countenance of their cavalry, and the fire of a numerous and well ſerved artillery, which was placed in the center of their camp. They loſt in this bloody action at leaſt 7000 men, killed, wounded, and priſoners, together with many cannon. The Auſtrian account allowed their own loſs in killed and wounded to amount to near 5000.

The King of Pruſſia, in retiring from Hohkirchen, in fact only altered the poſition of his right wing, which fell back as far as Weiſſenburg. His left ſtill remained at Bautzen. This poſition was nearly as good as the former. The great loſs, was the loſs of reputation which always attends a defeat, and the loſs of two great generals which attended this in particular. M. Keith was a Scotchman born. He engaged with his brother the Lord Marſhal in the rebellion of 1715. Being

Being obliged to relinquifh his country on this occafion, he entered into the troops of Spain, and afterwards paffing into Ruffia, he obtained a confiderable command, and performed many fignal fervices in their wars with Turkey and Sweden; and ferved them alfo in peace by feveral embaffies. But finding the honours of that country no better than a fplendid fervitude, and not meeting with thofe rewards, which his long and faithful fervices deferved, he left that court for one where merit is better known and better rewarded; and having been employed fince the beginning of the war, in a diftinguifhed command in the King of Pruffia's armies, he fell at laft in a fervice that was worthy of him.

If the King of Pruffia loft fome reputation in fuffering himfelf to be furprifed in this affair; he fully retrieved it by his extraordinary conduct in the courfe of the action, and his admirable efforts after it. On the whole, perhaps, when all circumftances are confidered, the King of Pruffia will appear greater in this defeat, than in any victory he ever yet obtained. The wing of his army that was attacked, was furprifed at a diftance from him, the two generals that commanded it flain in the firft onfet, his other principal generals wounded, the whole wing in confufion without a leader; to come, in thefe defperate circumftances, in hafte from another quarter; to recover all; twice to repulfe the enemy, and at laft to retire, overborn only by numbers and fatigue, without being purfued, is fuch an inftance of great generalfhip, as perhaps has never been exceeded.

Whilft thefe things were doing in Saxony, the Ruffians made no farther attempts on the fide of Brandenburg; they remained in their camp near Landfperg, until the 21ft of September; when after feveral feigned motions, made to cover their real defign, they began their retreat towards Pomerania, where they arrived on the 26th.

It was impoffible that they fhould keep their ground in that province during the winter, unlefs they could fecure fome fea-port, from whence they might be fupplied with provifions. The little town of Colberg was very opportune for that purpofe, as it is a fea-port on the Baltic, and fo meanly fortified, that the reduction of it appeared to be as eafy as expedient. On the 3d of October, they formed the fiege of this inconfiderable place, with a body of 15,000 men. But fuch was the bravery of Major Heydon the governor, and fuch the incapacity of the Ruffians for operations of this nature, that this little town, defended only by a rampart, without any outwork, and lined with a very feeble garrifon, held out againft the repeated attacks of the enemy twenty-fix days, and then obliged them to raife the fiege, without any fuccours whatfoever from without. Oct. 29. This was the laft enterprife of the Ruffians. Their vaft army retired with difgrace, firft from Brandenburg, and then from Pomerania; not having been able to mafter one place of ftrength in either country; but having deftroyed with the moft favage barbarity in both the open towns and defencelefs villages; leaving as ftrong impreffions of con-

tempt

tempt for their incapacity, as of horror for their cruelty.

After the defeat which the king received at Hohkirchen, he omitted no meaſures to prevent the enemy from making any material advantage of it. He perceived clearly, that the advantage they propoſed to derive from it, was to cover the operations of their armies in Sileſia; and that they had no longer any ſerious deſign upon Saxony during this campaign. The King therefore made no ſcruple to reinforce his army by conſiderable detachments from that of Prince Henry, which were brought up by that Prince himſelf. And as he ſaw that Neiſs, the ſiege of which had been already formed and proſecuted with great vigour, muſt certainly ſurrender if it were not ſpeedily ſuccoured, he reſolved to march into Sileſia.

To the execution of this deſign the greateſt difficulties ſtarted up on all ſides. The army of M. Daun lately victorious, had no other buſineſs than to intercept him. To fight was dubious; to avoid it, hard. If he could even avoid a battle, he had much to apprehend from the efforts of the enemy to harraſs him on his march. If he ſhould be ſo happy as to eſcape or to conquer theſe difficulties, yet his march entirely uncovered Saxony, and abandoned that moſt intereſting poſſeſſion, very poorly defended, to all the force of two powerful armies.

On the other hand, if the conſideration of Saxony ſhould detain him in his preſent ſituation, Sileſia ran the ſame riſque, and the ſame or greater diſadvantages muſt enſue to his affairs, by ſuffering the Auſtrians to obtain a footing there. This dilemma, which would have rendered a meaner genius entirely inactive, and hindered him from taking any reſolution, only obliged the King of Pruſſia to take his reſolution with the greater ſpeed, and to execute it with the greater vigour.

On the 24th of November at night, he quitted his camp at Dobreſchutz, and making a great compaſs, he arrived, without any obſtruction from the enemy, in the plain of Gorlitz. A body of the Auſtrians had in vain endeavoured to ſecure this poſt before him; thoſe that arrived were defeated, with the loſs of eight hundred men. By this happy march, all the advantages of M. Daun's ſtudied poſition, of all the fruits his boaſted victory at Hohkirchen, were loſt in a moment, and an open paſſage to Sileſia lay before the King. He purſued his march with the greateſt diligence. General Laudon, with 24,000 men, was ſent to purſue him. That active general continually harraſſed his rear guard; but the King continued his march without interruption, and ſuffered him to take many little advantages, rather than, by delaying to conteſt ſmall matters, to endanger a deſign, which might be deciſive of the whole campaign.

On the other hand, Daun, not content with the obſtacles which General Laudon threw in the King's way, ſent a large body of horſe and foot by another route to reinforce the army, which under the generals Harſch and de Ville had formed the ſiege of Neiſs, and the blockade of Coſel. But he perceived that all theſe meaſures would probably prove ineffectual, as his principal project, which was to cover Sileſia, had been defeated. He therefore turned his views towards Saxony, and ſatisfying himſelf with detaching General Laudon, which might create an opinion that the whole

whole Austrian army pursued, he followed the King no farther than Gorlitz; which place he immediately quitted, and having by forced marches gained the Elbe, he passed

Nov. 6. that river at Pirna, and advanced towards Dresden. At the same time the army of the Empire, by its motions, having obliged the Prussian army, then extremely weakened by the detachments that had been drawn from it, to retire from its post before Dresden, some miles to the westward of that city, cut off their communication with Leipsic, whilst M. Daun attempted to cut off their communication with Dresden; but they found means to throw themselves into that city, and afterwards to retire to the other side of the Elbe. The Austrians and Imperialists began at once to invest those two important places; another party advanced towards Torgau, and attempted that town. It seemed utterly impossible to prevent the Austrians from becoming masters of Saxony, who in a manner covered the whole country with their forces.

In the mean time, the King of Prussia drew nearer and nearer to Neiss. The siege of that fortress was commenced on the 4th of August; on the 3d of October it was completely invested; and the place was pushed on one side with the greatest vigour, and on the other maintained with the most consummate skill and bravery, until the approach of the King of Prussia obliged the Austrians, on the 1st of November, to raise the siege, leaving a considerable quantity of military stores behind them. The same terror obliged the parties employed in the blockade of Cosel, to leave that place at liberty, and to fall back, together with the armies of the generals Harsch and de Ville, into Bohemia, and the Austrian Silesia.

The King of Prussia, when he had thus by the report of Nov. 9. his march, without fighting, driven his enemies out of Silesia, lost not a moment to return by the same route, and with the same expedition to the relief of Saxony. Two bodies of his troops had moved for the same purpose out of Pomerania, one under Count Dohna, and one under General Wedel. The corps under Wedel had thrown itself into Torgau, repulsed the Austrians, who had attempted that place, and pursued them as far as Eulenburg. The grand operation of the Austrians was against Dresden. M. Daun, with an army of 60,000 men, came before that city, on the very day on which the King of Prussia began his march to oppose him, so that he might well imagine his success certain against a place meanly fortified, and defended only by 12000 men. The same day he began to cannonade it, and his light troops, supported by the grenadiers of the army, made a sharp attack upon the suburbs. The governor Count Schmettau saw that from the weakness of the suburbs, it would prove impossible for him to prevent the enemy from possessing himself of them by a *coup de main*; and if they succeeded in this attempt, the great height of the houses, being six or seven stories, and entirely commanding the ramparts, would render the reduction of the body of the place equally easy and certain. These considerations determined him to set these suburbs on fire.

It is well known that the suburbs of Dresden compose one of the finest towns in Europe, and are greatly

greatly superior to that which lies within the walls. Here the most wealthy part of the inhabitants reside, and here are carried on those several curious manufactures for which Dresden is so famous. Count Daun foresaw this consequence of his attempt. He endeavoured to intimidate the governor from this measure, to which he knew the cruel reason of war would naturally lead him, by threatening to make him personally answerable for the steps he should take; but Count Schmettau answered with the firmness that became a man of honour and a soldier, that he would answer whatever he should do, and would not only burn the suburbs, in case M. Daun advanced, but would likewise defend the city itself street by street, and at last even the castle, which was the royal residence, if he should be driven to it. When the magistrates were apprised of this resolution, they fell at the feet of Count Schmettau, and implored him to change his mind, and to have mercy on that devoted part of their city. The part of the royal family, who remained in Dresden, joined their supplications to those of the magistrates; they prayed him to spare that last refuge of distressed royalty, and to allow at least a secure residence to those, who had been deprived of every thing else. All entreaties were vain. Schmettau continued firm in his resolution. He told them that their safety depended on themselves, and on M. Daun; that if he made no attempts, the suburbs should be still secure; but that if he took any farther steps, the necessity of his master's service, and his own honour, wuold compel him to act very disagreeable to the lenity of his disposition. The magistrates retired in despair. Combustibles were laid in all their houses.

At three o'clock next morning, the signal for firing the suburbs was given; Nov. 10. and in a moment, a place so lately the seat of ease and luxury, flourishing in traffic, in pleasures, and ingenious arts, was all in flames. A calamity so dreadful need no high colouring. However, as little mischief attended such a combustion as the nature of the thing could admit. Very few lost their lives; but many their whole substance. When this was done, the Prussian troops abandoned the flaming suburbs, and retired in good order into the city.

M. Daun saw this fire, which whilst it laid waste the capital of his ally, made it more difficult for him to force it, he sent in some empty threats to the governor. But the Saxon minister at Ratisbon made grievous complaints to the Diet of what he represented as the most unparalleled act of wanton and unprovoked cruelty, that had ever been committed. The emissaries of the court of Vienna spread the same complaints; and they made no scruple to invent, and to alter facts in such a manner as to move the greatest pity towards the sufferers, and the greatest indignation against the King of Prussia. All these, however, were in a short time abundantly confuted, by the authentic certificates of the magistrates of Dresden, and of those officers of the court, who were perfectly acquainted with the transaction. By these certificates it appears that only two hundred and fifty houses were consumed. Though this was a terrible calamity, it was nothing to the accounts given in the gazettes of the Austrian faction.

By

2

By these certificates it appears alſo, that the people were not ſurpriſed, but had ſufficient notice of the governor's intentions, to enable them to provide for their ſafety. In a word, all the charges of cruelty againſt the Pruſſian commander, and ſoldiery, were fully overthrown.

This fire made a *coup de main* impracticable; regular operations demanded time, and the King of Pruſſia was now in full march towards Saxony. M. Daun retired from before the place on the 17th. The King after croſſing Luſatia, paſſing the Elbe, and joining his troops under Count Dohna and General Wedel, arrived triumphantly at Dreſden on the 20th. The armies of M. Daun and the Empire gave way towards Bohemia, into which kingdom they ſoon after finally retreated, without enterpriſing any thing further. Six ſieges were raiſed almoſt at the ſame time; that of Colberg, carried on by General Palmbach, under the orders of Marſhal Fermor; that of Neiſs, by M. de Harſch; that of Coſel; that of Dreſden, by Marſhal Daun; the blockade of Torgau, by M. Haddic; and that of Leipſic, by the Prince of Deux-Ponts.

About the time that the Auſtrians retired into winter quarters, the French did the ſame; and the Hanoverians permitted them to do it without moleſtation, the ſeaſon being too far advanced, and their army perhaps not of ſufficient ſtrength for offenſive operations; and Prince Ferdinand kept the field no longer. The Britiſh troops had no occaſion of ſignalizing their bravery during this year; but without a battle the nation ſuffered a very conſiderable loſs, and was touched with a very deep and general ſorrow. The Duke of Marlborough died in Munſter, the 20th of October, of a fever, contracted by the fatigues of the campaign. Never did the nation loſe in one man, a temper more candid and benevolent, manners more amiable and open, a more primitive integrity, a more exalted generoſity, a more warm and feeling heart. He left all the enjoyments, which an ample fortune and an high rank could beſtow in the public eye; and which every milder virtue, every diſpoſition to make and to be made happy, could give in a domeſtic life: he left theſe for the ſervice of his country, and died for its defence, as he had lived for its ornament and happineſs.

If we compare the events of this year with thoſe of the laſt, we ſhall find in the actions of the preſent year, perhaps ſomething leſs of that aſtoniſhing eclat; fewer battles; not ſo many nor ſo ſtriking revolutions of fortune; but we may diſcover upon all ſides far greater management, and a more ſtudied and refined conduct; more artful movements, a more judicious choice of poſts, more quick and vigorous marches. If in the laſt year, the King of Pruſſia was the hero of the imagination, he is this year the hero of the judgment; and we have, I think, reaſon to admire him upon juſter principles. Obliged to evacuate Moravia, he throws himſelf into Bohemia, and executes a retreat with all the ſpirit of an invaſion. He marches more than an hundred miles thro' an enemy's country, followed and harraſſed by large armies, who are unable to obtain any advantages over him. Gaining at length his own territories, he engaged the vaſt army of the Ruſ-

ſians

ſians and defeats it. He is unable to follow his blow, but he diſables them from ſtriking any blow againſt that part of his dominions, which he is obliged to leave. Whilſt he is engaged with the Ruſſians on the frontiers of Poland, the Auſtrians and Imperialiſts enter Saxony. Before they can do any thing deciſive, the King is himſelf ſuddenly in Saxony, and by his preſence, at once diſconcerts all their projects. The ſcene is again changed, they ſurpriſe him in his camp at Hohkirchen, two of his generals are killed, his army defeated, his camp is taken. They attack Sileſia with a formidable army. Notwithſtanding his late defeat; notwithſtanding the great ſuperiority of his enemies; notwithſtanding the advantage of their poſts; he makes an amazing ſweep about all their forces, eludes their vigilance, renders their poſitions unprofitable; and marching with an aſtoniſhing rapidity into the remoteſt parts of Sileſia, obliges the Auſtrian armies to retire with precipitation out of that province. Then he flies to the relief of Saxony, which his enemies had again profited of his abſence to invade; and again by the ſame rapid and well conducted march, he obliges them to abandon their prize. Defeated by the Auſtrians he acquired by his conduct all the advantages of the moſt compleat victory. He guarded all his poſſeſſions in ſuch a manner, as to enable them all to endure his abſence for ſome ſhort time; and he conducted his marches with ſuch ſpirit, as did not make it neceſſary to them to hold out any longer; he made twice the circuit of his dominions, and in their turn he relieved them all.

Nor was the conduct of Prince Ferdinand of Brunſwick leſs worthy of admiration. Placed at the head of a body of troops, who were but lately obliged to lay down their arms, he found the enemy in poſſeſſion of the whole open country, and of all the ſtrong places in it. Commencing the campaign in the midſt of a ſevere winter, without any place of ſtrength in his hands, he drove the enemy from all thoſe they held. He obliged them to repaſs the Rhine, he followed and defeated them in a pitched battle. Being afterwards obliged by the great force of France on its own frontier, and the numerous armies they had in different places, to repaſs the Rhine; he defeated Lippe againſt numbers greatly ſuperior, and though they defeated a part of his army, they were not able to turn their victory to the leaſt advantage. Prince Ferdinand's campaign may well paſs for a perfect model of defenſive operatiens.

The Auſtrians, in taking winter quarters, diſpoſed their forces ſo as to form a chain of an amazing length, from the frontiers of Moravia paſſing through Bohemia, all along the ſkirts of Sileſia and the borders of Saxony. There the Imperial army joined this chain, and continued it through Thuringia and Franconia, where it was united to the quarters of the Prince de Soubiſe. Theſe troops had fallen back from Heſſe-Caſſel, finding themſelves unable to maintain their ground in the landgraviate. The Prince de Soubiſe's cantonments extended weſtward along the courſe of the Maine and Lahn, to meet thoſe of M. de Contades which ſtretched to the Rhine, and continued the chain beyond it quite to the

the Maese, so as to command the whole course of the Rhine, on both sides, both upward and downward. Prince Ferdinand was unable to extend himself to such a length; and especially found it impracticable to establish quarters on the other side of the Rhine; but he disposed his troops in the most advantageous manner in the bishopricks of Munster, Paderborn, and Hildesheim, and in the landgraviate of Hesse-Cassel. The several bodies may all unite with ease, and support each other. To preserve a communication between this and the Prussian army, as well as to break some part of that formidable chain of the enemy, the King sent some bodies of his troops into Thuringia, who dispossessed the army of the Empire of several of their posts there, and they now threaten to penetrate still farther.

The King of Prussia, when he had a second time driven the Austrians and Imperialists out of Saxony, resolved to keep no measures with that unhappy country. He declared that he was resolved no longer to consider it as a deposit, but as a country which he had twice subdued by his arms. He therefore ordered those of the King of Poland's privy council, who still remained at Dresden, to retire at a very short warning. But if the King of Prussia had a right, as perhaps he had, to consider Saxony as a lawful conquest, he certainly seemed not to consider the people as subjects, when he continued to exact the most severe contributions; and in a manner too very little becoming a lawful sovereign; for he surrounded the exchange with soldiers, and confining the merchants in narrow lodgings on straw beds, he obliged them by extreme suffering, to draw bills on their foreign correspondents for very large sums. This city had been quite exhausted by former payments, and had not long before suffered military execution. An enemy that acted thus, had acted severely; but when a country is entirely possessed by any power, and claimed as a conquest, the rights of war seem to cease; and the people have a claim to be governed in such a manner as becomes a just prince; especially when no extreme necessity in his affairs compels him to these rigorous courses. To retaliate on these miserable people some part of the cruelties committed by the Russians on his dominions, seems to be very unreasonable, as it is but too obvious, that the barbarity of that people could not be restrained, however it might be exasperated by the total destruction of Saxony. Such retaliations are odious and cruel. We heartily wish we could praise the King of Prussia as much for his temperate use of his conquest, as for those wonderful and heroic qualities by which he obtained it. We might be considered as partial in our account, if we had omitted to take notice of what is alledged against the King of Prussia, when we have spoken so fully of the outrages committed by his enemies. It is now time to turn our eyes from this great theatre towards lesser events, but such as will employ us altogether as agreeably: the operations of the British fleets and armies in Europe and America against the French.

CHAP.

CHAP. XIII.

The burning of the ships at St. Malo. Taking of Cherbourg. Defeat at St. Cas. Operations in America. Siege and taking of Louisbourg. English army defeated at Ticonderoga. They take Frontenac The French abandon Fort du Quesne. Conclusion of the annals of the Year 1758.

IN the beginning of this year, the good condition of our navy and our army; the spirit and popularity of the ministry; the wise choice of commanders, in contempt of vulgar and trivial maxims; the prevalence of the contrary to all these among the enemy gave us the best grounded hopes of a vigorous and successful campaign. Concerning the theatre of our operations there was some doubt. In was the opinion of some, that our push in Europe should be made on the side of Germany; and that we ought to strengthen the army of Prince Ferdinand with such a respectable body of troops, as might enable that finished commander to exert all his talents, and improve to the utmost the advantages he had already obtained over the French. They imagined, that if an early and considerable reinforcement were sent to the Prince, whilst the French army was yet in a distressed condition, and if in this condition that should receive any considerable blow, they would find it extremely difficult to retrieve it: and receiving this blow, on the frontier of their own territories, the Prince might carry the war into France itself; and thus very probably bring matters to a speedy decision. That in pursuing this plan a diversion on the coast of France was by no means excluded: and that on the contrary it must, on this plan, be attended with consequences infinitely more important than it could otherwise; that otherwise, France might laugh at the little desultory efforts of an handful of men, who were to be embarked and disembarked with great difficulty and hazard, and which would always be obliged to fly at the first approach of an enemy. That whilst the French had only an army, greatly inferior in number to engage on the side of Germany, they would always find themselves to be able to act abroad, and defend themselves at home.

On the other hand it was strongly urged, that we ought to make the destruction of the French marine our great object, and to consider all continental operations only in a secondary light That in sending a large body of English troops to the King's army on the Rhine, we must necessarily weaken our efforts in America, and on the coast of France; and by drawing away all our forces, we must shake that internal security, which invigorated all our operations abroad. That whilst we maintained an army of 50,000 foreigners in Germany, it would be the greatest imprudence to send also a large body of our own national troops into the same country, and by that means not only squander away our men, but employ almost every penny granted for the land service, out of Great Britain; a method which could not fail of exhausting us in a very short time. That the force already in Germany was sufficient to keep the French engaged, and that the proposed expeditions to France would,

would, by attacking the coaſt, now in one part, now in another, and keeping all parts in continual alarms, neceſſarily detain a very conſiderable part of their forces at home, and thus make a powerful diverſion, whilſt it was purſuing what ought to be the grand perpetual object of all our operations, the deſtruction of the French maritime power.

The latter opinion prevailed; but it was however ſo far modified by the arguments on the other ſide, that after ſome time a few regiments were ſent into Germany, as we have before related. Theſe and better reaſons, no doubt, determined the operations on the coaſt of France; but whilſt the neceſſary preparations were making, their deſtination was kept an inviolable ſecret; and now, as they had the year before, inſpired France with no little terror. Two ſquadrons, by the latter end of May, were in readineſs for ſailing. The greater under Lord Anſon, the ſmaller under Commodore Howe, which was ſo deſigned to convoy the tranſports, and to favour the landing and reimbarkment. The land forces conſiſted of ſixteen battalions, and nine troops of light horſe: they were commanded by the late Duke of Marlborough. They ſailed from Portſmouth; but as ſoon
June 1.
as the fleet ſet ſail, the ſquadron of my Lord Anſon ſeparated from the reſt, and bore off to the Bay of Biſcay, in order to ſpread the alarm more widely, and to obſerve the French ſquadron in Breſt. The other part of the fleet, which was commanded by Commodore Howe, with the tranſports, arrived without any accident in Cancalle Bay, at a ſmall diſtance from the city of St. Malo. Here the troops landed without oppoſition, 5th.
and having fortified a poſt near Cancalle, (a poſt by nature well fitted for defence) for the ſecurity of their retreat, they marched in two columns to St. Maloes. When the army arrived there it was ſoon viſible, that the town, ſtrongly ſituated on a peninſula, communicating with the main land only by a long and narrow cauſeway, was by no means a proper object of a *coup de main*; and though for want of outworks, it was ill qualified to ſuſtain a regular ſiege; yet our forces were, for want of ſtrength and artillery ſufficient, altogether as ill qualified for ſuch an operation. They were therefore contented with ſetting fire to about an hundred ſail of ſhipping, many of them privateers, 8th.
which lay under the cannon of the town, and to ſeveral magazines filled with naval ſtores. The damage was very conſiderable; yet, what is to be remarked, the enemy did not fire a ſingle ſhot on the detachment employed in this ſervice. Having nothing more to do on this ſide, they retired to Cancalle; and reimbarked with as little oppoſition as they met 12th.
with at landing; the land and ſea commanders having made all the diſpoſitions with great judgment.

Before the fleet returned, they reconnoitred the town of Granville on the coaſt of Normandy; but finding that a large body of troops were encamped in the neighbourhood, they made no attempt there. From thence they moved towards Cherbourg, and made the proper diſpoſitions for landing near that place; but a hard gale blowing in to the ſhore, and the tranſports beginning to fall foul four on each other, it became extremely hazardous to attempt landing. Befides, the provifion was near exhaufted, and the foldiers by being fo long cooped up in the tranfports, were grown fickly. It became highly neceffary to return home; and they arrived at St. Helen's on the 29th of June.

The fuccefs of this expedition, by which the French fuffered largely, with fcarce any lofs on our fide, though it fufficiently anfwered the intention of this armament, fell fomewhat fhort of the expectations of the public, who had formed much greater hopes than it was poffible for the nature of fuch enterprifes to fulfil. However, their hopes were again revived; by feeing that every thing was prepared for another expedition, and that our armies and fleets were to be kept in conftant action during the fummer. The time was now come when we were to turn the tables upon France, and to retaliate by real attacks, the terrors which had been raifed by her menaces of an invafion. The Duke of Marlborough had now taken the command of the Englifh forces in Germany; and General Bligh fucceeded him in this command. Prince Edward refolved to go upon the expedition, and to form himfelf for the fervice of his country under fo brave and able a commander as Howe. It is eafy to imagine, how much the fpirit, the prefence and example of the gallant young Prince, who went with the utmoft cheerfulnefs through all the detail of a midfhipman's duty, infpired both into the feamen and the troops.

On the firft of Auguft, the fleet fet fail from St. Helen's. In a few days they came to anchor before Cherbourg. The French had drawn a line ftrengthened by forts, along the moft probable places for landing. They had drawn down three regiments of regular troops, and a confiderable body of militia to the fhore, and had in all appearance threatened a very refolute oppofition to the defcent of the Englifh forces. But the commodore difpofed the men of war and bomb ketches fo judicioufly, and made fo fharp a fire upon the enemy, that they never ventured out of their intrenchments; fo that the landing was effected in excellent order and with very little lofs. Aug. 6. The French who made fo poor an oppofition to the landing, had ftill many advantages from the nature of the ground which they occupied; but they neglected them all; and abandoning by a moft fhameful defpair their forts and lines on the coaft, they fuffered the Englifh to enter Cherbourg the day after the landing, without throwing the leaft obftacle in their way. It muft be remembered too that the whole number of the Englifh forces on this expedition, was rather fhort of 6000 men.

Cherbourg is on the land fide an open town; neither is it very ftrongly defended towards the fea. The harbour is naturally bad. But the place is well fituated, in the midft of the channel, for protecting the French, and annoying the Englifh commerce in the time of war, and perhaps for facilitating an invafion on England itfelf. Monfieur Belidor the famous engineer, had demonftrated its importance, and propofed a plan for the improvement and defence of the harbour, as well as for the fortifications of the town. The plan was approved and partly put in execution by the building of a mole, digging a bafon, and making fluices and flood gates with excellent materials and at a vaft expence. The work had been for a confiderable time difcontinued; but in this expedition, that work of fo much ingenuity, charge, and labour, was totally deftroyed. Whilft our humanity regrets the unhappy neceffity of war, we cannot help thinking that the Englifh nation was freed by the fuccefs of this expedition, from what might one day be caufe of no trivial alarms.

When this work of deftruction was over, all the veffels in the harbour burned, and hoftages taken for the contributions levied on the town, the forces reimbarked
16th. with great fpeed and fafety without any interruption from the enemy, and with the fame expedition, care and conduct, as they had been firft landed; the army having continued ten days unmolefted in France.

The nation exulted greatly in this advantage, efpecially as it almoft accompanied the news of our glorious fucceffes in America. Nothing was omitted to give the action its utmoft eclat; the brafs cannon and mortars taken at Cherbourg were drawn from Kenfington to the Tower, quite through the city, in great pomp and order, adorned with ftreamers,
Sep. 16. attended by guards, drums, mufic, and whatever elfe might draw the attention of the vulgar. They who cenfured this proceffion as too oftentatious, did not confider how forcibly things of this nature ftrike upon ordinary minds, and how greatly they contribute to keep the people in good humour to fupport the many charges and loffes that are incident to the moft fuccefsful war.

The fleet when it left Cherbourg, was driven to the coaft of England; but the troops were not difembarked; it was refolved, that the coaft of France fhould have no refpite; and accordingly they failed towards St. Malo, and landed in the bay of St. Lunar at a fmall diftance from the town of St. Malo. This choice of a place for landing, muft neceffarily have furprifed all thofe who remembered upon what reafons the attempt againft that place had been fo recently laid afide. There was no other object of fufficient confideration near it. The town was at leaft in as good a pofture of defence as it had been then; and the force which was to attack it had fince then been confiderably leffened. There is undoubtedly fomething very unaccountable, as well in the choice as in the whole conduct of this affair. The perfons in the principal commands, fhifted the blame from one to another. There is nothing more remote from our defign, than to fet up for judges in matters of this nature; or ungeneroufly to lean on an officer, who meaning well to the fervice of his country, by fome misfortune or miftake fails in fuch hazardous and intricate enterprifes. We fhall be fatisfied with relating the facts as they happened.

As foon as the troops were landed in the bay of St. Lunar, it became evident that the defign againft St. Malo was utterly impracticable. Other objects were then propofed, but they all feemed equally liable to objection. Whilft they debated concerning a plan for their operations, the fleet was in the

the greateſt danger. The bay of St. Lunar is extremely rocky; and the experience of the people of the country, together with what he ſaw himſelf, convinced the commodore that it was impoſſible to remain any longer in this road with tolerable ſafety. Therefore he moved up to the bay of St. Cas, about three leagues to the weſtward.

The fleet was ſeparated from the land forces; but it was ſtill eaſy to preſerve a communication between them; and as no attack was yet apprehended, they made no ſcruple to penetrate farther into the country. In two days they arrived at the village of Matignon, having had ſeveral ſkirmiſhes with ſmall bodies of the enemy, who from time to time appeared on their flanks, and who always diſappeared when they were briſkly encountered. By this time the Duke d'Aiguillon, governor of Brittany, was advanced within ſix miles of the Engliſh army, with a body of twelve battalions and ſix ſquadrons of regular troops, and two regiments of militia. This determined the council of war to retreat; they wanted but three miles to the bay of St. Cas. But in this little march a conſiderable time was conſumed, and the French army was cloſe upon them before they could be compleatly reimbarked. A very ſteep hill formed a ſort of amphitheatre about the bay of St. Cas, where the embarkation was making; but before the laſt diviſion, which conſiſted of all the grenadiers of the army, and the firſt regiment of guards, could get off, the French had marched down this hill, through an hollow way, and formed themſelves in a long line againſt the few Engliſh troops that remained. There remained in this exigency only the expedient of aſſuming a bold countenance, and attacking them with vigour. The bravery of our troops on this deſperate occaſion, was worthy of a better fortune. The ſhips and frigates ſeconded their efforts, and made a ſevere fire upon the enemy. All was to no purpoſe; their ammunition was at laſt ſpent; the enemies numbers prevailed; our little body attempted to retreat, but they fell into confuſion, they broke, an horrible ſlaughter followed, many ran into the water, and met their fate in that element. The ſhore was covered with dead bodies. General Dury was drowned. Sir John Armitage, a young volunteer of great fortune and hopes, was ſhot through the head. Several officers, men of large fortune and conſideration, fell. At length the firing of the frigates ceaſed, and the French immediately gave quarter. About 400 were made priſoners, 600 were killed and wounded.

In the midſt of this carnage, in the midſt of a fire that ſtaggered the braveſt ſeamen who managed the boats, Commodore Howe exhibited a noble example of intrepidity and fortitude, by ordering himſelf to be rowed in his own boat through the thickeſt of the fire, to encourage all that were engaged in that ſervice, and to bring off as many men as his veſſel could carry.

This affair diſpirited the people of England, and elated the people of France, far more than an affair of ſo little conſequence ought to have done. It was in fact no more than the cutting off a rear guard. There is often more bloodſhed in ſkirmiſhes in Germany, which make no figure in the Gazettes. And

 certainly,

certainly, if our expeditions to the coast of France were planned with any judgment, on our part we had rather reason to congratulate ourselves that we were able to land three times on that coast, with so inconsiderable a loss. The French indeed had reason to magnify this loss; and they did greatly magnify it in order to console their people, who had seen their trade suffer so much, and their country so long insulted with impunity.

Whatever our successes were on the coast of France, they did not affect us in the same manner with those which we had in America. From this part of the world we had long been strangers to any thing, but delays, misfortunes, disappointments, and disgraces. But the spirit which had been roused at home, diffused itself into all parts of the world where we had any concern, and invigorated all our operations.

Admiral Boscawen with a powerful fleet of men of war, and several transports, sailed for Halifax, from England Feb. 19th. He had the chief command of the expedition against Louisbourg, and in particular the direction of the naval operations. General Amherst, from whose character great things were expected, and who justified these expectations, was to command the land forces. These amounted to about 4000 men, including some light troops, fitted for the peculiar service of the country. The whole fleet, consisting of 151 ships, set sail from the harbour of Halifax. On the second of June, they appeared before Louisbourg. They were six days on the coast before a landing was found practicable; such a prodigious surf swelled all along the shore, that no boat could possibly live near it. The French not trusting to this obstacle, had drawn entrenchments in every part where it might be possible to land, supported them with batteries in convenient places, and lined them with a numerous infantry. At length the surf though violent, at best, was observed to be somewhat abated, and the admiral and general did not lose a moment to avail themselves of this first opportunity of landing; they made all their dispositions for it with the highest judgment. They ordered the frigates towards the enemies right and left, to rake them on their flanks. Then the troops were disposed for landing in three divisions. That on the left was commanded by General Wolfe, and was destined to the real attack. The divisions in the center to the right, were only designed for feigned attacks to draw the enemies attention to all parts, and to distract their defence. June 8.

When the fire of the frigates continued about a quarter of an hour, General Wolfe's division moved towards the land; the enemy reserved their shot until the boats were near the shore, and then directed the whole fire of their cannon and musquetry upon them. The surf aided their fire. Many of the boats overset, many were broke to pieces, the men jumped into the water, some were killed, some drowned; the rest supported and encouraged in all difficulties, by the example, spirit, and conduct of their truly gallant commander, gained the shore, took post, fell upon the enemy with such order and resolution, that they soon obliged them to fly in confusion. As soon as this post was made good, the center moved towards the left, and the right followed the center, ſo that the landing was compleated, though not without much time and trouble, in an excellent order, and with little loſs.

The operations of a ſiege are too minute and unintereſting to make a detail of them agreeable to readers, who are not converſant in the art military. The operations againſt Louisbourg for ſeveral days went on very ſlowly, owing entirely to the prodigious ſurf and the rough weather, which made it extremely difficult to land the artillery, ſtores, and inſtruments to be employed in the ſiege; however, the excellent conduct of the generals Amherſt and Wolfe, by degrees overcame all the difficulties of the weather, which was extremely unfavourable, the ground which was rugged in ſome places and boggy in others, and the reſiſtance of the garriſon which was conſiderable. The French had five men of war of the line in the harbour, who could bring all their guns to bear upon the approaches of the Engliſh troops. The firſt thing done was to ſecure a point called the light-houſe battery, from whence they might play upon theſe veſſels, and on the batteries on the other ſide of the harbour. General Wolfe performed the ſervice with his uſual vigour and celerity, and took poſſeſſion of
12th. this and all the other poſts in that quarter. His fire from this poſt on the 25th ſilenced the iſland battery, which was that moſt immediately oppoſed to his; but the ſhips ſtill continued to bear upon him until the 21ſt of the following month, when one of them blew up, and communicating the fire to the two others, they alſo were in a ſhort time conſumed to the water edge. This was a loſs not to be repaired; the approaches drew near the covered way, and things were in a good condition for making a lodgement in it; the enemies fire was conſiderably ſlackened: the town was conſumed to the ground in many places, and the works had ſuffered much in all. Yet the enemy ſtill delaying to ſurrender, gave occaſion to add one brave action to the others which had been diſplayed during the courſe of this ſiege. The admiral, who had all along done every thing poſſible to ſecond the efforts of the land forces, notwithſtanding the ſeverity of the weather, reſolved on a ſtroke, which by being deciſive of the poſſeſſion of the harbour, might make the reduction of the town a matter of little difficulty. He reſolved to ſend in a detachment of 600 ſeamen in boats, to take or burn the two ſhips of the line which remained, and if he ſhould ſucceed in this, he propoſed the next day to ſend in ſome of his own great ſhips who might batter the town on the ſide of the harbour. This was not more wiſely planned by the admiral, than gallantly and ſucceſsfully executed by Captain Laforey. In ſpite of the fire from the ſhips and the batteries, he made himſelf July 25. maſter of both theſe ſhips, one he towed off, the other as ſhe ran aground, was ſet on fire.

This ſtroke, in ſupport of the ſpirited advances of the land forces, was concluſive. The July 26. town ſurrendered the next day. The garriſon were priſoners of war, and amounted with the irregulars and ſeamen to 5637.

The taking of Louisbourg was an event the most desired by all our colonies; that harbour had always been a receptacle convenient to the enemies privateers, who infested the English trade in North America. It was the most effectual blow which France had received from the commencement of the war. By the taking of Louisbourg, she lost the only place from whence she could carry on the cod fishery; and the only place she had in a convenient situation for the reinforcements that were sent to support the war in the other parts of America; and with Louisbourg fell the island of St. John's, and whatever other inferior stations they had for carrying on the fishery towards Gaspesie and the bay de Chaleurs, which our ships soon after this event entirely destroyed. It is incredible how much this success in America, joined to the spirit of our other measures, operated to raise our military reputation in Europe, and to sink that of France, and consequently how much it influenced our most essential interests, and those of our allies.

The plan of our operations in America were, however, by no means confined solely to this object, important as it was. Two other attempts were proposed: the first attempt was with a great force to drive the French from Ticonderoga and Crown Point; in which, if we could succeed, the enemy would lose their posts from which they were in the best condition to molest our colonies, and by losing them, would lay open an easy road into the very heart of their settlements in Canada. The second attempt was to be made with a considerable, though an inferior force, from Pensylvania against Fort du Quesne: the success of this attempt would establish us in the possession of the Ohio, and break off the connection between Canada and Louisiana.

General Abercrombie, commander in chief of our forces in America, conducted the first of those expeditions. He embarked upon Lake George with near 16000 troops, regulars and provincials, and a numerous artillery, on the 5th of July; and after a prosperous navigation, arrived the next day at the place where it had been proposed to make the landing. They landed without opposition. The enemies advanced guards fled at their approach. The English army proceeded in four columns to Ticonderoga. As the country through which their march lay is difficult and woody, and the guides which conducted the march to this unknown country, were extremely unskilful, the troops were bewildered, the columns broke and fell in upon one another. Whilst they marched out in this alarming disorder the advanced guard of the French, which had lately fled before them, was bewildered in the same manner; and in the same disorder fell in with our forces. A skirmish ensued, in which this party was quickly defeated with the loss of near 300 killed and 148 prisoners. The loss on the English side was inconsiderable in numbers; but great in consequence. Lord Howe was killed. This gallant man, from the moment he landed in America, had wisely conformed and made his regiment conform to the kind of service which the country required. He did not suffer any under him to encumber themselves with superfluous baggage;

gage; he himself set the example, and fared like a common soldier The first to encounter danger, to endure hunger, to support fatigue; rigid in his discipline, but easy in his manners, his officers and soldiers readily obeyed the commander, because they loved the man; and now at the moment when such abilities, and such an example were the most wanted, was fatally lost a life which was long enough for his honour, but not for his country. It adds indeed to the glory of such a death, and to the consolation of his country, that we still possess the heir of his titles, his fortunes, and virtues, whilst we tremble to see the same virtues exposing themselves to the same dangers *

Excepting this loss, the army had hitherto proceeded successfully. In a little time they appeared before

July 8. Ticonderoga. This is a very important post, and as strongly secured. The fort is situated on a tongue of land between Lake George and a narrow gut, which communicates with the Lake Champlain. On three sides it is surrounded with water; and for a good part of the fourth it has a dangerous morass in front; where that failed, the French had made a very strong line upwards of eight feet high, defended by cannon, and secured by 4 or 5000 men. A great fall of trees with their branches outward, was spread before the entrenchment for about an hundred yards.

The general caused the ground to be reconnoitred; and the engineer made so favourable a report of the weakness of the retrenchment, that it appeared practicable to force it by musquetry alone. A fatal resolution was taken, in consequence of this report, not to wait the arrival of the artillery, which on account of the badness of the ground, could not be easily brought up, to attack the enemy without loss of time They were confirmed in this precipitate resolution, by a rumour that a body of 3000 men were on their march to join the French at Ticonderoga, and very shortly expected to arrive.

When the attack began, the difficulty of the ground and the strength of the enemies lines which had been so little foreseen, was but too severely felt. Although the troops behaved with the utmost spirit and gallantry, they suffered so terribly in their approaches, and made so little impression on the entrenchment, that the general seeing their reiterated and obstinate efforts fail of success, being upwards

* Soon after the news of Lord Howe's death arrived, the following advertisement appeared in the public papers; an application worthy of a Roman matron, in the virtuous times of the republic, and which could not fail of success, where the least spark of virtue existed:

'To the gentlemen, clergy, freeholders, and burgesses of the town and 'county of the town of Nottingham.

'As Lord Howe is now absent upon the public service, and Lieutenant 'Colonel Howe is with his regiment at Louisbourg, it rests upon me to 'beg the favour of your votes and interests, that Lieutenant Colonel Howe 'may supply the place of his late brother, as your representative in parlia'ment.

'Permit me therefore to implore the protection of every one of you, as the 'mother of him, whose life has been lost in the service of his country.'

Albemarle Street, Sept. 14, 1758. CHARLOTTE HOWE.

upwards of four hours expoſed to a moſt terrible fire, thought it neceſſary to order a retreat, to ſave the remains of the army. Near 2000 of our men were killed, wounded and taken priſoners ; the number of the taken being very inconſiderable. This precipitate attack was followed by a retreat as precipitate ; inſomuch that our army gained their former camp to the ſouthward of Lake
July 9. George, the evening after the action.

To repair the misfortune of this bloody defeat, General Abercrombie detached Colonel Bradſtreet with about 3000 provincials againſt Fort Frontenac. The colonel with great prudence and vigour, ſurmounting great difficulties, brought his army to Oſwego, where he embarked on the Lake Ontario, and arrived at Frontenac the 25th of Auguſt. This fort ſtands at the communication of Lake Ontario with the river St. Lawrence, the entrance into which river it in ſome manner commands. However, for a poſt of much moment, it was poorly fortified, and poorly garriſoned. It was taken without the loſs of a man on our ſide, in leſs
Aug. 27 than two days after it had been attacked. The garriſon conſiſting of 130 men were made priſoners, nine armed ſloops were taken and burned; and a large quantity of proviſions amaſſed there for the uſe of their garriſons to the ſouthward, was deſtroyed. The fort was demoliſhed. Colonel Bradſtreet having performed this important ſervice, returned. Many were of opinion, that ſo fine a poſt ought to have been kept and ſtrongly garriſoned ; others thought that it would be impoſſible to preſerve a place at ſuch a diſtance from our own eſtabliſhments.

It is very poſſible, that the ſucceſs of Colonel Bradſtreet greatly facilitated that of the expedition under General Forbes. The general had had a very tedious and troubleſome march, through a country almoſt impracticable, very little known, and continually harraſſed on his route by the enemies Indians. An advanced guard of this army, conſiſting of about 800 men under Major Grant, had moſt unaccountably advanced cloſe to Fort du Queſne, with a deſign as it ſhould ſeem of reducting the place by a *coup de main* ; but the garriſon ſuddenly ſallying out and attacking them warmly on all ſides, killed and made priſoners many of this party, and diſperſed the reſt. This was however their laſt ſucceſs ; for the body of the army being conduced with greater ſkill and circumſpection, baffled all their attempts ; ſo that the French being convinced by ſeveral ſkirmiſhes that all their efforts to ſurpriſe the troops, or interrupt their communication were to no purpoſe, and being conſcious that their fort was not tenable againſt a regular attack, they wiſely abandoned the
place after deſtroying their Nov. 24
works ; and fell down the Ohio, to the number of 4 or 500 men, towards their moſt ſouthern ſettlements. General Forbes once more erected the Engliſh flag on
Fort du Queſne. Without 25th.
any reſiſtance we became maſters in the third year after the commencement of hoſtilities of that fortreſs, the contention for which had kindled up the flames of ſo general and deſtructive a war. This place with its maſters has changed

its name, and is called Pittsbourg, with a propriety which does not need to be pointed out.

Notwithstanding the unhappy affair at Ticonderoga, the campaign of 1758 in America was very advantageous, and very honourable to the English interest. Louisbourg, St. John's, Frontenac, and du Quesne reduced, remove from our colonies all terror of the Indian incursions, draw from the French those useful allies, free our frontiers from the yoke of their enemies forts, make their supplies difficult, their communications precarious, and all their defensive or offensive operations uneffective; whilst their country uncovered of its principal bulwarks, lies open to the heart, and affords the most pleasing prospects of success to the vigorous measures which we may be assured will be taken in the next campaign. General Amherst is now commander.

It would be doing great injustice to the spirit and conduct of the ministry, not to observe, that they omitted to distress the enemy in no part, and that their plans of operation were as extensive as they were vigorous.

Mar. 9. Two ships of the line with some frigates, were sent early in the spring to the coast of Africa, to drive the French from their settlements there. They entered the river Senegal, and in spite of the obstruction of a dangerous bar, which the ships of war could not pass, they obliged the French fort which commands the river to surrender. May 1. And on the 29th of December following. Commodore Keppel, with the assistance of some troops under the command of Lieutenant-Colonel Worge, made himself master of the island of Goree and its forts; the garrison surrendering at discretion to his majesty's squadron. By these successes, we have taken from the enemy one of the most valuable branches of their commerce, and one the most capable of abundant improvement. *

From

* The river Senega, or Senegal, is one of those channels of the river Niger, by which it is supposed to discharge its waters into the Atlantic ocean: The river Niger, according to the best maps, rises in the east of Africa; and after a course of 300 miles, nearly due west, divides into three branches, the most northerly of which is the Senegal, as above; the middle is the Gambia, or Gambra; the most southern, Rio Grande. Senegal empties itself into the Atlantic ocean in 16 north lat. The entrance of it is guarded by several forts, the principal of which is Fort Lewis, built on an island of the same name. It is a quadrangle fort, with two bastions, and of no inconsiderable strength. At the mouth of the river is a bar; the best season for passing it, is from March to August, or September, or rather from April to July, because the tides are then highest. The English had formerly settlements here, out of which they were driven by the French, who have engrossed the whole trade from Cape Blanco to the river Gambia, which is near 500 miles. The Dutch were the first who settled Senegal, and built two forts. The French made themselves masters of them in 1678. In 1692 the English seized them; but next year the French retook them, and have kept them ever since. They built Fort Lewis in 1692, and have beyond it a multitude of other settlements, extending 200 leagues up the river. The principal commodities which the French import from this settlement, are that

From the East Indies we have this year heard nothing remarkable. It does not seem that the French, notwithstanding the great struggle they made to send out a strong armament under General Lally, have been in a condition to enterprise any thing. It is said, and probably with good foundation, that the greatest part of its force was dwindled away with sickness during the voyage. Our naval force was exerted with spririt and effect in the Mediterranean. The French found that the possession of Minorca could not drive us from the dominion of the Mediterranean, where Admiral Osborn gave the enemies maritime strength such blows, as they must long feel, and which merited him the greatest of all honours, to be joined with the conquerors of Louisbourg, in the thanks of the representative body of their country. But as these, although very important, are detached affairs, we imagined it better to give them in our Chronicle; as they could not so well come into the body of this work, without interrupting the series we propose to carry on.

The coming year seems big with great events. In Germany the affairs of the rival powers of Prussia and Austria, appear to be more nearly ballanced than at any time since the beginning of the war. Their force is as great as ever, and their animosity is noway lessened. Great steps are taken to assemble powerful armies on the Rhine; whilst Great Britain has sent out two considerable armaments, one to the West Indies, the other to Africa; the success of which must go a great way towards determining the issue of the war. Other great preparations are also making on the part of Great Britain. In the mean time, the Dutch, enraged at the captures of their ships, make complaints, and threaten armaments. The death of the Princess of Orange, which happened at a most critical juncture, adds more perplexity to affairs in that quarter. If we look to the southward, the clouds seem gathering there also. The imminent death of the King of Spain, will be an event fruitful of troubles. In this affair the King of Sardinia, the house of Austria, and the house of Bourbon, will find themselves concerned; to say nothing of the maritime powers. In a word, the flame of war threatens to spread in every part of Europe. What revolutions in politics these things will make, what new connections they will create, what old they will dissolve, what changes they will create in the fortunes of the present belligerent powers, or what disposition to peace or war they may produce, will be the subject of our next volume.

If the reader should perceive many faults and inaccuracies in this work, let him remember the disadvantages we labour under. Our accounts are taken from the

that valuable article gum senega, hides, bees-wax, elephants teeth, cotton, gold dust, negro slaves, ostrich feathers, ambergris, indigo, and civet.

At present we are obliged to buy all our gum senega of the Dutch, who purchase it from the French; and they set what price they please on it. But as the trade to Africa is now open, by this important acquisition, the price of this valuable drug, which is so much used in several of our manufactures, will be much reduced.

public

public ones of the year, which are themſelves often inaccurate, often contradictory. We find it very difficult to trace the true cauſes of events, which time can only draw from obſcurity. It is hard to find a connection between the facts, upon whoſe authenticity we may depend. And in the maſs of materials of a dubious authority, it is equally hard to know what ought to be choſen, to make out ſuch a connection. Yet with all theſe difficulties, we are of opinion, that the reader will find ſome entertainment, as well as ſome help to his memory, from reading a connected ſeries of thoſe very remarkable and intereſting events which this war has produced, and which he has hitherto no where ſeen but in a looſe detached manner. If we can do this, we are ſatisfied: for we do not pretend to give the name of hiſtory to what we have written.

THE

THE CHRONICLE.

JANUARY.

1st. A Fine equeſtrian ſtatue of his preſent majeſty king George, by Van Noſt, was erected on St. Stephen's Green, Dublin On the front of the pedeſtal is the following inſcription :

Georgio Secundo
Magnæ Britanniæ Franciæ
et Hiberniæ
Regi
Forti et Reipublicæ
Maxime fideli
Patriis virtutibus
Patrem Secuto
S P Q D
A. D. 1758.
Thomas Mead, Prætore Urbano.
Michaele Sweny, Gulielmo Forbes, } Vice-comitibus.

7th. By a letter from Captain Bray, commander of his majeſty's armed veſſel the Adventure, received this day at the Admiralty, there is an account of the taking the Machault privateer of Dunkirk, with 14 nine pounders, and 182 men. Captain Bray ſoon after the engagement began, ordered the helm to be put hard-aport, which had the deſired effect of laying her athwart hawſe, her bowſprit coming in between the Adventure's main and mizen maſts. They immediately paſſed the end of the mizen-top-ſail ſheet through the enemy's bobſtay, and made it faſt; but fearing to loſe ſo good an opportunity, and that they would get clear, Captain Bray and the pilot got a hawſer, and paſſed it three times round the Machault's bowſprit and the capſton on the Adventure's quarter-deck, ſo that the action depended chiefly on the ſmall-arms, which was very ſmart about an an hour. She then ſtruck her colours, but upon boarding her, began to fire again, which was ſoon ſilenced. She had killed and wounded 40 men, with the loſs only of one man killed, and two wounded on board the Adventure.

This evening 70 men on board the Namur in Portſmouth harbour forced their way into the dock, and from thence ſet out for London, in order to lay their complaints before the lords of the Admiralty; 15 of whom attempted to procure an audience, but were all ordered to be put in irons and carried back in order to be tried by a court martial for mutiny. It is reported that the badneſs of their proviſion was the cauſe of their complaint.

13th. A cup and ſalver intended to be preſented to Captain Lockhart, was ſent this day to Lloyd's to be viewed by the merchants. It was curiouſly chaſed and emboſſed with the ſeven French privateers, his own ſhip and arms. The ſalver is 26 inches diameter, with the following inſcription :

The

The gift of the two public companies,
The under-writers and merchants of the city of London,
To Capt. John Lockhart, commander of the Tartar,
For his signal service in supporting the trade,
By distressing the French privateers in the year 1757.

The merchants of Bristol presented him also with a gold cup, worth 100 l.

This day a committee of the subscribers to a fund for supplying the poor in the city of York with corn at a lower rate than the markets, began to deliver out the same, when 334 families were served with the best of corn at 1s. a peck, or 4s. the bushel.

14th. By a letter from Captain Lockhart to the Admiralty, there was advice that his majesty's ships Edinburgh, Dreadnought, Augusta, and a sloop, had blocked up the harbour of Cape Francois for some weeks: that on the 15th of October, all the French squadron sailed to drive the English off the coast; and the next day the two squadrons came to a close engagement, which continued till night, when the French squadron, having the land breeze, by the help of their frigates, were towed to port, greatly disabled, and the Opiniatre dismasted. They had 300 men killed, and as many wounded. This advice Captain Lockhart received from the crew of a St. Domingo-man, which he had taken; and it has since been confirmed by a letter in Lloyd's Evening-post, directly from the spot. The same advices from the Admiralty take notice likewise of the taking of two French ships both laden with provisions for Louisbourg. The prisoners say, that they sailed from l'Isle d'Aix, in company with three other merchant-ships, laden with provisions for Louisbourg, under convoy of the Prudent and Capricieux, and the Tripon and Heroine frigates, the two former of which parted company with them the day before they were taken. The frigates made their escape from our ships by its falling little wind, before which his majesty's ships outsailed them greatly; but there is reason to believe the other merchant ships are taken by the ships that were left in chase of them.

18th. A farmer upon Budgley Common, between Southampton and Redbridge, seeing a man with a blue coat, red waistcoat, and red plush breeches, very ragged, lying on the ground in a very weak condition: took him into his waggon, carried him to his house, gave him victuals and drink; but being full of vermin, made him up a bed of straw in the waggon, under the waggon-house, and covered him with sacks. Next morning he found him dead. He had an ensign's commission in his pocket, dated in March last, appointing him, as supposed, an ensign to an independent company of invalids at Plymouth; but no money in his pocket, except one half-penny.

The following message from the King was presented by Mr. Secretary Pitt to the house.

George R.

'His majesty having ordered the 'army, formed last year in his 'electoral dominions, to be put 'again into motion from the 28th 'of November last, and to act with 'the utmost vigour against the 'common enemy, in concert with

'his

'his good brother and ally the 'King of Pruſſia; and the exhauſted and ruined ſtate of that electorate, and of its revenues, having 'rendered it impoſſible for the ſame 'to maintain and keep together 'that army, until the further neceſſary charge thereof, as well as 'the more particular meaſures now 'concerting for the effectual ſupport of the King of Pruſſia, can be 'laid before this houſe; his majeſty, relying on the conſtant zeal 'of his faithful Commons, for the 'ſupport of the Proteſtant religion, 'and of the liberties of Europe, 'againſt the dangerous deſigns of 'France, and her confederates, finds 'himſelf, in the mean time, under 'the abſolute neceſſity of recommending to this houſe the ſpeedy 'conſideration of ſuch a preſent 'ſupply, as may enable his majeſty, in this critical exigency, to 'ſubſiſt and keep together the ſaid 'army.'

In conſequence of this meſſage, 100,000 l. was unanimouſly granted, to be taken immediately out of the ſupplies of laſt year unapplied, and to be remitted with all poſſible diſpatch.

21ſt. A court-martial was held on board the Newark, for the trial of the 15 mutineers belonging to the Namur man of war, who all received ſentence of death.

Information having been given to the Lord Lieutenant of Ireland, that ſeveral officers were recruiting in that kingdom from Great Britain, without the knowledge of the government there, his excellency ſignified his pleaſure to ſuch officers that they ſhould immediately deſiſt from raiſing men in that kingdom, and that they do immediately diſcharge all ſuch as they have already enliſted.

By letters from Conſtanti-
nople, we heard that the 30th.
caravan of pilgrims, returning from Mecca, had been attacked by a large body of Arabs, who had deſtroyed, as it is ſaid, from 50 to 60,000 perſons. This deſperate and unprecedented proceeding is ſuppoſed to have taken its riſe from the Arabs being diſguſted on account of the removal of the Paſcha of Damaſcus to Aleppo, who was greatly eſteemed by them, as a generous able man, and the Kiſlar Aga's having put into his room a man of different principles; who deprived them of ſome part of their dues, which they receive from the pilgrims. As the chief of the black eunuchs was the cauſe of all that has happened by that change, which he effected merely to ſerve his own intereſted views, the Grand Seignor ordered his head to be ſent for from Rhodes, where he was lately exiled, and on its arrival was expoſed to public view.

Captain Wallace of the King George of Briſtol, took up at ſea, off Bermudas, ſix men, the crew of the ſchooner Nancy of Boſton, one Gavian, maſter; the veſſel in a hard gale had overſet, but, after they had cut away their main-maſt, ſhe righted: but a ſea ſoon after beat in her ſtern, and having a quantity of bricks abaft, her ſtern ſunk and her head ſtuck upright, and then the people got on her bow. After the ſtorm abated, they got ſome mackrel out of the veſſel, and an iron inſtrument to ſtrike fiſh, and making an awning of one of the ſails, which they fixed to the bowſprit, they lived there 46 days before Captain Wallace met them, one of them died ſoon, and two others are deprived of their ſenſes.

The

The Lord Chief Juſtice of the King's-bench declared that court's opinion of the caſe of the bank note ſtolen out of the mail, and paid away by the robber, who received the full value of Mr. Miller, at the poſt-office at Hatfield, and then travelled on the ſame road in a four-wheel poſt-chaiſe and four horſes, and at the ſeveral ſtages paſſed off ſeveral other bank notes he had taken out of the mail at the ſame time; all which, at the requeſt of the owner, who ſent them by the poſt, were ſtopt by Mr. Rice, caſhier of the bank, and an action ſuffered to be brought againſt Mr. Rice, for recovery of the money; when after very learned pleadings on both ſides, it was moſt ſolemnly determined, 'That any perſon paying a valuable conſideration for a bank note to bearer, in a fair courſe of buſineſs, has an undoubted right to recover the money of the bank.' The pretext for ſtopping them at the bank was, becauſe they had been altered, the figures of 11, which denoted the date, having been by the robber dexterouſly converted to a 4.

This day being appointed for the execution of the 15 ſeamen, belonging to the Namur, the boats from every ſhip in commiſſion, manned and armed, attended, and rowed guard round the Royal Anne. A little before 12 o'clock the priſoners were brought up, in order to be executed, and the halters were fixing, when they were informed his majeſty had ſhewn mercy to 14, but they were to draw lots who ſhould be the man that was to ſuffer death. Matthew M'Can, the ſecond man that drew, had the unfortunate chance; and accordingly, at a gun fired as a ſignal, he was run up to the yard-arm, where he hung for near an hour. The reprieved were turned over to the Grafton and Sunderland, bound to the Eaſt Indies. It is ſaid, the cauſe of the mutiny was only the diſlike they had to quit the Namur, on board which ſhip Admiral Boſcawen, when he took upon him the command of the intended expedition, hoiſted his flag, and was to bring the crew of his former ſhip with him.

FEBRUARY.

1ſt. Monſieur Rene Briſon, ſecond captain of the Prince de Soubiſe, who formerly made his eſcape from where he reſided on his parole of honour, went into France, and was ſent back by order of the French king, made a ſecond attempt to eſcape out of Porcheſter caſtle, where he had been confined ever ſince his return. He had bribed the centinels on duty, but his attempt being ſuſpected by the officers of the priſon, they planted others at a diſtance, who immediately apprehended him, and carried him back to the caſtle.

4th. A marble buſt of Doctor Claudius Gilbert, formerly vice provoſt of Dublin college in Ireland, was ſet up in that college.—This excellent perſon, beſides other valuable donations, bequeathed to that college a collection of books, conſiſting of 13000 volumes, choſen with great diſcernment and care. His buſt is placed at the head of theſe. It is the workmanſhip of Mr. Verpoil; and for the expreſſion and elegance does great honour to the taſte and ſkill of the ſtatuary.

6th. It was ordered by the lords ſpiritual and temporal, in the parliament of Ireland aſſembled, That the king at arms, attended by by his proper officers, do blot out and deface all ensigns of honour, borne by such persons as have no legal title thereto, upon their carriages, plate, and furniture, and to make regular returns of their proceedings therein to the clerk of parliament.

10th. His majesty's ship Lancaster being paid at Spithead, among the trades-people that carried goods on board, were a great many Jews, who had large quantities of valuable effects with them; the Jews not meeting with the success they desired, were resolved to go on shore: it blew very hard, and they had a sailing boat, which they had hired for that purpose. About 20 Jews, and a few other people, got into her with their effects, but they had not gone far, when by gibeing the sail, they were overset. The ships boats immediately put off, and took up 9 or 10 of them. Nine Jews were drowned, and two died after they were brought on board.

13th. Extract of a letter from Portsmouth.

" Yesterday arrived here, with a messenger belonging to the admiralty, in the greatest haste, a person who was immediately introduced, by orders from above, to Admiral Boscawen; of whom the following particulars have transpired. This person was some time since master of an English vessel, trading from port to port in North America, particularly up the river St. Laurence; but being taken by the enemy, has been prisoner with the General Montcalm and others near three years, who would not admit of any exchange for him, on account of his extensive knowledge of all the coast, more particularly the strength and soundings of Quebec and Louisbourg; they therefore came to a resolution to send him to Old France, in the next packet boat, there to be confined till the end of the war. He was accordingly embarked (the only Englishman) and the packet put on board. In their voyage he was admitted to the cabbin, where he took notice one day, they bundled up the packet, and put it into a canvas bag, having previously thereto made it ready to be thrown overboard, upon any danger of being taken.

They were constrained to put into Vigo for some provisions, as also to gain some intelligence of the English in those seas, and there found one or more English men of war at anchor; upon which he thought it a proper opportunity of putting the following scheme in execution. One night taking the opportunity of all, but the watch, being in a sound sleep, he took the packet out of the bag, and having fixed it in his mouth, he silently let himself down into the bay; and to prevent noise by swimming, floated upon his back into the wake of the English man of war, where he secured himself by the hawser; and upon calling out for assistance, was immediately taken on board, and the packet entire. The captain examined him, treated him with great humanity, gave him a suit of his own cloaths, scarlet trimmed with black velvet, which he here appeared in, transcribed the packet, which is said to be of the utmost importance, in regard to our success in North-America, and then sent him over land, with the copy of the packet to Lisbon; from whence he was brought to Falmouth in a sloop of war, and immediately set out post for London.

Upon

Upon his arrival in town, he was examined by the proper persons in the administration, and rewarded with a present supply; and by his own desire was immediately sent to Portsmouth, to go out on board Admiral Boscawen's own ship, upon the present expedition to North-America, where he is to have the command of a sloop of war.

19th. Admiral Boscawen, with the fleet under his command, sailed from St. Helen's for North-America. The Invincible, one of his fleet, of 74 guns, Captain Bentley, missed her stays, and run upon a flat on the east of St. Helen's. Her men, guns, stores, &c. were taken out, but that fine ship was quite lost.

One of the ships lately arrived from the east country, shipped such a quantity of water, and in the late cold weather it froze to that degree, that the captain computed he had above forty tons of ice on board. Four of his men perished by the cold. They were obliged to cut their way through the ice into the hold of the ship.

21st. There was as great a market for fat cattle at Sevenoaks in Kent as was ever known, notwithstanding which they sold at a high price, from 14 to 20l. a head.— By an authentic list it appears, that there passed through Islington turnpike for Smithfield market, from Jan. 1, 1754, to Jan. 1, 1755, oxen 28,9[illegible]2, sheep 267,565; and from Jan. 1, 1757, to Jan. 1. 1758, oxen 30,952, sheep 200,180. By which it appears, that there is a decrease of more than 67,[illegible]00 sheep in this last year, and an increase only of about 2000 oxen, which is by no means a just proportion; so that on this principle the increase of the price of meat may be accounted for.

Extract of a letter from Rear-Admiral Cotes to Mr. Cleveland, dated on board his majesty's ship the Marlborough, November 9, 1757, in Port-Royal Harbour.

"The 25th of last month, Captain Forrest, in his majesty's ship the Augusta, with the Dreadnought and Edinburgh under his command, returned from their cruize off Cape Francois. Captain Forrest gives me the following account of an action that happened the 21st, between the ships under his command, and seven French ships of war.

At seven in the morning, the Dreadnought made the signal for seeing the enemy's fleet coming out of Cape Francois; we made sail to discover them plain; and at half past eight made seven sail of large ships, a schooner, and a pilot-boat. I then made the signal for the line a-head, and shortened sail, to let the enemy come up, and to preserve the weather gage. At noon saw with great certainty they were four ships of the line, and three large frigates. I then made the signal for the Captains Suckling and Langdon, who agreed with me to engage them: accordingly we bore down, and about twenty minutes after three, the action began with great briskness on both sides, and continued for two hours and an half, when the French commodore made a signal, and one of the frigates immediately came to tow him out of the line, and the rest of the French ships followed him. Our ships had suffered so much in their masts, sails, and rigging, that we were in no condition to pursue them. Both officers and seamen behaved with the greatest resolution the whole time of the action, and were unhappy at the conclusion of it, that the ships were not in a condition to follow the French, who had ſrigates to tow them off. I am informed the French, on this occaſion, had put on board the Sceptre her full complement of guns, either from the ſhore, or out of the India ſhip; and had alſo mounted the Outarde ſtore-ſhip with her full proportion of guns; and had taken not only the men out of the merchant ſhips, but ſoldiers from the garriſon, in hopes their appearance would frighten our ſmall ſquadron, and oblige them to leave their coaſt clear for them to carry out their large convoy of merchant ſhips; but our captains were too gallant to be terrified at their formidable appearance; and ſo far from avoiding them, that they bore down, and engaged with the greateſt reſolution and good conduct. And I have the pleaſure to acquaint their lordſhips, that the captains, officers, ſeamen, and marines, have done their duty on this occaſion, much to their honour; and I hope their good behaviour will be approved by their lordſhips."

William Page, who had not long before taken his tryal at the Old Bailey, and at Hertford aſſizes, for divers robberies on the highway, and was acquitted at both places, was, after a ſhort trial at Rocheſter aſſizes, found guilty for robbing the late commiſſioner Farrington, about two years ago, on the evidence of the ſervant.

27th. Richard William Vaughan, late a linen-draper at Stafford, was committed to Newgate, for counterfeiting the notes of the bank of England. He had employed ſeveral artiſts to engrave the different parts of the note, by one of whom the diſcovery was made. He had filled up to the number of 20, and depoſited them in the hands of a young lady, whom he courted, as a proof of his being a perſon of ſubſtance. This is the firſt attempt of the kind that ever was made.

30th. Mrs. Dennington, a quaker of eighty years of age, at Harefield in Middleſex, was baptized, and admitted a member of the church of England.

MARCH.

1ſt. His grace the Duke of Richmond, ordered a room at Whitehall to be opened for the uſe of thoſe who ſtudy painting, ſculpture, and engraving, in which is contained a large collection of original plaiſter caſts from the beſt antique ſtatues and buſts now at Rome and Florence, where any painter, ſculptor, carver, or other artiſt, to whom the ſtudy of theſe geſſes may be of uſe, will have liberty to draw, or model, at any time; and upon application to the perſon that has the care of them, any particular figure will be placed in ſuch a light as the artiſt ſhall deſire. And any young man or boy, above the age of twelve years, may alſo have the ſame liberty, by a recommendation from any known artiſt. On Saturdays, Meſſrs. Wilton and Capriani are to attend to ſee what progreſs each has made, to correct their drawings and models, and to give them ſuch inſtructions as ſhall be thought neceſſary. There will be given at Chriſtmas and Midſummer annually to thoſe who diſtinguiſh themſelves by making the greateſt progreſs, the following premiums: a figure will be ſelected from the reſt, and a large ſilver medal will be given for the beſt deſign of it, and another for the beſt model in baſſo relievo.

relievo. A ſmaller ſilver medal for the ſecond beſt deſign, and one for the ſecond beſt baſſo relievo. The ſervant who takes care of the room has ſtrict orders not to receive any money.

4th. The court martial on Commodore Pye at Portſmouth ended. He was charged for malepractices in the management of his command abroad; but the court was pleaſed to acquit him of that charge, and only reprimanded him for a neglect in not acquainting the naval officer, that a ſchooner which he bought coſt 200 l. currency, for which the naval officer had, by miſtake, charged 200 l. ſterling; and alſo for having interfered in purchaſing naval ſtores, the naval officer being upon the ſpot.

6th. A court of enquiry at Portſmouth began and ended on board the Royal George, concerning the loſs of his majeſty's ſhip Invincible. The principals examined were the pilots, who made it appear, that the loſs of her was owing to no miſconduct in the maſter, and declared, that, had the ſhip been their own, they ſhould have behaved juſt as he had done; whereupon the maſter was ſet at liberty.—Other accounts take notice that the ſands on which ſhe was loſt, were higher than uſual.

Florence Henſey, M.D. was committed to Newgate, charged with high treaſon.

9th. About 200 ſailors, armed with clubs, went to the back of the Point at Portſmouth to a public-houſe, which they pulled almoſt down; they threw the beds and furniture about the ſtreet, and ſtove all the beer in the cellar; after which they came into the town, and went into ſeveral public-houſes, broke the windows, ſtove the butts of beer, and did other conſiderable damage.

11th. The powder mills belonging to Mr. Smith at Hounſlow blew up; but happily no lives were loſt. This accident, no doubt, gave riſe to the following paragraph in the Reading Mercury of this day: 'Reading, March 12. Laſt night, 'about nine o'clock, a ſlight ſhock 'of an earthquake was felt at Colebrook, Maidenhead, and other 'places between London and this 'town, but we do not hear of 'any damage it has done. It was 'alſo perceived here.

Mr. Henry Raine, of St. George Middleſex, having in his life-time built and endowed an hoſpital for forty girls taken out of the charity ſchool, and maintained; by his will, dated October 17, 1736. bequeathed 4000 l. in 3 per cent. annuities to truſtees to accumulate and improve the growing dividends until the ſame ſhall produce yearly 210 l. to be diſpoſed of in marriage portions to two maidens brought up in his hoſpital, (viz. 100 l. and 5 l. for a wedding dinner each) who ſhall have continued there four years, attained the age of 22, and be beſt recommended by the maſters or miſtreſſes, whom they may have ſerved, for piety, induſtry, and a conſtant conformity to the eſtabliſhed church. The truſtees have given notice, that the ſum deſtined for this laudable purpoſe is compleated, and by an advertiſement ſummoned the maidens educated in the ſaid hoſpital, to appear on the 4th of next month, with proper certificates of their paſt behaviour and preſent circumſtances, in order that ſix may be ſelected of the moſt deſerving, to draw lots on the firſt of of May for the prize of 100 l. to be paid on the 5th of November following as her marriage portion, to an honeſt man, a member of the church of England, reſiding in the pariſhes of St. George, St. Paul Shadwell, or St. John, Wapping, and approved by the truſtees; at which time another girl will be added to the five who ſhall have drawn blanks before; and to her who ſhall then draw the prize will be paid 100 l. on her marriage the firſt of May following; the remaining five to continue intitled to a chance twice in every year, when a new candidate will be admitted, that every girl educated in this hoſpital, and careful of her character, may have a chance for this noble donation.

13th. Miſs Bab. Wyndham, of Saliſbury, ſiſter of Henry Wyndham, Eſq; of that city, a maiden lady of ample fortune, ordered her banker to prepare the ſum of 1000 l. to be immediately remitted, in her own name, as a preſent to the king of Pruſſia.

14th. A notorious impoſtor was detected at Edinburgh. When taken up, he had four pair of thick coarſe ſtockings, a pillow under his waiſtcoat, and, by an affected motion in his head and hands, has had the addreſs for ſome time paſt, to paſs upon the inhabitants as both dropſical and paralytical, and a very great object of charity. When freed of his dreſſings, he comes out to be a ſtrong well made fellow, and was immediately ſent to the caſtle, as very fit to ſerve as a ſoldier.

Mr. Smelt, one of the engineers belonging to the board of ordnance, is now at Tinmouth caſtle, having orders to repair the old works, build barracks for 1000 men, and to erect new batteries towards the ſea, in order to defend and be a ſafeguard to the ſhips when at anchor in the road.

17th. A moſt ſhocking murder was committed at Hambleton on the Hill, a village near Oakham in Rutlandſhire, upon the bodies of Anne Woods and Robert Broome, two poor aged cottagers, by John Swanſon of that neighbourhood. Woods had employed Broome to trim a hedge, in a ground not far from her houſe; Swanſon, being of the ſame occupation, and envious to ſee another preferred to himſelf, went to the hedge with a hatchet under his arm; but before he had got three parts of the way, he met the old woman returning home from the man; and, without any previous ſalutation, knocked her down with his hatchet. He then went to the place where the poor man was at work, knocked him down in the like manner, chopt off his head with the hatchet, opened his body, and plucked out his heart, which he wrapt up with the head, in a piece of old rag. He then returned to the dead corpſe of the woman, cut down her ſtays before, opened her body, and pulling out her heart, bound up both the hearts and head together, which he carried home, and hid in a cheſt under his own bed. The officers of the pariſh, receiving information that Broome was murdered, immediately turned their ſuſpicions upon Swanſon, and went the ſame night to Swanſon's houſe, and, being admitted, charged him with the murder, who, after ſtanding dumb about three minutes, con-

confeſſed the whole; and that Robert Broome's head, and both hearts, lay concealed under his bed. He was ſecured immediately and committed to Oakham goal.——It appears by all the circumſtances of this murder, that the man was mad, and ought to have been confined long before.

Admiralty-Office.

Extract of a letter from Commodore Holmes to Mr. Cleveland, dated from on board the Seahorſe at anchor off Embden, March 21, 1758.

" It is with the greateſt pleaſure that I acquaint my lords commiſſioners of the admiralty of the ſucceſs of his majeſty's ſhips in this river. The enemy had not ſuffered the buoys to be laid this year, thinking by that means to obſtruct any attempts for the recovery of Embden at ſea. It was therefore, with equal ſurprize and concern, that they obſerved the arrival of his majeſty's ſhips Seahorſe and Strombolo; and after having doubled the number of their workmen upon the batteries they had begun, they ſet about raiſing three more towards the ſea, with all expedition, expecting to be attacked from that quarter. On the 17th, the Seahorſe and Strombolo anchored between Delfzeil and Knock, and, on the 18th they came to their ſtation between Knock and Embden, by which the enemy ſaw themſelves cut off from all communication down the river. They continued working on their batteries towards the ſea, but at the ſame time made all the neceſſary preparations for evacuating the place.—The garriſon conſiſted of, French foot of Prince D'Eu's regiment, 1300.—Horſe of General Luſignan's regiment, 300.—Ditto of the regiment Belleſont du Roy, 300.—Ditto Orleans, 400—Ditto Bourbon Buſſet, 300.—Auſtrain foot of the regiment of Prince Charles of Lorraine, and Colonel Van Pflatz, 1100.—Two companies of artillery, of 60 men each, 120.—In all 3720.—On the 19th, at ſix in the morning, the French troops were under arms, and marched out of the town before night. And, on the 20th, the Auſtrians began their march at nine in the morning. About noon, and not before, I had intelligence of theſe operations, and that they had been tranſporting their baggage and cannon up the river, in ſmall veſſels over-night; and that one of them was laying round a point of land, at ſome diſtance from us, to go up by the next tide. So ſoon as we could ſtem the tide, I diſpatched the armed cutter Acrias, and two of my boats, in purſuit of the enemy. They came up with the veſſel we had intelligence of, and took her. I reinforced them by another boat, and the whole detachment commanded by Captain Taylor continued the chace up the river. The enemy at this time lined both ſides of it, and gave the firſt fire on the boats, who were then coming up with three of their armed veſſels. The fire was briſkly returned on our ſide; and in ſight of their army, and under their fire, Captain Taylor came up with one of them, attacked her, ran her a-ground, and carried her, after ſome firing on both ſides. The officers and men left the veſſel to recover the ſhore, in attempting of which, ſome of them were dropt by the fire from the boat. The other two veſſels, which had the cannon on board, got clear under favour of the night, and cover of their army. The first *vessel taken, had the son of Lieutenant*-Colonel Schollheins, of Prince Charles of Lorraine's regiment, and one corporal and one pioneer on board, with some baggage belonging to his father. There was some money found, which, partly from the specie, and partly from the manner of its being made up, was concluded to be pay for the troops, and therefore detained. together with the corporal and pioneer, and all the little implements of war they had with them. As for the lieutenant-colonel's son, he is but a boy, and not of an age to be regarded as an enemy; for which reason I have sent him ashore to be returned to his father, with all his and his father's things; and have wrote to his father, that, upon his giving me his honour that the money is truly his private property, it shall be returned. The other vessel that was taken, had on board Major de Bertrand, M. Von Longen, commissary of war; M. Trajane, adjutant de la place; N. Le Bouffe, lieutenant of artillery, and a guard of private men, with three hostages, which they had carried off from Embden, viz. Eodo Wilhelm Zur Michlen, doctor of laws, president of the college de Quarantes, and administrator of the royal and provincial college at Aurich; Baron Von Hane, of Leci, administrator at Embden; and Haiko George Eden, administrator of Leer. M. Eodo Wilhelm Zur Michlen, received a shot in the vessel during the scuffle, but *it is not dangerous. From him I* had the account already given to their lordships, of the happy effect the presence of his majesty's two ships have produced, by occasioning the sudden evacuation of the enemy out of the town of Embden."

An account arrived, that on the 28th of February, between Cape de Gatt and Carthagena, Admiral Osborn fell in with M. du Quesne in the * Foudroyant of 80, the Orpheus of 64, the Oriflame of 50, and the Pleiade of 24 guns, which were the four ships sent from Toulon to reinforce M. de Clue at Carthagena. On seeing the English squadron, they immediately dispersed and steered different courses. About seven in the evening, Captain Storr in the Revenge of 64, supported by Captain Hughes in the Berwick of 64, and Captain Evans in the Preston of 50 guns, took the Orpheus, commanded by M. de Harville, with 502 Men. Captain Gardiner, in the Monmouth of 64, supported by Captain Stanhope in the Swiftsure of 70, and Captain Hervey, in the Hampton-court of 64 guns, about one in the morning, took the Foudroyant, on board of which was the Marquis de Quesne, chef d'Escadre, with 800 men. Captain Rowley, in the Montagu, of 60, and Captain Montagu, in the Monarch of 74 guns, run the Oriflame shore, under the castle of Aiglois; and had it not been for

* The length of Le Foudroyant, at Gibraltar, taken from her carpenter's account, is,

	Feet Fr.		Feet Eng.	In.
From her stern to the taffarel ——— ———	171	=	185	3
Length of her keel ——— ——— —	144	=	156	

being 12 feet longer than an English first rate; her extreme breadth about 50 feet, nearly the same with our first rate.

violating the neutrality of the coaſt of Spain, they would certainly have deſtroyed her. The Pleiade, of 24 guns, got away by mere out-ſailing our ſhips

In this action Captain Gardiner was killed *, and Captain Storr loſt the calf of one of his legs. The very gallant and brave behaviour of the officers and ſeamen on this occaſion, deſerve the higheſt commendations; particularly that of Lieutenant Carket, of the Monmouth, who ||, after the captain's death, engaged and diſabled the Foudroyant in ſuch a manner, as to oblige her to ſtrike as ſoon as the other ſhips came up; for which ſervice Admiral Oſborn gave him the command of the Foudroyant as a reward.

28th. At York aſſizes which ended the 25th, four perſons were found guilty of high treaſon in obſtructing the militia act, and received ſentence of death accordingly; two of the Weſleydale rioters were likewiſe convicted for violently taking away meal on the highway in returning from market; about twenty priſoners more were tried for riots, ſome of whom were continued, others fined and impriſoned, and others admitted to bail. Great lenity was ſhewn by the judges and jury, where the priſoners did not appear to act with premeditation.

It is reported, that at a quarry near Fullwell-Hills near Sunderland, the ſkeleton of a man was found, which meaſured nine feet and upwards.

A P R I L.

3d. Came on to be tried at Kingſton aſſizes before the Hon. Sir Michael Foſter, Knight, and a ſpecial jury of gentlemen of the county of Surry, the tryal by way of indictment againſt Martha Grey, for obſtructing certain footways, leading from Eaſt-Sheene thro' Richmond Park. The defendant declined entering into the merits, but reſted her defence on an objection to the indictment, that Eaſt-Sheene, which in the indictment was laid to be in the pariſh of Wimbleton, was in the pariſh of Mortlake; but it appearing to the ſatisfaction of the judge and jury, that Mortlake was not a pariſh, but a chapelry in Wimbleton; the jury found the defendant guilty.

11th. Between the hours of 10 and 11, at night, the temporary wooden bridge, built for the convenience of carriages and paſſengers, whilſt London-bridge was widening and repairing, was diſcovered to be on fire, and continued burning till noon the next day, when the ruins fell into the Thames. An advertiſement was publiſhed by Mr. Secretary Pitt, with the offer of his majeſty's pardon to the diſcoverer of the perpetrators of ſo vile and wicked an action (it be-

* Captain Gardiner was ſhot thro' the arm the firſt fire; and ſoon after as he was encouraging his people, and enquiring what damage they had ſuſtained between decks, he received a ſecond wound, by a muſket ball, in his forehead, which proved fatal to him.

|| The Monmouth had 150 men killed and wounded; the Foudroyant 200. The loſs of maſts on both ſides brought on a cloſe engagement, which laſted till the Swiftſure came up. M. du Queſne refuſed, however, to deliver his ſword to the captain of the Swiftſure; but gave it with great politeneſs to Lieutenant Carket.

ing

ing ſuppoſed to be done wilfully and maliciouſly) and the city offered a reward of 200 l. for the ſame purpoſe. The Lord Mayor licenſed 40 boats extraordinary to work on the three ſucceeding Lord's days, whoſe ſtations were advertiſed in the public papers, and great numbers of hands were ſet to work to make a paſſage over the remains of the old bridge. This unhappy accident proved very detrimental to the inhabitants on each ſide the bridge, and put a great ſtop to the trade of London and Southwark. The inhabitants of the Borough were alſo greatly diſtreſſed, by the deſtroying the troughs, which conveyed water to them during the repairing of the bridge.

Baron Kniphauſen, miniſter plenipotentiary from the King of Pruſſia, had his firſt audience of his majeſty, and, on the 13th, of the Prince of Wales and the Princeſs Dowager.

17th. A proof was made at Paris of a cannon of a new invention, which fires ſixty times in ten minutes without ſpunging. With a proper charge of powder it carries 100 weight of lead, and one man may bear its carriage. Another cannon of like conſtruction has been broved in Pruſſia.

19th. London-bridge was opened for foot-paſſengers, in the reparation of which above 500 workmen were conſtantly employed, Sundays not excepted.

James White, aged 23, and Walter White, his brother, aged 21, were executed at Kennington Common, for breaking open and robbing the dwelling houſe of farmer Vincent of Crauley. They acknowledged the juſtice of their ſentence, but laid their ruin to an accomplice, who, they declared, decoyed them from their labouring work, by telling them how eaſily money was to be got by thieving.—While the unhappy wretches were hanging, a child about nine months old was put into the hands of the executioner, who nine times, with one of the hands of each of the dead bodies, ſtroked the child over the face. It ſeems the child had a wen on one of its cheeks, and that ſuperſtitious notion, which has long prevailed, of being touched as before mentioned, is looked on as a cure.

20th. Was held the anniverſary meeting of the ſons of the clergy, at which were preſent his grace the Lord Archbiſhop of Canterbury, preſident, and the Lord Chief Juſtice Willes, vice-preſident of the corporation, the Right Honourable the Lord Mayor, the Biſhops of Ely, Lincoln, Carliſle, Saliſbury, Rocheſter, Litchfield, Cheſter, Glouceſter and St. David's, and moſt of the aldermen. The ſermon was preached by the Reverend Dr. Ibbetſon, archdeacon of St. Alban's, and the collection in the whole (including a bank note of 100l. given by Samſon Gideon, Eſq;) amounted to 1066 l. 14 s. which is above 150 l. more than laſt year.

The money collected on Tueſday	306	18	0
Yeſterday at St. Paul's	207	1	6
At Merchant Taylors Hall	552	14	6
	£. 1066	14	0

Extract of a letter from Kenſington in Connecticut.

" On the third inſtant, about ſun-riſe, at this place was a fog of ſo ſtrange and extraordinary an appearance, that it filled us all with amazement. It came in great bodies,

dies, like thick clouds, down to the earth, and in its way, ſtriking againſt the houſes, would break and fall down the ſides in great bodies, rolling over and over. It reſembled the thick ſteam riſing from boiling wort, and was attended with ſuch heat, that we could hardly breathe. When firſt I ſaw it I really thought my houſe had been on fire, and ran out to ſee if it was ſo ; but many people thought the world was on fire, and the laſt day come. One of our neighbours was then at Sutton, 100 miles to the eaſtward, and reports it was much the ſame there."

21ſt. In conſequence of an application to parliament on account of the late unhappy accident, a reſolution paſſed the houſe, "That a ſum not exceeding "15,000 l. be granted to his majeſty, to be applied towards the "rebuilding London-bridge."

The Right Reverend Dr. Thomas Secker, Lord Biſhop of Oxford, was confirmed at Bow-church Lord Archbiſhop of the cathedral and metropolitan church of Canterbury, by the Moſt Reverend the Lord Archbiſhop of York, and the Right Reverend the Lords Biſhops of Durham, Worceſter, Ely, Bath and Wells, Lincoln, Hereford, Carliſle, and Salisbury, being appointed his majeſty's commiſſioners for that purpoſe.

It was this day reſolved, that towards the ſupply granted to his majeſty, the ſum of 4,500,000 l. be raiſed by annuities after the rate of 3 1-half per cent. for 24 years, the intereſt to commence from July 5 ; and 500,000 l. by way of lottery, at 3 per cent. the intereſt to commence from the 5th of January, 1756.

Payments of annuities.	Payments on lottery.
10 per c. Ap. 29	10 per c. Ap. 29.
15 - - - May 30	10 - - June 20
15 - - - June 28	20 - - July 18
15 - - - July 27	20 - - Auguſt 19
15 - - Auguſt 30	20 - - Sept. 20
15 - - Sept. 27	20 - - - Oct. 20
15 - - Oct. 29	

Three per cent. to be allowed for anticipating the payments on the annuities ; nothing on the lottery, but to have the tickets as ſoon as they can be got ready. Thoſe who had ſubſcribed for 500 l. were allowed 450 l. in annuities, and 50 l. in lottery tickets.

30th. The Hon. Mr. Finch and the Hon. Mr. Townſhend having propoſed, after the example of his grace the Duke of Newcaſtle, to give two prizes of fifteen guineas each to two ſenior batchelors of arts, and the like to two middle batchelors of the univerſity of Cambridge, who ſhall compoſe the beſt exerciſes in latin proſe, to be read publickly on a day hereafter to be appointed near the commencement: the vice chancellor gives notice, that the ſubjects for this year are, for the ſenior batchelors : *Utrum ſumma hominum felicitas juxta Epicurum in ſenſum delectationibus præcipue ponatur.* For the middle batchelors: *Utrum diverſarum gentium mores & inſtituta a diverſo eorum ſitu explicari poſſint.*

Ages of ten perſons now living in the pariſh of Boughton under Blean in the county of Kent.

	Years.	qu.
Thomas Hawkins, Eſq; in Naſh-Park	81	1
A woman at the Oaſts in the Park	80	1
Carry over	161	2

Brought

Brought over	161	2
Richard Drury, at the ſame place	72	0
His wife	78	0
Farmer Kingſland, joining to the Park	78	0
Hammon Gooding, near the ſame place	78	0
Goody Blakenbury, eaſt of the Park	96	0
Thomas Burley, a little farther	81	2
Mrs. Ovendon	81	2
Mrs. Spurgeon	78	0
In all	804	2

The following remarkable account is given by an officer on board a French Eaſt-Indiaman, in a letter to a friend at the Hague.

Jan. 20, 1757.

"Juſt before we ſailed from Pondicherry, fires broke out on the ſurface of the ſea, three leagues from that place, with the utmoſt impetuoſity, throwing up pumice-ſtones, and other combuſtibles, and forming an iſland of a league long, and of the ſame breadth, which increaſed to a conſiderable height, with a volcano, making a moſt hideous noiſe, like thunder, or great guns, and a cloud proceeding from it, breaking into ſmall rain of ſand inſtead of water. This prodigy was firſt ſeen by a ſhip's crew belonging to Pondicherry, who thought at firſt it had been a water-ſpout; but coming nearer it, ſaw a prodigious flaſhing of fire, which ſmelt of brimſtone, and heard a moſt aſtoniſhing noiſe; afterwards a vaſt quantity of fiſh was perceived dead on the ſea, and appeared broiled. Sailing a little further, they met with ſuch quantities of pumice-ſtones, that it was hardly poſſible to make through them; at the ſame time they diſcerned land, but it appeared to them as a cloud of fire and ſmoke on the ſurface of the ſea, and the cloud aſcending into the air, diſtilled in ſhowers of rain, which brought abundance of ſand on their ſhip's deck, and being nigh the flaſhes of fire, and hearing the noiſe, they were under great conſternation; but it pleaſed God to ſend them a little breeze of wind that brought them from it. Another ſhip ſailed round it, and they were ſo becalmed, that the aſhes proceeding from the vaſt fire fell on their deck, and they were in great danger of being burnt."

25th. The judges report of the ſeven rioters convicted at the late York aſſizes, was laid before his majeſty, when the two ringleaders, Cole for obſtructing the militia act, and Berry for violently taking away corn, were ordered for execution, four of them to be tranſported for life, and one pardoned.

26th. Began the ſale of the capital collection of Italian, Flemiſh and Dutch paintings, of Sir Luke Schaub, and continued the two following days, at Mr. Langford's, in the great piazza, Covent-garden. The whole collection was ſold for 7784l. 5s. many of the pictures ſelling for very extraordinary prices, particularly a landſcape and figures of Claude Lorraine, for 105l.—A man pipeing and his children dancing, by Le Nain, for 180l. 12s.—Our Saviour and St. John, by Guido, for 157l. 10s—St. Sebaſtian, by Guerchino, for 54 l. 12s.—Our Saviour healing the lame, by Rubens, for 79l. 16s.—A landſcape with figures and cattle, by D. Teneirs, for 120 l. 15 s.—Sigiſmunda weeping over the heart of Tancred, by Correggio, for 404l. 5s.—A laughing boy,

boy, by Vandyck, for 126l.—The baptifm of our Saviour, by Albano, for 120l. 15s.—Our Saviour afleep, and the Virgin watching over him, by Guido, for 328l. 13s. — The Virgin, with Jefus afleep in her lap, by Vandyck, for 211l. 1s.— Boors at cards, by D. Teniers, for 85l. 1s. — Four pieces, by Paul Brill, Rubens, Gillis, and Van Breughel, for 551l. 5s. — Jacob parting from Laban, by F. Baffano, for 115l. 10s. — Departure of Rinaldo from Armida, by Le Brun, for 73l. 10s. — A landfcape and figures, by G. Pouffin, for 109l. 4s. — The Virgin, our Saviour, and St. John, by Correggio, for 220l. 10s. —A converfation of boors, by D. Teniers, for 157l. 10s. —Tent of Darius, by Le Brun, for 127l. 1s.—St. Peter repenting, by Guido, for 288l. 15s. — A capital picture of an holy family, by Raphael, for 703l. 10s.

29th. Whitehall. An exprefs arrived with advice that Schweidnitz furrendered on the 16th inftant, and the garrifon was forced to furrender itfelf prifoners of war. It confifted of 230 officers, and 3200 private men. The blockade has befides coft the enemy 3500 men, who have perifhed by difeafes.

The firft ftone of a new bridge, to be built in purfuance of an act of parliament, from Brentford to Kew, was laid in the prefence of a great number of perfons of quality and diftinction.

M A Y.

1ft. The truftees of Raine's hofpital met in purfance of their advertifement, and having felected fix maidens educated therein, who were ftrongly recommended by their mafters and miftreffes, the lot was drawn according to the will of the founder, in the prefence of a polite and numerous affembly, for the prize of 100l. for a marriage portion, which fell upon Anne Netherland, who went out of the hofpital in the year 1743, and is to be married on the 5th of November next, when 5l. as by him directed, will be expended on a wedding dinner; and the five unfuccefsful girls will, with another then to be added, draw again for 100l. to be paid on May-day following.

3d. A young lady, who at New-market had laid a confiderable wager, that fhe could ride 1000 miles in 1000 hours, finifhed her match in a little more than two thirds of the time. At her coming in, the country people ftrewed flowers in her way.

8th. Florence Henfey, M. D. who had been fome time in cuftody, for holding a treafonable correfpondence with the enemy, was brought before the court of King's-bench, and ordered to prepare for trial the firft of June.

The Marquis du Quefne, chef d'Efcadre, lately taken prifoner in the Foudroyant, arrived in London.

9th. At the anniverfary meeting of the prefident and governors of the London lying-in hofpital in Alderfgate-ftreet, the collection at church and at hall amounted to 611l. 10s.

10th. Was held the annual general meeting of the hofpital for the maintenance of expofed and deferted young children, when a general committee for the year enfuing was elected by ballot. It appears, that fince this charity has been made general by parliamentary provifion, near 6000 infants have

have annually been taken in; one third of whom, nearly, have died at nurfe. A matter that merits a parliamentary enquiry.

12th. Ladders and gates were affixed to Eaft-Sheen gate in Surry, in order for foot people to go into Richmond Park; and alfo at Ham gate (purfuant to a verdict laft affizes at Kingfton); fo that her Royal Highnefs the Princefs Amelia has at length given up this long contefted affair for the eafe and convenience of the inhabitants.

13th. Admiralty-Office. In purfuance of the King's pleafure, Lord Anfon, Vice-Admiral of Great Britain, and Admiral of the White, was appointed commander in chief of a fleet, now fitting for the fea.—Advice is received from Rear-Admiral Broderick, that on the 13th of laft month, his majefty's fhip Prince George of 80 guns, in which the Rear Admiral hoifted his flag, took fire at half an hour after one in the afternoon, in lat. 48: and after burning to the water's edge, the remnant of her funk at a little before fix in the evening. The admiral fays, he could not then give a particular account of the people on board, being about 780; but he feared the number loft exceeded the number faved.

His majefty's fhip Windfor, of 60 guns, Captain Faulkner, with the Efcorte frigate, being fent to intercept two French frigates and three ftore-fhips from Dunkirk road to the weftward, on the 27th paft fell in with them about 16 leagues from the Ram-Head, when the two frigates brought to in a line, as if they intended to receive him, and the ftore-fhips continued ftanding to the weftward. When the Windfor came within about two gun fhot of the frigates, they made all the fail they could towards the coaft of France: upon which Captain Faulkner fent the Efcorte after the ftore-fhips, while he gave chace to the frigates, and continued it till four in the afternoon; when finding they greatly outfailed him, he gave it over, and made after their convoy, which could then but juft be difcerned from the poop. The next morning at day-light only one of them was to be feen, which the Windfor came up with and took. She is called the St Peter, of near 400 tuns burthen, and her cargo confifted of provifions, and 1000 ftand of arms, intended for Quebec. Another of thefe ftore-fhips was fallen in with, the fame day, by a fquadron of his majefty's fhips to the weftward, commanded by Captain Douglas in the Alcide. She is called the Baden, is about the fame fize with the other, and laden with provifions.

On the 29th about three o'clock in the afternoon, Captain Pratten feeing a fail to the S. W. made a fignal for the Dorfetfhire, of 70 guns and 520 men, commanded by Captain Denis, to give chace; and foon after obferving the chace to be a large fhip, difpatched the Achilles, of 60 guns, commanded by the honourable Captain Barrington, after her, and then followed them with the reft of the fquadron. About feven o'clock the Dorfetfhire came up with the chace, which proved to be the Raifonable, a French fhip of war of 64 guns, and 630 men, and Captain Denis began to engage her very clofely, and they continued warmly engaged till about nine o'clock, when the enemy's fhip, commanded by the Prince de Mombazon, chevalier de Rohan,

Rohan, ſtruck, having ſuffered greatly in her hull, and had 61 men killed, and 100 men wounded. She was going from l'Orient to Breſt, a new ſhip, not above four or five months off the ſtocks. The Dorſetſhire's maſts, yards, and ſails, were greatly ſhattered. She had 15 men killed, and 21 wounded, in the action; and one of the wounded is ſince dead.

By the French accounts, the Raiſonable, with the Hero, Formidable, and Intrepide, and two frigates, were deſigned for Canada; to which place and Louisbourg they have ſent ſeveral little ſquadrons, at different times; one under M. de Beauſſier, ſailed to the latter place on the 5th of April.

One Robert Anderſon was carried on board the Norfolk man of war, Commodore Brett, in the Downs, by the maſter of a Deal boat. The account he gave was this; that about three months ago, he was trapanned into the Iriſh brigades in the French King's ſervice; that about two o'clock on the 11th in the morning, when he was relieved from his poſt of centry by the water ſide at Graveling, he ſeized a ſmall boat within ten yards of his box, came down the canal two miles, in which he paſſed two captains guards, and ſeveral advanced poſts: that he then ſeized a fiſhing-boat, and ſet ſail for our coaſt, with the ſmall boat in tow; and that he ſteered directly for the Downs, with an intention to run into Ramſgate, where his wife lives; but was boarded by the Deal boat as above. He has brought muſket, bayonet, and all his accoutrements with him; is a very likely fellow, a gardener by trade, and all the knowledge he had of a boat was from being often a fiſhing for his amuſement. He ſteered by the ſtars till day-light, and then had the ſight of our coaſt. He had planned his deſign three weeks before, and had made himſelf perfectly maſter of the canal from conſtant obſervation, and knew by the ſame means the ſtated times when the fiſhermen arrived. Sir Piercy, with his wonted good-nature, ordered the boat to be ſold for the man's benefit.—— This account is taken from part of a letter from an officer on board the Norfolk, and what corroborates it, is, an imperfect relation from Broad-Stairs, of the arrival there of a French fiſhing boat, with two Engliſhmen in it, and a German, a ſoldier in the French King's ſervice, who aſſiſted the Engliſhmen to make their eſcape, and for whoſe uſe the boat was put up to auction, and ſold for 9 l. 5 s.

17th. Twelve flat-bottomed boats, of a new conſtruction, were launched at Portſmouth, to be employed in landing the troops then going on the enterpriſe to France. They carry 63 men each, are rowed with 12 oars, and draw not above two feet water.

18th. A young grenadier, aged about 27, was ſhot at Plymouth for deſertion; what is remarkable, being to receive 500 laſhes by the ſentence of a regimental court-martial, he choſe to appeal to a general court-martial, who inſtead of confirming his former ſentence, inflicted that of death. The young man ſuffered with great fortitude, having done nothing, he ſaid, to offend his Saviour.

19th. By an advertiſement it appeared, that 933 l. 7s. 6d. had been ſubſcribed to carry Mr. Fielding's plan into execution.

By

3

20th. By an advertiſement relating to Mr. Dingley's plan, it appears, that 3114 l. 17s. had been ſubſcribed to carry it into execution.

Four French ſhips, part of ſeventeen, which ſailed the firſt inſtant from Bourdeaux, laden with proviſions and ſtores for Canada, and ſaid to be under convoy of a large privateer of 54 guns, and two frigates, were brought into Falmouth by Commodore Keppel's ſquadron.

21ſt. An account was received of a dreadful fire at Bridge-Town in Barbadoes, which in February laſt had conſumed 120 houſes; and beſides that the crops in that iſland were very ſhort, having had little rain in the ſeaſon.

A waggon was burnt on Saliſbury-plain, laden with the whole rich wardrobe, ſcenery, and apparatus of the Bath theatre; beſides the entire property of each performer belonging to it. Some miles before the waggon reached Saliſbury, a ſervant of the theatre told the driver that the wheel would take fire, intreating him to ſtop and unload; but the fellow ſtill perſiſted in keeping on his way, and gave for reaſon, that he had driven twelve miles with his wheels ſmoaking. About three miles from this city, the flame burſt out, and before ten boxes could be preſerved, the whole waggon was conſumed. The damage is ſaid to amount to 2000 l.

23d. Two Stonehaven boats being out a fiſhing about ſix leagues from the land, a large French privateer brought aboard both their crews, uſed them civilly, paid them for their fiſh, and after detaining them ſome hours, diſmiſſed them when about nine miles from land. The fiſhermen report, that this ſhip mounts 40 guns, and carries 300 men, beſides marines. There were no ranſomers on board, and it appears that ſhe had juſt begun her cruize. [Stonehaven is about ten Scotch miles from Aberdeen.]

A diſcovery of the higheſt utility has lately been made at Edinburgh, and already ſufficiently confirmed by a number of ſucceſsful experiments: Dr. Francis Hume has inoculated for the meaſles, and has produced a diſeaſe free from all alarming ſymptoms.

30th. At a ſtore-cellar in Pall-Mall, Mrs. Hucks's cooper, and a chairman, who went down after him, were both ſuffocated, as ſuppoſed by the ſteam of 40 butts of unſtopped beer. [It might be of uſe to the public if ſome of our ingenious correſpondents would account for this accident.]

The following account of the ages of ten perſons in the borough of Hoath in Kent, eight of whom lived within a quarter of a mile of each other, and the other two but at a ſmall diſtance, is atteſted by good authority; Thomas Darby 89 years and a half; Richard Steed 87; William Chandler 77 and a half; Anne Chriſtian 76; William Brice 72 and a half; Suſanna Wix 87; Jane Thompſon 76; Amy Matthews 82 and a quarter; Elizabeth Brice 74; and Thomas Carey 78; in all 806 years and three quarters.

A ſociety has been lately erected at Glaſgow, under the name of the Glaſgow charitable marine ſociety; the end of which is to provide for ſuch ſeamen as ſhall become old, or diſabled in the ſervice of the merchants of that city; and alſo to afford relief for their poor

widows

widows and children. A truly laudable charity.

The West-India mail brought a confirmation of the news we had heard before of the Buckingham and Cambridge attacking and levelling with the ground, a small fort in Grand Ance bay on the island of Martinico, and destroying three privateers, and converting the fourth into a tender. But what does the greatest honour to Captain Tyrrel, the commodore, is the following incident; when the fort was demolished, a village situated close by it was a strong temptation to men flushed with victory to attack, and they sollicited warmly for leave to destroy it; but their brave commander replied, 'Gentlemen, it 'is beneath us to render a number of poor people miserable, 'by destroying their habitations 'and little conveniencies of life; 'brave Englishmen scorn to distress 'even their enemies when not in 'arms against them:' This prevailed, and saved the lives of the innocent villagers.

His Catholic majesty was pleased to declare the Conde de Fuentes, who is appointed ambassador to Great Britain, a grandee of Spain, and one of the gentlemen of his bed chamber.

J U N E.

1st. The felons in Newgate intended for transportation, in order to make their escape, had sawed thro' eight iron bars, each as thick as a man's wrist, except enough to keep them together, and filled up the notches with dirt and iron rust to prevent a discovery, but not succeeding in their attempt, the ring-leaders were chained to the floor, as is usual. —There has been a scheme much talked of for pulling down this goal, and rebuilding it in a stronger and more commodious manner.

Florence Hensey, M. D. was brought to trial at the court of King's-bench in Westminster-hall, on an indictment for high treason, before the Lord Chief Justice Mansfield, the Judges Dennison, Foster, and Wilmot: The council for the crown were the attorney and sollicitor-general, Sir Richard Lloyd, Mr. Norton, Mr. Parratt, Mr. Gould, and Mr. Serjeant Pool. The council for the prisoner were Mr. Moreton, and the Hon. Mr. Howard,

Several of his letters were produced in evidence against him, in one of which he sollicits employment from a fellow-student at Leyden, who is promoted in France, and professes great regard for the French nation, offering his best services not only from interest but inclination.

In the course of the trial it appeared, that soon after the declaration of war in 1756, he became a pensioner to France, and agreed for 100 guineas a year, to give the best intelligence he could of the state of affairs, in this kingdom. But a difference afterwards arising about his salary, which he represented as too small, and as an argument in his favour, said he belonged to a club in the Strand (from which he could gain great intelligence) at which they always drank French wine at dinner: the correspondence appears to have been some time discontinued: but in January 1757, it was agreed, that the doctor should receive 20 guineas a month, on condition of sending intelligence every post, but to forfeit a guinea for every omisſion; he received however no more than one monthly payment, and they gave for reaſon, that his intelligence was nothing but extracts from the news-papers.

The plan for carrying on this correſpondence was the following: The doctor wrote a common letter with ink, and between each line the ſecrets of England in lemon juice. This was incloſed under three or four different covers, directed to different perſons, in the ſecret, who conveyed them from one hand to another, till the firſt incloſed came to the principal for whom it was deſigned. He had a brother who is a jeſuit, and was chaplain and ſecretary to the Spaniſh ambaſſador at the Hague, from whom our reſident at that court gained a knowledge of ſome ſecrets relating to England, even before he had received any account thereof from his own court. This put him upon enquiry, and he ſoon learnt that the ſecretary had a brother, a phyſician in London, from whom poſſibly he might get intelligence; ſuſpicion being thus raiſed, the doctor was watched, and twenty-nine of his letters ſtopt.

From theſe letters it appeared, that he gave the French the firſt account of Admiral Boſcawen's ſailing to North America, and of the taking the Alcide and Lys, with every minute circumſtance relating to it; and from that time, of the ſailing of every fleet, and its deſtination; and was ſo minute as to give an account even of the launching of a man of war; he alſo gave an account of all difficulties relating to raiſing money: and particularly deſcribed the ſecret expedition in 1757, aſſuring them it was intended againſt Rochfort or Breſt, but gave his opinion for the former. And in one of his letters he particularly adviſed a deſcent of the French upon our coaſt, as the moſt certain method of diſtreſſing the government by affecting the public credit, and mentioned the time when, and the place where it would be moſt proper.

The trial began at half an hour after ten in the morning, and ended at half an hour after eight in the evening; when the jury, after ſtaying out about half an hour, brought him in guilty. He is a native of Ireland, aged about 44, and has a diploma from the univerſity of Leyden to practiſe phyſic.

There were 131 gentlemen from different places in the county of Middleſex ſummoned on the jury, and near 100 anſwered to their names. The doctor objected againſt fifteen, and the council for the crown againſt three.

14th. This day Florence Henſey, M. D. was brought to the bar of the court of King's-bench to receive ſentence, when Lord Manſfield, after a very moving ſpeech, pronounced ſentence in the uſual form, to be hanged, drawn, and quartered at Tyburn, on Wedneſday the 12th of July next.

Mr. Lee, a wealthy farmer, at Wroxeter in Northamptonſhire, being complained to by his neighbours for keeping a vicious bull, inſiſted upon it that he was not vicious, and went to him himſelf to convince them of it, when the bull immediately ran at him, and killed him upon the ſpot.

16th. The honourable houſe of commons reſolved, that an humble addreſs ſhould be preſented to his majeſty (by ſuch members of that houſe as are of the privy council) to repreſent, that the ſalaries

laries of most of the judges in his majesty's superior courts of justice in this kingdom, are inadequate to the dignity and importance of their offices; and therefore to beseech his majesty, that he would be graciously pleased to advance any sum not exceeding 11,450l. to be applied in augmentation of the salaries of such judges, and in such proportions as his majesty should think fit for the present year; and to assure his majesty that the house would make good the same to his majesty.

17th. The king has been pleased to appoint the Right Honourable George William Earl of Bristol, to be his majesty's ambassador extraordinary and plenipotentiary to the Catholic King.

[The reciprocal appointment of ambassadors by the courts of Madrid and London, destroys at once the credit of the reports industriously propagated of late, of our being upon the eve of a Spanish war.]

Came on in the court of King's bench in Westminster-hall, before Lord Chief Justice Mansfield, the trial on an information against Doctor Shebbeare, for writing a pamphlet, called a Sixth Letter to the people of England; when, after a short hearing, he was found guilty, and is to receive sentence next term.

19th. A journeyman barber that lived at Wandsworth, being under some discontent of mind, cut his throat from ear to ear. There was a note found by him, with these words: "I have wronged no man, nor never designed it; and am now gone before God."

22d. Was the hottest press for seamen on the Thames that has been known since the war began, no regard being had to protections, and upwards of 800 swept away. The crew of the Prince of Wales, a letter marque ship, stood to arms, and saved themselves by their resolution.

Matthew West, butcher, prisoner in the New Goal, 27th. and ringleader of those felons, who lately endeavoured to escape from that goal, got himself loose from an iron collar, in which his neck was fastened, and his arms extended, although he was chained down to the floor in the condemned room. When he got himself disengaged from the floor, he had the resolution to wring the collar from his neck, by fixing it between two of the bars of the goal window, and by main strength broke it short in two.

Some workmen have lately dug up near Colonna, where it is thought the ancient city of Laubicum stood, (about 14 miles from Rome) an antique Venus of white marble, thought to be of more exquisite workmanship than even the Venus of Medicis, and fine bust of Lucius Verus, with several vases, lamps, coins, and other antiquities; and a Greek inscription has been discovered near the great building, importing that there was in that place a library.

Ended the sessions at the 29th. Old Bailey, when Jacob Romart, a jeweller, for the murder of Theodore Wentworth, a fellow workman; and Henry Carrier, for publishing as true, an acceptance to a bill of exchange, with intent to defraud, received sentence of death; and 21 for transportation.

J U L Y.

Jacob Romart was carried 1st. from Newgate to Tyburn, and executed

executed for the muder of Theodore Wentworth. He was a native of Norway, 28 years of age, and very unhappy in his temper: in his confinement he had taken little care to make a proper defence on his trial, and was regardless afterwards what became of him, being possessed of a spirit of obstinacy scarcely to be paralleled: he refused to acknowledge that he repented of the crime: but insisted he had a commission from God for what he did. It appears from the ordinary of Newgate's account that he was a gloomy, visionary enthusiast; that he had twice fasted for an extraordinary length of time; and that Wentworth had been too free in joking with a man of his temper, though, when he received his death's wound, no words had passed between them.

Arrived at St. Helen's Commodore Howe, with his squadron of men of war and all the transports. They were obliged to proceed to St. Helen's for want of provisions for the men, and forage for their horses.

On the 7th the troops disembarked and encamped, the foot on the Isle of Wight, and the horse on South-sea common, at Portsmouth; They had 1200 sick, occasioned by the inclemency of the weather.

About eight o'clock at night, George (alias Captain) Forrester, committed some time since to Bristol goal for forgery, and Captain Moliere, a Frenchman, for stealing a diamond ring, assisted by several other felons, attempted to make their escape out of the goal. The sheriff, with some invalids, came to the assistance of the jailer, and were obliged to fire thrice among them before they would surrender, after which they were all properly secured. One of the shot went in at Forrester's right breast, and came out through his back, and lodged in the partition.

4th. A reprieve was brought to Newgate for Dr. Hensey, respiting his sentence for a fortnight, early in the morning, but however not so soon as to prevent the assembling of a great concourse of people to see him executed, who committed some disorders. The doctor has since been two or three times under examination, and it is said has made great discoveries.

5th. Admiral Saunders arrived at Spithead from the Streights, in the Monmouth, with the Revenge, Foudroyant, and Orpheus, and brought home with him above 1000 French prisoners. The Foudroyant is a surprizing 84 gun ship, her guns are on two decks, her lower tier monstrously unwieldy, and not easy to be worked, the shot weighing very little short of fifty pounds each. Notwithstanding their superiority in bulk, our thirty-two pound shot are thought by all judges to be on a par with them, and of as much efficacy when they take place. Her larboard side is most terribly mauled, there are seventy shot-holes on that side plugged up; she came home under jury masts: Her lower tier abaft the main-mast are fine brass guns, several of which have very fine bustos in an oval compartment of Lewis XIV. The Orpheus is a fine large 64 gun ship, she is peppered very well too, her masts very much wounded: It is surprizing how they stood home. She also has several fine brass guns. The prisoners were put on board the Boyne, and from thence conveyed to Porchester castle.

An

8th. An old lodging-houſe in Plumb-tree-court, Broad St. Giles's, fell down, by which accident ſeveral poor wretches were cruſhed to death, and many more deſperately maimed. There being other houſes in the court in the like tottering condition, the mob aſſembled in a few days afterwards, and pulled them down.

17th. Sir John Barnard, Kt. father of the city, and alderman of Bridge ward without, deſired the court of aldermen would permit him to reſign his gown on account of his age and bad ſtate of health; to which, after much reluctance, and many importunities uſed by the aldermen preſent to the contrary, the court conſented.

John Cole, who at Chelmsford aſſizes received ſentence of death for the murder of Martha Adams, at her houſe at Eſcott in the hundred of Eſſex, was this day executed at Chelmsford, when John Loads, who came to ſea the execution, was charged by Cole at the gallows as being acceſſary in the ſaid murder; he was immediately apprehended, and had before a magiſtrate, where he confeſſed his guilt, and was committed to Chelmsford goal.

18th. An experiment was made with the light horſe and flat-bottomed boats, from the South-ſea beach, near Portſmouth, where the horſe lie encamped; 12 horſes were put on board a boat, which had a platform laid in it railed round. They were carried to Spithead, and laid along-ſide a tranſport three miles from the beach, and were ſlung, and hoiſted into the ſhip, and re-imbarked into the boats with great eaſe. Several guns were fired to try the horſes, which they bore very patiently, only ſnorting a little at the ſmoak flying about them. They were landed on the beach again in extreme good order.

His Royal Highneſs Prince Edward, who had been ſome 24th. time indiſpoſed, arrived at Portſmouth, and embarked on board the Eſſex, Commodore Howe's own ſhip, in which he ſails as a volunteer in the intended expedition againſt France. His Royal Highneſs went from the dock-yard in the Eſſex's twelve-oared barge, attended by Lord George Sackville, and Admiral Holbourne. His Royal Highneſs had the ſtandard of England flying in the bow of the boat. Admiral Holbourne's barge followed with his flag flying in the bow of his boat, and all the captains according to their ſeniority, which made a very agreeable appearance.

Was held a court of common council at Guildhall, 25th. when, upon the motion of John Paterſon, Eſq; it was reſolved, *nem. con.* "That Sir John Barnard, Knt. ſo juſtly and emphatically ſtiled the father of this city, having lately (to the great and laſting regret of this court) thought proper to reſign the office of alderman, the thanks of this court be given him for having ſo long and ſo faithfully devoted himſelf to the ſervice of his fellow-citizens: for the honour and influence which this city has, upon many occaſions, derived from the dignity of his character, and the wiſdom, ſteadineſs, and integrity of his conduct: for his firm adherence to the conſtitution, both in church and ſtate, his noble ſtruggles for liberty, and his diſintereſted and invariable purſuit of the true glory and proſperity of his king and country, uninfluenced by power, anawed by clamour, and unbiaſſed by the prejudice of party."

Sir Robert Ladbroke, at the ſaid court declared his aſſent to take upon him the office of father of this city, and the aldermanſhip of Bridge ward without.

A motion was made by the ſaid gentleman, that the thanks of the court of aldermen ſhould be given to Sir John Barnard, which was agreed to, and expreſſed in the following terms:

'It is unanimouſly agreed and 'ordered, that the thanks of this 'court be given to Sir John Barnard, Knt. late one of the aldermen, and father of this city, for 'his conſtant attendance and ſalutary counſels in this court, his 'wiſe, vigilant, and impartial administration of juſtice, his unwearied zeal for the honour, ſafety, and proſperity of his fellow-citizens, his inviolable attachment 'to the laws and liberties of his 'country, and for the noble example he has ſet of a long and 'uninterrupted courſe of virtue in 'private as well as public life.'

This day a further reſpite for Dr. Henſey was brought to Newgate till the 8th of November.

The ſociety for the encouragement of arts, manufactures, and commerce, having propoſed two medals for planting acorns for timber; a gold medal was this day adjudged to his grace the Duke of Beaufort, for planting the largeſt quantity; a ſilver medal to Philip Carteret Webb, Eſq; for the next largeſt quantity; and a ſilver medal likewiſe to John Berney, Eſq; for planting the third largeſt quantity.

26th. At a committee of Chriſt's hoſpital, Sir John Barnard regſined the preſidentſhip of that houſe, on account of his great age and infirmities.

31ſt. On the 5th of this month, Cardinal Charles Rezzonico, biſhop of Padua, a Venetian, was elected pope. He was born on the 7th of March 1693, and was formerly auditor of the Rota. He was made cardinal by Clement XII. on the 20th of October 1737, at the nomination of the republic of Venice. He had the title of St. Mara d' Ara Cœli (the principal convent of the Cordeliers) and was protector of the Illyrian nation, the Pandours. He is ill-favoured and hunch-backed; but of a ſtrong vigorous conſtitution; a freſh complexion, walks well and firm; the honeſteſt man in the world; a moſt exemplary eccleſiaſtic; of the pureſt morals; devout, ſteady, learned, diligent; in ſhort, worthy to ſucceed the great Benedict XIV. though no body, certainly, ever thought he would be called to ſucceed him.

The following is a true copy of the manifeſto, which his grace the Duke of Marlborough publiſhed in Brittany on the 7th of June, the ſecond day after the landing of the troops at Cancalle.

"We the high and mighty Prince Charles Duke of Marlborough, Marquis of Blandford, Earl of Sunderland, Baron Churchill, Knight of the moſt noble order of the Garter, Privy-counſellor to his Britannic Majeſty, Grand Maſter of the Ordnance, and Commander in chief of his forces, &c.

"Make known to all the inhabitants of Brittany, that the deſcent on their coaſt with the powerful army under our command, and our formidable armament by ſea, is not made

made with an intention to make war on the inhabitants of the country, excepting thofe who fhall be found in arms, or fhall otherwife oppofe the juft war, which we wage againft his majefty the moft Chriftian king.

"Be it known, therefore, to all who will remain in peaceable poffeffion of their habitations and effects, that they may ftay unmolefted in their refpective dwellings, and follow their ufual occupations; and that, excepting the cuftoms and taxes which they pay to the king. nothing will be required of them, either in money or merchandizes, but what is abfolutely neceffary for the fubfiftence of the army; and that for all the provifions they fhall bring in, they fhall be paid ready money.

"On the contrary, if notwithftanding this declaration which we have been pleafed to make, the inhabitants of the towns or villages carry away their furniture, effects, or provifions, and abandon their houfes or dwellings, we fhall treat fuch delinquents as enemies, and deftroy by fire and fword, or fuch other methods as fhall be in our power, their towns, villages, dwellings, or houfes. Given at the head quarters at Parame.

June 7, 1758. MARLBOROUGH."

By his grace's command, BRYANT.

His grace fent at the fame time the following letter to the magiftrates and echevins of St. Maloes.

GENTLEMEN,

"We being in poffeffion of all the country between Dinan, Rennes, and Doll, as far as St. Malo, and finding that all the inhabitants of the towns and villages in this extent of country have abandoned their habitations, probably to avoid the payment of the ufual contributions: and as we are informed that the inhabitants have, by your orders, been compelled to go to St. Malo, we give you notice, that if they do not return peaceably to their houfes, and fend their magiftrates to our head quarters to fettle the contributions, we fhall think ourfelves obliged to fet fire to them without further delay.

MARLBOROUGH."

AUGUST.

1ft. In the paft month of July, by an exact meafurement, above five inches of rain fell in London, a quantity furpaffing any in the fame month perhaps in the memory of man. The mean depth in England, one year with another, is about 23 inches and an half, of which a larger proportion ufually falls in the winter months.

A loan to his majefty, in his quality of Elector of Hanover, for two hundred thoufand pounds, was opened at the bank; which was immediately filled by the following gentlemen.

	£.
Sir Jofhua Vanneck —	50000
Meffrs. Backwell, Hart, and Co — —	50000
Samfon Gideon, Efq; —	40000
Nicholas Magens, Efq;	20000
George Amyand, Efq;	15000
Bartholomew Burton, Efq;	15000
Thomas Marin, Efq;	5000
Jofeph Salvadore, Efq;	5000
	200000

And Meffrs. Amyand, Backwell, Burton, and Magens, are appointed truftees for the management of the faid loan.

A great number of fowls, beafts, &c. which came over in the Weft-India fleet, were brought to St.

James's, presents to his Royal Highness the Duke of Cumberland.

2d. At Wigton, there was such a fall of rain, as has not been known in the memory of the oldest man living. It swelled the rivulets to such a degree in that town and neighbourhood, that five bridges within two miles of the town were swept away by the flood. In several houses of the town the water was six feet deep the day after the flood.

6th. Two powder-mills at Hounslow blew up with about 600 weight of powder.

The lords of the admiralty received information, that a Dutch ship, having on board the baggage of the Marquis de Pignatelly, minister from the court of Spain to the court of Denmark, and several of his domestics, was, on the 30th of June last, boarded three times, by the crews of three different English privateers; that some of the crews armed with cutlasses, pistols and hatchets, forced open the hatchways, and went into the said ship's hold, and there broke open two trunks belonging to the Marquis de Pignatelly, wherein were rich cloaths, and laced liveries, which they carried away to their ship: and that whilst they were so doing the crew of another English vessel joined, upon which the said crews committed very great outrages, by breaking open all the said Marquis de Pignatelly's cases, and trunks, and taking and carrying away all the valuable effects, which were in six of the said cases and trunks, and destroying or damaging the rest of those effects; and then falling upon his, the said minister's officers, beat them in a very cruel and shameful manner, and stripping them of their cloaths, carried them off, together with their letters of credit and a bill of exchange. Their lordships, therefore, in order to discover and bring to justice the persons guilty of the piratical offences above-mentioned, are pleased to promise a reward of 500l. without any deduction, unto, or amongst such person or persons, as shall, within three months from this time, discover any two or more of the offenders, concerned in committing the piracies above mentioned.

Advice was received, that an unsuccessful attempt had been made on the island of Goree, near the river Senegal; but that the ships who had attacked it, had lost but a few men, and received very little damage. 8th.

The same day an account was received of the burning the Rose, a French man of war of 40 guns, by the Monmouth, Captain Hervey, in the island of Malta, of which insult the Maltese complain loudly.

The Magdalen hospital in Goodman's fields for the reception of penitent prostitutes was opened, when fifty petitions were presented, and several of the penitents admitted. 10th.

This day a company of labourers, headed by some farmers, assembled in a riotous manner, and pulled down a bridge that was building near Norwich, and after having levelled it with the ground, they broke up the road, and then dispersed.

At Poole, in the county of Montgomery, whilst the court of great sessions was sitting in the hall there over the market place, an alarm was given that the floor gave way; which occasioned 11th.

to

so great crouding at the door and stairs, that six of the common people were trampled to death, and many others bruised.

12th. The assizes at Lancaster ended, when many capital offenders were tried. On the first day of the assize an account was received of prodigious riots and tumults, in and about Manchester, that near 10,000 manufacturers had left off working, and entered into a combination to raise the price of wages by force; that large sums of money were collected, and paid into the hands of some of the leaders, for the maintenance of the poorer sort while they refused to work; that they insulted and abused such as would not join in the combination; that incendiary letters were dispersed, and threats of vengeance denounced against all who should oppose them; that business was at a stand, the magistrates were afraid to act, and every thing seemed in great confusion. Lord Mansfield adapted part of his charge to the importance of the occasion, and the grand jury, upon strong evidence, singled out 17 or 18 of the ring-leaders, against whom they found bills of indictment; after which they unanimously joined in a request to his lordship to give them in writing that charge, the effects of which they had so powerfully felt upon themselves, and which, if made public, they had reason to hope would be equally felt by others in this critical period; but whether this request was complied with, or not, is not said.

16th. A captain of a privateer was taken into the custody of the marshal of the admiralty, near the Royal Exchange, on an information for committing several outrages on neutral vessels in the British channel.

17th. Came on at the high court of admiralty, before Sir George Lee, Knt. several trials with regard to Dutch and Danish ships taken by our privateers; and it appearing to the satisfaction of the court, that their cargoes were French property, four were condemned as lawful prizes; and the court gave orders that the freights of three of them should be paid, and the ships set at liberty: but a Dutch vessel taken by the Hawk privateer, and carried into Gibraltar, had both ship and cargo condemned; she is a very valuable prize.

Richard Houseman of Knaresborough, was committed to York castle on suspicion of murdering Daniel Clark, of the same place, shoemaker, about 14 years ago: the discovery was remarkable. Some workmen digging about St. Robert's Cave, near Knaresborough, found the remains of a body, which they supposed to have been murdered; and as Daniel Clark had suddenly disappeared, and was generally thought to have been murdered, they imagined it might be his body, and therefore apprehended Houseman, and carried him before a justice, as it was recollected that he was one of the last persons seen in Clark's company. On his examination he said that the body found was not Clark's body, for Clark was buried in another place, which he mentioned, and accordingly the remains of another body was there found, on which he was committed as above. And one Engene Aram was also committed on suspicion of being an accomplice.

A prayer

27th. A prayer of thanksgiving for the taking of Louisbourg, was used in the churches and chapels throughout the kingdom.

Some wicked incendiaries having attempted to set fire to the new temporary bridge, a strong guard is placed to prevent their design.

Four ships sailed from Whitby on the Greenland fishery; one was lost in the ice, one returned without any fish, and two brought home three whales between them. Two ships of Edinburgh returned with five large whales, and four others returned empty. The Oswald, of Borrowstowness, returned with two large whales. Many have arrived at the port of London with various success.

On the 11th instant a vessel arrived at Cork from Fyal, bound for Bremen; she sailed from Rio de Janeiro in last January, and was there in October, when General Lally, with five French men of war and two frigates, put in there in his way to the East Indies. His fleet had lost above 1000 men from their sailing from France, and was then so sickly, that General Lally was heard to say that he could not undertake any thing against the English settlements without a reinforcement. On his proceeding from thence, he left an officer behind, who took his passage in the above ship for Europe, and died on the voyage. On examining his papers a large packet of letters was found, directed for the French ambassador at Lisbon, to be forwarded to Versailles, which letters were last night forwarded to their Excellencies the Lords Justices of this kingdom. The above vessel on her passage met with eleven Spanish men of war, on the 24th of July, in lat. 40. 7. long. 23. 25. from London, standing to the S. E. Note, the said ships were all clean, and every one of them had new sails.

Heads of an act passed last sessions, to permit the importation of salted beef, pork, and butter, from Ireland, for a limited time.

That it shall be lawful to import salted beef, pork, and butter, from Ireland, for six months, to commence the 24th of June, and expire the 24th of December 1758, without being subject to any penalties, forfeitures or other duties, on the landing thereof, except 1s. 3d. per ct. weight for beef or pork, and 4d. per ct. weight for butter; the same to be paid to the Exchequer, as part of the duties on salt, laid by the act of 5 Geo. II. If any should be landed before duty is paid, the importer, besides the forfeiture of the said commodities, is to forfeit also 20 s. per barrel, and so in proportion for any greater or lesser quantity, half to the king, half to the informer. No bounty to be allowed on the exporting it from England.

New York, June 19.

Captain Smith arrived at Newhaven the 7th instant, in 25 days from Antigua, and reports that about a week before he sailed, Commodore Moore with 7 ships of the line, and two frigates, sailed from thence on some secret design, thought to be against St. Domingo.

New York, July 3.

A few days since a flag of truce (it is said of 30 men) came into Fort Edward, from Canada, to demand the return of the brave Colonel Peter Schuyler, of New Jersey, agreeable to engagement, Mons. Montcalm having rejected the proposals that were offered with regard

gard to his exchange: and the colonel, we hear, ſet out yeſterday for Albany.

A woman, who uſed to paſs for a perſon of quality, and went by ſeveral different names, and kept ſervants in livery, was committed to the Gate-houſe for embezzling the goods entruſted with her in her ready-furniſhed lodgings in Dean-ſtreet, Soho. She was carried to goal in a chair, attended by one of her footmen.

A quarrel happening in Thomas-ſtreet, Drury-lane, between John Garland, a bricklayer's labourer, and Thomas Lockwood, a fruiterer; the former uſed the latter ſo cruelly, that he left him for dead, and made his eſcape. Lockwood was carried the ſame night to the Middleſex hoſpital, where he died yeſterday morning.

28th. A man was obſerved to walk to and fro at Tower-wharf for near an hour; and when it was quite dark he went into the farthermoſt boat, threw himſelf from thence into the river, and was drowned. He was a tall, thin, well dreſſed man.

A ſervant maid at Execution-dock, delivered herſelf of a child, which being ſoon diſcovered by the people of the houſe, ſearch was made, and the infant was found torn in two, wrapt up in a flannel petticoat, and hid under her bed. She is ſecured.

30th. A remarkable carriage ſet out from Alderſgate-ſtreet for Birmingham, from which town it arrived the Thurſday before, full of paſſengers and baggage, without uſing coomb, or any oily, unctuous, or other liquid matter whatever, to the wheels, or axles; its conſtruction being ſuch, as to render all ſuch helps uſeleſs. The inventor has engraved on the boxes of the wheels, theſe words, FRICTION ANNIHILATED, and it is aſſured that the carriage will go as long and as eaſy, if not longer and eaſier, without greaſing, than any of the ordinary ſtage carriages will do with greaſing. If this anſwers in common practice, it is perhaps the moſt uſeful invention in mechanics that this age has produced.

A diſpute happened between ſome officers of the cuſtoms and the maſter of a veſſel arrived from Ireland with ſalt beef, pork, bacon and neats tongues, which two laſt articles were objected to, as being an infringement of the act of parliament paſſed for allowing ſalted proviſions to be brought from Ireland; but the ſame being referred to the proper commiſſioners, it was agreed, that the intent and meaning of the ſaid act was, for importing all ſalted pork and beef whatever from that kingdom; and that bacon, tongues, and hams, were parts of beef and pork. [This is a miſtake, but the point is now ſettled by an amendment to the act this ſeſſion.] 29th.

Between nine and ten at night, a fire broke out among ſome new cordage, very near the ſtore-houſe in his majeſty's yard at Deptford, on which all the alarm bells were rung, and the gates ſet open, when great numbers of the artificers went to give their aſſiſtance, by whom it was ſoon extinguiſhed. There is great reaſon to believe that this fire was not accidental; the ſpot where the diſcovery was made is not 25 feet diſtance from a new 74 gun ſhip on the ſtocks, and within 16 feet of great quantities of combuſtibles, 30th.

bustibles, such as resin, turpentine, &c. which were in cellars under the store-house, the largest and most valuable of any belonging to the navy; so that from a loss of these stores, with the disappointment that must have naturally followed, the damage done to the service would have been very great; but all this was happily prevented by the great vigilance of the officers, and the uncommon readiness and activity of the workmen of the yard, who on this occasion performed wonders, by removing almost instantaneously great pieces of timber, &c. and in separating and rolling off large coils of cordage, several of which were then on fire; so that in less than an hour the whole was extinguished, to the inexpressible joy of 3000 spectators.——The commissioners of the navy have since promised 500l. reward to any person concerned in this wicked affair, who shall make discovery thereof, except the person who set the said place on fire.

SEPTEMBER.

5th. A fire broke out in the Amsterdam galley, a new ship of 250 tons burthen, in the port of Limerick in Ireland, by which she was immediately consumed, and by the explosion of some gunpowder, the sails and rigging were blown upon a cottage upon the shore, and burnt it to the ground. She had some bale goods on board, and was to have taken in a lading of beef and pork for St. Eustatia.

6th. Whitehall. The King having been pleased to order the colours taken at Louisbourg, which were lately brought to the palace at Kensington, to be deposited in the cathedral church of St. Paul; proper detachments of horse and foot grenadiers were ordered to parade at Kensington at ten o'clock, and marched before his majesty in the following order:

A serjeant, and twelve horse grenadiers.

A field officer, and officers in proportion.

A detachment of fourscore of the horse grenadier guards.

Then eighty of the life-guards, with officers in proportion, with their standard, kettle drums and trumpets.

Then a serjeant and twelve grenadiers of the foot guards

Then eleven serjeans of the foot guards carrying the eleven French colours, advanced.

Then the four companies of grenadiers of the foot guards closed the march.

In this manner they proceeded from Kensington through Hyde-Park, into St. James's Park, and through the stable yard St. James's, into Pall-mall, and so on to the west gate of St. Paul's, where the colours were received by the dean and chapter, attended by the choir; about which time the guns at the Tower, and in St. James's Park were fired, were fired.

These colours are put up near the west door of the cathedral, as a lasting memorial of the success of his majesty's arms, in the reduction of the important fortress of Louisbourg, and the islands of Cape Breton and St. John.

7th. Two bricklayers labourers in digging at the back of Mr. Pearson's house in Broad-street, discovered two vessels with ancient coins to a considerable value.

At

At the anniversary feast of the natives of Gloucestershire, held at Gloucester, for the putting out of poor boys to trades, 157 l. was collected by the gentlemen for that laudable purpose.

10th. Soon after morning service at St. John, Wapping, the neighbourhood was alarmed with the cry of fire, which spread a general consternation among the inhabitants The house of Mr. Hughes, sail-maker, adjoining to Gun dock, was all in flames in an instant, and communicated itself to a biscuit baker's adjoining, and with irresistible fury burnt down 15 houses on both sides the way before water could be had to supply the engines, it being then ebb-tide. Numbers of the unhappy sufferers had their goods carried off by persons who pretended to assist them in their distress, some of whom are in custody. A large ship that was repairing at Gun-dock, was set on fire, and her rigging and tops burnt away, and had they not taken the precaution to cut away her bowsprit, the vessel must have been entirely burnt, as she lay close to the houses.

11th. A gentleman was stopt in Holborn about 12 at night by two footpads, who, on the gentleman's making resistance, shot him dead, and then robbed him. Some of the villains have been since apprehended.

12th. In the afternoon, the Shrewsbury man of war joined the Unicorn and Lizard, and soon got sight of a great number of small coasting vessels, under convoy of the Calipso and Thetis frigates, and an armed snow, working for Brest. The greatest part escaped by running into the pass of Fouilinguet; but the Lizard got between the pass and the frigates, and engaged them both bravely for above two hours, when the Thetis sheered off, and run in for the rocks at the mouth of Poul Davit, and the Calipso with about twenty of the small craft run in upon the rocks near Point de Leven, where it was supposed they must all perish, it being a lee shore, and the swell of the sea very great. The Lizard had one man killed and eight wounded.

14th. His majesty's ships Kingston and Burford arrived at Plymouth from Louisbourg, with the transports, having the garrison of Louisbourg on board under their convoy.——His majesty was pleased to make a present of 500l. to the Captains Amherst and Edgecombe, who jointly brought the news of the taking of this important fortress; and to order a further sum to each of those gentlemen to purcase a sword and ring.

15th. While two serjeants and a corporal were employed in making up cartridges in the exchange at Morpeth, the powder took fire, and above 1000 cartridges were blown up. The three men were terribly burnt, and the recovery of one of the serjeants is despaired of. The windows of the exchange were much shattered, and the consequences would have been still more dreadful, had not 3000 cartridges, and two sacks of powder which were upon the table, providentially escaped.

16th. The cannon and mortars taken at Cherbourg passed by his majesty, and set out from Hyde-Park, and came through the city in grand procession, guarded by a company of matrosses, with drums

drums beating and fifes playing all the way to the Tower, where they arrived about four o'clock in the afternoon. There were 23 carriages, drawn by 229 horses, with a postilion and driver to each carriage, in the following manner; the first drawn by 15 grey horses, with the English colours and the French underneath; seven ditto, drawn by 13 horses each; nine ditto, by 9 horses each; three ditto, by 7 horses each; one ditto, by five horses; then the two mortarts, by nine horses each. These pieces are finely ornamented with the arms of France, and other hieroglyphics, such as trophies, &c. finished in a masterly manner: their names, exact weight, and nearly their bore, are as under:

Cannon	wt	Inches in bore	Cannon	wt.	Inches in bore
Hecube	4090	6	Antonin	5740	6
Nitocris	4080	do	Insensible	5660	do
Emerillon	5320	do	Malfaisant	5500	do
Temerare	5680	do	Vanqueur	5690	do
Augusta	5770	do	Juste	5470	do
In the second line.					
Ulysse	2353	4	Sage	4346	5
Foudroyant	3311	5	Violente	4150	do
Renomyne	3367	do	Furieuse	4160	do
Laborieux	3302	do	Imperieuse	4160	do
Diligence	3960	do	Devineresse	4000	do
Moresque	3980	do			

The two mortars had not their weight expressed. All the pieces except six remain nailed up, as they were taken at Cherbourg.

Eleven seamen accused of being concerned in the practices compained of by the Dutch and Danes, and for the discovery of whom the government offered a considerable reward, were brought up the river by a king's cutter, and are since committed to the Marshalsea prison. One of their accomplices has made himself an evidence, and has impeached several not yet taken.

19th. The foot forces employed in the late expedition against St. Maloes, were disembarked at Cowes in the Isle of Wight, and marched directly for Newport, near which they encamped, with orders to hold themselves in readiness at a moment's warning. The light horse disembarked at Portsmouth, and marched to the quarters allotted them at Southampton, Petersfield and Chichester, &c.

21st. His Royal Highness Prince Edward, having arrived at Kew from Portsmouth the day before, waited upon the King at Kensington in his uniform. His majesty received him graciously, and encouraged him to behave valiantly. There is another expedition against France on foot, in which the Prince is to be engaged.

25th. The boat-builders at Portsmouth received fresh orders to put in hand directly a number of flat-bottomed boats, to replace those that are destroyed in the bay of St. Cas. They are to be compleated in ten days, about which time, it is supposed, the troops will be ready to embark.

26th. The soldiers of the first battalion of the first regiment of guards, began their march from the Isle of Wight for London. They were met on the road by proper officers, with cloathing and other necessaries, of which they were in great want. A draught from the guards has already been made to supply their place, as well as of those who were killed or taken prisoners in the late skirmish on the coast of France.

A farmer near Blandford in Dorsetshire ploughing up part of an inclosed field, the ploughshare struck against an earthen vessel or

urn,

urn, and broke it in two, being quite rotten : it was full of ashes and pieces of human bones, among which was the head of a javelin, or spear, of an uncommon size and fashion, much too heavy to be wielded easily by any common man, weighing thirteen pounds and an half, and twenty-eight inches long, the socket three inches and a quarter in diameter. There was also in the same vessel an helmet of brass, which seemed to have been curiously wrought, but was quite decayed by time, the rust having eaten holes through it. Its diameter was twelve inches and three quarters, and it weighed near eleven pounds.

28th. Four tea dealers were tried before the commissioners of excise, and fined in the penalty of 10 l. per pound for selling bohea tea coloured for green tea; the colouring used for this purpose is supposed to be Dutch pink, which will make bohea tea of a fine green.

Was issued a decree of the Aulic council of the Empire, enjoining all directors of circles, all imperial towns, and the noblesse of the Empire, to send to Vienna an exact list of all those who have disobeyed the Avocatoria of the emperor, and who, as the decree expresses it, adhere to the Elector of Brandenburgh's rebellion, among whom the Elector of Hanover is particularly mentioned. It is declared that their revenues shall be sequestrated, and they punished in honours, body, and goods.

29th. A letter to the admiralty from Captain Kirk, commander of his majesty's ship Lynn, convoy to the Jamaica fleet, consisting of 147 sail, was made public, complaining of the disregard paid to his signals by many of the merchantmen, and of the obstinate and untowardly behaviour of others, by which the fleet suffered much; but more particularly complaining of the irregularities committed by several of the crews in the Spanish settlements, where they were obliged to put in for water, by which much offence was given to the governor of the Havanna, and much injury done to the poor people, whose cattle and hogs they killed and carried off in numbers without reserve, after they had hospitably shewn them where they might be supplied with water.

30th. The plague at Smyrna has continued to rage with so much violence this summer, that by letters received from thence there is advice, that there are scarce people enough left in the neighbourhood of that city to gather in the fruits of the earth.

Bitter complaints have lately been made by the Spaniards against the conduct of our privateers, which have lately seized some of their ships under pretence of having French property on board.

By advices received from Genoa, the chief of the malecontents, de Paoli, has entered the province of Cape Corso, in the island of Corsica, and with 2000 men laid siege to Rogliano, to facilitate the surrender of which, he has caused the city of Bastia to be blockaded with 1500 men.

There are divers accounts from English gentlemen of credit in France, which represent the usage of the poor prisoners there as intolerable; one, in particular, remarks, that the number that has perished by the wretchedness of their

their condition in that country, exceeds that of the killed by sea and land during the present war.

OCTOBER.

1st. His Portuguese majesty coming out of the country in the evening, attended by three of his domestics, was set upon by three fellows near Belem, in a lonesome place; two of them had muskets, and the third had a blunderbuss loaded with small shot; one was discharged at the coachman, who is very much wounded; the king is very dangerously wounded in several parts of his body and face, and his right arm is so much shattered, that it is thought his majesty will never have the use of it; the footman was miserably wounded. None are permitted to see the king but the physicians and surgeons, and ministers of state. The queen transacts all public business during his majesty's indisposition.

A part of the battalion of militia for the county of Dorset, commanded by Edward Hooper, Esq; was reviewed near Cranborn by the Right Honourable the Lord Lieutenant of the county. The men were dressed in their uniform, made a handsome appearance, and performed their exercise with great dexterity.

In other counties so few gentlemen have offered to serve in the militia, that the act has been obliged to be suspended until next year.

2d. The corps of an undertaker and pawnbroker near Moorgate, was interred in Islington church yard, attended by a company of the artillery, who were to perform the usual ceremony of firing over his grave, as he was a member of their body: but in the procession of the funeral a mob arose, and committed such enormous outrages, out of resentment to the deceased, that the clergyman who officiated had great difficulty to perform his office. It is said that he died worth several thousand pounds, and that he had left upwards of 200 l. to pay to the debtors in prison at his suit, a groat a day each for their maintenance, according to the act of parliament. The crowd was so great that several persons were much hurt.

6th. John Houls, a farmer at Longhope in Gloucestershire was convicted of drawing a narrow-wheeled waggon on the turnpike road with more than four horses, and paid the penalty of 5 l. and his servant who drove the horses was also convicted in the same penalty, and for want of ability to pay the same, was sent to the house of correction for a month; which, 'tis hoped, will be a caution to others.

8th. A great storm of wind at W. and W. by S. did considerable damage to the shipping in the Downs, at Portsmouth, and in many other places on the sea coast. At the Isle of Wight, a fish of an enormous size, supposed to be a whale, was cast on shore near Athenfield rocks in that island, where he disembogued daily large quantities of oil into the sea. He was upwards of sixty-six feet in length, and had part of an hawser or cable hoisted round his tail, so that it is supposed he was cut loose from the stern ftern of fome fhip, to prevent her finking.

9th. A fellow was committed to the New Goal in Southwark for felling adulterated tea in the Borough; a vile practice that feems to have got footing in the fhops of fome confiderable dealers in this city, feveral grocers having being lately convicted before the commiffioners of excife of felling dyed tea, and dying it with pernicious drugs, and fined in large fums. Perhaps the legiflature may take this practice under confideration.

11th. Lord Frederick Cavendifh, and Sir Charles Gilmore, Bart. arrived at court on their paroles of honour, to fettle the exchange of prifoners.

The Briftol merchant fhip, with wine, grocery, and fpirits, ran aground in the road of Liverpool, and fince bulged. Part of her lading was put on fhore on the Welch fide, where the populace, notwithftanding all that could be done to prevent it, broached the wine and fpirits, got immoderately drunk, and committed the moft violent outrages.

Doctor de Caftro, a member of the Royal College of Phyficians, and fellow of the Royal Society of London, feparated himfelf from the community of the Jews, by a letter which he wrote to the elders of the fynagogue in the following words:

'Gentlemen,

'The different opinion and 'fentiments I have entertained 'long ago, entirely diffenting from 'thofe of the fynagogue, do not 'permit me any longer to keep 'the appearance of a member of a 'your body; I now therefore take 'my leave of you, hereby re'nouncing exprefsly that commu'nion in which I have been con'fidered with yourfelves. I do not 'however renounce the intercourfe 'I may have with you in the ge'neral fociety of men of honour 'and probity, of which character 'I know many among you, and 'whom, as fuch, I fhall always 'efteem.

'I have fent the key of my 'drawer, that you may difpofe of 'my place.

J. De Castro Sarmento.

30th. The public was in great pain for the Admirals Bofcawen and Hardy, who with four fhips of the line, from Cape-Breton, were left to the weftward of Scilly in fight of fix large French fhips of war; fome fhots were exchanged, but the French were far from feeking an engagement, and our admirals arrived fafe a few days after.

NOVEMBER.

7th. Doctor Henfey was further refpited during his majefty's pleafure.

The Dublin trader, Captain White, who failed about the latter end of laft month from Park-Gate, and was loft, had on board for the linen merchants in Ireland about 70,000 l. in money, and 80,000 l. in goods; above fixty paffengers, among whom were the Earl of Drogheda and his fecond fon, and feveral other perfons of fortune.

14th. Began the drawing of the lottery at Guildhall, when № 38,500, as firft drawn ticket, was intituled to 500 l.

Admiralty-Office. Captain Saumarez, of his majefty's fhip Antelope, having received intelligence in in King-Road, on the 31ſt paſt, that a French ſhip of war was lying in Lundy-Road, he weighed and went in queſt of her, and though the wind was contrary, and blew hard, he beat down channel, and, on the firſt inſtant, ſaw her at anchor at Ilfracombe. Upon diſcovering the Antelope, ſhe weighed and ſtood toward her, and upon coming pretty near, hoiſted her colours, and ſeemed prepared to engage, but ſoon after hauled them down. When the Antelope came within gun-ſhot, ſhe fired at the French ſhip, which ſhe not returning, Captain Saumarez ſent a boat with his firſt lieutenant, to know if they had ſurrendered; but finding the boat did not return, he bore down upon her ſtern, and aſked if ſhe had ſtruck, and was anſwered they had. She proved to be the Belliqnieux, pierced for 66 guns, and had 64 mounted, with 417 men.

21ſt. No. 49,711 was drawn at Guildhall, a prize of 10,000l.

A rule was given in the great cauſe ſo long depending between the Honourable James Anneſley, Eſq; and Richard the preſent Earl of Angleſey, for paſſing publication by Mr. Anneſley's clerk in court; that is, cloſing the examination of witneſſes, and reſting the determination of the cauſe on the merits of the evidence given in.

23d. Both houſes of parliament met at Weſtminſter, when the ſeſſions was opened by commiſſion, and the Lord Keeper by his majeſty's command made this ſpeech;

My Lords and Gentlemen,

In purſuance of the authority given to us by his majeſty's commiſſion under the great ſeal, amongſt other things to declare the cauſes of his holding this parliament, his majeſty has been graciouſly pleaſed to direct us to aſſure you, that he always receives the higheſt ſatisfaction, in being able to lay before you any events, that may promote the honour and intereſt of his kingdoms.

That, in conſequence of your advice, and enabled by the aſſiſtance which you unanimouſly gave him, his majeſty has exerted his endeavours to carry on the war, in the moſt vigorous manner, in order to that deſirable end, always to be wiſhed, a ſafe and honourable peace. It has pleaſed the Divine Providence to bleſs his majeſty's meaſures and arms with ſucceſs in ſeveral parts; and to make our enemies feel, that the ſtrength of Great Britain is not to be provoked with impunity.

We have it alſo in command from his majeſty to acquaint you, that the conqueſt of the ſtrong fortreſs of Louisbourg, with the iſlands of Cape Breton and St. John; the taking of Frontenac, of the higheſt importance to our operations in North America; and the reduction of Senegal; cannot fail to bring great diſtreſs upon the French commerce, and colonies; and, in proportion, to procure great advantages to our own. The nation has alſo been made ſenſible, that whilſt their forces are ſent forth to invade and ravage the dominions of their neighbours, their own coaſts are not inacceſſible to his majeſty's fleets and armies. This they have experienced in the demolition of their works at Cherburg, erected at a great expence, with a particular view to annoy this country; and in the loſs of a great number of ſhips

ſhips and veſſels: but no treatment, however injurious to his majeſty, could tempt him to make retaliation on the innocent ſubjects of that crown.

In Germany, his majeſty's good brother the King of Pruſſia, and Prince Ferdinand of Brunſwick, have found full employment for the armies of France, and her confederates; from which our operations, both by ſea, and in America, have derived the moſt evident advantage. Their ſucceſſes, owing, under God, to their able conduct, and the bravery of his majeſty's troops and thoſe of his allies, have been ſignal and glorious.

His majeſty has further commanded us to obſerve to you, that the common cauſe of liberty and independency is ſtill making noble and vigorous efforts, againſt the unnatural union formed to oppreſs it. That the commerce of his ſubjects, the ſource of our riches, has, by the vigilant protection received from his majeſty's fleet, flouriſhed in a manner not to be paralleled during ſuch troubles.

In this ſtate of things, his majeſty, in his wiſdom, thinks it unneceſſary to uſe many words to perſuade you to bear up againſt all difficulties; effectually to ſtand by, and defend his majeſty; vigorouſly to ſupport the King of Pruſſia, and the reſt of his majeſty's allies; and to exert yourſelves to reduce our enemies to equitable terms of accommodation.

Gentlemen of the Houſe of Commons,

The uncommon extent of this war, in different parts, occaſions it to be uncommonly expenſive. This his majeſty has ordered us to declare to you, that he ſincerely laments, and feels deeply for the burdens of his people. The ſeveral eſtimates are ordered to be laid before you; and his majeſty deſires only ſuch ſupplies, as ſhall be requiſite to puſh the war with advantage, and to be adequate to the neceſſary ſervices.

My Lords and Gentlemen,

His majeſty has, in the laſt place, graciouſly commanded us to aſſure you, that he takes ſo much ſatiſfaction in that good harmony which ſubſiſts amongſt his faithful ſubjects, that it is more proper for him now to thank you for it, than to repeat his exhortations to it. This union, neceſſary at all times, is more eſpecially ſo in ſuch critical conjunctures; and his majeſty doubts not, but the good effects we have found from it, will be the ſtrongeſt motives to you to purſue it.

28th. Dr. Shebbeare received ſentence for a libellous pamphlet, intitled, A Sixth Letter to the People of England: he is fined five pounds; to ſtand in the pillory Dec. 5, at Charing-Croſs; to be confined three years; and then to give ſecurity for his good behaviour for ſeven years, himſelf bound in 500 l. and two others in 250 l. each.

In the Canterbury Mercury of this day's date, there is an account of the diſcovery of ſome remarkable human ſkeletons, near the road-ſide, at a place called Breech-Down; the firſt was found by a labourer in widening the road, and had round his neck a ſtring of beads of various forms and ſizes, from the bigneſs of a pigeon's egg to that of a pea: by his ſide lay three inſtruments of war, one a kind of ſcymeter, the ſecond what the Scots call a dirk, and the third a ſpear. Near the ſame place were afterwards found ſeven other ſkeletons, all ranged in good order at about a yard apart, and about two feet under ground; but neither of theſe had any thing to diſtinguiſh them. How theſe bodies came to be depoſited in this place affords matter of ſpeculation to the curious.

A melancholy affair happened on board a Scotch veſſel, laden with corn, which was juſt come up the river; and lay off Tower-wharf: the captain, on their coming up, would have had his people go on ſhore, and refreſh themſelves, which they refuſed, and remained on board. Soon after (whether through wantonneſs, or cruelty, is not known) ſome fellows got on the deck, faſtened their hatches, ſtopped up their funnel, cut their cables, and ſet them adrift. In running down with the tide, ſhe fell foul of a tier of ſhips, the people of whom ſeeing her without any body on the deck, ſuſpected ſomething, and going down into the cabin, found three men lying dead, and the captain and a boy near expiring. The funnel, &c. being ſtopped, occaſioned ſuch a ſmoke, as ſuffocated the three poor fellows; the captain is pretty well recovered, but there are very little hopes of the boy.

29th. Came on to be argued before the Lord Chief Baron of the Exchequer, and a ſpecial jury of gentlemen, a cauſe which has been depending above twelve months in that court; wherein Edward Burrow, Eſq; collector of his majeſty's cuſtoms at Hull, on the part of the king, was plaintiff, and a Dutch merchant defendant, touching the ſeizure of a Dutch veſſel, for importing French brandy into the port of Hull; when after many learned arguments on both ſides, (during the ſpace of ſix hours) a verdict was given for the plaintiff without the jury ever ſtirring out of court.

By the ſaid determination it is to be hoped a ſtop will be put to this particular trade of our good friends the Dutch.

DECEMBER.

Dr. Shebbeare ſtood on the pillory, purſuant to his ſentence. 5th.

Dr. Henſey was farther reſpited to January 21. 6th

N° 72,570 in the preſent lottery, was drawn a prize of 10,000 l. 12th.

The drawing of the lottery was finiſhed, when N° 30,135 being the laſt drawn ticket, is entitled to 1000 l.

An oak in Langley woods near Downton, Wilts, ſuppoſed to be near 1000 years growth, was ſold for 40 l. It was the property of the Biſhop of Saliſbury, meaſured 6 feet 2 inches in diameter, and contained about 10 ton of timber.

On the 11th inſtant the old caſtle of Douglas, in Scotland, the reſidence of the Duke of Douglas, was conſumed by fire.

Sunday night, the 26th ult. about nine o'clock, a very remarkable meteor appeared in the firmament, and paſſed over the city of Edinburgh with great velocity. It was of a conic form, and in appearance about four or five inches diameter at the baſe, and as it went along, numbers of ſparks fell from it, like thoſe of a rocket when its force is ſpent. A moſt ſurprizing light iſſued from it, ſo ſtrong, that while it laſted, which was for five or ſix ſeconds, one

eaſily

eafily could perceive the moft minute thing upon the ftreet. This meteor was likewife feen in feveral parts of the neighbourhood, and in appearance was much the fame as above defcribed.

This meteor was alfo feen at Dublin, Newcaftle, Plymouth, and by three gentlemen in Chelfea-fields, near London.

Mr. Speaker, in purfuance of the refolution of the 6th inftant, addreffed himfelf to Admiral Bofcawen, and gave him the thanks of the houfe, as he ftood in his place, in the following terms:

Admiral Bofcawen!

The houfe have unanimoufly refolved, that their thanks fhould be given to you for the fervices you have done to your King and Country in North-America; and it is my duty to convey their thanks to you.

I wifh I could do it in a manner fuitable to the occafion, and as they ought to be given to you, now ftanding in your place, as a member of this houfe.

But were I able to enumerate and fet forth, in the beft manner, the great and extenfive advantages accruing to this nation from the conqueft of Louisbourg, with the iflands of Cape Breton and St. John, I could only exhibit a repetition of what has already been, and is, the genuine and uniform fenfe and language of every part of the kingdom.

Their joy too has been equal to their fentiments upon the interefting event: and in their fentiments and joy they have carried their gratitude alfo to you, Sir, as a principal inftrument in thefe moft important acquifitions.

You are now therefore receiving the acknowledgements of the people, only in a more folemn way—by the voice, the general voice, of their reprefentatives in parliament—The moft honourable fame that any man can arrive at, in this, or any other country. It is, on thefe occafions, a national honour, from a free people; ever cautioufly to be conferred, in order to be the more efteemed—to be the greater reward; and which ought to be referved for the moft fignal fervices to the ftate, and the moft approved merit in them; fuch as this houfe has ufually, and very lately, made their objects of public thanks.

The ufe, I am perfuaded, you will make of this juft teftimony, and high reward of your fervices and merit, will be the preferving in your own mind a lafting impreffion of what the Commons of Great Britain are now tendering to you, and in a conftant continuance of the zeal and ardour for the glory of your King and Country, which have made you to deferve it.

In obedience to the commands of the houfe I do, with great pleafure to myfelf, give you the thanks of the houfe for the fervices you have done to your King and Country in North America.

To which Admiral Bofcawen anfwered.

Mr. Speaker!

I am happy in having been able to do my duty: but have not words to exprefs my fenfe of the diftinguifhing reward, that has been conferred upon me by this houfe; nor can I enough thank you, Sir, for the polite and elegant manner, in which you have been pleafed to convey to me the refolution of the houfe.

And then the Speaker acquainted the houfe, that, in obedience to their commands, he had fignified to

Admiral Oſborn their thanks, and had received the following anſwer:

Sir, I want words to expreſs my ſenſe of the honour the houſe of Commons has been pleaſed to confer upon me, and only hope that you, Sir, will be as gracious to me in repreſenting my gratitude to that auguſt aſſembly, as you have been in acquainting me with their favourable acceptance of my ſervices. I have done no more than my duty. I have only been the humble, though happy, inſtrument of executing the wiſe meaſures directed by his majeſty.

I have no title, Sir, to any glory, but what is common to me as a ſeaman, and as an Engliſhman zealous for the ſervice of my country, which is pleaſed to reward me with this inſtance of their approbation. From the ſituation of my health, Sir, I can flatter myſelf with having but few opportunities of employing the remainder of my life, in grateful exertion of my abilities for the honour and intereſt of my country. But as the houſe of Commons is ſo glorioufly watchful to encourage the greateſt merit, by rewarding the leaſt, England can never want good officers; and however honoured I am by this diſtinction, may my ſervices be the moſt inconſiderable, that ſhall be thus acknowledged. I am, with the greateſt reſpect, Sir,

Your moſt obedient, and
Dec. 8. moſt humble ſervant,
1758. HENRY OSBORN.

The Engliſh priſoners, taken at St. Cas, arrived at Dover from France.

29th. At night about twelve o'clock, a ſtove of gun-powder at the Powder-mills on Hounſlow-heath, belonging to Samuel Underhill, Eſq; took fire, and blew up; as the quantity of powder that then lay drying therein was great, conſiſting of 17 ct. weight, the exploſion was extremely violent and alarming, inſomuch that his dwelling-houſe was conſiderably damaged thereby, and, though at near 300 yards diſtance from the works, ſeveral of the windows thereof were ſhattered to pieces, ſome furniture thrown down, particularly a repeating clock, part of the glaſs of a ſaſh window was forced upon a bed, in which a gentleman then lay aſleep, but happily no perſon received any hurt. What might be the cauſe of this accident is unknown to any one. In many parts the ſhock was felt, and ſuppoſed to be that of an earthquake.

Tranſlation of a paragraph of a diſpatch wrote by M. da Cunha, ſecretary of ſtate in Portugal for foreign affairs and at war, dated Belem, Sept. 12.

'Laſt Sunday the King had a 'fall in his palace, by which he 'was conſiderably hurt in his right 'arm. He was let blood on Mon'day, and is at preſent better. His 'majeſty, being prevented by this 'accident from attending to pub'lic affairs for ſome days, has em'powered the queen to ſign diſ'patches, and other inſtruments 'during his illneſs.'

From Liſbon advice has been received, of a moſt wicked and daring attempt on the life of the King of Portugal. No clear and authentic account has yet been received, either of the particulars of the action itſelf, or the motives to it. Several perſons of the moſt diſtinguiſhed rank in that kingdom, have been already ſecured for this conſpiracy; yet every thing concerning it is ſtill involved in an impenetrable darkneſs, which all reaſonings

ings and conjectures have hitherto conſpired to make only more obſcure. During the courſe of the enſuing year, we hope to receive ſome farther light, ſo as to enable us to give our readers a ſatisfactory account of this very extraordinary affair.

After the remarkable tranſactions of the year, ſomething of the remarkable turns of humour, whether real or fictitious, which diſplay themſelves in the public papers, will not we hope prove diſagreeable to our readers.

From the Daily Advertiſer.

A Young lady, juſt come out of Derbyſhire, ſtrayed from her guardian; ſhe is remarkably genteel and handſome; ſhe has been brought up by a farmer, near Derby, and knows no other but they are her parents; but it is not ſo, for ſhe is a lady by birth, though of but little learning; ſhe has no cloaths with her, but a riding habit ſhe uſed to go to market in; ſhe will have a fine eſtate, as ſhe is an heireſs, but knows not her birth, as her parents died when ſhe was a child, and I had the care of her, ſo ſhe knows not but I am her mother; ſhe has a brown ſilk gown that ſhe borrowed of her maid, that is dy'd ſilk, and her riding dreſs a light drab, lined with blue tammy, and it has blue loops at the button holes; ſhe has out-grown it; and I am ſure that ſhe is in great diſtreſs both for money and cloaths; but whoever has relieved her, I will be anſwerable, if they will give me a letter where ſhe may be found; ſhe knows not her own ſirname; I underſtand ſhe has been in Northampton for ſome time; ſhe has a cut in her forehead. Whoever will give me an account where ſhe is to be found, ſhall receive twenty guineas reward. Direct for M. W. at the George Inn, Derby.

Ladies! A young gentleman, aged 25, eaſy in fortune, happy in temper, of tolerable parts, not ſuperficially polite, but genteel addreſs, ſome knowledge of the world, and little acquaintance with the Fair, preſumes to offer his ſervice to one, not exceeding ten years older than himſelf, of good-nature, and affable diſpoſition, abſolutely miſtreſs of at leaſt 1000l. will find the utmoſt ſincerity from one, who would make it the ultimate end of his ambition to render the marriage ſtate truly happy. Any lady who has ſpirit enough to break through the idle cuſtoms of the age, and not give trouble out of mere curioſity, inclined to anſwer this, may leave a line for X. O. at Gregg's coffee-houſe in York-ſtreet, Covent-garden, ſhall receive immediate anſwer, and be waited on in perſon, at any time and place ſhe ſhall appoint. The moſt inviolable ſecrecy and honour will be punctually obſerved.

A ſingle gentleman, in a very good way of buſineſs, and can make 200 per cent. advantage of it, and free from debts, about 26 years of age, and is what the flatterer calls genteel, and rather handſome, of a chearful diſpoſition, and a very affable temper, not at all given to drinking, gaming, or any other vice that a lady can take umbrage at; one that would rather endeavour to get a fortune than ſpend one, has been in moſt parts of England, and is very well acquainted with London, and no ſtranger to the fair ſex, but entirely ſo to any one he would prefer for a wife. As he has not been ſo happy as to meet with a lady that ſuits his diſpoſition, as yet; a chearful diſpoſition, and free from the modern vices; one that is of the church of England, and has no objection to going there on the ſabbath, and to take ſome care for a future happineſs; one that would think herſelf rather happier in her huſband's company, than at public places; one that would more conſult the intereſt of her family than the glaſs in a morning; to be neat in perſon and apparel; and as to the lady's perſon it will be more agreeable to have it what the world calls agreeable than a beauty; with any fortune not leſs than 500l. at her own diſpoſal, except ſhe has good intereſt, then leſs will be agreeable. Any lady this may ſuit, will be waited on by directing a line to G. C. at Peele's coffee-houſe in Fleet-ſtreet.

Inviolable ſecrecy may be depended on, as the gentleman does not chuſe a ſeven years ſiege.

A perſon of character, candour, and honour, who has an intire knowledge of the world, and has great intimacy with both ſexes among the nobility, gentry, and perſons of credit and reputation; and as it oftens happens, that many deſerving perſons of both ſexes are deprived of the opportunity of entering into the ſtate of matrimony, by being unacquainted with the merits of each other, therefore upon directing a line for A. Z. of any one's intention of entering into the above ſtate, to the advantage of each, to be left at Mr. Perry's, Miller's-court, Aldermanbury, ſecrecy and honour will be obſerved in bringing to a concluſion ſuch their intention. Any perſon who ſhall ſend a letter, is deſired to order the bearer to put it into the letter box for fear it may be miſlaid: and it is deſired, that none but thoſe who are ſincere would make any application on the above ſubject.

In the Edinburgh Courant of the 28th ult. is the following extraordinary advertiſement.

Glaſgow, Oct. 23.

We Robert M'Nair, and Jean Holmes, having taken into conſideration the way and manner our daughter Jean acted in her marriage, that ſhe took none of our advice, nor adviſed us before ſhe married, for which reaſon we diſcharged her from our family, for more than twelve months; and being afraid that ſome or other of our family may alſo preſume to marry without duly adviſing us thereof; we, taking the affair into our ſerious conſideration, hereby diſcharge all and every one of our children from offering to marry without our ſpecial advice and conſent firſt had and obtained; and if any of our children ſhould propoſe or preſume to offer marriage to any, without as aforeſaid our advice and conſent, they in that caſe ſhall be baniſhed from our family twelve months; and if they ſhould go ſo far as to marry without our advice and conſent, in that caſe they are to be baniſhed from the family ſeven years; but whoever adviſes us of their intention to marry, and obtains our conſent, ſhall not only remain children of the family, but alſo ſhall have a due proportion of our goods, gear, and eſtate, as we ſhall think convenient, and as the bargain requires;

quires.; and further, if any of our children ſhall marry clandeſtinely, they, by ſo doing, ſhall loſe all claim, or title, to our effects, goods, gear, or eſtate; and we intimate this to all concerned, that none may pretend ignorance.

A General BILL of all the Chriſtenings and Burials in London, from Dec. 13, 1757, to Dec. 12. 1758.

Chriſtened		Buried	
Males	7347	Males	8932
Females	6862	Females	8644
	14209		17576

Decreaſed in the Burials this Year 3737.

Died under 2 Years of Age			5971
Between 2	and	5	1795
5	and	10	717
10	and	20	556
20	and	30	1362
30	and	40	1589
40	and	50	1606
50	and	60	1368
60	and	70	1208
70	and	80	961
80	and	90	370
90	and	100	68
		102	2
		103	1
		104	1
		106	1
			17576

The following remarkable incident was too long, and indeed of too extraordinary a nature, to be inſerted among the common articles of the Chronicle; and as it does not naturally fall under any other head of the work, we have therefore choſen to place it here, at the end of the occurrences of the year.

An account of ſome threatening letters ſent to the Duke of Marlborough, and a proſecution which his Grace carried on againſt William Barnard, ſuppoſing him to have written them.

ON the 29th of November his Grace the Duke of Marlborough received the following letter, from an unknown hand.

To his Grace the Duke of Marlborough, with care and ſpeed.

"My Lord, xxviii Nov.

As ceremony is an idle thing upon moſt occaſions, more eſpecially to perſons in my ſtate of mind, I ſhall proceed immediately to acquaint you with the motive and end of addreſſing this epiſtle to you, which is equally intereſting to us both. You are to know, then, that my preſent ſituation in life is ſuch, that I ſhould perfer annihilation to a continuance in it. Deſperate diſeaſes require deſperate remedies; and you are the man I have pitched upon, either to make me, or to unmake yourſelf. As I never had the honour to live among the Great, the tenour of my propoſals will not be very courtly; but let that be an argument to enforce a belief of what I am now going to write. It has employed my invention for ſome time, to find out a method to deſtroy another, without expoſing my own life: that I have accompliſhed, and defy the law. Now for the application of it. I am deſperate, and muſt be provided for. You have it in your power, it is my buſineſs to make it your inclination to ſerve me; which you muſt determine to comply with, by procuring me a genteel ſupport for my my life, or your own will be at a period before this session of parliament is over. I have more motives than one, for singling you at first upon this occasion; and I give you this fair warning, because the means I shall make use of are too fatal to be eluded by the power of physic. If you think this of any consequence, you will not fail to meet the author on Sunday next, at ten in the morning, or on Monday (if the weather should be rainy on Sunday) near the first tree, beyond the stile in Hyde Park, in the foot walk to Kensington. Secrecy and compliance may preserve you from a double danger of this sort; as there is a certain part of the world, where your death has more than been wished for upon other motives. I know the world too well to trust this secret in any breast but my own. A few days determine me, your friend or enemy. FELTON.

"You will apprehend, that I mean you should be alone; and depend upon it, that a discovery of any artifice in this affair will be fatal to you. My safety is insured by my silence, for confession only can condemn me."

In consequence of this letter, his Grace went to the place appointed at ten o'clock on the Sunday morning. He was on horseback, had pistols before him, and, as he was without a great coat, his star was easily to be seen. He was without any attendant, but had a friend in the Park, who kept at such a distance, as scarce to be noticed. When he first came up to the tree he saw no body, either at it or near it, whom he could suspect to be the person. He continued some time about the same spot, but no body appearing, he rode away. It happened, that when he came to Hyde Park Corner, and turned his horse, he saw some body stand loitering, and looking at the water, over the bridge, within twenty yards of the tree; this induced him to ride back, which he did very gently, and, passing by the person, expected him to speak to him, but was disappointed. He passed by him a second time, and the person still taking no notice, his Grace made him a bow, and asked, if he had not something to say to him. He replied, 'No; 'I don't know you.' His Grace then said, 'I am the Duke of 'Marlborough; now you know me; 'I imagine you have something to 'say to me.' He replied, 'No; I 'have not:' and his Grace then rode away.

The next day, or the day after, the Duke received a second letter, as follows:

To his Grace the Duke of Marlborough.

"MY LORD,

You receive this as an acknowledgement of your punctuality, as to the time and place of meeting on Sunday last, tho' it was owing to you, that it answered no purpose. The pageantry of being armed, and the ensign of your order, were useless, and too conspicuous. You needed no attendant: the place was not calculated for mischief, nor was any intended. If you walk in the west isle of Westminster Abbey, towards eleven o'clock on Sunday next, your sagacity will point out the person, whom you will address, by asking his company to take a turn or two with you. You will not fail, on enquiry, to be acquainted with the name, and place of abode; according to which directions, you will please to send fend two, or three, hundred pound bank notes, the next day, by the penny-poft. Exert not your curiofity too early; it is in your power to make me grateful on certain terms. I have friends who are faithful, but they do not bark before they bite. I am, &c. F."

The Duke was pleafed to attend a fecond time, at the place and hour appointed, and walked five or fix minutes in the Abbey before he faw any body that he fufpected. He then faw the fame perfon whom he had feen before in Hyde Park. He came in with a good-looking man, who had the appearance of a fubftantial tradefman, and they went about, looking on the monuments. After fome time the ftranger went into the choir, and the perfon whom he had feen before, turned back, and came towards the Duke. The Duke then afked him, if he had any thing to fay to him, or any commands for him? and he replied, 'No, my Lord, I have not.' The Duke then faid, 'Sure you 'have?' But he replied again with the fame words, 'No, my Lord.' The Duke then left him, and as he continued to walk up and down one fide of the ifle, his Grace walked up and down the other, to give him a little more time; but he did not fpeak. The Duke had then feveral perfons difguifed in the Abbey, who were to have taken up the perfon he was to meet if the fignal had been given; but the Duke did not give it, becaufe, though he was very fure the perfon he had fpoke to was the fame he had feen in the Park, yet he chofe rather to run a farther rifk himfelf, than to take up an innocent man.

Very foon after this his Grace received a third letter, as follows.

To his Grace the Duke of Marlborough.

"My Lord,

I am fully convinced you had a companion on Sunday. I interpret it as owing to the weaknefs of human nature; but fuch proceeding is far from being ingenuous, and may produce bad effects, whilft it is impoffible to anfwer the end propofed. You will fee me again foon, as it were by accident, and may eafily find where I go to: in confequence of which, by being fent to, I fhall wait on your Grace, but expect to be quite alone, and to converfe in whifpers; you will likewife give your honour, upon meeting, that no part of the converfation fhall tranfpire. Thefe, and the former terms complied with, enfure your fafety: my revenge in cafe of non-compliance (or any fcheme to expofe me) will be flower, but not lefs fure; and ftrong fufpicion, the utmoft that can poffibly enfue upon it: while the chances would be tenfold againft you. You will poffibly be in doubt after the meeting, but it is quite neceffary the outfide fhould be a mafk to the in. The family of the Bloods is not extinct, though they are not in my fcheme."

This letter, by the expreffion "you will fee me again foon, as "it were by accident," feems to intimate, that the writer had not only feen the Duke, but that the Duke had feen the writer fo as to know and remember him; for how elfe could his Grace fee him "as "it were by accident," fo as to note him, and find out whither he went?

His

His Grace, however, did not fee either the perfon he had feen before or any other perfon whom he had the leaft reafon to fuppofe to be the writer of the letters; but about two months afterwards he received the following letter as from another hand.

To his Grace the Duke of Marlborough.

"May it pleafe your Grace,

I have reafon to believe that the fon of one Barnard, a furveyor in Abingdon Buildings, Weftminfter, is acquainted with fome fecrets that nearly concern your fafety; his father is now out of town, which will give you an opportunity of queftioning him more privately; it would be ufelefs to your Grace, as well as dangerous to me, to appear more publicly in this affair.

Your fincere friend,
ANONYMOUS.

"He frequently goes to Storey's-gate coffee-houfe."

About ten days after the receipt of this letter, the Duke fent a perfon, whofe name is Merrick, to Storey's-gate coffee-houfe, to tell Mr. Barnard, that the Duke defired to fpeak with him. The meffage was delivered to Mr. Barnard on Tuefday the 25th of April, in the evening; and he fent word by the meffenger, Mr. Merrick, that he would wait upon his Grace on Thurfday morning following, at half an hour after ten.

On Thurfday morning, at the time appointed, he went, and the Duke, who inftantly knew him to be the perfon he had feen before in the Park and the Abbey, took him into a room, and fhut the door. He then asked him, as he had done at their former meetings, whether he had any thing to fay to him? and he faid, he had nothing to fay. The Duke then recapitulated all the letters, beginning with the firft, and Barnard liftened with attention and furprife, but without any appearance of fear. The Duke obferved, that it feemed to him a ftrange thing to find fuch letters as thefe written with the correctnefs of a fcholar; to which Barnard replied, "That a man might be very learned and very poor:" to which he might have added, that he might be very daring and very wicked. The Duke then fhewed him the fourth letter, in which his name was mentioned; upon which Barnard faid, "It was very odd; my father was then out of town." This fpeech the Duke thought remarkable: becaufe, though Barnard faid his father was then out of town, the letter was without a date. The Duke then told him, that if he was innocent, it behoved him, more than his Grace, to difcover the writers of the letters, efpecially the laft; upon which, he gave the Duke a fmile, and went away.

How thefe circumftances came to the knowledge of Mr. Fielding does not appear; but Fielding foon after took Mr. Barnard into cuftody, and he was tried the laft feffions at the Old Bailey, for fending a threatening letter, contrary to the ftatute.

In the account of the trial, as it is printed in the feffions paper, there is no mention of any evidence to prove the letters to be Mr.

Mr. Barnard's hand-writing *, nor indeed any evidence to prove that he was the writer of them, except his being in Hyde-park, and in the Abbey, at the times when the writers of the firſt and ſecond letters appointed the Duke to meet him there.

It ſeemed, however, to be incumbent upon Mr. Barnard, to ſhew how he came to be at thoſe places juſt at thoſe times; and this he has done in a very particular manner, ſupported by very credible teſtimony.

He proved, that on the Sunday morning mentioned in the firſt letter to the Duke, his father ordered him to go to Kenſington to the ſollicitor of the turnpike, to know whether the treaſurer of the turnpike had not paid ſome money for his uſe: That in conſequence of this order, he did go to Kenſington, ſaw the ſollicitor of the turnpike there, dined afterwards with his uncle, at his houſe at Kenſington, in company with ſeveral other perſons, to whom he related the particulars of the Duke's coming up to him in Hyde-Park, and aſking if he had any thing to ſay to him. This is atteſted by Barnard the father, who gave him orders to go to Kenſington, by the perſon to whom he went, by his uncle, with whom he dined, and ſeveral others that were at the ſame table.

As to his being in the Abbey, he proved that Mr. James Greenwood, a relation, a brewer at Deptford, being at breakfaſt with him, on the Sunday mentioned in the ſecond letter, at his father's, where he had lain the night before, deſired to get himſelf dreſſed and go with him into the Park: That he did not comply till after much ſollicitation; and that when they came to the end of Henry the VIIth's chapel, Mr. Barnard would have gone into the Park without going through the Abbey, if Mr. Greenwood had not inſiſted on the contrary, as he had never ſeen General Hargrave's monument. This Mr. Greenwood was that good-looking man whom the Duke ſays he ſaw come into the Abbey with Mr. Barnard. As Barnard had told Greenwood the ſtrange circumſtance of the Duke's ſpeaking to him in the Park, Greenwood, as ſoon as he ſaw the Duke, whom he knew, told Barnard who he was; for Barnard, being very near ſighted, had not ſeen him, and if he had, would not have known him. Mr. Greenwood obſerving the Duke to come up to him, and paſs him ſeveral times, ſuppoſed he had a mind to ſpeak to Mr. Barnard, but would not do it till he was alone; and for that reaſon he left him, and went into the choir. Theſe facts are atteſted by Mr. Greenwood, the only perſon to whom they could be known; and it ſhould be obſerved, that Mr. Barnard could not appoint a meeting on theſe days, in conſequence of his having buſineſs which at thoſe times would call him to the places mentioned, becauſe he did not know of his going either to the Park or the Abbey, till the very day on which he went.

Mr. Barnard alſo proved, by

* The three letters are ſaid to have been written in print hand, which accounts for there being no comparing the writing in the letters with his father's books, or with any other writing under his hand.

unex

unexceptionable witneſſes, that he mentioned the ſtrange circumſtances of the Duke's meeting and ſpeaking to him, both in the Park and in the Abbey, among his friends and acquaintance, openly on the day when they happened, and very frequently afterwards: that his father is eſtabliſhed in a very reputable and profitable buſineſs, in which his ſon is likely to ſucceed him, being extremely capable of the employment, and very diligent in it. It is alſo proved, by ſeveral perſons of the higheſt character, particularly Dr. Markham, the preſent worthy maſter of Weſtminſter ſchool, that he is in plentiful circumſtances, very far from being in any exigence which might urge him to obtain money at ſuch a riſk, not only of his reputation but his life; that his conduct had always been irreproachable; and his fidelity often tried.

The fourth letter ſtill remains an inſcrutable myſtery. No man could imagine, from what Mr. Barnard had ſaid from time to time, concerning the Duke's behaviour to him, that 'he was acquainted with ſome ſecrets which nearly concerned his Grace's ſafety;' and why any perſon, who might hear that the Duke had received threatening letters, without knowing from whom, ſhould mention Mr. Barnard, cannot eaſily be gueſſed. The only conjecture that ſeems probable, if on ſuch an occaſion a conjecture may be allowed, is, that ſome officious perſon, who had received ſome ſlight information of the Duke's buſineſs at the Abbey, and obſerved him ſpeaking to Mr. Barnard, might watch him home, and, taking for granted that if he ſhould, in conſequence of this information, be detected in any evil deſign, the informer, whenever he ſhould think fit to reveal himſelf, would be rewarded, might be induced to make the information at a venture, and conceal himſelf till the event ſhould be known.

As to the Duke, he appears to have acted with the utmoſt tenderneſs and generoſity through the whole affair, to have undertaken the proſecution purely from public principles, and to have been more deſirous that the priſoner ſhould appear innocent than guilty.

SUP-

SUPPLIES granted by Parliament for the service of the year 1758.

	£.	s.	d.
DECEMBER 8, 1757.			
1. That 60,000 men be employed for the sea service for 1758, including 14,845 marines.			
2. That a sum not exceeding 4l. per man, per month, be allowed for maintaining them, for 13 months, including the ordnance for sea service	3120000	0	0
DECEMBER 15.			
1. That a number of land forces, including 4008 invalids, amounting to 53,777 effective men, commission and non-commission officers included, be employed for the service of 1758.			
2. That for defraying the charge of the said number of land forces for guards and garrisons, and other his majesty's land forces in Great Britain, Guernsey, and Jersey, for 1758, there be granted a sum not exceeding	1253368	18	6
3. For the pay of the general, and general staff-officers, and officers of the hospitals for the land forces, for 1758	37452	3	4
4. For maintaining his majesty's forces and garrisons in the plantations and Gibraltar, and for provisions for the garrisons in Nova Scotia, Newfoundland, Gibraltar, and Providence, for 1758	623704	0	2
5. For defraying the charge of four regiments of foot, on the Irish establishment, serving in North America and the East-Indies, for 1758 —	43968	4	2
	1958493	6	2
DECEMBER 20.			
1. For the charge of the office of ordnance for land service, for 1758 — —	181505	10	0
2. For defraying the extraordinary expence of the board of ordnance for land service, not provided for by parliament — —	210301	17	3
3. To make good the sum which had been issued by his majesty's orders in pursuance of the address of that house — — —	31000	0	0
	422807	7	0
JANUARY 23, 1758.			
1. For a present supply in the then critical exigency, towards enabling his majesty to subsist, and keep together, the army formed last year in his			

	£.	s.	d.
electoral dominions, and then again put into motion, and actually employed against the common enemy in concert with the King of Prussia, agreed to *nem. con.*	100000	0	0
2. For the ordinary of the navy, including half-pay to the sea officers, for 1758	224421	5	8
3. Towards carrying on the works of the hospital for sick and wounded seamen, building at Hasler near Gosport, for 1758	10000	0	0
4. Towards carrying on the works of the hospital for sick and wounded seamen, building near Plymouth, for 1758	10000	0	0
5. Towards the support of the royal hospital at Greenwich, for the better maintenance of the seamen of the said hospital, worn out and become decrepit in the service of their country	10000	0	0
	354421	5	8
JANUARY 31.			
1. Upon account of the reduced officers of the land forces and marines, for 1758	35602	0	0
2. For defraying the charge for allowances to the several officers and private gentlemen of the two troops of horse guards, and regiment of horse, reduced, and to the superannuated gentlemen of the four regiments of horse guards, for 1758	3098	17	11
3. For the paying of the pensions to the widows of such reduced officers of the land forces and marines, as died upon the establishment of half-pay in Great Britain, and who were married to them before Dec. 25, 1716, for 1758	2226	0	0
	40926	17	11
FEBRUARY 6.			
Towards the buildings, rebuildings, and repairs of his majesty's ships, for 1758	200000	0	0
FEBRUARY 23.			
For defraying the charge of 2120 horse, and 9900 foot, together with the general and staff officers, the officers of the hospital, and officers, and others, belonging to the train of artillery, the troops of the Landgrave of Hesse-Cassel, in the pay of Great Britain, for 60 days, from Dec. 25, 1757, to Feb. 22, 1758, both inclusive, together with the subsidy for the said time, pursuant to treaty	38360	19	10¾
MARCH 7.			
Towards enabling the governors and guardians of the hospital for maintenance and education of exposed			

and

	£.	s.	d.
and deserted young children, to receive all such children, under a certain age to be by them limited, as shall be brought to the said hospital, before Jan. 1, 1759; and also towards enabling them to maintain and educate such children as were then under their care, and to continue to carry into execution the good purposes for which they were incorporated; and that the sum granted should be issued and paid for the use of the said hospital, without fee or reward, or any deduction whatsoever	40000	0	0
MARCH 13.			
Towards paying off and discharging the debt of the navy	300000	0	0
MARCH 21.			
1. To make good the deficiency of the grants for the service of the year 1757	284802	1	0¾
2. For defraying the charge of 2120 horse, and 9900 foot, together with the general and staff-officers, the officers of the hospital, and officers, and others, belonging to the train of artillery, the troops of the Landgrave of Hesse-Cassel, in the pay of Great Britain, for 60 days, from Feb. 23, 1758, to April 23 following, both inclusive, together with the subsidy for the said time, pursuant to treaty	38360	19	10¾
3. Upon account for out-pensioners of Chelsea-hospital, for 1758	26000	0	0
	349163	0	11½
APRIL 6.			
1. To enable his majesty to defray the like sum raised in pursuance of an act made in the last session of parliament, and charged upon the first aids or supplies, to be granted in the then current session	800000	0	0
2. Upon account for supporting and maintaining the settlement of the colony of Nova Scotia, for 1758	9902	5	0
3. Upon account for defraying the charges incurred by supporting and maintaining the said colony in 1756, and not provided for by parliament	6626	9	9½
4. Upon account for defraying the charges of the civil establishment of the colony of Georgia, and other incidental expences attending the same, from June 24, 1757, to June 24, 1758	3557	10	0
	820086	4	9½

April 20.

	£.	s.	d.
1. To enable his majesty to make good his engagements with the King of Prussia, pursuant to a convention between his majesty and the King of Prussia, concluded April 11, 1758 —— ——	670000	0	0
2. For defraying the charge of 38,000 men of the troops of Hanover, Wolfenbuttle, Saxe-Gotha, and the Count of Bukkeburgh, together with that of general and staff-officers, actually employed against the common enemy, in concert with the King of Prussia, from Nov. 28, 1757, to Dec. 24, 1758, inclusive, to be issued in advance every two months, in like manner as the pay of the Hessian forces then in the service of Great Britain, the said body of troops to be mustered by an English commissary, and the effective state thereof to be also ascertained by the signature of the commander in chief of the said forces, the further sum of —— —— ——	463084	6	10
3. In full satisfaction for defraying the charges of forage, bread-waggons, train of artillery, and train of provisions, wood, straw, &c. and all other extraordinary expences, contingencies, and losses whatsoever incurred, and to be incurred, on account of his majesty's army, consisting of 38,000 men actually employed against the common enemy, in concert with the King of Prussia, from Nov. 28 last, to Dec. 24 next, inclusive, the said sum to be issued from time to time, in like proportions as the pay of the said troops —— ——	386915	13	2
4. For defraying the extraordinary expences of the land forces, and other services incurred in 1757, and not provided for by parliament ——	145454	15	0½
5. For defraying the charge of what remained to be paid, for 2120 horse, and 9900 foot, together with the general and staff-officers, the officers of the hospital, and officers, and others, belonging to the train of artillery, the troops of the Landgrave of Hesse-Cassel, in the pay of Great Britain, for 365 days, from Dec. 25, 1757, to Dec. 24, 1758, both days inclusive, together with the subsidy for the said time, pursuant to treaty —— ——	165175	4	10½
6. To be applied towards the rebuilding of London-Bridge —— —— ——	15000	0	0
	1845629	19	10½

	£.	s.	d.
MAY 2.			
Upon account towards defraying the charge of pay and cloathing for the militia for 1758, and for defraying such expences as were actually incurred upon the account of the militia in 1757 —	100000	0	0
MAY 4.			
Towards carrying on the works for fortifying and securing the harbour of Milford —	10000	0	0
JUNE 1.			
1. For reimbursing to the province of Massachuset's bay, their expences in furnishing provisions and stores to the troops raised by them, for his majesty's service, for the campaign in 1756 — —	27380	19	11½
2. For reimbursing to the colony of Connecticut, the expence of furnishing provisions and stores to the troops raised by them, for his majesty's service, for the campaign in 1756 — —	13736	17	7
3. For reparing the parish church of St. Margaret's Westminster — — —	4000	0	0
	45117	17	6½
JUNE 8.			
To enable his majesty to defray any extraordinary expences of the war, incurred, or to be incurred, for the service of 1758; and to take all such measures as may be necessary to disappoint or defeat any enterprizes or designs of the enemies, and as the exigency of affairs may require —	800000	0	0
JUNE 10.			
1. Upon account to be paid to the East-India company, towards enabling them to defray the expence of a military force in their settlements, to be maintained by them, in lieu of the battalion of his majesty's forces withdrawn from those settlements —	20000	0	0
2. To be employed in maintaining and supporting the British forces and settlements upon the coast of Africa — — —	10000	0	0
	30000	0	0
Sum total of the grants made by the committee of supply — —	10475007	0	1

Granted in the same session by an address, as follows.

June 16, it was upon motion resolved, That an humble address should be presented to his majesty, to represent, that the salaries of most of the judges in his majesty's superior courts of justice in this

K 2 king-

	£.	s.	d.
kingdom, were inadequate to the dignity and importance of their offices; and therefore to beseech his majesty that he would be graciously pleased to advance any sum, not exceeding 11,450l. to be applied in augmentation of the salaries of such judges, and in such proportions as his majesty, in his great wisdom, should think fit, for the present year; and to assure his majesty, that the house would make good the same to his majesty. And on the 19th, the Earl of Thomond reported to the house, that the said address had been presented to his majesty, and that he had commanded him to acquaint the house, that he would give directions as thereby desired; consequently we must add to the above total	11450	0	0
Sum total of the grants of last session	10486457	0	1

From the foregoing articles of supply, it is observed that for the support of our connections on the continent, the following sums have been granted

	£.	s.	d.
Jan. 23, article I.	100000	0	0
Feb. 23	38360	19	10¾
March 21, art. II.	38360	19	10¾
April 20, art. I.	670000	0	0
—— art. II.	463084	6	10
—— art. III.	386915	13	2
—— art. V.	165175	4	10½
Sum total	1861897	4	8

As soon as the house had agreed to the resolutions of the committee of supply of Dec. 8, 1757, it was resolved, that the house would next morning resolve itself into a committee of the whole house, to consider of ways and means of raising the supply granted to his majesty; from which time this committee was continued to June 12, 1758, and in that time the following resolutions were agreed to in the committee, and all upon the report agreed to by the house, as follows.

December 12, 1757.

That the duties on malt, mum, cyder, and perry, be continued and charged upon all malt which shall be made, and all mum which shall be made or imported, and all cyder and perry which shall be made for sale within the kingdom of Great Britain, from June

£. s. d.

June 23, 1758, to June 24, 1759. The produce of which is computed at, and granted for — 750000 0 0

That the ſum of 4s. in the pound, and no more, upon lands, tenements, hereditaments, and perſonal eſtates, and alſo the ſum of 4s. in the pound upon offices and penſions, be raiſed in that part of Great-Britain, called England, Wales, and town of Berwick upon Tweed, within the ſpace of one year, from March 25, 1758; and that a proportionable ceſs, according to the 9th article of the treaty of union, be laid upon that part of Great Britain, called Scotland — — — 2037874 1 10

Of which ſum, there was, by the bill brought in and paſſed in purſuance of this reſolution, the ſum of 1,989,920l. 8d. to be raiſed in England, &c. and 47,954l. 1s. 2d. to be raiſed in Scotland.

DECBMBER 20.

1. That the ſum remaining in his majeſty's Exchequer, diſpoſable by parliament, of the produce of the ſinking fund for the quarter ended Oct. 10, 1757, be iſſued and applied towards making good the ſupply of this ſeſſion — — 93371 11 $7\frac{3}{4}$

2. That there be iſſued and applied, out of ſuch monies as ſhall or may ariſe of the ſurplus, exceſſes, or overplus monies, and other revenues compoſing the ſinking fund, the ſum of — 300000 0 0

393371 11 $7\frac{3}{4}$

APRIL 18, 1758.

That the ſum remaining in his majeſty's Exchequer, diſpoſable by parliament, of the produce of the ſinking fund, on April 5, 1758, be iſſued and applied towards making good the ſupply this ſeſſion 492400 8 3

APRIL 22.

1. That the ſum of 4,500,000l be raiſed by annuities, at 3l. 10s. per cent. per ann. and the ſum of 500,000l. by a lottery, to be attended with annuities, redeemable by parliament, after the rate of 3l. per cent. per ann. the ſaid ſeveral annuities to be transferable at the bank of England, and charged upon a fund to be eſtabliſhed in this ſeſſion of parliament for payment thereof; and for which the ſinking fund ſhall be a collateral ſecurity; and that every perſon ſubſcribing for 500l. ſhall be intitled to 450l. in annuities, and 50l. in lottery tickets, and ſo in

£. s. d.

proportion for a greater or leſſer ſum; that the ſaid lottery ſhall conſiſt of tickets of the value of 10l. each, in a proportion not exceeding eight blanks to a prize, the blanks to be of the value of 6l. each; the blanks and prizes to bear an intereſt after the rate of 3l. per cent. per ann. to commence from Jan. 5, 1759; and that the ſum of 4,500,000l. to be raiſed by annuities, bear an intereſt after the rate of 3l. 10s. per cent. per ann. from July 5, 1758; which ſaid annuities ſhall ſtand reduced to 3l. per cent. per ann. after the expiration of 24 years, to be computed from July 5, 1758; and ſhall afterwards be redeemable in the whole or in part, by ſums not leſs than 500,000l. at one time, ſix months notice having been given firſt of ſuch payment or payments reſpectively; that any ſubſcriber may, on or before April 29 inſtant, at five o'clock in the afternoon, make a depoſit of 10l. per cent. on ſuch ſums as he ſhall chuſe to ſubſcribe towards raiſing the ſaid ſum of 5,000,000l. with the caſhiers of the bank of England, as a ſecurity for his making the future payments on the days herein after appointed. On the 5,000,000l. 10l per cent. depoſit on or before April 29 inſtant, on the whole five millions. On 4,500,000l. in annuities. 15 per cent. on or before May 30 next—15 per cent, on or before June 28 next—15 per cent. on or before July 27 next—15 per cent. on or before Auguſt 30 next—15 per cent. on or before September 27 next—15 per cent. on or before October 26 next—On the lottery for 500,000l. 20 per cent. on or before June 10 next.—15 per cent. on or before July 10 next.—15 per cent. on or before Auguſt 19 next.—20 per cent. on or before September 9 next.—20 per cent. on or before October 9 next. Which ſeveral ſums ſo received ſhall by the ſaid caſhiers be paid into the receipt of the Exchequer, to be applied, from time to time, to ſuch ſervices as ſhall then have been voted by this houſe in this ſeſſion of parliament, and not otherwiſe. That any ſubſcriber paying in the whole, or any part of his ſubſcription, previous to the days appointed for the reſpective payments, ſhall be allowed a diſcount after the rate of 3l. per cent. per ann. from the days of ſuch reſpective payments to the reſpective times, on which ſuch payments are directed to be made; and that all ſuch perſons, as ſhall make their full payments on the ſaid lottery, ſhall have their tickets delivered as ſoon as they can conveniently be made out ——— ——— ——— 5000000 0 0

2d. That

	£.	s.	d.
2. That there be iſſued and applied out of ſuch monies, as ſhall or may ariſe of the ſurpluſſes, exceſſes, or overplus monies, and other revenues, compoſing the ſinking fund, the ſum of ———	1606076	5	$1\frac{1}{4}$
	6606076	5	$1\frac{1}{4}$

SATURDAY, April 29.

1. That there ſhould be paid yearly the ſum of 1s. in the pound of all ſalaries, fees, and perquiſites of offices and employments in Great Britain, and on all penſions and other gratuities payable out of any revenues belonging to his majeſty in Great Britain, exceeding the value of 100l. per ann.

2. That there ſhall be paid for, and upon every dwelling-houſe inhabited, which now is, or hereafter ſhall be erected, within the kingdom of Great Britain, the yearly ſum of 1s. over and above all duties chargeable thereupon, to commence from the fifth day of this inſtant April 1758.

3. That there ſhall be paid for every window, or light, in every dwelling-houſe, inhabited or to be inhabited, within the kingdom of Great Britain, which ſhall contain 15 windows or lights, or upward, the yearly ſum of 6d. for each window or light in ſuch houſe, over and above all duties chargeable thereupon, to commence from the fifth day of this inſtant April, 1758.

MAY 2.

1. That the annuities, payable purſuant to the reſolution of this houſe of April 22 laſt, be charged upon the ſeveral additional rates and duties upon offices and penſions, and upon houſes and upon windows or lights, which were granted by the reſolutions of this houſe of Saturday laſt.

2. That an act made in the 9th year of the reign of his preſent majeſty, entituled, "An Act for further "encouraging and regulating the Manufacture of "Britiſh made Sail Cloth, and for the more effec-"tual ſecuring the Duties now payable on Foreign "Sail Cloth imported into this Kingdom," which was to continue in force from June 24, 1736, for the term of five years, and from thence to the end of the then next ſeſſion of parliament, and which by ſeveral ſubſequent acts made in the 13th and 24th years of the reign of his preſent majeſty, was further continued until Dec. 25, 1757, and from thence to the end of the then next ſeſſion of parliament, is near expiring, and fit to be continued.

£. s. d.

3. That an act made in the 4th year of the reign of his present majesty, entituled, "An Act for "granting an Allowance upon the Exportation of "British made Gunpowder," which was to continue in force for five years from June 24, 1731, and from thence to the end of then next session of parliament, and which by several subsequent acts made in the 10th, 16th, and 24th years of the reign of his present majesty, was further continued until June 24, 1757, and from thence to the end of the then next session of parliament, is near expiring, and fit to be continued.

4. That an act made in the 6th year of the reign of his present majesty, entituled, "An Act for the better securing and encouraging the Trade of his Majesty's Sugar Colonies in America," which was to continue in force for five years, to be computed from June 24, 1733, and to the end of the then next session of parliament, and which by several subsequent acts made in the 12th, 19th, 26th, and 29th years of the reign of his present majesty, was further continued until June 24, 1759, is near expiring, and fit to be continued.

5. That so much of an act made in the 15th and 16th years of his present majesty's reign, entituled, "An act to impower the Importers or Proprietors of "Rum or Spirits of the British Sugar Plantations, to "land the same before Payment of the Duties of "Excise charged thereon, and to lodge the same in "Warehouses at their own Expence, and for the "relief of Ralph Barrow, in respect to the Duty on "some Rock Salt lost by the Overflowing of the Ri-"vers Weaver and Dane," as relates to the landing of rum or spirits of the British sugar plantations before payment of the duties of excise, and to the lodging of the same in warehouses at the expence of the importers or proprietors thereof; which was to continue in force until Dec. 29, 1749, and from thence to the end of the then next session of parliament, and which by an act made in the 23d year of the reign of his present majesty, was further continued from the expiration thereof until Sept. 29, 1757, and from thence to the end of the then next session of parliament, is near expiring, and fit to be continued.

MAY 9.

1. That the duty of 6d. per ounce Troy on all silver plate, made or wrought, or which ought to be touched

	£.	s.	d.
touched, aſſayed, or marked in this kingdom, granted by an act made in the ſixth year of his late majeſty's reign, ſhall, from and after June 1, 1758, ceaſe, determine, and be no longer paid.			
2. That in lieu thereof, the ſum of 40 s. yearly, ſhall, from and after June 1, 1758, be paid to his majeſty, for a licence to be taken out by every perſon trading in, ſelling or vending gold or ſilver plate.			
3. That the ſums to be paid for the ſaid licences, ſhall be applied to the ſame uſes and purpoſes, as the preſent duty on ſilver plate made or wrought in this kingdom, is now liable, and appropriated unto, and in the ſame manner.			
May 11.			
That all drawbacks now payable on the exportation of ſilver plate, ſhall, from and after June 1, 1758, ceaſe and determine.			
June 1.			
That from and after July 5, 1758, no perſon ſhall be permitted to ſell by retail, any ſweets or made wines, without having firſt taken out a licence for retailing wine.			
June 10.			
That there be raiſed by loans of Exchequer bills, to be charged on the firſt aids to be granted the next ſeſſion of parliament, the ſum of —— ——	800000	0	0
Theſe were all the reſolutions, or proviſions made by this commitee, amounting in the whole to —	11079722	6	10
So that they exceed the ſum total granted by the committee of ſupply in the ſum of —— ——	593265	6	9

To this we subjoin a State of the National Debt, provided or unprovided for by Parliament, as it stood Jan 11. 1757, *and* Jan. 11, 1758, *together with an Account of the Produce of the Sinking Fund in that Year, and to the Payment of what Debts contracted before* Dec. 25, 1716, *the said Fund has been applied.*

EXCHEQUER.	*Amount of the national debt on* Jan. 11, 1759. £. s. d. q.	*Increased between* Jan. 11, 1759, *and* Jan. 11, 1758. £.	*Paid off within that time.* £. s. d. q.	*Account of the national debt on* Jan. 11, 1758. £. s. d. q.
Annuities for long terms, being the remainder of the original sum contributed and unsubscribed to the South-Sea company	1836275 17 10 3/4			1836275 17 10 3/4
Ditto for lives, with the benefit of survivorship, being the original sum contributed	180100			180100
Ditto for two and three lives, being the sum remaining after what is fallen in by deaths	83055 14 10 3/4		500	82555 14 10 3/4
Exchequer bills made out for interest of old bills	2200			2200
Note, The land taxes and duties on malt, being annual grants, are not charged in this account, nor the 1,000,000 l. charged on the deductions of 6d. per pound on pensions, &c. nor the sum of 800,000 l. charged on the supply, anno 1758.				
EAST-INDIA Company.				
By 2 acts of parliament 9 Will. III. and 2 other acts 6 and 9 Annæ, at 3l. per cent. per ann.	3200000			3200000
Annuities at 3l. per cent. 1744, charged on the surplus of the additional duties on low wines, spirits, and strong waters	1000000			1000000
BANK of ENGLAND.				
On their original fund at 3l. per cent. from August 1, 1743	3200000			3200000
For cancelling Exchequer bills, 3 Geo. I.	500000			500000
Purchased of the S. S. company	4000000			4000000
Annuities at 3l. 10s. per cent. charged on the duties on coals, &c. since Lady Day, 1719	1750000			1750000
Ditto charged on the surplus of the funds for lottery, 1714	1250000			1250000

	l.	s.	d.			l.	s.	d.
Ditto 1746, charged on duties on licences for retailing spirituous liquors, since Lady Day, 1746	986800					986800		
Ditto at 3l. per cent. charged on the sinking fund, by the acts 25, 28, 29 and 31 Geo. II.	13537821	5	1 ¼			10537821	5	1 ¼
Ditto charged on the said fund by the act 25 Geo. II. viz. At 3l. 10s. per cent. 14984455l. 18s. 4d. At 3l. per cent. 2716867l. 18s.	17701323	16	4			17701323	16	4
Ditto at 3l. 10s. per cent. charged on ditto	1500000					1500000		
Ditto at 3l. per cent. charged on the stamp duties, &c. by the act 30 Geo. II.				3000000		3000000		
Memorandum. The subscribers of 100l. to the lottery 1745, were allowed an annuity for one life at 9s. a ticket, which amounted to 22,500l. but is now reduced, by lives fallen in, to 19,570l. 15s. And the subscribers of 100l. to the lottery 1746, were allowed an annuity for one life of 18s. a ticket, which amounted to 45,000l. but is now reduced by lives fallen in, to 40,023l. 10s. And also the subscribers of 100l. for 3l. per cent. annuities, 1757, were allowed an annuity for one life of 1l. 2s. 6d. a year, which amounted to 33,750l. which annuities are an increase of the national debt, but cannot be added thereto, as no money was advanced for the same.								
SOUTH-SEA Company.								
On their capital stock and annuities, 9 Geo. I.	2502309	13	11 ½			2502309	13	11 ½
Annuities at 3l. per cent. charged on the sinking fund	2100000					2100000		
	74780886	8	2 ¼	3000000	500	77780386	8	2 ¼

There was remaining in the Hands of the late and present Treasurers of the NAVY *on* Dec. 31, 1757, *in Money as undermentioned and may be reckoned towards satisfying the following Debt of the Navy.*

In what treasurers hands.	*In* MONEY.	*Wear and tear ordinary and transp.* £. s. d.	*On the* HEADS *of* *Seamens wages.* £. s. d.	*Victuals.* £. s. d.	*Total.* £. s. d.
Right Hon. George Dodington, Esq; first treasurership.	In money.	5743 6 $\frac{1}{4}$	1951 5 9	34 18 2 $\frac{1}{2}$	7761 10 4
	Ditto towards the debt for sick and hurt seamen	—	38 4 $\frac{1}{4}$	—	
Right Hon. Henry Legge, Esq.	In money	6746 3	2423 16 10 $\frac{3}{4}$	2895 3 7 $\frac{1}{2}$	12120 16 2 $\frac{1}{4}$
	Ditto towards the debt for sick and hurt seamen	—	55 15 5	—	
Right Hon. George Grenville, Esq; first treasurership.	In money	4725 12 2 $\frac{1}{4}$	4483 6 4 $\frac{3}{4}$	5125 18 6 $\frac{3}{4}$	13344 5 6 $\frac{3}{4}$
	Ditto towards the debt for sick and hurt seamen	—	1009 8 5	—	
Right Hon. George Dodington, Esq; second treasurership.	In money	11449 13 3 $\frac{1}{2}$	1945 1 6	1507 5 3 $\frac{1}{2}$	15978 15 2
	Ditto towards the debt for sick and hurt seamen	—	1076 15	—	
Right Hon. George Grenville, Esq; second treasurership.	In money	34180 5 10	29058 3 9 $\frac{1}{4}$	14219 4 4 $\frac{1}{2}$	83493 16 6 $\frac{1}{2}$
	Ditto towards the debt for sick and hurt seamen	—	6036 2 7	—	
		62844 17 7	48077 16 1	23782 10 $\frac{1}{2}$	154705 3 8 $\frac{1}{2}$

There remained on Dec. 31, 1757, to come in of the supplies of the year 1757, including 10,000l. for Plymouth hospital, 19850l. 7s. 9d. $\frac{1}{2}$.

An ESTIMATE *of the* DEBT *of his Majesty's* NAVY *on the Heads hereafter mentioned, as it stood on* Dec. 31, 1757.

HEADS *of the Naval Estimates.*	Particulars. £.	s.	d.	Total. £.	s.	d.
Wear and tear, ordinary and transports.						
DUE, to pay off and discharge all the bills registered in the course of the navy for stores, freight of transports, &c. supplied for the service thereof —	686708	9				
To pay off and discharge bills registered on the said course for premiums allowed by act of parliament — — —	2987	17	7			
To freight of transports and tenders, and for stores delivered into his majesty's several yards, &c. for which no bills were made out on the aforesaid Dec. 31, as also to several bills of exchange	289735	7	5	1196715	14	
To his majesty's yards and rope-yards, for the ordinary and extraordinary	205795					
For the half-pay to sea officers, according to an establishment made by his late majesty in council on that behalf — — — — —	11489					
Seamens Wages.						
Due, to pay the men, &c. unpaid on the books of ships paid off	221402	15	11 1/4			
To ships in sea pay, on the aforesaid Dec. 31, 1759 — —	1643888			1914184	15	6 1/4
To pay off and discharge all the bills entered in course for slop-cloaths bedding for seamen, surgeons necessaries, bounties to widows and orphans of men slain at sea, &c. —	48893	19	7			
Victualling debt as per estimate received from those commissioners, viz.						
Due, for short allowance to the companies of his majesty's ships in pay, and which have been paid off — — —	14211	11	7			
For paying off all the bills entered on their course — —	327336	8	8			
For provisions delivered, and services performed, for which no bills were made out on the aforesaid Dec. 31, 1757 — — — —	43966	10	4	412711	17	
For necessary-money, extra-necessary-money, bills of exchange and contingencies	7062		3			
To the officers, workmen, and labourers employed at the several ports —	20135	6	3			
Sick and wounded, the debt of that office as per estimate received from those commissioners, viz.						
Due, for the quarters and cure of the sick and hurt seamen set on shore from his majesty's ships at the several ports, and for prisoners of war and contingencies relating to the said service	—			93910	10	3 1/2
The total amounts to the sum of — — —				3617522	16	10 3/4
From whence deducting the money in the treasurers hands	134705	3	8 1/2			
As also the money that remained to come in of the supplies of the year as on the other side	19850	7	9 1/2	154555	11	6
The debt of the navy will be then — — — —				3462967	5	4 3/4

	£.	s.	d.	£.	s.	d.
Brought over				3462967	5	4 $\frac{3}{4}$
N. B. In this debt is included for charge of transports between Jan. 1, 1757, and Dec. 31, following	314832	4	1			
And it appears by an account received from the commissioners of the victualling, that the expence of victuals supplied the soldiers between Jan. 1, 1757, and Dec. 3, following, amounts to	61304	9	7 $\frac{3}{4}$	376136	13	8 $\frac{3}{4}$
For which sum of 376,136l. 13s. 8d. $\frac{3}{4}$ no provision has been made by parliament, but if thought fit to be granted, as the like service was provided for in former years.						
The nett debt of the navy will then be				3086830	11	8

An ACCOUNT *of the Produce of the Sinking Fund, and to the Payment of what Debts contracted before* Jan. 11, 1758, *the said Fund has been applied.*

Dr.	£.	s.	d.		£.	s.	d. q.
THE Exchequer is to cash on the sinking fund, Jan. 11, 1757					306300	11	4 $\frac{1}{4}$
To the produce of the sinking fund between Jan. 11, 1757, and Jan. 11, 1758, viz.							
Surplus of the aggregate fund	952285	19	2	$\frac{3}{4}$			
Surplus of the general fund	606530	15	2	$\frac{1}{4}$			
South-Sea company fund	159452	19	1	$\frac{1}{2}$			
					1718249	13	6 $\frac{1}{2}$
Monies brought to this fund pursuant to the act 25 George II.							
Of the duty on wrought plate	7583	19	2	$\frac{1}{2}$			
Additional duty on paper	31382	17	9				
Surplus of the duties on wines	38477	15	1	$\frac{1}{2}$			

Per contra Cr.	£.	s.	d.
By monies issued between Jan. 11, 1757, and Jan. 11, 1758, viz.			
By the Bank of England for subscribed annuities, at $3\frac{1}{2}$ and 3l. per cent. for 12 months interest and charges of management, to Oct. 10, 1757	615845	19	10
By ditto for ditto, at 3l. per cent. for 12 months interest and management, to Jan. 5, 1758	320913	17	10 $\frac{1}{4}$
By ditto for annuities, 1756, at $3\frac{1}{2}$ per cent. for 12 months interest and management, to Jan. 5, 1758	54311	19	9
By ditto for ditto, upon sundry annuities.	4020	6	9 $\frac{1}{4}$

Duty on glafs, and additional duty on fpirits	33867	8	5 ½			
Surplus of the additional duty on fpirits	122726	3	2 ½			
Duty on houfes and windows	129814	2	4			
Duty on coaches	46463	14	10 ¾			
Additional duty on poundage	314072	18	3 ½			
				724388	12	3 ¼
Duty on fweets	10288	19	9			
Duty on falt	232811	2	11 ½			
				243100	2	8 ½
Surplus of the additional duty on paper, foap, and coals	28136	0	10			
Duty on coals	13431	1	4 ½			
				41567	2	2 ½
Additional duty on cards and dice	6934	12	11			
Ditto on ale-licences	60325	18	1			
New duty on plate	20331	17	1 ½			
				87593	8	1 ½
				3121198	17	2 ½

By the South-Sea company for annuities 1757, for 12 months intereft and management, to January 5, 1758	64181	5	
By cafh taken to make good the deficiency of the annuity funds 1757	7546	12	10
In full of 1300,000l. granted for the fervice of the year 1756	362530	10	2
In full of 1200,000l. granted for ditto 1757	1200000		
In part of the fupply 1758, to make good the civil lift	31000		
	2660350	12	2 ½
Balance, Jan. 11. 1758	460848	5	
	3121198	17	2 ½

STATE PAPERS.

Hague.

ON the 22d Dec. 1758, Major General Yorke delivered the following memorial to the deputies of the States General.

" High and mighty Lords,

" I had the honour to acquaint you at the conference I obtained of your high mightineſſes on the 7th inſtant, that the king my maſter had authorized and inſtructed me to enter into a negotiation with ſuch perſons as your high mightineſſes ſhould think proper to nominate for that end; but that, as the affair required a minute diſcuſſion, it would be impoſſible to terminate it without ſome farther explanations. It is with the higheſt pleaſure that I this day open our conferences on this important ſubject; and I flatter myſelf that if your high mightineſſes are as deſirous of a reconciliation as his majeſty is, it will ſoon be happily concluded.

By the two reſolutions of Sept. 12, and Sept. 25, which were delivered to me the day following, your high mightineſſes thought proper to make ſome difficulty of receiving the declaration which I had the honour to preſent to you, in the king's name, againſt the trade carried on by your ſubjects to the French colonies in America, for the account of thoſe very colonies. If his majeſty, on being informed thereof, commanded me to declare that he could not depart from his preceding declaration, it was becauſe he thought this claim had no foundation in the treaties ſubſiſting between him and the republic. Beſides, ſhould the perſons concerned in this trade even be able to wreſt the ſenſe of treaties ſo as to deceive their friends, and make the obſtructing of it by England paſs for a grievance, ſtill his majeſty is perſuaded that their high mightineſſes will ſee with pleaſure that his majeſty ſets aſide the diſcuſſion of this treaty, which is connected with ſo many others, and ſets himſelf wholly to do the ſubjects of his ancient allies all the ſervice, and to grant them every favour that ſhall not notably prejudice the welfare and ſafety of his people. It is in this light that his majeſty conſiders the trade, directly or indirectly, to the French colonies in America.

His majeſty is at war with the moſt chriſtian king: he cannot hope to get out of it with ſafety, or obtain a ſpeedy and laſting peace, which is his majeſty's ſole aim, if the princes who have declared themſelves neuter, inſtead of contenting themſelves with trading as uſual, without any riſk, aſſume a right of carrying on that trade of the king's enemies, which is not allowed them in time of peace. The injuſtice of this proceeding is too apparent to require more to be ſaid on it: one may venture to appeal to your high mightineſſes own conduct in the like caſe. A trade of this natuee was never ſuffered by you; and it hath been op-

opposed by the *Salus Populi* in all countries, in like circumstances.

His majesty sees with pleasure the trade of his neighbours flourish, and would behold its increase with satisfaction, if its prosperity were not repugnant to this primary law. But he likewise persuades himself, that never, for the sake of some transient profit to individuals, will his ancient allies be the first to injure England in this essential part. Considering the thing in this light, I cannot doubt but your high mightinesses will give the king the pleasure to hear that they, for their subjects, have honestly abandoned it, and that this stumbling block is for ever removed. In settling this point, his majesty commands me to include in it the change, commonly called Overscheepen, which is made of a French vessel into a Dutch vessel, when the former dares not continue her course, and endeavours to save herself by carrying neutral colours, in order to avoid seizure at sea by the king's ships. Your high mightinesses while you acknowledge the justice of my first demand, cannot refuse the second; since that would be to declare, that you treat with good faith, whilst, at the same time, a more dangerous door would be left for fraud. Such a conduct is unworthy of the equity of your high mightinesses, especially in the present case, when the question is the prevention of any object of future dispute, and the restoration of harmony and good neighbourhood between the two powers.

The last point of my instructions, which relates to the amicable demands made by his majesty to your high mightinesses, requires a more minute consideration. I cannot enter upon that subject yet; but reserve it till afterwards. I must, nevertheless, observe to you, that the king has seen, not without pain, yet without giving them any molestation, a great number of Dutch ships pass by his harbours, since the commencement of the war, laden with all sorts of materials for building and repairing his enemies fleets. His majesty asks that certain articles of naval stores may be comprehended in the class of contraband: but he will so settle it with your high mightinesses, as that the inoffensive trade of your subjects to the North of Europe (if I may use that term) shall not be involved in this article. Your high mightinesses, who are yourselves a maritime power, and know how to contend for and defend your prerogatives as such, must always allow that in the present war against France, it is both the king's interest, and his duty, not only to hinder the marine of his enemy from becoming too formidable, but also to employ all means to weaken it. Can it be disputed that naval stores are not, in this view, as prejudicial as balls and gunpowder.

Let France be without ships, and her warlike stores will never make England uneasy. The importance of this article is so evident, that the king ventures to refer it to the judgment of your high mightinesses. These, my lords, are my instructions with regard to the satisfaction which the king would think himself entitled to require from the friendship and justice of the republic, if he had no other foundation for his

his claim. But I have already informed you, that it is his majeſty's ſincere deſire to unite his own ſafety with the convenience of your high mightineſſes; which makes it unneceſſary for me to enlarge on this head.

In this repreſentation of the points on which I have orders to inſiſt with your high mightineſſes, I have endeavoured to follow the method which you yourſelves have begun to put in practice; that is to ſay, firſt to ſtate the claim, and afterwards propoſe the expedients.

I come now to the articles of your reſolutions of the 25th of September laſt.

I. As to the demand contained in the firſt article, I muſt obſerve to your high mightineſſes, that this very treaty, which you ſo ſtrongly inſiſt on, preſcribes the manner of proceeding in caſe of ſeizure or detention; and that you cannot claim the exerciſe of an extra-judicial power by his majeſty, whoſe hands are tied with regard to his own ſubjects by the laws, and with regard to foreigners by treaties. If there have been any irregular ſentences, either the judge muſt have been miſled by appearances at the hearing of the cauſe, or delays were made, of which there was juſt reaſon to complain. The ſupreme court, eſtabliſhed for judging in the laſt reſort, hath always been ready to reviſe and correct abuſes, if at any time any could be diſcovered in the ſentences of the inferior courts. But your high mightineſſes will give me leave to obſerve, that it is very extraordinary, that not one appeal hath yet been thrown in, notwithſtanding the aſſurances given to your high mightineſſes by many perſons. This is a fact at which every body in England is aſtoniſhed. And, doubtleſs, had the appellants been deſirous to be heard, the number of complaints would have been greatly diminiſhed.

Mean while, to aſſiſt and relieve the ſubjects of your high mightineſſes as much as poſſible, and to avoid confounding the innocent with the guilty, his majeſty hath juſt now ordered an exact liſt to be delivered to him of all the Dutch veſſels detained in his harbours, in order to call thoſe to an account who may have brought them in on frivolous pretences; to oblige them to releaſe them, and to haſten the finiſhing of the trials in general. If there remains any thing more to be done for the further facility and ſecurity of the navigation of the republic, it will readily be agreed to by his majeſty. The nation is deſirous to ſecond the king's good intentions on this head. I flatter myſelf that theſe aſſurances will be ſufficient to diſſipate thoſe ill-grounded fears which poſſeſs certain perſons in theſe provinces. A mutual confidence and a deſire to avoid any ſubject of animoſity are highly requiſite in treating of matters of ſuch importance, and of ſuch a complicated nature.

II. As to the ſecond article of the ſaid reſolution, I almoſt dare venture to aſſure your high mightineſſes, that if you cordially intereſt yourſelves in his majeſty's ſituation in the preſent war, and diſcover a readineſs to grant the points which he thinks he hath a right to require of you, you will receive all poſſible ſatisfaction and ſecurity. It is his majeſty's intention

tention that the subjects of your high mightinesses should fully enjoy all the privileges and immunities resulting from the treaty of 1674, so far as the tenor of it is not derogated from by the present accommodation.

III. As to the third article, as soon as your high mightinesses shall have agreed with his majesty on the points which I have mentioned in his name, it will be easily settled.

IV. The fourth article contains complaints for which perhaps there is too much foundation, by the violence committed by English privateers, or vessels pretending to be such. His majesty is sincerely grieved that such disorders should have been committed to the disgrace of his subjects. The whole nation joins with the *king* in endeavouring to suppress those robberies. I take the liberty to communicate to you the orders issued by the admiralty of Great Britain against such behaviour: and, for the honour of the merchants of London, I must add the advertisement published by them, offering a reward for discovering the offenders. His majesty intreats your high mightinesses to assist him on this occasion, by exhorting your subjects to bring to justice the authors of those offences; in which they may depend on the utmost protection and encouragement. As to the rest, the king is astonished, that after so many applications made here for obtaining proofs of the facts alledged, not one, notwithstanding the reward offered, is gone over to England to give evidence.

I take the liberty to refer to the contents of my first article for an answer to the fifth resolution of your high mightinesses; only adding, that his majesty will with pleasure agree to any method that shall be proposed to him for authenticating the genuineness of ship-papers, in which point too many abuses have been committed."

Hague, Aug. 2.

The Count d'Affry, the French ambassador, presented the following memorial to the States General, July 25.

"High and Mighty Lords,

"On the repeated sollicitations which M. de Berkenrode hath been ordered to make, and on those which the counsellor pensionary hath often made, particularly of late, that the king my master would be graciously pleased to grant a bounty on herrings taken by the Dutch and imported into France; his majesty authorises me to declare to your high mightinesses, that he is disposed to grant your subjects such bounty; which shall be immediately settled at Paris, agreeably to the instructions which your high mightinesses shall be pleased to send on that head to Mr. Berkenrode your ambassador.

The king my master has determined to grant this favour to the republic, from his friendship for her, and his assurance that the republic will never depart from that system of equity and neutrality, which she hath adopted with regard to the present war."

The Count d'Affry, the French ambassador, presented to the States General a memorial on Jan. 25. ult. from which we shall give such extracts as are a reply to Colonel Yorke's memorial.

"Your high mightinesses were informed in the month of July last, that the king my master, and the empress queen of Hungary and

Bohemia, had agreed to put French garrisons into Ostend and Nieuport. Their majesties, in order to give your republic a fresh proof of their friendship and confidence, were pleased, at that time, to command their respective ministers to communicate to your high mightinesses, by the president of your assembly, their just reasons for taking this resolution. Accordingly I waited on him the 18th of July, with Baron Reischach, and we declared to him: That, the empress queen, being under an absolute necessity of employing all her forces to defend her hereditary dominions in Germany, was obliged to withdraw her troops from Ostend and Nieuport. That, it was of the more importance to provide for the safety of those two places, as there was great reason to believe that the court of London, which sought only to spread the war, and perpetuate it, had formed a design to seize them; and as the port of Ostend was even blocked up by several English men of war and frigates. That, in these circumstances the empress queen applied to the king, as her ally nearest at hand, to furnish troops which might be substituted in Ostend and Nieuport, in the room of the empress queen's, there to remain only whilst it should be judged necessary and convenient for their reciprocal interests. That the empress queen had reserved to herself, and in those two towns, the free and entire exercise of all the rights of property and sovereignty; such as the administration of justice, the collecting of the revenue and taxes, and the disposition even of the artillery and stores of all sorts. (Your high mightinesses know that accordingly the Count de la Mothe d'Hugues, who commands the king's troops at Ostend and Nieuport, took an oath to the empress queen, before the Count de Cobentzel, her minister plenipotentiary.) That, the friendship of the king, and the empress, for your high mightinesses, was a full security for their majesties constant attention to maintain the best understanding with your republic, and to prevent the regulation in question from doing it any prejudice, or giving it the least uneasiness.

It is by express command of the king my master, and to declare to your high mightinesses, That the introduction of French garrisons into Ostend and Nieuport had no other motive than what I have just mentioned in this memorial: That, his majesty's troops shall remain there only to the end of this present war: and that they shall even march out sooner if the empress queen desire it, and they shall march out that very moment that she shall intrust the guard of those two places to her own troops. The necessity of attending to their preservation is the more indispensable, as your high mightinesses cannot, doubtless, be ignorant that if the Low Countries have any thing to apprehend for their safety and quiet, it is against England alone that the powers interested therein ought to take precautions. It is needless to enter into particulars on this head. It is sufficient to apprize your high mightinesses, that one of the projects of that crown is to carry the war into the neighbourhood of your republic; and it is but too probable that the neutrality and territory of your high mightinesses would perhaps be no more regarded on this occasion, than the law of nations, treaties, and paroles of of honour have been hitherto. The king perſuades himſelf, that after a declaration ſo preciſe, which his majeſty has been induced to make only by his affection for your republic, your high mightineſſes will, from a juſt notion of the methods which the court of London is inceſſantly employing, to make your high mightineſſes ſhare in the calamities and dangers of a war, which his majeſty undertook with regret, and not till he was forced thereto by the moſt unjuſt and unexpected aggreſſion; and which he continues only from his fidelity to his engagements, and to fulfil the duty impoſed upon him by his quality of guarantee of the laws and liberties of the Germanic body."

Tranſlation of the famous memorial preſented to the States General by two hundred and ſixty-nine merchants, which is kept very ſecret in Holland.

"We the underſigned merchants, inſurers, and others, concerned in the commerce and navigation of the ſtate, moſt humbly repreſent, That the violences and unjuſt depredations committed by Engliſh men of war and privateers on the veſſels and effects of the ſubjects of the ſtate, are not only continued, but daily multiplied; and cruelty and exceſſes carried to ſuch a height, that the petitioners are forced to implore the aſſiſtance of your high mightineſſes, that the commerce and navigation of the republic, which are the two ſinews of the ſtate, may ſuffer no interruption, and be protected in the moſt efficacious manner, in order that the being of the ſtate may be preſerved, and that it may be kept from compleat and final ruin.

The petitioners ſhall not inſert here a long recital of their ſhips that have been illegally ſtopped and ſeized, nor of the piracies and violences that have been committed for a conſiderable ſpace of time, on the ſubjects of the republic; nor of the acts of inhumanity with which they were often attended, even ſo far, that leſs cruelty might have been expected from a declared enemy, than they have ſuffered from the ſubjects of a power with whom the ſtate is connected by the moſt ſolemn treaties of friendſhip. The whole is public and notorious.

Nor will the petitioners enlarge on the inſults offered to the Dutch flag, in contempt of your high mightineſſes, the natural protectors of the ſubjects of the republic. The facts are known to your high mightineſſes.

But the petitioners beg leave to repreſent, with all due ſubmiſſion, that they cannot forbear to lay their juſt complaints before your high mightineſſes, who are the protectors of their perſons, their eſtates, their commerce, and navigation; and to lay before you the indiſpenſable neceſſity of putting a ſtop, as ſoon as poſſible, to thoſe depredations and violences. The petitioners offer to contribute each his contingent, and to arm, at their own charge, for the ſupport and protection of their commerce and navigation.

The petitioners flatter themſelves that their toils, and the riſk to which their effects are expoſed on the ſeas, will have their proper influence on the general body of the ſtate, ſince the traders of this country, finding themſelves left to the diſcretion of a part of that nation with whom the ſtate is moſt intitimately connected, thousands of tradesmen and others, who are connected with merchants that have hitherto carried on a flourishing trade, will be reduced to distress and poverty; those connections ceasing by the extinction of the estates of merchants, who have always approved themselves faithful to their country, these will be forced to abandon it, to their great regret, and seek shelter and protection elsewhere; which will give a mortal blow to the principal members of the state.

For these just causes, the petitioners have recourse to your high mightinesses, most humbly imploring them, both in their own names, and in the name of a multitude of unhappy people, who are on the point of being stript of all their effects, of sinking into the utmost distress, and being reduced to beggary, that it may please your high mightinesses to grant to commerce and navigation such speedy, vigorous, and effectual protection, that the faithful subjects of this free state may enjoy their possessions in full security.

And your petitioners, &c."

Memorial which the Princess Gouvernante presented to the States General on the 7th of June, relating to the proposed augmentation of their land forces.

"High and Mighty Lords,

"My quality, my duty, and my inclination, lead me to make the following representation to your high mightinesses. I had the honour to represent to you, when the war began to be kindled between France and England, about the limits of their territories in America, that this war would undoubtedly be transferred from that part of the world to Europe, and that prudence required that an augmentation should be made in the land forces of the state, in order to reinforce the garrisons of the frontier towns, and cover the territories of the republic from invasion.

I farther foresaw, that Europe, being made the theatre of war, several camps would be formed in Flanders, on the banks of the Rhine, and in the dutchy of Cleves. The event having shewn the justness of these conjectures, I again insisted upon the necessity of making this augmentation, that the republic might be in a condition to cause her neutrality to be respected, and to prevent her territories from being made the seat of war.

The provinces of Guelders and Overyssel, frighted at the danger with which those provinces are threatened by the proximity of two formidable armies, have resolved to demand that the affair of the augmentation of the republic's forces may be taken into serious consideration by the other provinces, and have requested me to join my sollicitations to theirs, that this augmentation may take place; which I do the more readily, as I am equally sensible with them of the extent of the danger, that threatens the republic, especially since the Hanoverian army crossed the Rhine. This augmentation is the more necessary, as it behoves the state to be able to hinder either army from retiring into the territories of the state if it should be defeated: for in that case the conqueror, being authorised to pursue his enemy wherever he can find him, would bring the war into the heart of our country. None of the powers at war could be offended at the

the efficacious measures taken by the republic to cause her neutrality to be respected; and to hinder her territories from being made the theatre of war. The good faith of the Dutch is well known; and from the assurances already given, those powers will rest satisfied, that the Dutch had no bad intention, and that their design is not to take part in the present troubles, but wholly to keep the war at a distance, and prevent their country from being the seat thereof.

Agreeable, therefore, to the request of the provinces of Guelders and Overyssel, I join my sollicitation to theirs, that your high mightinesses would take this affair into serious consideration, and that in regard to the crisis in which the republic is at present, this augmentation may take place.

I conclude these representations with praying the God of all understanding to preside in your deliberations, and that he would inspire you with vigorous resolutions proportioned to the dangers that threaten the state, and conformable to my desires and wishes."

In the answer which the Princess Regent gave, on the 7th of December, to the fourth deputation of the merchants, she said, among other things, 'That she beheld the state 'of trade with concern; that she 'was as much moved at it as any 'of the merchants; that its want of 'protection was not her fault, but 'that of the towns of Dort, Harlem, Amsterdam, Tergaw, Rotterdam, and the Brielle; that, 'had it not been for those towns, 'the forces of the state, by sea 'and land, would have been on a 'better footing; and that she had 'never ceased to protect trade; a 'proof of which was the letter of 'the king her father, wherein his 'majesty says, *The affair of the* '*Dutch is now under consideration*; '*and Yorke will speedily receive* '*the necessary instructions for settling* '*it amicably. Some method shall be* '*thought of to curb the insolence of* '*the privateers.* That she was informed, that Mr. Yorke had asked 'a conference to treat of this matter; and that she hoped the negotiation would be attended with 'success.'

The deputies were afterwards referred by her royal highness to M. de la Larrey, who now does the business that was formerly done by M. de Back. The merchants laboured much to persuade this minister, that the augmentation of the land forces, and the equipment of a fleet, were matters quite distinct from each other, as light is from darkness; that there was no pressing motive for the augmentation; whereas innumerable reasons rendered the fitting out of a fleet a matter of the most urgent necessity. M. de Larrey contented himself with saying, that the want of a sufficient fleet was not owing to her royal highness; that opinions differed on this head; and that it was a seetled point at present, not to fit out a fleet without augmenting the army.

Whatever may be in this, four days after the speech was delivered, her royal highness carried it to the assembly of the States General, addressing herself to them in these words:

" High and Mighty Lords,

" It would be injustice to that zeal and vigilance for the safety of the state, of which your high mightinesses have long given me convincing proof, to endeavour to excite you now to greater zeal and vigilance? It is from this persuasion I appear in the assembly of your high mightinesses, to represent to you, that, seeing your earnest and repeated efforts to induce the provinces of Holland and West Friseland, of Zealand, and of Friseland, to agree to the proposed augmentation of the land forces, and equipment of a fleet, have been ineffectual, your high mightinesses will be pleased to consider of a way to put an end to this affair, and the sooner the better, in order, on one hand, to satisfy the strong and well-grounded instances of the provinces of Guelders, Utrecht, Overyssel, and Groningen; and on the other, to comply with the ardent just desire of the commercial inhabitants of this country; who, *though* I had informed them of the negotiation between Great Britain and your high mightinesses to accommodate the differences that have arisen, and of my own assiduity to forward an equitable accommodation, and of the consequences of the steps I thought it my duty to take, have, *nevertheless*, sent me a deputation for the fourth time to insist on a very considerable augmentation of the naval forces of the state.

This deputation consisted of forty merchants; a number that merits attention no less than the speech they read to me, of which a great number of copies, printed before-hand, were immediately distributed in all parts. I shall make no remarks upon that speech; only that the drift of it did not tend to facilitate the negotiations begun with England, nor to induce the nation to prefer a convention, to a rupture, with that crown. I shall enter no farther into this subject, choosing rather to refer the whole to the sound and penetrating judgment of your high mightinesses, who may also see by that speech, that it is more than time to finish the deliberations on the motion for augmenting our forces both by sea and land, on which I have always insisted with the greatest earnestness; as without it, I am convinced in my conscience, the state is, and will always remain, exposed to all sorts of misfortunes and danger, both now and hereafter."

In consequence of this speech, the States General sent, the same day; the following letter to the States of Holland and West Friseland.

"Noble and Mighty Lords,

"The princess gouvernante having come to our assembly this morning, in consequence of a deputation of the merchants, who had waited on her a few days before; to insist on a considerable augmentation of our naval forces, her royal highness again represented to us the urgent necessity of coming to a determination both with regard to the augmentation proposed by land, and with regard to an equipment by sea; two points, upon which her royal highness has always most earnestly insisted, and without which the state is, and will remain, exposed to all sorts of misfortunes and dangers, both at present and for the future.

We thought proper to send a copy of the said proposition to your noble mightinesses, and also to the states of the provinces of Zealand and Friseland; and at the same time, to represent to you, that it is now time, if ever, to consider seriously of those two points as soon as possible, and carry

carry them into effect by a salutary and unanimous resolution. It would be both superfluous and tiresome again to point out to your noble mightinesses the dangerous situation of the republic from the war which hath been kindled and rages all over Europe, and which hath spread to the very frontiers of this state: nor is there the smallest prospect of seeing it extinguished next year, as we are informed from all sides, that the principal powers concerned are taking all the necessary measures for making it rage next campaign with greater fury, if possible, than ever.

Every one, who considers how uncertain the consequences of a war between powerful neighbours may be to a state surrounded on all sides by foreign troops, must allow, that it were greatly to be wished the republic were in a proper posture of defence whilst the war is on its frontiers. All who know that the happiness of our country depends upon the safety of trade, must be equally convinced, that an armament by sea is absolutely necessary in this critical conjuncture, when our navigation is disturbed in a manner unheard of; and that the neglect of our naval forces at this time, would be wholly unjustifiable. We have always considered the zealous efforts of your noble mightinesses, from time to time, to induce your confederates to consent to this armament, as highly reasonable; and as far as in us lay, we always endeavoured to second them.

Nor can we disapprove of the step taken by the merchants in carrying their complaints on this head where they ought to be carried, when it is done in a proper and decent manner: but as it is the duty of wise and faithful rulers to extend their care not only to a part of the subjects, but also to all in general; and as the principal aim of a sovereign ought to be, on one side, to watch over the happiness of his subjects, and on the other to protect them against all violence from without, we think that in such a situation as that of the republic at present, an augmentation of the troops of the state, for the defence of the frontiers, is unavoidable, as well as an equipment by sea for the security of trade; and that they ought to go hand in hand. The states of the provinces of Guelders, Utrecht, Overyssel, and Groningen, join with her royal highness and us in the same opinion, and accordingly have always insisted, by divers letters and propositions, on those two points so essential to the public interest.

We doubt not but the said states will explain themselves to your noble mightinesses on this head, and at the same time signify their readiness to interest themselves in the welfare of the trading inhabitants, in case your noble mightinesses will also effectually provide for the safety of their inhabitants.

When we reflect, that not only the interest of the republic in general requires that it be put in a proper state of defence both by sea and land, but that we can see no way of determining this matter, unless, by a reciprocal indulgence, one of the confederates comply with the sentiments of the other, we leave your noble mightinesses to judge, whether by a longer delay in coming to a conclusion, both with regard to the augmentation of the land forces and

and the equipment of a fleet, room will not be given for a schism and dangerous division among the confederates, the consequences of which would be very deplorable, while the republic in the mean time will remain a defenceless state, both by sea and land, and depend upon the arbitrary power of its neighbours.

We therefore most earnestly intreat your noble mightinesses, as you value the safety of the country, and all that is dear to you, as you regard the protection of the good inhabitants, and as you value the concord and good harmony, which at all times, but especially in the present danger, is of the last necessity, that you will seriously reflect upon the exhortations of her royal highness, and on the instances of the majority of the confederates, and take a wise and salutary resolution with regard to the proposed augmentation of the land forces; so that this augmentation, together with an equipment by sea, may, the sooner the better, be unanimously brought to a conclusion.

Thus concluding, noble and mighty lords, we pray God Almighty to keep your mightinesses in his holy protection, &c. &c."

Hague, Nov. 7.

A deputation of the most eminent merchants of Amsterdam arrived here; and after visiting the pensionary and the president of the week, waited on her royal highness the princess regent, to whom they delivered the following memorial.

"The merchants of this province, who have the honour to obtain an audience of your royal highness for the third time, find themselves obliged to renew their complaint of the great damage which their vessels and cargoes continue to suffer by the English. The deputies therefore take the liberty to put your royal highness in mind, That the first time that their confidence in your highness's equity, led them to have recourse to you, their principals, who had the justest ground of complaint, foresaw at that time the total ruin of our navigation and commerce: That, on that account, your royal highness graciously promised powerfully to support their just complaints in the assembly of the States General, and even to make remonstrances in your own name to the British court, provided the losses were properly attested: That the merchants of the province immediately drew up a list of the vessels that had been carried either into the ports of Great Britain, or those of her colonies, with an estimate of the value of the cargoes, and a detail of the enormous robberies committed by English privateers on board those vessels; the whole accompanied with original and credible attestations: That, not content with having respectfully delivered those incontestible proofs to their high mightinesses, and to your royal highness in private, the body of merchants took the liberty to present in writing, and verbally, how much it imported the welfare of the provinces to take proper measures for putting an end to such unjust depredations, and for obtaining reparation for so great losses. That in the second audience which your royal highness was pleased to give them, upon fresh complaints, your royal highness declared, that the subsequent damage

damage exceeded what you could have believed. That your royal highness, in your astonishment, added, in terms full of cordial affection, that if things should continue as they were, your dear country, in whose welfare you took so much concern, having adopted it alone for *your* country, would be ruined. That you would employ your utmost endeavours to obtain reparation of past losses, and would immediately take such means for that end, as should be consistent with the honour of the republic, and the advantage of commerce, which should always have your protection; and that you would justify the sincerity of your promises by facts.

That the deputies on their return home, made a report of the success of their commission to their principals, who were equally pleased, and certain of seeing the face of affairs soon changed; but their joy and expectation is turned into bitterness, which is the more sensibly felt, as they now again find themselves under a necessity of importuning your royal highness for the third time, by exhibiting a list of seventy of their ships taken by the English since that time, amounting to near thirteen millions of florins: That these vessels have been condemned, some in the three kingdoms, others in the British colonies, and elsewhere, under the most frivolous pretences, in contempt of all law, contrary to justice and reason, as well as the treaties in force between the two nations: That being informed an accommodation was negotiating with the British ministry, the body of merchants flattered themselves they should obtain by this treaty, an indemnification of their great losses: but that not one merchant had as yet reaped the smallest fruit from this negotiation.

That with grief they behold their hopes of protection diminish daily, rather than increase: That it is to be feared the evil will grow worse and worse, and rise to the utmost height: That several ships of war, which have returned to the ports of the republic from their voyages, have been disarmed and laid up, without being replaced by others: That it is evident to a demonstration, that the aforesaid illicit practices must give a mortal blow to commerce in general, and to our country in particular: That thousands of persons, who were possessed of great wealth, or in easy circumstances, are thereby fallen to decay; and if a speedy remedy be not applied, not only eminent merchants, but swarms of retail traders, will infallibly be ruined: That by this decay of trade many hundred mechanics are deprived of work, particularly those employed in the silk way, in sugar-houses, dying, &c. who consequently languish in idleness.

That at present (and what will it be in the middle of winter?) a great number of creditable tradesmen are forced to subsist on the charity of their respective companies, and of the hospitals: That the number of these necessitous people increases daily, whilst the revenues of the charitable foundations decrease, because they are obliged to give alms to such numbers, and because they are deprived of the contributions they used to receive in better times: That it is natural for every one, who foresees a threatening loss, to attend rather

rather to his own preservation, than to the assistance of those whose unhappy lot has rendered them objects of compassion: That frugality, thus prevailing over liberality, people continue to feel the misfortunes of others, but are little disposed to give them any relief: That, considering on one hand all these disasters, and on the other the welfare of commerce and of their country, the body of merchants have thought it their duty again to represent to your royal highness, that if redress doth not soon succeed to their complaints, it is to be feared, that in case the ships expected home should be taken like the others, want of means will force the merchants to give up trade.

For these reasons, being persuaded of your royal highness's clemency, they presume to claim the performance of the promises you were pleased to make them at their second audience; promises so agreeable, so full of tenderness and regard, and so much confided in by them, that they still expect to feel the effects of them. Accordingly they most humbly supplicate your royal highness to be graciously pleased to concur in the necessary measures for saving the commercial subjects of the republic from a calamity that is arrived at its utmost period; and to consider, that, if the restitution of the ships and cargoes be delayed, the one will go to decay, and the other be spoilt. They moreover conjure your royal highness to interpose your good offices in such a manner, that the English nation may make good the immense losses they have suffered, and abstain from doing them farther damage, to the hazard of totally ruining the republic.

The merchants cannot forbear laying before your royal highness the firm resolution taken by his highness the late Prince of Orange, your illustrious husband, of most laudable memory, to employ, had Heaven been pleased to prolong his days, every method to restore the trade which these provinces carry on by Hamburg, to its former flourishing state. They most humbly recommend to your royal highness this branch of trade which hath cost them such heavy impositions during so many years, and of which they will be able to continue the payment, when by the interposition of your royal highness, they shall be so happy as to enjoy her protection in this respect, which is not more necessary than ardently desired. If that should fail, the merchants must declare upon their honour, that the commerce of these provinces in general will be at an end; and that, notwithstanding their zeal for the welfare of the commonwealth, they will be unable to pay taxes much less necessary.

To these humble supplications, the merchants add the most sincere prayers for the prosperity of your royal highness's family, whom moreover they request to preserve their common rights and liberties, purchased at so dear a rate, and to maintain them against those who seek to make the republic suffer."

They write from Holland, that the princess gouvernante, when she went to the assembly of the States General, and delivered the famous me-

memorial of the merchants, expressed herself to the following purport.

"That she came not to the assembly to stir up the zeal of their high mightinesses for the preservation of their country, of which they had given evident proofs on every occasion; but to intreat them to take into their serious consideration, the augmentation of the land forces, which was so necessary in the present critical circumstances of the state, in order to guard its frontiers from insult. That with regard to the fourth deputation of the merchants, and the speech, of which she had delivered to them a copy, she had as yet made no remarks on it, only that it was not expressed in proper terms to bring things to an amicable conclusion, notwithstanding the assurances she had given the merchants. That she hoped, by her repeated sollicitations, to bring matters to an happy issue in England; that she therefore laid it before their high mightinesses, and left it to them to do in that affair as they should think proper: That the time became more and more urgent, for thinking of the safety of the republic: That if the equipment proposed by the merchants should be judged necessary, it ought immediately to be carried into execution jointly with the augmentation of the land forces, that the state might be put on a respectable footing by sea and land: That she therefore hoped that on her sollicitation, and that of the provinces of Guelders, Utrecht, Overyssel, and Groningen, their mightinesses would exhort the province of Holland to desist from its opposition to the said augmentation; and that all the confederates would unanimously consent to those two points, so essential at all times, but especially in the present circumstances."

Translation of a rescript sent by Count Kaunitz, prime minister to the empress queen, to the imperial ministers at the several courts of the empire.

"The unfortunate issue of the last campaign, gave the enemy a fine game to play. He had it in his power, from the beginning of spring, to form his plan of offensive operations as he thought best. We, for our part, could only have one principal object, namely, the putting our army on a proper footing, and endeavouring to make in time every other disposition for defence. This was accomplished, no labour or money being spared, to the great surprize of the enemy himself: in a few months our army was put on such a footing, that it did not hesitate to present itself before the enemy. At the same time a negotiation was commenced with Russia, to induce that court to march, even in the winter, a body of 30,000 men straight into Moravia. That court was so complaisant as to declare, that they would march a body of 30,000 fresh troops, either to be employed in Moravia, or to reinforce the imperial army of Russia, and so push the operations of the war with vigour. Their march was left to the option of the court of Vienna. Though at that time our own defensive operations were not brought to maturity, their imperial majesties, in consideration of the common cause, generously receded from their first demand, and signified that the reinforcement in question ought rather to join the imperial army of Russia, that it might continue to act vigorously.

The

The crown of France was at the ſame time required to ſend, purſuant to treaty, an auxiliary body of 24,000 men at leaſt. It is unneceſſary to mention the intereſting circumſtances of things at that preciſe period when this corps ought to have marched; and though, ſome time after this, it was very uncertain what turn the ſiege of Olmutz would take, the court of Vienna itſelf inſiſted upon poſtponing the march of thoſe ſuccours till another time; and laboured to concert new meaſures to divert the unforeſeen ſtorm, that threatened to burſt over the eſtates of the patriotic and well-intentioned members of the empire: a point which hath been effectually accompliſhed.

What was done on our ſide, during the ſiege of Olmutz, is generally known. The enemy retired through Bohemia: and ſcarce had we enjoyed the ſmiling proſpect of our hereditary ſtates being entirely delivered from them, when, after mature deliberation, a reſolution was taken at Vienna, by no means to march the imperial and royal army into Sileſia; but to carry it directly into Luſatia, as ſoon as the enemy, in abandoning Bohemia, ſhould direct his march that way. The principal motives which determined us to take this reſolution, were, among others, that by ſuch a motion our army drew nearer to thoſe of Ruſſia and Sweden; that it opened a communication with thoſe armies, and the enemy would be moleſted in the center of his poſition. Advice was immediately given to the Ruſſian generals of this reſolution, and they were left to draw up what plan of operations they ſhould think proper.

In the mean time the imperial army of Ruſſia, and the body of reſerve, had drawn near the eſtates of the enemy. In a council of war it was debated whether they ought to advance ſtraight to Francfort on the Oder, or towards Lower Sileſia, or penetrate by the Wartha into the New Marche. Several difficulties were ſtarted with regard to the two former projects, both with regard to the ſubſiſtence, and the neceſſity of preſerving a communication with the kingdom of Pruſſia. The third project was therefore made choice of, and executed; which the court of Vienna learnt with the greater ſatisfaction, as it had conceived ſome uneaſineſs concerning the march of the Ruſſian army towards Francfort on the Oder, or towards Sileſia; ſeeing that with regard to the firſt caſe, the corps of general Dohna was already aſſembled in that part; and on the other hand, the King of Pruſſia in retiring from Bohemia, was marching to Sileſia; ſo that he would have it in his power at once to employ his whole force joined to Dohna's corps, againſt the Ruſſian army; and this army, by marching towards Landſberg, would be removed from the Pruſſians, and would moreover have the Oder and the Wartha before it.

The firſt news of the part taken by the Ruſſian generals was received at Vienna, at the time that Marſhal Daun was already advanced with his army towards Gorlitz, and almoſt at the ſame time that undoubted intelligence was received from ſeveral quarters, that the King of Pruſſia in perſon was in full march with a body of 15 or 16,000 men to join General Dohna, and on the 12th of Auguſt, arrived near Lignitz.

It

It was the lefs poffible to prevent or hinder this march, as the enemy had, through his own country, a much fhorter road, than we had, and could fcarce be at any lofs for fubfiftence; that, befides the Ruffian army, by its march to Landfberg, was removed farther from our army, which had on its flank, on the fide of Silefia, an army of 30,000 of the enemy's troops.

In thefe circumftances, the following points were taken into confideration. Whether, for the good of the common caufe, the marfhal ought not to march forward with his whole army, either towards Berlin, or towards Francfort on the Oder; or whether he ought to direct his operations towards Silefia, or towards Saxony. It was confidered that the firft of thefe projects could be regarded as a *coup de main* only, and by no means as a decifive blow: and there were the fewer motives to follow it, as it was eafy to imagine that the King of Pruffia would give battle to the Ruffians before we could, for want of fubfiftence, get into the Lower Lufatia with our whole force.

It feemed at the fame time highly improper to transfer the theatre of war into Silefia, becaufe nothing effential would thereby be gained, and it would give to the troops of the enemy that were left in Silefia, an opportunity of taking an advantageous camp near fome fortrefs in that dutchy, and fo protract our operations. The court, therefore, as well as Marfhal Daun, thought it would be beft to march toward Saxony. It was thought that by taking this ftep effential advantages would be gained, or that at leaft the enemy would be forced, by the apprehenfion of fuffering a very fenfible lofs, to bring all his forces into Saxony, againft the imperial and royal army; and the combined army, and by that means the Ruffians and Swedes, as well as the bodies of forces left on the frontiers of Bohemia and Moravia, under the generals Harfch and De Ville, would have their hands much more free, to act efficacioufly.

The real advantage that muft refult from all this, doubtlefs confifted in diflodging the army under Prince Henry, and delivering Drefden and the greateft part of Saxony.

To attain this important end, M. Daun's firft project was to advance with his whole army ftraight to Meiffen, there crofs the Elbe, and at once march up to the enemy, at the fame time that he fhould be attacked by the combined army, and thus deprived of an opportunity of throwing himfelf into Drefden. But at that time, that is to fay, on the 3d of September, Sonneftein was not yet in our poffeffion, and the enemy had taken fuch an advantageous pofition, oppofite to the combined army, that it was thought fcarce feafible, and highly dangerous, for this to make the firft attack; and yet unlefs it did fo, Prince Henry would ftill have it in his power to throw himfelf into Drefden, whilft the imperial and royal army paffed the Elbe near Meiffen, and to maintain himfelf on this fide of the river, and open a communication with the king.

Marfhal Daun did not think it confiftent with the dignity of arms, or the intereft of the fervice, to make ufelefs marches, and to take infignificant pofitions. Nor did he think it prudent to remove to a greater

greater diſtance, either from the Ruſſians or the Swedes, or even from Luſatia or Sileſia; he therefore ſuddenly took a reſolution to draw near to the combined army, and to direct his march towards Stolpen; and this the rather, as the city of Dreſden could not be attacked in form, and as the news of an entire defeat (as it was falſely called) of the Ruſſian army, was received at the ſame time. It was therefore very natural to imagine, that the King of Pruſſia would haſten back with a conſiderable army, and render the ſiege of Dreſden of no effect.

As ſoon as the imperial and royal army had fixed its camp at Stolpen, the field marſhal employed himſelf in reconnoitring the poſition of the enemy, and in forming new plans to give him an effectual blow. On the 9th he held a conference with the Prince of Deux-Ponts, at which he propoſed a deſign, a little too bold perhaps; namely, that this prince ſhould attack the enemy next day; that for this end he (the marſhal) would approach that very night to the Elbe, paſs it between the enemy's camp and Dreſden, laying bridges between two fires at a ſmall diſtance from each other; and carry over his whole army; attack the enemy, and cut him off from Dreſden. The Prince of Deux-Ponts entered wholly into this plan; only he found it impoſſible to make the attack next day, becauſe the time was too ſhort to make the neceſſary diſpoſitions, call in the detached poſts, and employ them where neceſſary.

Though the marſhal inſiſted with the more vehemence on the neceſſity of making haſte, as we had received ſure accounts, that the king was on his march with a conſiderable body, and there was not a moment to loſe, he ſaw himſelf forced, however, by the obſtacles juſt mentioned, to defer the attack till the 11th. It was agreed therefore, that in the night between the 10th and the 11th, the imperial and royal army ſhould approach to the Elbe, and lay bridges over it, that the combined army ſhould advance in order of battle, and make thoſe movements on the flanks which ſhould be deemed proper; and that at day-break it ſhould venture to make the attack. This plan of operations was executed, excepting the attack; for Marſhal Daun received the ſame day, the 10th, certain intelligence that the king was arrived near Dreſden with a conſiderable body, and that the reſt of the enemy's troops were not far off. On this account, it was, after mature deliberation, judged to be an enterpriſe too raſh to attempt to paſs ſuch a river as the Elbe, between the army of Prince Henry, and the city of Dreſden, and that at a time when there was another army behind them; that in caſe of any misfortune the imperial and royal army would be expoſed to total ruin. The marſhal, agreeably to his uſual foreſight and experience in war, came over to this opinion, and ſaw himſelf obliged to ſignify to the prince of Deux-Ponts, even the very night in which the attack was to have been made, that difficulties had occurred in relation to the attack which had been concerted, and even in ſome meaſure begun.

Thus one principal project, namely, the ſpeedy expulſion of Prince Henry, failed. We could not, however, have hindered him from joining the king a little further down the river, and from oppoſing the

the ſiege of Dreſden. But, on the other hand, we obtained the whole of the ſecond principal object, that is to ſay, the drawing the enemy's forces into Saxony, and accordingly he brought into Saxony the greateſt part of thoſe troops he had in Sileſia, as well as a numerous body from General Dohna's army; and thereby he has left himſelf more and more expoſed in other parts.

Such is the true plan of the preſent campaign; and though the iſſue of it be not as yet intirely ſatisfactory, and ſuch as might be deſired, the imperial court enjoys, at leaſt, the ſincere ſatisfaction of reflecting, that according to the change of circumſtances, it inſtantly took the moſt vigorous reſolutions, and that it was never deficient in any thing that might contribute to the good of the common cauſe, and that it is ſtill making at preſent preparations from which it may hope for the moſt happy conſequences. I expect to be ſoon able to give you an account of them, being, &c".

Declaration delivered the 12th of June to all the foreign miniſters at Peterſburgh.

"The empreſs having engaged in the preſent war, in order to ſuccour her allies, has their intereſts as much at heart as her own: her majeſty therefore could not, without ſome concern, hear of the convention concluded the 11th of April laſt in London, between the King of Great Britain and the King of Pruſſia, as the Britiſh court thereby pretends not only to make the war kindled up by that prince her own quarrel, but, in all appearance, a firm reſolution is alſo taken to give no ſatiſfaction to the powers ſo unjuſtly attacked and ſo grievouſly wronged, and to carry on the war to the laſt extremity. 'Tis doubtleſs on this principle, that the continual devaſtations exerciſed by the King of Pruſſia, even in ſome neutral ſtates, are varniſhed over with the name of defence, or ſupport of the liberties of the Germanic body; that the oppoſition made by the empreſs queen againſt a total invaſion of her hereditary dominions, is termed a dangerous deſign upon the proteſtant religion; and, in fine, that the aſſiſtance given to that princeſs by her allies, is repreſented as an aggreſſion againſt the empire.

It is true, that in the ſaid convention her imperial majeſty of all the Ruſſias is not mentioned by name. But the King of Pruſſia having already publiſhed laſt year, as ſoon as the Ruſſian troops entered Pruſſia, a particular declaration againſt her majeſty (a ſtep which he did not take againſt France when her army entered his territories, though it was notorious that ſhe, as well as Ruſſia, had no other deſign but to ſuccour their allies) he has thereby plainly ſhewn that he endeavours if poſſible, to make the war waged in his German dominions common to the whole empire; and that, on the contrary, by entirely excluding Pruſſia, he ſtrives to perſuade neutral princes that he is actuated by nothing but the intereſt of the empire, and that it is only in this object he deſires their concurrence. As to the conſervation of Pruſſia perhaps he thinks himſelf ſingly ſtrong enough to make ſure of it; or that, in ſacrificing it, he ſeeks to to represent the part the empress takes in this war as a matter quite foreign to the common cause, and no way connected with it, to the end, that the allies may less mind it, and in return, that his party may appear the stronger for it. But besides that this artifice cannot impose upon any body; the empress hopes that, with the help of God, her troops will soon enter the provinces of the King of Prussia that make part of the German empire.

And as on this occasion one must expect to meet with all the false imputations, which the empress's allies are obliged to bear, as if the empire was invaded, its liberties infringed, and the protestant religion menaced; her majesty declares in the most solemn manner, that having taken part in the present war only by virtue of her anterior engagements, and after her reiterated declarations, that she would not look with indifference on any invasion that should be made by the King of Prussia, in the dominions of her allies, but would assist, with all her power, the party attacked, did not produce the effect that was hoped from them; and considering the firm resolution taken by the enemies of her allies to continue an unjust war, she also becomes more and more steady in he. design, as well as in her sincere desire to act unanimously with them, and to assist them efficaciously and vigorously, in order to procure just satisfaction to the parties aggrieved, and to settle the general peace on terms that may be productive of a solid and lasting tranquillity. That, towards attaining so salutary an end, the troops of her imperial majesty will endeavour to penetrate in to the King of Prussia's German dominions as far as possible: that every one may persuade themselves beforehand, that on this occasion there will be no violation of the laws and liberties of Germany; but, on the contrary, that even the inhabitants of the enemy's countries shall experience, each in their station, as far as circumstances may permit, the effects of her imperial majesty's benignity, as appears already by the permission she has given for carrying on a free trade, even in the places that may become the seat of war: That as on the occasion of the new motions the Russian troops are going to make in favour of the empress's allies, they will be indispensibly obliged to pass through the territories of the republic of Poland, her imperial majesty's renews the assurances she has more than once given, that neither in this occasional passage, nor in any other circumstance, will they ever dream of violating the rights and liberties of the republic, whose tranquillity will ever be dear to the empress: in fine, that whatever may be the always uncertain events of war, her imperial majesty can beforehand affirm, that her fortitude shall not be shaken by them; that she never will recede from the engagements she has entered into with her allies, nor to treat separately about a truce of peace; but that her majesty will faithfully and punctually perform whatever she has once promised and declared."

Translation of the brief, which the pope addressed to the empress queen, when he conferred upon her

her the title of Apoſtolical Queen of Hungary.

"The Roman pontifs, whom we have ſucceeded notwithſtanding our want of merit, wiſely neglected not, greatly to their honour, amidſt different regulations, paternally to diſtinguiſh and load with favours, as occaſion offered, the countries ſituated on the frontiers of the perpetual enemies of the Chriſtian name, and always regarded thoſe countries as the bulwarks, which alone could ſecure Chriſtianity from hoſtile invaſions. We have regarded in the ſame light, the moſt flouriſhing kingdom of Hungary, poſſeſſed by our dearly beloved daughter in Chriſt; which, both by its ſituation and the bravery of the people, is the moſt proper for the propagation of the Chriſtian luſtre and name. All the world knows how the noble Hungarians have contributed, by their valour, to the extending and defending the Chriſtian religion; and how often, and with what ſucceſs, they have fought againſt its hereditary enemy. Who knows not the ſignal and almoſt incredible victories which they have gained, when Chriſtendom was in danger of being totally ruined and overwhelmed?

Theſe actions are generally known. They are recorded in the moſt authentic annals, and will be tranſmitted down to the moſt diſtant poſterity. Mean while we ought to call to mind St. Stephen, that valiant ſovereign of Hungary, whoſe memory is precious to the church; which has been inſcribed in the catalogue of the ſaints, and whom we particularly reverence. We talk, even in theſe parts (to the honour of the Hungarian nation) of his virtues, his piety, and his magnanimity. The princes who have ſucceeded him, have exerted themſelves at all times to imitate his virtuous example.

No wonder, then, that the ſovereign pontifs, having regard to the ſincere and unſhaken attachment of the princes and kings of Hungary to the catholic faith, and calling to mind the ſervice, they have done to the holy ſee, have, from time to time, heightened their merit, and granted them particular privileges. Among other privileges, their kings enjoyed that of having a croſs carried before them by a biſhop, when they appeared in public on ſolemn occaſions, as the moſt eminent ſign of their apoſtleſhip; a particular conceſſion of the holy ſee, which would thereby ſhew that the Hungarian nation, and its kings, gloried only in the croſs of our Saviour Chriſt, and have always been wont to fight and overcome for the catholic faith, under this holy banner.

The kings of Hungary have alſo, at divers times, acquired the privilege of being decorated and honoured with the glorious and magnificent title of Apoſtolic kings, though the true origin of this cuſtom, and the authenticity of ſuch a high prerogative, cannot be preciſely diſcovered.

We, for our part, though we cannot manifeſt the true ſpirit of our predeceſſors, have, nevertheleſs, made it our conſtant endeavours to follow their ſentiments. We cannot, we imagine, more advantageouſly diſtinguiſh the beginning of our pontificate, than by conferring all poſſible honours, and the utmoſt ſplendor on thoſe princes and kings whom we know to be attached to the holy ſee; and therefore we have thought proper to contribute particularly to the exaltation of your Apoſtolic majeſty, and of your kingdom of Hungary. We cannot do this more effectually, than by confirming, as far as in us lies, by our papal authority and power, this apoſtolical denomination. We therefore, of our own proper motion, certain knowledge, and plenitude of apoſtolic authority, inveſt, honour, and decorate your majeſty, as Queen of Hungary, and your ſucceſſors in that kingdom, with the title and denomination of Apoſtolic Queen; willing that all, and every one, ſhall name and acknowledge you, and your ſucceſſors, for Apoſtolic Queen.

Receive then, dearly beloved daughter in Chriſt, this title joyfully; not, however, as a mark of that power, which the vanity of the age, and a deceitful ambition may invent, but as a ſymbol of a chriſtian ſubmiſſion to Jeſus Chriſt, by whom alone the true glory of your kingdom can ſubſiſt for ever. This title you receive as a teſtimony or recompence of your zeal for the propagation of the catholic religion; a zeal, which hath been tranſmitted to you by a long ſeries of anceſtors, which you have kept up, and which increaſes in you more and more. Tranſmit this title of honour and ſplendor to the beſt and beſt beloved of ſons, that ſon who ſhall poſſeſs the whole glory of his mother's inheritance. Receive this brief as the pledge and the firſt-fruits of the paternal love and affection, which we bear towards your Apoſtolic majeſty; and we give you, dearly beloved daughter in Chriſt Jeſus, moſt tenderly our apoſtolic benediction.

Rome, Auguſt 25."

Tranſlation of the inſtructions given by the States of Courland and Semigallia to Mr. Schopping, whom they ſent as their deputy to Warſaw, about the election of a new duke.

"1. He ſhall, with the moſt profound reſpect, aſſure his majeſty, our moſt gracious king and lord paramount, of the inviolable obedience and fidelity of theſe dutchies, and moſt humbly recommend them to his majeſty's paternal benevolence and protection.

2. He ſhall moſt reſpectfully beſeech his majeſty, and the moſt illuſtrious republic, to procure the releaſe of the unfortunate duke and his family.

3. His excellency Count Malachowſki, high chancellor of the crown, having written to the ſtates, that it was in vain to hope any longer for the releaſe of that duke and his male iſſue; and M. Simolin, miniſter-reſident from her majeſty the empreſs of all the Ruſſias in theſe dutchies, having declared and confirmed the ſame thing, by order of his court, adding, that her imperial majeſty of all the Ruſſias, would be glad to ſee his royal highneſs Prince Charles of Poland elected Duke of Courland; and her imperial Czariſh majeſty having given the like inſtructions to her miniſter at Warſaw; the deputy muſt alſo repreſent to the high chancellor of the crown, that, according to the

the precise terms of the constitutions of our government, the assembly of the states cannot attempt any thing against the investiture of the dutchies; and that so long as the king and republic do not declare the seat to be vacant, we must, according to our laws, continue to pray for our unfortunate lord and his family.

4. But, whereas his royal highness Prince Charles has gained the veneration of all hearts by his great qualities, and his gracious deportment, both in going to and returning from Petersburgh, the deputy is to make known the inclination of the states for this prince, in case the seat of the dutchies be declared vacant and intimate that they should deem themselves very happy if his royal highness would make profession of the confession of Augsburgh, and thereby impower them humbly to beseech his majesty to grant him the sovereignty of these dutchies.

5. This being supposed, then, if his royal highness will be pleased, according to custom, previously to secure to the country, all its civil and religious rights, the deputy shall declare that the states will not hesitate a moment to take advantage of the dispositions of the empress of all the Russias in favour of this prince, and will entreat her to grant him the sovereignty of these dutchies.

6. But since, according to the compacts of subjection, the guaranties of religion, and other documents, these dutchies must have as heretofore a Teutonic magistracy of the confession of Augsburgh; as no change can be made in this respect, without failing in the assurances given and confirmed upon oath; and as Gothard, first Duke of Courland, did keep to himself, in quality of grand master, the whole administration of ecclesiastic affairs, which the protestant princes have also done, in consequence of the compacts of subjection, whose authority ought to be immutable, according to the constitutions of the government; the deputy shall constantly and most strenuously insist on this object, most humbly representing the firm persuasion of the states that his majesty and the illustrious republic will take into consideration the said assurances given to this country by his majesty's predecessors, and will preserve the Teutonic magistracy which it has had ever since its subjection to the republic, viz. a prince of the confession of Augsburgh.

7. As for the rest, the states will always continue with the most inviolable loyalty to live under the gracious supremacy of his majesty and the illustrious republic of Poland, and never will they wish for a duke that is not agreeable to their gracious lord paramount. This is what the deputy shall declare; and he is desired to conform exactly to his instructions, without deviating therefrom in any one point. Whereupon we wish him a good journey, and a happy issue to his negotiation."

[These instructions are signed by Christopher Frederick Sacken, governor; Otho Christopher von der Hoon, chancellor; Henry Christian Offenberg, burgrave; Francis George Frank, marshal; all members of the great council; and also by twenty-five deputies of the parishes of Courland.

 The

The dyet of Poland breaking up without settling any one national affair, the Courlanders are just where they were before; for though the Empress of Russia and King of Poland may declare the seat of their duke to be vacant, the republic must concur in this verdict before it can be filled up; and should these two sovereigns attempt by force to carry an election in Courland in favour of Prince Charles, it might possibly occasion an insurrection in Poland. Besides, the change of religion required for qualifying him to be a candidate, is another bar to his preferment: But this might, perhaps, be got over with help of a *dispensation from* Rome, allowing him to keep covenants with his subjects only till he should be able to break them.]

Translation of the Universalia issued by the King of Poland, for the assembling of a general dyet of the states at Warsaw.

"Augustus III. by the grace of God, King of Paland, Grand Duke of Lithuania, &c.

In the horrid calamities which have so long afflicted our hereditary dominions, the happiness and prosperity of the republic is the greatest alleviation we can find to the grief with which we are penetrated.

In 1756, about the time that was fixed for the ordinary dyet, the whole force of the enemy came and fell upon our hereditary dominions, and at one instant presented us with a prospect of all the misfortunes that were afterwards to ensue to that unhappy country.

This idea, painful as it was, would not so deeply have wounded our paternal breast, if the army of an enterprizing neighbour, which surrounded us on all sides, had not prevented us from coming to you at the time appointed for the assembling of the states of the republic; for the sight of that assembly, and of a people that have been ever dear to us, would have assuaged our other sorrows.

The tenor of the laws empowers us to convoke the general dyet this year at Warsaw, in order to treat there of the several necessities of the republic; therefore waving the consideration of the toil attached to this obligation, and animated only with the pleasing hopes of the public good, which, through your unanimity, may perhaps result from thence to the country, we fix the said ordinary dyet at Warsaw on the 2d of October 1758; the ante-comitial dyet at the usual place on the 21st of August; and that of the generality for the 18th of the same month.

As in former dyets we never proposed any thing relating to our own private interests, or those of our royal family, so we now solemnly protest, that we have no such views in this, and that we are very far from seeking our own advantage to the prejudice of Poland, by wanting to involve it in the present fatal troubles of the rest of Europe.

It is by so upright a conduct that we hope to silence all those, who, by secret and artful insinuations, endeavour to destroy the confidence that subsists between ourselves and the states of the republic, and render suspicious our most salutary measures for your welfare, that they may perpetuate disorder in the country, over-

overturn the basis of public deliberations, and on the ruins of Poland erect trophies of glory to foreign nations, whose interest it may be to foment and keep up these divisions.

Zeal for the public good alone, the motive that has always influenced our actions hitherto, will direct and animate all our deliberations at the approaching dyet. And without insisting now upon any particular propositions, we are ready even to go contrary to natural subordination, in conforming ourselves, though we are the father of the country, to the desires of its dear children, provided that, laying aside every other sentiment, the three estates of the republic will unanimously concur in every thing that shall be found for the good of the country."

Memorial concerning the destroying of the suburb of Dresden.

"Marshal Daun having taken advantage of the king's absence, who was gone to fight the Russians, to fall upon Saxony with all his forces, in the month of July last, the army of the empire having entered it on another side by Peterswalde, Count Schmettau governor of Dresden, thought that place in such imminent danger, that he found himself indispensibly obliged to take every possible measure to guard against a surprize, and to hinder the Austrians from carrying the place by a *coup de main*. An enterprize of this nature would have been the more easy, as most of the houses of the suburbs, from the gate of Pirna, to that of Wilsdorff, absolutely command the body of the town, both by their prodigious height, being six or seven stories high, and by their proximity to the rampart. From this consideration Count Schmettau caused it to be declared to the court by M. de Bose, chief cup-bearer, that as soon as the enemy should make a shew of attacking Dresden, he should find himself under the disagreeable necessity of burning the suburbs, and that for that end he had just put combustible matters in the highest houses, and those next to the rampart, that his orders for that purpose might be speedily executed, whenever the reasons of war obliged him to issue them in his own defence. The same declaration was made to the magistrates, the governor having sent for the burgo-master to come to him. The court and the city earnestly implored, that this misfortune might be averted from the inhabitants; but the governor insisted that it would be indispensibly necessary to come to that extremity, if the enemy themselves would pay no respect to the royal residence; and caused every thing to be got ready for the execution of his threats.

Meanwhile, the city, as well as the states of Saxony, who were then assembled at Dresden, sent a deputation to M. de Borcke, the king's minister, to intreat him to intercede with the governor in their behalf. M. de Borcke, after conferring with Count Schmettau, answered them, that it depended on the court and the city themselves, to prevent the attacking of Dresden; but that if the Austrians should attack it, it would be impossible to spare the suburbs, the houses of which commanded the rampart, the governor having exprefs orders to defend himfelf till the laft extremity. The minifter at the fame time pointed out to them the imminent danger to which the city and the caftle, and even the royal family, would be expofed, if he fhould be forced to come to that extremity, as the fire of the fuburbs could not fail, without a miracle, to reach the town, and make terrible havock: He at the fame time conjured the deputies of the ftates, to ufe their utmoft endeavours to divert the ftorm, and not to confider the governor's declaration as a vain threat, for he could affure them upon his honour, that upon the firing of the firft cannon againft the town, they would fee the fuburbs on fire.

Marfhal Daun happily changed his refolution upon the king's approach, who was returning victorious from Zorndorff; and the governor of Drefden, yielding to the intreaties of the inhabitants, ordered the combuftible matters with which he had filled the houfes to be removed. But Marfhal Daun returning a fecond time into Saxony, appeared again, namely on the 6th of November, within fight of Drefden, with a formidable army. This army having made a motion on the 7th, and taken a camp on this fide Lockowitz, the governor, who could no longer doubt that his views were againft the capital, caufed the combuftible matters to be quickly replaced in the houfes of the fuburbs which furrounded the town ditch, and command the rampart. The court was immediately informed of it by M. de Bofe, the chief cupbearer, whom Count Schmettau charged to reprefent again to his court, that if the enemy's army fhould approach the fuburbs, he would that inftant fet fire to them. It was anfwered, that as the court, its hands being tied, was obliged to acquiefce in all, and wait the laft extremities, the governor was free to do whatever he thought he could anfwer.

The fame day (Nov. 8.) at noon, the enemy's advanced troops attacked the huffars and independent battalions which were pofted at Streiffen and Gruene-Wiefe. This fkirmifh continued till night came on, and made the governor judge that it might have confequences, as the enemy might eafily repulfe thofe advanced pofts, and enter pell-mell with them into the fuburb. He therefore detached next day (the 9th) in the morning colonel Itzenplitz with 700 men, and fome pieces of cannon, and pofted them himfelf in the redoubts that furrounded the fuburb, that, in cafe of need, they might fupport the huffars and the independent battalions. About noon he fent for the magiftrates of the town; put them in mind of what he had faid to them in the month of July laft; and told them, that the enemy having evidently a real defign againft Drefden, he gave them notice for the laft time, that on the firft appearance of an Auftrian in the fuburbs, they would be fet on fire. The magiftrates anfwered by only fhrugging their fhoulders, and deploring the misfortune of their fellow citizens. The governor told them, that they had nothing to do but to apply to the court, who alone could avert the calamity.

About noon the Auftrian vanguard attacked the advanced pofts; re-

repelled the huffars, whofe number was too fmall to make refiftance, and even forced them, as well as Monjou's independent battalion, to quit the great garden and gain the fuburbs. The enemy immediately attacked the fmall redoubts where 700 men of the garrifon had been pofted, forced three of them, and penetrated to Zinzendorf-houfe, and even made fuch progrefs, that an Auftrian foldier was killed on the draw-bridge of Pirna gate, and fome cannon were obliged to be fired on Zinzendorf-houfe to drive out the Auftrians. During this attack, the enemy's cannon played into the town, and feveral fix-pounders fell in the arfenal, in the Prince's hotel, and in the houfes of Loos, Mnifceck, and Counfellor Fritfch. One ball even fell before the houfe of Marfhal Count Rutowfky.

Notwithftanding this declared attack againft the town and fuburbs, no houfe was yet on fire; a plain proof that there was little inclination *to proceed to that extremity*. The cannon of the rampart forced the enemy to retire; and before night even all the redoubts of which they had got poffeffion were retaken.

Mean while the army of General Itzenplitz marched through the town, paffed the Elbe, and encamped under the cannon of the new town; and General Meyer was ordered to defend the fuburbs with his independent battalions, and four others, and to fet fire to them after giving notice to the inhabitants. One of this general's officers told the governor, about midnight, that he heard men at work, and that the enemy feemed to be erecting batteries and planting cannon; accordingly, all who were fent out beyond the barriers to reconnoitre, had a fmart fire to fuftain. Thefe preparations, added to the preceding affair, giving room to think that at day-break the enemy would make a vigorous attack, and make themfelves mafters of the fuburbs, into which the cannon of the town could not difpute their entrance, by reafon of the height of the houfes, the governor had no other meafures to take but thofe which the intereft of his mafter, reafons of war, and his own honour, dictated. The fignal was given by General Meyer, and immediately, at three in the morning of the 10th, the greateft part of the fuburbs of Pirna, the houfes adjoining to the ditch, and two in the fuburb of Wilfdorff, were in flames. The fix battalions with the 700 men, entered the town by the three gates, which were immediately barricaded; and after fix in the morning there was not a Pruffian in the fuburbs, as the inhabitants of the town can teftify. The ftory of the *frequent fallies of the Pruffians* to light up what was not yet confumed, is void of all foundation. It is likewife abfolutely falfe that the inhabitants had not timely notice given them. Thefe atrocious calumnies are fufficiently confuted by the annexed certificates of the chief cup-bearer de Bofe, and of the magiftrates. As to the red-hot bullets fired upon the inhabitants, the lighted waggon, the children thrown into the fire, thefe are fo many horrible lies, which will fall of themfelves, when the aforefaid certificates of the court, the magiftrates, and the judges of the fuburbs are feen. The order given to the burghers to remain quiet in their houfes was intimated only to the magiftrates of the city, in the month

month of July; and not to thofe of the fuburbs; and there was nothing in this but what is ufual. What hath been faid to the contrary, is, in fhort, fo falfe, that the court of Drefden was pleafed to thank the governor for the good order he caufed to be obferved during thofe troubles; as will appear by the annexed letter of De Bofe the chief cup-bearer.

It only remains that we fhould fay fomething of the meffages that paffed between Marfhal Daun and Count Schmettau, by the intervention of Colonel Sawoifky. After the firft compliments, M. de Sawoifky told the governor, that Marfhal Daun was extremely furprifed at the burning of the fuburbs; that he (Sawoifky) was defired to enquire whether it was by order that this was done in a royal refidence, which was a thing unheard of among chriftians; and that he hoped the city of Drefden would not be treated in the fame manner. The marfhal then made his compliments to the court; and added, that the governor fhould be refponfible in his perfon for what had been done, or for what might be done, againft this royal refidence.

The colonel received for anfwer, in prefence of lieutenant-general Itzenplitz, that the governor had the honour to be known to the marfhal; that he had orders to defend the town to the laft man; that his excellency was too well acquainted with war, to be ignorant that the deftruction of the fuburbs, which the marfhal had attacked, was according to rule: that as to what concerned the town, it depended upon his excellency, fince if he attacked it, the governor would defend himfelf from houfe to houfe, and from ftreet to ftreet; and that the whole infantry of the army was ready to defend the city.

On the 11th, the governor having learnt from feveral burghers of the fuburbs, who, at their own requeft, had been brought into the town with their effects by water, that the enemy had thrown into the flames, or maffacred without pity, fome defencelefs people belonging to the Pruffian army, who had remained behind, particularly a furgeon; fent at noon Captain Collas with a trumpet to the marfhal, with orders to tell him, that his excellency's well-known character did not permit it to be believed that fuch cruelties were committed by his order; and therefore to demand to whom they were to be afcribed: that as to the deftruction of the fuburbs, Colonel Sawoifky had already carried an anfwer on that head to the marfhal, but that this opportunity was taken to declare to his excellency, that if he defired to fave the reft of the fuburbs, he muft hinder his troops from appearing in them; that no body had the prefervation of the town and fuburbs more at heart than the governor, as far as was confiftent with his duty, and his honour: that the houfes would not have been fet on fire, had not the troops of his army forced their way into the fuburbs, and even fired feveral cannon into the town (which M. Daun pretended not to know; faying, that it had been done without his orders;) and that the combuftible matters were ready to confume what was left of the fuburb, in cafe his troops fhould again enter it. The court took advantage of of this meſſage to aſk a paſſport from M. Daun for bringing ſome ſheep and fire-wood into the town.

His excellency anſwered to theſe three heads, That he had no irregular troops with him; and that he had forbid any perſon of his army to approach the ſuburbs; that he did not apprehend any exceſſes had been committed; but in caſe there had, he deſired to know the number of the perſons maſſacred; that he was the more aſtoniſhed at thoſe complaints, as he never ſuffered ſuch diſorders; that he abhorred them, and that perhaps the burghers had no foundation for what they had ſaid. As to the ſuburbs, M. Daun anſwered, that he would not ſuffer rules to be preſcribed to him; that it depended upon him to ſend troops into the ſuburbs, as he ſhould judge proper, and the governor might do as he pleaſed; but that he hoped that in the mean while no more families would be made wretched; and that he had forbid his troops, on ſevere penalties, to enter the ſuburbs to pillage. As to the demand made by the court, he anſwered, that he would particularly attend to it; and aſſured them of his profound reſpects.

On the 12th his excellency ſent an officer with a permit to deliver the ſheep and fire-wood for the court, which were to be brought into the town by Pruſſians; and Captain Collas was ſent to regulate this affair. The captain, in paſſing through the ſuburbs, ſhewed the lieutenant ſent by M. Daun the maroders of his troops, both foot and huſſars, who exceeded 200; and the officer promiſed to make a report of it to the marſhal. The reſt of the time, to the 26th, that the enemy's army retired, paſſed in amazing tranquillity.

C. Count de Schmettau.

Dreſden, Dec. 5, 1758.

No. I. Letter from M. de Boſe, chief cup-bearer, to Count Schmettau.

I have the honour to acquaint your excellency, in anſwer to what you wrote me this day, I muſt own that ever ſince you had the government of Dreſden, I informed you of all that his royal highneſs charged me to tell you in his name, and I have likewiſe reported to his highneſs your excellency's anſwers.

As to the firſt point, I alſo remember very well that your excellency charged me, in the month of July, to repreſent in your name to his royal highneſs, that if Marſhal Daun ſhould attack the city, you muſt ſet fire to the ſuburbs, particularly the houſes that adjoined to the ditch; into which houſes your excellency immediately ordered combuſtibles to be put. I alſo remember, that upon the ſollicitations which his royal highneſs made, by me, to your excellency, you ordered them to be removed when Marſhal Daun retired; and of this alſo I made an humble report.

It is alſo true, that when Marſhal Daun was at Lockowitz, on the 8th of November laſt, your excellency charged me to acquaint his royal highneſs in your name, that if the marſhal ſhould approach nearer the town and attack it, you ſhould be obliged to burn the ſuburbs, and the houſes adjoining to the town ditch. Although I made ſeveral remonſtrances to your excellency from the court, you declared,

clared, that you was ordered by the king your maſter to defend yourſelf to the laſt extremity, and that you could not change your meaſures, unleſs Marſhal Daun ſhould be prevailed with not to attack the town. To which I anſwered, in his royal highneſs's name, That he knew nothing of Marſhal Daun's deſigns; that he could not intermeddle in the operations of war, and would conſequently be obliged to endure what he could not hinder.

Laſtly, it is well known that your excellency, during the fire, took every poſſible meaſure in the town to prevent thoſe exceſſes and diſorders, which might have been apprehended; and his royal highneſs charged me to return you his thanks for it. I have the honour to be, &c.

Joachim Frederick de Boſe.

Dec. 4, 1758.

No. II. Certificate of the Magiſtrates of Dreſden.

In conſequence of orders received from his excellency Count Schmettau, lieutenant-general and governor, we certify what we know concerning the burning of the ſuburbs, viz.

That it was about the end of July when combuſtibles were put into the new built houſes on the counterſcarp; that upon the repreſentation made thereupon to his excellency, by the court and the magiſtrates, he anſwered, that our court itſelf had given its conſent to it; and that if the enemy did not approach he would not cauſe the houſes to be burnt. Though we have ſince heard that thoſe combuſtibles were taken away, no perſon ever told us, nor have we ever heard that any one ſuffered the leaſt damage thereby.

On the 2d of November, at noon, his excellency ordered the burgomaſters and magiſtrates to come to him, and told us, that he was commanded by the king, his maſter, to defend the place to the laſt extremity; that though the new works were ſufficiently provided with men, he ſhould be obliged, if the enemy ſhould force them, to ſet fire to the houſes, and had already given orders accordingly. Though we made the moſt preſſing intreaties that he would ſpare the town, repreſenting that it did not belong to the magiſtrates, but to his majeſty the King of Poland, and that it was the reſidence of an elector; his excellency anſwered, that he would not alter his meaſures, were it the reſidence of the emperor himſelf; that it was not our fault; and that we might apply to our court, who had drawn thither the enemy. Upon which he ſent us away, and would not hear our remonſtrances.

Being returned to the town-houſe, we apprized the judges of the Fiſhmongers and Ram quarters, of the danger with which the ſuburbs were threatened; we enjoined them to give notice to the judges of the other quarters to repair to the town-houſe; and we told thoſe who attended there, that their ſuburbs were in the greateſt danger of being ſet on fire; that they muſt warn their burghers to be on their guard; to provide themſelves with inſtruments againſt the fire, and mutually to aſſiſt each other in caſe of any misfortune, ſince no aſſiſtance could be expected from the town. We have heard, ſince the

the misfortune happened, that this order was executed.

This fire burnt 252 houses of the jurisdiction of the magistrates, which have been entirely consumed, and two more were much damaged. Thirty-one houses of the jurisdiction of the Bailiwic were likewise intirely burnt down.

Two persons were burnt to death, two killed, three hurt by the fire, and two wounded by the soldiers.

We never heard, in any shape, of a waggon full of goods which they were endeavouring to save, and which it was pretended was covered with combustibles, and so set on fire; nor of ninety persons said to have perished at the Hart, nor of the Austrian troops, who, it is pretended, assisted in extinguishing the flames. Dresden, Dec. 4, 1758.

(L.S.) The Magistrates of Dresden.

No. III. Certificate of the Judges of the suburb of Dresden.

We the judges of the suburb of Dresden, certify and attest, that at the time of the calamity that hath just happened, things passed in this manner.

1. In the month of July combustibles were placed on the counterscarp, and removed in the month of August following, without doing the least damage.

2. They were replaced there a second time on the 7th of November, about six in the evening. On the 7th, about three in the afternoon, the magistrates ordered all the judges to attend them. Accordingly Simon Steltzner, judge; John Christian Dittritch, alderman; John Michael Faber, and John Christian Kretschmar, judges, attended, and were told (being enjoined at the same time to acquaint the other judges with it) to provide the houses with water, to give notice to the landlords, and keep the pumps ready, and endeavour to assist one another, because, if any misfortune should happen, the people of the town could not come to our assistance, nor could we go to theirs; and of this we informed all the burghers.

3. On the 8th and 9th the Austrian army approached the town; and on the 9th the Austrian hussars forced their way to the suburb of Pirna and to Zinzindorf-house.

4. On the 10th, at two in the morning, fire was set to the quarters of Pirna, Ram, and Wilsdorff, which consumed

7	houses in the Fishmongers quarter.
141	—— in Ram quarter.
82	—— in Pirna quarter.
1	—— in Halbe Gasse quarter.
2	—— in Seethor quarter.
9	—— in Poppitz quarter.
23	—— in the Bailiwic quarter.
1	The excise-house, as also the excise-house and guard-house at Pirna gate, and the excise and guard-houses at Seethor.
266	houses in all.

Persons who lost their lives, or were hurt.

In Ram quarter. Two persons burnt.

In Pirna quarter.

A burgher, named Kammerling, killed by a cannon-ball fired from the town, and buried at Pirna.

A girl of fourteen wounded, who was removed to Pirna.

A widow

A widow wounded, carried into the town.

In Poppitz quarter.

One woman killed by the independent battalion.

There have been therefore in all, two persons burnt, a man and a woman greatly advanced in years, and whom it was impossible to save; two killed, and two wounded.

What has been said of a waggon is false; and it is equally false that 90 persons perished at the Hart; only four persons in all having lost their lives, as we have just mentioned.

The 10th, in the morning, there were found before Wilsdorff gate, among some straw, which had been unloaded there and laid before the houses, some parcels of gunpowder, which a burgher threw into the water. Two rooms in the house called Jungfer Palais were set on fire; but it was soon extinguished.

Lastly, it is false that the Austrian carpenters assisted us in extinguishing the fire. We never saw one of them.

We certify that all the above is strictly conformable to truth.

Simon Steltzner, judge;
John Christopher Groll,
Godefroi Schneider,
C. Benjamin Stamm.
John Daniel Karichs,
John Michael Faber
John Christ. Grohmann,
John George Seyffert,
John Gottfried Peter,
John Christ. Kretscmar.

Dresden, Dec. 4, 1758.

The Saxon account of the damage done by the burning of the suburbs of Dresden, referred to in the several passages of the foregoing memorial, is contained in the following

Translation of a memorial presented on the 24th Nov. to the dyet of the empire, by the Saxon minister.

It was reserved for the history of the war, which the King of Prussia hath kindled in Germany, to transmit to future ages an action of such a nature as is that, which, according to the authentic advices that have been received by the undersigned minister of his majesty the King of Poland, Elector of Saxony, Lietenant General Schmettau, the Prussian governor of Dresden, hath just now ordered and executed in that royal residence and in the suburbs. The proceeding is so atrocious, that he thought it his duty, without waiting for his master's orders, most humbly to give notice of it to the laudable dyet of the empire. Those advices are dated the 14th ult. and are to the following effect:

" The Austrian army having on the 9th instant forced the Prussian corps under General Itzenplitz to decamp from Gorlitz, and driven Meyer's independent battalion out of the Great Garden, General Schmettau, governor of Dresden, ordered the burghers to carry a vast quantity of straw into the suburbs, which was put into the houses in trusses. He made the inhabitants perfectly easy by making the strongest protestations to them, That they had nothing to fear; and ordered them to remain quiet within doors; and that no person should be seen in the streets in the night, for fear of danger in case the enemy should make an attack.

At two in the morning a cannon was fired. On this signal the gunners and the soldiers of the independent

dependent battalion difperfed themfelves in the ftreets of the Pirna and Wilfchen fuburbs, broke open the doors of the houfes and fhops, fet fire to the ftraw, added frefh quantities of it, and increafed the flames by torches of pitch, and afterwards fhut the houfes.

By the violence of the flames, which was kept up by red-hot balls fired into the houfes and along the ftreets, the whole was inftantly on fire. Thofe who wanted to run out of their houfes were in danger of being killed by the fire of cannon and fmall arms. There were even foldiers in the ftreets, who pufhed down with their bayonets fuch as were endeavouring to fave their perfons or effects. By this means a multitude of people of all ages, who inhabited thofe populous fuburbs, perifhed amidft the flames, and under the ruins of houfes. The number of thofe who were killed in the fingle inn the fign of the Golden Hart, amounted to ninety; and upwards of two hundred of the principal houfes have been reduced to afhes. Humanity is fhocked at the thought of the cruelties committed this night and the two following days. A fhoemaker, who was running away with his infant on a pillow, to fave it from being burnt to death, was met by a volunteer, who fnatched the pillow from him, and threw the babe into the flames. Many perfons, and even fome of diftinction, after lofing all their effects, were forced to make their efcapes in their fhirts, through gardens, to the neighbouring villages. Others, who had faved a part of their beds and bedding in a garden, faw it fet on fire, before their eyes, with torches. Some poor people fayed their cloaths and a few other things in the church-yard; but even there did the red-hot balls follow them, and fet on fire their little furniture, and even the coffins of the dead. One man had got his things into a waggon; the Pruffians ftopt it, covered it over with pitch, and fet it on fire.

On the following days, fuch as ventured to return to the fuburbs to fave a part of what they had loft, were fired at. Pruffian foldiers fallied out of the city, from time to time, to fet one houfe on fire after another; many of thefe men were feized by the Auftrian huffars and Croats, who difcovered fo much humanity and tendernefs on this occafion, that they were feen, with tears in their eyes, readily parting with their own allowance of bread to give to the ftarving fufferers; they even gave them money; and ventured through the flames with them, honeftly to affift them in faving their effects.

The Auftrian army beheld thefe horrible acts, and was filled with indignation and rage. Its generals melting with compaffion, tried every method to remedy them. They fent 300 carpenters into the fuburbs to endeavour to extinguifh the flames. The Auftrians brought away all the inhabitants that had taken refuge in the Great Garden, and very generoufly fet open to them their magazines. The general officers even made a confiderable collection for them. Field-Marfhal Count Daun, with a view to ftop the horrid ravages of the enemy, fent M. Zawoifky, a colonel in the Polifh fervice, with a trumpet, to General Schmettau, the Pruffian governor of that capital, to reprefent to him, that thefe proceedings were quite unheard of in civilized nations, among Chrifti-

2 ans,

ans, and even among Barbarians; and to declare to him, that he ſhould be reſponſible for them in his perſon, as well as for all that might happen to the royal family, the rather as he had no reaſon given him for them; as he had not been ſummoned, nor had one inch of ground in the ſuburbs been taken, nor one muſket fired into the town. To which the Pruſſian governor anſwered, That he was a ſoldier; that he acted according to the articles of war, without troubling himſelf about the royal family, or the fate of the town; and that what he did was by expreſs order of his maſter.

There remains to be added to theſe afflicting advices, that the enormities committed even in the royal reſidence were equal to thoſe in the ſuburbs. We have been already informed that perſons perfectly innocent have been expoſed to the moſt rigorous treatment, and that ſeveral houſes have been pillaged.

What moderation ſoever ſhall be uſed in judging of theſe horrible exceſſes commited by the Pruſſian troops in a royal and electoral reſidence, ſtill it muſt be acknowledged that this conduct is very ſtrange, and altogether ſingular. For there was neither reaſon nor neceſſity for committing a devaſtation ſo horrible, and accompanied with the ſhedding ſo much innocent blood. It ſhould ſeem that pains were taken to ſtifle the voice of humanity, to fill the numerous royal family, reſiding in that unfortunate city, with the greateſt terror, and to put their lives in danger.

It is unneceſſary for me to enlarge farther by obſerving to the laudable dyet of the empire, that beſides the cruelties committed on this occaſion, the regard due to the perſons of ſovereigns, their families, and reſidences, a regard which men have ever held ſacred and inviolable, was trampled on.

John George Ponickau.

Tranſlation of the memorial preſented on the 27th of November, to the dyet of the empire, by M. de Plotho, the Brandenbourg miniſter, in anſwer to that of the Saxon miniſter.

There is not perhaps an inſtance of ſuch a denunciation to the dyet of the empire, as that which was made in relation to what preceded the burning of the ſuburbs of Dreſden, by the Saxon miniſter, in a memorial dated November 24, in which all the facts ſet forth are founded on advices pretended to be moſt authentic: yet it hath not been judged proper to venture to tell whence, or from whom, thoſe advices were received, that the aſſembly of the empire, and the impartial world might judge with certainty, what degree of credit they deſerved.

The Saxon electoral miniſtry ought not therefore to be ſurpriſed, if on this occaſion, their miniſterial credit ſhould receive ſome check; and if blind zeal ſhould not meet with a blind credulity.

We are therefore obliged, on our part, to give, as the Saxon miniſter hath done, but ſtrictly adhering to truth, the authentic preliminary advices received from our court.

[Here Baron Plotho inſerts, word for word, the relation of what paſſed at Dreſden, and before that city, from the 8th of November, till the ſending of M. Sawoiſky. See page 168, &c.]

M. Plotho proceeds thus:

From

From this genuine relation of what preceded the affair, every one will easily judge that nothing was done but what necessity and the exigency of war required. It is certainly most natural, that when siege is laid to a town which is a royal residence, he that defends it should employ the same precautions in its defence that are used in ordinary fortresses: and we cannot conceive on what foundation the besieged can be required to use tenderness when none is shewn by the besiegers; this would be to carry complaisance too far.

Mean while, all this, alas! is the deplorable effect of the war; and those who will not agree to gentle methods, but demand fire and sword, and insist on it, see their wishes and their desires fully, and more than fully, accomplished.

The undersigned can, nevertheless, most solemnly assure, with the greatest truth, that the King of Prussia, from his great love to mankind, always feels the greatest emotion of soul, and the most exquisite concern at the sight of the profuse effusion of blood, the devastation of cities and countries, and the inconveniences of war, by which so many thousands are overwhelmed: and if his sincere and honest inclination to procure peace to Germany, his dear country, could have prevailed, or been listened to, in any shape, the present war, attended with so much bloodshed, and ruinous to so many countries, would have been prevented and avoided.

Those therefore, who stirred up the present war, and who instead of extinguishing it without shedding of blood, took measures by which oil was thrown on the flames, and the fire rendered fiercer, have to answer to God for such a profuse effusion of blood, for the ruin and devastation of so many countries, and for the loss of the lives and effects of so many innocent persons.

Ehrich Christopher
Baron PLOTHO.

On the 26th of July, M. Le Chevalier Drucour, Governor of Louisbourg, surrendered that place by capitulation, on the following articles, viz.

I. The garrison of Louisbourg shall be prisoners of war, and shall be carried to England in the ships of his Britannic majesty.

II. All the artillery, ammunition, provisions, as well as the arms of any kind whatsoever, which are at present in the town of Louisbourg, the islands of Cape-Breton and St. John, and their appurtenances, shall be delivered without the least damage, to such commissaries as shall be appointed to receive them, for the use of his Britannic majesty.

III. The governor shall give his orders that the troops which are in the island of St. John, and its appurtenances, shall go on board such ships of war as the admiral shall send to receive them.

IV. The gate called Port Dauphire, shall be given up to the troops of his Britannic majesty, tomorrow at eight o'clock in the morning, and the garrison, including all those that carried arms, drawn up at noon, on the Esplanade, where they shall lay down their arms, colours, implements and ornaments of war. And the garrison shall go on board, in order to be carried to England in a convenient time.

V. The same care shall be taken of the sick and wounded that are in the

the hospitals, as of those belonging to his Britannic majesty.

VI. The merchants and their clerks that have not carried arms, shall be sent to France, in such manner as the admiral shall think proper.

Louisbourg, 26th July, 1758.
(Signed) Le Chevalier de Drucour.

Two hundred and twenty-one pieces of cannon, eighteen mortars, with a considerable quantity of ammunition and stores had been found in the place, and it was expected that more would be found. The following is the return of the state of the garrison when it capitulated.

State of the garrison of Louisbourg the 26th of July 1758, when it capitulated.

Names of Regiments.	Officers.	Soldiers fit for duty.	Sick and wounded.	Total.
Twenty-four companies of marines of the usual garrison and two of the artillery	79	746	195	1017
Second battalion of Volontaires Etrangers	48	402	86	526
Second battalion of Cambise	38	466	104	608
Second battalion of Artois	32	407	27	466
Second battalion of Bourgogne	30	353	31	414
Total of the garrison	214	2374	453	3031
Sea officers, private men, and marines fit for duty, with the sick and wounded, belonging to the ships	135	1124	1347	2606
Total prisoners				5637

All the French men of war that were in the harbour have been taken and destroyed, viz.

Prudent, 74 guns, burnt by the boats of the fleet, under the Captains Leforey and Balfour.

Entreprenant, 74 guns, blown up and burnt, by a shot from the marine battery.

Capricieux and Celebre, both 64 guns, burnt by the Entreprenant.

Bienfaisant, 64 guns, taken by the boats of the fleet, and towed from under the walls of the town into the east harbour, by Captain Balfour.

Apollo, 50 guns, Chevre, Biche, and Fidelle frigates, sunk by the enemy across the harbour's mouth, to prevent the fleet's going in.

Diana, 36 guns, taken by his majesty's ship Boreas.

Echo, 26 guns, taken by his majesty's ship Juno.

Of his majesty's forces were killed and wounded as follows.

KILLED.

Royal. Lieut. Fenton, Lieutenant Howe.

Gen. Amherst's. Lieut. Nicholson, Lieut. Campbell.

Gen. Forbes's. Capt. Earl of Dundonald.

Gen. Webb's. Ensign Godfrey Rowe.

Col.

Col. Monckton's. Lieut. Hart.

Col. Fraser's. Capt. Bailey, Lieut. Cuthbert, Lieut. Fraser, Lieut. Murray.

Capt. Rogers's Rangers. Ensign Francis Caruthers.

10 Non-commission officers.

146 Private men.

Artillery. 1 gunner, and 3 matrosses.

WOUNDED.

Col. Bastide, engineer in chief.

Royal. Lieut. Fitz-Simmons, Lieut. Bailey, Lieut. Ashe, Ensign Waterson.

Gen. Amherst's. Lieut. Hamilton, Lieut. and Adjutant Mukins, Ensign Moneypenny.

Gen. Forbs's. Capt. Rycaut, Lieut. Francis Tew.

Gen. Whitmore's. Lieut. Pierce Butler, Lieut. John Jermyn, Lieut. William Hamilton.

Gen. Bragg's. Captain Browne.

Gen. Otway's. Lieutenant Allan, Lieut. Brown, Lieut. and Adjutant Cockburn, Ensign Armstrong.

Gen. Hodgson's. Lieut. Lilly.

Gen. Webb's. Lieut. Hopkins.

Col. Anstruther's. Capt. Smith.

Col. Fraser's. Captain Donald M'Donald, Lieutenant Alexander Campbell, Lieutenant John M'Donald.

7 Non-commission officers.

2 Drummers.

315 Private men.

Artillery. 1 corporal, 1 gunner, 3 matrosses.

Translation of a letter from the Chevalier Drucour, late governor of Louisbourg, to a friend at Paris, dated Andover, October 1, 1748.

Infandum, regina, jubes—I wish, Sir, I could erase from my memory the four years I passed at Louisbourg. The bad state of the place, the impossibility of making it better, the subsistence of a garrison and inhabitants supported there at the king's expence, and threatened with famine once a month, gave no little uneasiness and anxiety to all who are charged therewith. This situation——— *manet alta mente repostum.* Many old officers, from all the provinces of the kingdom, have been witnesses of my conduct; and I dare assert that it was never impeached. But he who views objects at a distance only, may judge differently. I hope, Sir, this was not your case; but that you said, 'It must 'have been impossible for Drucour to act otherwise.' Of this I cannot so easily convince you till I have the pleasure of seeing you. Mean while, know that twenty-three ships of war, eighteen frigates, sixteen thousand land forces, with a proportionable train of cannon and mortars, came in sight on the first of June, and landed on the 8th. To oppose them, we had at most but 2500 men of the garrison, and 300 militia of the burghers of the town and St. John's island; a fortification (if it could deserve the name) crumbling down in every flank, face, and courtine, except the right flank of the king's bastion, which was remounted the first year after my arrival. The covered-way was covered as much as it could be, and yet was commanded and enfiladed throughout, as well as the dauphin and king's bastions. In the harbour were five men of war. This was our force. The succours I expected from Canada did not arrive till the end of the ſiege; and conſiſted of about 350 Canadians only, including 60 Indians.

The enemy was at firſt very ſlow in making his approaches; for on the 15th of July, he was three hundred toiſes from the place. He was employed in ſecuring his camp by redoubts and epaulements, thinking we had many Canadians and Indians behind him. We, on our parts, uſed every method to deſtroy and retard his work; both by the fire of the place and that of the ſhips in the harbour. The commodore of thoſe ſhips warmly ſollicited leave to quit the place; but knowing the importance of their ſtay to its ſafety, I refuſed it. It was our buſineſs to defer the determination of our fate as long as poſſible. My accounts from Canada aſſured me, that M. de Montcalm was marching to the enemy, and would come up with them between the 15th and 20th of July. I ſaid, then, 'If the ſhips leave the harbour on the 10th of June (as they deſire) the Engliſh admiral will enter it immediately after;' and we ſhould have been loſt before the end of the month; which would have put it in the power of the generals of the beſiegers to have employed the months of July and Auguſt in ſending ſuccours to the troops marching againſt Canada, and to have entered the river St. Lawrence at the proper ſeaſon. This object alone ſeemed to me of ſufficient importance to require a council of war, whoſe opinion was the ſame with mine, and conformable to the king's intentions. The ſituation of the ſhips was not leſs critical than ours. Four of them were burnt, with two corps of caſerns, by the enemy's bombs. At laſt, on the 26th of July, no ſhips being left, and the place being open in different parts of the king, the dauphin, and the queen's baſtions, a council of war determined to aſk to capitulate.

I propoſed much the ſame articles as were granted at Portmahon: But the generals would liſten to no propoſals, but our being priſoners of war. I annex this letter, and my anſwer, by which you will ſee that I was reſolved to wait the general aſſault, when Mr. Prevot, commiſſary-general and intendant of the colony, brought me a petition from the traders and inhabitants, which determined me to ſend back the officer who carried my former letter, to make our ſubmiſſion to the law of force; a ſubmiſſion which, in our condition, was inevitable. This condition was ſuch, that, for eight days, the officers had not, any more than the private men, one moment's reſt, nor indeed any place in which to take reſt. In all beſieged towns there are entrenchments where thoſe who are not on duty may retire, and be covered from the enemy's fire; but at Louiſbourg we had not a ſafe place even for the wounded; ſo that they were almoſt as much expoſed every minute of the four and twenty hours, as if they had been on the covered-way. Nevertheleſs the men did not murmur in the leaſt, nor diſcover the ſmalleſt diſcontent; which was owing to the good example and exact diſcipline of their officers. None deſerted but foreigners, Germans; one of whom prevented an intended ſally. As he had gone over

over to the enemy two hours before, it was not thought prudent to make it. The burning of the ships and of the caserns of the king's and queen's bastions hindered our making another. A third had not better success; we proceeded no farther than the glacis of the covered-way, having missed the quay of a small passage which it behoved us to turn in order to take the enemy in flank: so that of four sallies, which were intended, one only succeeded, in which we made 30 grenadiers, and two officers prisoners, besides those that were killed, among whom was a captain. We had about 330 killed and wounded during the course of the siege, including officers. The crews of the king's ships are not comprehended in that number.

As to the landing, it must have been effected, by sacrificing lives in one part or another; it being impossible to guard such an extent of coast with a garrison of 3000 men, and leave men in the place for the daily duty. We occupied above two leagues and a half of ground in the most accessible parts: but there were some intermediate places we could not guard; and it was precisely in one of these that the enemy took post.

The captain of a ship strikes when his vessel is dismasted, his rigging cut to pieces, and several shot received between wind and water. A governor of a town surrenders the place when the breaches are practicable, and when he has no resource by entrenching himself in the gorges of bastions, or within the place. Such was the case of Louisbourg. Add to this, that it wanted every necessary for such operations: General Wolfe himself was obliged to place centinels on the ramparts; for the private men, and the sutlers entered through the breaches and gaps, with as much ease, as if there had been only an old ditch. Of 52 pieces of cannon, which were opposed to the batteries of the besiegers, 40 were dismounted, broke, or rendered unserviceable. It is easy to judge what condition those of the place were in. Was it possible, in such circumstances, to avoid being made prisoners of war? I have the honour to be, &c.

Le Chevalier de Drucour.

General Amherst's letter to the Governor of Louisbourg referred to above.

'In answer to the proposal I have just now had the honour to receive from your excellency, by the Sieur Loppinot, I have only to tell your excellency, that it hath been determined by his excellency Admiral Boscawen and me, that his ships shall go in to-morrow to make a general attack upon the town. Your excellency knows very well the situation of the army and the fleet; and as his excellency the admiral, as well as I, is very desirous to prevent the effusion of blood, we give your excellency one hour after receiving this, to determine either to capitulate as prisoners of war, or to take upon you all the bad consequences of a defence against this fleet and army.

Boscawen.
Jeff. Amherst.'

The Governor's answer to General Amherst.

'To answer your excellencies in as few words as possible, I shall have the honour to repeat to you that my resolution is still the same; and that I will suffer the consequences, and sustain the attack you speak of.

Le Chevalier de DRUCOUR.'

A piece extracted from authenic documents of the French administration in Hanover.

One Gautier, a farmer of Paris, arriving at Hanover some days before Christmas, and there fixing his office, there appeared a decree of council of the King of France, dated the 18th of October, 1757, the tenor of which is as follows.

Extract from the registers of the council of state.

The king having, by a result of council of the 11th of this instant, charged John Faidy, citizen of Paris, to take upon him, on his majesty's account, the direction, receipt, and administration of the duties and revenues, of what nature soever they may be, without any exception, and under what denomination soever they may be levied and collected, belonging to his majesty in the electorate of Hanover, the countries, states, provinces, towns, districts, commonalties, and administrations, conquered from the King of England, Elector of Hanover, that have been subjected to his majesty since the beginning of this year's campaign, or may hereafter be subjected, to receive and bring to account all such persons as have had the direction, receipt and administration of all the said revenues of what kind soever they may be, since the conquest of the electorate of Hanover, the countries, states, towns, districts, commonalties and administrations, conquered from the King of England, Elector of Hanover, for all the sums which they shall have received; to bring, in like manner, to account all persons, who, before the electorate of Hanover, and the other conquered countries passed under his majesty's dominion, were employed in the direction and receipt of the revenues of the country, whether they farmed them on a lease for a certain term, or had the receipt and direction thereof, for the account of the preceding sovereign: In short, to receive of the said persons the sums due from them for the value of their farms, as well as from those who have had the direction thereof, for the revenues previous to the possession taken for, and in the name of his majesty, of the said electorate of Hanover, the countries, states, provinces, towns, districts, commonalties, and administrations: And it being his majesty's will, that the said John Faidy be put into immediate possession of the said direction and general administration, the report having been heard of the Sieur Boulogne, counsellor in ordinary to the royal council, comptroller general of the finances, the king in council has ordered, and does hereby order, that in the interim, till letters patent, sealed and registered, where necessary, shall be issued forth, in consequence of the result of the council of the 11th instant, the said John Faidy be put into possession of the direction, receipt, and administration of all the revenues and duties, of what nature soever they be, without any exception, and under what denomination soever

ever they have been received, levied, and collected, or may hereafter be ſo, in the electorate of Hanover, countries, ſtates, provinces, towns, diſtricts, commonalties, and adminiſtrations, conquered from the King of England, Elector of Hanover, from the time they have been ſubjected to his majeſty: It is his majeſty's will, that the receipt, direction, and adminiſtration of all the revenues whatſoever, be in the hands of the ſaid John Faidy, his receivers, directors, attornies, clerks, and others appointed by him; and for that purpoſe, that all the regiſters, accounts, papers, eſtimates, and documents, relating to the receipt, direction, and maintenance of the ſaid duties and revenues, be delivered to him by thoſe, in whoſe cuſtody they ſhall be found, or who ſhall have been employed in the receipt and direction of the ſaid revenues, whether they have enjoyed the ſame as farmers upon a leaſe for a certain term, or have been employed in the receipt and direction thereof on account of the preceding ſovereign, before the electorate or other countries conquered from the King of England, Elector of Hanover, paſſed under the dominion of his majeſty, and by thoſe, who, ſince the poſſeſſion taken of the ſaid country, have directed, adminiſtred, and received the revenues of the ſaid electorate, countries, provinces, towns, diſtricts, commonalties, and adminiſtrations: It is his majeſty's will and order, that all thoſe, who have been employed in the receipt and direction of the ſaid revenues, under what title ſoever, be obliged to account to the ſaid John Faidy, or to the directors, receivers, and caſhiers, appointed by him, for all receipts by them made, and to pay the ſums due from them, whether as farmers, directors, or receivers, whereto they ſhall be obliged by the ordinary methods uſed in the king's revenues and affairs, upon complaints exhibited againſt them by the ſaid John Faidy, or his attornies: His majeſty orders, that the receivers, of whatſoever kind they may be, be likewiſe obliged to produce and deliver to the ſaid John Faidy, or his attornies, upon their giving receipts, the accounts they have given in, their regiſters, land-rolls, and other deeds, by virtue whereof they have received and collected the duties and revenues of the preceding ſovereign, and that the ſaid receivers ſhall account for what they have received, and ſhall pay the ſums ſtill remaining due from them, under pain of being obliged thereto by the aforeſaid methods: His majeſty empowers the ſaid John Faidy to remove the receivers, and all other perſons, who ſhall have been employed in any part of the direction, receipt, and adminiſtration of the duties and revenues, of what nature, and under what denomination ſoever they may be, of the electorate of Hanover, ſtates, countries, provinces, towns, diſtricts, commonaltes, and adminiſtrations, and to place others in their room, his majeſty reſerving to himſelf the power of ordering the vouchers of thoſe in employment, who may be removed, to be produced, and to provide for the reimburſing them the money they ſhall prove to have paid, in the manner he ſhall judge proper: His majeſty orders, that all perſons, of what rank and condition ſoever, who have been entruſted under the preceding government with titles, papers, accounts, regiſters, eſtimates, and in general, any thing relative to the direction, receipt, and adminiſtration of the revenues of the electorate of Hanover, the countries, ſtates, provinces, towns, diſtricts, commonalties, and adminiſtrations, already conquered from the King of England, Elector of Hanover, or thoſe that may hereafter be ſo, to communicate the ſame to the ſaid John Faidy, his attornies, directors, and officers, and to deliver them authentic copies of all he papers they ſhall deſire to have, without any exemption for o doing, under pain of diſobedience: His majeſty in like manner orders, under the ſame penalties, that the magiſtrates of the towns, thoſe of the diſtricts and commonalties, the perſons who are at the head of the particular adminiſtrations of the ſtates and provinces, ſhall deliver, upon the firſt requiſition of the ſaid John Faidy, his attornies, directors, and officers, eſtimates, certified by them, of the produce of ſix years, reckoning from the firſt of January 1751, to the laſt of December 1756, of the duties and revenues which the ſaid towns, diſtricts, commonalties, and ſtates of the provinces, are in poſſeſſion of; that they likewiſe deliver to the ſaid John Faidy, his attornies, directors, and officers, ſtates, certified by them, of the ſums they ſhall have paid to the preceding ſovereign during the ſaid ſix years, and ſtates of the charges neceſſarily incurred during the ſaid term, independent of the ſums they have paid: It is his majeſty's intention and will, that the ſaid John Faidy be put into poſſeſſion and enjoyment of the houſes, offices, and utenſils, hitherto made uſe of in the direction and general management of the duties and revenues of all kinds, with the direction and adminiſtration whereof he is charged, payment being made by him to the proprietors of the houſes for the rent thereof, upon the footing they ſhall agree: His majeſty likewiſe orders, that the receivers, clerks, and in general all thoſe who are actually employed in the direction and general management of the duties and revenues of all kinds, of the electorate of Hanover, countries, ſtates, provinces, towns, diſtricts, commonalties, and adminiſtrations, may, after having been authorized thereto by the ſaid John Faidy, his directors and attornies, continue to act in their employments, without being obliged to take any new oaths, and that thoſe, who ſhall replace them, or come in upon a freſh eſtabliſhment, ſhall be admitted without any charges to take the oath and diſcharge the duty of the employments to which they ſhall be named, upon the ſimple preſentation of the ſaid John Faidy, or of his directors and attornies, or upon the commiſſions which ſhall be delivered to them; His majeſty orders, that the ſtates, towns, and adminiſtrations, commonalties, farmers upon leaſe, the directors of the duties and revenues, treaſurers, receivers general, and particular caſhiers, and in general all thoſe who ſhall be accountable and indebted to the duties and revenues, of what nature ſoever they be, comprehended in the direction and adminiſtration with which the ſaid John Faidy is charged, ſhall be well and truly acquitted and diſcharged

towards

towards his majeſty and all others, of whatſoever they ſhall be found to owe, by producing receipts from the ſaid John Faidy, his attornies, receivers, and general caſhiers, of the accounts they ſhall have given in at the time they ſhall be ballanced and acquitted: It is his majeſty's will, that any diſputes that ſhall ariſe with regard to the direction, receipt, and general adminiſtration of the duties and revenues, of what nature ſoever they be, of the electorate of Hanover, countries, ſtates, provinces, towns, diſtricts, commonalties, and adminiſtrations, wherewith the ſaid John Faidy is charged, appurtenances and dependencies thereof, be brought before the intendant and commiſſary, who has the department of the conquered country, and adjudged by him, ſaving an appeal to the council, his majeſty reſerving to it the determination thereof, and forbidding the ſame to all courts and judges: His majeſty enjoins the ſaid intendant and commiſſary of the ſaid department, to ſupport the execution of the preſent decree, which ſhall be executed, notwithſtanding all oppoſition and hindrances, of which, if any ſhould happen, his majeſty reſerves to himſelf and his council the cognizance, and forbids the ſame to all courts and judges.

Done at the king's council of ſtate, held at Verſailles the 18th of the month of October, 1757.

(Signed) EYNARD.

and compared with the paraphe.

It appears from the date of this decree, and by what is ſaid therein, that, in the weeks immediately ſubſequent to the convention of Bremervorde, the council of Verſailles was already employed in framing it; and the ſaid decree implies in clear and preciſe terms, that it was determined in the council of Verſailles, to change the government and ſyſtem of the electorate of Hanover, notwithſtanding what was expreſsly promiſed by the capitulation made the 9th of Auguſt, 1757, upon the ſurrender of the capital, and that the adminiſtration herein mentioned, with which the ſaid John Faidy is charged, was to extend itſelf to the countries which might hereafter be conquered.

If this confeſſion, made by the crown of France itſelf, cannot but be conſidered as an undeniable proof, that the ſame crown had a premeditated deſign of making an ill uſe of the ceſſation of arms, in order to proceed in taking poſſeſſion of the provinces they had not yet ſeized upon, when the ceſſation of arms was concluded, and bring to utter deſtruction the electorate of Hanover, without leaving the ſovereign thereof any method of preſerving it; neither can any one diſpute, but that great weight is hereby added to the motives, which have induced the king, our ſovereign, to take up arms afreſh, and which have already been laid open to the eyes of the public.

Lewis Fra. Armand du Pleſſis, Duke de Richelieu, General of the French army in Germany.

The breaking of the capitulation of Cloſter-ſeven, in ſpite of the moſt ſolemn treaty, and the word of honour given by the generals, renders void the treaty made with the country of Hanover, when the

the king's army entered it; and this infraction of good faith requires the greateſt rigour toward the Hanoverian army, now actually in hoſtilities.

Wherefore we order, that all the goods, and all other effects of what nature ſoever, belonging to all the officers or others actually with the ſaid Hanoverian army, be confiſcated to the king's uſe, and that the adminiſtrator general of the conquered countries take poſſeſſion thereof; in order to collect the revenues ariſing therefrom, which are to be added to the contributions, and to make uſe of them in the moſt advantageous manner for his majeſty, in whatever places of the conquered countries they may be ſituated.

We ſtrictly require monſieur le Duc de Randan, commander in the country of Hanover, and all other commanders, to enforce the execution of theſe preſents, and to ſupport the ſame as far as it may concern them.

Done at Zell, Dec. 22, 1757.
(Signed) The Marſhal Duc de Richelien.
And underneath, Le Lurez.

Conditions of a ſubſidy treaty, delivered on the 18th of October, in the name of the Landgrave of Heſſe Caſſel, to his excellency the Abbe Count de Bernis, miniſter for foreign affairs, by M. Packbelle, the duke de Deux-Ponts' miniſter.

His moſt ſerene highneſs the Landgrave of Heſſe Caſſel, deſires nothing more ardently, than to attach himſelf wholly to France, and to make a treaty with the king for that end. It ſhould ſeem that it might be concluded on the following conditions:

I. The baſis and foundation of it ſhall be the laws and conſtitutions of the empire, and the treaties of Weſtphalia, of which his majeſty is a guarantee.

II. The landgrave ſhall enter into no engagement againſt the king and his allies, and ſhall never give any troops to ſerve againſt France or her allies, nor give any aſſiſtance directly or indirectly, to the enemies of his majeſty and of his allies.

III. He ſhall never give his vote in the general or particular aſſemblies of the empire contrary to his majeſty's intereſt. On the contrary he ſhall employ his influence jointly with France, to put an end to the troubles of the empire.

IV. For this end his moſt ſerene highneſs ſhall put his troops which have ſerved in the Hanoverian army, into the pay of France, on conditions that ſhall be agreed on, this condition particularly, that they ſhall not ſerve in the preſent war againſt his Britannic majeſty.

V. His majeſty ſhall, in return, as ſoon as the treaty is ſigned, reſtore to the landgrave his eſtates; and all things ſhall be put in the condition they were in before the French troops entered them.

VI. Thoſe eſtates ſhall not only be evacuated by the French as ſoon as the treaty is ſigned, but they ſhall in conſequence thereof be exempted from winter quarters, and from all further contributions, either in money, grain, forage, wood, cattle, or any thing elſe, though already impoſed on the ſubjects of Heſſe: but his majeſty ſhall likewiſe cauſe ready money to be paid for proviſions, and every kind of ſubſiſtence, of which his troops may ſtand in need in Heſſe; upon condition, however, that in conſidera-

tion

tion of all this, the landgrave ſhall take no toll for warlike ſtores and proviſions, and other effects of that nature, which may paſs through his country.

VII. The king ſhall guaranty all the eſtates which his moſt ſerene highneſs poſſeſſed before the French ſeized them, and all the rights of the houſe of Heſſe Caſſel.

VIII. His majeſty ſhall guaranty to that prince the act of aſſurance given him by his ſon the hereditary prince with regard to religion; and ſhall not ſuffer it to be violated by any perſon, or under any pretext.

IX. The moſt chriſtian king ſhall uſe his intereſt with the emperor and the empreſs queen, that, in conſideration of the immenſe loſſes and damages his moſt ſerene highneſs hath ſuffered ſince the French entered his country, and of the great ſums he loſes with England, in arrears and ſubſidies, by this accommodation with his moſt chriſtian majeſty, he may be excuſed from furniſhing his contingent to the army of the empire, and from paying the Roman months granted by the dyet of the empire.

X. If, in reſentment of this convention, the eſtates of his moſt ſerene highneſs ſhall be attacked, the king ſhall give the moſt ſpeedy and efficacious ſuccours.

Tranſlation of a memorial preſented in November to the dyet of the empire, by Baron Gimmengen, electoral miniſter of Brunſwick Lunenbourg.

His imperial majeſty hath been pleaſed to communicate to the dyet of the empire, by a pretended moſt gracious decree of the Aulic council, dated the 28th of Auguſt laſt, mandates iſſued the 21ſt of the ſame month, on pain of the ban of the empire, and with avocatory letters thereto annexed, againſt his majeſty the King of Great Britain, my moſt gracious maſter, and alſo againſt ſome others of the moſt reſpectable princes of the Germanic empire.

There is not an example of this kind in the hiſtory of the empire. His Britannic majeſty, during the one and thirty years of his glorious reign, hath obſerved ſo unimpeachable a conduct towards all his coeſtates of the empire, without diſtinction of religion, that no prince of the empire hath received greater proofs of eſteem and confidence than he can produce. His majeſty hath, as much as the weakeſt ſtates, always obſerved right and juſtice.

On the death of the emperor Charles VI. he beheld the time, which will be a famous æra in the hiſtory of the houſe of Auſtria, when the crown of France poured numerous armies into the empire to exterminate that houſe, and make itſelf maſter of Germany. His majeſty, in his double capacity of king and elector, put himſelf in the breach; he led in perſon the auxiliary army of her majeſty the empreſs queen, the greateſt part of which was compoſed of his own troops: at the battle of Dettingen he expoſed his ſacred perſon for that princeſs, and his royal highneſs the Duke of Cumberland his ſon, ſtill bears the ſcars of wounds there received.

The year 1745, when his preſent imperial majeſty was choſen Emperor, is ſtill recent in the memory of all the ſtates of the empire, as well as the pains which his Britannic majeſty took upon that occaſion. He purchaſed the preſerva-

tion

tion of the houſe of Auſtria, which was effected by the peace of Aix-la-Chapelle, with the blood of his ſubjects, and by means of the moſt important conqueſts of his crown. He hath endeavoured to maintain the imperial crown in that houſe, by negotiations for the election of a king of the Romans. The treaty of ſucceſſion concluded with the Duke of Modena, and the aggrandiſement reſulting from it to the houſe of Auſtria, was owing to his majeſty's *friendſhip for it.*

Inſtead of a recompence, inſtead of performing the tender proteſtations of regard and gratitude, which his majeſty then received from her majeſty the empreſs qneen, and which *his* magnanimity hinders him *from* making public; inſtead of the obſervation due to the moſt ſolemn treaties, her majeſty the empreſs queen refuſes him the aſſiſtance which ſhe ought to give him againſt an invaſion, proceeding wholly from the hatred of France, which his Britannic majeſty has drawn upon himſelf by his friendſhip to that princeſs; and his imperial majeſty even denies him the dehortatorial letters he ſollicited. The court of Vienna ſigns a treaty with the crown of France, in March 1757, at a time when his majeſty's troops were quiet in his own dominions, by which the French troops were to paſs the Weſer the 10th of July, and enter the electorate of Hanover. She joins her troops to thoſe of that crown, and ravages the king's dominions worſe than the French troops had done. The ſame Duke of Cumberland who was wounded at Dettingen in defending her imperial majeſty, is obliged to fight at Haſtenbeck, againſt the troops of that princeſs which attacked the king's dominions.

The empreſs queen ſends commiſſaries to Hanover, who are to ſhare, and actually did ſhare, with the crown of France in the contributions. She rejects all propoſals of peace; ſhe diſmiſſes the king's miniſters from her court; and after the divine Providence, according to its righteous ways, had, by a victory granted to the king's army, delivered the electorate from its enemies, when we were endeavouring to hinder the French troops from entering it a ſecond time, as they threatened, and as all the world knows, his imperial majeſty, who, by virtue of the capitulation which he has ſworn, ought 'to protect the empire, and 'at all times conſider the electors 'as its internal members and main 'pillars, and oppoſe the entrance 'of foreign troops deſtined to op- 'preſs the ſtates of the empire,' finds it his duty, without making the leaſt mention of this invaſion by the French troops, to require his majeſty to withdraw his troops from the countries where they then were, to put a ſtop to all his warlike preparations, and by that means again open a paſſage for the French army to enter his German dominions. His imperial majeſty thinks proper to recal the king's troops, to releaſe them from their allegiance, and duty to his majeſty; to enjoin them never more to obey his orders, but to abandon their colours, their ſervice, and their poſt; threatening the ſaid troops with puniſhment, in body, honour, and eſtates; and the king himſelf with being put under the ban of the empire, which is not in the power of the emperor; and em-

employing in the proceedings on this occasion, a style proper only to be used to a Tuscan or an Austrian subject.

The public has already judged of these proceedings, and history will transmit them to posterity, without disguise, but with indelible colours.

His Britannic majesty still retains the same veneration for the Germanic body: that respect peculiar to the house of Brunswick Lunenbourg, which will always hold it inviolable, is become habitual to his majesty in particular: accordingly he again hath recourse, in quality of elector, to the dyet of the empire by means of this memorial, though previously reserving to himself a power to do it hereafter in a more ample manner. The records of the empire shew what he has done for Germany in such a manner, that at least it cannot yet be forgotten in that country. He hopes that upon this occasion it will have some weight, the rather as his high co-estates will easily consider, that what is now endeavoured to be done to his majesty, may one day, and perhaps sooner than they think, be done to themselves.

His majesty, as elector, is charged, 1st. With not conforming to the resolution taken the 17th of January, and the 9th of May, last year; but on the contrary, refusing his concurrence, and declaring for a neutrality. 2dly, With giving succours, aid and assistance to his majesty the King of Prussia, entering into an alliance with that prince, joining his troops to those of Prussia, under the command of a general in the service of his Prussian majesty, of sending English troops into Germany, and making them take possession of the city of Embden, and employing the auxiliary troops of some other states of the empire: And, 3dly, It is complained that contributions had been exacted in his majesty's name of divers states of the empire.

With regard to the first charge, it is very true, in the deliberations held at the dyet of the empire the beginning of last year, it was given as his majesty's opinion, as well as that of most of his Protestant co-estates, that the present troubles should be amicably terminated. His majesty in giving this opinion, had, as usual, no other view than what equity and the good of the Germanic empire seemed to him to require. Whatever judgment shall be formed of the unhappy war that hath broke out, the public will always remember, that by a bare declaration of her majesty the empress queen, 'That she would not attack his Prussian majesty,' the rupture would have been avoided, and the effusion of much blood, as well as the desolation of Germany, prevented. The states that have suffered by the calamities of the war, may judge whether the way that was taken was the shortest for the re-establishment of peace so much to be desired; and whether it were not to be wished that laying aside all private views, his Britannic majesty's proposal had been followed.

It is true, his majesty took no part in the resolutions, which were contrary to his sentiments. But the laws of the empire have not thereby received the least infringement. The question, whether *in*

mate-

materia collectarum, the majority be ſufficient, has been referred *ad comitia imperii*, by the *inſtrumentum*, *P. W. Art.* §. v. 52. and is yet undecided. It is not by the plurality of voices that it can be there determined, but only by means of an amicable accommodation; ſince otherwiſe that reference would have been a very uſeleſs courſe; and it is well known, at the negotiations for the peace of Weſtphalia, what was the tendency of the opinion of the catholic ſtates, which formed the majority; thoſe very ſtates, and all other members of the empire, ought however to conſider well, whether it be their eſſential intereſt to acknowledge, in the preſent caſe, that every ſtate in the empire is obliged to ſubmit it to the majority of votes, in matters of conſent, as in the preſent caſe; which the principal catholic electors have in other caſes denied; and which will certainly be retorted upon them in proper time.

But whatever principles ſhall be aſſumed, with regard to this queſtion, nothing is more evident, than that, conſidering circumſtances and the ſituation of the affair then and now in queſtion, his majeſty could never be required to give his troops to comply with thoſe reſolutions of the empire. All Germany knows, though the decree of the Aulic imperial council ſays not a word about it, that at the very time when thoſe reſolutions were taken, his majeſty's electoral dominions were moſt unjuſtly threatened with an invaſion by France. In the month of March that year, the court of Vienna ſigned a convention with France, by virtue of which the enemy was to paſs the Weſer in the month of July, and enter the king's territories. This invaſion was made accordingly. The empreſs queen joined her own troops to thoſe of France; and in return ſtipulated by ſolemn treaties, ſigned beforehand, to have half of the contributions that ſhould be exacted. The damage which the king's ſubjects ſuffered by the firſt invaſion, excluſive of the ſums which the provinces were to furniſh (and which have been paid out of the royal demeſnes) amounted to ſeveral millions. And ſtill the unjuſt rage of his majeſty's enemies was not exhauſted. The French army, which entered on the other ſide under the command of the Prince de Soubiſe, in company with the troops of Wirtemberg, which the reigning duke, a thing of which there is no example, led himſelf, under a French general, againſt a co-eſtate, hath again invaded, for the ſecond time, his majeſty's dominions and thoſe of his allies; exacted inſupportable contributions; carried off the king's officers, entirely foraged the country, and plundered ſeveral places, and committed the greateſt diſorders, whilſt the court of Vienna boaſts of having ordered this invaſion (the ſole end of which was to ravage the king's dominions and thoſe of Heſſe) as an effect of its magnanimity, and as a merit with the Germanic body.

If in ſuch circumſtances his majeſty ſhould be required to ſuſpend the preparations he has begun, and join the troops that he wants for his own defence to thoſe, which, from the arbitrary views of the court of Vienna, are led againſt his

his Pruſſian majeſty by a prince who doth not belong to the generality of the empire, and on whom the command hath been conferred without a previous concluſum of the Germanic body; the right of the ſtates of the empire to defend themſelves when ſuch defence ſquares not with the views of the imperial court, ought, at the ſame time, to be ſettled. It is hoped that things are not yet come to this paſs in Germany. Self-defence is the moſt urgent duty. The reſolutions of the empire cannot deprive the meaneſt man, much leſs a free ſtate, and an elector of the empire, of his right; nor require him to join the troops he wants for that end, to thoſe, which jointly with the troops of France, have invaded his country, and ſhared in the contributions there extorted.

In the ſecond place, his majeſty doth not deny that he hath entered into an alliance with the king of Pruſſia, which is entirely conformable to the rules of right: but as he is accountable to God alone for what he doth as king, on the other hand, in the report made of what he has done as elector, the times which preceded hath been confounded with thoſe that followed the French invaſion. From the beginning of the laſt year his majeſty took every method to ſhew, that the only thing he aimed at, without taking part, otherwiſe, in the war, was to oppoſe the French foreign troops, knowing they were ſent only to invade his electorate, as indeed they have employed themſelves almoſt wholly in ruining eſtates comprehended under the guaranty of the empire, as well thoſe of the Duke of Saxony of the Erneſtine line, of the Duke of Brunſwick Wofenbuttel, the Landgrave of Heſſe-Caſſel, and the Count of Lippe-Schaumburg, as thoſe of his majeſty. This juſt intention, founded on the laws, from which his majeſty hath been ſo far from derogating in the ſmalleſt matter, that no inſtance thereof hath been, or can be brought, did not, nevertheleſs, hinder the French troops, who were furniſhed with the emperor's letters requiſitorial, from entering Germany in the avowed quality of auxiliary troops to the empreſs queen, in company with thoſe of the houſe of Auſtria and the elector Palatine. The empire hath already been informed, on the third of *December* laſt year, of the firſt propoſals made, both to the imperial court, and the court of France, for an amicable determination of differences; propoſals, which could not have been rejected, had not an hoſtile attack been *reſolved on*. Theſe offers, which from the manner in which they were received, his majeſty hath reaſon to regret that he ever made, leave no ſhadow of plauſibility to the reproaches that may be made on account of the engagement that enſued, in whatever light the king of Pruſſia's cauſe may be conſidered. His majeſty is, indeed, fully perſuaded, that he might, at any time, have entered into an alliance with that prince for their common defence; but no one can doubt, that, in this urgent neceſſity, when he was left alone, he had a right to ſeek aſſiſtance where it could be got. No fault can poſſibly be found with that which the King of Pruſſia gave him to deliver the electoral ſtates of Brunſwick, and thoſe of Wolfenbuttel, Heſſe, and Bucke-

Buckebourg. The very nature of this deliverance, and the prudence and bravery with which it hath been effected, have acquired immortal glory to his most serene highness Duke Ferdinand of Brunswick-Lunenbourg (who doth not command the King's army as a Prussian general) a glory, which is the greater, as it is more laudable for that prince to have delivered from such heavy and unjust oppression the dominions of a king from whose family he is descended, and principalities in which he drew his first breath, where his ancestors have reigned, and where the duke his brother still reigns. It is with an equally just right that this duke, with the Duke of Saxe-Gotha, the Landgrave of Hesse-Cassel, and the Count of Schaumbourg-Lippe, put their troops into his majesty's pay. Posterity will hardly believe, that at a time when Austrian, Palatine, and Wirtemberg auxiliaries were employed to invade the countries belonging to states of the empire, other members of the Germanic body who employed auxiliaries in their defence, were threatened with the ban. His majesty ordered the English troops to be sent over, and possession to be taken of Embden, in his quality of king; and hath no occasion to give account thereof to any. Mean while the laws of the empire permit the states thereof to make use of foreign troops in their own defence; they forbid only the introduction of them into the empire to invade the dominions of another, as the empress queen hath done.

In the third and last place, his majesty the King of Great Btitain, Elector of Brunswick-Lunenbourg, sent ministers, particularly to the Palatine court and that of Cologne, to divert them from joining in the designs of France against his dominions. It cannot therefore be doubted, that it would have been highly agreeable to him, if those courts had taken measures that would have freed him from the burthen of the war. But none can expect that his majesty should with indifference see himself treated as an enemy by his co-estates. The Elector of Cologne and the Bishop of Liege had no troops that were wanted in the French army: but in consideration of subsidies, opened to it the gates of their towns, and gave it all the assistance in their power; without which that army could not at that time have proceeded so far as the electoral estates, where the Austrian and Palatine troops behaved much worse than the French themselves. How can it be expected that his majesty, after God hath blessed his arms with success, should not resent this treatment? The laws of the empire forbid the attacking of the states of the empire; but they permit defence against, and the pursuit of those who by their invasion have violated the public peace.

If the crown of France be free to ravage the dominions of the Duke of Brunswick and the Landgrave of Hesse-Cassel, because they have given the king auxiliary troops: if the empress queen may, for the assistance she hath lent the French king to attack the king's dominions, appropriate to herself half of the contributious raised there; his majesty ought to be equally permitted to make those states, who have favoured the unjust enter-

enterprizes of his enemies, feel the burden of the war.

These are facts notorious to the whole empire: his majesty hath too good an opinion of the penetration of his high co-estates, to doubt of their perceiving the importance of them, and laying to heart what the merit he has acquired with the empire might have required, and still requires; and therefore his majesty expects that the dyet will, by way of advice, propose to his imperial majesty, to annul his most inconsistent mandates; and not only take the most effectual measures to protect the electorate and the countries of his majesty, and those of Brunswick-Wolfenbuttel, Hesse-Cassel, and Lippe-Schaumbourg, and procure them a proper indemnification; but also give orders for those proceedings against the empress queen, as archdutchess of Austria, the elector palatine, and the duke of Wirtemberg, which her majesty, without being required to do it, puts in force against his Britannic majesty, Elector of Brunswick-Lunebourg. For which end the undersigned most humbly requests your excellencies to ask immediately necessary instructions from your principals.

Can it be said, that this was approving of a convention, and demanding an explanation so important and so contrary to its true meaning. His majesty the King of Denmark had too great regard for the king, to think it just to engage him to subscribe to that, as a consequence of the treaty signed at Closter-seven. If Marshal Richelieu did not mean by his pretended words of honour, the assurance not to begin hostilities before the rupture of the negotiation, we own we know not what he meant, at least that is the sense in which we have ever understood those expressions, and in which we have executed the convention. The French ministry know very well, that the chief point is to determine how long the obligation of the treaty ought to subsist, according to the views of the contracting parties. 'Hence, say they, it is evident, 'that the expression of final reconciliation is made use of in 'Article III. only to denote that 'Bremen and Verden were to 'remain in the hands of the 'French till that final reconciliation should happen. This is 'the same thing as if it had been 'stipulated, that the French should 'remain in possession of that 'country till a peace. That the 'Duke of Cumberland knew very 'well that his most christian majesty had formerly refused to 'treat with him about a neutrality for Hanover; that he had 'therefore left out the condition 'of a separate reconciliation, fearing that his proposal might have 'caused the convention to be rejected, which he had so much 'interest and honour to obtain. 'That it is plain, from the preamble to the convention, that 'the intention of it was to hinder 'the countries of Bremen and Verden from being any longer the 'theatre of the war.'

His royal highness, the Duke of Cumberland, so far from being convinced of the impossibility of obtaining a separate accommodation for the king, knew that the court of Vienna had promised her utmost efforts to bring it about, and had even, for that purpose, sent a courier to Versailles to hasten its conclusion. These promises were the more to be depended on, as France had all along pretended in her writings, that her sole motive in not acceding to these proposals, was because she was not willing to do it *without the concurrence of her allies*. The final reconciliation of the two sovereigns, namely, the king as elector, and the king of France, had certainly no relation to a general peace. The proposals made to France of an accommodation, and known both to Marshal Richelieu and Count Lynar, could leave no difficulty as to the true sense of the term of a final reconciliation. She may exaggerate, as much as she will, the dangerous situation, and the extremity to which the king's army was reduced, when the suspension of arms was concluded; but the event could not have been more fatal than that which France wanted to bring about; as the intention of the two contracting parttes; for by her principles the states of the king would have remained in the hands of the enemy, as long as the court of Versailles should have thought proper to keep them; the auxiliary troops would have been disarmed, and those of the king exposed to total destruction. It is plain that the preamble to the convention speaks only of the reasons which induced his Danish majesty to interpose in that affair. The king gives them that justice which they deserve, and looks upon the care of the King of Denmark as a proof of his inestimable friendship, and at the same time as an effect of his humanity, and of the generous concern which his Danish majesty took to prevent the effusion of blood, and to stop the scourge of war; but by this also the king is persuaded, that the court of Copenhagen never intended to become an instrument to France, to make the king submit to the severe terms which the latter wanted to impose upon him, under pretence of the convention, and by means of pretended necessary explanations.

The disarming of the Hessians is properly the rock on which the convention split, so the French spare no pains to give a colour to this pretence. 'The Duke of 'Brunswick, say they, ratified, 'without any alteration, the con'vention signed at Vienna, relating 'to the disarming of his troops. 'The landgrave had formally 'demanded to be treated as that 'prince. It was not natural to 'trust to a considerable body of 'troops, which submitted only 'through fear, and it was a silly 'precaution to take away the 'means of offence, without be'ing sure of taking away the in'clination. It follows evidently 'from the terms of the conven'tion, that these troops being 'disbanded, they were disingag'ed from all connexions with the 'King of England, Elector of 'Hanover, who consequently had 'no right to retain them, and to 'steal away the son of the Duke 'of Brunswick. The only condi'tion which the Hanoverian ge'neral had a right to demand 'for the auxiliary troops, was, 'that they should not be re'garded as prisoners of war; and 'he could not pretend but that

'they

'they had been disarmed, The 'condition of disarmed troops is 'by no means equal to that of 'troops prisoners of war.'

It is not our purpose here to examine the negotiations which, it is pretended, the Landgrave, and the Duke of Brunswick entered upon with the court of France; but every one knows that these princes thought themselves in no wise bound by what passed. The design of sowing diffidence among the allies, which France had certainly in view, by alledging these pretended negotiations, will not have its desired effect. Nor will we trouble ourselves to examine, whether the prudence and interest of the court of Versailles required the disarming of the auxiliary troops: Though that court has long adopted it as a maxim to consult only her own interest, and to give no other reason but her own convenience, without considering whether it would be impossible to reconcile these motives with the laws of justice and equity. These are not, however, sufficient means to justify, to the eyes of the public, the pretensions formed with regard to the auxiliary troops.

Nor need we enter into explanations with France about the manner in which the Brunswick troops were retained, nor of that which concerns his royal highness the hereditary Prince of Wolfenbuttel. It would be very easy to free ourselves from all reproach on that head. It is sufficient that these two articles were amicably terminated with his royal highness the Duke of Brunswick. The question between the king and France is, whether the king had reason to oppose the disarming of the auxiliary troops, and whether he had a right to keep them in his pay. We need only see the convention to decide in favour of the affirmative. It does not contain one word which can naturally mean a disarming; nor does it contain any tacit consent to this pretence. It is, indeed, stipulated, that the troops should not be considered as prisoners; but if it could be concluded from hence that the disarming had been granted, it must at the same time be owned, that the convention delivered up these troops to the mercy and discretion of France. The French ministry themselves would not go upon so strange a supposition.

These troops, in quality of troops, and consequently armed, were to return home, and there to find quarters. It was in consequence of this regulation that advice was given of the convention to the sovereigns of the auxiliary troops. It is absurd to say, that by this means they had been disbanded. The landgrave's troops remained, notwithstanding, in the pay of Great Britain, and the troops of the Duke of Brunswick and Gotha, and also those of the Count de la Lippe, never lost their quality of subsidiary troops of the king, as elector. To maintain the contrary, would be to say, that his majesty, in quality of king and elector, had the power of revoking the treaties of subsidy concluded between them, without consulting these princes, a power which his majesty does not pretend to, and which the Duke of Cumberland neither had, nor could have, a design to make use of. The true sense of the convention certainly was, that during the continuance of the ſuſpenſion of arms, theſe troops ſhould remain quiet in their reſpective countries, and at the expiration of the ſuſpenſion they ſhould be at liberty to renew their ſervices by virtue of treaties, and in conſequence of their quality of ſubſidiaries, which was by no means deſtroyed. This having happened, it would be uſeleſs to examine the extent of the articles of the convention, with regard to the deſtination of the Heſſian troops in the pay of England.

The French miniſtry make but a very ſhort anſwer to the accuſations of their having broke the convention, ſet forth in the *Motives* and General Zaſtrow's letter of Nov. 14. They ſay, 'That none of the 'reaſons alledged could occaſion 'the breaking of the convention; 'that no ſtipulation had been made 'for the caſtle of Schartzfeld, nor 'the reſtitution of priſoners; that 'no mention had been made of 'the treatment of the conquered 'countries; and, laſtly, that the 'things ſet forth in M. Zaſtrow's 'letter did not happen till after the 'convention had been firſt broken 'by the Hanoverians.'

When one of the contracting parties thinks itſelf authoriſed to break a treaty, and no recourſe can be had to a ſuperior judgment, it is moſt natural for the other to think itſelf equally diſengaged from all obligation. It is true, that in the treaty of Cloſter-ſeven no mention had been made of priſoners of war; but this point was adjuſted ſix days after, by the act of accommodation concluded at Bremeworde, the 16th of September 1757, between General Sporcken and General Villemur.

The ſuſpenſion of arms had put an end to the hoſtilities of all ſorts which the French army could commit againſt the king, in quality of elector; but was it not an hoſtility to take by aſſault the caſtle of Schartzfeld, to plunder it, and carry off the garriſon priſoners of war? Was it not an hoſtility to redouble, after ſigning the convention, the exactions and violences towards the king's ſubjects, inſtead of granting them the relief which they expected? When a people ſubmits and ceaſes to make reſiſtance, they have a natural right to a milder treatment from the conqueror, than another which is ſtill in fear of hoſtilities. The ſubjects of the electorate tried, though impoſſible, to ſatisfy the exactions that were impoſed upon them; their reſignation only multiplied the moſt exorbitant demands, accompanied with threatnings, which but too plainly ſhewed, that the total ruin and deſtruction of the country would be the conſequences of a convention concluded to prevent this misfortune. Laſtly, if the other breaches by the French had not exiſted before the open breaking of the convention, General Zaſtrow would have no reaſon to complain of them in his letter of the 14th of November.

They pretend to juſtify themſelves by ſaying, 'That the pretence of diſarming the Heſſians 'had been taken away by the 'king's complaiſance, in deſiſting 'from that condition; that what 'was ſaid in the *Motives* was 'falſe; that France had but very 'lately ſoftened her language on 'that head; that as early as the '2d of November, Marſhal Richelieu had declared his having

'deſiſted

'desisted from them, by virtue of 'his full powers, and that in case 'the Hanoverian general had no 'pretence left for executing the 'convention of Closter-seven.' On the 17th of October, 1757, Count Lynar wrote to his majesty's electoral minister, that Marshal Richelieu's courier was returned from Versailles with instructions, which expresly said, the court would hear of no terms of peace; that it was resolved to hold to the scheme of explanation; and lastly, that it would less than ever desist from the condition of disarming the Hessians, and that it had rejected the offer of his Danish majesty, to receive these troops into his territories.

It was therefore necessary to come to a determination on this head, or to wait to see the war kindled up a-fresh. The battle of Rosbach happened on the 5th of November, soon after the arrival of that letter. The king could not foresee that France would then change her tone; he saw himself obliged to take measures, in consequence of the declarations which he had been informed of, by the letter of October 17, nor could he afterwards change them, when it at length pleased the court of Versailles to come down, though very little, from her unjust pretensions. On one hand, he had already addressed himself to his Prussian majesty, and on the other, the proceedings of France shewed but too plainly, that he had reason to be diffident of her fidelity. Besides, it is not true, that she desisted from the disarming of all the auxillary troops. In Marshal Richelieu's letter of November 9, he makes only mention of the Hessians, and is silent with regard to the fate of the troops of Brunswick; lastly, she never pronounced her pretensions to keep the states of the king till a general peace.

It is plain, that during the continuance of a negotiation, and before every thing be regulated and concluded, the two parties have a power to renounce their engagements. If all difficulties had been removed by the convention of Closter-seven, what need was there of a new negotiation? France persisting to want further clauses, and explications to be added to it, gave the king an incontestible right to declare himself according to the nature of the subject and circumstances.

Not content with having combated the motives, which engaged the king to take up arms, they criticise violently upon the manner in which that was executed. 'Had 'there been, say they, any honour'able way of withdrawing from 'the execution of that solemn act, 'it would have been to declare it 'void, by putting themselves in 'the same position they were be'fore it was concluded; but in'stead of that the most odious 'means were made use of to vio'late that capitulation successively 'and with impunity. The time 'was spun out for three months, 'to find an opportunity to break 'the convention. The French 'army was suffered to go to Hal'berstadt, and they waited till it 'was separated by the bad season. 'They seized the opportunity of a 'repulse to come out of the limits 'prescribed them, under pretence 'of extending their quarters. They 'afterwards took advantageous 'posts, under pretences equally 'contrary to the convention. They 'made all the dispositions for the 'siege of Harbourg, without any 'previous declaration of war; and 'having made all these preparations, and when they thought 'the enemy sufficiently weakened 'and deceived, to fight them with 'advantage, they declared that hostilities were to be commenced, 'and that they considered the convention as broken, while they 'were marching against them, 'and attacking their posts.'

The more the author of the Parallel exhausts his rhetoric in this sort of declamation, so much the less regard doth he pay to truth. It is certain and incontestible, that the Hanoverians conformed on their part, in every respect, to the convention, as it was signed. It was neither the king's generals, nor Marshal Richelieu, who caused it to be broken by their declarations; but the court of Versailles, which would not look upon the convention as obligatory, unless it should be extended to the disarming of the auxiliary troops, and unless the king would leave his country to the discretion of his enemies, till a general peace. The king, therefore, had the same right to look upon this affair as depending upon the resolution of the respective courts, and to take his measures accordingly. He made use of that right. It was natural not to commit hostilities as long as Count Lyner's negotiation lasted; but that minister, as the court of Versailles well knows, could never bring about negotiations of peace, which was, however, the true intention of the suspension of arms. Could it be thought strange, if the king, by virtue of the right which the inflexible severity of his enemies gave him, determined himself, according to the events that happened, and the victory gained over the French army at Rosbach? This event, however, did not influence his majesty's resolutions. If any one will but calculate the date of these events, he will be convinced of the contrary. The battle of Rosbach happened on the 5th of November, and the motions of the Hanoverian army were renewed on the 26th of the same month. The king could not have been informed at London, in so short a time, of that success, to give orders to his minister, to sollicit the consent of his Prussian majesty, with regard to Prince Ferdinand, to whom the king offered the command of the army, so as to receive the King of Prussia's answer to hear of the prince's arrival, and cause hostilities to be renewed. If the rules of good faith had not been scrupulously observed, the French army might have been reduced to a more dangerous situation than it really was. In what a critical situation would it have found itself, if the king's troops, as they were fully authorized to do, had marched, on the first discovery of the design to disarm the auxiliary troops, and, at the same time that the battle of Rosbach happened, and when Marshal Richelieu was at Halberstadt with his army, had attacked him in the rear? The operations of the army did not begin till after the King of Prussia was gone into Silesia, and when the French were not only upon their guard, but the first columns of their army had even advanced beyond Lunenbourg, with design to obtain, by open force, the unjust conditions proposed by the court of Versailles. As to the pretended preparations for the siege of Harbourg, we know nothing at all of them. We do not deny but the quarters of the troops were extended; but that we were obliged to do it through unavoidable neceſſity, the quarters deſtined to receive only the Hanoverian troops, not being, at the ſame time, ſufficient for thoſe of Heſſe and Brunſwick alſo, which by a natural conſequence of the proceedings of France, could not be ſeparated from the body of the army. Neither of the two French detachments were ſurprized; the two armies were aſſembled when the ſcene of operations was again opened, and in this reſpect they were in the ſame ſituation as at Cloſter-ſeven. Nor was it in the year 1757, but the year following, that the French army was driven out of his majeſty's German dominions. The victory gained at Roſbach, the bad ſeaſon, the diſeaſes, and decreaſe of the French army, events which never followed from the king's reſolutions, could not oblige his majeſty to maintain a convention, which in itſelf was not binding, and which France would not acknowledge as ſuch, when it was a proper time.

We flatter ourſelves we have fully anſwered the reproaches of the court of Verſailles; at leaſt none of the objections that relate to the deciſion of the ſubject, have been wilfully forgot. We do not pretend to anticipate the judgment of the public; we leave it to pronounce, after having ſeen a true repreſentation of his Britannic majeſty's conduct, whether the miniſtry of Verſailles are in the right, when they ſay, 'That ſuch odious 'principles and proceedings can 'only be owing to the artifices and 'evil counſels of ſome corrupt miniſters.' We will not trouble ourſelves to anſwer this abuſive language: nor will we retort it, but paſs over the above, as well as many other reproaches equally odious and trifling. The French miniſtry cannot be ſo ignorant of the judgment, which their own nation forms of their principles, to doubt, that we might, if we had a mind, reproach them with their evil counſels and meaſures, equally ruinous to France and Germany, in a manner which, even in France itſelf, would not fail to make an impreſſion. It is, however, neceſſary to add two remarks on what has been ſaid. Our days have produced a phænomenon, of which hiſtory does not furniſh us with an example; we have ſeen the houſes of Auſtria and Bourbon, uniting their forces to give chains to Europe, and eſpecially to Germany. Providence does not want means to prevent this misfortune. This dominion ſo eagerly ſought for could not be exerciſed in concert, if they ſhould make themſelves maſters of it. That alliance, the firſt years of which have flowed with rivers of blood, will occaſion no leſs bloodſhed, when it comes one day to be broken; but the violent tumults, and the imminent dangers, with which the politic ſyſtem of Europe, and ſo many kingdoms and ſtates are threatened during this criſis, merit the moſt ſerious attention of thoſe who are at the helm of government. Eſpecially it is manifeſt, that the Proteſtant religion is in inevitable danger, notwithſtanding the falſe proteſtations given to the profeſſors of it. The pretended ſchemes of ſecularization aſcribed to his Britannic majeſty and the King of Pruſſia, are ſo ill-founded, that they are taken upon the authority of an obſcure work, every page of which ſhews the author to have no right to be a negotiator of peace. Never had the Catholic religion leſs to fear than at a time when its arms are united, and diſſention reigns among the Proteſtants. It is not the ſame with regard to what the latter have to fear from their enemies. The deſigns of the court of Vienna to render the Catholic religion predominant in Germany, have been plainly exhibited by the reflections, and the advices of a very able miniſter, who certainly would not have impoſed upon his court, and who had his information from the fountain-head. The juſtice of his diſcoveries has been proved by the event, for we ſee not one Catholic ſtate of the empire, but what have bowed the neck to his new ſyſtem, out of a zeal for religion, notwithſtanding the real diſadvantages that muſt naturally follow. It is only anſwered to theſe arguments, that the treaty of Verſailles has been founded upon the treaty of Weſtphalia. But are not the courts which have contracted theſe new engagements, free to change them at pleaſure, and according to circumſtances? Beſides, if the Proteſtant ſtates, as they pretend, are bound to adopt the treaty of the peace of Weſtphalia, in what ſenſe the Catholics pleaſe to give it, it is but too clear, that the Proteſtants are already diveſted of the moſt important privileges, granted to them by that treaty.

All the king's meaſures will ever tend to the general ſafety of Europe, to the liberty and independence of the empire, and the maintainance of the Proteſtant religion. Neither the misfortune with his eſtates of Germany have ſuffered, nor the baſe treatment which he hath received from the court of Vienna, nor the conduct of ſeveral of his co-eſtates, which favour the unjuſt deſigns of that court, will ever be able to divert him from an end ſo worthy of himſelf. He hopes that the Divine Providence will continue to bleſs the arms which he has taken up in his own defence, and that it will make this the means of procuring peace to the empire, and alſo of blaſting the wicked deſigns of thoſe who have brought into it the flame of war, and have opened a ſcene of calamities, of which we have not ſeen an inſtance ſince the peace of Weſtphalia.

Extracts from the manifeſto of the court of France, lately publiſhed by authority at Paris.

This ſophiſtical and ſcurrilous piece conſiſts of three parts: the firſt contains what they call preliminary eclairciſſements: the ſecond is called, Parallel of the king's conduct with that of the King of England, Elector of Hanover: and the third contains the vouchers of the facts mentioned in the two former.

The firſt labours to prove the juſtice of the king's ſending his armies into Germany, and attacking the Elector of Hanover and Landgrave of Heſſe-Caſſel; and the reaſoning in it would have ſome foundation, if they had proved, that the King of Pruſſia was the firſt aggreſſor, and conſequently the firſt infractor of the peace of the empire. But this they take for granted, ſo that the whole is founded upon a *petitio principii*, or what we call a begging the queſtion, therefore deſerves no notice.

As to the ſecond part, after ſome ſcurrilous ſtrictures upon the conduct

duct of Hanover, with relation to the convention of Closter-seven, they proceed as follows.

" As it is chiefly from the king's alliance with the Empress Queen of Hungary and Bohemia, that the King of England, Elector of Hanover, has sought to take advantage for stirring up the states of Germany against their most Christian and Imperial Majesties, and cover with a specious pretext his pernicious attempts against the quiet and safety of the empire; the first thing must be to deface the false impressions intended by him to be made on the public.

To this end it will be demonstrated, that this alliance which his Britannic majesty has pretended to be so very unnatural and so dangerous for the Germanic liberty, has, on the contrary, been quite natural; that the kings of England and Prussia have themselves rendered it necessary, and that if the liberty of the empire is threatened with the greatest dangers, it is from those who have attacked it, and who in contempt of the Germanic constitutions, and of whatever among sovereigns is most sacred, labour to oppress it, and not from those who defend it, pursuant to their engagements, in conformity to the resolutions of the empire, and at the hazard of their own safety.

It is manifest that on the first hostilities in North America of the King of England against the French, the king formed the design of confining himself to his own defence against the English, in order, were it possible, to preserve to Europe in general, and the empire in particular, the advantages of peace, of which he found himself deprived by the injustice and ambition of his enemies.

But very different were the thoughts of other powers; the King of Prussia, dazzled, as he himself owns, by the King of England's glittering promises, quitted the alliance of France; and suddenly came to light a particular treaty betwixt the courts of London and Berlin, containing the most dangerous views, and which, among other objects, imposed laws on the princes of Germany, interdicting them the liberty of foreign succours, which is reserved to them by the Germanic constitutions, in case of their being attacked.

These two courts indeed gave out that this treaty tended only to the support of the tranquillity of Germany, and that it was the motive for the clause expressing, that they would suffer no foreign troops to enter it under any pretence whatever; but as the empire had in no wise commissioned them with this care, and the King of Prussia, in concert with the King of England, was making immense preparations of war, at a time when he had no enemies to fight, it was easy to judge, that the real scope of a clause so contrary to the Germanic constitutions, was to hinder any opposition coming from without Germany to the war which those two princes had determined to kindle within, if they should not find the court of Vienna favourable to the project of exciting a general war, in which France might be implicated.

If the expression of this clause drew a suspicion on their views, they were entirely laid open by the

the omiſſion of another; that is, by their affectation of not inſerting into the treaty of Weſtminſter the neutrality of the Low Countries, in favour of the empreſs queen, at the ſame time as that of Germany. The public ſoon ſaw into this artifice. The King of England having, to no purpoſe, uſed all his endeavours with that princeſs, for drawing her into the ſcheme of the general war which he was concerned and reſolved to bring on the continent; their Britannic and Pruſſian majeſties contrived the expedient of leaving expoſed the Low Countries, then very thin of troops, and by this bait to incline France to attack them. The drift of theſe two princes in the ſuppoſition of ſuch an event was to reap a double advantage from it, to alienate the Dutch from the neutrality, and to join the empreſs queen to their meaſures by the neceſſity of defending herſelf.

The good faith of the king and the empreſs queen fruſtrated this deceptive project; the king did not think it juſt to fall on the Low Countries, becauſe the Engliſh made war on him; the empire held it unworthy of her to join in the deſign of kindling a general war to ſerve the exceſſive ambition of England, at the expence of France, againſt whom ſhe had no cauſe of complaint, and to the prejudice of the quiet and ſafety of the empire.

In theſe circumſtances, the king and the empreſs, abandoned at the ſame time by their principal allies, could no longer remain under an incertainty of their reſpective deſigns: the empreſs's territories lay open towards France, as likewiſe towards the King of Pruſſia, and the King of England Elector of Hanover; his majeſty, on his ſide, might fear that this critical conjuncture would at length oblige the empreſs to yield to the ſollicitations and menaces of the King of England. The ſimilarity of their moſt Chriſtian and Imperial majeſties ſituation, that of their zeal for the general tranquiliity, the mutual ſentiments of eſteem with which they had long before inſpired each other, made them open their eyes. They at length perceived, that the private ambition of princes continually inſtigating one againſt the other, was the mean cauſe of their variances, and of the wars which had ſo long deſolated Europe; and eſpecially Germany: and in order to deſtroy the very root of the evil, their majeſties united together in a treaty of friendſhip, purely defenſive, and in a convention of neutrality for the Low Countries, and their reſpective dominions.

Thus had the kings of England and Pruſſia the art of bringing about by their conduct what, for ſeveral centuries paſt, all the efforts of policy had in vain been labouring at, and what, for the tranquillity of the empire, the beſt inclined part of Germany had always deſired. Thus their ambition and infidelity proved both the natural and neceſſary cauſe of the union of the courts of France and Vienna; there, and there only, it is to be ſought for.

All the illuſory ſuſpicions, all the imaginary fears, which the kings of Pruſſia and England have endeavoured to infuſe into the public againſt the union of thoſe two powers, as comprehending

ing the deſign of injuring the rights of the princes of the empire, and of exalting the Roman Catholic religion on the ruin of the Proteſtant, are mere chimeras, forged by the vexation of not having been able to arm the courts of France and Vienna againſt each other as formerly, and by a ſtrong impatience to remedy that diſappointment, by ſtirring up the Proteſtant princes againſt thoſe courts, under the maſk of religion.

The difference of the conduct of the king from that of the kings of England and Pruſſia, need but be conſidered, to know the difference of their intentions, and to be convinced of the truth of what is here alledged. His majeſty, as it is before noticed, and as all the world has perceived, has omitted nothing, that the American diſturbances might not reach the continent of Europe; and whilſt their Britannic and Pruſſian majeſties left no ſtone unturned for drawing the war into the empire, and ſubverting its laws, his majeſty was intent on keeping off the conflagration, and preſerving thoſe laws from utter deſtruction.

It is with this motive, that by means of the convention of neutrality which the king has concluded with the empreſs queen for the Low Countries, and of the declaration given him by the States General of the United Provinces, he has ſecured peace in that part of Europe, which had hitherto been moſt expoſed to the flame of war; which had generally, if not always, communicated it to Germany, and which by their Britannic and Pruſſian majeſties had been left to the diſcretion of France.

It is likewiſe with the ſame motive, that the king and the empreſs have made known to all Europe, that the principal object of their union was the maintenance of the laws and conſtitution of Germany; that in conſequence thereof the two courts have taken for the baſis of the treaty of Verſailles the peace of Weſtphalia, which is the ſureſt barrier of the Germanic liberty: and that his majeſty, together with Sweden, joint guarantee of this peace, has declared to all the empire, that he would uſe his utmoſt efforts for maintaining the rights of the ſtates, and particularly of the three religions eſtabliſhed in Germany.

Had the kings of England and Pruſſia been poſſeſſed with the ſame zeal for the peace of Europe as his majeſty, the treaty of Verſailles, the neutrality of the Low Countries, and that of Holland, could not have raiſed in them that paſſionate reſentment which they have ſhewn at it, and the empire would ſtill enjoy the moſt profound calm, ſecured from the ſtorms which have broke out in America; but the projects of thoſe princes were not compatible either with the quiet of Europe, or that of the empire; they could not do without a continental war.

The ill ſucceſs of the unjuſt and violent enterprizes of the King of England againſt France, both in America and Europe, having changed the brilliant expectations with which that prince's miniſters had flattered the Britiſh nation into real loſſes for the preſent,

ſent, and apprehenſions for the future, they have been forced to have recourſe to freſh expedients for allaying the reſentment of that nation, and eſpecially for getting from it ſuch an augmentation of ſubſidies, of which the Elector of Hanover ſhould come in for a part; the way which has ſeemed to them the fitteſt for ſettling their affairs, has been to throw thoſe of others in confuſion, and at any rate to kindle a war in Germany.

The King of England and his miniſters have done ſo much juſtice to the king, as to conclude, that in caſe of any attack made on the principal ſtates of the empire to which he was united, or of any violation of the Germanic laws and conſtitutions, his majeſty's fidelity towards his allies, his quality of guarantee of the treaty of Weſtphalia, his conſtant zeal for the quiet and ſafety of Germany, would induce him to take part in this war, and that by this diverſion they ſhould weaken the efforts which France was obliged to make by ſea, for defending itſelf againſt the Engliſh.

The court of Hanover has not forgot its advantages in the plan which it has formed for itſelf. As the intereſts of the Britiſh nation have for a long time been ſubordinate to the elector's conveniency, it had two views relative to the latter; the firſt of procuring to his electoral highneſs large ſubſidies, by arming the Hanoverians for ſupporting the King of Pruſſia's enterprizes, and thus weaken the king's operations for the defence of the liberty of the empire, and that of the ſtates of the allies.

The ſecond view has been to convert the war of Germany into a religious war, in order to gain to themſelves the ſupport of the Proteſtant princes; hence a double advantage was to reſult; if theſe princes by their ſuccours facilitated the execution of the deſigns of their Britannic and Pruſſian majeſties, an increaſe of authority and power was thus procured to the Elector of Hanover, to the detriment of his neighbours, both Catholic and Proteſtant; and this is known to have long been the favourite object of his ambition; if, on the other hand, the ſucceſſes ſhould fail, a greater part of the damages to be ſuſtained was to be thrown on the allied princes.

A project of ſuch danger to the empire could not be executed but with the concurrence of the King of Pruſſia, and this the King of England has obtained by ſoothing the ambition of that prince with the hopes of a new acquiſition at the expence of the empreſs queen, who was to be chaſtiſed for having dared to refuſe aſſiſting in the execution of the unjuſt projects of the King of England, Elector of Hanover. His Pruſſian majeſty the more readily came into thoſe views, as from the ideas which he had formed on the conjunctures of Europe at that time, and particularly on the ſituation of Saxony and Bohemia, as defenceleſs, he imagined that he ſhould penetrate to Vienna itſelf, without meeting with any obſtacles of ſtrength to ſtop him; that there he ſhould dictate the conditions of peace; that, in fine, he ſhould give laws on the continent, whilſt his Britiſh majeſty did the like on the ocean; and that to the

public

public the success would sufficiently justify the enormity of the attempt, and all the odious practices made use of for its accomplishment.

Such have been the projects of the two kings; such is the whole mystery of this unjust war, set on foot by those princes, in contempt of the faith of treaties, and of the laws of the empire. It would be in vain for the King of England, Elector of Hanover, to alledge, as he before has, that he had no hand in this war, and that he even disapproved of it; the contrary is not only demonstrated by facts, but there are still other proofs, which attest that he was the first promoter of it, and they are such as cannot be disputed, proceeding directly from the Kings of England and Prussia; these two princes have laid each other open in the declarations which passed betwixt them in the month of September last.

In that of the King of Prussia, on the intelligence he had received of a neutrality proposed by the Duke of Cumberland to the Marshal de Richelieu, he expresses himself thus:

"I just now hear that the business of a neutrality for the electorate of Hanover is not yet dropped; can your majesty have so little constancy and firmness, as to be discouraged by a few cross events? Are affairs so far gone that they cannot be retrieved? Consider the step which your majesty proposes to take, and that which you made me take. You are the cause of all the misfortunes now impending over me. I should never have departed from the alliance with France but for your many magnificent promises. I do not repent of the treaty which I have made with your majesty; but after having drawn on me most of the forces of Europe, do not meanly leave me to the mercy of my enemies. I make account that your majesty will call to mind your engagements, which have been renewed no longer ago than the 26th of the last month, and that you will not hearken to any accommodation in which I am not included." *

The King of England's answer to this declaration confirms the truth of its contents, as this prince does not contradict the charge brought against him of being the cause of the war in Germany; and after clearing himself but very indifferently of the reproach made him for entering on a negotiation for the electorate of Hanover, he concludes with these words:

"In such a critical situation whatever might have been the success of arms, his majesty is determined steadily to concur with the King of Prussia in the most efficacious measures for disappointing the iniquitous and oppressive designs of their common enemies; and the King of Prussia may assure himself, that the crown of Great Britain will continue religiously to fulfil its engagements with his Prussian majesty, and support him with vigour and constancy."

The King of Prussia's declaration, and the King of England's answer, having been inserted in the public papers without any contradiction from them, their authenticity is not to

* *N. B.* This letter was disowned, and declared to be supposititious, by an article in the Berlin Gazette, after the Hanoverians had resolved to renew hostilities.

to be queſtioned, nor conſequently the credit of what they contain.

To theſe proofs it cannot but be pertinent to add ſome obſervations on the endeavours put in practice for inſtigating the Proteſtants of Germany againſt France, under the falſe prete ce that it has deſigns pernicious to their religion.

To carry this point, the moſt odious devices are daily employed. Licentiouſneſs has, very lately, been carried ſo far as to inſert in the public news-papers fictitious facts, and no leſs ridiculous than injurious, in order to impoſe on the good faith of the Proteſtant ſtates, and arm them againſt the French troops; but the motives of thoſe who have invented ſuch fables, and the means they make uſe of for gaining them credit, have evidenced to the whole empire, that the intent of making a religious war of that which has been ſtirred up merely by ambition, is only to aſſociate the Proteſtants in Germany in the bad cauſe taken in hand, and by their ſuccours and at their expence, procure a facility of carrying it through.

The ſtates of Saxony are particularly a proof and inſtance of this truth; the Pruſſians have by the moſt flagitious injuſtice forcibly made themſelves maſters of Saxony, which has been the nurſery of the Proteſtant religion, and where it ſubſiſts in the greateſt vigour; yet have they there, againſt the ſovereign of the country, againſt his family and his ſubjects, committed ſuch violences as are ſhocking to human nature.

The territories of the Duke of Mecklenburgh have had the ſame fate. The Pruſſians entered it ſword in hand without any reaſon, and in contempt of the public peace. The duke they have obliged to ſeek refuge at Lubeck; the fortreſſes they have taken poſſeſſion of; and by deſpotic orders, without any payment, have made themſelves be ſupplied with the corn and forage; the young men have been forced away from their parents, to inliſt them and make them ſerve agaiaſt their own ſovereign; in a word, without the ſlighteſt complaint againſt the Duke of Mecklenburgh, his dutchy is treated by the Pruſſians like a conquered country. In fine, to perſuade the Proteſtants of Germany that their religion is threatened, martyrs of it have been made; and the authors of all theſe violences would have them be eſteemed as preparatory acts of the zeal with which they are animated for the defence of that religion.

One muſt be void of common ſenſe to be caught by ſuch coarſe-ſpun artifices! The three religions of the empire, and particularly the Proteſtant, cannot have any more ſure guarantees of their rights than thoſe of the peace of Weſtphalia; as in theſe are united both the intereſt and will to provide for the conſervation of them.

This peace the king has taken for the baſis of his treaty with the empreſs queen. He has, jointly with Sweden, declared, that he would maintain the Germanic liberty, and particularly the rights of the three religions rendered ſacred by the treaties of Weſtphalia; and his majeſty here renews the authentic declaration, that he never entertained a deſign of doing the leaſt hurt to either of thoſe three religions; and that he will, with the greateſt punctuality, fulfil the engagements which, on that head, he has entered into with the crown of Sweden; what greater ſecurity

would

would the Proteſtant ſtates have, ſhould they after this ſuffer themſelves to be drawn into real calamities by an imaginary fear; a fear ſuggeſted to them merely as a veil to ſuch ambitious views as are highly detrimental to the whole empire?

After this diſcuſſion, let us reaſſume the thread of the events. When the war, which had been meditated by the King of England, Elector of Hanover, in concert with the King of Pruſſia, had broke out in Germany; the ideas which theſe two princes had formed from the king's fidelity to his engagements, were not miſtaken. The ſtates of the empire attacked by the King of Pruſſia, together with the princes, who had moſt at heart the Germanic ſyſtem, applied for aſſiſtance to his majeſty, both as an ally of the empire and guarantee of the treaty of Weſtphalia, as in virtue of his alliances merely defenſive with ſeveral courts of Germany; and tho' the king was engaged in a perſonal and onerous war with England, he did not heſitate to form the generous reſolution of employing the greateſt part of his forces in the defence of his allies, and the maintenance of the laws of the empire, and of the Germanic ſyſtem, threatened with a total ſubverſion from their Britannic and Pruſſian majeſties, both as kings and electors.

Sweden being joint guarantee of the peace of Weſtphalia, together with the king, was required to make good its guaranty; and ſuch was its magnanimity, its regard to honour and good faith, that immediately it formed the ſame reſolution.

The king at the ſame time ſignified to the empire, that he would act up to his quality of guarantee; he expreſsly aſſured it that he would ſupport the liberty of the three religions jointly with Sweden, which has always been the moſt declared protectreſs of the Proteſtant religion; and his majeſty made all the neceſſary preparations for fulfilling his engagements, by ſending a conſiderable body of troops to the Lower and Upper Rhine.

The King of England was conſcious, that every kind of reaſon authoriſed his majeſty not to make the chimerical diſtinction he was for eſtabliſhing betwixt his quality of king and that of elector, eſpecially when one raiſes a war and pays the coſts, and the other takes upon him the execution of it. It was a critical conjuncture for that prince, as great part of the Hanoverian troops, by the allurement to the ample ſubſidies which the elector had got from the parliament, and under the colour of defending the Britiſh nation, had been drawn over to England; but this nation ſending them back, the elector was afraid that France would march a detachment of its army into the electorate of Hanover, before the Hanoverians, who were to return into Germany, ſhould get back.

It was in theſe moments of incertitude and dread, that the elector cauſed ſome inſinuations to be made for a neutrality of his German dominions.

The king and the empreſs queen, animated with an equal zeal for the good of the empire, were deſirous that the war ſhould not ſpread to the ſtates forbearing to aſſiſt the infractor of the public peace, and with this view her imperial majeſty ſollicited the king to grant a neutrality for the elector of Hanover.

The

The proposal was not without difficulty; the forced situation of that prince, and the instance of the neutrality in 1741, no sooner concluded than violated by the Hanoverians, raised suspicion of the sincerity of the insinuation made by his ministers. It was natural to apprehend that their own drift was to disturb the operations of the then opening campaign, to procure his electoral highness time for stirring up a part of the princes of Germany against the king and the empress, and then to join all their troops to his, in order, at the first favourable opportunity, safely to fall on the French army.

These reflections, in themselves so just, and of which the solidity was confirmed by past experience in a like circumstance, certainly deserved great regard; but the king's deference for an ally in all respects so faithful and respectable as the empress queen, together with the fear that his majesty might one day be reproached with having rejected a measure which seemed to promise a more speedy restoration of the peace of the empire, prevailed in his mind above every other consideration, and he consented that her imperial majesty should offer on his part a neutrality for the Hanoverian states.

The elector answered it in the memorial of the 20th of February, hereto annexed, but it will be seen that the loftiness with which his electoral highness expresses himself in it, and the invectives against France scattered throughout it, with so little decency, do not indicate very sincere intentions towards a neutrality. The truth is, this prince had almost at the same time asked and obtained from his parliament subsidies for the King of Prussia, and likewise for assembling an army composed of his electoral troops and those of his allies, under the name of an army of observation, in order to support the cause of the infractor of the public peace against the king's troops, which had been sent to the assistance of her allies, and the defence of the liberty of the empire. The Duke of Cumberland had already been appointed for commanding this army, and the 8000 Hanoverians were on the point of passing from England into Germany, so that there seemed to remain no hope for the success of the negotiation; yet did the empress, on fresh insinuations from the elector, desire that the king would impower her to make new trials with that prince. The courts of Russia and Denmark added to them their good offices; they offered their guaranty, and the king was pleased again to come into this fresh negotiation, and condescend to the conditions which alone could render the neutrality solid and lasting; and of which a copy is annexed to this memorial.

The elector's fresh overtures having no more sincerity in them than the former, this second trial had no better fate than the first; the Elector of Hanover clamoured against the conditions proposed, and especially rejected that of the *free passage through his dominions*, and the possession of Hamelen for a cautionary town, as unjust, contrary to his honour, and containing suspicious views; yet that he might not seem totally to renounce the neutrality, his electoral highness proposed to accept of it, provided that instead of the king's troops passing through his dominions, they should take their way thro' the countries of Cassel, Brunswick, Gotha and Weimar;

mar; but this rout being naturally longer and more difficult, it could not be accepted of; and from this time the elector took occasion to break off the negotiation, and throw the blame on the pretended injustice of the French conditions."

Then, after giving several reasons why the King of England, Elector of Hanover, ought to have accepted of the terms offered, and why they could not accept of the terms he proposed, they proceed thus.

"From the concurrence of all these reasons it results, that the Elector of Hanover in his overtures for a neutrality, aimed only at getting time; that he never intended to accept of it, and that he has refused it unjustly and on false pretences. It results further, that the King of England, Elector of Hanover, having been the author of this war, and having, to the neutrality offered him, preferred the party of supporting the King of Prussia's cause, and to take up arms against the king's and empress queen's troops, he has declared himself the aggressor against their most christian and imperial majesties, and an accomplice of the breach of the public peace, and that he was to be treated as such by the king by the empress, and by the empire.

This proposition, besides its adherent justice, has acquired a new degree of force by the behaviour of the Hanoverian troops, both with regard to those of the king and of his allies. The first far from confining themselves according to the assurance given of it by the elector in public instruments, to the defence of the territories of the electorate in case of a design to attack them, entered with open force into the states of the Elector of Cologne, where those of France were: they pillaged the subsistences destined for the French army, carried off the grains and forage, dispersed the troops of the empire's contingent; in a word, they have committed all kinds of violences in the states of the Elector of Cologne, the king's ally; yet would not his majesty begin hostilities against the Elector of Hanover; and even, if possible, to avert them from his dominions, he caused a demand to be made by the Marshal d'Etrees to the Hanoverian general, of a *free and amicable passage* through his electoral highness's territory; but that prince had already dispersed manifestoes against the entrance of the French troops into Westphalia; and the Duke of Cumberland sent answer by General Sporken, that he was ordered to attend to the defence and conservation of the states of the King of Prussia and of his allies, and to hinder the passage of any foreign troops through the said states.

At length the Hanoverians having provoked his majesty's troops by hostilities of every kind, the moment came for repelling force by force, and to make them and their allies repent of their outrages; and victory seconded the justice of the king's arms, by the successive advantages which the French troops obtained over them."

They then come to the convention of Closter-seven, as follows:

"But the king's generous sentiments have never shone with greater lustre than in the capitulation of Closter-seven. The Hanoverian army being forced to fly before that of the Marshal de Richelieu, had been obliged, as its last shift, to betake itself to Stade. In a more dangerous condition it could not be. It was the concern of of the Duke of Cumberland, general of the Hanoverians, besides fearing the just discontent of his allies, which was near breaking out, to save his troops from the total destruction with which they were threatened, to secure the treasure of the king his father, and to hinder the dutchies of Bremen and Verden from becoming the theatre of war, and to exempt all the King of England's dominions in Germany from the miseries consecutive to a general defeat, and which by a concurrence of circumstances would have been but too justifiable.

It was no favourable conjuncture for softening the victor. The King of England was sending away a very strong squadron, with land forces, for a descent, with a design of making themselves masters of Rochefort, or at least to burn the docks, the store-houses; in a word, to commit all possible hostilities on the coast of France.

Besides many subjects of apprehensions for the defeated party, there was one of greater weight than all the others; past experience seemed to have inspired a grounded mistrust of any proposal from the King of England, Elector of Hanover; of this the Duke of Cumberland had recent proofs. After he had been obliged to retreat into the dutchy of Bremen, he had proposed a neutrality, and it was refused him; he had acquainted the French ministry, that he was authorised by full powers from the king his father, to treat of a peace, of a neutrality, or of a preliminary accommodation; and the king, faithful to his allies, would hearken to no proposal but in concert with them.

From all these reasons, the Duke of Cumberland did not believe that he should be able, by himself, to obtain the capitulation, which alone could secure him from all the several dangers he had to fear; but being informed of the king's great regard for the King of Denmark, his ally, he implored the assistance of that prince, and got a cessation of arms to be proposed to the Marshal de Richelieu by the negotiation of the Count de Lynar, the King of Denmark's minister, and under his Danish majesty's guaranty.

On this proposal the marshal deliberated which was best for the empire, to grant or refuse the capitulation. By the latter he answered the king's just vengeance; in the former he considered the advantages of keeping the Hanoverians and their allies inactive during the remainder of the war, and consequently of reserving his troops for marching without delay to Halberstadt, and by the celerity of his operations to hasten the evacuation of Saxony, and the restoration of the peace in Germany. As the king's sentiments were perfectly known to him, he immediately preferred that measure which he judged might be most beneficial to the empire and the allies of France, and he granted the capitulation or military convention which the Duke of Cumberland offered to him through the Count de Lynar. It was concluded at Closter-seven on the 8th of September; and the execution of it was secured both by the Marshal de Richelieu's word of honour and that of the Duke of Cumberland, lodged in the Count de Lynar's hands, and by the engagement of the King of Denmark's guaranty accepted by the two generals.

As

As in the firſt moment of the concluſion, ſeveral particulars and explanations in favour of the Hanoverians and their auxiliaries had been omitted, the Duke of Cumberland two days after, and by the mediation of the Count de Lynar, deſired ſuch omiſſions might be ſupplied by ſome ſeparate articles, which Marſhal Richelieu made no difficulty of granting."

After ſome remarks on this convention, they proceed thus:

"The king, ſuch was his zeal for his allies and for the empire, approved of the Marſhal de Richelieu's conduct, and to ſtrengthen the capitulation, propoſed the adding of ſome explications, which ſhould ſo clearly fix its meaning, as to obviate any miſinterpretations. Theſe explications were of the following tenor.

1. That the ceſſation of hoſtilities ſhould laſt during the whole time of the preſent war.

2. That the Hanoverian troops which were to go on the other ſide of the Elbe into the dutchy of Lawenburg, ſhould not come out of it, and together with the troops remaining on this ſide, ſhould not commit any hoſtility neither againſt the king, nor againſt his allies; and that the French troops likewiſe ſhould not commit any hoſtilities againſt them.

3. That no Engliſh troops ſhould be admitted into the dutchies of Bremen and Verden.

4. That the troops, both the Hanoverians and thoſe of the auxiliaries, ſhould not ſerve during the preſent war, either againſt the king, or againſt his allies, nor join thoſe of the King of England, nor thoſe of his allies.

Had there on the ſide of the court of Hanover been the ſame good faith as on the king's ſide, theſe explications would have met with no difficulty.

The ſenſe they offer had been contained in the conventions of the 8th and 10th of September, either in equivalent terms, or by a natural inference; and ſo juſt were they, that the Count de Lynar, to whom they were delivered, judged them to be the true meaning in which the convention had been underſtood, and the court of Copenhagen was of the ſame opinion."

They then endeavoured to ſhew, that theſe explications were virtually contained in the convention, that, though not agreed to, the convention remained in full force, and that the Daniſh miniſter was of this opinion. After this they go into a long and tedious account of the behaviour of the Hanoverians, Heſſians, and Wolfenbuttlers, and the methods which the Hanoverian generals took to deceive the French general, by making him believe, that they were reſolved to obſerve punctually the convention, while at the ſame time they were concerting with the King of Pruſſia, and preparing to recommence hoſtilities, as ſoon as they ſhould find a favourable opportunity, by the French army's being diſperſed into winter quarters; and this ſecond part they conclude as follows.

"One reflection ſhall put a period to this detail. If the Duke of Cumberland aſked to capitulate, it was becauſe he found himſelf in a critical poſition, and juſtly feared that, ſhould the Marſhal de Richelieu attack him, he would ruin the Hanoverian army irretrievably, and make himſelf maſter of the town of Stade, and of the depoſitum lodged there. Had not his ſituation been ſo dangerous in every reſpect, can it be ſuppoſed that a prince, whoſe courage all Europe has beheld, would have aſked to capitulate at the head of an army of near 40,000 men, under the cannon of the town, and in a poſt of difficult acceſs and well intrenched? But this prince, whoſe capacity gave him to perceive, that no retreat remained for him in caſe he ſhould be beaten, preferred the glory of ſaving the king his father's troops, and thoſe of his allies, to the vain honour of fighting the king's army, without any grounded hope of ſucceſs. The more of his ſelf-love he had by this ſtep ſacrificed to the good of the king his father, the more ſacred and inviolable did the capitulation, which he had aſked and obtained, become to him. It is unqueſtionable in the rules of honour and war, that a capitulation is never to be aſked of an enemy till at an extremity; but when reduced to it, it is not lawful to employ thoſe arms againſt him, which by promiſe were to be laid down. Honour would look on ſuch a procedure with indignation; and if private perſons deteſt a treachery of this nature, is it not ſtill more unworthy of ſovereigns, who are the protectors of good faith, and who are more concerned than private perſons to preſerve their glory and reputation?

Accordingly the Duke of Cumberland, by laying down his military employments, was for ſaving himſelf the infamy of breaking ſuch ſacred engagements; he has proved by that ſtep that he is incapable of being ſo far wanting to himſelf; but in ſheltering his own honour, why has he not been afraid of expoſing that of the king his father?

If the King of England, Elector of Hanover, on his receiving advice of the capitulation, had diſowned the Duke of Cumberland his general and ſon, ſtill would the king have had cauſe of complaint, military conventions not requiring a ratification; but, at leaſt, there would have been in this proceeding an appearance of good faith; but to temporize during near three months, in ſeeking occaſion for breaking the capitulation with impunity, let the French army march away for Halberſtadt, wait till it was ſeparated in the bad ſeaſon, lay hold of the circumſtances of a check to come out of the preſcribed limits, under pretence of extending quarters, afterwards take advantageous poſts, equally contrary to the convention; make every diſpoſition for the ſiege of Harburg, without any previous declaration of war; and when all theſe preparations are made, and the enemy is thought to be ſufficient weakened and deceived, to be fought with advantage, to declare to him, that hoſtilities are to be renewed, and that the capitulation is looked on as broken, at the very ſame moment that the troops are marching to him, and his poſts are attacked; to engage one prince, by ſeducement, to violate this capitulation, and to hinder another by open force from executing it; to impriſon the general of the latter, and detain his troops, and take away his ſon from him: to make him ſerve as an inſtrument to the treachery; this is trampling on the law of nations, on the laws of juſtice, honour, and good faith; rights of the ſovereignty of the ſtates of the empire; the ties of nature and of blood; it is to fear neither the judgment of cotemporaries, or of poſterity; it is wilfully branding one's life and memory with an indelible mark of infamy;

in a word, it is daring to ſet up and give a ſanction to the pernicious maxim, "That every means is lawful to obtain one's end."

Principles and procedures ſo heinous are to be attributed only to the artifices and evil councils of corrupt miniſters. To ſuſpect princes themſelves of them, would be wanting to the reſpect due to them.

After the preceding faithful repreſentation of the king's conduct, and that of the King of England, Elector of Hanover, all Europe, and eſpecially Germany, may eaſily judge of the difference of the intentions of theſe two princes; and it is hoped, that they will impute the blame of the conſequence of this war to thoſe only, who, in contempt of all laws and all rules, have again taken up arms to hinder the concluſion of it.

This is the cauſe of all ſovereigns, but eſpecially that of the empire; it being the bad faith of the Hanoverians which has retarded the ſucceſs of the king's operations for reſtoring the peace of Germany; and their unjuſt and violent proceedings, both towards the king and the Duke of Brunſwick, are a freſh breach of the public peace, and of the treaties of Weſtphalia.

The king will omit nothing to acquit himſelf of what he owes to his dignity, injured by the outrage done him by the court of Hanover. As to the Germanic body, his majeſty will redouble his efforts for preſerving it from the new dangers with which it is threatened; and fulfil the engagements he has entered into both with his allies and the empire. He is perſuaded that the electors, princes, and ſtates, will do juſtice to the uprightneſs and generoſity of his ſentiments; and he with the greater confidence hopes they will ſecond his meaſures and operations, as, agreeably to the wiſh and reſolution of the dyet, they tend only to ſuccour the allies of France, to maintain the Germanic ſyſtem, and to reſtore order and peace in Germany."

Verſailles, December
the 30th, 1757.

In the appendix to the Parallel of the Conduct of the two Kings is the following letter (dated Nov. 27, 1757) to Prince Ferdinand from the reigning Duke of Brunſwic his brother, who ſent a copy of it to Marſhal Richelieu. It ſhews that Prince Ferdinand contributed greatly to the juſt reſentment which hath been ſhewn of the French infraction of the treaty of Cloſter-ſeven. It ſerves, too, to diſcover that duke's character, and his high eſteem of his brother Ferdinand.

SIR,

I know you too well to entertain a doubt that the ſituation we are in with reſpect to each other gives you pain; nor can you have any doubt that it gives me concern: indeed it afflicts me greatly. Mean while, my deareſt brother, I could never have believed, that it would be you who ſhould carry away from me my eldeſt ſon: and how great is my mortification to find myſelf under the hard neceſſity of telling you, that this ſtep is contrary to the law of nations, and the conſtitution of the empire; and that if you perſiſt in it, you will diſgrace your family, and bring a ſtain upon your country, which you pretend to ſerve. The hereditary prince my ſon was at Hamburgh by my order; you have carried him to Stade. Could he diſtruſt his uncle, an uncle, who hath done ſo much honour to his houſe! Could he believe that this uncle would deprive him of liberty; a liberty never refuſed to the loweſt officer. I ordered him to make a tour to Holland: could not the loweſt officer have done as much? Let us ſuppoſe for a moment, that my troops, among whom he ſerved, were to have ſtaid with the Hanoverians, would it not ſtill have been in my power to give an officer leave of abſence, or even leave to reſign his commiſſion? And would you, my dear brother, hinder your brother, the head of your family, and of ſuch a family as ours, to exerciſe this right with regard to a ſon who is the hereditary prince, of whoſe rights and prerogatives you cannot be ignorant? It is impoſſible that you could have conceived ſuch deſigns without the ſuggeſtion of others. Thoſe who did ſuggeſt them have trampled on the rights of nature, of nations, and of the princes of Germany: they have induced you to add, to the infraction of all theſe, the moſt cruel inſult on a brother whom you love, and who loves you. Would you have your brother lay his juſt complaints againſt you before the whole empire, and all Europe? Is not your proceeding without example! What is Germany become. What are its princes, and what is our houſe, in particular, become! Is it the intereſt of the two kings, the cauſe of your country, and my cauſe, that you pretend to ſupport? —I repeat it, brother, that this deſign could never have been framed by you. I again command my ſon to purſue his journey, and I cannot conceive that you will give any obſtruction. If you ſhould (which I pray God avert!) I ſolemnly declare to you, that I ſhall not be conſtrained by ſuch means, and that I ſhall never forget what I owe to myſelf.

As to my troops, you may ſee what I have written on that head to the Hanoverian miniſtry. The Duke of Cumberland, by the convention of Cloſter-ſeven, diſmiſſed them and ſent them home: the ſaid miniſtry gave me notice of this convention as what bound me: the march of the troops was ſettled: an incident happening, they halted; the obſtacle being removed, they were to have continued their march. The court of Hanover will no longer be bound by the convention; whilſt I not only accepted it on their word, but have alſo, in conformity to their inſtructions, negotiated at Verſailles and Vienna*.

After

* It ſhould ſeem that the Hanoverian miniſtry, foreſeeing what would happen, adviſed the Duke of Brunſwick, even before the convention of Cloſter-ſeven was concluded, to make his peace with France; for that convention was ſigned Sept. 10. and the duke's miniſter ſigned at Vienna the following treaty with France, ten days after; a ſpace too ſhort to ſend from Brunſwick to Paris and from Paris to Vienna.

1. The king ſhall keep poſſeſſion of the cities of Brunſwick and Wolfenbuttel, whilſt the war laſts; and the general of his majeſty's forces ſhall make uſe of the artillery, arms, and military ſtores, in the arſenals of thoſe two towns.

2. The Duke of Brunſwick ſhall, when his troops return from the Duke of Cumberland's camp, diſband them in his own country. Their

arms

After all this, they would have me contradict myself, break my word, and intirely ruin my estate and my honour. Did you ever know your brothrr guilty of such things? It is true, that I have, as you say, sacrificed my all; or rather, I have been sacrificed. The only thing left me is my honour: and in the unhappy contrast of our situations, I lament both you, and myself, that it should be from you, my dear brother, I should receive the cruel advice to give up my honour. I cannot listen to it: I cannot recede from my promise; my troops, therefore, must return home, agreeably to what the Duke of Cumberland and the Hanoverian ministry stipulated with regard to me in the strongest manner. I am afraid that the true circumstances of things are concealed from you.

Not to detain your express too long, I shall send you by the post copies of all I have written to the Hanoverian ministry. It will grieve your honest heart to read it. I am, with a heart almost broken, yet full of tenderness for you, your, &c.

Blanckenbourg, Nov. 27, 1757.

The

arms shall be deposited in the aforesaid arsenals; and the general and subaltern officers of the said troops shall take an oath not to serve against the king, or his allies, during the present war.

The Duke of Brunswick shall, nevertheless, be permitted to keep, if he pleases, for the guard of his person and castles, a battalion of foot, and two squadrons of horse.

3. The regulations made by Marshal Richelieu, and the intendant of his army, shall subsist on their present footing.

4. The Duke of Brunswick shall furnish his contingent in money and troops, agreeably to the laws of the empire; his troops shall immediately join those which the Germanic body has assembled, and he shall order his minister at Ratisbon to vote conformably to the resolutions of the dyet approved and confirmed by the emperor. On these conditions the Duke of Brunswick shall be restored to the king's favour; all due respect shall be paid to his most serene highness, and all the princes and princesses of his house; neither his revenues nor his treasure shall be touched, nor shall the administration of justice, civil or ecclesiastical, be exacted, and winter quarters only shall be demanded for the general officers and regiments which shall winter in the Duke of Brunswick's country.

The aforesaid conditions of a formal convention being presented to me in the name of his most christian majesty, by his excellency the Count de Stainville, his ambassador at the imperial court, and in the name of the empress queen by his excellency Count Kaunitz, chancellor of state; and notwithstanding my pressing remonstrance and sollicitations to get some of the articles changed or mitigated, having received for answer that they were the *ultimatum*, I declare, by virtue of the full powers received from his most serene highness, my most gracious master, that I accept the aforesaid conditions; and acknowledge them to be binding. In witness whereof I have hereto set my name and arms.

Vienna, September 20, 1757.

L. S BERNARD PAUL DE MOLL.

The King of England's conduct as Elector of Hanover; in answer to the Parallel of the conduct of the King of France, with that of the King of England, Elector of Hanover.

The conduct of his majesty the King of Great Britain, Elector of Brunswick and Lunenbourg, with regard to the troubles of the empire, give no reason to think that France could hope to be a gainer by a parallel of that conduct with her own. She has, however, undertaken this comparison. The public has seen the memorial published by France under the title of *A Parallel of the King's conduct with that of the King of England, relative to the breach of the capitulation of Closter-seven by the Hanoverians.*

In the introduction to this piece we are assured, that it was merely from moderation, and to avoid the kindling of animosities, that the publication of it was so long delayed. Indeed, in several places of this piece, the style and expressions are far from being conformable to that regard which crowned heads, though at war, owe one to another. As to the things themselves, so little regard is paid to truth, that we are certain they will not have the promised effect.

His Britannic majesty has too great a value for the judgment which the public forms of the actions of the greatest monarchs, and which posterity will make with still greater freedom, not to let them know the motives upon which he has acted, and which render his conduct irreproachable. It is, therefore, with the greatest readiness, that he seizes an opportunity which France furnishes him, to expose them to the view of Europe. Very different from those who have attacked him with animosity, he will use the language of moderation. The truth, set in its proper light, carries so strong conviction with it, that it loses nothing by a simple and dispassionate relation. It will be sufficient simply to relate what is past, to make appear which side justice is on, and to whom are to be imputed the torrents of blood that have been spilt, and which in all probability will yet dye the earth.

The troubles appeased by the late treaty of Aix la-Chapelle, are too recent to be yet forgot. France, which, notwithstanding the continual wars which Lewis XIII Lewis XIV and Lewis XV. made on the empire, notwithstanding the desolations which she has caused, and the provinces which she has taken from it, thinks, however, that she may give herself the title of *Ancient Friend and Ally of the Empire*; France, which makes no scruple to advance that the private ambition of princes, who continually excited the two houses of France and Austria against one another, was the chief cause of their divisions, and of the wars which so long desolated Europe, and especially Germany; France without being excited thereto, attempted, at the death of the Emperor Charles VI. to make herself mistress of that superiority of dominion which she always had in view. She should have obtained her end, had she been able to divide the estates of the house of Austria, among the different princes who formed pretensions to them, and

and of whom none would have been in a condition to make head againſt France. To defeat this project, the king then took part with the houſe of Auſtria, when attacked on all ſides, and abandoned by every power. He took that part with a greatneſs of ſoul, which, though forgot at Vienna, and repaid with ingratitude, will never be forgot in hiſtory, that generous monarch fought in perſon for the cauſe of his ally, ſacrificed the blood of his ſubjects, the treaſures, and even the moſt important conqueſts of his crown, to prevent the ruin with which ſhe was threatened on all hands. The effects of theſe meaſures are known to the whole world. It is true, that the empreſs queen yielded up by the moſt ſolemn treaties the dutchy of Sileſia to the king of Pruſſia; but the numerous armies which that princeſs keeps on foot in the preſent war, ſufficiently ſhew that the houſe of Auſtria has preſerved ſince the peace of Aix la-Chapelle, the power which was thought neceſſary to maintain the ballance of Europe, in hopes that, conformable to the laudable example of Leopold I. Joſeph I. and Charles VI. ſhe would make uſe of this power in defence of the common liberty.

The concluſion of theſe troubles convinced France that ſhe could never expect to ſucceed in her deſigns, while Great Britain preſerved by her commerce, ſufficient force vigorouſly to oppoſe her. Scarce therefore was the peace of Aix-la-Chapelle concluded, when ſhe ſought out other ways to execute her projects which that peace had defeated. With this view, ſhe began to diſturb the Engliſh, to hem in her colonies in the new world on all ſides, in contempt of the cleareſt articles of the peace of Utrecht, in order to put them in the moſt critical ſituation, and take away the ſtrongeſt ſupport of the liberties of Europe.

It is not our purpoſe here to defend the rights of the king in theſe differences, they have been made ſufficiently manifeſt: but we cannot help remarking, that the cauſe of the Britiſh crown ought naturally to be that of all thoſe who muſt expect their independency from the common liberty. We may eaſily ſee what would infallibly happen in Germany and elſewhere, ſhould France, with the forces ſhe has at land, ever get poſſeſſion of the ſovereignty of the ſea.

His majeſty therefore had good grounds to expect the aſſiſtance of other powers in the differences we have juſt mentionod; but he was far from deſiring to involve them unneceſſarily in that affair; on the contrary, he did all in his power to maintain peace on the continent.

None but ſuch as are unacqaainted with the maritime force of England, can believe that, without a diverſion on the continent, to employ part of the enemy's force, ſhe is not in a condition to hope for ſucceſs, and maintain her ſuperiority at ſea. England had, therefore, no intereſt to foment quarrels or wars in Europe; but for the ſame reaſon, there was room to fear that France would embrace a different ſyſtem: accordingly ſhe took no pains to conceal her views, and her envoys declared publicly, that a war upon the continent was inevitable, and that the king's dominions

in

in Germany would be its principal object. France did not confine herself to bare declarations; in the autumn of the year 1755 we saw the French troops assemble upon the Moselle, and the Upper Rhine. It could not be affirmed that these troops were destined to maintain peace, and with defensive views only, as no one could think of carrying the war into France. These grand preparations could therefore have no other end, but that of carrying the war elsewhere herself, and of entering the territories of the empire. The king, in these circumstances, first addressed himself in quality of king and elector, to the imperial and royal court. It was certainly the empress queen whom this affair principally regarded. His Britannic majesty expected of her, as king and elector, that she would call to remembrance the times not long elapsed, and also the accomplishment of the treaties which the king had fulfilled with the most scrupulous exactness. He might above all have expected, in quality of elector, that his imperial majesty would execute faithfully what he had promised by his capitulation.

He might perhaps have obtained the assistance of the court of Vienna, had he been willing to enter into the views which the ministers of that court had sufficiently made known; but the king thought them as improper for answering his intention to maintain peace in Europe, as contrary to justice. Hence the dry and unsatisfactory answers which he received from Vienna; answers which sufficiently discovered the new plan that court was pursuing, and which was totally different from that to which the house of Austria had been so often indebted for its preservation.

Such were the circumstances when a favourable opportunity offered for concluding with his Prussian majesty the treaty of Westminster, Jan. 16, 1756. The two contracting monarchs considered it as a sure means to maintain peace in Europe, and especially in Germany. Then it was that France saw the hopes vanish with which she had flattered herself, of being assisted by the king of Prussia in her views against the peace of Europe. No body then thought, that the court of Vienna would, in order to obtain its ends, make an alliance with that of Versailles, and throw itself into the danger which must inevitably follow. It seemed, therefore, natural to hope, that France would abandon a scheme which she wanted allies to execute, and that the peace of the empire would continue undisturbed. This is as evident as what the French have advanced in their memorial, in order to throw a false gloss upon the treaty of Westminster, is weak, and void of probability. It is there said 'That the kings of England 'and Prussia had no enemies to 'contend with when the treaty of 'Westminster was concluded.' But is not the contrary known to all the world? Had not France already assembled troops in 1755, and threatened to attack the king's German dominions? This piece adds, 'That the King of Great 'Britain had reasons to wish for 'a war upon the continent: That 'the operations of France by sea 'would thereby be weakened: 'That the Hanoverian troops 'would obtain subsidies: That

'endea-

'endeavours were used to turn the 'war in Germany into a religious 'war, in order to gain the assistance of the Protestant princes: 'That the concurrence of the king 'of Prussia was obtained by flattering his ambition with the 'hopes of a new aggrandisement, 'at the expence of the empress 'queen: and that the King of 'Prussia, in a public news-paper, 'reproaches the King of Great 'Britain as being the first mover 'of this war.'

If the question, which of the two powers is to be considered as the author of the war in Germany, is to be decided by the advantages to be reaped from it by such party, the impartial public would be at no loss to give its judgment. They must be very ignorant, indeed, who imagine that the forces of England are not able to resist those of France, unless the latter be hindered from turning all her efforts to the sea. In case of a war upon the continent, the two powers must pay subsidies; only with this difference, that France can employ her own land forces and aspire at conquests. Nothing can be more odious, or more groundless, than the reproach of the pretended design to procure subsidies to Hanoverian troops.

The king defrayed the expences of the campaign of 1757 at his own proper charge, and except the payment which the Hessian troops received from England, that crown contributed only 200,000 l. sterling to that campaign; a sum which, it is easy to see, was sufficient but for a small part of the necessary expences. Had it been in the power of the king to shun this war, the Hanoverian troops would have had no need of subsidies. Can it be imagined, that the king would have desired to purchase these subsidies at the price of the danger to which he exposed his German dominions, in case the French armies should penetrate to the heart of the empire? Every one may easily see what the Protestants had to expect from the court of Versailles. It was not, therefore, without reason that this object was recommended to the consideration of the Protestant powers and states of the empire: but the king was so far from using this motive to excite a war on the continent, that he had nothing more at heart than to prevent it.

The King of Prussia has published to the world the reasons that forced him to take arms. We leave the impartial to judge, whether these reasons were not sufficient of themselves, without any view of aggrandisement, to kindle up a war between that prince and the empress queen; at least it can never be imputed to the king, who exposed his sacred person, and also the blood and treasure of his subjects, to save the house of Austria, that he occasioned the present troubles, that lay waste the empire, with a view to distress that house.

The French ministry are very sensible of all the weakness of these pretended conjectures. Hence they have recourse to a letter which his Prussian majesty is said to have written to the king. Can there be a more formal acknowledgement that they want solid proofs, than their having recourse to a writing which bears the most evident marks of falsity and forgery; and which only have proceeded from the wicked hearts of those who are not ashamed to use venal pens,

pens, to forge pieces purposely to impose upon the abused and credulous public, and to answer the sinister ends which they hoped to make of it at a proper time and place?

It is said also, in the memorial of the court of France, 'That 'the clause contained in the treaty 'of Westminster to oppose the 'introduction of foreign troops 'into Germany, is contrary to 'the right which the states have 'to make alliances with foreign 'powers; and that it had France 'principally in view: That his 'Britannic majesty was not ignorant, that, by virtue of his defensive treaties, and his guaranty 'of those of Westphalia, the King 'of France would be obliged, at 'the requisition of those states, to 'send troops to their assistance, 'in case of their being attacked: 'and that the engagement made 'to oppose those troops, was a 'most unjust declaration of war.'

The second article of the treaty of Westminster absolutely destroys this objection. It speaks only of troops that should come *to disturb the peace of the empire*; for what other troops could be then thought of? To suppose a design had been formed to attack Saxony and Bohemia, and to exclude the entrance of lawful succours, is to assert the very thing that is called in question, and, considering the evidence to the contrary, is intirely void of all proof. It is objected in the last place, 'That in the treaty of Westminster the neutrality of 'the Low Countries, in favour of 'the empress queen, was not inserted with that of Germany: 'That the public soon discovered 'the artifice; and that it was the 'intention and design of the 'contracting parties to excite 'France, by this fact, to attack 'those countries, in order, by 'that means, to kindle up a general war.'

The reason why the Austrian Netherlands were not comprehended in that treaty is very clearly explained in a separate article. His Prussian majesty was not obliged by the peace of Dresden, to guaranty these countries. Besides, what reason could there be for such a guaranty for the empress queen, who had signified on several occasions, that she feared nothing from France? Was it not in the power of his most christian majesty not to attack the countries in question; or did the treaty of Westminster give him a right to invade them? At least, if he had taken so unjust a resolution, it is plain that his Britannic majesty would not have been answerable for the event. However, the peace of these provinces was no less secured by that treaty, than if they had been expresly included. France would naturally avoid carrying the war thither, at a time, when, by her own confession, she was abandoned by her ally, and engaged in a burthensome war. She would have been afraid of drawing upon her Austria, Holland, and other powers, who, both by virtue of treaties, and also from motives of self-interest, must, in that case, have taken part in the war.

Nothing then can be more unexceptionable than the king's conduct with regard to the treaty of Westminster, which will be for ever an irreproachable witness of the care he took to maintain the peace of Europe.

France took quite different measures: her numerous land forces per-

persuaded her that it was her interest to make war on the continent. Her envoys made no secret of her design, as we have already observed. The preparations which she made, and the troops which she assembled in 1755 upon the Upper Rhine and the Moselle, were a convincing proof of the blow which she meditated. She even induced the empress queen to make a treaty with her, signed at Versailles the first of May 1756. Nothing can be less difficult than to discover the views of the courts of Vienna and Versailles, in making that alliance, and the consequences which they promised themselves from that system. France wanted to punish the King of Prussia for having dared to dispute the dependence which she exacts from all the courts in Europe, and for having made with England a treaty, which, though inoffensive, was inconsistent with the views of the French ministry.

She above all flattered herself, that by the measures she had pursued, by the war which she was going to make on the continent, and by the invasion of the king's German dominions, he would be brought to make a peace prejudicial to his crown, or in case he refused to come into that, designs might be accomplished, that would include the ruin of the house of Hanover. These are not mere conjectures. They are the sentiments of a person whose penetration, and the confidence which the allied courts justly put in him, enabled him to discover the truth, and who had the intelligence which he sent to his court, from the fountain head.

The following is part of a letter from Count Fleming, dated July 29, 1756. 'If the court of 'London does not separate itself 'from the King of Prussia, and 'make peace with France on the 'best terms possible, the latter 'will go on from success to success, and from scheme to scheme, 'which may in the end become 'fatal to the house of Hanover.' The court of Vienna, which the king had so faithfully succoured, and which, in consequence of the most solemn treaties, ought to have defended the electorate of Hanover, made so little opposition to its being invaded, that Count Fleming gave the followiug opinion of it in a letter, dated June 12, 1756. 'I think (says he) 'that it would not be ill-timed, 'if France, the more to embarrass 'the King of Prussia, should send 'an army of 60,000 men into 'the country of Hanover; which 'would greatly facilitate its designs.' The same minister informs his court of his reasons for thinking so, and of the court of Vienna's motive for refusing to succour the king in case of a hostile invasion, in a letter dated May 10, 1756, being the very day the treaty of Versailles was signed. 'It plainly appears (says he) 'that since the court of Vienna 'cannot have the King of Prussia 'for the object of the war, it 'will no longer run the risque with 'England, against France, which 'it looks upon as a much less 'dangerous enemy than the King 'of Prussia.'

His dispatch of June 9, 1756, gives the following account why it did not yet fear France so much as the King of Prussia: 'Nevertheless, 'thelefs, (fays he) it is but too 'remarkable, that it wants to get 'rid of all thefe difficulties, and is 'bent on giving a different face 'to the affairs of religion in the 'empire, and to conquer Silefia.' In a difpatch of the 16th of the fame month, he fays, 'I am more 'and more perfuaded, that the 'reflections, which I have made 'in my former letters, and efpe-'cially in that of the 9th inftant, 'are not without foundation, and 'I can no longer doubt that the 'court where I am has formed a 'fcheme, the principal objects of 'which are, religion, and the re-'covery of Silefia.'

Laftly, he tells us the manner in which this fcheme was to have been executed, in a letter well worthy of attention, dated July 8, 1756.

'They know very well, (fays 'the count) that it is neceffary 'to purfue without interruption, 'the meafures already begun, that 'they may beable to play a double 'game, and put themfelves in fo 'good a condition, that the King 'of Pruffia fhall be thereby oblig-'ed by fupporting his armaments, 'and the augmentation made or to 'be made, either to wafte away 'by little and little, or, to pre-'vent that inconvenience, fuffer 'himfelf to run into fome preci-'pitate refolution, which to me 'feems to be the very thing they 'expect.'

It is in confequence of thefe defigns, and by thefe means, that Germany is become the unhappy theatre of war. Does Europe at prefent fay that this is to be laid to the king's account, or to whom does juftice afcribe it?

The conduct of the king, after the war broke out, was the fame; always juft and irreproachable. The harmony between him and his Polifh majefty fubfifted upon its former footing; he defired peace, and though he neither could nor would engage the King of Pruffia to neglect the neceffary means of defence, he did not fail to remonftrate to that monarch, not to ufe them but in the utmoft neceffity. The king was at peace with the emprefs queen; he had no hand in the war between Pruffia, Auftria, and Saxony, nor had he ever been follicited by the King of Pruffia to take part in it. This has been declared, on different occafions, as well to the court of Vienna and the dyet of the empire, as to the principal courts of Germany, by minifters fent exprefsly for that purpofe.

At a comitial deliberation of the 10th of January 1757, the king, as elector, gave it as his opinion, that the empire fhould interpofe its mediation to appeafe, in an amicable manner, the troubles in which it was involved. All thefe things are publicly known, nor can any one have the face to alledge the leaft ftep, the leaft meafure from which the contrary can be inferred.

The winter which followed, hindered France from fending her troops in 1756 againft the dominions of his Britannic majefty; but at the fame time it opened a new fcene by the neutrality offered the king for thefe dominions. After fhewing what paffed upon this occafion, we fhall draw from them the confequences which naturally follow. On the fourth of January 1757, Count Kaunitz declared to Baron Steinberg, the Hanoverian minifter minister at Vienna, that he had a proposal to make to him which he did not expect; that the empress queen had ordered him to give him a memorial (which the count at the same time presented) and that she desired that his court would return an answer to it as soon as possible. This memorial remarks, that, in offering that neutrality, all the securities and just and reasonable indulgences and conditions were required for the empress and her allies, which ought to follow from such an engagement. Nothing could be more natural than for the king to desire an explanation of those equivocal terms, which were susceptible of any meaning that might be put upon them. He did so, in an answer, conformable to the same language which he had always used in quality of elector, and repeated, with that freedom and uprightness from which he never departed, his resolution to stop the French troops, and to take no other share in the war. These assurances would have been sufficient, if there had really been no design to injure the king's dominions, and those of his allies, as long as, in quality of elector, he remained neuter.

The court of Vienna had previously answered, that it would treat with France concerning that affair; but it at the same time signed a convention with the Count d'Etrees, by virtue of which the French army was to pass the Weser the 10th of July. This circumstance, after the testimony which M. d'Etrees himself has given of it, cannot be called in question.

Instead of the explanation that was expected, the Count de Colloredo sent to London in the month of April to Baron de Munchausen his Britannic majesty's electoral minister, the scheme of a treaty of neutrality; wherein not only a passage for the combined army was demanded, but it was also said, that the king had delivered up his strong places to foreign troops; that he should not augment nor assemble his own; but should disperse them in such a manner as should be agreed on. The king by submitting to these terms, was no longer master of his own country, nor of his own troops, and voluntarily disarmed himself. The French ministry, however, have not scrupled to annex to their Parallel the piece which contains such strange propositions. The consequences were such as the court of Vienna might naturally expect, and which after signing the convention with the Count d'Etrees, it might desire. The king broke off a negotiation which only shewed the arrogance of the courts which had begun it.

The reader is now able to judge of that part of the memorial of the court of France, that regards this article. It first endeavours to render the king suspected by his allies, when it says, 'That he 'had given insinuations for the 'neutrality of his German dominions, and that afterwards he had 'proposed to admit of it, provided that the French troops, instead of passing thro' his dominions, were made to pass through 'the countries of Cassel, Brunswick, 'Gotha, and Weimar.'

Certainly the author of the French memorial, when he wrote this, forgot that the king's answer an-

annexed to the Parallel, destroys both these reproaches. The king there owns with what satisfaction he received the offer which had been made him, and speaks of it as a proposal not coming from him, but solely from the empress queen: 'His majesty (says that 'paper) has heard, with as great 'pleasure as regard for her ma-'jesty the empress queen of 'Hungary and Bohemia, that her 'imperial and royal majesty 'wanted to hinder the countries 'belonging to his Britannic ma-'jesty in Germany, from being 'involved in the present troubles. 'The king also declares, that he 'persisted in the resolution to take 'all possible measures to keep out 'foreign troops from his possessions, 'and from their neighbourhood, 'more effectually to prevent the 'danger which might threaten 'them.'

The French army would not have been far from the king's territories, had he followed the path which was marked out for him. After sending this explanation to the court of Vienna, it was necessary to wait for its answer before passing to other proposals. This answer was only received in the scheme of the convention; and the court of Vienna must own, that the negotiation was then absolutely broken off.

The court of France is very sensible that these objections have nothing to do with the principal affair; but that the question properly is, whether the king was obliged to accept the neutrality offered him? Whether his refusal of it justifies their proceedings afterwards towards his dominions, and those of his allies? And whether the conditions offered him are not the clearest proof of the unjust designs the French had against him? Thus they seek to excuse themselves; but nothing can be more weak than that pretended justification. 'The king, 'it is said, was obliged to permit 'the French army to have a pas-'sage through his dominions; it 'could take no other rout; the 'conditions offered had nothing 'in them unjust, dishonourable nor 'dangerous, as it was proposed 'to put the fortress of Hamelen 'into the hands of the Empress 'of Russia, or of the King of 'Denmark.'

Nothing can be worse founded than the pretended obligation of the king, to permit the French army a passage thro' his dominions. According to the law of nations, and that of the states of the empire with regard to foreign powers, no state can be forced to grant a passage to the troops of another state thro' its territories; much less ought that passage to be demanded, when it might give occasion or pretence to bring the theatre of the war into the country, where it would get footing. The laws of the empire do not allow the emperor to introduce foreign troops into Germany, without the consent of the states. In the case wherein, by the constitution of the empire, the states are obliged to allow such passage, it is not to be done with prejudice of danger to the countries. For this reason it is ordained, that first of all, the person to whom the troops belong shall give security, to cause the troops to march in small bodies, without causing any damage to the coun-

try,

try, and paying for every thing that ſhall be furniſhed them for their ſubſiſtence.

To apply theſe regulations to the paſſage demanded of the king. The empire had not conſented to the introduction of the French troops. France had lately ſignified to the dyet, that ſhe thought it juſt to take what revenge ſhe could of the king's ſtates in Germany, on account of the differences that had ariſen in America. It was not France that could give ſuch ſecurity; ſhe demanded the king to deliver up his fortreſſes, to diſarm himſelf, and leave it to the diſcretion of France, whether ſhe ſhould think proper, under pretence of a paſſage, to exerciſe her declared revenge, and ruin the electoral ſtates as much as ſhe could by an open war. The very demand of a paſſage ſufficiently proves, that this was the deſign of France. She needs only throw an eye upon a map to be convinced, that the ſhorteſt way to go from France to Saxony and Bohemia, which were then the theatre of the war, was not to paſs thro' the territories of the king in Germany, nor thoſe of his neighbours. It is no wonder that France finds the conditions, which ſhe propoſed to the king, neither diſhonourable, unjuſt or dangerous. Having imbibed ideas of deſpotiſm, ſhe thinks, that all other powers ought to conſider every thing that ſhe thinks fit to impoſe upon them, as equitable, juſt, and proper. Delicate with regard to her own honour, ſhe would have others to be indifferent about theirs; but ſuch notions will never alter the nature of things, nor hinder every one from being perſuaded, that there is nothing more hard, more unjuſt, or more incompatible with the dignity of a free ſtate of the empire, than to ſee that power, that ſtrength, and authority, for which ſhe is alone indebted to providence, taken from her by the hand of a ſtranger. The ſtates of the empire may ſee, from this example, of what nature the paſſage is, which the court of France thinks ſhe has a right to demand as a guarantee of the treaty of Weſtphalia, and with the approbation of the court of Vienna. The imperial town of Cologn has experienced it in this war, and perhaps the time is nearer at hand than they expect, when thoſe, whoſe zeal for their religion, the ſubſidies which they receive, and other views, make them look upon the ſufferings of their co-eſtates with a careleſs indifference, will themſelves ſhare the ſame fate in their turns.

We flatter ourſelves that we have ſaid enough to ſet the conduct of the king and that of France, with regard to the neutrality, in a clear light. We have ſeen that the king ſeized the offer that was made him to repeat the aſſurances that he would endeavour, on his ſide, to maintain peace in Germany. That, on the contrary, the courts of Vienna and Verſailles have been, from the beginning, very equivocal and ſuſpicious; that while they made a ſhew of procuring the neutrality of the electorate, they ſigned a convention, by which the combined armies were to enter the electorate after the 10th of July; and laſtly, that the conditions propoſed to the king, were ſo hard ſo dangerous, and ſo inconſiſtent with his honour, that they were only intended to make him reject them, to give them a prea pretence for executing the resolution they had taken to invade his majesty's dominions, in contempt of the laws of equity and justice.

This fatal design was soon put into execution. Was the public ignorant what the king's territories have suffered by that invasion, we could give it a long detail on this head. The suburbs of Zell burnt, the town of Hoy almost reduced to ashes, without any reason of war, so many villages plundered, so many towns ravaged, almost all the horses of the country carried away, the country foraged, exactions amounting to immense sums, indecencies committed with regard to the king's principal officers: all these horrors will transmit to the latest posterity, the remembrance of an invasion equally unjust and cruel. If France could justify her conduct in the eyes of the world, she would not fail to give valid reasons for the invasion of the electorate; but no such thing appears in the paper published in her defence. It is true, she alledges the war of England, and hostilities commenced, as she says, by the Hanoverians; but she yet barely touches upon these two articles; she sees that this would be an open violation of the best established maxims of the law of nations, and would involve the empire in continual wars, if it might be maintained that the states of which it was composed, could be attacked for quarrels that regard only their sovereigns in quality of foreign powers.

If the approach of a numerous French army ought not to be considered as a declaration of war, at last, they cannot deny, but that before the two armies were near enough to come to blows, Marshal d'Etrees committed the first act of hostility in the county of Bentheim, of which the king was in possession, and which France thought she could put into the hands of the count of that name, by virtue of the authority which she arrogated of supreme judge of the empire. To colour these violences, she had no other pretence left but the quality of guarantee of the peace of Westphalia. She pretends that, to perform this obligation, she might send troops into Germany; that the King of Prussia had invaded Saxony and Bohemia, that the king and his allies, by supporting the cause of his Prussian majesty with an army, had formally declared themselves adherents to the breaker of the public peace, and consequently their countries ought to be treated as those of enemies.

It is true that it is against the Landgrave of Hesse-Cassel, that this pretence of guarantee is chiefly urged; but as no better reason is alledged to justify the invasion of the different states of the empire, as the king besides considers the conduct of his serene highness the Landgrave of Hesse-Cassel as both just and glorious, and as he never pretends to separate the cause of that prince from his own; *this reason*, which France gives for her conduct, ought not to be left unanswered.

The Parallel supposes that the King of Prussia was the aggressor in the war with her majesty the empress queen, and that he had not sufficient reason to take up arms in his own defence. How many things might be urged in answer to this imputation? Count Fleming's remarkable letter of the 28th of July 1756, speaks in a very different strain. But as it is not our design at present to justify the King of Prussia, who has no need of a foreign

reign pen to defend him, we ſhall, for a moment, ſuppoſe the accuſation againſt him well founded. To come at the end propoſed, it will be ſufficient to make two remarks, which will wholly expoſe the emptineſs of the pretence which France has thought proper to make uſe of. Firſt, it is notoriouſly falſe, that the king as elector, or any of the other princes his allies, had taken any part in the differences between the King of Pruſſia and the houſe of Auſtria, before they were invaded by the French. The king had, on ſeveral occaſions, declared, that he had no deſign to interfere in the war, and that all his views and meaſures ſhould only be to keep out of his poſſeſſions and their neighbourhood the foreign troops with which they were threatened. Nothing can be more comformable to theſe declarations than the meaſures that have been purſued, nor can any thing be alledged to infer the contrary. At the deliberations of the dyet of the 10th of January, the king, and his allies, voted for an amicable accommodation, and did not join in the meaſures approved by the majority. But the peace of Weſtphalia ſtipulates that all mild methods ſhall be tried before the guarantees are authorized to take up arms. It ſecures to the ſtates of the empire an entire liberty of voting, and leaves the deciſion of that queſtion to the dyet, ſo that the majority of voices determines with regard to collections and contributions neceſſary for the expences of a war. If then France wanted to take advantage of her quality of guarantee of the peace of Weſtphalia, ſhe ought not to have uſed any other means but thoſe preſcribed by treaty, and propoſed by his Britannic majeſty; but ſo far from that ſhe pretends to aſſume the right of executing the concluſions of the empire, and uſurps a more extenſive power than the emperor himſelf in Germany. But in the ſecond place, nothing is a ſtranger proof of the monſtrous abuſes which France has made of the guaranty of that treaty, than her conduct in the king's territories, when ſhe ſaw herſelf able to ſpeak and act as their miſtreſs. If there be any one who doubts that ſhe had a deſign to revenge herſelf upon the king's German dominions for the differences in America, by ſpoiling, ruining, and deſtroying his territories, and thoſe of his allies, and by putting it out of their power to ſuccour the Proteſtant religion, and the liberty of Germany, it is ſufficiently demonſtrated to them by this conduct. Scarce were the French troops in poſſeſſion of the country, but, not content with raiſing heavy contributions, ſhe took upon her the regulation of the revenues, and poured in a croud of placemen and commiſſioners, who followed the army, to whom the adminiſtration was entruſted. The country changed its maſter, and in all the ordinances publiſhed in the name of the intendant, or of the generals, it was ſtiled a country of his moſt chriſtian majeſty; the town of Hamelen was even ſummoned to take the oaths of allegiance to the King of France. Notice was given to his Britannic majeſty's miniſters of ſtate, that by virtue of a convention ſigned between France and the empreſs queen, the revenues and contributions ariſing from the electorate ſhould be divided between the two powers; even all the conquered countries, and thoſe that ſhould be conquered, belonging to the king, as Elector of Hanover, were farmed out to a citizen of Paris, which was notified by a public edict to the whole electorate, and would have been soon put in execution.

To maintain that these privileges which a guarantee of the treaty of Westphalia hath a right to; to pretend that France had no other view but to execute the laws of the empire, and to put the King of Poland again in possession of Saxony, is contrary to the impression which plain facts must make upon the minds of the most prejudiced. It would be needless to attempt overthrowing a pretence, of which all the world sees the weakness; a pretence of which France did not avail herself when she saw herself in possession of Hanover; a pretence, in short, which she has refused in the plainest manner by her conduct, when the king, as elector, caused proposals of peace to be made to her.

We come now to examine the rest of these measures, the convention of Closter-seven, and the objections to which it has given occasion.

On reading what the court of France says of the convention, one would think that this is the article on which she laid the greatest stress. It is plain, however, that the plan which it has followed in this affair is most unjustifiable, and that the king's conduct here, as in every other respect, is void of all just censure. To prove this we shall, as the most proper way, relate the whole matter of fact. We shall first shew it to the public in the most natural light, and then answer the objections made by France.

After the affair of Hastenbeck on the 26th of July 1757, wherein the two armies, though very unequal in numbers, fought long with doubtful success till the weakest was obliged to retreat, by reason of the too great superiority of the enemy's troops over those of the Duke of Cumberland; the greatest part of the king's German territories, and also those of the Landgrave of Hesse-Cassel and of the Duke of Brunswick, fell into the enemy's hands, who made them feel all the hardships of war. They, however, always pretended, that these misfortunes were a consequence of the measures taken by his majesty, who would not grant the peace intended for his states, and those of his allies. His majesty then resolved, in quality of elector, to make proposals of peace to the empress queen and the court of France. He saw that the efforts which he had made to stop the French army had been ineffectual; his paternal heart was sensibly affected to see the oppression and ruin of his faithful subjects.

The severity with which they acted with regard to his allies, excited in his soul sentiments of the most sincere compassion; he then repeated his former declarations, that he would observe the most strict neutrality as elector, during the troubles of Germany, and promised to separate his army, on condition that his states, and those of his allies, were delivered from the yoke under which they groaned. These offers were absolutely all that the courts of Vienna and Versailles had demanded, and the latter especially could not reject them, without taking off the mask, discovering her design to make conquests in Germany, and of destroying, contrary to all the laws of nations, the electorate of Hanover, incorporated with the empire, and taking no part in these quarrels on account of the war in America. The two courts had as yet given no definitive answer, when his royal highness the Duke of Cumberland, by the mediation of Count de Lynar, concluded the truce of Sept. 8, 1757. We only know that the court of Vienna had assured Baron de Steinberg, envoy from the king, as elector, to that court, that when the first overtures were made of a peace, it had given orders to Count de Strahremberg to support them at Versailles. That convention bore, that hostilities should cease on both sides; and that the auxiliary troops should return into their own countries: that the Hanoverians should be placed in the part of his majesty's dominions which should be assigned them, and that the French should possess the rest till a final reconciliation. The most remarkable of these separate articles is that wherein it is declared, that the allies *should not be looked upon at prisoners of war.*

It needs but little attention to discover the nature and end of this convention: it is a suspension of arms, a military regulation, which the French minister himself drew up: it was to continue till the issue of a negotiation, begun by his Britannic majesty in the quality of Elector of Hanover, and upon the declaration of the courts of Vienna and Versailles which was expected. This was the reason why it was not thought necessary to fix the time the suspension of arms was to last. It was drawn up by the generals of the two armies, who mutually agreed that it might be concluded without the ratification of the two courts: and, indeed, they might well agree to a truce, which was to last only for a short time; but it is impossible to suppose that they had power to make a treaty by which, without the ratification of the sovereigns, the king's dominions should be delivered up into the hands of foreigners, till a general peace, of which there was not the least appearance. It is a thing unheard of to give the general of an army so extensive an authority.

The conduct of Hanover, immediately after it was signed, shews still more clearly the meaning and end of the convention: not only the instructions given to the king's envoys, but the original letters which remain in the hands of the most respectable ministers who were employed in this affair, testify to the whole world the truth of what we have here advanced. His royal highness the Duke of Cumberland in the first memorial, delivered to Count de Lynar, informs him, 'That he had a view to procure, 'by means of the convention, a 'suspension of arms on both sides, 'as the first means of a reconcilia-'tion.' Baron de Schwegeld, his Britannic majesty's minister, writes the 10th of September, the same day the convention was signed, to Baron de Bernstorff, his Danish majesty's minister of state, as follows; 'I need not enter into a 'detail of negotiation of which 'your excellency will be already 'fully informed by Count de Ly-'nar. You will see, Sir, by the 'account which he will give you, 'that nothing but the hopes that 'this first step would serve as a 'foundation and introduction to 'other measures, made us over-'look numberless considerations, 'which otherwise would have me-'rited the most serious considera-'tion in many respects.' Baron de Steinberg, minister of state, wrote in the following terms to the Count de Lynar, who had sent the scheme of explanation. This letter is dated

September 28. 'Your excellency 'has too well obferved, during 'your refidence here, how faithfully we have acted, and how ardently we have defired to continue 'the negotiation begun, to pave 'the way to were particular explanations, and to the relief which 'the ftates of the king ftand fo 'much in need of. Your excellency, I fay, has too well obferved all this, to make the leaft 'doubt, that the hopes which you 'gave occafion to, in your letter 'of the 27th, are not entirely 'agreeable to the miniftry, who 'are under the greateft obligations 'to your excellency for the zeal 'which you fhew in this affair, and 'the care which you have promifed to take. As to a more particular convention mentioned to 'us by your excellency, I fhall 'conform entirely to what his royal 'highnefs the Duke of Cumberland 'fhall fignify on that head. I add, 'however, that the king's minifter has feen, with great pleafure, the efforts which your excellency, who hath fo fure and extenfive a knowledge, hath made 'to bring things to a formal 'negotiation. And as there is the 'greateft reafon to think, that the 'exhibition of full powers will, 'with this view, be infifted upon, 'the miniftry make no doubt 'but your excellency will take 'all poffible care to caufe thofe of 'Marfhal Richelieu, or of any 'other, to extend farther than to a 'negotiation, *ad interim*, and confequently to an entire conclufion 'of the accommodation which they 'have in veiw. The articles contained in your excellency's fcheme 'of explanation will furnifh fufficient arguments on this head, 'as every fufpenfion of arms undetermined with regard to time, 'firft fuppofes that the principal 'negotiation will follow, and that 'equitable terms will be granted 'on both fides. The promife of 'the king, the Duke of Brunfwick, 'and the Landgrave of Heffe, 'not to employ their troops during the prefent troubles, muft be 'founded upon the hopes, that in 'confideration thereof their ftates 'fhall be delivered from the oppreffion under which they at prefent groan, and that no pretences 'fhall be made to put off this condition till a general peace, which 'a feries of unforefeen events, of 'which the prefent year has furnifhed fo great a number, may long 'prevent.'

Laftly, it is plain that France herfelf underftood the convention in the very fame fenfe. For whether the hands of the Hanoverians were tied up by the fufpenfion of arms concluded at Clofter-feven, till a general peace, or whether this ftate of inaction was only to laft till it fhould be feen whether the king, as elector, could obtain a particular accommodation: In the former cafe, and if that obligation exifted already, why did France infift upon having it ftipulated by the fcheme of explanation propofed by Count de Lynar. And in the other, the king muft have been at liberty to put an end to the truce when there were no hopes left of obtaining a particular peace. In a word, if we but fimply confider the convention of Clofter-feven, both thefe points are inconteftible. If the convention was a fufpenfion of arms, a military regulation, the duration of which depended upon the fuccefs of the propofals for a particular peace, it might then be revoked when the courts of

Vienna

Vienna and Verſailles had rejected theſe propoſals. If, on the contrary, it was a formal treaty, by virtue of which the king's dominions were to remain in the enemy's hands, till an entire reconciliation of the ſovereigns, which was at a great diſtance, it required the ratification of the king, which had never been obtained.

The court of France has furniſhed the king with many other reaſons for regarding the convention as null and void. Scarce was the news of it received at Paris, but they thought they had gained the point ſo long deſired, and that they were able to make the king accept the moſt unſupportable terms They not only declared, that they would abſolutely hear no terms of peace, but even proteſted againſt the validity of the convention, and refuſed to accept the guaranty of the King of Denmark, unleſs the troops ſhould take a ſolemn engagement not to ſerve during the war againſt France or her allies. This is formally declared in the poſtſcript to a letter to Count de Lynar. Another equally authentic proof of this fact, is found in a letter of Marſhal Richelieu to General de Zaſtrow. The diſarming of the troops was alſo inſiſted upon, though by the advice of France herſelf, the convention had obſerved a profound ſilence on that head. This pretenſion was ſo obſtinately maintained, that the propoſal made without the concurrence of his Britannic majeſty, by his majeſty the King of Denmark, to receive theſe troops into his dominions, was rejected.

The weight of the yoke impoſed upon the electorate of Hanover was doubled, by giving it in farm to a citizen named Faidy: ſo that the ſentiments of humanity which a people reduced to the laſt extremity might expect from ſome placemen of France, were more effectually ſtifled by the avarice of the farmer, whoſe intereſt rendered him deaf to prayers and remonſtrances. To leave no doubt of the ambitious views of the court of Verſailles; to ſhew that it expected to make new conqueſts over the king, the ſaid Jean Faidy obtained by patent the farm *of the territories of his Britannic majeſty, which were conquered or to be conquered.*

The convention was infringed in numberleſs other reſpects by France, of which an ample account was given in a piece, intitled, *Previous expoſitions of the reaſons which induced his Britannic majeſty, in quality of Elector of Hanover, to take up arms againſt the French army, which is again in motion.*

The king's territories and thoſe of his allies were threatened with the moſt ſevere treatment. They even threatened to raiſe and reduce to aſhes the royal palaces, and thoſe of the king's miniſters, in caſe they ſhould make the leaſt difficulty to ſubſcribe blindly to the will and orders of the court of France. Of this Count Lynar's letter gives ſufficient proof. As to the court of Vienna, it ſpared no pains to ſecond the unjuſt deſigns of its ally. After the example of the latter, it declared that it was not a ſeparate peace that would be ſought: and that the king might not change his premeditated deſign of putting the laſt hand to it, the Aulic and Imperial Councils ought to interpoſe on this occaſion. The Prince of Tour-Taxis had alſo the credit and influence at Vienna, precifely in thefe circumftances, to bring about the moft unjuft and illegal proceedings againft his Britannic majefty in the affair of the pofts.

The king eafily perceived to what the threatenings of his enemies tended. They wanted to throw an indelible ftain upon his arms, by difarming the auxiliary troops, who had no other refource left but either to difband or enter into the French armies. The Hanoverian troops were confined in fo narrow a fpace, that it would have been impoffible for them to fubfift long, but muft have perifhed in mifery. Befides, the king, by fubfcribing to the new terms which they wanted to impofe upon him, could not afterwards have claimed the affiftance of the Britifh nation for that electorate. The revenues of his German dominions would have been feized, and the country exhaufted in fuch a manner, that nothing could have been expected from it in a long courfe of years. The king would then have feen himfelf unable to maintain either his own or fubfidiary troops, which by a natural confequence he had been forced to difband. Then would his majefty's enemies have accomplifhed the dangerous fchemes which Count Fleming foretold, *might one day become fatal to the houfe of Hanover.*

Let any one but examine this picture, whofe natural colours are much ftronger than here reprefented; let him but liften to the voice of reafon, juftice, and equity; let him, in fhort, but put himfelf in the king's place, it will be impoffible for him to hefitate a moment, what part the king had to take in thefe circumftances. The court of France itfelf acknowledged, that the laft conditions propofed did not exift in the treaty of Clofter-feven, as it wanted them to be granted by new conventions. The king had therefore an undoubted right to reject them. France alfo maintained, that the convention, before it could become obligatory, wanted the ratification of his moft chriftian majefty. The king, therefore, had an equal power to grant his, or to refufe it. Was he to renounce this power, and abandon his country and people to the difcretion of an enemy, who fought their total ruin and deftruction?

The king, then, took the moft juft meafures, and the moft agreeable for his own dignity and prefervation; the only meafures which the arrogance of his enemies had permitted him to take; meafures, in fhort, which, however dangerous and uncertain they then appeared, could not poffibly prove more fatal, than the equally heavy and fhameful yoke which France wanted to impofe upon the king, by the new convention. He refolved to try, what was poffible, to deliver his eftates, and thofe of his allies, from tyranny and oppreffion, and for this purpofe, and to defend himfelf, to join in quality of elector, with his Pruffian majefty. He ordered a perfon of confidence to be fent to that monarch, to defire him to permit Prince Ferdinand of Brunfwick, a prince of the blood-royal, to take the command of his army. This was the firft of Nov. and confequently five days before the battle of Rofbach, when Major General Count de Schulembourg departed from Stade, to go to the King of Pruffia. In the mean time, the

the generals and ministers had not yet received orders to commence hostilities. The king would not permit them to pursue any measures which might give France room to think that he was disposed to enter into her views. General Zastrow's letter, annexed to the Parallel shews that they conformed exactly to his majesty's intentions, and they signified that they thought the king was resolved henceforward to regard the convention as null and void. As soon as we were sure of a general, a resolution was taken to march against the enemy. Duke Ferdinand gave notice of this to Marshal Richelieu, by a letter of the 28th of November.

The king gave all the world an account of the just motives of this conduct in a memorial published the 26th of that month, and hostilities were renewed on both sides. This is the justest idea that can be given of an event, which will serve as an eternal monument of France's manner of acting as soon as she thinks she has the superiority on her side; her conduct will convince all the states of the empire, that there is nothing to be gained by yielding to her, and that her pride, and the abuse of her strength, increase in proportion as they become abject.

We shall examine as we go along, and dissipate the falshoods with which the court of France has sought to amuse the public, with regard to this event, and the sophistry which she has made use of for her justification. It is impossible, in doing this, not to fall into some repetitions. The French ministry begin with an exaggerated description of the condition of the Hanoverian army at the signing of the convention. It is said in the Parallel, 'That the generous sentiments of the King of France were never more conspicuous than in the capitulation of Closter-seven: That the Hanoverian army, forced to fly before that of Marshal Richelieu, had been obliged to retire to Stade, where it was in the most dangerous situation.'

It will be easily granted, that at the time of making the convention, we had no hopes of soon delivering the king's dominions, and those of his allies, by force of arms, because we saw an army making head against us greatly superior to ours in number. But had not Marshal Richelieu reason, on the other hand, to fear a reverse of fortune, if he was resolved to drive an army of forty thousand men to despair, whose valour he had experienced at the affair of Hastenbeck? Besides, it was that marshal, and not the Duke of Cumberland, who was informed of the march of the King of Prussia against the Prince of Soubise. So there is not the least mention made of the haste with which the French army flew to the assistance of the latter, immediately after signing the convention. As to the rest, it is impossible to conceive that this convention can serve as an example of the generous sentiments of his most christian majesty. They ingenuously own, that Marshal Richelieu granted the capitulation of his own accord, without consulting his court. As to the new conditions proposed by the court of Versailles, and with which she connected her ratification, it would be absurd to maintain that they were dictated by sentiments of generosity.

The

The court of France ſaw very well that ſhe could not claim the right of refuſing the capitulation of the treaty of Cloſter-ſeven, without giving the ſame right to his Britannic majeſty. In order, therefore, to throw a falſe gloſs upon the explanation of the treaty, it pretends, 'That the King of 'France, out of his zeal for his 'allies and the empire, approved 'of the conduct of Marſhal Richelieu; and to render the capitu-'lation more ſolid, his majeſty 'propoſed to add to it ſome expla-'nations, to fix the ſenſe of it in 'ſo clear a manner, as to obviate 'every falſe interpretation; expla-'nations which the court of Co-'penhagen and count Lynar had 'found conformable to the true 'ſenſe of the capitulation.'

But this tale is abſolutely contrary to the true ſtate of things. The court of France declared, that it would not acknowledge the validity of the convention, unleſs the new terms which is intended to add were agreed to, and the auxiliary troops were diſarmed. This circumſtance, which is moſt clearly related in Count de Lynar's letter, which is known to the court of Copenhagen, and which was the cauſe that the guaranty of that court was not ſought, is alſo mentioned in Marſhal Richelieu's own letter, annexed to the Parallel. His words are as follow: 'His Daniſh ma-'jeſty having offered to guaranty 'them (the articles of the conven-'tion) the king my maſter thinks, 'that before he ſigns his accep-'tance of them, it will be proper 'to obviate ſome obſcurities which 'might occaſion difficulties in the 'execution, which has been ſuſ-'pended reciprocally upon words 'of honour, to make no alteration 'in their ſubſtance, and always to 'execute them, when both ſides 'have come to an underſtanding 'relating to any doubts that may 'ariſe.'

CHA-

CHARACTERS.

WE have ſet apart this article, for ſome remarkable characters of thoſe, whether in the politial or the literary world, whether living or dead, who have been diſtinguiſhed by ſuch talents as merit the public attention. The three firſt are drawn by hands altogether worthy of their ſubjects; neither are the others contemptibly executed. If the firſt of theſe pictures inclines ſomewhat towards panegyric, and if the ſecond ſhould be thought to partake of ſatire, the reader will not therefore think either of them leſs juſt.

An eſſay towards the character of the King of Pruſſia, tranſlated from the French of M. Maupertuis.

THE moſt faithful and ſcrupulous hiſtorian would be the beſt panegyriſt of Frederick King of Pruſſia. I pretend to be neither; I only attempt the out-lines of his character, which even co-temporary jealouſy, envy and malignity, are forced to admire, and which more impartial poſterity, if it can believe, will almoſt adore.

By the mere natural ſtrength and ſuperiority of his genius, without experience, he broke out at once, a general and a hero. He diſtinguiſhed with preciſion what inferior minds never diſcover at all, the difference between great difficulties and impoſſibilities, and being never diſcouraged by the former, has often ſeemed to execute the latter.

Indefatigably laborious and active, coolly intrepid in action, he diſcerns, as by intuition, ſeizes with rapidity, and improves with ſkill, the ſhort, favourable, and often deciſive moments of battle. Modeſt and magnanimous after victory, he becomes the generous protector of his ſubdued, and captive enemies. Reſolute and undejected in misfortunes, he has ariſen ſuperior to diſtreſſes, and ſtruggled with difficulties, which no courage, no conſtancy but his own would have reſiſted, nor could have ſurmounted.

But as he cannot always command the ſucceſs which he always deſerves, he may perhaps be obliged to yield at laſt to the ſuperior numbers of almoſt all Europe combined againſt him; their legions may perhaps conquer, but his virtues muſt triumph.

As a king, he is a *man*, a citizen, a legiſlator, and a patriot. His own extenſive mind forms all his plans of government, undebaſed by ſelfiſh miniſterial intereſts and miſrepreſentations. Juſtice and humanity are his only miniſters. *

In

* The following account, the truth of which is not diſputed, will ſerve to give ſome idea of that great prince in that part of his character.

An Engliſh lady being poſſeſſed of actions [ſhares] in the Embden company, and having occaſion to raiſe money on them, repaired to Antwerp, and made

In his own dominions he has reformed the law, and reduced it to equity, by a code of his own digesting. He has thrown cavil out

made application for that purpose to a director of the company, established there by the King of Prussia, for the managing all affairs relating thereto. This person very willingly entered into treaty with her; but the sum he offered to lend, being far short of what the actions would bear, and also insisting on forfeiture of her right in them, if not redeemed in twelve months, she broke off with him, and had recourse to some merchants at Antwerp, who were inclinable to treat with her on much more equitable terms. The proceeding necessarily brought the parties before this director, for receiving his sanction, which was essential to the solidity of the agreement; and he, finding he was like to lose the advantage he had flattered himself with, disputed the authenticity of the actions, and thereby threw her into such discredit, as to render all attempts to raise money on them ineffectual. Upon this the lady wrote a letter by the common post to his majesty of Prussia, accompanied with a memorial, complaining of the treatment she had received from the director; and likewise inclosed the actions themselves, in another letter to a friend at Berlin. By the return of the post, his majesty condescended to answer her letter; and the actions were returned authenticated, which so restored her credit, that in a few hours all difficulties were removed, relating to the transaction she had in her hand; and it is more than probable, the director has felt his majesty's resentment for his ill behaviour.

A translation of the lady's letter.

SIRE,

Having had the happiness to pay my court to your majesty, during a pretty long residence at Berlin, and to receive such marks of favour from their majesties the queens, as I shall ever retain a grateful sense of, I presume to flatter myself that your majesty will not be offended at the respectful liberty I take, in laying before you my complaints against one Van Ertborn, a director of the Embden China company, whose bad behaviour to me, as set forth in my memorial, hath forced me to make a very long and expensive stay at this place: and as the considerable interest I have in that company may further subject me to his caprices, I cannot forbear laying my grievances at the foot of your majesty's throne, most respectfully supplicating your majesty, that you would be graciously pleased to give orders that this director should not act towards me for the future, as he hath done hitherto.

I hope for this favour from your majesty's sovereign equity; and I shall never cease offering up my ardent prayers for the prosperity of your glorious reign; having the honour to be, with the most respectful zeal, SIRE,

Your majesty's most humble,
most obedient,
and most devoted servant,
* * * *.

Translation of his Prussian *majesty's answer.*

Madam,

I received the letter, of the 19th instant, which you thought proper to write me, and was not a little displeased to hear of the bad behaviour of one of the directors of the Asiatic company of Embden towards you, of which you were forced to complain. I shall direct your grievances to be examined, and have just now dispatched my orders for that purpose, to Lentz, my president of the chamber of East-Friesland. You may assure yourself the strictest justice shall be done you that the case will admit. God keep you in his holy protection.

Potsdam, FREDERICK.
Feb. 26, 1756.

out of the ſhifting and wavering ſcales of juſtice, and poized them equally to all.

Indulgent to the various errors of the human mind, becauſe tainted with ſo few himſelf, he has eſtabliſhed *univerſal toleration* ; that deciſive characteriſtic of true religion, natural juſtice, ſocial benevolence, and even good policy. He equally abhors the guilt of making martyrs, and the folly of making hypocrites.

Greatly above all narrow local prejudices, he has invited and engaged, by a *general indiſcriminating uaturalization*, people of all nations to ſettle in his dominions. He encourages and rewards the induſtrious, he cheriſhes and honours the learned ; and *man as man*, wherever oppreſſed by civil, or perſecuted by eccleſiaſtical tyranny, finds a ſure refuge in his ſentiments of juſtice and humanity, which the purple robe has not been able to ſmother.

A philoſopher undazzled with the ſplendor of the heroic parts of this character, may perhaps inquire after the milder and ſocial virtues of humanity, *and ſeek for the mnn* —— He will find both the man and the philoſopher too in Frederick, unallayed by the king, and unſullied by the warrior.

A patron of all liberal arts and ſciences, and a model of moſt. In a more particular manner cultivating, adorning and adorned by the *belles lettres*. His early and firſt attempt was a refutation of the impious ſyſtem of Machivael, that celebrated profeſſor of political iniquity ; nobly conſcious that he might venture to give the world, that public pledge of his future virtue. His memoirs, intended to ſerve only as materials for a future hiſtory of the houſe of Brandenbourg, are ſuch as muſt neceſſarily defeat his own purpoſe, unleſs he will write the hiſtory too, himſelf. There are alſo ſpecimens enough of his poetical genius, to ſhew what he might be as a poet, were he not ſomething greater and better.

Neither the toils of war, nor the cares of government engroſs his whole time, but he enjoys a conſiderable part of it in familiar and eaſy converſation with his equals, *men*. There the king is unknown, and what is more, *unfelt*. Merit is the only diſtinction, in which his unaſſerted, but confeſſed, and undecided ſuperiority, flatters a mind formed like his much more delicately, than the always caſual, and often undeſerved, ſuperiority of rank and birth.

But not to ſwell an eſſay towards a character, to the bulk of a finiſhed character ſtill leſs to that of a hiſtory ; I will conclude this ſketch with this obſervation : Many a private man might make a great king, but where is the king who could make a great private man, except FREDERICK ?

The following character of M. de Voltaire, is ſaid to have been written by a P—— ce.

M. De Voltaire is below the ſtature of a tall man, or, in other words, he is a little above thoſe of a middling ſize : he is extremely thin, and of an aduſt temperament, hot and atrabilious ; his viſage is meagre, his aſpect

ardent

ardent and penetrating, and there is a malignant quicknefs in his eye; the fame fire that animates his works appears in his actions, which are lively even to abfurdity; he is a kind of meteor, perpetually coming and going with a quick motion, and a fparkling light that dazzles our eyes. A man thus conftituted cannot fail of being a valetudinarian: the blade eats away the fcabbard; gay by complexion, grave by regimen; open without franknefs, politic without refinement, fociable without friends: He knows the world, and he forgets it; in the morning he is Ariftippus, and Diogenes at night; he loves grandeur, and defpifes the great; with his fuperiors his carriage is eafy, but with his equals conftrained; he is firft polite, then cold, then difgufting. He loves the court, yet makes himfelf weary of it; he has fenfibility without connections, and is voluptuous without paffion. He is attached to nothing by choice, but to every thing by inconftancy. As he reafons without principle, his reafon has its fits like the folly of others. He has a clear head, and a corrupt heart; he thinks of every thing, and treats every thing with derifion. He is a libertine without a conftitution for pleafure, and he knows how to moralize without morality. His vanity is exceffive, but his avarice is yet greater than his vanity; he therefore writes lefs for reputation than money, for which he may be faid both to hunger and thirft. He is in hafte to work that he may be in hafte to live: he was made to enjoy, and he determines only to hoard. Such is the man, and fuch is the author.

There is no other poet in the world, whofe verfes coft him fo little labour: but this facility of compofition hurts him becaufe he abufes it; as there is but little for labour to fupply, he is content that little fhould be wanting, and therefore almoft all his pieces are unfinifhed. But tho' he is an eafy, an ingenious, and elegant writer of poetry, yet his principal excellence would be hiftory, if he made fewer reflections, and drew no parallels, in both of which however, he has fometimes been very happy. In his laft work he has imitated the manner of Bayle, of whom, even in his cenfure of him, he has exhibited a copy. It has long been faid, that for a writer to be without paffion, and without prejudice, he muft have neither religion nor country, and in this refpect Mr. Voltaire has made great advances towards perfection. He cannot be accufed of being a partifan to his nation; he appears on the contrary to be infected with a fpecies of madnefs fomewhat like that of old men, who are always extolling the time paft, and bitterly complaining of the prefent. Voltaire is always diffatisfied with his own country, and lavifh in his praife of thofe that are a thoufand leagues off. As to religion, he is in that refpect evidently undetermined, and he would certainly be the neutral and impartial being, fo much defired for an author, but for a little leaven of anti-janfenifm which appears fomewhat too plainly diftinguifhed in his works. Voltaire has much foreign and much French literature; nor is he deficient in that mixed erudition which is now fo much in fafhion. He is a politician,

litician, a naturalift, a geometrician, or whatever elfe he pleafes; but he is always fuperficial, becaufe he is not able to be deep. He could not, however, flourifh as he does upon thefe fubjects without great ingenuity. His tafte is rather delicate than juft; he is an ingenious fatyrift, a bad critic, and a dabler in the abftracted fciences. Imagination is his element, and yet, ftrange as it is, he has no invention. He is reproached with continually paffing from one extream to another; now a *Philanthropift*, then a cynic; now an exceffive encomiaft, then an outrageous fatyrift. In one word, Voltaire would fain be an extraordinary man, and an extraordinary man he moft certainly is!

Anecdotes of the life of Baron Montefquieu, author of the Spirit of Laws.

From the French of M. D'Alembert.

CHarles de Secondat, Baron of la Brede and Montefquieu, prefident *à mortier* in the parliament of Bourdeaux, member of the French academy, of the royal academy of fciences and belles lettres at Berlin, and of the royal fociety of London, was defcended of a noble family in Guienne, and born at the caftle of la Brede, near Bourdeaux, on the 28th of January, 1689. His father was a younger brother, and ferved fome time in the army, from which he foon retired, Young Montefquieu gave early proofs of his fuperior talents, and his father was diligent to improve them. At the age of twenty he was employed in preparing the materials of his *Spirit of Laws*, by judicious extracts from the immenfe volumes that compofe the body of civil law. Jurifprudence, though lefs dry to him than to moft who apply to it, becaufe he cultivated it as a philofopher, was not fufficient for his extenfive and active genius. He entered, at the fame time, into the depths of the moft important and delicate fubjects ||, and treated them with that judgment, decency, and juftnefs, which diftinguifh all his writings.

His father's brother, prefident *à mortier* of the parliament of Bourdeaux, who was the eldeft branch of the family, lofing his only fon, left his fortune and his office to M. Montefquieu, who had been admitted a counfellor in the parliament of Bourdeaux, Feb. 14, 1714, and was received prefident *à mortier* July 13, 1716. In 1722, during the king's minority, he was deputed by the parliament to make remonftrances againft a new oppreffive tax. He difcharged this commiffion with fo much boldnefs and addrefs, that the tax was abolifhed. April 3, 1716, he was admitted a member of the infant academy of Bourdeaux, and diverted the fociety from the ftudy of the fine arts, which can feldom be cultivated to advantage but in the capital, to the more ufeful ftudy of phyfic.

|| This was a tract in the form of letters; defigned to fhew that the idolatry of moft of the Pagans did not deferve eternal damnation.

In

In 1721, when he was 32 years of age, he publiſhed his firſt work, intitled, Perſian Letters [*Lettres Perſannes*.] In theſe he expoſes with great ſprightlineſs and energy, the cuſtom of the French, to treat the moſt trifling things with ſerioufneſs, and turn the moſt important into ridicule; their converſation ſo noiſy and frivolous; their languor, even in the lap of pleaſure; their prejudices and their actions in continual contradiction to their underſtanding; their ardent love of glory joined to the moſt profound homage to the idol of court-favour; their courtiers ſo ſervile, and yet ſo vain; their outward politeneſs to, and their innate contempt of foreigners, or affected partiality towards them; the extravagance of their taſte, than which nothing can be more contemptible, except the eagerneſs of all Europe to adopt it; their barbarous diſdain of the moſt reſpectable occupations of a citizen, namely, commerce and the adminiſtration of juſtice; their literary diſputes, ſo warm and yet ſo uſeleſs; their rage of writing without thought, and judging without knowledge. To this lively portrait he oppoſes, in the apologue of the Troglodites, a repreſentation of England, which he calls a virtuous nation made wiſe by misfortunes.

Though this piece had the greateſt ſucceſs, it was not owned by the author. There were ſeveral free expreſſions in it, relating not to the eſſentials of Chriſtianity, but to things that many people ſtudy to confound with Chriſtianity; concerning the ſpirit of perſecution, with which ſo many Chriſtians have been animated; the temporal uſurpations made by the clergy; and the exceſſive multiplication of monaſteries, which leſſens the number of ſubjects in the ſtate, without increaſing the ſincere worſhippers of God. Theſe and ſome other points being miſrepreſented to the miniſtry, when M. de Monteſquieu ſtood candidate for a place in the French academy, vacant by the death of M. de Sacy, it was ſignified to the members, that the king would not approve of the election of the author of the *Lettres Perſannes*. M. de Monteſquieu ſaw the conſequence of this blow, to his perſon, his family, and the tranquillity of his life. He conſidered perpetual excluſion from the academy, eſpecially from ſuch motives, as an injury. He waited on the miniſter; repreſented that, for private reaſons, he did not acknowledge himſelf to be the author of the *Lettres Perſannes*; but that there was nothing in them he was aſhamed of; and that he ought to have been judged not upon the repreſentation of an informer, but upon a candid peruſal of his work *. The miniſters did what they ought to have done at firſt: they read the book, and liked the author, and learned where to place their confidence. France retained a ſubject whom ſuperſtition and calumny

* Voltaire ſays (Siecle de Louis XIV. edit. 1756.) that Monteſquieu cauſed a new edition of his book to be printed off in a few days; in which he either omitted or ſoftened whatever could give offence to Cardinal Fleury, and carried the book to him himſelf. The Cardinal, who ſcarce ever read, curſorily looked into ſome parts of it, and the air of confidence Monteſquieu aſſumed, joined to the ſollicitations of ſome perſons of high rank, made him drop his oppoſition.

were

were on the point of making her lofe. For M. de Montefquieu declared, that after fuch an affront, he would feek among ftrangers, who held out their arms to receive him, that fecurity and quiet, and perhaps thofe recompences, which he might have hoped for in his own country. He was received into the academy, Jan. 24, 1728.

The new academician was the more deferving of that title, as he had a little before quitted every other employment to follow entirely his genius and tafte. He was fenfible that he could be more ferviceable to his country, and to mankind by his writings, than by deciding, in obfcurity, private contentions. He, therefore, determined to fell his place; and ceafing to be a judge, devoted his time to letters only.

But to be ufeful to different nations, it was neceffary that he fhould know them. With this view he fet out on his travels. He went firft to Vienna, where he often faw the celebrated Prince Eugene. This hero fo fatal to France (to which he might have been ufeful) after bringing Lewis XIV. into jeopardy, and humbling the Ottoman pride, lived, in time of peace, without pomp, a lover and encourager of letters, in a court where little honour is paid to them, and fet an example to his mafters to patronife them.

M. de Montefquieu went next to Hungary, an opulent and fertile country, inhabited by a proud and generous people, the fcourge of tyrants, and the fupporters of their fovereigns. As this country is little known, he is very full on it in the account of his travels, which are not yet publifhed. He went next to Italy. At Venice he faw the famous Law, who had nothing left of his former grandeur, but projects that were happily deftined to die with him, and a diamond which he often pledged to raife money to play at games of chance. One day the converfation turned on the famous fyftem invented by Law, the æra of the ruin and the opulence of many people in France, and of a remarkable corruption of manners in that kingdom. Law met with oppofition to his fcheme from the parliament of Paris, who are the immediate depofitaries of the laws during a minority. M. de Montefquieu afked him why he did not try to gain them by that which proves infallible in England, money? 'The members of 'your parliament, replied Law, 'have lefs fire and generofity than 'my countrymen; but they have 'more integrity *.' Another perfon not lefs famous, whom Montefquieu faw often at Venice, was Count Bonneval. This man, fo well known by his adventures, which were not yet brought to their final period, pleafed to have a judge that deferved fo well to hear him, took great pleafure in giving M. de Montefquieu a de-

* M. D'Alembert's remark on this paffage, is as follows:
'We fhall add, without any prejudice from national vanity, than a body, 'which is free for a fhort time only, muft refift corruption better, than a body 'which is always free: the firft, if it fells its liberty, lofes it; the fecond only 'lends it (if I may be allowed the expreffion) and exercifes it even in pledging 'it. Thus the vices and virtues of nations arife from circumftances and the 'nature of the government.'

 tail

tail of his very extraordinary life, of the military actions he had a part in, and the characters of the generals and minifters he had known. Montefquieu often recalled to mind thofe converfations, and related many paffages of them to his friends.

From Venice he went to Rome. In this ancient capital of the world, which is ftill fo in fome refpects, he particularly attended to that by which it is at prefent diftinguifhed, the works of Raphael, Titian, and Michael Angelo. He had never particularly ftudied the fine arts: but the expreffion that fhines forth in the mafter-pieces of that kind, never fails to ftrike every man of genius. Accuftomed to attend to nature, he knows her when he fees her imitated; as a good likenefs ftrikes all to whom the original is familiar.

After travelling through Italy, M. de Montefquieu went to Switzerland, and carefully examined the vaft countries that are watered by the Rhine. There remained nothing more in Germany for him to fee; for Frederick was not yet come to the crown. After ftaying fome time in the United Provinces, which are an admirable monument of what *Induftry* can do animated by the love of *Liberty*, he came over to England, where he refided two years. He had nothing to regret, but that he did not come fooner, Locke and Newton were both dead. But he had often the honour to wait on their protectrefs, Queen Caroline, who cultivated philofophy on the throne, and had a juft relifh for M. de Montefquieu's converfation. He was equally well received by the nation; who in this inftance did not want to have the example fet them by the court. At London he formed connections with men accuftomed to meditation, who qualified themfelves for fo great actions by ftudy. From them he informed himfelf of the nature of the Englifh government, and acquired a perfect knowledge of it. Germany, he faid, was fit only to travel in, Italy to refide in, England to think in, and France to live in.

On his return to France, he retired for two years to his feat at la Brede, and put the laft hand to his work, of the caufes of the rife and fall of Rome, *Sur la caufe de la grandeur, & de la decadence des Romains*; which appeared in 1734. It might juftly have been entitled, *The Roman Hiftory, for the ufe of Statefmen and Philofophers.*

How much reputation foever he might have gained by this and his former works, he had, as yet, only cleared the way for a much greater undertaking, that which ought to immortalife his name, and render his memory refpectable to future ages. He had long before this time formed the defign of it: he had meditated on the execution of it for twenty years, or rather his whole life was one continued meditation. He firft made himfelf, as it were, a ftranger in his own country, that he might know it better. He next vifited Europe, and with the deepeft attention ftudied the characteriftics of the different nations by which it is inhabited. The famous ifland, which glories fo much in its laws, and makes fuch a bad ufe of them, was to him, in this long tour, what the ifle of Crete was formerly to Lycurgus, a fchool where he improved in knowledge, without approving of the whole. In fine, he had examined and judged nations and eminent men that no longer exift, but in the annals of the world. Thus he gradually rose to the highest title a wise man can arrive at, that of Legislator of nations.

If he was animated by the importance of his subject, he was discouraged by its extent: he abandoned and resumed it several times. And length, encouraged by his friends, he mustered all his strength, and gave the public his *Spirit of Laws*.

Among the authors by whom he was assisted, and from whom he borrowed some of his sentiments, the principal are the two of deepest meditation, Tacitus and Plutarch: but, though a philosopher who reads two, may dispense with many others, Montesquieu neglected or slighted none that could be of use. *The Spirit of Laws* discovers immense reading: and the judicious use which the author made of the prodigious mass of materials will appear still more surprizing, when it is known that he was almost wholly deprived of sight, and obliged to make use of other peoples eyes.

Though M. de Montesquieu did not long survive the publication of his *Esprit des Loix*, he had the satisfaction to see the beginning of its effects upon the French nation; the natural love of the French to their country, turned to its proper object; a taste for commerce, agriculture, and the useful arts, beginning to spread throughout that kingdom; and that general knowledge of the principles of government, which renders the people more attached to what they ought to love.

Neverthelefs a multitude of pieces appeared in France against his book. The anonymous author of a periodical work, who imagined himself the successor of Paschal, because he succeeded to his opinions, thought to ruin M. de Montesquieu, but was the occasion of new lustre being cast on his name, as a man of learning, by provoking him to write a *Defence of his Spirit of Laws*. This work may serve as a model on account of the moderation, truth, and humour that appear throughout the whole of it. M. de Montesquieu could easily have rendered his adversary odious; but he chuse rather to make him ridiculous. What adds to the value of this excellent piece, is, that the author, without thinking of it, has in it drawn a true picture of himself: those who knew him imagine they hear him speak; and posterity, when they read his *Defence*, will see that his conversation was not inferior to his writings.

While the insects thus buzzed about and molested him in his own country, M. Dassier, famous for his medals of illustrious men, went from London to Paris, 1752, to strike a medal of M. de Montesquieu. M. de la Tour, also, an eminent painter, was very desirous to paint the author of the *Spirit of Laws*: but M. de Montesquieu constantly refused, in a polite manner, his pressing solicitations. M. Dassier met with the same difficulties at first: 'Don't you think (said he one day to Montesquieu) 'that 'there is as much pride in refusing 'my request, as there would ap-'pear in granting it?' Disarmed by this pleasantry, he suffered M. Dassier to do what he pleased.

He was at last in peaceable possession of the glory he so justly acquired, when he was taken ill in the beginning of February. His health, naturally delicate, had long before begun to break by the slow and almost imperceptible effects of his close study, the chagrin given

R 2 him

him on account of his work, and the multiplicity of company that crowded to him at Paris. His end was worthy of his life. Oppreſſed by grievous pain, and at a diſtance from a family he loved, he breathed his laſt with the tranquility of a good man, conſcious of having devoted his talents to the ſervice of virtue and mankind. He died on the 10th of February, 1755, univerſally and ſincerely regretted. 'His virtues (ſays Lord Cheſterfield) 'did honour to human nature, his writings juſtice. A 'friend to mankind, he aſſerted 'their undoubted and unalienable 'rights and freedom, even in his 'country, whoſe prejudice in matters of religion and government 'he had long lamented, and endeavoured (not without ſome ſucceſs) to remove. He well knew, 'and juſtly admired the happy 'conſtitution of this country, where 'fixed and known laws reſtrain 'monarchy from tyranny, and liberty from licentiouſneſs. His 'works will illuſtrate his name, 'and ſurvive him as long as right 'reaſon, moral obligation, and the 'true ſpirit of laws ſhall be underſtood, reſpected, and maintained.'

With regard to his private life. In company he was always pleaſant and gay: his converſation, by the many men and nations he had converſed with, was ſprightly, agreeable, and inſtructive. It was abrupt, like his ſtyle; full of piquant ſallies, without bitterneſs or ſatire. Nobody told a ſtory with more life, readineſs, and grace, and leſs formality; he knew that the concluſion of a pleaſant ſtory is the chief point, and he haſtened to it, and produced the deſired effect, without having promiſed it. The pleaſure found in his company was not the effect of his temper and genius, but of a kind of regimen, alſo, which he obſerved in his ſtudies: though capable of deep and long-continued meditation, he never exhauſted his ſtrength; but always quitted labour before he felt any ſenſation of fatigue.

Nothing does more honour to his memory, than his œconomy; which was thought too great in an age of avarice and diſſipation when its motives were not perceived, nor if perceived, could have been felt. Beneficent, and conſequently juſt, M. de Monteſquieu would take from his family nothing of what he gave to relieve the diſtreſſed, nor of the large expences occaſioned by his long travels, the diſorder in his eyes, and the printing of his works. He left to his children the inheritance of his father, without diminution, and without increaſe.

He married in 1715, Jane de Lartigue, daughter of Pierre de Lartigue, lieutenant-colonel of the regiment of Maulévrier; by whom he had two daughters, and a ſon, who by his character, his manners, and his writings, hath ſhewn himſelf worthy of ſuch a father.

We omitted to mention in its place ſome of the author's leſs conſiderable works, which ſerved him for relaxation. The moſt remarkable of theſe is the *Temple de Gnide*, which appeared ſoon after the *Lettres Perſannes*. In this piece he paints the delicacy and naivety of paſtoral love, as it appears in a mind uncorrupted by the commerce of the world. He concludes in the preface, in which he repreſents the work as a tranſlation from the Greek, with theſe words: 'If grave 'people ſhould deſire of me a leſs 'frivolous work, I can ſatisfy 'them

'them: I have been employed 'for these thirty years on twelve 'pages, which are to contain all 'that we know of metaphyſics, 'politics, and morals; and all 'that very great authors have 'forgotten in the volumes they 'have written on thoſe ſciences.

Some remarkable paſſages of the life and death of the celebrated Dr. Boerhaave.

IT was the daily practice of that eminent phyſician, Dr. Boerhaave throughout his whole life, as ſoon as he aroſe in the morning, which was generally very early, to retire for an hour to private prayer, and meditation on ſome part of the ſcriptures.—He often told his friends, when they aſked him how it was poſſible for him to go through ſo much fatigue? that it was *This* which gave him ſpirit and vigour in the buſineſs of the day. *This* he therefore recommended as *the beſt rule* he could give; for nothing, he ſaid, could tend more to the health of the body, than the tranquility of the mind; and that he knew nothing which could ſupport himſelf, or his fellow creatures, amidſt the various diſtreſſes of life, but a well-grounded confidence in the Supreme Being upon the principles of chriſtianity. This remark of the doctor's is undeniably juſt; for a benevolent manner of acting, and a true greatneſs of ſoul, can never flow from any other ſource than a conſciouſneſs of the divine favour and aſſiſtance.--This was ſtrongly exemplified in his own illneſs in 1722, which can hardly be told without horror, and by which the courſe of his lectures as well as his practice was long interrupted. He was for five months confined to his bed by the gout, where he lay upon his back without daring to attempt the leaſt motion, becauſe any effort renewed his torments, which were ſo exquiſite, that he was at length not only deprived of motion but of ſenſe.---Here his medical ART was at a ſtand, nothing could be attempted, becauſe nothing could be propoſed with the leaſt proſpect of ſucceſs. But having (in the ſixth month of his illneſs) obtained ſome remiſſion, he determined to try whether the juice of fumitory, endive, and ſuccory, taken thrice a day in a large quantity (viz. above half a pint each doſe) might not contribute to his relief, and by a perſeverance in this method he was wonderfully recovered. This patience of Boerhaave's was founded not on vain reaſonings, like that of which the *Stoicks* boaſted, but on a religious compoſure of mind, and chriſtian reſignation to the will of GOD.

Of his ſagacity and the wonderful penetration with which he often diſcovered and deſcribed, at the firſt ſight of a patient, ſuch diſtempers as betray themſelves by no ſymptoms to common eyes, ſuch ſurprizing accounts have been given as ſcarcely can be credited, though atteſted beyond all doubt.--Yet this great maſter of medical knowledge was ſo far from a preſumptuous confidence in his abilities, or from being puffed up by his rich , that he was condeſcending to all, and remarkably diligent in his profeſſion; and he often uſed to ſay that the life of a patient (if trifled with, or neglected) would one day be required at the hand of the phyſician.---He always called the poor his beſt patients, for God, ſaid he, is their pay-maſter.

The activity of his mind ſparkled viſibly in his eyes.--He was always chearful, and deſirous of promoting every valuable end of converſation; and the excellency of the chriſtian religion was frequently the ſubject of it; for he aſſerted on all *proper* occaſions, the divine authority and ſacred efficacy of the ſcriptures; and maintained, that *they only* could give peace of mind, that ſweet and ſacred peace which paſſeth all underſtanding; ſince none can conceive it, but he who has it; and none can have it, but by divine communication. He never regarded calumny, nor detraction, (for Boerhaave himſelf had enemies) nor ever thought it neceſſary to confute them, '*They are* '*ſparks*, ſaid he, *which if you do* '*not blow, will go out of them*'*ſelves*.'--*The ſureſt remedy againſt* '*ſcandal, is* TO LIVE IT DOWN '*by a perſeverance in well-doing*; '*and by praying to God that he* '*would cure the diſtemper'd minds* '*of thoſe who traduce, and injure* '*us*.' An excellent method this: eſpecially as it keeps our minds contented and unruffled, whilſt the hearts of our enemies are overflowing with rancour, envy, and other diabolical paſſions.

He was not to be over-awed, or depreſſed by the preſence, frowns, or inſolence of great men, but perſiſted on all occaſions in doing what was right, regardleſs of the conſequences.---He could, too, with uncommon readineſs, and almoſt to a certainty, make a conjecture of men's inclinations and capacity by their aſpect---A ſagacity perhaps unequalled, and which often ſurprized even his moſt intimate acquaintance, though they ſo well knew his talents.

Being once aſked by a friend, who had often admired his patience under great provocations, whether he knew what it was to be angry, and by what means he had ſo entirely ſuppreſſed that impetuous and ungovernable paſſion? Dr. Boerhave anſwered, with the utmoſt frankneſs and ſincerity, that he was *naturally* quick of reſentment, but that he had, by daily prayer and meditation, at length attained to this maſtery over himſelf. But this he ſaid was the work of *God's Grace*; for he was too ſenſible of his own weakneſs to aſcribe any thing to himſelf, or to conceive that he could ſubdue paſſion, or withſtand temptation *by his own natural power*: he attributed every good thought, and every laudable action to the Father of goodneſs.

To the will of God he paid an abſolute ſubmiſſion, without endeavouring to diſcover the *reaſons* of his unſearchable determinations; and this he accounted the firſt and moſt inviolable duty of a chriſtian.

About the middle of the year 1737 he felt the firſt approaches of that fatal illneſs, which brought him to the grave, viz. a diſorder in his breaſt, which was at times very painful; often threatened him with immediate ſuffocation; and terminated in an univerſal dropſy; but during this afflictive and lingering illneſs, his conſtancy and firmneſs did not forſake him. He neither intermitted the neceſſary cares of life, nor forgot the proper preparations of death. About three weeks before his diſſolution, when the Rev. Mr. Schultens, one of the moſt

most learned and exemplary divines of the age, attended him at his country house, the doctor desired his prayers, and afterwards entered into a most remarkably judicious discourse with him on the spiritual and immaterial nature of the soul; and this he illustrated to Mr. Schultens with wonderful perspicuity, by a description of the effects which the infirmities of his body had upon his faculties; which yet they did not so oppress or vanquish, but his soul was always master of itself, and always resigned to the pleasure of its maker---and then he added, "*He who loves* GOD *ought to think* "*nothing desireable but what is most* "*pleasing to the supreme goodness.*" These were his sentiments, and such was his conduct in this state of weakness and pain; as death approached nearer, he was so far from terror or confusion, that he seemed less sensible of pain, and more chearful under his torments, which continued till the 23d day of September, 1738, on which he died (much honoured and lamented) between four and five in the morning, in the 70th year of his age---often recommending to the by-standers a careful observation of St. John's precepts concerning the love of GOD, and the love of *Man*, as frequently inculcated in his first epistle, particularly in the 5th chapter.

Such were the qualities of the great BOERHAAVE.----So far was this truly eminent man from being made impious by philosophy, or vain by his extraordinary genius for physic, that he ascribed all his abilities to the bounty, and all his goodness to the grace of GOD.---- May his example extend its influence to his admirers and followers! May those who study his writings as a physician, imitate his life as a christian! And thus, while they are endeavouring after his medical knowledge, be aspiring likewise to his exalted piety, as he was so admirable a pattern of patience, fortitude, chearfulness, charity, candour, humility, and devotion.

His funeral oration was spoken in Latin before the university of Leyden, to a very numerous audience, by Mr. Schultens, and afterwards published at their particular desire.

After these remarkable characters, in which the advantages of birth or education have joined to adorn and perfect natural genius, we present the reader with as remarkable an instance of the power of natural capacity and application contending with every difficulty, and without any of these advantages arriving at a very high point of erudition. After this we have placed one of the most curious accounts that perhaps ever was published. As in the case of John Ludwig, one sees the triumph of industry and perseverance over all the obstacles of a hard fortune: in the case of the lady who suffered by the small pox, we have a strong instance of the power of these virtues in overcoming even natural defects, in supplying the want of several of the senses themselves, and of those senses too which are the general inlets of knowledge.

An account of John Ludwig,

IT is usual for the commissaries of excise in Saxony to appoint a peasant in every village in their diſtrict to receive the exciſe of the place, for which few are allowed more than one crown, and none more than three. Mr. Chriſtian Gothold Hoffman, who is chief commiſſary of Dreſden and the villages adjacent, when he was auditing the accounts of ſome of theſe peaſants in 1753, was told that there was one John Ludwig among them, a ſtrange man; who, though he was very poor and had a family, was yet continually reading in books, and very often ſtood the greateſt part of the night at his door, gazing at the ſtars.

This account raiſed M. Hoffman's curioſity, and he ordered the man to be brought before him. Hoffman, who expected ſomething in the man's appearance that correſponded with a mind ſuperior to his ſtation, was greatly ſurprized to ſee the moſt ruſtic boor he had ever beheld. His hair hung over his forehead down to his eyes, his aſpect was ſordid and ſtupid, and his manner was, in every reſpect, that of a plodding ignorant clown. Mr. Hoffman, after contemplating this unpromiſing appearance, concluded, that as the ſuppoſed ſuperiority of this man was of the intellectual kind, it would certainly appear when he ſpoke; but even in this experiment he was alſo diſappointed. He aſked him, if what his neighbours had ſaid of his reading and ſtudying was true? and the man bluntly and coarſely replied, "What neighbour has told you that I read and ſtudied? If I have ſtudied, I have ſtudied for myſelf, and I don't deſire that you or any body elſe ſhould know any thing of the matter." Hoffman, however, continued the converſation, notwithſtanding his diſppointment, and asked ſeveral queſtions concerning arithmetic and the firſt rudiments of aſtronomy; to which he now expected vague and confuſed replies. But in this too he had formed an erroneous prognoſtic; for Hoffman was ſtruck not only with aſtoniſhment but confuſion, to hear ſuch definitions and explications as would have done honour to a regular academician in a public examination.

Mr. Hoffman, after this converſation, prevailed on the peaſant to ſtay ſome time at his houſe, that he might further gratify his curioſity at ſuch times as would be moſt convenient. In their ſubſequent conferences he propoſed to his gueſt the moſt abſtracted and embarraſſing queſtions, which were always anſwered with the utmoſt readineſs and preciſion. The account which this extraordinary perſon gives of himſelf and his acquiſitions, is as follows:

John Ludwig was born the 24th of February, 1715, in the village of Coſſe-daude, and was, among other poor children of the village, ſent very young to ſchool. The Bible, which was the book by which he was taught to read, gave him ſo much pleaſure, that he conceived the moſt eager deſire to read others, which, however, he had no opportunity to get into his poſſeſſion. In about a year his maſter began to teach him to write, but this exerciſe was rather irkſome than pleaſing at firſt; but when the firſt difficulty was ſurmounted, he applied to it with great alacrity, eſpecially as books were put into his hand to copy as an exerciſe; and he employed himſelf almoſt night and day, not in copying particular paſſages only, but in forming collections of ſentences, or events that were connected with each

each other. When he was ten years old, he had been at ſchool four years, and was then put to arithmetic, but this embarraſſed him with innumerable difficulties, which his maſter would not take the trouble to explain, expecting that he ſhould content himſelf with the implicit practice of poſitive rules. Ludwig, therefore, was ſo diſguſted with arithmetic, that after much ſcolding and beating he went from ſchool, without having learnt any thing more than reading, writing, and his catechiſm.

He was then ſent into the field to keep cows, and in this employment he ſoon became clowniſh, and negligent of every thing elſe; ſo that the greateſt part of what he had learnt was forgotten. He was aſſociated with the ſordid and the vicious, and he became inſenſibly like them. As he grew up he kept company with women of bad character, and abandoned himſelf to ſuch places as were within his reach. But a deſire of ſurpaſſing others, that principle which is productive of every kind of greatneſs, was ſtill living in his breaſt; he remembered to have been praiſed by his maſter, and preferred above his comrades when he was learning to read and write, and he was ſtill deſirous of the ſame pleaſure, though he did not know how to get at it.

In the autumn of 1735, when he was about twenty years old, he bought a ſmall Bible, at the end of which was a catechiſm, with references to a great number of texts, upon which the principles contained in the anſwers were founded. Ludwig had never been uſed to take any thing upon truſt, and was therefore continually turning over the leaves of his bible, to find the paſſages referred to in the catechiſm; but this he found ſo irkſome a taſk, that he determined to have the whole at one view, and therefore ſet about to tranſcribe the catechiſm, with all the texts at large brought into their proper places. With this exerciſe he filled two quires of paper, and though when he began, the character was ſcarce legible, yet before he had finiſhed it was greatly improved; for an art that has been once learnt is eaſily recovered.

In the month of March 1736, he was employed to receive the exciſe of the little diſtrict in which he lived, and he found that in order to diſcharge this office, it was neceſſary for him not only to write, but to be maſter of the two firſt rules of arithmetic, addition and ſubſtraction. His ambition had now an object, and a deſire to keep the accounts of the tax he was to gather, better than others of his ſtation, determined him once more to apply to arithmetic, however hateful the taſk, and whatever labour it might require. He now regretted that he was without an inſtructor, and would have been glad at any rate to have practiſed the rules without firſt knowing the rationale. His mind was continually upon the ſtretch to find out ſome way of ſupplying this want, and at laſt he recollected that one of his ſchool-fellows had a book, from which examples of ſeveral rules were taken by the maſter to exerciſe the ſcholars. He, therefore, went immediately in ſearch of this ſchool-fellow, and was overjoyed to find upon enquiry, that the book was ſtill in his poſſeſſion. Having borrowed this important volume, he returned home with it, and beginning his ſtudies as he went along, he he purfued them with fuch application, that in about fix months he was mafter of the rule of three with fractions.

The reluctance with which he began to learn the powers and properties of figures was now at an end; he knew enough to make him earneftly defirous of knowing more; he was therefore impatient to proceed from this book to one that was more difficult, and having at length found means to procure one that treated of more intricate and complicated calculations, he made himfelf mafter of that alfo before the end of the year 1739. He had the good fortune foon after to meet with a treatife of geometry, written by Pachek, the fame author whofe arithmetic he had been ftudying; and finding that this fcience was in fome meafure founded on that which he had learnt, he applied to his new book with great affiduity for fome time; but at length, not being able perfectly to comprehend the theory as he went on, nor yet to difcover the utility of the practice, he laid it afide, to which he was alfo induced by the neceffity of his immediate attendance to his field and his vines.

The fevere winter which happened in the year 1740, obliged him to keep long within his cottage, and having there no employment either for his body or his mind, he had once more recourfe to his book of geometry; and having at length comprehended fome of the leading principles, he procured a little box ruler and an old pair of compaffes, on one point of which he mounted the end of a quill cut into a pen. With thefe inftruments he employed himfelf inceffantly in making various geometrical figures on paper, to illuftrate the theory by a folution of the problems. He was thus bufied in his cot till March, and the joy arifing ftom the knowledge he had acquired was exceeded only by his defire of knowing more.

He was now neceffarily recalled to that labour by which alone he could procure himfelf food, and was befides without money to procure fuch books and inftruments as were abfolutely neceffary to purfue his geometrical ftudies. However, with the affiftance of a neighbouring artificer, he procured the figures which he found reprefented by the diagrams in his book, to be made in wood, and with thefe he went to work at every interval of leifure, which now happened only once a week, after divine fervice on a Sunday. He was ftill in want of a new book, and having laid by a little fum for that purpofe againft the time of the fair, where alone he had accefs to a bookfeller's fhop, he made a purchafe of three fmall volumes, from which he acquired a complete knowledge of trigonometry, After this acquifition he could not reft till he had begun to ftudy aftronomy; his next purchafe therefore was an introduction to that fcience, which he read with indefatigable diligence, and invented innumerable expedients to fupply the want of proper inftruments, by which he was not lefs fuccefsful than Robinfon Crufoe, who in an ifland, of which he was the only rational inhabitant, found means to fupply himfelf not only with the neceffaries but the conveniencies of life.

During his ftudy of geometry and aftronomy, he had frequently met with the word *philofophy*, and this became more and more the object of his attention. He conceived that

that it was the name of ſome ſcience of great importance and extent, with which he was as yet wholly unacquainted; he became therefore impatient in the higheſt degree to get acquainted with philoſophy; and being continually upon the watch for ſuch aſſiſtance as offered, he at laſt picked up a book, called *An introduction to the knowledge of God, of man, and of the univerſe.* In reading this book he was ſtruck with a variety of objects that were equally intereſting and new.

But as this book contained only general principles, he went to Dreſden and enquired among the bookſellers, who was the moſt celebrated author that had written on philoſophy. By the bookſellers he was recommended to the works of Wolfius written in the German language; and Wolfius having been mentioned in ſeveral books he had read, as one of the moſt able men of his age, he readily took him for his guide in the regions of philoſophy.

The firſt purchaſe that he made of Wolfius's works, was his logic, and at this he laboured a full year, ſtill attending to his other ſtudies, ſo as not to loſe what he had gained before. In this book he found himſelf referred to another, written by the ſame author, called Mathematical Principles, as the fitteſt to give juſt ideas of things, and facilitate the practice of logic; he therefore enquired after this book with a deſign to buy it, but finding it too dear for his finances he was obliged to content himſelf with an abridgment of it, which he purchaſed in the autumn of 1743. From this book he derived much pleaſure and much profit, and it employed him from October 1743 to February 1745.

He then proceeded to metaphyſics, at which he laboured till the October following, and he would fain have entered on the ſtudy of phyſics, but his indigence was an inſuperable impediment, and he was obliged to content himſelf with his author's morality, politics, and remarks on metaphyſics, which employed him to July 1746; by this time he had ſcraped together a ſum ſufficient to buy the phyſics, which he had ſo earneſtly deſired, and this work he read twice within the year.

About this time a dealer in old books ſold him a volume of Wolfius's Mathematical Principles at large, and the ſpherical trigonometry which he found in this book was a new treaſure, which he was very deſirous to make his own. This however coſt him incredible labour, and filled every moment that he could ſpare from his buſineſs and his ſleep for ſomething more than a year.

He proceeded to the ſtudy of Kahrel's Law of Nature and Nations, and at the ſame time procured a little book on the terreſtrial and celeſtial globes. Theſe books with a few that he borrowed were the ſources from which he derived ſuch a ſtock of knowledge, as is ſeldom found even among thoſe who have aſſociated with the inhabitants of a univerſity, and had perpetual acceſs to public libraries.

Mr. Hoffman, during Ludwig's reſidence at his houſe, dreſſed him in his own gown with other proper habiliments, and he obſerves that this alteration of his dreſs had ſuch an effect, that Hoffman could not conceive the man's accent or dialect to be the ſame, and he felt himſelf ſecretly inclined to treat him with more deference than

when

when he was in his peaſant's dreſs, though the alteration was made in his preſence and with his own apparel.

It happened alſo that before Ludwig went home there was an eclipſe of the ſun, and Mr. Hoffman propoſed to his gueſt that he ſhould obſerve this phænomenon as an aſtronomer, and for that purpoſe furniſhed him with proper inſtruments. The impatience of Ludwig till the time of the eclipſe is not to be expreſſed; he had hitherto been acquainted with the planetary world only by books and a view of the heavens with the naked eye; he had never yet looked thro' a teleſcope, and the anticipation of the pleaſure which the new obſervation would yield him, ſcarce ſuffered him either to eat or ſleep; but it unfortunately happened, that juſt before the eclipſe came on, the ſky became cloudy, and continued ſo during the whole time of its continuance; this misfortune was more than the philoſophy even of Ludwig could bear; as the cloud came on he looked up at it in the agony of a man that expected the diſſolution of nature to follow; when it came over the ſun, he ſtood fixed in a conſternation not to be deſcribed, and when he knew the eclipſe was paſt, his diſappointment and grief were little ſhort of diſtraction.

Mr. Hoffman ſoon after went in his turn to viſit Mr. Ludwig, and take a view of his dwelling, his library, his ſtudy, and his inſtruments. He found an old crazy cottage, the inſide of which had been long blacked with ſmoke; the walls were covered with propoſitions and diagrams written with chalk. In one corner was a bed, in another a cradle, and under a little window at the ſide, three pieces of board, laid ſide by ſide over two truſſels, made a writing table for the philoſopher, upon which were ſcattered ſome pieces of writing paper containing extracts of books, various calculations and geometrical figures; the books which have been mentioned before were placed on a ſhelf with the compaſs and ruler that have been deſcribed, which with a wooden ſquare and a pair of ſix inch globes, conſtituted the library and muſæum of the truly celebrated John Ludwig.

In this hovel he lived till the year 1754, and while he was purſuing the ſtudy of philoſophy at his leiſure hours, he was indefatigable in his day labour as a poor peaſant, ſometimes carrying a baſket at his back, and ſometimes driving a wheel-barrow, and crying ſuch garden ſtuff as he had to ſell about the village. In this ſtate he was ſubject to frequent inſults, "ſuch as patient merit takes of the unworthy," and he bore them without reply, or any other mark either of reſentment or contempt, when thoſe who could not agree with him about the price of his commodities uſed to turn from him with an air of ſuperiority, and call him in deriſion *ſilly* clown and a *ſtupid* dog.

Mr. Hoffman, when he diſmiſſed him, preſented him with a hundred crowns, which has filled all his wiſhes, and made him the happieſt man in the world: with this ſum he has built himſelf a more commodious habitation in the middle of his vineyard, and furniſhed it with many moveables and utenſils, of which he was in great want; but above all he has procured a very conſiderable addition to his library, an article ſo eſſential to his happineſs,

neſs, that he declared to Mr. Hoffman, he would not accept the whole province in which he lived upon condition that he ſhould renounce his ſtudies, and that he had rather live on bread and water than withhold from his mind that food which his intellectual hunger perpetually required.

An account of ſome remarkable particulars that happened to a lady after having had the confluent kind of the ſmallpox.

IN the courſe of this diſeaſe, during which the lady was attended by the late Sir Hans Sloane, ſeveral threatening ſymptoms appeared, which, however, were at length overcome; and the patient, being thought out of danger, took ſeveral doſes of ſuch purgative medicines as are uſually adminiſtered in the decline of the diſeaſe, without any bad conſequence.

But in the evening of the day on which ſhe had taken the laſt doſe that was intended to be given her on that occaſion, ſhe was ſuddenly ſeized with pains and convulſions in the bowels; the pain and other ſymptoms became gradually leſs violent, as the force of the medicine abated, and by ſuch remedies as were thought beſt adapted to the caſe, they ſeemed at length to be intirely ſubdued.

They were, however, ſubdued only in appearance; for at eleven o'clock in the forenoon of the next day they returned with great violence, and continued ſome hours; when they went off, they left the muſcles of the lower jaw ſo much relaxed, that it fell down, and the chin was ſupported on the breaſt. The ſtrength of the patient was ſo much exhauſted during this paroxyſm, that ſhe lay near two hours with no other ſign of life than a very feeble reſpiration, which was often ſo difficult to be diſcerned, that thoſe about her concluded ſhe was dead.

From this time the fits returned periodically every day, at about the ſame hour. At firſt they ſeemed to affect her nearly in the ſame degree; but at length all the ſymptoms were aggravated, the convulſions became more general, and her arms were ſometimes convulſed alternately; it alſo frequently happened that the arm which was laſt convulſed remained extended and inflexible ſome hours after the ſtruggles were over. Her neck was often twiſted with ſuch violence, that the face looked directly backwards, and the back part of the head was over the breaſt; the muſcles of the countenance were alſo ſo contracted and writhed by the ſpaſms, that the features were totally changed, and it was impoſſible to find any reſemblance of her natural aſpect by which ſhe could be known. Her feet were not leſs diſtorted than her head, for they were twiſted almoſt to diſlocation at the inſtep, ſo that ſhe could not walk but upon her ancles.

To remove or mitigate theſe deplorable ſymptoms, many remedies were tried, and, among others, the cold bath; but either by the natural effect of the bath, or by ſome miſmanagement in the bathing, the unhappy patient firſt became blind, and ſoon afterwards deaf and dumb. It is not eaſy to conceive what could increaſe the miſery of deafneſs, dumbneſs, blindneſs, and frequent paroxyſms of excruciating pain; yet a very conſiderable aggravation was added, for the loſs of

her

her ſight, her hearing; and her ſpeech, was followed by ſuch a ſtricture of the muſcles of her throat that ſhe could not ſwallow any kind of aliment, either ſolid or liquid. It might reaſonably be ſuppoſed that this circumſtance, though it added to the degree of her miſery, would have ſhortened its duration; yet in this condition ſhe continued near three quarters of a year, and during that time was ſupported, in a very uncommon manner, by chewing her food only, which having turned often, and kept long in her mouth, ſhe was obliged at laſt to ſpit out. Liquors were likewiſe gargled about in her mouth for ſome time, and then returned in the ſame manner, no part of them having paſſed the throat by an act of deglutition: ſo that whatever was conveyed into the ſtomach, either of the juices of the ſolid food, or of liquids, was either gradually imbibed by the ſpongineſs of the parts, which they moiſtened, or trickled down in a very ſmall quantity along the ſides of the veſſels.

But there were other peculiarities in the caſe of this lady, yet more extraordinary. During the privation of her *ſight* and *hearing*, her *touch* and her *ſmell* became ſo exquiſite, that ſhe could diſtinguiſh the different colours of ſilk and flowers, and was ſenſible when any ſtranger was in the room with her.

After ſhe became blind, and deaf, and dumb, it was not eaſy to contrive any method by which a queſtion could be aſked her, and an anſwer received. This however was at laſt effected, by talking with the fingers, at which ſhe was uncommonly ready. But thoſe who converſed with her in this manner, were obliged to expreſs themſelves by touching her hand and fingers inſtead of their own.

A lady, who was nearly related to her, having an apron on, that was embroidered with ſilk of different colours, aſked her, in the manner which has juſt been juſt deſcribed, if ſhe could tell what colour it was? and after applying her fingers attentively to the figures of the embroidery, ſhe replied, that it was red, and blue, and green, which was true, but whether there were any other colours in the apron, the writer of this account does not remember. The ſame lady having a pink-coloured ribbon on her head, and being willing ſtill farther to ſatisfy her curioſity and her doubts, aſked what colour that was? her couſin, after feeling ſome time, anſwered, that it was pink colour, this anſwer was yet more aſtoniſhing, becauſe it ſhewed not only a power of diſtinguiſhing different colours, but different kinds of the ſame colour; the ribbon was not only diſcovered to be red, but the red was diſcovered to be of the pale kind, called a pink.

This unhappy lady, conſcious of her own uncommon infirmities, was extreamly unwilling to be ſeen by ſtrangers, and therefore generally retired to her chamber, where none but thoſe of the family were likely to come. The ſame relation, who had by the experiment of the apron and ribbon diſcovered the exquiſite ſenſibility of her *touch*, was ſoon after convinced by an accident, that her power of *ſmelling* was acute and refined in the ſame aſtoniſhing degree.

Being one day viſiting the family, ſhe went up to her couſin's chamber, and after making herſelf known, ſhe intreated her to go down,

down, and ſit with her among the reſt of the family, aſſuring her, that there was no other perſon preſent; to this ſhe at length conſented, and went down to the parlour door; but the moment the door was opened, ſhe turned back, and retired to her own chamber much diſpleaſed, alledging, that there were ſtrangers in the room, and that an attempt had been made to deceive her. It happened, indeed, that there were ſtrangers in the room, but they had come in while the lady was above ſtairs: ſo that ſhe did not know they were there. When ſhe had ſatisfied her couſin of this particular, ſhe was pacified; and being afterwards aſked how ſhe knew there were ſtrangers in the room, ſhe anſwered, by the ſmell.

But though ſhe could by this ſenſe diſtinguiſh in general between perſons with whom ſhe was well acquainted, and ſtrangers, yet ſhe could not ſo eaſily diſtinguiſh one of her acquaintance from another without other aſſiſtance. She generally diſtinguiſhed her friends by feeling their hands, and when they came in they uſed to preſent their hands to her, as a means of making themſelves known; the make and warmth of the hand produced in general the differences that ſhe diſtinguiſhed, but ſometimes ſhe uſed to ſpan the wriſt and meaſure the fingers. A lady, with whom ſhe was very well acquainted, coming in one very hot day, after having walked a mile, preſented her hand, as uſual; ſhe felt it longer than ordinary, and ſeemed to doubt whoſe it was; but after ſpanning the wriſt, and meaſuring the fingers, ſhe ſaid, "It is Mrs. M. but ſhe is "warmer to-day than ever I felt "her before."

To amuſe herſelf in the mournful and perpetual ſolitude and darkneſs to which her diſorder had reduced her, ſhe uſed to work much at her needle; and it is remarkable, that her needle-work was uncommonly neat and exact; among many other pieces of her work that are preſerved in the family, is a pincuſhion, which can ſcarce be equalled. She uſed alſo ſometimes to write, and her writing was yet more extraordinary than her needle-work; it was executed with the ſame regularity and exactneſs; the character was very pretty, the lines were all even, and the letters placed at equal diſtances from each other; but the moſt aſtoniſhing particular of all, with reſpect to her writing, is, that ſhe could by ſome means diſcover when a letter had by ſome miſtake been omitted, and would place it over that part of the word where it ſhould have been inſerted, with a caret under it. It was her cuſtom to ſit up in bed at any hour of the night, either to write or to work, when her pain or any other cauſe kept her awake.

Theſe circumſtances were ſo very extraordinary, that it was long doubted whether ſhe had not ſome faint remains both of hearing and ſight, and many experiments were made to aſcertain the matter; ſome of theſe experimets ſhe accidentally diſcovered, and the diſcovery always threw her into violent convulſions. The thought of being ſuſpected of inſincerity, or ſuppoſed capable of acting ſo wicked a part as to feign infirmities that were not inflicted, was an addition to her miſery which ſhe could not bear, and which never failed to produce an agony of mind not leſs viſible

visible than those of her body. A clergyman, who found her one evening at work by a table with a candle upon it, put his hat between her eyes and the candle, in such a manner that it was impossible she could receive any benefit from the light of it if she had not been blind. She continued still at her work, with great tranquility, till putting up her hand suddenly to rub her forehead, she struck it against the hat, and discovered what was doing; upon which she was thrown into violent convulsions, and was not without great difficulty recovered. The family were, by these experiments, and by several accidental circumstances, fully convinced that she was totally deaf and blind, particularly by sitting unconcerned at her work, during a dreadful storm of thunder and lightening, though she was then facing the window, and always used to be much terrified in such circumstances; but Sir Hans Sloane, her physician, being still doubtful of the truth of facts, which were scarce less than miraculous, he was permitted to satisfy himself by such experiments and observations as he thought proper: the issue of which was, that he pronounced her to be absolutely deaf and blind.

She was at length sent to Bath, where she was in some measure relieved, her convulsions being less frequent, and her pains less acute; but she never recovered her speech, her sight, or her hearing, in the least degree.

Many of the letters, dated at Bath, in some of which there are instances of interlineations with a caret, the writer of this narrative hath seen, and they are now in the custody of the widow of one of her brothers, who, with many other persons, can support the facts here related, however wonderful, with such evidence as it would not only be injustice, but folly, to disbelieve.

The following characters of Lord Somers, the Duke and Dutche of Marlborough, Lord Godolphin, Lord Sanderland, Lord Wharton, Lord Cowper, the Earl of Nottingham, and Sir Robert Walpole, are extracted from the history of the four last years of the queen, by Dr. Swift, who professes to describe those qualities in each of them, which few of their admirers will deny, and which appeared chiefly to have influenced them in acting their several parts upon the public stage: 'For I do 'not intend (says he) to draw 'their characters entire, which 'would be tedious and little to the 'purpose; but shall only single out 'these passions, acquirements, and 'habits, which the owners were 'most likely to transfer into their 'political schemes, and which 'were most subservient to the 'designs they seemed to have in 'view.'

These characters and the history from whence they have been extracted, are far from giving us a very just idea of the times, or the persons they profess to describe; they may be read very usefully notwithstanding this defect. For they may serve as a striking example of the melancholy effects of prejudice, and party zeal; a zeal, which whilst it corrupts the heart, vitiates the understanding itself; and could mislead a writer of so penetrating a genius as Doctor Swift, to imagine that posterity would accept satire in the place

place of hiſtory, and would read with ſatisfaction a performance in which the courage and military ſkill of the Duke of Marlborough is called in queſtion. The real character of thoſe great men, was not what the low idolatry of the one faction, or the malignity of the other would repreſent it. They were men, who with great virtues and great talents, mixt with ſome human infirmities, did their country much ſervice and honour. Their talents were a public benefit; their failings ſuch as only affected their private character. The diſplay of this mixture had been a very proper taſk for an impartial hiſtorian; and had proved equally agreeable and inſtructive to the reader, in ſuch hands. But theſe characters before us, have all the ſigns of being written, as Tacitus calls it, recentibus odiis. *In all other reſpects the piece ſeems to be a work not unworthy of its author; a clear and ſtrong, though not an elevated ſtile; an entire freedom from every ſort of affected ornament; a peculiar happineſs of putting thoſe he would ſatirize in the moſt odious and contemptible light, without ſeeming directly to intend it.*

Theſe are the characteriſtics of all Swift's works, and they appear as ſtrongly in this as in any of them. If there be any thing different in this performance, from the manner of his works publiſhed in his life-time, it is, that the ſtile is in this thrown ſomething more backwards, and has a more antique caſt. This probably he did deſignedly, as he might think it gave a greater dignity to the work. He had a ſtrong prejudice in favour of the language as it was in Queen Elizabeth's reign; and he rated the ſtile of the authors of that time a little above its real value. Their ſtile was indeed ſufficiently bold and nervous, but deficient in grace and elegance.

THE Lord Somers may very deſervedly be reputed the head and oracle of that party: he hath raiſed himſelf by the concurrence of many circumſtances, to the greateſt employments of the ſtate, without the leaſt ſupport from birth or fortune: he hath conſtantly, and with great ſteadineſs, cultivated thoſe principles under which he grew. The accident which firſt produced him into the world, of pleading for the biſhops, whom King James had ſent to the Tower, might have proved a piece of merit as honourable as it was fortunate; but the old republican ſpirit which the revolution had reſtored, began to teach other leſſons; that ſince we had accepted a new king from a calviniſtical commonwealth, we muſt alſo admit new maxims in religion and government: but ſince the nobility and gentry would probably adhere to the eſtabliſhed church, and to the rights of monarchy as delivered down from their anceſtors; as it was the practice of thoſe politicians to introduce ſuch men as were perfectly indifferent to any or no religion, and who were not likely to inherit much loyalty from thoſe to whom they owed their birth. Of this number was the perſon I am now deſcribing. I have hardly known any man with talents more proper to acquire and preſerve the favour of a prince, never offending in word or geſture, which are

are in the higheſt degree courteous and complaiſant, wherein he ſet an excellent example to his collegues, which they did not think fit to follow; but this extreme civility is univerſal and undiſtinguiſhed, and in private converſation, where he obſerveth it as inviolably as if he were in the greateſt aſſembly, it is ſometimes cenſured as formal: two reaſons are aſſigned for this behaviour; firſt, from the conſciouſneſs of his humble original, he keepeth all familiarity at the utmoſt diſtance, which otherwiſe might be apt to intrude; the ſecond, that being ſenſible how ſubject he is to violent paſſions, he avoideth all incitements to them, by teaching thoſe he converſes with, from his own example, to keep a great way within the bounds of decency and reſpect; and it is, indeed, true, that no man is more apt to take fire upon the leaſt appearance of provocation, which temper he ſtrives to ſubdue with the utmoſt violence to himſelf: ſo that his breaſt has been ſeen to heave, and his eyes to ſparkle with rage, in thoſe very moments, when his words, and the cadence of his voice were in the humbleſt and ſofteſt manner; perhaps that force upon his nature, may cauſe that inſatiable love of revenge, which his detractors lay to his charge, who conſequently reckon diſſimulation among his chief perfections. Avarice he hath none; and his ambition is gratified, by being the unconteſted head of his party. With an excellent underſtanding, adorned by all the polite parts of learning, he hath very little taſte for converſation, to which he prefers the pleaſure of reading and thinking; and in the intervals of his time amuſeth himſelf with an illiterate chaplain, an humble companion, or a favourite ſervant.

Theſe are ſome few diſtinguiſhing marks in the character of that perſon who now preſideth over the diſcontented party: although he be not anſwerable for all their miſtakes; and if his precepts had been more ſtrictly followed, perhaps their power would not have been ſo eaſily ſhaken. I have been aſſured, and heard him profeſs, that he was againſt engaging in that fooliſh proſecution of Dr. Sacheverel, as what he foreſaw was likely to end in their ruin; that he blamed the rough demeanour of ſome perſons to the queen, as a great failure in prudence; and that when it appeared, her majeſty was firmly reſolved upon a treaty of peace, he adviſed his friends not to oppoſe it in its progreſs, but find fault with it after it was made, which would be a copy of the like uſage themſelves had met with after the treaty of Ryſwick; and the ſafeſt, as well as the moſt probable way of diſgracing the promoters and adviſers. I have been the larger in repreſenting to the reader ſome idea of this extraordinary genius, becauſe whatever attempt hath hitherto been made with any appearance of conduct, or probability of ſucceſs, to reſtore the dominion of that party, was infallibly contrived by him: and I propheſy the ſame for the future, as long as his age and infirmities will leave him capable of buſineſs.

The Duke of Marlborough's character hath been ſo variouſly drawn, and is indeed of ſo mixed a nature a nature in itſelf, that it is hard to pronounce on either ſide without the ſuſpicion of flattery or detraction. I ſhall ſay nothing of his military accompliſhments, which the oppoſite reports of his friends and enemies among the ſoldiers have rendered problematical: but if he be among thoſe who delight in war, it is agreed to be, not for the reaſons common with other generals. Thoſe maligners who deny him perſonal valour, ſeem not to conſider, that this accuſation is charged at a venture; ſince the perſon of a wiſe general is too ſeldom expoſed to form any judgment in the matter: and that fear, which is ſaid to have ſometimes diſconcerted him before an action, might probably be more for his army than for himſelf. He was bred in the height of what is called the tory principle, and continued with a ſtrong biaſs that way, till the other party had bid higher for him than his friends could afford to give. His want of literature is in ſome ſort ſupplied by a good underſtanding, a degree of natural elocution, and that knowledge of the world which is learned in armies and courts. We are not to take the height of his ambition from his ſolliciting to be general for life: I am perſuaded his chief motive was the pay and perquiſites, by continuing the war; and that he had then no intentions of ſettling the crown in his family, his only ſon having been dead ſome years before. He is noted to be maſter of great temper, able to govern or very well to diſguiſe his paſſions, which are all melted down or extinguiſhed in his love of wealth. That liberality which nature has denied him, with reſpect of money, he makes up by a great profuſion of promiſes; but this perfection ſo neceſſary in courts, is not very ſucceſsful in camps among ſoldiers, who are not refined enough to underſtand or to reliſh it.

His wife the dutcheſs may juſtly challenge her place in this liſt. It is to her the duke is chiefly indebted for his greatneſs and his fall; for above 20 years ſhe poſſeſſed, without a rival, the favours of the moſt indulgent miſtreſs in the world, nor ever miſſed one ſingle opportunity that fell in her way of improving it to her own advantage. She hath preſerved a tolerable court-reputation, with reſpect to love and gallantry; but three furies reigned in her breaſt, the moſt mortal enemies of all ſofter paſſions, which were ſordid avarice, diſdainful pride, and ungovernable rage; by the laſt of theſe often breaking out in ſallies of the moſt unpardonable ſort, ſhe had long alienated her ſovereign's mind, before it appeared to the world. This lady is not without ſome degree of wit, and hath in her time affected the character of it, by the uſual method of arguing againſt religion, and proving the doctrines of chriſtianity to be impoſſible and abſurd. Imagine what ſuch a ſpirit, irritated by the loſs of power, favour, and employment, is capable of acting or attempting, and then I have ſaid enough.

The next in order to be mentioned is the Earl of Godolphin. It is ſaid, he was originally intended for a trade, before his friends preferred him to be a page at court, which ſome have very un-

unjuftly objected as a reproach. He hath rifen gradually in four reigns, and was more conftant to his fecond mafter King James, than fome others who had received much greater obligations; for he attended the abdicated king to the fea-fide, and kept conftant correfpondence with him till the day of his death. He always profeffed a fort of paffion for the queen at St. Germain's; and his letters were to her in the ftyle of what the French call double entendre. In a mixture of love and refpect he ufed frequently to fend her from hence little prefents of thofe things which are agreeable to ladies, for which he always afked King William's leave, as if without her privity; becaufe if fhe had known that circumftance, it was to be fuppofed fhe would not accept them. Phyfiognomifts would hardly difcover, by confulting the afpect of this lord, that his predominant paffions were love and play; that he could fometimes fcratch out a fong in praife of his miftrefs with a pencil and card; or that he hath tears at command, like a woman, to be ufed either in an intrigue of gallantry or politics. His alliance with the Marlborough family, and his paffion for the duchefs, were the cords which dragged him into a party, whofe principles he naturally difliked, and whofe leaders he perfonally hated, as they did him. He became a thorough convert, by a perfect trifle, taking fire at a nickname (Volpone) delivered by Dr. Sacheverel, which he applied to himfelf: and this is one among many inftances given by his enemies, that magnanimity is none of his virtues.

The Earl of Sunderland is another of that alliance. It feems to have been this gentleman's fortune to have learned his divinity from his uncle, and his politics from his tutor (Dr. Trimnel, fince bifhop of Winton). It may be thought a blemifh in his character, that he hath much fallen from the height of thofe republican principles with which he began; for in his father's life-time, while he was a member of the houfe of commons, he would often among his familiar friends refufe the title of lord (as he hath done to myfelf) fwear he would be never be called otherwife than Charles Spencer, and hoped to fee the day when there fhould not be a peer in England. His underftanding, at the beft, is of the middle fize: neither hath he much improved it, either in reality, or, which is very unfortunate, even in the opinion of the world, by an overgrown library. It is hard to decide whether he learned that rough way of treating his fovereign from the lady he is allied to, or whether it be the refult of his own nature. The fenfe of the injuries he had done, renders him (as it is very natural) implacable towards thofe to whom he hath given great caufe to complain; for which reafon he will never forgive either the queen, or the prefent treafurer.

The Earl of Wharton hath filled the province allotted him by his collegues, with fufficiency equal to the ableft of them all. He hath imbibed his father's [the earl, his father, was a rigid Prefbyterian] principles in government, but dropt his religion, and took

up

up no other in its ſtead; excepting that circumſtance, he is a firm Preſbyterian. He is perfectly ſkilled in all the arts of managing at elections, as well as in large baits of pleaſure for making converts of young men of quality, upon their firſt appearance; in which public ſervice he contracted ſuch large debts, that his brethren were forced, out of mere juſtice, to leave Ireland at his mercy, where he had only time to ſet himſelf right. Although the graver heads of his party think him too profligate and abandoned, yet they dare not be aſhamed of him; for beſides his talents abovementioned, he is very uſeful in parliament, being a ready ſpeaker, and content to employ his gift upon ſuch occaſions, where thoſe who conceive they have any remainder of reputation or modeſty are aſhamed to appear. In ſhort, he is an unconteſtible inſtance to diſcover the true nature of faction; ſince being over-run with every quality which produceth contempt and hatred in all other commerce of the world, he hath notwithſtanding been able to make ſo conſiderable a figure.

The Lord Cowper, although his merits are later than the reſt, deſerveth a rank in this great council. He was conſiderable in the ſtation of a practiſing lawyer: but as he was raiſed to be a chancellor and a peer, without paſſing through any of the intermediate ſteps, which in the late times have been the conſtant practice, and little ſkilled in the nature of government, or the true intereſts of princes, further than the municipal, or common law of England; his abilities, as to foreign affairs, did not equally appear in the council. Some former paſſages of his life were thought to diſqualify him for that office, by which he was to be the guardian of the queen's conſcience: but theſe difficulties were eaſily overruled by the authors of his promotion, who wanted a perſon that would be ſubſervient to all their deſigns, wherein they were not diſappointed. As to his other accompliſhments, he was what we uſually call a piece of a ſcholar, and a good logical reaſoner, if this were not too often allayed by a fallacious way of managing an argument, which makes him apt to deceive the unwary, and ſometimes to deceive himſelf.

The laſt to be ſpoken of in this liſt, is the Earl of Nottingham, a convert and acquiſition to that party ſince their fall to which he contributed his aſſiſtance. I mean his words, and probably his wiſhes; for he had always lived under the conſtant viſible profeſſion of principles, directly oppoſite to thoſe of his new friends: his vehement and frequent ſpeeches againſt admitting the Prince of Orange to the throne, are yet to be ſeen; and although a numerous family gave a ſpecious pretence to his love of power and money, for taking an employment under that monarch; yet he was allowed to have always kept a reſerve of allegiance to his exiled maſter, of which his friends produce ſeveral inſtances, and ſome while was ſecretary of ſtate to King William. His outward regularity of life, his appearance of religion, and ſeeming zeal for the church, as they are an effect, ſo they are the excuſe of that ſtiffneſs and formality with which his nature is fraught. His aduſt complexion diſpoſeth him to rigour and ſeverity, which his admirers palliate with the name of zeal. No man had ever a ſincerer countenance, or more truly repreſenting his mind and manners. He hath ſome knowledge in the law, very amply ſufficient to defend his property at leaſt: a facility of utterance, deſcended to him from his father, and improved by a few ſprinklings of literature, hath brought himſelf, and ſome few admirers, into an opinion of his eloquence. He is every way inferior to his brother Guernſey, but chiefly in thoſe talents which he moſt values and pretends to; over whom, nevertheleſs, he preſerveth an aſcendant. His great ambition was to be the head of thoſe who were called the church-party: and, indeed, his grave ſolemn deportment and countenance, ſeconded by abundance of profeſſions for their ſervice, had given many of them an opinion of his veracity, which he interpreted as their ſenſe of his judgment and wiſdom; and this miſtake laſted till the time of his defection: of which it was partly the cauſe; but then it plainly appeared, that he had not credit to bring over one ſingle proſelyte, to keep himſelf in countenance.

The following character is alſo by the ſame hand, and an inſtance equally ſtrong, of the ſame party blindneſs.

Sir Robert Walpole was a perſon much careſſed by the oppoſers of Queen Anne and her miniſtry, having been firſt drawn into their party by his indifference to any principles, and afterwards kept ſteady by the loſs of his place [of ſecretary at war.] His bold forward countenance, altogether a ſtranger to that infirmity which makes men baſhful, joined to a readineſs of ſpeaking in public, hath juſtly intitled him, among thoſe of his faction, to be a ſort of leader of the ſecond form. The reader muſt excuſe me for being ſo particular about one, who is otherwiſe altogether obſcure.

It is not foreign to the plan of this article to inſert the following deſcription of the court and perſon of Q. Elizabeth, from the journey into England, of Paul Hentzer, in 1598.

Minds of a much deeper turn than the author of this itinerary ſeems to have been, may find matter of agreeable reflection in his account of England, as it appeared under Q. Elizabeth. That great princeſs had as much ſtate and magnificence in her court, as wiſdom and ſteadineſs in her government. She knew that it was neceſſary to ſtrike the imaginations, as well as to purſue the real intereſts of her people. Thus ſhe threw a veil over the foibles of her perſonal character, and prevented the weak vanity of an old coquette from eclipſing the virtues of a great Queen. Our traveller is a very minute painter; but even minute things, where they concern great characters, ſeem to quit their nature, and become things of conſequence; beſides that they bring us nearer to the times and perſons they deſcribe. It will be equally agreeable in the character of the Engliſh, to trace the difference which increaſe of riches, refinement, and even time itſelf

hate

have made in the manners and taſtes of the people; and no leſs ſo to obſerve, that ground-work of character which is the ſame in the people of thoſe days and of ours, and which no accidental circumſtances are able totally to alter.

WE arrived next at the royal palace at Greenwich, reported to have been originally built by Humphrey Duke of Glouceſter, and to have received very magnificent additions from Henry VII. It was here Elizabeth, the preſent queen, was born, and here ſhe generally reſides, particularly in ſummer, for the delightfulneſs of its ſituation. We were admited, by an order Mr. Rogers had procured from the lord chamberlain, into the preſence chamber, hung with rich tapeſtry, and the floor, after the Engliſh faſhion, ſtrowed with hay, through which the queen paſſes in her way to chapel: at the door ſtood a gentleman dreſſed in velvet, with a gold chain, whoſe office was to introduce to the queen any perſon of diſtinction, that came to wait on her: it was Sunday, when there is uſually the greateſt attendance of nobility. In the ſame hall were the Archbiſhop of Canterbury, the Biſhop of London, a great number of counſellors of ſtate, officers of the crown, and gentlemen, who waited the queen's coming out; which ſhe did from her own apartment, when it was time to go to prayers, attended in the following manner: firſt went Gentlemen, Barons, Earls, Knights of the garter, all richly dreſſed, and bareheaded; next came the chancellor bearing the ſeals in a red ſilk purſe, between two; one of which carried the royal ſcepter, the other the ſword of ſtate, in a red ſcabbard ſtudded with golden fleurs de lis, the point upwards; next came the queen, in the ſixty-fifth year of her age, as we are told, very majeſtic; her face oblong, fair, but wrinkled; her eyes ſmall, yet black and pleaſant; her noſe a little hooked; her lips narrow, and her teeth black (a defect the Engliſh ſeem ſubject to, from their too great uſe of ſugar); ſhe had in her ears two pearls, with very rich drops; ſhe wore falſe hair, and that red; upon her head ſhe had a ſmall crown, reported to be made of ſome of the gold of the celebrated Lunebourg table: her boſom was uncovered, as all the Engliſh have it till they marry; and ſhe had on a necklace of exceeding fine jewels; her hands were ſmall, her fingers long, and her ſtature neither tall nor low; her air was ſtately, her manner of ſpeaking mild and obliging. That day ſhe was dreſſed in white ſilk, bordered with pearls of the ſize of beans; and over it a mantle of black ſilk, ſhot with ſilver threads; her train was very long, the end of it borne by a marchioneſs; inſtead of a chain ſhe had an oblong collar of gold and jewels. As ſhe went along in all this ſtate and magnificence, ſhe ſpoke very graciouſly, firſt to one, then to another, whether foreign miniſters, or thoſe who attended for different reaſons, in Engliſh, French, and Italian; for, beſides being well ſkilled in Greek, Latin, and the languages I have mentioned, ſhe is miſtreſs of Spaniſh, Scotch, and Dutch: whoever ſpeaks to her, it is kneeling; now and then ſhe raiſes ſome with her hand. While we were there, W. Slawata, a Bohemian baron, had letters to preſent to her; and ſhe, after pulling off her glove, gave him her hand to kiſs, ſparkling with rings and jewels, a mark of particular favour. Wherever ſhe turned her face, as ſhe was going along every body fell down on their knees. The ladies of the court followed next to her, very handſome, and well-ſhaped, and, for the moſt part, dreſſed in white; ſhe was guarded on each ſide by the gentlemen penſioners, fifty in number, with gilt battle-axes. In the anti-chapel, next the hall, where we were, petitions were preſented to her, and ſhe received them moſt graciouſly, which occaſioned the acclamation of *Long live Queen Elizabeth!* ſhe anſwered it with, *I thank you my good people.* In the chapel was excellent muſic; as ſoon as it, and the ſervice was over, which ſcarce exceeded half an hour, the queen returned in the ſame ſtate and order, and prepared to go to dinner. But, while ſhe was ſtill at prayers, we ſaw her table ſet out with the following ſolemnity: a gentleman entered the room bearing a rod, and along with him another who had a table-cloth, which, after they had both kneeled three times, with the utmoſt veneration, he ſpread upon the table; and, after kneeling again, they both retired. Then came two others, one with the rod again, the other with the ſalt-ſeller, a plate, and bread; when they had kneeled, as the others had done, and placed what was brought upon the table, they too retired with the ſame ceremonies performed by the firſt. At laſt came an unmarried lady (we were told ſhe was a counteſs) and along with her a married one, bearing a taſting knife; the former was dreſſed in white ſilk, who, when ſhe had proſtrated herſelf three times, in the moſt graceful manner, approached the table, rubbed the plates with bread and ſalt, with as much awe as if the queen had been preſent: when they had waited there a little while, the yeomen of the guard entered, bareheaded, cloathed in ſcarlet, with golden roſes upon their backs, bringing in at each turn a courſe of twenty-four diſhes, ſerved in plate, moſt of them gilt; theſe diſhes were received by gentlemen in the ſame order they were brought, and placed upon the table, while the lady taſter gave to each of the guard a mouthful to eat of the particular diſh he had brought, for fear of poiſon. During the time that this guard, which conſiſts of the talleſt and ſtouteſt men that can be found in all England, being carefully ſelected for this ſervice, were bringing dinner, twelve trumpets, and two kettle drums, made the hall ring for half an hour together. At the end of all this ceremonial, a number of unmarried ladies appeared, who, with particular ſolemnity, lifted the meat off the table, and conveyed it into the queen's inner and more private chamber, where, after ſhe had choſen for herſelf, the reſt goes to the ladies of the court. The queen dines and ſups alone, with a very few attendants; and it is very ſeldom that any body, foreigner or native, is admitted at that time, and then only at the interceſſion of ſomebody in power.

Deſcription of Theobalds and Nonſuch, from Hentzer.

THeobalds belongs to Lord Burleigh the treaſurer. In the gallery was painted the genealogy of the kings of England; from

from this place one goes into the garden, encompassed with water, large enough for one to have the pleasure of going in a boat, and rowing between the shrubs; here are a great variety of trees and plants, labyrinths made with a great deal of labour, a *jet d'eau*, with its bason of white marble, and columns and pyramids of wood and other materials up and down the garden: after seeing these, we were led by the gardener into the summer-house, in the lower part of which, built semi-circularly, are the twelve Roman emperors in white marble, and a table of truck-stone; the upper part of it is set round with cisterns of lead, into which the water is conveyed through pipes, so that fish may be kept in them, and, in summer time, they are very convenient for bathing: in another room for entertainment, very near this and joined to it by a little bridge, was a noble table of red marble. We were not admitted to see the apartments of this palace, there being nobody to shew it, as the family was in town attending the funeral of their lord.

Nonsuch is a royal retreat, in a place formerly called Cuddington, a very healthful situation, chosen by K. Henry VIII. for his pleasure and retirement, and built by him with an excess of magnificence and elegance, even to ostentation; one would imagine every thing that architecture can perform, to have been employed in this one work: there are every where so many statues that seem to breathe, so many miracles of consummate art, so many charts that rival even the perfection of Roman antiquity, that it may well claim and justify its name of Nonsuch, being without an equal, as the poet sung,

> *This which no equal has in art or fame,*
> *Britons deservedly a Nonsuch name.*

The place of itself is so encompassed with parks full of deer, delicious gardens, groves ornamented with trellis work, cabinets of verdure, and walks so embrowned with trees, that it seems to be a place pitched upon by Pleasure herself, to dwell in along with Health.

In the pleasure and artificial gardens are many columns and pyramids of marble, two fountains that spout water, one round the other, like a pyramid, upon which are put small birds that stream water out of their bills: in the grove Diana is a very agreeable fountain, with Actæon turned into a stag, as he was sprinkled by the goddess and the nymphs, with inscriptions.

There is besides another pyramid of marble, full of concealed pipes, which spout upon all who come within their reach.

From the same itinerary we shall present our readers with the manner of celebrating harvest-home in England, in our author's time.

AS we were returning to our inn, we happened to meet some country people celebrating harvest-home; their last load of corn they crown with flowers, having besides an image richly dressed, by which perhaps they would signify Ceres; this they keep moving about, while men and women, men and maid servants, riding through the streets in the cart, shout as loud as they can, till they arrive at the barn; the farmers here do not

not bind up their corn in ſheaves, as they do with us, but directly as they have reaped or mowed it, put it into carts, and convey it into their barns.

He gives the following account of the manners of our anceſtors.

THE Engliſh are ſerious, and like the Germans, lovers of ſhow: liking to be followed whereever they go by whole troops of ſervants, who wear their maſters arms in ſilver, faſtened to their left arms; a ridicule they very deſervedly lay under. They excel in dancing and muſic, for they are active and lively, though of a thicker make than the French. They cut their hair cloſe on the middle of the head, letting it grow on either ſide. They are good ſailors, and better pirates, cunning, treacherous and thieviſh; above * 300 are ſaid to be hanged annually at London. Beheading with them leſs is leſs infamous than hanging. They give the wall as the place of honour. Hawking is the general ſport of the gentry. They are more polite in eating than the French, devouring leſs bread, but more meat, which they roaſt in perfection. They put a great deal of ſugar in their drink. Their beds are covered with tapeſtry, even thoſe of farmers. They are often moleſted with the ſcurvy, ſaid to have firſt crept into England with the Norman conqueſt. Their houſes are commonly of two ſtories, except in London, where they are of three and four, though but ſeldom of four; they are built of wood, thoſe of the richer ſort with bricks; their roofs are low, and where the owner has money, covered with lead.

They are powerful in the field, ſucceſsful againſt their enemies, impatient of any thing like ſlavery; vaſtly fond of great noiſes that fill the ear, ſuch as the firing of cannon, drums, and the ringing of bells, ſo that it is common for a number of them, that have got a glaſs in their heads, to go up into ſome belfry, and ring the bells for hours together, for the ſake of exerciſe. If they ſee a foreigner very well made, or particularly handſome, they will ſay, it is a pity he is not an Engliſhman.

The two following pieces having appeared within the laſt year, and the firſt throwing ſome light on ancient cuſtoms, and the latter containing ſome particulars of a very remarkable perſonage, we thought it beſt to inſert them here.

Order of King Henry VIII. *for the ſupply of Lady Lucy's table, taken from a collection of letters and ſtate papers, from the original manuſcripts of ſeveral princes and great perſonages in the two laſt centuries. Compiled by L. Howard, D. D.*

HENRY. By the King.

WE wol and comaunde you to allowe dailly from hensforth, unto our right dere and wel beloved, the lady Lucye, in-

* Although it is likely that the people being then poor to what they are now, were more addicted to theft, as it uſually happens; yet this account of executions muſt certainly be exaggerated. As to the cunning and treachery he mentions, it ſeems never to have been the real character of the Engliſh.

to her chambre, the dyat faire hearafter ensuyng:

Furst, Every morning at brekefast, oon chyne of beyf at our kechyn, oon chete loff and oon mannchet at our panatrye barr, and a galon of ale at our buttrye bar:

Item, At dyner, a pese of beyf, a stroke of roste, and a rewarde at our said kechyn, a cast of chete bread at our panatrye barr, and a galon of ale at our buttrye barr:

Item, At after none, a mannchet at our panatrye barr, and half a galon of ale at our buttrye barr:

Item, At supper, a mess of porage, a pese of mutton, and a rewarde at our said kechyn, a cast of chete bred at our panatrye, and a galon of ale at our buttrye:

Item, At after-supper, a chete loff and a mannchet at our panatrye barr, a galon of ale at our buttrye bar, and half a galon of wine at our seller barr:

Item, Ev'ry morning at our wood-yard, four tall shyds and twoo faggots:

Item, At our chaundrye barr in winter, ev'ry night, oon picket and four syses of waxe, with eight candells, white lights, and oon torch:

Item, At our picker-house, weekly, six white cuppas:

Item, At ev'ry time of our removal, oon hool carte for the carriage of her stuff:

And these our letters shall be your sufficient warrant and discharge in this behalfe, at all tymes hereafter. Given under our segnet at our manour of Esthampstede, the 17th day of July, the 14th yere of our reign.

To the lord steward of our houshold, the treasurer, comptroller, cofferer, clerks of the greene clothe, the clerks of our kechyn, and all other our hed officers of our said houshold, and to ev'ry of them.

The character of Oliver Cromwell may be seen in the following extract from the said state papers.

To his highness, the Lord Protector of the common wealth of England, Scotland, and Ireland.

The humble petition of Marjery, the wife of William Beacham, mariner.

SHEWETH,

THAT your petitioner's husband hath been active and faithful in the wars of this commonwealth, both by sea and land, and hath undergone many hazards by imprisonment and fights to the endangering of his life, and at last lost the use of his right arm, and is utterly disabled from future service, as doth appear by the certificate annexed, and yet he hath no more than forty shillings pension from Chatham by the year:

That your petitioner having one only sonne, who is tractable to learn, and not having wherewith to bring him up, by reason of their present low estate, occasioned by the publique service aforesaid:

Humbly prayeth, That your Highness would vouchsafe to present her said sonne Randolph Beacham, to be scholler in Sutton's hospital called the Charter-house.

OLIVER, P.

We referre this petition and certificate to the commiſſioners of Sutton's hoſpital.

July 28, 1655.

Copy of a letter ſent by Oliver to his ſecretary on the above petition.

You receive from me this 28th inſtant, a petition of Marjery Beacham, deſiring the admiſſion of her ſon into the Charter-houſe. I know the man, who was employed one day in a very important ſecret ſervice, which he did effectually to our great benefit, and the commonwealth's. The petition is a brief relation of a fact, without any flattery. I have wrote under it a common reference to the commiſſioners, but I *mean* a great deal more, that it *ſhall* be *done*, without *their debate*, or *conſideration of the matter*, and ſo do you privately hint to * * * * *

I have not the particular ſhining bauble or feather in my cap, for crouds to *gaze at*, or *kneel to*, but I have power and reſolution for foes to *tremble at*; to be ſhort, I know how to *deny* petitions; and whatever I think proper, for outward form to refer to any officer or office, I expect that ſuch my compliance with cuſtom ſhall be alſo looked upon as an indication of my will and pleaſure to have the thing done. See therefore that the boy is admitted.

Thy true friend,

July 28, 1655. OLIVER, P.

An account of the origin, and manners, and cuſtoms of the Calmucks and Coſſacks, who have lately committed ſuch outrages on the ſubjects of the King of Pruſſia. From an account given by the Chevalier de Polignac, Secretary to King Staniſlaus; written in 1750.

As this is a good account of two very remarkable nations, which the preſent troubles have brought much into converſation, we thought it naturally referable to this head.

THAT theſe people are Tartars, and that the Tartars are of Scythian original, is evident from their ſentiments and manners at this day. The Scythians ſacrificed to their gods the priſoners taken in war. The Tartars do not indeed deprive their priſoners of life, but they make death preferable, by ſelling them to maſters that equal themſelves in cruelty. The ancient Scythians lived on mares milk, applied themſelves to the feeding of cattle, and neglected tillage. They had no other habitations but tilted waggons, which were drawn from paſture to paſture, as herbage failed and neceſſity required. Their cloathing was the ſkins of beaſts. They made uſe of poiſoned arrows. To croſs a river they filled ſacks with cork, on which they placed themſelves, and were drawn over by horſes which they held by the tail. They had no written laws, but adminiſtered juſtice according to the natural dictates of reaſon. Theſe cuſtoms ſtill ſubſiſt, with little variation, among the Tartars. There was one very ſingular cuſtom among the Scythians: when two friends wanted to ſwear a laſting friendſhip, they made inciſions in their fingers, and

and received the blood in a cup. Both dipt the point of their swords in it, and lifting them to their heads, eagerly sucked it. When the modern Tartars take an oath, they dip their sabres in water, which they afterwards drink. The barbarity of some of their customs appears to have been softened by time: but one thing that has remained invariable in the character of these people, is their rage of invading the neighbouring nations upon every opportunity that offers, and often of falling upon one another, when they are confined in their own country by superior force or fear. Their wars, their incursions, their ravages, differ in nothing from those of the Scythians. We may apply to them what the prophet Jeremiah said, speaking of the irruption of their ancestors into Judea: *Their chariots are as a whirlwind; their horses are swifter than eagles, and their quiver is as an open sepulchre*, iv. 13.

Asia hath often felt that they have lost nothing of the brutal impetuosity of their ancestors. Their success is less surprizing than that continuance of their valour, which, though not always sufficient to preserve their conquests, still kept up in them a desire to recover them. Thus, though expelled China in 1368, after possessing it above a century, they never ceased their efforts to recover it, and in 1644 reduced it in such a manner, that they have no reason to apprehend a second expulsion. The exploits of Tamerlane *, the chief of one of their rulers, are well known. He was equal to Cæsar in courage, and not inferior to Alexander in good fortune. He conquered the Indies, subdued Persia, vanquished the Turks, and ravaged all Egypt. His name and his reputation have reached nations to whom his country is still unknown.

The Tartars are generally divided into three distinct powers: the first are those known by the name of Tartars; the second are the Calmucks; and the third the Moungals.

The Tartars properly so called, live to the west of the Caspian sea. The most considerable of them are the Usbecs; the Kara-Kallpacks; the Nagais who are subject to Russia; the Baskirs, who also hold of that empire; and the Daghestans, who depend on no power, and who are more savage than any of those just named.—The Nagais, who at present occupy the lands of Astrachan, between the Jaïck and the Wolga, and the Baskirs, who are situated in the eastern part of the kingdom of Casan, between the Wolga and the river Kama, formerly received tribute from Russia, which the Great Duke of Muscovy carried to them annually on his own horses. He was obliged to walk on foot, followed by the principal persons of his court, to meet the persons who came to demand this tribute, who were the poorest and most wretched of all the tribes. John or Iwan, Duke of Muscovy, surnamed the Great, was the first, who, to free himself from this shameful mark of servitude, attempted to bring the Tartars under subjection. His son Basil continued to reduce them; but the final blow was given them by John Basilides, a prince detested for his barbarity, but resolute and

* The Orientals call him Timur-lang, that is, Tamur the lame. He in fact halted, by reason of a wound received in his youth. He was born in 1432, and reigned six and thirty years, and died at the age of 63.

valiant,

valiant. He extended his power even over the moſt diſtant of their hords.

The Kan of the Calmucks, who occupy a great part of the country, which lies between the Moungal and the Wolga, is ſo rich and powerful, that it is ſaid he can bring an army of an hundred thouſand men into the field. There is always a body of them in the Ruſſian army. I have ſeen them, and can therefore deſcribe them. They are rather ſhort than tall; but ſtrong, robuſt, courageous, and inured to fatigue. Their complexion is tawny; their faces flat, and their noſes ſunk to a level with their cheeks; only their two noſtrils are ſtriking, becauſe larger than their eyes; theſe are ſo ſmall, that they could not be perceived, if they were not extremely black and brilliant. They have ſcarce any beard; and their hair, of which they wear only a tuft on the crown of the head, is rough like a horſe's mane. They wear a round bonnet with a border of fur, in the Poliſh manner, and a kind of looſe coat of ſheep ſkins, which comes down to the middle of their leg. They ſerve only on horſeback; their arms are a bow which is larger, and arrows which are longer than uſual. It is ſaid that their arrows are ſo ſharp pointed, and that they make them fly with ſuch force, that they will pierce a man through. They carry alſo a fuſee, which hangs by their ſide; and a lance, which they handle with great dexterity. They are all pagans: the name Calmucks is a kind of nick-name given them by the Mahometan Tartars, with which they are much offended. They want to be called Mogouls

Thoſe Tartats who are at preſent called Moungals, are ſituated, on one ſide, between theſe laſt people and the ſea of Japan; and on the other between China and Siberia. It is of little importance to mention their ſeveral tribes.

Thoſe that lie next to Poland, and who by their incurſions into that kingdom, have made themſelves better known than the others, are called Little Tartars, to diſtinguiſh them from thoſe of Aſia. Like theſe they are divided into ſeveral hords, each forming a different nation: The Kubans; the Tartars of the Crimea or Perecop; the hord of Oczakow; and that of Büoziack.

Beſides theſe four ſpecies of Little Tartars, there is another very ſingular one, of which it may not be improper to take notice. They are ſituated in the heart of Lithuania. Some tribes of this people formerly threatened that dutchy: Vitoldus, uncle of Flagellon, a bold and haughty prince, marched againſt them, and ſucceeded. He led captive into Lithuania many thouſands of thoſe Tartars of both ſexes. He treated them mildly, and aſſigned them lands near Vilna to cultivate, which their poſterity poſſeſs at this day. They have retained Mahometaniſm, and all their ancient cuſtoms; but they are leſs barbarous than thoſe of the Crimea and its neighbourhood. They love work, are very ſober, and of inviolable fidelity. The grandees of Poland are fond of having them in their ſervice. They have eſcorted me in many journeys, and it is from them I have received the following portrait of the preſent Tartars, who were originally one and the ſame people with themſelves. They come into the world with their eyelids

lids closed together so fast, that for some days they cannot open them. They are thick-set, with broad shoulders, and extremely strong and vigorous. They have a short neck and large head, a flat face almost round, a large forehead well shaped, bright eyes, a short nose, a little mouth, white teeth, an olive complexion, rough black hair, and scarce any beard. They clip the hind part of their head, leaving only a tuft before. They never till the ground, and are strangers to all the arts of luxury and effeminacy. They know nothing of the sciences. Their laws are simple; and are derived from plain good sense, as much as from custom. Gentle and affable among themselves, they are so likewise to those whom trade brings into their country. They have no law-suits nor quarrels among them. If any one has a claim upon another, he goes to one of the principal men, called Murzas, who determines it without long discussion, and without formality. Prejudiced in favour of the principles of Mahomet's law, which they profess, they abhor all Christians; and in their invasions, covering their avarice with a religious motive, they make a merit of causing Christians to feel all the ferocity of their character.

They are brought up very hardy. Destined to a life of toil, they are inured to it from their infancy. Mothers often wash their children in cold water, mixed with salt, to harden their skins; hence, in the depth of winter they swim across rivers without suffering any inconvenience. They teach them to be marksmen, they receive no food after they are seven years old, but what they kill with their arrows.

Their cloathing is sheep skins. In winter, they wear the wool next to them; but in summer, or when it rains, they wear the other side next them. The Kan and all his family are cloathed in silk, which they usually receive in presents from the neighbouring nations, particularly Poland; and the officers wear cloth. They wear no turban, but bonnets of the Polish fashion.

Their arms are a crooked sabre, a lance, and a bow. They are afraid of fire-arms. They fight at a distance, and even in their flight, they let fly their arrows; but if they cannot avoid a close fight, they use their sabres with such dexterity, that it is not easy to parry them. In their flight, they are very swift, and their pursuers run a great risk, not so much from their arrows, as from their unexpected return. They all carry a knife and an awl to make leather straps to bind their prisoners. They often poison the points of their arrows.

Their horses are extremely brisk and nimble runners; and as indefatigable as their riders; but they make no shew; the Tartars often make them travel fifty or sixty miles without halting. They cut the cartilage which separates their nostrils, that, breathing more easily they may be less apt to give out, however violently they may be rode. They always lead several in their hands, and when one is tired, they spring on the back of another without stopping a moment.

The usual food of these Tartars, and that of which they are most fond, is horse flesh. Bread and mutton are reserved for the rich, and for the wealthy burghers, that live in their towns without ever taking the field. The poorer sort bake

bake under ashes, cakes made of millet, barley, or Sarrazin corn, which grows spontaneously. The Poles call this bread Tatarka. Tho' some become servants to others, yet most of them choose rather to seek their food by rapine, than to earn it by an ignominious subjection. It is scarce conceivable, considering their indefatigability in war, how lazy and slothful they are in their families, where they spend their days in the most contemptible indolence. When they kill a horse, they first thrust a knife into his throat, and carefully saving the blood, they mix it with flour of millet, and make a kind of pudding, which they hold to be delicious. They afterwards cut the horse into four quarters. The master reserves one only for himself, and sends the other three as presents to his friends or neighbours, who make returns in kind.

Their usual drink is water. In some parts of their country there is none, and they either have not the sense to dig pits, or they neglect it through indolence. Snow, however, in the winter, supplies the defect. Those who live more comfortably than the rest, make a kind of drink of boiled millet. It is of the consistence and colour of milk, and drank to excess will intoxicate. However, they esteem nothing comparable to mares milk, which they chiefly use when they cross desarts to make war. Being Mahometans, they abstain from wine, or drink it only by stealth; but they think the frequent use of brandy no breach of their laws.

When they find themselves indisposed, they open a vein of a horse, drink the blood hot, and fatigue themselves as much as possible, by galloping*. If any one is so weak that he cannot use this exercise, two of them get on horseback, and holding him each by an arm, make him ride at full speed. There are few ailments which they do not actually cure, or believe they cure, by this remedy. Without any other occasion, than to appease their hunger or thirst, when they have nothing else, they bleed their horses and drink the blood. This likewise was the custom of the ancient Scythians. They all carry millet of meal with them when they go to war, They mix it with water; and this supports them in their painful marches, and extremely refreshes them in the great heats. Polish lords, who have been obliged to follow them, have often experienced what I say; and it is upon their testimony I relate it.

Ever ready to make incursions among their neighbours, because they have no other way of supplying themselves with what they want, they are not apprehensive of being attacked in their turn. They trust to the power of the Turks for their protection.

When they are preparing for an expedition, they send their horses for some time to grass in the fields to fatten: their Kan holds council with the Galga, or general of the army: they assemble their chief Murzas: they draw up the plan of operations, or rather of the ravages to be commited. If the Kan commands

* Persons of credit have assured me (says M. Polignac) that when Charles XII. was at Bender, the Swedes of his retinue having neither surgeons nor physicians to attend them in their illness, made use of this remedy, and were all cured by it.

mands in perſon, all muſt march with him; none muſt ſtay even to guard their country; nor are the infirmities of old age admitted as an excuſe. On theſe occaſions, the army amounts, as I have ſaid, to 100,000 men, and 2 or 300,000 horſes; for each Tartar has two or three.

They croſs rivers in a very extraordinary manner. Every one gathers ruſhes or reeds, which he faſtens to two long poles, and makes a kind of raſt, on which he places his cloaths and arms. He ties theſe poles to the tail of one of his horſes, whoſe mane he holds with one hand, and holding a rod in the other to guide the horſe, he ſwims with his feet, and paſſes the river quite naked. As to the reſt, theſe rafts, though made in haſte, are ſo well joined and ſo firm, that they carry ſafely ſuch of their ſlaves as cannot ſwim.

If they have effects which water might damage, they kill four horſes that are nearly of a ſize; and preſerving the ſkins whole, after taking out the fleſh and bones, they blow them like bladders, and place them on ſledges, or waggons, of which they take off the wheels. Several Tartars ſwim at the ſides to ſecure this floating machine, which is drawn by two horſes, each of which hath a conductor to guide him to ſhore.

They are more eager to make incurſions in winter than in ſummer, becauſe in that ſeaſon they find in the houſes of the peaſants, all the proviſions which in ſummer they muſt collect in the fields, and the rivers and marſhes being frozen, they can go any where without hindrance; the ſnow too renders the roads more convenient for their horſes, which they never ſhoe. The feeding of their horſes gives them no more trouble than the feeding of themſelves; they require neither proviſions nor magazines.

Moſs, bark of trees, and poor herbs, are to them as good, and ſupport them as well as the choiceſt forage; and in the winter they ſeek their food under ſnow, which they remove with their feet.

The Tartars in their expeditions never follow the uſual beaten paths. They always chooſe the leaſt known and moſt difficult roads; and to cover their march ſtill more, they never make fires in their camp. By theſe means, they ſurprize even theſe who are moſt upon their guard againſt theſe incurſions.

When they arrive within three or four leagues of the country into which they intend to penetrate, they halt for ſome days to reſt. They then divide into three bodies; two of which compoſe the main body of their army: the third is ſubdivided, and forms a large detachment at each ſide. In this order they enter the country. The center advances in a parallel line with the right and left; but the whole marches night and day, without halting above an hour at moſt.

After marching ſixty or eighty leagues into the country (which tract they ſpare at preſent, paſſing through it only as travellers) the two wings are ordered to diſperſe themſelves ſix leagues round. Divided again into ten or twelve brigades, of above 5 or 600 men each, and theſe into ſeveral others as they advance, they make what haſte they can to pillage the country; and joining again by degrees, and in the ſame order in which they ſeparated, they carry the booty to the main body of the army, which during this time kept together to repel the inhabitants, who might aſſemble to attack them. Two new corps are detached to ſcour the parts where the former had been; and in the inſtant theſe return, a third detachment is ſent out to gather the gleaning the others may have left.

Theſe barbarians ſpare none, They cut the throats of infants and old people; but men and women, boys and girls, they compel to follow them. The number of their captives hath ſometimes exceeded 50,000. They generally burn the houſes they have plundered, and turn the moſt pleaſant and fruitful countries into a frightful deſart.

The ſame havock which they make round the places they fix for the limits of their incurſions, they make alſo in their return in thoſe parts which they ſpared at firſt, provided they be not purſued. When they paſs the frontiers and get to a place of ſafety, they repoſe themſelves and divide the booty, of which one tenth is always reſerved for the Kan. They cruelly ſeparate all the members of one family; the huſband from the wife, the children from the parents, alloting them to different perſons, and ſelling them into different countries. They ſell many of them to the Turks, who employ them on board their gallies; but they reſerve the young women to be the unfortunate victims of their brutality. Tho' they arrive in a country all together, yet in going back they march in ſeveral diviſions, that thoſe who follow them, ſeeing ſeveral tracks, may not know preciſely which road they have taken. On theſe occaſions, the Coſſacks, who have almoſt as much ferocity, and no leſs love of plunder, generally lay ambuſcades for them. They wait for them in defiles, or even in the midſt of plains, where they march in *tabort*; that is the name they give to their manner of travelling between two rows of waggons, which encloſe them: and from thence they fire on the Tartars with ſmall arms. It ſeldom happens, but that the whole army is put into diſorder. They fly in ſuch confuſion, that one runs over another, without reſpect even to their leaders. Each runs whither his fears carry him: and if they are purſued, they gradually throw away all they carry. They ſtrew effects in the way, to amuſe the enemy. They throw away even their arms, and often, without ceaſing to run, they cut the girts of their ſaddles, and let them fall off, in order to relieve their horſes, that they may run more ſwiftly.

The following remarkable part was acted in Dublin, by a perſon who has acted very remarkable parts wherever he has appeared; who has good humour enough to make a life of diſſipation and frolick, ſerve as a ſort of merit; who has great talents for mimickry, without being an actor, and who has a conſiderable ſhare of wit and humour, which could acquire him the reputation of a writer. But he has made more noiſe than many who have had a larger ſhare of theſe talents, which is all he ſeems to deſire. In a word, he is the moſt ſingular man in this age, and is able to appear in a greater variety of characters than any body elſe, becauſe he has no character of his own.

From

From Drontheim in Norway, having also visited in his tour the cities of Petersburgh, Hamburgh, Amsterdam and London, (from which last capital he is just arrived) Ulam Smolenzo Czernznigorff, the celebrated Laplander, born within the confines of the Artic circle.

HE tells things past, present and to come, by means of a quobdas, kannus or drum, handed down from nine generations from his great anceltor Ulan Gorff, who in the reign of Swein, King of Norway, was burnt for being a wizard, being charged by some missionaries with having a familiar, but was in reality no other than a Gam, or good genius, which is a constant attendant on the chief sire of each tribe of the Laplanders, and most of the aborigines or old inhabitants of Scandinavia, and all the regions of the north.

His life hath been devoted to the study of astrology ; and he hereby informs the learned, that his chief reason of his present visit to these southern regions of the globe, is to have the opportunity of beholding and observing the expected amazing comet, or blazing star, whose appearance was predicted by him in his Ephemeris Sepentrionalis, published at Copenhagen and Stockholm in 1743, the transit of which, being by him and Dr. Halley laid down to be south of the equinoctial line, could not be observed in his own country, the latitude or altitude of the *pole being there 73 degrees north,* consequently the comet's path being below the horizon of Lapland, that stupendous phænomenon will be invisible to all the inhabitants thereof.

He begs leave to acquaint the public, that he hath by frequent converse with some Bramins (who, by means of the Russian caravans from China and India, have passed from the east into Norway) acquired all the wisdom of the oriental Magi or Gymnosophists, the same as that of the ancient soothsayers, modern rosycrusians, or followers of Peter Lully, the first European professor of the cabalistical and hermetic arts, derived originally from the Pythagorean sect ; and hath, according to the unalterable rule and law of the original founder, condemned himself to a septennial silence and cessation of speech, but utters his responses in writing, void of all ambiguity, and easy to be comprehended by the meanest capacity.

He therefore professes and understands all the mysteries of chyromanchy, alectiomanchy, and catoptromanchy, he having a magical glass to be consulted upon some extraordinary occasions. He can also divine either by hydromanchy or negromancy, and is fully possessed of the art, called by the Greeks, oneiocritica, or the interpretation of dreams : and will prove to the virtuosi, that he hath the true selinites lac lunæ, or moonstone, proper for the making of talismans, only to be found genuine near the dreadful volcano of Mount Hecla in Iceland ; and though he also hath in his museum several of the mystical knots and magical darts of his countrymen, the *Samoides and Finlanders, he sticks chiefly to his* drum.

From all which it is evident, (even to the literati themselves) that

that he can inform mankind whether life be happy or unhappy? Suits at law, who ſhall overcome? If the party is to be rich, and how wealth may lawfully be obtained? He anſwers to all queſtions relating to love, gallantry and marriage, as what manner of perſon one ſhall be courted by, and be married unto? Whether at preſent batchelor, maid, huſband, wife, widower, or widow? Whether the party be beloved or not? Children, their number and ſex; alſo the diſeaſes, croſſes, accidents, or other fortunate and unfortunate adventures and events, he, ſhe, or they ſhall meet with, or be incident unto, with the means of preventing and avoiding them; and can foretell moſt people's buſineſs, even before they deliver any queſtions; all which he performs with due regard to honour and the ſtricteſt ſecrecy.

*** He ſells prolific drops for barrenneſs in women, the true arcanum by which the northern hive hath anciently poured forth its ſwarms over the reſt of Europe, the uſe of them counteracting the inclemency of that climate, and invigorates cold and languid conſtitutions. Price of the bottle half a guinea, with compleat directions for uſe.

††† He hath a few remaining bottles of his grand coſmetic waſh, for the invention of which her Serene Highneſs the Archdutcheſs of Livonia preſented him with a veſt of ſables; and honoured him with a ſeal ring from her own finger, and 500 Livonian ducats. Price of this ineſtimable ſecret one guinea.

He is to be ſpoke with at his lodgings at Mr. Tucker's, a portrait-painter, at the houſe with the Venetian window in Uſher's ſtreet, the back of Uſher's quay, from the hours of ſeven till nine, on the evenings of Mondays, Tueſdays, Thurſdays and Fridays only, the other parts of his time being devoted to aſtrology and the ſtudy of the occult ſciences, when he will not be interrupted on any account whatſoever.

Dublin, Dec. 14.

Yeſterday morning the learned world was deprived of one of its moſt uſeful ornaments by the death of the celebrated Lapland philoſopher and viruoſo, Ulan Smolenzco Czernznigorff, who is greatly lamented by perſons of all ranks, ſexes, and diſtinctions. His diſſolution, which was long ſince predicted by himſelf, was occaſioned by an atrophy contracted by intenſe ſtudy. He was attended by ſeveral eminent phyſicians, whom he diſcovered by his art, to have miſtaken the ſtate of his caſe. Many divines remarkable for their learning and piety, waited alſo upon him, and exhorted him to make a full and ample confeſſion of his miſdeeds, as they were perſuaded that he had certainly practiſed the black art, and dealt with the devil, and more eſpecially, as he gave each of them a ſuccinct account of all their moſt ſecret tranſactions; but he perſiſting to the laſt, that all his knowledge was obtained by means of the Gam or good genius, that inhabited his drum, they denounced an anathema againſt him, and refuſed him the rites of their function. He has given all the product of his gain, ſince his arrival in this kingdom, to charitable uſes, and bequeathed many legacies, particularly his quobdas or drum, to be placed in our muſeum. To his

his trufty and well-beloved faithful fervant Peter, has left a great number of original letters and queries from doctors of divinity, phyfic and law, lords and efquires, ladies, widows, lawyers, kept-miftreffes, politicians, courtezans, attornies, waiting-women, civil and military officers, belles, beaux, fpruce curates, and many others of all ranks, ages, denominations, and fexes; together with feveral horofcopes ready drawn for perfons, who he underftood by his art, intended to favour him with their company, many of which laft will be fent by the faid Peter to their refpective owners. The memoirs of feveral tranfactions that befel him, fince his arrival in this metropolis, being a compleat fecret hiftory of all the private intrigues, anecdotes, &c. thereof, he hath ordered to be printed under the infpection of an eminent bookfeller who lately went to vifit him, fo that the public may fhortly expect to fee feveral curious, ufeful and truly valuable difcoveries, the benefit of which works is to go alfo to his man Peter. It appears by a fketch, found among his papers, that he had formed the plan of an academy for inftructing the youth of this kingdom in the Pythagorean philofophy; and particularly in the judicious *Art of holding the tongue*, which it is thought would prove of great and fingular advantage to feveral perfons who fpeak in public; and that fo ufeful an inftitution may not be loft, it is hoped, that fuch gentlemen as have the reputation of this country at heart, will appoint fome place of meeting to confider of proper ways and means to carry this important defign into execution.

EXTRAORDINARY ADVENTURES.

PERHAPS the human mind can have no entertainment at once more congenial and more useful to it, than such stories as compose the following article; stories of extraordinary distresses, and wonderful deliverances. In the former part our humanity is cultivated; in the latter is inspired a spirited hope and a trust in Providence, which may enable us to act with resolution in the trying emergencies of life. They have the effect which Aristotle attributes to good tragedy, in correcting the passions by terror and pity. They give us striking examples of the resources in which ingenious distress is fruitful; and instances are remarkable of magnanimity and virtue, sometimes even in rude minds, and where it might least be expected. For these reasons we have not confined ourselves wholly to the publications of this last year, for narratives of that kind, but have collected from those of the preceding, such as we thought most memorable.

A genuine narrative of the sufferings of the persons who were confined in the prison called the Black Hole, in Fort William at Calcutta, in the kingdom of Bengal, after the surrender of that place to the Indians in June 1756, *from a letter of J. Z. Holwell, Esq; to William Davis, Esq;*

THE ill conduct of Drake, the late governor of Calcutta, who had, among other things, unjustly imprisoned a very considerable merchant of the country, whose name was Omychund, and who was a Gentoo, having drawn the resentment of the viceroy upon the factory, he marched against it in person, with a very considerable force, and laid siege to the fort.

Drake, who had brought on this misfortune, no sooner saw it approach, then he deserted his station, and left the gentlemen of the factory and the garrison to shift for themselves. As soon as Drake was gone, Mr. Holwell, from whose letter this account is taken, took the command upon himself, and resolved to defend the place as long as he was able. This voluntary opposition of Mr. Holwell incensed the viceroy against him; and supposing, that he would not have undertaken a work of supererogation, attended with such fatigue and danger, upon disinterested principles, he made no doubt but that there were very great treasures in the fort, in which he was deeply concerned as a proprietor; he therefore pushed on the siege with great vigour.

A very good account of the whole transaction is given by Mr. Holwell himself, in the following manner.

"The suba, or viceroy of Bengal, and his troops, were in pos-

possession of the fort, before six in the evening. At a third interview with him, before seven, he repeated his assurances to me, on the word of a soldier, that no harm should come to us: and, indeed, I believe his orders were only general, that we should for that night be secured; and that what followed was the result of revenge and resentment in the breasts of the lower Jemmautdaars, or Serjeants (to whose custody we were delivered) for the number of their order killed during the siege. Be this as it may, as soon as it was dark, we were all, without distinction, directed by the guard set over us, to collect ourselves into one body, and sit down quietly under the arched Veranda, or Piazza, to the west of the Black-hole prison, and the barracks to the left of the court of guard. Just as it was dark, about 400 or 500 men, who were drawn up upon the parade, advanced, and ordered us all to rise and go into the barracks. We were no sooner all within them, than the guard advanced to the inner arches and parapet wall; and, with their muskets presented, ordered us to go into the room at the southernmost end of the barrack, commonly called the Black-hole prison. Few amongst us, the soldiers excepted, had the least idea of the dimensions or nature of a place we had never seen; for if we had, we should, at all events, have rushed upon the guard, and been, as the lesser evil, by our own choice cut to pieces.

Amongst the first that entered were myself, Messieurs Baillie, Jenks, Cooke, T. Coles, Ensign Scott, Revely, Law, Buchanan, &c. I got possession of the window nearest the door, and Messieurs Coles and Scott into the window with me, they being both wounded (the first I believe mortally.) The rest of the above mentioned gentlemen were close round about me. It was now bout eight o'clock.

Figure to yourself, my friend, if possible, the situation of a hundred and forty-six wretches, exhausted by continual fatigue and action, crammed together in a cube of eighteen feet, in a close sultry night, in Bengal, shut up to the eastward and southward (the only quarters from which air could reach us) by dead walls, and by a wall and door to the north, open only to the westward by two windows, strongly barred with iron, from which we could receive scarce any the least circulation of fresh air.

What must ensue, appeared to me in lively and dreadful colours, the instant I cast my eyes round and saw the size and situation of the room. Many unsuccessful attempts were made to force the door; for having nothing but our hands to work with, and the door opening inward, all endeavours were vain and fruitless. . . . .

Amongst the guards posted at the windows, I observed an old Jemmautdaar near me, who seemed to carry some compassion for us in his countenance. I called him to me, and pressed him to endeavour to get us separated, half in one place, and half in another, and that he should in the morning receive a thousand rupees for this act of tenderness. He withdrew; but in a few minutes returned, and told me it was impossible. I then thought I had been deficient in my offer, and promised him two thousand: he

 with-

withdrew a ſecond time, but returned ſoon, and (with, I believe, much real pity and concern) told me, that it could not be done but by the ſuba's order, and that no one dared awake him.

We had been but few minutes confined before every one fell into a perſpiration ſo profuſe, you can form no idea of it. This brought on a raging thirſt, which increaſed in proportion as the body was drained of its moiſture.

Various expedients were thought of to give more room and air. To obtain the former, it was moved to put off their cloaths: this was approved as a happy motion, and in a few minutes, I believe every man was ſtripped (myſelf, Mr. Court, and the two young gentlemen by me excepted.) For a little time they flattered themſelves with having gained a mighty advantage; every hat was put in motion to produce a circulation of air, and Mr. Baillie propoſed that every man ſhould ſit down on his hams. This expedient was ſeveral times put in practice, and at each time many of the poor creatures, whoſe natural ſtrength was leſs than that of others, or who had been more exhauſted and could not immediately recover their legs, as others did when the word was given to riſe, fell to riſe no more; for they were inſtantly trod to death, or ſuffocated. When the whole body ſat down, they were ſo cloſely wedged together, that they were obliged to uſe many efforts, before they could put themſelves in motion to get up again.

Before nine o'clock every man's thirſt grew intolerable, and reſpiration difficult. Efforts were made again to force the door, but in vain. Many inſults were uſed to the guard to provoke them to fire in upon us. For my own part, I hitherto felt little pain or uneaſineſs, but what reſulted from my anxiety for the ſufferings of thoſe within. By keeping my face between two of the bars I obtained air enough to give my lungs eaſy play, though my perſpiration was exceſſive, and thirſt commencing. At this period, ſo ſtrong a urinous volatile effluvia came from the priſon, that I was not able to turn my head that way, for more than a few ſeconds at a time.

Now every body, excepting thoſe ſituated in and near the windows, began to grow outrageous, and many delirious: *Water*, *water*, became the general cry. And the old Jemmautdaar before mentioned, taking pity on us, ordered the people to bring ſome ſkins of water. This was what I dreaded. I foreſaw it would prove the ruin of the ſmall chance left us, and eſſayed many times to ſpeak to him privately to forbid its being brought: but the clamour was ſo loud, it became impoſſible. The water appeared. Words cannot point to you the univerſal agitation and raving the ſight of it threw us into. I flattered myſelf that ſome, by preſerving an equal temper of mind, might out-live the night; but now the reflection, which gave me the greateſt pain, was, that I ſaw no poſſibility of one eſcaping to tell the diſmal tale.

Until the water came, I had myſelf not ſuffered much from thirſt, which inſtantly grew exceſſive. We had no means of conveying it into the priſon, but by hats forced through the bars; and thus

myſelf

myself and Meffieurs Cole and Scott (notwithftanding the pains they fuffered from their wounds) fupplied them as faft as poffible. But thofe who have experienced intenfe thirft, or are acquainted with the caufe and nature of this appetite, will be fufficiently fenfible it could receive no more than a momentary alleviation; the caufe ftill fubfifted. Though we brought full hats within the bars, there enfued fuch violent ftruggles, and frequent contefts to get at it, that before it reached the lips of any one, there would be fcarcely a fmall tea-cup full left in them. Thefe fupplies, like fprinkling water on fire, only ferved to feed and raife the flame.

Oh! my dear Sir, how fhall I give you a conception of what I felt at the cries and ravings of thofe in the remoter parts of the prifon, who could not entertain a probable hope of obtaining a drop, yet could not diveft themfelves of expectation, however unavailing! and calling on me by the tender confiderations of friendfhip and affection, and who knew they were really dear to me! Think, if poffible, what my heart muft have fuffered at feeing and hearing their diftrefs, without having it in my power to relieve them: for the confufion now became general and horrid. Several quitted the other window (the only chance they had for life) to force their way to the water, and the throng and prefs upon the window was beyond bearing; many forcing their paffage from the further part of the room, preffed down thofe in their way, who had ftrength, and trampled them to death.

From about nine to near eleven, I fuftained this cruel fcene and painful fituation, ftill fupplying them with water, though my legs were almoft broke with the weight againft them. By this time I myfelf was near preffed to death, and my two companions, with Mr. William Parker (who had forced himfelf into the window) were really fo. . . .

For a great while they preferved a refpect and regard to me, more than indeed I could well expect, our circumftances confidered; but now all diftinction was loft. My friend Baillie, Meffrs. Jenks, Revely, Law, Buchanan, Simpfon, and feveral others, for whom I had a real efteem and affection, had for fome time been dead at my feet; and were now trampled upon by every corporal or common foldier, who, by the help of more robuft conftitutions, had forced their way to the window, and held faft by the bars over me, till at laft I became fo preffed and wedged up, I was deprived of all motion.

Determined now to give every thing up, I called to them, and begged, as the laft inftance of their regard, they would remove the preffure upon me, and permit me to retire out of the window, to die in quiet. They gave way; and with much difficulty I forced a paffage into the center of the prifon, where the throng was lefs by the many dead, (then I believe amounting to one third) and the numbers who flocked to the windows; for by this time they had water alfo at the other window.

In

In the Black-hole there is a platform * corresponding with that in the barrack: I travelled over the dead, and repaired to the further end of it, just opposite to the other window. Here my poor friend Mr. Edward Eyre came staggering over the dead to me, and with his usual coolness and good nature, asked me how I did? but fell and expired before I had time to make him a reply. I laid myself down on some of the dead behind me, on the platform; and, recommending myself to heaven, had the comfort of thinking my sufferings could have no long duration.

My thirst grew now insupportable, and the difficulty of breathing much increased; and I had not remained in this situation, I believe, ten minutes, when I was seized with a pain in my breast, and palpitation of heart, both to the most exquisite degree. These roused and obliged me to get up again; but still the pain, palpitation, thirst, and difficulty of breathing increased. I retained my senses notwithstanding; and had the grief to see death not so near me as I hoped; but could no longer bear the pains I suffered without attempting a relief, which I knew fresh air would and could only give me. I instantly determined to push for the window opposite to me; and by an effort of double the strength I had ever before possessed, gained the third rank at it, with one hand seized a bar, and by that means gained the second, though I think there were at least six or seven ranks between me and the window.

In a few moments the pain, palpitation, and difficulty of breathing ceased; but my thirst continued intolerable. I called aloud for *Water for God's sake.* I had been concluded dead; but as soon as they found me amongst them, they still had the respect and tenderness for me, crying out, *Give him water, give him water!* nor would one of them at the window attempt to touch it until I had drank. But from the water I had no relief; my thirst was rather increased by it; so I determined to drink no more, but patiently wait the event; and kept my mouth moist from time to time by sucking the perspiration out of my shirt-sleeves, and catching the drops as they fell, like heavy rain from my head and face; you can hardly imagine how unhappy I was if any of them escaped my mouth.

I came into the prison without coat or waistcoat; the season was too hot to bear the former, and the latter tempted the avarice of one of the guards, who robbed me of it when we were under the Veranda. Whilst I was at this second window, I was observed by one of my miserable companions on the right of me, in the expedient of allaying my thirst by sucking my shirt-sleeve. He took the hint, and robbed me from time to time of a considerable part of my store; though after I detected him, I had even the address to begin on that sleeve first, when I thought my reservoirs were sufficiently reple-

* This platform was raised between three or four feet from the floor, open underneath; it extended the whole length of the east side of the prison, and was above six feet wide.

nished;

niſhed; and our mouths and noſes often met in the conteſt. This plunderer I found afterwards was a worthy young gentleman in the ſervice, Mr. Luſhington, one of the few who eſcaped from death, and ſince paid me the compliment of aſſuring me, he believed he owed his life to the many comfortable draughts he had from my ſleeves. Before I hit upon this happy expedient, I had, in an ungovernable fit of thirſt, attempted drinking my urine; but it was ſo intenſely bitter, there was no enduring a ſecond taſte, whereas no Briſtol water could be more ſoft or pleaſant than what aroſe from perſpiration.

By half an hour paſt eleven, the much greater number of thoſe living were in an outrageous delirium, and the others quite ungovernable; few retaining any calmneſs, but the ranks next the windows. They all now found, that water, inſtead of relieving, rather heightened their uneaſineſſes; and, *Air, air*, was the general cry. Every inſult that could be deviſed againſt the guard, all the opprobrious names and abuſe that the ſuba, Monickchund, &c. could be loaded with, were repeated to provoke the guard to fire upon us, every man that could, ruſhing tumultuouſly towards the windows, with eager hopes of meeting the firſt ſhot. Then a general prayer to Heaven to haſten the approach of the flames to the right and left of us, and put a period to our miſery. But theſe failing, they whoſe ſtrength and ſpirits were quite exhauſted, laid themſelves down and expired quietly upon their fellows: others who had yet ſome ſtrength and vigour left, made a laſt effort for the windows, and ſeveral ſucceeded by leaping and ſcrambling over the backs and heads of thoſe in the firſt ranks; and got hold of the bars, from which there was no removing them. Many to the right and left ſunk with the violent preſſure, and were ſoon ſuffocated; for now a ſteam aroſe from the living and the dead, which affected us in all its circumſtances, as if we were forcibly held by our heads over a bowl of ſtrong volatile ſpirit of hartſhorn, until ſuffocated; nor could the effluvia of the one, be diſtinguiſhed from the other; and frequently, when I was forced by the load upon my head and ſhoulders, to hold my face down, I was obliged, near as I was to the window, inſtantly to raiſe it again, to eſcape ſuffocation.

I need not, my dear friend, aſk your commiſeration, when I tell you, that in this plight, from half an hour after eleven till near two in the morning, I ſuſtained the weight of a heavy man, with his knees on my back, and the preſſure of his whole body on my head; a Dutch ſerjeant, who had taken his ſeat upon my left ſhoulder, and a Topaz * bearing on my right; all which, nothing could have enabled me long to ſupport, but the props and preſſure equally ſuſtaining me all around. The two latter I frequently diſlodged, by ſhifting my hold on the bars, and driving my knuckles into their ribs; but my friend above ſtuck faſt, and as he held by two bars, was immoveable.

The repeated trials and efforts I made to diſlodge this inſufferable incumbrance upon me, at laſt quite exhauſted me, and towards two o' clock,

* A black chriſtian ſoldier; uſually termed ſubjects of Portugal.

clock, finding I muſt quit the window, or ſink where I was, I reſolved on the former, having borne, truly for the ſake of others, infinitely more for life, than the beſt of it is worth.

In the rank cloſe behind me was an officer of one of the ſhips, whoſe name was Carey, and who behaved with much bravery during the ſiege, (his wife, a fine woman, tho' country born, would not quit him, but accompanied him into the priſon, and was one who ſurvived.) This poor wretch had been long raving for water and air; I told him I was determined to give up life, and recommended his gaining my ſtation. On my quitting, he made an attempt to get my place; but was ſupplanted.

Poor Carey expreſſed his thankfulneſs, and ſaid, he would give up life too; but it was with the utmoſt labour we forced our way from the window (ſeveral in the inner ranks appearing to me dead ſtanding †.) He laid himſelf down to die: and his death, I believe, was very ſudden; for he was a ſhort, full, ſanguine man: his ſtrength was great, and I imagine had he not retired with me, I ſhould never have been able to have forced my way.

I was at this time ſenſible of no pain, and little uneaſineſs. I found a ſtupor coming on apace, and laid myſelf down by that gallant old man, the reverend Mr. Jervas Bellamy, who lay dead with his ſon the lieutenant, hand in hand, near the ſouthernmoſt wall of the priſon.

When I had lain there ſome little time, I ſtill had reflection enough to ſuffer ſome uneaſineſs in the thought, that I ſhould be trampled upon, when dead, as I myſelf had done to others. With ſome difficulty I raiſed myſelf and gained the platform a ſecond time, where I preſently loſt all ſenſation: the laſt trace of ſenſibility that I have been able to recollect after my lying down, was, my ſaſh being uneaſy about my waiſt, which I untied and threw from me. Of what paſſed in this interval to the time of my reſurrection from this hole of horrors, I can give you no account.

When the day broke, and the gentlemen found that no intreaties could prevail to get the door opened, it occurred to one of them (I think to Mr. Secretary Cooke) to make a ſearch for me, in hopes I might have influence enough to gain a releaſe from this ſcene of miſery. Accordingly Meſſrs Luſhington and Walcot undertook the ſearch, and by my ſhirt diſcovered me under the dead upon the platform. They took me from thence, and imagining I had ſome ſigns of life, brought me towards the window I had firſt poſſeſſion of.

But as life was equally dear to every man (and the ſtench ariſing from the dead bodies was grown ſo intolerable) no one would give up his ſtation in or near the window: ſo they were obliged to carry me back again. But ſoon after Captain Mills, (now captain of the company's yacht) who was in poſſeſſion of a ſeat in the window, had the humanity to offer to reſign it. I was again brought by the ſame gentleman and placed in the window.

At this juncture the ſuba, who had received an account of the havock

† Unable to fall by the throng and equal preſſure round.

vock death had made amongst us, sent one of his Jemmautdaars to enquire if the Chief survived. They shewed me to him; told I had appearance of life remaining; and believed I might recover, if the door was opened very soon. This answer being returned to the suba, an order came immediately for our release, it being then near six in the morning.

As the door opened inwards, and as the dead were piled up against it, and covered all the rest of the floor, it was impossible to open it by any efforts from without; it was therefore necessary that the dead should be removed by the few that were within, who were become so feeble, that the task, tho' it was the condition of life, was not performed without the utmost difficulty, and it was 20 minutes after the order came, before the door could be opened.

About a quarter after six in the morning, the poor remains of 146 souls, being no more than three and twenty, came out of the Black-hole alive, but in a condition which made it very doubtful whether they would see the morning of the next day; among the living was Mrs. Carey, but poor Leech was among the dead. The bodies were dragged out of the hole by the soldiers, and thrown promiscuously into the ditch of an unfinished ravelin, which was afterwards filled with earth."

Mr. Holwell, Mr. Court, Mr. Walcot, and Mr. Burdet, were ordered into the custody of an officer, and the rest were immediately set at liberty, except poor Mrs. Carey, whose youth and beauty caused her to be detained for the conqueror, or some officer of state.

Mr. Holwell when he came out of the prison, was in a high fever, and not able to stand; he was, however, sent for to be examined by the viceroy, and was in this condition carried to his presence. It was some time before he could speak, but as soon as he was able, he began to relate the sufferings and death of his unhappy companions. The viceroy, without taking any notice of this tale of distress, stopt him short, by telling him, that he had been informed, there was treasure to a very considerable value secreted in the fort, and that if he did not discover it, he must expect no mercy. Mr. Holwell replied, that he knew of no such treasure; and then began to remind him of his assurance the day before, that no hurt should come either to himself or his friends. To this remonstrance he paid no more regard than he had done to the complaint, but proceeded in his enquiry concerning the treasure; and when he found no intelligence could be got, he ordered the general of his houshold troops, whose name was Mhir Muddon, to take charge of Mr. Holwell as his prisoner.

Among the guard that marched before Mr. Holwell, when he went out from the presence of the viceroy, there was a man who carried a large Moratta battle-ax on his shoulder, which occasioned a report, first, that his head was to be struck off, and afterwards that the sentence was executed.

It happened unfortunately, that Mr. Holwell, in the hurry and confusion of the siege, after the fort had been deserted by Drake, forgot to set Omychund, the black merchant, whom Drake had injuriously imprisoned, at liberty. This neglect

glect Omychund resented as an act of wilful injustice, and Mr. Holwell is of opinion, that if it had not been for Omychund's insinuations, he should have been discharged with the rest, notwithstanding the offence he had given to the viceroy by defending the fort; and the notion that prevailed of his being privy to the concealment of money; and in this opinion he says he is confirmed by the confinement of the three gentlemen, who were detained with him, who were all of them persons against whom Omychund was known to have conceived a particular resentment.

Mr. Holwell, and his associates in captivity, were conveyed in a kind of coach, drawn by oxen, called a hackery, to the camp, where they were loaded with fetters, and lodged in the tent of a Moorish soldier, which being no more than 4 feet by 3 feet, they were obliged to lie, sick as they were, half in and half out the whole night, which happened to be very rainy; yet the next day their fever happily came to a crisis, and boils broke out on every part of their bodies, which, though they were extremely painful, were the certain presages of their recovery. The next day they were removed to the coast, and by order of general Mhir Muddon, were soon after sent by sea to Maxadavad, the metropolis of Bengal, to wait the viceroy's return, and be disposed of as he should farther determine.

At Maxadavad they arrived, after a voyage of 13 days, in a large boat, in which they had no better provision than rice and water, and no softer bed than some bamboos laid on the bottom timber of the vessel; they were, besides, exposed alternately to excessive heat and violent rains, without any covering but a bit of old mat and some scraps of sacking. The boils that covered them were become running sores, and the irons on their legs had consumed the flesh almost to the bone.

When they arrived at Maxadavad, Mr. Holwell sent a letter to Mr. Law, the chief of the French factory, with an account of their distress, and Mr. Law with great politeness and humanity, sent them not only cloaths, linnen, provision and liquors, in great plenty, but money.

About 4 o'clock on the 7th of July, they landed, and after marching a considerable way as a spectacle to the multitude that thronged round them, they were deposited under an open shed, not far from the place.

In this place they received every possible relief, not only from the great kindness of the French and Dutch chiefs, but from the Arabian merchants.

On the 18th of July, the viceroy arrived, and the prisoners then learned that he had enquired for them, in order to set them at liberty before he left Calcutta, and was offended with Mhir Muddon for having so hastily removed them to Maxadavad. He did not, however, order their immediate discharge when he arrived, which it is natural to suppose he would have done, if they had been detained in custody contrary to his inclination.

On the 25th they were conducted to the palace, to have an audience, and to know their fate; but they could have no audience that day, which, as it happened, was a favourable circumstance, for

at

at night the viceroy's grandmother sollicited their liberty, at a feast, to which she was invited on his safe return, and the viceroy promised that he would release them on the morrow.

On the morrow, about five in the morning, they were waked, and told that the viceroy would in a few minutes pass by to his palace of Mooteejeel. Upon this intelligence they got up, and when the viceroy came in sight, they paid him the usual homage, and uttered their benediction aloud. He looked at them with strong marks of compassion in his countenance, and ordering his litter to stop, he called them to him, and having heard a short extemporary petition, which was spoken by Mr. Holwell, he made no reply, but ordered two of his officers to see their irons instantly struck off, and conduct them safely wherever they chose to go, giving them a strict charge to see that they suffered no injury or insult by the way.

This act of mercy, however late, or from whatever motive, was the more meritorious, as great pains were taken by some time-serving sycophants to prevent it: they told the viceroy, that Mr. Holwell, notwithstanding his losses, was still possessed of enough to pay a considerable sum for his freedom, to which the viceroy nobly replied, "If he has any thing left, let him keep it; his sufferings have been great, and he shall have his liberty."

Mr. Holwell and his friends being thus dismissed, immediately took boat, and soon after arrived safe at the Dutch settlement at Corcemadad, where he afterwards embarked for England.

An authentic narrative of the loss of the Doddington Indiaman, and of the adventures of those on board who survived the shipwreck; from the journal of one of the surviving officers.

THE Doddington, Captain Samson, sailed from the Downs on the 23d of April 1755, in company with the Pelham, the Houghton, the Streatham, and the Edgecourt, all in the service of the East-India company, and in about seven days got clear of the channel; during this time Captain Samson perceived that his ship sailed faster than any of the others, and he was unwilling to lose the advantage of this superiority by keeping them company: he therefore stood on alone, and having very soon lost sight of them, he made Bonavista, one of the Cape de Verd islands, lat. 16 North, on the 20th of May, and on the 21st he got into Porto Prior bay. It now appeared either that he had been mistaken in supposing his ship to outsail the rest of the fleet, or that he had lost time by the course he had steered, for he found the Pelham and the Streatham had reached the bay two hours before him. The Houghton arrived soon afterwards, but the Edgecourt did not come in till the 26th.

On the 27th of May, the Doddington, Pelham, Streatham, and Houghton, having taken in their water, proceeded on the voyage together, leaving the Edgecourt in the road; they continued in company steering S. by E. $\frac{1}{4}$ E. till the 28th, when Capt. Samson thinking the course too far easterly, ordered the Doddington to be kept South, which

which again ſeparated her from the reſt of the fleet, and after a fine voyage of ſeven weeks ſhe made the land of the Cape of Good Hope. Having juſt doubled the Cape, a new departure was taken from de Agulhas on the 8th of July; and the veſſel having ſteered eaſtward about twenty-four hours, between the latitude of 35 d. 30 m. and 36 d. the captain ordered her to be kept E. N. E.

In this courſe ſhe continued till about a quarter before one in the morning of Thurſday, July 17, when ſhe ſtruck: the officer from whoſe journal this account is taken, was then aſleep in his cabin, but being ſuddenly awaked by the ſhock, he ſtarted up in the utmoſt conſternation, and made all the haſte he could to get upon deck; here all the terrors of his ſituation ruſhed upon him at once; he ſaw the men daſhed to and fro by the violence of the ſea that rolled over them, and the ſhip breaking to pieces at every ſtroke of the ſurge; he crawled over, with great diffi-culty, to the larboard ſide of the quarter-deck, which lay the higheſt out of water, and there he found the captain, who ſaid very little more than they muſt all periſh; in a few minutes a ſea parted them, and he ſaw him no more. He made a ſhift to get back to the quarter-deck, but he was very much bruiſ-ed, and the ſmall bone of his left arm was broken; all the reſt of the ſhip was under water, and ſhattered to pieces. In this dreadful ſituation, expecting every moment to be ſwal-lowed up, he heard ſomebody cry out, *Land!* upon this he looked eagerly about him, but though he ſaw ſomething which he ſuppoſed was taken for land, he believed it only the range of the ſea on the other ſide of the breakers; at the ſame moment the ſea broke over him with great violence, and not only forced him from his hold, but ſtunned him by a violent blow upon his eye. Though from this time he lay inſenſible till after day light, yet he continued upon the wreck, and when he recovered he found himſelf made faſt to a plank by a nail that had been forced into his ſhoulder. Beſides the pain that he felt from his wounds and bruiſes, he was now ſo benumbed with cold, that he could ſcarce move either hand or foot; he called out as loud as he could, and was heard by the people on the rocks, but they could give no aſſiſtance, ſo that it was a conſi-derable time before he could diſen-gage himſelf and crawl on ſhore.

This ſhore was a barren uninha-bited rock, in the lat. of 33 d. 44 m. South, and diſtance about 250 leagues Eaſt of the Cape of Good Hope. Here were now met Mr. Evan Jones, chief mate, Mr. John Collet 2d, Mr. William Webb 3d, and Mr. S. Powell 5th mate; Ri-chard Topping, Carpenter; Neal Bothwell and Nathaniel Chiſholm, quarter-maſters; Daniel Ladova, the captain's ſteward; Henry Sharp, the ſurgeon's ſervant, Tho-mas Arnold, a black, and John Mackdowal, ſervants to the cap-tain; Robert Beaſeley, John King, Gilbert Chain, Terence Mole, Jo-nas Roſenbury, John Glaſs, ——— Taylor, and Hendrick Scantz, ſeamen; John Yets, midſhipman; and John Liſter, Ralph Smith, and Edward Dyſoy, matroſſes. Theſe perſons, being 23 in number, were all that remained of 270 ſouls that were on board when the ſhip ſtruck.

Their firſt care was to ſearch among the things which had been

thrown

thrown upon the rocks from the ſhip, for ſomething to cover them, in which they ſucceeded beyond their hopes. The next thing they felt the want of was fire: and this was not ſo eaſily ſupplied; ſome of them attempted to kindle two pieces of wood, by rubbing them together, but without ſucceſs; others went peeping out among the rocks to pick up ſomething that might ſerve for a flint and ſteel; after long ſearch they found a box that contained two gun flints and a broken file; this was a joyful acquiſition, but ſtill they had nothing that would kindle from a ſpark, and till ſomething like tinder could be procured, the flint and ſteel were uſeleſs; a farther ſearch was therefore undertaken with inexpreſſible ſollicitude and anxiety; a caſk of gunpowder was at laſt diſcovered, but to their great diſappointment it proved to be wet; however, upon a near examination, a ſmall quantity was found at the bottom of the caſk, which had ſuffered no damage. Some of this they bruiſed on a linnen rag, which ſerved them very well for tinder, and a fire was ſoon made; the bruiſed and wounded gathered about it, and the reſt went in ſearch of other neceſſaries, without which the rock could afford them but a ſhort reſpite from deſtruction. In the afternoon a box of wax-candles, and a caſe of brandy were brought in; both were extremely welcome, eſpecially the brandy, of which every one thought it adviſeable to take a dram. Soon after ſome others of the party returned with an account that they had diſcovered a caſk almoſt full of freſh water, which was yet of more conſequence than the brandy, and Mr. Jones brought in ſome pieces of ſalt-pork, and ſoon after ſome others arrived driving before them ſeven hogs, which had come on ſhore alive; ſome caſks of beer, water, flour, were alſo ſeen at a diſtance, but it was not then poſſible to get them over the rocks. The approach of night made it neceſſary to provide ſome ſhelter, all hands therefore were employed to make a tent of ſome canvas that had been thrown on ſhore, which was at laſt effected, though it was ſo ſmall for want of more ſail-cloth, that it would not hold them all. The iſland was much frequented by a kind of water-fowl ſomething larger than a duck, called a gannet, and the higheſt part of it was covered with their dung; upon this part they were obliged to build their tent, for fear of being overflowed, and they placed thoſe who could not walk, under the tent, and kindled a fire near them; but as they had paſſed the day without food, they paſſed the night without reſt; for beſides, that they were ſunk a foot in the fowl's dung, the night was ſo tempeſtuous that the wind blew about their fire, and before it could be ſcraped together again, the rain put it out.

In the morning, which was Friday, July the 18th, thoſe that were able went again about the rock, to ſee what could be ſaved from the wreck, but to their great mortification, they found all the caſks which they had ſeen the night before, except one of beer, and one of flour, ſtaved to pieces againſt the rocks; ſoon after theſe were ſecured the tide flowed up, and put a ſtop to the work of that day. The company therefore was called together to eat their firſt meal,

meal, and ſome raſhers of pork were broiled upon the coals for dinner.

The ſitting down thus deſolate and forlorn, to a repaſt, which they uſed to ſhare in the convivial chearfulneſs, which naturally aroſe from the conſciouſneſs of preſent plenty, and the hope of future, ſtruck them with ſuch a ſenſe of their condition, that they burſt into paſſionate lamentations, wringing their hands and looking round them with all the wildneſs of deſpair. In ſuch tumult of mind, our thoughts hurry from one ſubject to another, to fix, if poſſible, upon ſomething that may afford comfort; and one of the company recollecting, that as the carpenter was among them, they might build a ſtrong ſloop, if they could procure materials and tools, mentioned this as a ſubject of hope to the reſt. Every man's attention was immediately turned upon the carpenter, who declared that he had no doubt but he ſhould be able to build a ſloop that would carry them all to ſome port of ſafety, if tools and materials could be found; at that time indeed, they had no rational proſpect of procuring either, any more than of being able to victual a ſloop, if they had had one ready built; yet they had no ſooner placed their deliverance one remove beyond total impoſſibility, than they ſeemed to think it neither improbable nor difficult; they began to eat without farther repining, and that moment the boat engroſſed their whole converſation; and they not only debated upon the ſize and manner of rigging her, but to what port they ſhould ſteer her. whether to the Cape or Delagoa.

As ſoon as they had finiſhed their repaſt, ſome went in ſearch of tools, others to mend the tent; no tools however were found that day.

Saturday, July 19, they ſecured four butts of water, one caſk of flour, one hogſhead of brandy, and one of their little boats, which had been thrown up by the tide, in a ſhattered condition; but they found no tools except a ſcraper.

Sunday, July 20, they had the good fortune to find a hamper, in which there were files, ſail-needles, gimblets, and an azimuth compaſs-card. They alſo found two quadrants, a carpenter's adze, a chiſſel, and three ſword blades, and a cheſt of treaſure. This ſearch was made very early in the morning, as there had been a prodigious ſurf rolling in all the day before, by which it was reaſonable to ſuppoſe ſomething would be thrown up. At ten o'clock they all aſſembled to prayers, and did not go out again till after dinner, when they found moſt of the packets of letters belonging to the king and the company; theſe they carefully dried and laid by.

The ſame day, as they were ſearching about the beach, they found the body of a gentlewoman, which they knew to be that of Mrs. Collet, the wife of their ſecond mate, who was then at a little diſtance from the ſpot. The mutual affection of this couple was remarkably tender, and Mr. Jones, the firſt mate, immediately ſtepped aſide to Mr. Collet, and found means to take him to the other ſide of the rock, while the other two mates, the carpenter, and ſome others, dug a grave in the bird's dung, in which they depoſited the body, reading over it the burial ſervice, from a French prayer-book, which had driven aſhore with her from the

the wreck. Having thus paid the debt of humanity to the dead, and concealed from Mr. Collet a ſight which would moſt ſenſibly, if not fatally, have affected him, they found means, after ſome days, to diſcloſe to him by degrees what they had done, and to give him the wedding-ring, which they had taken from her finger. He received it with great emotion, and afterwards ſpent many days in raiſing a monument over the grave, by piling up the ſquareſt ſtones he could find, on the top of which he fixed an elm plank, and inſcribed it with her name, her age, the time of her death, and ſome account of the fatal accident by which it was occaſioned.

On Monday, July 21, they ſecured ſome more water and pork, and found ſome timber, plank, cordage, and canvas. Theſe they ſecured with great joy for the boat, though as yet they were in want of many implements, without which it was impoſſible for the carpenter to work. He had juſt finiſhed a ſaw, but he had neither hammer nor nails. It happened, however, that one of the ſeamen, Hendrick Scantz, a Swede, having picked up an old pair of bellows, brought them to his companions, and told them, that he had been by profeſſion a ſmith, and that with theſe bellows and a forge, which he hoped they would be able, by his direction, to build, he could furniſh the carpenter with all the tools he would want, nails included, as plenty of iron might be obtained by burning the timber which had come on ſhore from the wreck. This account was received with a tranſport of joy; the ſmith immediately applied himſelf to mend the bellows, and the three following days were ſpent in building a tent and a forge, in bringing together the timber and plank for the carpenter's uſe, who was alſo buſy in getting ready the few tools he had, that he might begin the boat as ſoon as poſſible.

Thurſday, July 24, the carpenter, aſſiſted by Cheſholm the quarter-maſter, began to work upon the keel of the boat, which they had determined ſhould be a ſloop, thirty feet long, and twelve wide. This day alſo the ſmith finiſhed his forge and laid in a quantity of fir for fuel. From this time the carpenter and ſmith continued to work with indefatigable diligence, except when they were prevented by the weather; the ſmith having fortunately found the ring and nut of a bower anchor, which ſerved him for an anvil, ſupplied chiſſels, axes, hammers, nails, as they wanted, and the carpenter uſed them with great dexterity and diſpatch, till the 31ſt, when he fell ſick.

As the lives of the whole company depended upon the carpenter, they watched his recovery with the utmoſt impatience and anxiety, and to their unſpeakable joy he was ſo far recovered on the 2d of Auguſt, as to return to his work.

In the mean time the ſtores which they had ſaved from the wreck were ſo near exhauſted, that they came to an allowance of two ounces of bread a man per day, and had no ſalt pork, except what they were determined to keep to victual the boat; water alſo fell ſhort. In this diſtreſs they had recourſe to ſeveral expedients; they dug a well, in hopes to find a ſpring, but were diſappointed: they attempted to knock down ſome of the gannets that ſettled on the top of the rock, and in this they had ſome ſucceſs;

but they found the fleſh very rank, of a fiſhy taſte, and as black as a ſhoe. They alſo made a raft or float, called a catamaran, on which they propoſed to go out a fiſhing, with ſuch hooks and lines as had come aſhore. They killed alſo ſome ſeals, but all thoſe who eat of them were ſick.

When they were driven to great diſtreſs, they killed a hog, but they had generally ſucceſs in fiſhing on a float, and they ſometimes ſent out two at a time. It happened, however, that Mr. Collet the ſecond mate, and Mr. Yets the midſhipman, were very near being driven out to ſea on one of theſe floats, where they would inevitably have periſhed. —— On the 20th of Auguſt they had been fiſhing all the afternoon, till about four o'clock when they weighed, and endeavoured to come in again, but the wind ſuddenly freſhening up to the weſtward, they found, that inſtead of gaining a-head, they drove out very faſt. The people on ſhore perceived their diſtreſs, but knew not how to aſſiſt them; at laſt, however, they ſent out another float, with killicks and ropes, which they hoped would enable them to ride till the wind became more moderate; but the ſurf was ſo great, that it overſet three times, and the men were obliged to ſwim back. In the mean time, they ſaw their friends driving out to ſea at a great rate, and were juſt giving them up to inevitable deſtruction, when the carpenter ſent them word, that he would make the little boat ſo tight, that ſhe ſhould not take in water, faſter than one man could lave it out. This gave them freſh hope, and every one was ready to venture out for the deliverace of their friends. The carpenter diſpatched the boat in a quarter of an hour, and ſhe ſoon overtook the float, and took Collet and Yets on board. They ſoon found, however, that the water gained very faſt upon them, notwithſtanding their utmoſt efforts, and when ſhe came in, ſhe was ſo full of water, that in a few minutes ſhe muſt have ſunk.

As they were now afraid of venturing any more on the raft, the capenter went again to work on the little boat, and put her into compleat repair. Their ſucceſs in fiſhing was very uncertain; ſometimes they took great quantities, and ſometimes they took none. Nor were the ſupplies they gained on ſhore leſs precarious; the gannets would ſometimes ſettle in amazing numbers, like a cloud, and ſometimes they would totally diſappear for ſeveral days together. This made them very deſirous of finding ſome way to preſerve the food they caught, from putrefaction, that they might lay by the ſurplus of a fortunate day, to ſerve them when neither gannets nor fiſh were to be caught. They made ſeveral attempts to cure both their fiſh and their fowl by ſmoaking it, but without ſucceſs. They then attempted to make ſalt, but this had like to have been fatal to them all. The ſmith had mended a copper veſſel for the experiment, and they immediately began to work without knowing that their proceſs in ſalt-making would diſſolve the ſurface of the copper into verdigreeſe, and that this ſolution or ruſt of copper was poiſon. Salt, however, was procured, but the quality that made it poiſonous happened to abound in ſuch a degree, as to make it intolerably offenſive fenfive to the tafte; it was therefore thrown away, but thofe who had ventured to palate it, were feized with violent cholics, cold fweats, and reachings, which fufficiently convinced them of the danger they had efcaped.

Wednefday, Sept. 3. They had now been inhabitants of this defolate rock, ever fince the 17th of July, near feven weeks, and during this time they had often feen a great fmoke on the main land, which made them very defirous to fend the boat, to try what affiftance might be obtained from thence. On this day, therefore, Bothwell, Rofenbury, and Taylor, fet out on the difcovery, and at night the people on fhore made a large fire on the higheft part of the rock, as a fignal to them.

While they were waiting the return of the boat, they were all thrown into the utmoft confternation by an accident which happened to the carpenter, who unfortunately cut his leg with an adze, in fuch a manner that he was in great danger of bleeding to death, they having no furgeon among them, nor any thing proper to apply to the wound. At length, however, tho' with much difficulty, the blood was ftaunched, and the wound healed without any bad fymptom intervening.

Saturday, Sept. 6. The weather having been fair for 48 hours, they impatiently expected the return of the boat. At noon they became very uneafy at having feen nothing of her; but juft as they were fitting down to dinner, they were agreeably furprifed by two of their people, who came running over the rocks, crying out, *the boat! the boat!* They all ftarted up, overjoyed at the found, and ran to fee her come in, with great hopes that fhe had fucceeded; but they foon diftinguifhed, that fhe was rowed only by one man who plied both oars: they concluded, therefore, that the other two were loft or detained; but prefently they faw another get up from the bottom of the boat, where it was fuppofed he had lain down for a fhort refrefhment, and then the boat came forward fomewhat fafter, though ftill at a flow rate. The dinner was now entirely forgot, and after they had waited an hour on the beach with the utmoft impatience, the boat came in. The two men were Rofenbury and Taylor, who the moment they ftept on fhore, threw themfelves on their knees, and in fhort but earneft ejaculations returned thanks to God for having once more fet them fafe upon this place, which, barren and defolate as it was, they now confidered as an afylum from a fituation of much greater diftrefs. Having exerted their utmoft effort to bring the boat in, their ftrength forfook them at once, and they were not able to rife from the ground without affiftance.

As foon as they were got over to the tent, every body was bufy to procure them fome refrefhment, for they found that the boat was quite empty both of provifions and water. They dreffed them fome fifh, with as much hafte as they could, and perceiving that they were quite exhaufted with watching and labour, they left them when they had eaten their meal, without afking any queftions, and they immediately fell afleep. The behaviour of thefe honeft failors to their mefs-mates, was an uncommon inftance of hearty kindnefs, and generous felf-denial; the impatience of their curiofity muft have been both increafed and juftified in proportion as they were interefted in the account that was to gratify it; yet even this curiofity, in which life itfelf was concerned, they had the kindnefs and the fortitude to reprefs, rather than delay the refrefhment of others for its gratification.

The account which was given by the two adventurers when they awoke, was to this effect:

About three o'clock on the day they fet out, they got round a point, about fix leagues eaft of the rock *, as they approached, it had the appearance of a double point, which encouraged them to hope, that between the two points they fhould find an harbour; but in this hope they were difappointed, for they found a large furf all along the coaft. However, about five o'clock, having feen only one of the natives, they ventured to pull in for the fhore, but the moment they got into the furf, the boat overfet. By this accident poor Bothwell was drowned, and the other two, who reached the fhore in an exhaufted and feeble condition, were left deftitute of every kind of provifion, except a fmall keg of brandy. As foon as they had a little recovered their ftrength, they crawled along the fhore to feek for the boat, having no other hope of fhelter from the wild beafts, which might be expected to come abroad in the night. After fome fearch they found her, but they were too weak to get her up, and darknefs coming on, they were obliged to lie down upon the fand, with no other covering than the branches of a tree, and in this condition they paffed the night. As foon as the morning dawned, they went again to look for the boat, which the furf had driven from where they left her. As they walked along the coaft they faw a man and advanced toward him, upon which he ran away into the woods, that lay near the beach, and were very thick. They went on, and foon after difcovered the body of their companion Bothwell, which had been dragged up the fand a confiderable diftance from the water, and torn to pieces by fome wild beaft. This terrified them exceedingly, and having found the boat, the dread of paffing another night on fhore determined them immediately to return. They were, however, prevented in the attempt by a frefh gale at weft, and before they could put back, the boat overfet with them a fecond time, and drove with them along the fhore. After much ftruggling and fwimming, they got once more fafe on the land: but as they had now been fafting ever fince three o'clock the day before, they were fainting with hunger and fatigue. It happened, however, that they met with a fruit refembling an apple, which they eagerly gathered and eat, without knowing either its name or its quality. By good fortune it did them no harm; and being fomewhat refrefhed by their antedilu-

* It does not appear by any map, that in lat. 33. 40. 250 leagues eaft of the Cape, the fuppofed fituation of their rock, they could be within fix leagues of any part of the main land; they muft therefore be all miftaken in their reckoning.

vian repaſt, they made ſhift to haul the boat on ſhore, and turning it upſide down, they crept under it to ſleep, being thus very well ſheltered from the ſun, and ſecured againſt the wild beaſts. Thoſe who know the irreſiſtible power of ſleep, after long watching and exceſſive labour, will not conclude that their firſt ſlumber was ſhort, becauſe their ſituation was incommodious or inſecure; they waked, however, before the next morning, and peeping under the edge of the boat, they could diſcern the feet of ſeveral creatures, which by their claws they ſuppoſed to be tygers, paſs by them to and again. This was a ſufficient motive to remain in their reſting place till the morning, when they looked out again, and ſaw the feet of a man. Upon this diſcovery they came from under the boat, to the great aſtoniſhment of the poor ſavage, and two other men and a boy, who were at ſome diſtance. When they had got all together, and were a little recovered from their ſurpriſe, they made ſigns to the ſailors to go away, which they endeavoured to do, though they were able to move but very ſlowly. Before they had gone far from the boat, a conſiderable number of the natives ran down upon them with their launces. It happened that Roſenbury had picked up the maſt of the boat and a piſtol which had been waſhed on ſhore, as he went along; being thus armed, when the Indians came down upon him, and being beſides unable to run, he imprudently turned about, and exerting all his ſtrength, advanced towards them in a threatening manner, ſuppoſing they would have been ſeized with a pannic and retreated into the woods. It happened, however, that he was miſtaken; for inſtead of running away they ſurrounded him, and began to whet their launces. Taylor thought it was now time to try what could be done by ſupplication; he therefore threw himſelf on his knees, and in a piteous tone cried out for mercy; but Roſenbury took refuge in the water. The ſavages immediately came up to Taylor, and began to ſtrip him: he ſuffered them quietly to take his ſhoes and his ſhirt, but when they attacked his trowſers he made ſome reſiſtance, and by his geſtures, intreated they would not leave him quite naked, upon which they thought fit to deſiſt. They then made ſigns for Roſenbury to come to them, who was all this while ſwimming about in the ſea; but he refuſed, and made ſigns that they would kill him. They then pointed to Taylor, intimating that they had not killed him: upon this he came forward, and having firſt thrown them his piſtol, and all his cloaths but his ſhirt, he ventured to put himſelf in their hands. When he came up they offered him no violence, only held the boat's maſt and the piſtol to him, by way of deriding the folly of his attempt to fright them. They ſeemed to be very much pleaſed with the clothes, which they divided among them as far as they would go. Then they began to rifle the boat, and having taken all the rope they could find, and the hook by which the rudder hung to the ſtern-poſt, they began to knock the ſtern to pieces, for the iron which they ſaw about it. Next to knocking the poor wretches on the head, this was the worſt thing they could do, and, rough as they were, they burſt into tears

tears at the injury that was offered to their boat, and intreated the ſavages to deſiſt, with ſuch agony of diſtreſs that they ſuffered the boat to remain as they found it. Encouraged by this appearance of placability and kindneſs, and urged by hunger, they aſked by ſigns, for ſomething to eat; this requeſt was alſo granted, and having given them ſome roots, they again made ſigns for them to depart; upon which they once more launched their boat, and got into it, but the wind blowing ſtrong from the weſt, they could not put off. The natives perceiving that they were willing to comply with their deſires, but not able, covered them with the boat to ſleep under, and left them as they had found them. The next morning, the weather being fine, and the wind eaſterly, they launched the boat a third time, and returned back to the rock.

From this time till Sunday the 29th of September, the carpenter and ſmith continued to work upon the boat, and the people were buſy in getting in from time to time what was thrown up from the wreck, particularly cordage and canvas, to rig the boat, and ſome caſks of freſh water, which they were very ſollicitous to keep for ſea-ſtores, as their eſcape in the boat ſcarce depended leſs upon freſh water than upon the ſails themſelves. On this day, after they had been at prayers, a duty which was regularly and publicly performed every Sunday, the officers diſcovered that the cheſt of treaſure had been broke open, and the greater part of it taken away and concealed. It may perhaps be thought ſtrange, that the people, whom danger had made religious, ſhould at the ſame time be guilty of theft; but, upon this occaſion, it ſhould be remembered, that as ſoon as the ſhip is loſt, the ſailors loſe their pay, and the captain his command; every diſtinction and ſubordination that ſubſiſted on ſhip-board is at an end; and whatever is caſt on ſhore from the wreck is, by the ſailors, conſidered as common property. The men therefore, who thought fit ſecretly to take what they deemed their ſhare of this treaſure, were not, in their own opinion, guilty of diſhoneſty, but intended only to ſecure what they feared the officers would monopolize, and by this means prevent diſputes, which, in their circumſtances, might produce fatal effects. The officers, however, when they diſcovered what had been done, and found that nobody would own they knew any thing about it, propoſed to write the form of an oath, and adminiſter it ſeparately to every individual, the officers to take it firſt. But to this the majority immediately objected; for though they might not ſuppoſe they had committed a crime by taking the treaſure, they knew it would be not only immoral, but impious, to ſwear they had not taken it. As the minority were not in a condition to ſupport their motion, the affair was ſuffered to reſt, without farther enquiry or remonſtrance.

On the 6th of October they found a fowling-piece; this was a joyful acquiſition, and though the barrel was much bent, it was ſoon made ſerviceable by the carpenter, and uſed with great ſucceſs in ſhooting the birds, which before they had no way of taking but by knocking them down with a ſtick.

On

On Friday October 11, they perceived the gannets, which had of late forsaken them, to hover again about the rock in great numbers, and were in hopes they would settle to lay their eggs, in which, to their great joy, they were not disappointed; for after this time they were constantly supplied with eggs in great plenty, till the beginning of January, when the season of laying was past.

On Sunday October 20, Mr. Collet, Mr. Webb, and two others, ventured out once more on the float, but the wind springing up very fresh, the float broke loose, and drove them to the other side of the rocks. The wind still rising, and the sea running very high, it was impossible for the boat to put out; they were therefore obliged to remain all night among the seals on the rocks, without any shelter or refreshment. But in this situation, however dreadful, they received great comfort from reflecting how much more dreadful it would have been, if instead of being driven to the rocks, their float had been carried out to sea. It was noon the next day before the wind abated, and then the boat ventured off; but as the waves still ran high, it could bring in no more than two at a time, leaving the float behind them. They had now some rainy weather, which proved very acceptable, as they contrived to save some of the water for sea-stores; but they were still in great want of bread, having lived many days on short allowance. As a last resource, they thought of building an oven, for they had some barrels of flour, though they had no bread: in this attempt they succeeded, beyond their expectations, and were able to convert their flour into a tolerable biscuit.

This biscuit, however, was at length so near exhausted, that they were obliged to live upon a few ounces a day, without brandy, of which only a small quantity remained, and this they preserved inviolable for the use of the carpenter. They were also so short of water, that of this they were allowed but half a pint a day.

In this condition, however, they happily in a great degree preserved their health and vigour, and on the 16th of February they launched their boat, and called her the *Happy Deliverance*. On the 17th they got their little pittance of stores on board, and on the 18th they set sail from the rock, on which they had lived just seven months, and to which at parting they gave the name of *Bird Island*.

A wonderful and affecting account of the preservation of three persons buried above five weeks in snow sixty feet deep; by Dr. Joseph Bruni, professor of philosophy at Turin. From the Philos. Transactions.

A Small cluster of houses at a place called Bergemoletto near Demonte in the upper valley of Stura, was on the 19th of March 1755, entirely overwhelmed by two vast bodies of snow that tumbled down from a neighbouring mountain. All the inhabitants were then within doors, except one Joseph Rochia and his son, a lad of 15, who were on the roof of their house clearing away the snow which had fallen for three days incessantly. A priest going by by to mafs, advifed them to come down, having juft before obferved a body of fnow tumbling from the mountain towards them. The man defcended with great precipitation and fled with his fon, he knew not whither; but fcarce had he gone 30 or 40 fteps, before his fon, who followed him, fell down; on which looking back, he faw his own and his neighbours houfes, in which were 22 perfons in all, covered with a high mountain of fnow. He lifted up his fon, and reflecting that his wife, his fifter, two children, and all his effects were thus buried, he fainted away; but foon reviving got fafe to a friend's houfe at fome diftance.

Five days after, Jofeph being perfectly recovered, got upon the fnow, with his fon, and two of his wife's brothers, to try if he could find the exact place where his houfe ftood; but after many openings made in the fnow they could not difcover it. The month of April proving hot, and ;he fnow beginning to foften, he again ufed his utmoft endeavours to recover his effects, and to bury as he thought, the remains of his family. He made new openings and threw in earth, to melt the fnow, which on the 24th of April was greatly diminifhed He broke through ice fix Englifh feet thick, with iron bars, thruft down a long pole and touched the ground, but evening coming on, he defifted.

His wife's brother, who lived at Demonte, dreamed that night, that his fifter was ftill alive, and begged him to help her; the man affected by his dream, rofe early in the morning and went to Bergemoletto, where Jofeph was; and after refting himfelf a little, went with him to work upon the fnow, where they made another opening, which led them to the houfe they fearched for; but finding no dead bodies in its ruins, they fought for the ftable, which was about 240 Englifh feet diftant, which having found they heard a cry of, *Help, my dear brother*. Being greatly furprifed as well as encouraged by thefe words, they laboured with all diligence till they had made a large opening, through which the brother who had the dream immediately went down, where the fifter with an agonizing and feeble voice told him, *I have always trufted in God and you, that you would not forfake me*. The other brother and the hufband then went down, and found ftill alive the wife about 45, the fifter about 35, and a daughter about thirteen years old. Thefe they raifed on their fhoulders to men above, who pulled them up as if from the grave, and carried them to a neighbouring houfe: they were unable to walk, and fo wafted, that they appeared like mere fkeletons. They were immediately put to bed, and gruel of rye-flour and a little butter was given to recover them. Some days after the intendant came to fee them, and found the wife ftill unable to rife from bed or ufe her feet, from the intenfe cold fhe had endured, and the uneafy pofture fhe had been in. The fifter, whofe legs had been bathed with hot wine, could walk with fome difficulty; and the daughter needed no further remedies.

On the intendant's interrogating the women, they told him, that on the morning of the 19th of March they were in the ftable with

with a boy of ſix years old, and a girl of about thirteen: in the ſame ſtable were ſix goats, one of which having brought forth two dead kids the night before, they went to carry her a ſmall veſſel of rye-flour gruel; there were alſo an aſs and five or ſix fowls. They were ſheltering themſelves in a warm corner of the ſtable till the church bell ſhould ring, intending to attend the ſervice. The wife related, that wanting to go out of the ſtable to kindle a fire in the houſe of her huſband, who was clearing away the ſnow from the top of it, ſhe perceived a maſs of ſnow breaking down towards the eaſt, upon which ſhe went back into the ſtable, ſhut the door, and told her ſiſter of it. In leſs than three minutes they heard the roof break over their heads, and alſo part of the ceiling. The ſiſter adviſed to get into the rack and manger, which they did. The aſs was tied to the manger, but got looſe by kicking and ſtruggling, and threw down the little veſſel, which they found, and afterwards uſed to hold the melted ſnow, which ſerved them for drink.

Very fortunately the manger was under the main prop of the ſtable, and ſo reſiſted the weight of the ſnow. Their firſt care was to know what they had to eat. The ſiſter ſaid ſhe had fifteen cheſnuts in her pocket; the children ſaid they had breakfaſted, and ſhould want no more that day. They remembered there were thirty-ſix or forty cakes in a place near the ſtable, and endeavoured to get at them, but were not able for the ſnow. They called often for help, but were heard by none. The ſiſter gave the cheſnuts to the wife, and eat two herſelf, and they drank ſome ſnow water. The aſs was reſtleſs, and the goats kept bleating for ſome days; after which they heard no more of them. Two of the goats, however, being left alive, and near the manger, they felt them, and found that one of them was big, and would kid, as they recollected, about the middle of April; the other gave milk, wherewith they preſerved their lives. During all the time they ſaw not one ray of light, yet for about 20 days they had ſome notice of night and day from the crowing of the fowls, till they died.

The ſecond day, being very hungry, they eat all the cheſnuts, and drank what milk the goat yielded, being very near two pounds a day at firſt, but it ſoon decreaſed. The third day they attempted again, but in vain, to get at the cakes: ſo reſolved to take all poſſible care to feed the goats; for juſt above the manger was a hay-loft, whence through a hole the ſiſter pulled down hay into the rack, and gave it to the goats as long as ſhe could reach it, and then, when it was beyond her reach the goats climbed upon her ſhoulders, and reached it themſelves.

On the ſixth day the boy ſickened, and ſix days after deſired his mother, who all this time had held him in her lap, to lay him at his length in the manger. She did ſo, and taking him by the hand, felt it was very cold; ſhe then put her hand to his mouth, and finding that cold likewiſe, ſhe gave him a little milk; the boy then cried, *O my father is in the ſnow! Oh father, father!* and then expired.

In the mean while the goats milk diminiſhed daily, and the fowls

fowls ſoon after dying they could no longer diſtinguiſh night from day; but according to their reckoning the time was near when the other goat ſhould kid, which at length they knew was come, by its cries: the ſiſter helped it, and they killed the kid, to ſave the milk for their own ſubſiſtence: ſo they found that the middle of April was come. Whenever they called this goat, it would come and lick their faces and hands, and gave them every day two pounds of milk, on which account they ſtill bear the poor creatnre a great affection.

They ſaid, that during all this time, hunger gave them but little uneaſineſs, except for the firſt five or ſix days; that their greateſt pain was from the extreme coldneſs of the melted ſnow water, which fell on them, from the ſtench of the dead aſs, goats, fowls, &c. and from lice; but more than all from the very uneaſy poſture they were confined to, the manger in which they ſat ſquatting againſt the wall, being no more than three feet four inches broad.

After the firſt two or three days they had no evacuation by ſtool. The melted ſnow-water and milk were diſcharged by urine. The mother ſaid ſhe had never ſlept, but the ſiſter and daughter declared they ſlept as uſual.

Atteſted before the intendant by the ſaid women the 16th of May, 1755.

Extract of a letter from Portſmouth, Feb. 13, 1758.

YEſterday arrived here, with a meſſenger belonging to the admiralty, in the greateſt haſte, a perſon who was immediately introduced, by orders from above, to Admiral Boſcawen. The following particulars concerning him have tranſpired. He was ſome time ſince maſter of an Engliſh veſſel, trading from port to port in North America, particularly up the river St. Lawrence; but being taken by the enemy, has been priſoner with General Montcalm and others near three years, who would not admit of any exchange for him, on account of his extenſive knowledge of all the coaſt, more particularly the ſtrength and ſoundings of Quebec and Louiſbourg. They therefore came to a reſolution to ſend him to Old France, in the next pacquet-boat, there to be confined till the end of the war. He was accordingly embarked, (the only Engliſhman) and the pacquet put on board. In their voyage he was admitted to the cabin, where he took notice one day, that they bundled up the pacquet, and put it into a canvas bag, having previouſly made it ready to be thrown over-board, upon any danger of being taken.

They were conſtrained to put into Vigo for ſome proviſions, as alſo to gain ſome intelligence of the ſtrength of the Engliſh in thoſe ſeas; there they found one or more Engliſh men of war at anchor. The priſoner thought this a proper opportunity of putting the following ſcheme in execution. One night taking the opportunity of all, but the watch, being in a ſound ſleep, he took the pacquet out of the bag; and having fixed it in his mouth, he ſilently let himſelf down into the bay; and to prevent noiſe by ſwimming, floated upon his back into the

wake

wake of the English man of war, where he secured himself by the hawser, and upon calling out for assistance, was immediately taken on board with the pacquet. The captain examined him, treated him with great humanity, gave him a suit of his own cloaths, scarlet trimmed with black velvet, which he appeared in: transcribed the pacquet, which is said to be of the utmost importance in regard to our success in North America, and then sent him post over land with the copy of the pacquet to Lisbon; from whence he was brought to Falmouth in a sloop of war, and immediately set out post for London. Upon his arrival in town, he was examined by proper persons in the administration, and rewarded with a present supply; and by his own desire, was immediately sent to Portsmouth, to go out on board Admiral Boscawen's own ship, upon the present expedition to North America.

A faithful narrative of the dangers, sufferings, and deliverances of Robert Eastburn, and his captivity among the Indians in North America.

ROBERT Eastburn, with about thirty other traders, set out from Philadelphia for Oswego, early in the spring of the year 1756, and on the 28th of March arrived at Captain Williams's fort, where they proposed to take up their lodgings for that night; but Captain Williams informing them that there was not convenient room for them, they passed the night in a building called the Indian house, at a small distance from the fort.

At ten o'clock in the morning of the next day, Eastburn being still at the Indian house where he had lodged, was alarmed by a negro man, who came running down the road, crying out that several of the English had been taken by the enemy, who were coming forward. Eastburn not thinking himself safe at the Indian house, joined a small detachment, consisting of a serjeant and twelve men, whom Captain Williams had dispatched to see if the report of the negro was true, and having marched with them about a quarter of a mile, he heard the report of a musquet, which was instantly followed by the cries of a dying man. As soon as his first surprize was over, he advanced to discover the enemy, and soon perceived they were too well prepared for the reception of his party. In these circumstances of imminent danger, he placed himself behind a large pine-tree, which he saw at a small distance, and while the enemy were viewing his party, he discharged his piece among them, by which he wounded one and killed another; at the same time his party fired, but finding it impossible to make a stand against such a superiority of numbers, they retreated as soon as they had made their fire, and Eastburn's situation behind the tree being such as made it impossible for him to join them, he was compelled to retreat a different way.

Some of the Indians seeing him go off, followed his track in a light snow, but it is probable he might yet have escaped, if he had not unfortunately fallen into a deep bog, where he was soon discovered and surrounded.

He

He was taken out and dragged back to the main body, where he was inftantly ftripped of all his cloaths, except a flannel waiftcoat without fleeves ; a rope was then put round his neck, his arms were pinioned behind him, a band was faftened round his body, and a heavy load placed on his back; in this condition one of the favages ftruck him a fevere blow on his head, and then drove him through the woods before them.

He was foon after joined by 18 unhappy wretches, who had likewife been made prifoners by this party, which confifted of about 100 men : they did not purfue their route towards Capt. Williams's fort, becaufe Eaftburn, being afked by them concerning its ftrength, gave them fuch an anfwer as difcouraged them from attempting it. They determined, however, to deftroy another fort called Bull's fort fituated at the head of Wood's creek, which they foon effected, and except five perfons, put every foul they found in it to the fword.

After this exploit they retired to the woods and joined their main body, which confifted of 400 French and 500 Indians,commanded by one of the principal gentlemen of Quebec; as foon as they got together they threw themfelves on their knees, and returned thanks to God for their victory, an example, fays Eaftburn, well worthy of imitation.

They continued their march thro' the woods about four miles, and then it being dark, and feveral of the Indians being drunk, they encamped.

The Indians, according to their cuftom, foon made a fire, and ftrewed round it fome branches of green hemlock to fit upon; they then went up to Eaftburn, and untied his arms, after which they tied the two ends of a ftring that was faftened to the band which went round his middle to two trees; two of them then fat down on the green boughs, one on each fide of him, with the ftring that was faftened to his band under them, to prevent his efcape, and having covered him with an old blanket they went to fleep.

They encamped, and refted much in the fame manner the night following ; and the next morning, Sunday the 28th, they rofe very early and retreated haftily towards Canada, for fear of General Johnfon, who, as they were informed, was on his march againft them.

Eaftburn having on this occafion been fent for by the commanding officer, and afked many queftions, the officer at length difcovered that he was a fmith, a circumftance which probably induced his enemies to fpare his life, in hopes that he might be ufeful to them, and he was advifed to fettle at Canada and fend for his wife, with promifes of great advantages, which however he refufed. In his march he fuffered incredible fatigue and hardfhip, travelling almoft naked through deep fnow, and being frequently obliged to wade through rivers, the water of which wanted but little of being as cold as ice. Under thefe feverities he fell fick, and had the mortification to fee one of his friends, who was in the fame circumftances, killed and fcalped by the Indians, becaufe he was no longer able to keep pace with them: to him, however, they were more merciful, for perceiving that he could not fwallow their coarfe food,

food, they boiled him ſome chocolate, and ſeemed pleaſed when they perceived that he eat it.

But there were other circumſtances beſides cold, and nakedneſs, and ſickneſs, and fatigue, which made this march ſtill more dreadful to poor Eaſtburn. He was appointed to march behind an Indian, who had a large bunch of green ſcalps hanging at his back, which was increaſed as often as ſome ſtraggling wretch was overtaken, whoſe ſcalp was immediately added to the reſt. This object being perpetually before his eyes, while his ears, frequently wounded with the infernal yell which they called the dead ſhout, and which they never fail to utter when a victim falls into their hands, filled him at once with grief and horror, and aggravated the ſufferings of his body by ſuch anguiſh of mind as thoſe only can conceive who have felt.

After a march of ſeven days they arrived at Lake Ontario, where they were met by ſome French batteaus with a large ſupply of proviſions, of which they had been in ſo much want, that they had ſubſiſted during ſome part of their march upon horſe-fleſh, and had even devoured a porcupine without any other dreſſing than ſufficed juſt to ſcorch off the hair and quills.

Eaſtburn, after a tedious voyage with part of this company, arrived at Oſwegotchy, an Indian town, where he hoped to continue till warm weather, but to his inexpreſſible diſappointment, he was ordered the next day to proceed 200 miles farther down the ſtream.

To aggravate this misfortune, he was appointed to go in a batteau with eight Indians, one of whom was the very man he had wounded, when he fired from behind the pine the day he was taken. He contrived to eſcape the notice of this man by wrapping himſelf up in the old blanket that had been given him to ſleep under while they were in the boat, but when they went on ſhore he was diſcovered. The Indian caſt his eyes upon him with a kind of malignant joy, and immediately taking away his blanket ordered him to dance round the fire barefoot, and ſing the priſoners ſong. With this order Eaſtburn abſolutely refuſed to comply, becauſe, as he ſays, he thought the compliance ſinful; this ſo enraged the Indian, that he endeavoured many times to puſh him alive in the fire, which he avoided by jumping over it; and his enemy being weak with his wound, and not being ſeconded by his aſſociates, at length deſiſted from his attempts; and after a painful journey, ſometimes on the water, and ſometimes on the ſnow, they came at length to the upper part of Canada. Here it was Eaſtburn's hard fortune to be quartered at a Frenchman's houſe, where his old enemy, the wounded Indian, again appeared, and related to the Frenchman the circumſtance of his refuſing to dance and ſing. Upon this the good Frenchman aſſiſted his friend the Indian to ſtrip poor Eaſtburn of his flannel veſt without ſleeves, the only garment that was then left him. It was then inſiſted both by the Frenchman and Indian that he ſhould abſolutely dance and ſing, and upon his refuſal they uſed him with great cruelty, and would probably have murdered him, if he had not been reſcued from his per-

ſecutors

ſecutors by the compaſſion of ſome women, who had been witneſſes of his ill treatment.

On the 11th of April they came within ſight of the town of Conaſadanga, where they were ſoon ſurrounded by a large company of Indians, who ordered all the priſoners to dance and ſing; many complied, but Eaſtburn ſtill refuſed; he could not however avoid a very diſagreeable ceremony, which was performed immediately after the dance and ſong were ended.

The dancing and ſinging was as uſual performed in the middle of a large circle of Indians, at a conſiderable diſtance from an Indian houſe, the door of which was ſet open; as ſoon as the ſong was ended, the circle opened, and the priſoners were to run the gauntlet to this houſe; while they were running, the Indians continued a moſt vociferous ſhout, and beat them ſo violently upon the head that many dropped down, but when they had entered the houſe they were to be beaten no more. Eaſtburn received ſeveral blows in this diabolical race, which he felt long afterwards, but he was notwithſtanding one of the firſt that entered the aſylum: he was treated with great kindneſs by the women, who gave him and his companions boiled corn and beans, and warmed them at a good fire, though ſtill he was without cloaths.

After he had continued ten days at this place, he was ſent by water with a ſmall party of Indians to another town called Cohnewago, and obliged to leave all his companions behind him. When the party that eſcorted him came near the town, they ſhouted to give notice that they had a priſoner, upon which the whole town came out to meet him; as the batteau in which he was ſitting came near the ſhore, a young Indian rudely hauled him out of it into the water, which was knee-deep, and very cold. As ſoon as he had got on ſhore he was ſurrounded by a ring of Indians to the number of 500, who ordered him again to perform the ceremony of the ſong and dance, which was to be followed by the ſame race which he had run at his former lodging; he did not, he ſays, indulge this party by dancing any more than the others, but he acknowledged that he *ſtamped*, which, as he ſays, was to prepare him for his race, and after ſome time the Indians, either miſtaking this ſtamping for dancing, or diſpenſing with their command, made way for him to run. When he ſet off, about 150 boys, who had been prepared for that purpoſe, pelted him with ſtones and dirt; but he would not have received much damage from this volley, if an Indian, grudging him his good fortune, had not ſtopped him as he was running, and held him till the boys had armed themſelves with more dirt and ſtones; by this ſecond volley he was wounded in the right eye, and his head and face were ſo covered with dirt that he could not ſee his way; he was however again delivered by ſome women, who took pity on him, waſhed his wounds, and gave him food.

The next day he was brought to the center of the town, and there delivered to three young Indians to be adopted, and ſent 200 miles farther up the ſtream, to a town called Oſwegotchy.

Theſe young men as ſoon as they had received him, told him he he was their brother, and ſet out with him for the place of their deſtination.

When he arrived at Oſwegotchy he was adopted by an old Indian and his wife, who becauſe he refuſed to go to maſs, employed him in hard labour, and treated him with great unkindneſs. As he conſidered himſelf to be ſuffering for conſcience ſake, he ſubmitted without murmuring, and fulfilled his taſk, however ſevere, with ſuch diligence and aſſiduity, that the reſentment of his new parents ſubſided, and they treated him like their ſon.

After he had continued ſome time in this ſituation, he ſaw at Montreal ſome Indians who were in friendſhip with the Engliſh, and had come thither with ſome complaint to the governor, and he found means by ſome of theſe Indians to ſend a letter to his friends, informing them where he was, and in what ſituation.

It happened, however, that having been ſoon after detected in a project to eſcape, he was removed from this place to Cohnewago, under a ſtrong guard; but at Cohnewago he was in a better ſituation than before, for he worked at his trade with a French ſmith, who paid him 6 livres 5 ſous per week, and he alſo obtained leave of the captain of the guard to walk where he would.

After having worked ſome time at this place, he obtained leave to go to Montreal, where he hoped to get yet higher wages; and ſoon after his arrival there, he entered into partnerſhip with an Engliſh ſmith, and continued to work with him till he heard that the French had made themſelves maſters of Oſwego, and ſoon after ſaw the Britiſh ſtandards and priſoners brought into the town.

Eaſtburn looked upon theſe trophies of his enemies with a heavy heart, and as he was muſing on the misfortunes of himſelf and his countrymen, he diſcovered among the priſoners his own ſon, a lad about 17 years of age; the ſon at the ſame time fixed his eyes on his father, and the emotions of both were ſuch as can be better conceived than deſcribed, eſpecially as it was impoſſible for them at that time to come near enough to ſpeak to each other, and in ſome degree uncertain whether they ſhould ever meet again.

Eaſtburn, however, ſoon after had the good fortune to obtain his ſon's liberty. The officers belonging to Oſwego would fain have had them both with them, for they were to be ſent to Philadelphia: but this was not permitted to the father, becauſe he was an Indian priſoner, and the ſon refuſed to be releaſed without him. From theſe gentlemen, however, he received many acts of kindneſs, ſome giving him money, and others cloaths, which were yet more welcome.

Eaſtburn having continued with his ſon among the French, and the French Indians, till the 22d of July 1757, was then releaſed on a cartel, and arrived at Philadelphia after many hardſhips and delays for want of money, on the 26th of November following, where he was relieved with great liberality by thoſe to whom his merit and his ſufferings were known; for, though he was poor, he was a man of good repute, and much reſpected by his ſuperiors, particularly the reverend Mr. Tennant, who has written a recommendatory preface to the narrative of his ſufferings, from which this account is extracted, and which was publiſhed at Philadelphia for the benefit of himſelf and his family, who were in his abſence reduced to the moſt pitiable diſtreſs.

As the burning the Prince George man of war, Admiral Broderick's own ſhip, the fate of ſome part of the crew, and the extraordinary eſcape of ſome particulars, are moſt affecting events; we have given them in what appears to us the moſt affecting manner; in the words of thoſe who had themſelves a part in that terrible calamity.

From the Reverend Mr. Sharp, Chaplain.

Glaſgow, off Liſbon, April 20.

ON Thurſday the 13th inſt. at half an hour paſt one in the afternoon, word was paſſed into the ward-room, by the centry, that the fore part of our ſhip, the Prince George, was on fire. The lieutenants ran immediately forward, and myſelf, with many others, went directly on the quarter-deck, when we found the whole ſhip's crew was alarmed. The pumps were handed out, engines and buckets carried forward, and every immediate remedy applied. The admiral, with the lieutenants on watch, kept the quarter-deck, from whence he ſent ſuch orders as he thought moſt expedient for the preſervation of the ſhip, and the ſouls in her. Captain Payton, and the lieutenants, on ſearch, found that the fire broke out firſt in the boatſwain's ſtore-room, to which place large quantities of water were applied, but in vain; for the ſmoke was ſo very great and hot, that the poor creatures could not get near enough to the flames for their labour to have any effect. On which Captain Payton ordered ſcuttles to be made, that the water might be poured in by that means; but there he was defeated likewiſe, for only two carpenters could be found, and they had nothing to work with for a long time but a hammer and chiſſel each. The lower gun deck ports were then opened, but the water that flowed in was not ſufficient to ſtop the violence of the flames. He ordered likewiſe the powder room to be wetted, leſt the ſhip ſhould immediately be blown up, and every ſoul periſh in an inſtant. This had the deſired effect, and for ſome minutes we had glimmering hopes. I mention the above particulars, as I was below myſelf, worked with the men as long as I could ſtand it, went up for air, and returned again inſtantly, and conſequently an eye-witneſs, therefore declare them as facts. The fire ſoon increaſed, and raged violently aft on the larboard ſide; and as the deſtruction of the ſhip was now found inevitable, the preſervation of the admiral was firſt conſulted. Captain Payton came on the quarter-deck, and ordered the barge to be manned, into which the admiral entered with near forty more; for now there was no diſtinction, every man's life was equally precious. The admiral finding the barge would overſet, ſtripped himſelf naked, and committed himſelf to the mercy of the waves, and after toiling an hour he was at length taken up by a merchantman's boat. Captain Payton kept the quarter-deck

an

an hour after the admiral left it, when he happily got into a boat from the ftern ladder, and was put fafe on board the Alderney floop. I muft be deficient even to attempt a defcription of the melancholy fcene that was before me; fhrieking, cries, lamentations, bemoanings, raving, defpair, and even madnefs itfelf prefented themfelves. It was now high time to think of taking care of myfelf. I looked from every part of the fhip for my prefervation, and foon faw three boats off the ftern of the fhip. I went immediately to my cabin, and offered up my prayers to God, particularly thanking him for giving me fuch refolution and compofure of mind. I then jumped into the fea from one of the gun room ports, and fwam to a boat, which put me fafe on board the Alderney floop. There are near 300 people faved, and more might have been faved had the merchantmen behaved like human creatures; but they kept a long way to windward the whole time; and if poffible to their greater fhame be it fpoken, inftead of faving the men that fwam to their boats, they were employed in taking up geefe, fowls, tables, chairs, and whatever elfe of the kind came near them.

From Mr. Parry, an officer, dated as above.

ABout half paft one at noon, being in the office adjoining to the cabin, I faw the admiral run out, with two or three officers; on enquiring the caufe, I was alarmed with the fhip's being on fire forwards, and it was believed in the boatfwain's fore ftore-room; every method was taken to extinguifh it, but the fmoke was fo violent, that no perfon could get near enough to find where the fire was. About half paft two we made the fignal of diftrefs; but to render our fituation more wretched, the fog came on very thick, and the wind frefhed, and it was near four before the Glafgow and Alderney got intelligence of our condition; when they repeated the fignal, hoifted out their boats, and ftood towards us; but they not knowing we had taken care to float our powder, were under fad apprehenfions we might blow up, and therefore could not (confiftent with their own fafety) give us the affiftance our deplorable condition rendered us fo much in need of. We attempted to fcuttle the decks to let the water on the fire, but the people could not ftand a minute without being near fuffocated. About half paft four the fmoke increafed, and the flames began to break out; the admiral then ordered the boats to be hoifted out, got the barge out, and went off, promifing to bring a fhip along-fide of us. I obferved her fo full her gunwale was almoft with the water, and, in a few minutes after faw her fink at fome diftance a-ftern, and not above three or four were faved out of near forty, among whom it pleafed God to preferve the admiral. The weather was now become clear, but none of the merchantmen would come near us. Our officers behaved well, and endeavoured to keep the people to the pumps and drawing water, but they now were become quite ungovernable. About a quarter before five Captain Payton left the fhip, and promifed as the admiral; but was not able to accomplifh it. About five the long-

 boat

boat was endeavoured to be got out, in which were near a hundred people; but as they were hoiſting her out, one of the tackles gave way, by which ſhe overſet, and almoſt every ſoul periſhed. We were now reduced to the greateſt diſtreſs. You may have ſome idea of our miſerable condition, when I tell you the ſhip began to be in flames fore and aft, ſpreading like flax; people diſtracted, not knowing what they did, and jumping over-board from all parts. I was reduced to the melancholy choice of either burning with the ſhip or going over-board. Very few that could ſwim were taken up, and I that could not ſwim, muſt have little hopes indeed. About a quarter paſt five, I went into the admiral's ſtern gallery, where two young gentlemen were laſhing two tables together for a raft; I aſſiſted them, and one of them propoſed to make faſt the laſhing to the gallery, and lower ourſelves down to the tables, then cut the laſhing, and commit ourſelves to the mercy of Providence; we hoiſted over the tables, but being badly laſhed, one of them we loſt; as ſoon as the other was down, I propoſed to venture firſt, which they readily conſented to; there was now three boats a-ſtern, this was the time or never, down I went by the rope; but as there was a great ſwell of ſea, it was impoſſible for any one to follow me, and I was turned adrift. By the cries of the people from the ſhip to the boats, in about five minutes I was taken up, very near drowned *.

From a midſhipman, dated as above.

ON Thurſday the 13th, about half an hour paſt one in the afternoon, we were alarmed with fire in the boatſwain's fore ſtore-room, which put us all into great diſorder; and it being a very thick fog, we could not ſee one ſhip in the fleet. We kept firing guns of diſtreſs, and no ſhip appearing in ſight for an hour, we were all in the greateſt conſternation; but the fog then diſpelling, the Glaſgow hailed us, to whom we told our condition, and earneſtly begged of them to ſave our lives.

The fire ſtill increaſing, we were obliged to hoiſt out our boats, which from the confuſion were near three hours fixing to the tackles, &c. every body being engaged in preparing to ſave himſelf. The poop, ſtern, and quarter galleries, were lined with men and boys, crying out in a moſt moving manner to be aſſiſted. During this time out of twenty-three ſail of ſhips we had but three boats to our aſſiſtance, and thoſe would not come near the ſhip for fear of being ſunk, the poor fellows continually jumping over-board; great numbers of whom were drowned in our ſight.

We got our boats out, which never returned after going once. By this time the fire had communicated itſelf to the middle gun deck, and

* 715 complement.	260 ſaved.
30 paſſengers to Gibraltar.	485 loſt.
745	745

nobody

nobody could go down below, every one expecting his death every minute, either by fire or water, and were taking leave of each other. Soon after going out of the admiral's cabin, I ſaw the flames coming out in the hatchway of the upper gun deck; I returned immediately, and took my leave of the petty officers that were there, and went over the ſtarboard ſtern ladder, to ſave myſelf by ſwimming, and, thanks be to Almighty God! reached a boat, and was taken up.

I had juſt got clear of the ſhip, when the flames became general, and thoſe poor unhappy wretches that could not ſwim, were obliged to remain upon the wreck, with the fire falling down upon them. Shortly after the maſts went away, and killed numbers, and thoſe that were not killed by the maſts, thought themſelves happy to get upon them. But the ſhip rolling by reaſon of the great ſea, the fire had communicated itſelf to the guns, which ſwept them off the deck in great numbers, they being all loaded and ſhotted.

Such a terrible ſight the oldeſt men in the fleet ſay they never ſaw. Thus ended our unhappy ſhip, after burning about ſix hours and a half, who had as complete a crew, and was as well manned as any ſhip that ever ſailed from England.

Letter from the maſter of a merchant-man, under convoy of Admiral Broderick.

THurſday, April 13th, Uſhant bearing Eaſt, ſixty leagues diſtance, at noon I ſaw Admiral Broderick hoiſt a ſignal of diſtreſs; upon which I made what ſail I could and went down on him. At one in the afternoon I could diſcern the Prince George on fire; at two drew pretty near her, but thought they might have quenched the fire. At three o'clock I ſaw plainly there was no quenching it. I was within a hundred yards of her ſtern, but durſt not venture along-ſide, the ſea beating high; beſides, the going off of her guns, and danger of blowing up. At four in the afternoon the admiral was taken up ſwimming by a merchant-ſhip's boat, as then the ſhips that had boats were all out, and a good many of them loſt. The weather proving bad, towards night I was within piſtol ſhot, and there remained ſome time; and picked up four of her crew: and had not two of my men run away with my boat the night before we ſailed from St. Helen's, I am confident I could have ſaved ſixty or eighty of them at leaſt, as I was all the time nearer to them than any ſhip in the fleet. What made me venture ſo near was, that I knew my ſhip went well, and was under good command. At ſix, what a diſmal ſight! the maſts and ſails all in a blaze; hundreds of ſouls hanging by the ropes alongaſide, I could count fifty of them hanging over in the ſtern ladder, others in the ſea on oars and pieces of wood; a melancholy ſpectacle! beſides the diſmal cries from the ſhip, which ſtill ring in my ears. Half an hour paſt ſix the flames broke out at her broadſide, and in leſs than five minutes every bit of her was in flames, and ſo continued till ſeven, when ſhe overſet, but did not ſink. I then ran within twenty yards of her,

her, but my people compelled me to go further off, for fear of ſtriking on the wreck. All I can farther ſay of it, there never was a more ſhocking ſight; pray God that I may never ſee the like again! It was very grievous to me that I could not ſave more of her men, without running the riſk of ſharing her fate. The eighteenth of April the Glaſgow, a twenty gun ſhip, hoiſted the ſignal for all maſters of merchant-ſhips to come on board, where the admiral had his flag hoiſted, to know how many people we had ſaved amongſt us, and to deliver them up. By the then liſt it appeared, that the Admiral, Captain Payton, and about two hundred and fifty-three men were ſaved.

Lite-

Literary and Miſcellaneous Eſſays.

THIS head of our collection is not of ſo uniform a nature as the foregoing diviſions. But we have endeavoured at as much order in the diſpoſition of the ſeveral pieces which compoſe it, and the diverſity of the ſubjects would admit. The firſt piece we give is upon the ſubject of Taſte. It is ſaying enough in its praiſe, to ſay it is written by Monſ. de Monteſquieu, who ſo happily employed philoſophy to illuſtrate and improve the laws of all the nations of the world. So far as this piece goes, (for it is but a fragment) he employs philoſophy with equal happineſs to explain and improve the polite arts. As the piece is long, we have in ſome places abridged it. In ſome few places it may poſſibly ſeem a little obſcure. If any blame ſhould, on that account, be laid on the tranſlator, we muſt not forget that the excellent author himſelf, through an extreme refinement, was not wholly free from obſcurity.

An Essay on Taste.

TASTE, in the moſt general definition of it, without conſidering whether good or bad, juſt or not juſt, is that which attaches us to a thing by ſentiments; which does not hinder its being applied to intellectual things, the knowledge of which gives ſo much pleaſure to the ſoul, that it was the only happineſs that certain philoſophers could conceive. The ſoul receives her knowledge through her ideas and through her ſentiments; ſhe receives certain pleaſures thro' theſe ideas and theſe ſentiments. For although we oppoſe idea to ſentiment, yet when the ſoul ſees a thing, ſhe feels it; and there is nothing ſo intellectual, that ſhe does not ſee, or think ſhe ſees, and conſequently that ſhe does not feel.

Of curioſity.

Our ſoul is made for thinking; that is to ſay, for making diſcoveries. Such a being ought then to have curioſity; for as all things are in a chain, where each idea precedes one, and follows another idea, you cannot leave the ſight of one thing without having a deſire to ſee another; and if we had not this deſire of ſeeing more, we ſhould not have had any pleaſure in ſeeing what we do ſee. Thus when a part of a picture is ſhewn to us, our deſire to ſee the part which is yet concealed, is in proportion to the pleaſure we have had in what was ſhewn to us.

It is then the pleaſure we have in one object that leads us towards another. Hence it is, that the ſoul always ſeeks novelty, and is never at reſt. Thus will you be ſure to delight the ſoul, when you make

make it ſee many things, or more things than ſhe expected.

From this appears the reaſon why we are pleaſed when we ſee a garden that is very regular; and why we are alſo pleaſed when we ſee a ſpot that is rough and wild. The ſame cauſe produces theſe effects.

As we love to ſee a great number of objects, we would enlarge our view, we would be in many places, we would run over more ſpace. In fine, our ſoul hates to be bound, and ſhe would as it were enlarge the ſphere of her preſence. Thus is it a great pleaſure for her, to extend her view to a diſtance. But how ſhould ſhe do it? In towns our view is bounded by houſes; it is ſo in the country, by a thouſand obſtacles; ſcarcely can we ſee three or four trees. Art comes to our aid, and diſcovers nature, who hides herſelf from us. We love art, and we love it better than nature, that is to ſay, better than nature when it is hid from our eyes. But when we find fine ſituations, when our ſight at liberty can ſee at a diſtance rivers, hills, meadows, and their diſpoſitions which are, as one may ſay, erected for the purpoſe, ſhe is enchanted in quite a different manner, than when ſhe ſees the gardens of Le Notre; becauſe nature copies herſelf: whereas art has always a ſameneſs. It is for this reaſon that in painting we are better pleaſed with a landſcape, than with the plan of the fineſt garden in the world.

What commonly makes a great thought, is when a thing is ſaid, that makes us ſee a great number of other things; and diſcovers to us all at once, what we could not have expected to have attained but by long ſtudy.

Florus in a few words repreſents to us all the faults of Hanibal, "While," ſays he, "he might "have made advantage of the "victory, he choſe rather to "enjoy it." *Cum victoria poſſetati, frui maluit.*

He gives us an idea of the whole war of Macedon, in ſaying, "To enter it, was to conquer it." *Introiſſe victoria fuit.*

He gives us an entire view of the life of Scipio, when ſpeaking of his youth, he ſays, 'This ſhall be 'Scipio, who is growing up for 'the deſtruction of Africa.' *Hic erit Scipio, qui in exitium Africæ creſcit.* You imagine before your eyes a child, who is riſing up and growing like a giant. Finally he ſhews us the great character of Hanibal, the condition of the univerſe, and all the grandeur of the Roman people, when he ſays, "Hanibal, "driven from his country, ſought "through the univerſe an enemy "to the Roman people." *Qui profugus ex Africa hoſtem populo Romano toto orbe querebat.*

Of the pleaſure that order gives.

It is not ſufficient to ſhew the ſoul many things; they muſt be ſhewn in order; for then we recollect what we have ſeen; and we begin to imagine what we ſhall ſee. Our ſoul congratulates herſelf on her extent, and on her penetration. But in a work where there is no order, the ſoul at every turn, perceives that the order ſhe would eſtabliſh is diſturbed. The arrangement that the author has made, and that which we make for ourſelves, are confounded with

one

one another; the ſoul retains nothing, foreſees nothing, ſhe is humbled by the confuſion of her ideas, by the inanity that is left upon her; ſhe is fatigued to no purpoſe, and can taſte no pleaſure. For this reaſon, except when the deſign is to expreſs or ſhew confuſion, they always put an order even in confuſion itſelf. Thus the painters groupe their figures. Thus thoſe who paint battles, place the thing which the eye is to diſtinguiſh, in the front, and throw the confuſion in the bottom and deepenings of their pictures.

Of the pleaſures that variety gives.

But if order is neceſſary, ſo alſo is variety. Without this the ſoul languiſhes. For things that are alike, ſeem to her to be the ſame. And if one part of a picture was diſcovered to us, reſembling another which we had ſeen, that object would be new without ſeeming ſo, and would give no pleaſure: and as the beauties of the works of art, which reſemble thoſe of nature, conſiſt only in the pleaſures that they raiſe in us; they muſt be made, as much as poſſible, capable of varying theſe pleaſures. The ſoul muſt be ſhewn things ſhe has not ſeen; ſhe muſt have ſentiments impreſſed on her different from thoſe ſhe had before.

It is thus that hiſtory pleaſes us from the variety of its accounts; romance, from the variety of its prodigies; theatrical pieces, from the variety of paſſions, that they cauſe; and 'tis from hence that thoſe who know how to inſtruct us modify, as much as they can, the uniform tone of inſtruction.

A long uniformity makes every thing inſupportable; the ſame order of periods long continued, wearies in an harangue. The ſame number and the ſame cadences tires one in a long poem. If it is true, that a long alley is made from Moſcow to Peterſburgh, the traveller muſt be tired to death, ſhut up between the two ſides of that alley. And he who ſhould live for any time in the Alps, would come down diſguſted with the happieſt ſituations and the moſt charming proſpects.

The ſoul loves variety; but we have ſaid ſhe loves it only as ſhe is made for knowledge and diſcovery. She muſt then ſee; and variety muſt not prevent her ſeeing; that is, a thing muſt be ſimple enough to be ſeen, and have variety enough to be ſeen with pleaſure.

Some things ſeem to have great variety and have it not; and ſome ſeem uniform and have great variety.

The Gothic architecture ſeems to have great variety; but the confuſion of its ornaments fatigues by their littleneſs; which makes it impoſſible to diſtinguiſh any one from the reſt; and their number is ſo great that it is impoſſible for the eye to reſt on any of them. So that it diſpleaſes through the very means that were choſen to make it agreeable.

A Gothic building is a kind of ænigma to the eye; and the ſoul is embarraſſed, as when ſhe is preſented with an obſcure poem.

The Grecian architecture, on the contrary, ſeems uniform; but as it has the diviſions that are neceſſary, and as many as are neceſſary to let the ſoul ſee clearly ſo much as ſhe can without fatigue, and yet enough to employ her, ſhe has that variety which makes her look on it with pleaſure.

The

The Grecian architecture which has few and great divisions, imitates great things. The soul receives a certain dignity that reigns throughout.

Of the pleasures that symmetry gives.

I have said that the soul loves variety: yet in most things she likes to see a sort of symmetry; this seems a contradiction. I explain it thus.

One of the principal causes of the pleasures of the soul in seeing objects, is the ease with which she discovers them; and the reason why symmetry is so pleasing to the soul, is that it saves her trouble, that it eases her, and, as one may say, cuts off half the work.

From whence we may draw a general rule.—Wherever symmetry is useful to the soul and may assist her functions, it is agreeable to her; but wherever it is useless it becomes distasteful, because it takes away variety. Therefore things that we see in succession ought to have variety; for our soul has no difficulty in seeing them; those on the contrary that we see at one glance, ought to have symmetry. Thus at one glance we see the front of a building, a parterre, a temple; in such things there is always a symmetry, which pleases the soul by the facility it gives her of taking the whole object at once.

As the object that is to be seen at one glance ought to be simple, so it ought to be one, and the parts should all refer to the main object; it is for this too that symmetry is agreeable, it unites all the parts into one whole.

It is in nature that every whole should be finished; and the soul that sees the whole, will not that any part should be imperfect, and this again makes symmetry so lovely; there must be a sort of equal weight and ballance; and a building with one wing, or with one wing shorter than the other, is as far from being finished, as a body with one arm, or with one arm too short.

Of contrasts.

The soul loves symmetry — she loves contrasts also; this requires explanation. For example.——If nature demands that painters and sculptors should preserve a symmetry in the parts of their figures, she requires too on the other hand, that they should make a contrast in their attitudes. On foot set like the other; one member placed just like the other, are insupportable; the reason of which is, that this symmetry makes the attitudes almost always alike, as we see in the Gothic figures, which are by that means all alike. Thus there remains no longer any varieties in the productions of art. Moreover nature has not so formed us; she has given us motion, she has not fixed us in our actions and our manners like Pagods; and if men thus bound up and constrained are insupportable, what must such productions of art be?

The attitudes then must be contrasted, especially in works of sculpture, which from its natural coldness, admits of no fire by force of contrast and situation.

But as I have said, that the variety which they have endeavoured to put into the Gothic, has given it an uniformity, so it often happens that the variety which they have endeavoured at by means of the contrast, is become a symmetry and a vicious uniformi

This

This is perceivable, not only in certain works of ſculpture and painting; but alſo in the ſtyle of ſome writers, who in every phraſe, contraſt the beginning with the end, by a continual antitheſis, ſuch as St. Auguſtine, and other of the later Roman writers; and ſome moderns, as St. Evremont. The turn of phraſe always the ſame, and always uniform, is extremely diſpleaſing. This perpetual contraſt becomes a ſymmetry, and that affected oppoſition becomes uniformity.

The mind finds ſo little variety there, that when you have ſeen one part of the phraſe, you always gueſs the other: you ſee words that are oppoſed to one another, but oppoſed in the ſame manner; you ſee a turn in the phraſe, but it is always the ſame.

Many painters have fallen into the fault of mixing contraſts every where, and without art, ſo that when you ſee one figure, you gueſs immediately at the diſpoſition of the one that is near it. This continual diverſity became ſomething like it: whereas nature, who throws things into diſorder, never ſhews any affectation of continued contraſt; not to ſay that ſhe does not put all bodies in motion, and in a forced motion too. She is more varied than that; ſhe leaves ſome at reſt, and gives others different ſorts of motion.

Of the pleaſures of ſurprize.

That diſpoſition of the ſoul which always inclines her to different objects, makes her taſte all the pleaſures that come from ſurprize; which is a ſenſation pleaſing to the ſoul, both from the view itſelf, and from the quickneſs of the action; for ſhe ſees or feels a thing that ſhe did not expect, or in a manner ſhe did not expect.

A thing may ſurprize us, not only as it is marvellous, but alſo as new, and even as unexpected. And in this laſt caſe, the principal ſentiment is joined to an acceſſary ſentiment, founded on the thing's being new, or unexpected.

It is from hence that the game of hazard affects us; it lets ſee a continual ſucceſſion of unexpected events.

It is from hence too, that theatrical pieces pleaſe us; they ſhew themſelves by degrees, they conceal the events till they happen; always preparing for us new cauſe of ſurprize, and often ſtrike us in letting us ſee them ſuch as we might have foreſeen them.

Surprize may be produced by the thing, or by the manner of perceiving it; for we ſee a thing as greater or ſmaller, than it really is, or different from what it is, or we ſee the thing itſelf, but with an acceſſary idea that ſurprizes us, ſuch as the difficulty of making it; or the perſon who made it; or the time when it was made; or the manner in which it was made; or ſome other circumſtance that is joined to it.

Suetonius deſcribes the crimes of Nero with a coldneſs that ſurprizes us, in making us almoſt believe that he does not feel the horror of what he is relating; all at once he changes his ſtyle, and ſays, "The "univerſe having ſuffered this mon-"ſter for 14 years, at laſt gave him "up." *Tale monſtrum per quatuordecim annos perpeſſus terrarum orbis, tandem deſtituit.* This produces in the mind different ſorts of ſurprize; we are ſurprized at the change of the author's ſtyle; at the diſcovery of his

his different way of thinking; at his manner of telling in fo few words, the event of fo great a revolution, fo that the mind finds a great number of different fentiments that concur to fhake her, and to compofe a pleafure for her.

Of the different caufes which may produce a fentiment.

It muft be remarked, that a fentiment is not commonly produced in our foul by one fingle caufe. It is, if I may venture upon the term, a certain dofe, which at once produces ftrength and variety. Genius confifts in ftriking many organs at once; and if the feveral writers are examined, perhaps it will be feen, that the beft, and thofe who have pleafed moft, are thofe who have excited in the foul the greateft number of fenfations, at one and the fame time.

We love play becaufe it fatisfies our avarice; that is to fay, our defire of having more: it flatters our vanity by the idea of preference that fortune gives us, and of the attention that others pay to our fuccefs. It fatisfies our curiofity, in giving us a fpectacle. In fhort, it gives us the different pleafures of furprize.

Of delicacy.

Delicate people are thofe, who to every idea, or to every tafte, join many acceffary ideas, or many acceffary taftes. Grofs people have but one fenfation; their foul can neither compound nor diffolve; they neither add any thing to, nor take any thing away from what naturegives; whereas delicate people, who are in love, by compofition form almoft all the pleafures that are to be found in love. Polixene and Apicius carry to their tables, taftes that are unknown to us vulgar eaters: and thofe who judge the works of wit with tafte, have and make to themfelves an infinity of fenfations that other men are ftrangers to.

The *Je ne fai quoi*, in perfons and in things, is often an invifible charm, a natural grace, that cannot be defined, and which we have been forced to call the *Je ne fai quoi*. I take it to be an effect principally founded on furprize; we are touched by being more pleafed with a perfon than we at firft expected to be; and we are agreeably furprized to find thofe faults overcome, which our eyes pointed out to us, but which our hearts no longer acknowledge. This is the reafon why ugly women are very often poffeffed of the graces, and that it is but feldom that beautiful women have them. Graces are oftener found in the wit than in the face; for a fine face is feen at once, and fcarce any of it is concealed; but wit fhews itfelf by little and little, juft when it chufes, and juft as much as it chufes; it can conceal itfelf, and make its appearance give that fort of furprize which conftitutes the graces.

The graces are not fo much in the features of the face, as in the manners; for the manners are every inftant new, and may every moment create furprize.

Progrefs of furprize.

What makes the greateft beauty, is when a thing furprizes but moderately at firft, but keeps up that furprize, increafes it, and at laft leads to admiration. The works of Raphael ftrike but little at firft fight; but an extraordinary expref-

fion

fion, a ftrong colouring, an uncommon attitude of a worfe painter, feizes us at the firft glance, becaufe it is what we have not been ufed to fee. Raphael may be compared to Virgil, and the painters of Venice with their forced attitudes to Lucan: Virgil, more natural, ftrikes lefs at firft, to ftrike the more forcibly afterwards; Lucan ftrikes more at firft, and affects us lefs afterwards.

The exact proportion of the famous church of St. Peter, makes it not appear at firft fo great as it really is; for we do not fee immediately where to fix ourfelves to judge of its greatnefs. If it was lefs in breadth, we fhould be ftruck with the length; if it was fhorter, we fhould be ftruck with its breadth; but as we continue our examination it grows upon the eye, and the aftonifhment increafes. It may be compared to the Pyrenees, where the eye that thinks it fees all at firft, difcovers mountain behind mountain, and lofes itfelf more and more.

It often happens that our foul feels a pleafure when fhe has a fentiment that fhe cannot herfelf unfold, and that a thing feems to her abfolutely different from what it is, which gives her a fentiment of furprize, which fhe cannot get out of. This is an example of it. It is known that Michael Angelo feeing the Pantheon, which was the greateft temple at Rome, faid he would make one like it, but that he would place it in the air. Upon this model then he made the dome of St. Peter; but he made the pillars fo maffive, that that dome which is like a mountain over ones head, appears light to the eye that confiders it. The mind at the time remains uncertain, between what fhe fees, and what fhe knows, and remains furprized to fee a mafs a once fo vaft, and fo light.

Of the beauties which refult from a certain embarraffment of the foul.

The foul is often furprized from not being able to reconcile what fhe now fees, with what fhe has feen. There is a great lake in Italy called Lago Maggiore. It is a little fea, whofe fhores fhew nothing but what is entirely favage. Fifteen miles within the lake are two ifles of a quarter of a mile round, called the Barromes, which, in my opinion, is of all the world the fpot the moft delightful; the foul is aftonifhed in the romantic contraft, from a pleafing recollection of the wonders of Romana, where having paffed by rocks and a dry country, you find yourfelf in a fairy land. Contrafts always ftrike us, becaufe the two things always heighten one another.

Thefe forts of furpri s the pleafure that is found in all oppofitions, in all antithefes and fuch like figures. When Florus fays, "*Sora & algidum!* who would believe it had been formidable to us! Saticula and Corniculum were once provinces. We blufh for the Borilians and Virulani, but we triumphed over them. In fhort, Tibur our fuburb, Prenefte where our houfes of pleafure are, were once the objects of the vows we made at the Capitol." This author, I fay, fhews us at once the grandeur of the Romans, and the littlenefs of their beginnings, and thefe two things here raife our wonder.

It may be here remarked, how wide the difference is between the antithefis of ideas, and the antithefis of expreffion. The antithefis of expreffion is never concealed; that of of ideas is. One has always the ſame dreſs, the other changes when you pleaſe. The one is varied, the other is not.

The ſame Florus, in ſpeaking of the Samnites, ſays, "Their towns "were deſtroyed, that it is at this "day difficult to find the ſubject of "four and twenty triumphs." *Ut non facile appareat materia quatuor et viginti triumphorum.* And by the ſame words, that mark the deſtruction of that people, he lets us ſee the greatneſs of their courage and their firmneſs.

One of the things which pleaſes us moſt, is the ſimple, but it is alſo the moſt difficult ſtyle, becauſe it is preciſely between the noble and the mean; and is ſo near the mean, that it is very difficult to keep always on the brink of it without ſometimes falling into it.

The muſicians have owned, that the muſic which is eaſieſt ſung is moſt difficult to compoſe: a ſure proof that our pleaſures, and the art which gives them, lie between certain boundaries.

When a thing is ſhewn us with certain circumſtances or acceſſaries, which aggrandize it, it appears noble to us. This is more particularly obſervable in compariſons, where the mind ſhould always gain and never loſe; for the compariſon ſhould always add ſomething, to ſhew it in more grandeur; or if it is not grandeur that is required, more fine or more delicate.

When a thing is to be ſhewn fine, the ſoul would rather ſee a manner compared with a manner; an action with an action; than a thing with a thing; as an hero to a lion, a woman to a ſtar, a nimble man to a ſtag.

Michael Angelo is the maſter who has thrown ſomething noble into all his ſubjects. In his famous Bacchus, he has not, like the Flemiſh painters, ſhewn a tottering figure, and which is as it were in the air; that would be unworthy the majeſty of a god; he paints him firm on his legs: but he ſo happily gives him the gaiety of drunkenneſs, and ſuch a joy in ſeeing the liquor run that he pours into his cup, that there is nothing ſo admirable.

In the Paſſion, that is in the gallery at Florence, he has painted the Virgin ſtanding, who looks upon her crucified Son, without grief, without pity, without regret, without tears. He ſuppoſes her inſtructed in the great myſtery, and thereby makes her ſupport with grandeur the ſight of that death.

Julio Romano, in his chamber of giants at Mantua, where he repreſents Jupiter throwing down his thunder on them, lets us ſee all the gods affrighted; but Juno is near Jupiter, with an aſſured air ſhe points out to him a giant, againſt whom he ought to launch his thunder; by this he gives her an air of grandeur, that the other gods have not. The nearer they are to Jupiter, the more aſſured they are; and that is very natural, for in a battle, the fear ceaſes near him who has the advantage.

After this general theory of Taſte, an application of ſome of the moſt ſtriking rules, in the practice of one of the moſt agreeable of all arts, that of laying out gardens, will not prove diſagreeable to the reader. It will not be the leſs agreeable, that the obſervations are drawn from a country, which while it is ſo remote from us in ſituation, manners, and cuſtoms, preſerves ſo ſtrong a conformity

in

in this article, which the best ideas, which the improvement of taste has introduced amongst us in England. This piece, we may venture to say, is much the best which has ever been written on this subject.

Of the art of laying out gardens among the Chinese, by Mr. Chambers.

THE gardens, says he, which I saw in China, were very small; nevertheless from them, and what could be gathered from Lepqua, a celebrated Chinese painter, with whom I had several conversations on the subject of gardening, I think I have acquired sufficient knowledge of their notions on this head.

Nature is their pattern, and their aim is to imitate her in all her beautiful irregularities. The first consideration is the form of the ground, whether it be flat, sloping, hilly, or mountainous, extensive, or of small compass, of a dry or marshy nature, abounding with rivers and springs, or liable to a scarcity of water; to all which circumstances they attend with great care, chusing such dispositions as humour the ground, can be executed with the least expence, hide its defects, and set its advantages in the most conspicuous light.

As the Chinese are not fond of walking, we seldom meet with avenues or spacious walks, as in our European plantations. The whole ground is laid out in a variety of scenes, and you are led, by winding passages cut in the groves, to the different points of view, each of which is marked by a seat, a building, or some other object.

The perfection of their gardens consists in the number, beauty, and diversity of these scenes. The Chinese gardeners, like the European painters, collect from nature the most pleasing objects, which they endeavour to combine in such a manner, as not only to appear to the best advantage separately, but likewise to unite in forming an elegant and striking whole.

Their arts distinguish three different species of scenes, to which they give the appellations of pleasing, horrid, and enchanted. Their enchanted scenes answer, in a great measure, to what we call romantic, and in these they make use of several artifices to excite surprize. Sometimes they make a rapid stream, or torrent, pass under ground, the turbulent noise of which strikes the ear of the new comer, who is at a loss to know from whence it proceeds. At other times they dispose the rocks, buildings, and other objects that form the composition in such a manner, as that the wind passing through the different interstices and cavities, made in them for that purpose, causes strange and uncommon sounds. They introduce into these scenes all kinds of extraordinary trees, plants, and flowers, form artificial and complicated echos, and let loose different sorts of monstrous birds and animals.

In their scenes of horror, they introduce impending rocks, dark caverns, and impetuous cataracts rushing down the mountains from all sides; the trees are ill-formed, and seemingly torn to pieces by the violence of tempests; some are thrown down, and intercept the

courſe

course of the torrents, appearing as if they had been brought down by the fury of the waters; others look as if shattered and blasted by the force of lightening: the buildings are some in ruins, others half-consumed by fire, and some miserable huts dispersed in the mountains serve, at once, to indicate the existence and wretchedness of the inhabitants. These scenes are generally succeeded by pleasing ones. The Chinese artists, knowing how powerfully contrast operates on the mind, constantly practise sudden transitions, and a striking opposition of forms, colours, and shades. Thus they conduct you from limited prospects to extensive views; from objects of horror to scenes of delight; from lakes and rivers, to plains, hills, and woods; to dark and gloomy colours they oppose such as are brilliant, and to complicated forms simple ones; distributing by a judicious arrangement, the different masses of light and shade, in such a manner as to render the composition at once distinct in its parts, and striking in the whole.

Where the ground is extensive, and a multiplicity of scenes are to be introduced, they generally adapt each to one single point of view: but where it is limited, and affords no room for variety, they endeavour to remedy this defect, by disposing the objects so, that being viewed from different points, they produce different representations; and sometimes by an artful disposition, such as have no resemblance to each other.

In their large gardens they contrive different scenes for morning, noon, and evening; erecting, at the proper points of view, buildings adapted to the recreations of each particular time of the day: and in their small ones (where, as has been observed, one arrangement produces many representations) they dispose in the same manner, at the several points of view, buildings, which, from their use point out the time of day for enjoying the scene in its perfection.

As the climate of China is exceeding hot, they employ a great deal of water in their gardens. In the small ones, if the situation admits, they frequently lay almost the whole ground under water; leaving only some islands and rocks: and in their large ones they introduce extensive lakes, rivers, and canals. The banks of their lakes and rivers are variegated in imitation of nature; being sometimes bare and gravelly, sometimes covered with woods quite to the water's edge. In some places flat, and adorned with flowers and shrubs; in others steep, rocky, and forming caverns, into which part of the waters discharge themselves with noise and violence. Sometimes you see meadows covered with cattle, or rice-grounds that run out into the lakes, leaving between them passages for vessels; and sometimes groves, into which enter, in different parts, creeks, and rivulets, sufficiently deep to admit boats; their banks being planted with trees, whose spreading branches in some places, form arbours, under which the boats pass. These generally conduct to some very interesting object; such as a magnificent building; places on the top of a mountain cut into terrasses; a casine situated in the midst of a lake; a cascade; a grotto cut into a variety of apartments;

ments; an artificial rock; and many other ſuch inventions.

Their rivers are ſeldom ſtraight, but ſerpentine, and broken into many irregular points; ſometimes they are narrow, noiſy, and rapid; at other times, deep, broad, and ſlow. Both in their rivers and lakes are ſeen reeds, with other aquatic plants and flowers; particularly the lyen hoa, of which they are very fond. They frequently erect mills, and other hydraulic machines, the motions of which enliven the ſcene. They have alſo a great number of veſſels of different forms and ſizes. In their lakes they interſperſe iſlands; ſome of them barren, and ſurrounded with rocks and ſhoals; others enriched with every thing that art and nature can furniſh moſt perfect. They likewiſe form artificial rocks; and in compoſitions of this kind the Chineſe ſurpaſs all other nations. The making them is a diſtinct profeſſion: and there are at Canton, and probably in moſt other cities of China, numbers of artificers conſtantly employed in this buſineſs. The ſtone they are made of comes from the ſouthern coaſts of China: it is of a blueiſh caſt, and worn into irregular forms by the action of the waves. The Chineſe are exceeding nice in the choice of this ſtone, inſomuch that I have ſeen ſeveral tael given for a bit no bigger than a man's fiſt, when it happened to be of a beautiful form and lively colour. But theſe ſelect pieces they uſe in landſcapes for their apartments; in gardens they employ a coarſer ſort, which they join with a blueiſh cement, and form rocks of a conſiderable ſize. I have ſeen ſome of theſe exquiſitely fine, and ſuch as diſcovered an uncommon elegance of taſte in the contriver. When they are large they make in them caves and grottos, with openings, through which you diſcover diſtant proſpects. They cover them in different places with trees, ſhrubs, briars, and moſs; placing on their tops little temples, or other buildings, to which you aſcend by rugged and irregular ſteps cut in the rock.

When there is a ſufficient ſupply of water, and proper ground, the Chineſe never fail to form caſcades in their gardens. They avoid all regularity in theſe works, obſerving nature according to her operations in that mountainous country. The waters burſt out from among the caverns and windings of the rocks. In ſome places a large and impetuous cataract appears; in others are ſeen many leſſer falls. Sometimes the view of the caſcade is intercepted by trees, whoſe leaves and branches only leave room to diſcover the waters, in ſome places, as they fall down the ſides of the mountain. They frequently throw rough wooden bridges from one rock to another, over the ſteepeſt part of the cataract; and often intercept its paſſage by trees and heaps of ſtones, that ſeem to have been brought down by the violence of the torrent.

In their plantations they vary the forms and colours of their trees; mixing ſuch as have large and ſpreading branches with thoſe of pyramid figures, and dark greens with brighter, interſperſing among them ſuch as produce flowers, of which they have ſome that flouriſh a great part of the year. The weeping willow is one of their favourite trees, and always among thofe that border their lakes and rivers, being fo planted as to have its branches hanging over the water. They likewife introduce trunks of decayed trees, fometimes erect, and at other times lying on the ground, being very nice about their forms, and the colour of the bark and mofs on them.

Various are the artifices they employ to furprize. Sometimes they lead you through dark caverns and gloomy paffages, at the iffue of which you are, on a fudden, ftruck with the view of a delicious landfcape, enriched with every thing that luxuriant nature affords moft beautiful. At other times you are conducted through avenues and walks, that gradually diminifh and grow rugged, till the paffage is at length entirely intercepted and rendered impracticable, by bufhes, briars, and ftones; when unexpectedly a rich and extenfive profpect opens to view, fo much the more pleafing, as it was lefs looked for.

Another of their artifices is to hide fome part of a compofition by trees, or other intermediate objects. This naturally excites the curiofity of the fpectator to take a nearer view; when he is furprized by fome unexpected fcene, or fome reprefentation totally oppofite to the thing he looked for. The termination of their lakes they always hide, leaving room for the imagination to work; and the fame rule they obferve in other compofitions, wherever it can be put in practice.

Though the Chinefe are not well verfed in optics, yet experience has taught them that objects appear lefs in fize, and grow dim in colour, in propofition as they are more removed from the eye of the fpectator. Thefe difcoveries have given rife to an artifice, which they fometimes put in practice. It is the forming profpects in perfpective, by introducing buildings, veffels, and other objects, leffened according as they are more diftant from the point of view; and that the deception may be ftill more ftriking, they give a greyifh tinge to the diftant parts of the compofition, and plant in the remoter parts of thefe fcenes trees of a fainter colour, and fmaller growth, than thofe that appear in the front, or fore-ground; by thefe means rendering what in reality is trifling and limited, great and confiderable in appearance.

The Chinefe generally avoid ftraight lines; yet they do not abfolutely reject them. They fometimes make avenues, when they have any interefting object to expofe to view. Roads they always make ftraight, unlefs the unevennefs of the ground, or other impediments, afford at leaft a pretext for doing otherwife. Where the ground is entirely level, they look upon it as an abfurdity to make a ferpentine road; for they fay, that it muft either be made by art, or worn by the conftant paffage of travellers: in either of which cafes it is not natural to fuppofe men would chufe a crooked line, when they might go by a ftraight one.

What we call clumps, the Chinefe gardeners are not unacquainted with; but they ufe them fomewhat more fparingly than we do. They never fill a whole piece of ground with clumps; they confider a plantation as painters do a picture, and groupe their trees in the fame manner as thefe do their figures, having

having their principal and ſubſervient maſſes.

This is the ſubſtance of what I learnt during my ſtay in China, partly from my own obſervation, but chiefly from the leſſons of Lepqua. And from what has been ſaid it may be inferred, that the art of laying out grounds after the Chineſe manner is exceedingly difficult, and not to be attained by perſons of narrow intellects: for though the precepts are ſimple and obvious, yet the putting them in execution requires genius, judgment, and experience, ſtrong imagination, and a thorough knowledge of the human mind; this method being fixed to no certain rule, but liable to as many variations as there are different arrangements in the works of the creation.

Deſcription of Lough-lane, or the lake of Killarney, in the barony of Magunihy, in the county of Kerry, in Ireland. From Mr. Smith's ingenious account of that county, lately printed at Dublin.

THE mountain of Mangerton, which ſtands ſouth-eaſt of Lough-lane, is eſteemed one of the higheſt in this kingdom: by the experiment of the barometer, its altitude was found to be one thouſand and twenty yards, perpendicular, above the lake of Killarney, which is conſiderably higher than the ſea; for that lake in diſcharging itſelf, runs a courſe of ſome miles, and forms what is called the river Lane, before it joins the ocean. The mountains called the Reeks, which lie to the weſtward of Mangerton, ſeem, by the eye, to be rather higher than the mountain; but hills which are conical, and terminated in points, appear higher at a diſtance, than thoſe mountains which have a large ſurface on their tops: as ſteeples, which are terminated by ſpires, ſeem to be higher than thoſe covered with domes, the points of the former being, as it were, more hid and loſt in the atmoſphere, than the other. They are ſteeper than Mangerton, and have more terrible precipices, and declivities; ſo that it was in a manner impoſſible to determine the height by the barometer. On the weſt ſide of that mountain, is a large and deep hole, filled with water, which they call the Devil's punch-bowl: it overflows, and makes an agreeable caſcade, down the ſide of the mountain, in view of Mucruſs houſe, the ſeat of Edward Herbert, Eſq; by opening a large cut on the ſide of his baſon, there would be a broader, more conſtant, and nobler ſupply of water, which might afford a beautiful cataract, for the greateſt part of the year. This water ſupplies the mills for the iron works, and then falls into Lough-lane, which beautiful lake I am now about to deſcribe. One of the beſt proſpects which it affords, is on a riſing ground, near the ruined cathedral of Aghadoe: not but there are many other fine views of it, from every other ſide, but few of them take in ſo many particulars as may be obſerved from that ſtation. For from hence is to be ſeen, one of the moſt delicious landſcapes in Ireland; and, perhaps, few countries in Europe afford better. But this is ſuch a maſterpiece, that even the Pouſſins, Salvator Roſa, or the moſt eminent painter in that way, might here furniſh himſelf with ſufficient matter,

ter, not only to form one, but several entertaining profpects. From this eminence a furvey may be taken of the greateft part of this beautiful lake; and likewife of that ftupendous amphitheatre of mountains which are ranged along the oppofite fhore. Towards the fouth-eaft, ftands the above-mentioned mountain, called Mangerton, whofe feet the lake wafhes, and whofe fummit is generally loft in the clouds, it being, from the above-recited experiment, juftly efteemed one of the higheft mountains in Ireland. More towards the center lake, is an high mole, called Turk, whofe fides, down to the verge of the water, are beautifully cloathed with groves, of various kinds of trees. One part of this hill flopes away like a promontory, terminating in the lake, forming one fide of a canal, which is a paffage into the upper lake; as doth the point of another mountain called Glenna, the other fide of this ftrait, which is adorned alfo with foreft trees. As a fine contraft to this verdure, at the back of thefe mountains ftand others, fhaped into pyramids, being only naked rocks of a vaft height. The grandeur and magnificence of thefe mountains, not only entertain and furprize the fpectator, but he muft be alfo agreeably amufed, in contemplating the infinite variety of beautiful colouring they afford. For, in one part may be feen the gayeft verdure, blended with fcarlet fruit, and fnowy bloffoms, well known properties of the arbutus; and in other places, the moft elegant variety of brown and yellow tints, caufed by other kinds of trees and fhrubs, appears: all thefe are intermixed with rock-work; and to foften the whole, a deep, fmooth, and noble bafon of water, extends itfelf beneath this fcenery. But to give the reader an adequate idea of this place, would require the pencil of fome excellent painter, rather than the pen of any profe writer. To the weft of Glenna, ftands the lofty pike called Tomifh, variegated half way to its top, with a waving foreft; and down whofe fides, efpecially after rains, run very confiderable cataracts into the great lake. There are many other hills ftill running more weft, as far as the eye can trace for many miles: the neareft and moft furprizing for their loftinefs, are the Reeks already mentioned, whofe tops refemble fo many pinacles or rather fpires loft in the clouds. The water is light and pure, and notwithftanding the great variety of minerals, which furround this lake, it doth not feem to be impregnated with any of them. The ancient verfes of Ninius, who wrote in the ninth century, and which Mr. O-Flaherty, in his Ogygia, alfo cites, make mention of them.

Mamonia ftagnum, Lochlenius undique Zonis
Quatuor ambitur: prior eft ex ære, fecunda
Plumbea, de rigido conflatur tertia ferro:
Quarta renidenti pallefcit linea ftanno.

As for copper, few mines in Europe have produced fuch quantity of ore, as that work lately difcovered near Mucrufs; having afforded, in the fpace of a year after its working, three hundred feventy-five tons of ore, which produces from an ounce of the general fample, five penny weight,

eight

eight grains of copper, being considerably more than a fourth part of pure metal of a very fine quality; and the Briſtol company, to whom the proprietors of this work ſold it, muſt have extracted a greater proportion of copper, as it is well known, from the laws of attraction, that a large portion of ore will yield more on the aſſay, than a ſmall quantity. Lead ore hath been alſo diſcovered near this lake; and the adjacent mountains all abound with iron. As to tin ore, there hath been no diſcovery made yet to any purpoſe; although I do not queſtion, but it will be alſo found, for I have picked up ſmall ſpecimens of ore, which contain ſome tin, at no great diſtance from this lake; and thus far are the above ancient verſes verified. O-Flaherty alſo takes notice, that pearls have been found in this lake, "*Et in eo ſtagno margaritæ multæ reperiuntur, quas ponunt reges in auribus ſuis.*" But becauſe of the great depth of the lough, they are not ſo frequently found in it, as in the river Lane which runs out of it. As one ſide of this lake conſiſts of the abovementioned range of formidable hills, ſo the oppoſite ſide is adorned with a level and beautiful country, with the town of Killarney, and the habitations and improvements of ſeveral gentlemen, at different diſtances. But before I deſcribe theſe, it will be neceſſary to mention ſomewhat of the ſeveral iſlands, which lie beautifully ſcattered over the lake; as alſo of the ſurprizing echoes that it affords. The moſt noted of theſe iſlands is that of Roſs, which is rather a peninſula, being only ſeparated by a ſmall cut through a moraſs, from the main land, over which is a bridge. On it ſtands an ancient caſtle, formerly the ſeat of O-Donaghoe Roſs, which hath a new barrack adjoining to it. This place hath been, for ſome years paſt, a military garriſon, having a governor appointed for it, upon the eſtabliſhment. Before the caſtle, are a few old diſmounted iron guns, which give it ſomething of the air of a fortification. The caſtle had been flanked with round turrets, which, together with its ſituation, rendered it a place of ſome ſtrength. In the wars of 1641, it ſurrendered to Ludlow, who was attended in the expedition by Lord Broghill and Sir Hardreſs Waller; and was the laſt place that held out in Munſter againſt the Engliſh parliament. The greateſt part of this iſland is covered with wood; and it is no diſagreeable ſpot, for ſuch gentlemen of the army quartered here who are fond of fiſhing, hunting, or fowling. The iſland of Inniſfallen, is next to Roſs in quantity of land; in it are the ruins of a very ancient religious houſe, founded by St. Finian, ſirnamed the Leper, who flouriſhed towards the middle of the ſixth century. He is the patron ſaint of theſe parts, and to him the cathedral of Aghadoe is alſo dedicated. The remains of this abbey are very extenſive, although the walls in many places are levelled to the ground; its ſituation was extremely romantic and retired. Upon the diſſolution of religious houſes, the poſſeſſions of this abbey were granted to Captain Robert Collam. This iſland contains about twelve acres, and hath ſeveral very pleaſant coves, agreeably wooded, for landing upon it. It yields ſo great a profuſion of ſweet herbage, that the kine which are put into it to fatten, thrive ſo prodigiouſly, that their fat becomes a kind of rich marrow, in a very ſhort time. The more fleſhy parts are in a manner marbled with fat, but their tallow is too ſoft to make candles, tho' it is proper enough for ſoap. On the eaſt ſide of the iſland, the walls of an old chapel have been lately repaired by ſome gentlemen, who frequently uſe it as a banqueting-houſe. There are beſides timber trees, the remains of ſeveral fruit trees, as plumbs, pears, &c. which have outlived the deſolation that hath ſeized on the cells of thoſe recluſes who firſt planted them. Many of theſe trees had fruit ripe on them when I was in the iſland; the plumbs in particular, being of a large red kind, were very fine. Here are alſo the fruit of the ſorbus or ſervice tree, likewiſe the arbutus, and other ſhrubs, which were all planted by the monks, tho' the neighbouring inhabitants will have them to be the ſpontaneous production of the ſoil. In ſhort, it is a beautiful, romantic wilderneſs, decorated, at preſent, with theſe plantations, and its venerable ruins, which are no ſmall addition to the beauties of Loughlane. Rabbit-Iſland ſtands to the weſt of Innisfallen, and is chiefly remarkable for its quarries of good lime-ſtone. An infinite number of iſlands of a ſmaller ſize, ſpangle and adorn this lake, moſt of which are covered with the arbutus, and ſeveral other beautiful ſhrubs. One of them from a fancied repreſentation, reſembles, at ſome diſtance, the figure of an horſe, in a drinking poſture; another is called O-Donaghoe's priſon; and a third his garden. Moſt of them are of marble, cloathed with ever-green ſhrubs, growing out of the crevices of the rocks. Some of the iſlands in the upper lake are of ſuch a ſtupendous height, that they reſemble, at a diſtance, ſo many lofty towers ſtanding in the water, and being many of them crowned with wreaths of arbutus, repreſent the ruins of ſtately palaces. Their edges are ſo much worn by the daſhing of the water againſt their ſides, and by frequent rains waſhing away the earth, and time hath ſo disjointed many of the marble rocks, that ſeveral of them hang in a moſt ſurprizing and tottering manner, and repreſent a rude kind of confuſed architecture, almoſt without foundations. In others of them, the waters have worn paſſages ſufficiently large for boats to go through theſe tottering arches, which in ſome places (though they are of an immenſe weight) are only upheld by very ſlender pillars.

The arbutus which cloaths theſe iſlands, gives even the haggard winter the beautiful appearance of ſpring; for in that melancholy ſeaſon, this tree puts on its higheſt bloom; which rarely growing in other places, is more likely to be admired by ſtrangers in this. The preparation of charcoal, for the iron works, hath been the occaſion of a great deſtruction of this beautiful tree in other parts of the country: and it is ſaid, that even here, it ſuffered much by an accidental fire that laid waſte a great part of a foreſt. Its growth, upon rocks of marble, where no earth appears, and ſo high above the ſurface of the water, renders it a matter of both ſurprize and pleaſure*.

This

* The arbutus, ſaith Sir Thomas Molineux, (in the Philoſophical Tranſactions, No. 227) is not to be found any where, of ſpontaneous growth, nearer to

This tree is extremely agreeable in every different circumſtance of vegetation, for it hath, at one and the ſame time, ripe and green fruit upon its branches, which, as they approach to ripeneſs, from green become yellow, and at length terminate in a fine ſcarlet colour, reſembling in form a field ſtrawberry, though in ſize that of the beſt garden kind.

The bloſſoms grow in cluſters of ſmall white bells, not unlike thoſe of the lilly of the valley; aud in ſuch great abundance, as, in that reſpect alone, to be equal in beauty to the lauruſtinus, and in other reſpects, much ſuperior to it; for the agreeable verdure of the leaves, not much unlike the bay, the ſcarlet hue of the tender part of the ſtalk, and all the different ſtages of vegetation, at one and the ſame time, from the knitting fruit to perfect ripeneſs, cannot but be exceeding agreeable to the curious obſerver.

Upwards of forty iſlands in this lake are covered with an intermixture of theſe trees and other ſhrubs; beſides, at leaſt a fourth part of the aſcent of the mountains, the verges of whoſe baſes, like that of Mangerton, and others abovementioned, are waſhed by the water of this lake.

Thus having mentioned what was remarkable of the mountains which ſurround it, and of the lake itſelf, and its iſlands, I ſhall beg leave to apply the following lines of the poet, whoſe deſcription of the lake Pergus is no ill picture of Lough-lane.

———*Non illa plura cajiſtros*
Carmina Cignorum labentibus audit in undis.
Silva coronat aquas, cingens latus omne; ſuiſque
Frondibus, ut velo, Phœbêos ſubmovet ignes.
Frigora dant rami, Tyrios humus humida flores,
Perpetuum ver eſt.

Ovid. Metam. Lib. V.

The principal inhabitants of theſe lofty mountains, except a few woodmen, kept in theſe foreſts by the lord of the ſoil, are great herds of red deer: the chace of which affords a much higher gratification to the ſportſmen than in many other places. And when a ſtag is hunted near this lake, nothing is more agreeably ſurprizing, than the repeated echoes: it being ſcarce poſſible to diſtinguiſh the real clangor of the French horns, or the true cry of the dogs, from the numberleſs reverberations of them among the rocks and mountains.

The echoes which are cauſed by this ſport, reverberate the ſound in

to Ireland than the moſt ſouthern parts of France, Italy, and Sicily; and there too, it is never known but as a frutex or ſhrub; whereas in the rocky parts of the county of Kerry, about Lough-lane, and in ſome of the rocky mountains adjacent, where the people of the country call it the cane apple, it flouriſhes naturally to that degree as to become a large tall tree. Petrus Bellonius obſerves, that it doth ſo in mount Athos in Macedonia; and Juba is quoted by Pliny, as mentioning it as a thing extraordinary, that the arbutus grows to an high tree in Arabia. Dr. Molineux adds, that the trunks of the trees of Ireland have been frequently four feet and a half in circumference, or 18 inches diameter; and that the trees grow to about nine or ten yards in height, and in ſuch a plenty, that many of them have been cut down to melt and refine the ore of ſilver and lead mines diſcovered near Roſs caſtle.

in a manner not to be deſcribed, nor believed by any but by thoſe who have heard them; the whole duration of a ſingle ſound being near a minute; and yet the repercuſſions are innumerable, and the variety inconceivable. But the reader may from this imagine, that a moſt ſurprizing muſical effect muſt ariſe from the variety of notes iſſuing from the throats of a large pack of buck-hounds, enlivened by the chearing throats of the ſportſmen, and the noiſe of the horns.

From the mountains the ſtag often flies to the ſoil for refreſhment, where he is ſometimes taken by perſons who attend in boats to caſt a rope over the horns; or the poor animal is purſued to ſome iſland, where he is killed; or being refreſhed by ſwimming, is hunted again to the mountains; in all, and every of which places, particularly towards the upper lake, the echoes are prodigious grand.

But the moſt aſtoniſhing ſounds are thoſe made by the diſcharge of cannon, placed in a proper ſituation, upon the points of ſome particular iſlands, which may beſt anſwer to the concave ſides of the mountains. When the piece is firſt exploded, there is no return of any particular ſound for near a minute; but then a loud clap of thunder, which laſts for ſeveral ſeconds, enſues; and after a ſhort pauſe, a ſecond, and ſo on, for ſeveral repetitions; like volleys of ſmall arms, which are alternately anſwered from the neighbouring mountains and vallies, and at length die away, with a noiſe reſembling that of the waves of the ocean beating againſt a concave ſhore. Nothing would be more pleaſant than the ringing of a peal of bells, placed in a ſmall iſland in this lake, which would ſeem to be more numerous than all thoſe of a great city, by being anſwered by numberleſs imaginary bells from the neighbouring rocks. But this, with ſeveral other methods of improving the natural beauties of the lake, particularly the placing tame ſwans on it, and other embelliſhments, is ſubmitted to its owner: who, by adding, if poſſible, to its native elegancy, might render it more pleaſing to travellers, who may be induced, out of curioſity, to viſit it, and which would be of great advantage to the adjacent town of Killarney.

There have been but few countries in Europe that have not contrived means to draw a concourſe of people to viſit them, whoſe very travelling and intercourſe increaſe wealth and trade; and are a ſecret motive to induce inhabitants to come and ſettle in them.

A river falls from the upper into the lower lake, diſcharging itſelf between the mountains of Glenna and Turk, between which hills is one of the moſt romantic glins that can be conceived. The trees on both ſides ſeem to overſhadow this paſſage, which is a kind of watry defile for ſome miles in length, and admits of a conſiderable variety, being deep and ſmooth in ſome places, and in others rocky and ſhallow; at which laſt, the paſſengers diſembark, and the boat is forced by ſtrength of men's arms, under a kind of arch. The uſing of ſails is here dangerous, on account of the mountain ſqualls, their ſides hanging directly over the river, which, in this place, is almoſt too narrow even for oars. The ſtupendous rock, called the Eagle's Neſt, noted alſo for a fine echo, is commonly a place of refreſhment to

paſſen-

passengers, who here enjoy the grateful shade of the arbutus, yews, hollies, and many other trees, that cover the rocks in this canal, several of which hang dreadfully over its sides; and, no doubt, had a person sufficient leisure, thoroughly to search up the sides of this glin, and the adjacent places, which would require vastly more time, labour, and expence, than the encouragement given to works of this nature will afford, abundance of curious discoveries might certainly be made here in the botanical way, especially in the adjacent forests.

The boatmen have given imaginary names to these rocks, as to one the Man of War; a rock, which in some sort represents the hull of a large vessel, the mast and rigging of which is no other than a large branching yew at the top. Having, at length, passed this long and narrow strait, the upper lake is discovered, which is surrounded on all sides with mountains of an amazing height beautified also with woods. For here, according to Milton,

——Over head up grow
Insuperable height of loftiest shade,
Cedar, and pine, and fir, and branching palm,
A sylvan scene; and as the ranks ascend
Shade above shade, a woody theatre
Of stateliest view——
Luxuriant: Mean while murmuring waters fall
Down the slope hills, disperst, or in a lake,
——Unite their streams:
Paradise Lost, Book IV.

This upper lake is an oblong square, extending north and south, but is not a third of the area of the lower lake. The rocks and islands are here inhabited by eagles, ospreys, hawks, and other birds of prey; as are the forests on the adjacent mountains with red deer.

In certain easons very considerable water-falls and cascades tumble from the mountains into this upper lake, which with the echoes, and delightful scenery of the prospect, are also the chief entertainment of this place, as in the lower lake. In one of these islands travellers generally take a repast, for few people go so far into these wilds without laying in provisions before-hand. The manner of returning is, either back through the same scene, or on horseback over the mountain, on a new road, which was made by subscription of the principal gentlemen of the county.

Towards the southern part of the lake, situated on a kind of peninsula, stands Mucruss, the seat of Edward Herbert, Esq; a situation where nature, in her native attire, very little assisted by art, outdoes every thing that human fancy, supported with the highest expence, hath yet performed; for whether we first reflect on the delightful prospects that this seat affords, as the lofty mountains hanging over the lake, wooded almost to their summits; cascades pouring down from several of them, particularly that already noticed from Mangerton, which sends down a roaring torrent not far distant; the beautiful expanse of water which washes the verge of this gentleman's gardens and improvements, scattered over with islands, so wooded as to represent several well-cultivated spots; also a particular lake called Mucruss lake, divided by that peninsula from the great one; and on the opposite shore, a level, well im-

improved country: I ſay, whether we take in at one view all this inchanting ſcenery, or ſtop to admire the particular beauties of the ſeat itſelf, we ſhall find ſufficient matter for pleaſure and admiration. The natural appearance of this place, before it was adorned by any improvement, was that of a luxuriant garden, where a great variety of trees and ſhrubs, the produce only of a more favourable clime, flouriſhed ſpontaneouſly, as the arbutus, juniper, yew, buckthorn, ſervice, and others, found growing among the crevices of marble rocks; the ſeeds, and original plantation of which I ſuſpect to have been laid here, many centuries ago, by the monks of the adjacent abbeys; where, meeting with a ſoil and climate favourable to their preſervation and propagation, they have wonderfully flouriſhed ever ſince, without any aſſiſtance from art.

Theſe natural gardens, therefore, wanted little aſſiſtance to beautify them, except an incloſure towards the land, and the lopping away part of their luxuriance, to form avenues and walks through them, beſides the addition of ſuch exotics as have been but of late years introduced into Ireland; among which there have been planted a conſiderahle number of vines, which are now ſpreading their branches, and crawling up ſeveral ſloping rocks of variegated marble.

It was, indeed, an handſome compliment which was paid to this place, by a late Right Rev. Prelate *, whoſe high taſte in the beauties of art and nature, as well as goodneſs of heart, and ſolid learning, all the world equally admired and acknowledged; who being aſked what he thought of this ſeat, immediately anſwered, that the French Monarch might poſſible be able to erect another Verſailles, but could not with all his revenues lay out another Mucruſs.

The gardens of this ſeat extend to the ruins of an ancient friery called Irrelagh, i. e. on the lough, founded by Donald, ſon of Thady Mac Carty, in the year 1440, for Minorites, or conventual Franciſcans, and repaired by him in 1468, the year of his death. It was again re-edified in the year 1602, but ſoon after ſuffered to go to ruin. The walks are ſurrounded by a venerable grove of aſh-trees, which are very tall, and in ſome places grow ſpontaneouſly, from the ruins of the abbey. The choir, nave, and ſteeple ſtill remain entire, in which are ſeveral decayed tombs. The cloyſters are likewiſe entire, in which are ſeveral Gothic arches of ſolid marble, which incloſe a ſmall ſquare, in the center of which ſtands one of the talleſt yew-trees I have ever ſeen; its ſpreading branches, like a great umbrella, overſhadow the niches of the whole cloyſter, forming a more ſolemn and aweful kind of covering to it than originally belonged to the place. The ſteeple was ſmall, and capable of containing only a ſingle bell; and it is ſupported by a Gothic arch or vault. The bell was, not many years ago, found in the adjacent lough, and by the inſcription, was known to have belonged to this priory, which from the time of its foundation, hath been the cemetery of the Mac Carty-Mores,

* Dr. Berkley, the late Biſhop of Cloyne.

and other families. Upon the diſſolution of religious houſes, the revenues and ſcite of this abbey were granted to Captain Robert Collam, who aſſigned them to Biſhop Croſbie.

The town of Killarney is a ſmall thriving place, being conſiderably improved ſince the minority of its preſent owner, the Lord Viſcount Kenmare, who hath encouraged ſeveral inhabitants to ſettle in it, and hath erected ſome houſes for linen manufacturers, about a mile from the town. There are already four new roads finiſhed to this town, one from the county of Cork, which leads to that city; a ſecond from Caſtle-Iſland, which proceeds towards Limerick; the third is that to the river of Kenmare beforementioned; and a fourth is lately made to Caſtlemain; from which laſt place new roads have been carried to Tralee and Dingle. The neighbourhood of the mines affords employment for ſeveral people, and will conſequently cauſe a conſiderable ſum of money to be ſpent in it. A new ſtreet, with a large commodious inn, are deſigned to be built here; for the curioſities of the neighbouring lake have of late drawn great numbers of curious travellers to viſit it, and, no doubt, many more will go thither to partake of the diverſions and amuſements of that place, when they can be aſſured of being commodiouſly and cheaply entertained.

The principal ornament of Killarney is the ſeat and gardens of Lord Kenmare, planted with large nurſeries of fruit and timber trees. His lordſhip propoſes to enlarge a canal, which runs through his gardens, and to make it communicate with the lake, which will not only render them more beautiful, but will alſo add to the convenience of water-carriage to and from the lake. Not far from the houſe is a large and pleaſant park, well wooded, and ſtocked with deer, which he hath alſo in plenty in the foreſts of the adjacent mountains.

The natural hiſtory of Hartz Foreſt, in his Majeſty's German dominions, Written in German by H. Ebrens, M. D.

Of the cavern at Scharzfeld.

THE cavern at Scharzfeld is well worth ſeeing, being caves remarkable for ſeveral rarities; the country people called it the Dwarf-holes. It is ſituated in the Lower Hartz, in the county of Hohnſtein, in a wood not far from the caſtle of Scharzfeld. Whoever wants to ſee this cavern, goes to the village of Scharzfeld to look out for a guide. Then you proceed through a wood and a thicket, and coming near the cavern, you muſt get down by the knots and branches of a large tree with ſome trouble and danger, to come to the mouth of it. When you are on the ground, there appears to your view a large cleft in a rock, about fourteen feet high: the inſide of it is lined all about with a thick and ſhining *Drop-ſtone*. Now you advance a pretty way forwards, and muſt creep a conſiderable length, till you come into the ſecond cave, which for height and bigneſs is not inferior to the firſt. From hence you creep again with ſome trouble into the third, and from thence to the fourth cave, and ſo on; and in this manner, ſome guides ſay, one may go five or ſix Engliſh miles under ground, without coming to the end.

The

The cold is very intenſe in this cavern, and rather greater than in the Baumans cave. To let in ſome light, there are ſeveral round and ſquare holes in the roof, ſome of which are ſtopped up with ſtones and other rubbiſh. The common people imagine the dwarfs went in and out of theſe openings, but it is more probable they were made for air-holes. There are ſuch numbers of paſſages and turnings, that it is almoſt impoſſible to count them; ſome running forwards, ſome ſideways, and others a-croſs, all communicating with one another in the manner of a labyrinth, for which reaſon it is very difficult to find one's way out of it again without a guide. Moſt of theſe paſſages are as clean as if they were ſwept with a broom, and ſome are filled up with rubbiſh by thoſe that dug there, either for ore, or the foſſile unicorn.

The *Drop-ſtone* is found in ſeveral of theſe caves, although the top of the mountain where the cavern is, be a dry lime-ſtone. The water drops continually from the roof, ſo thick that it ſeems as if it rained; and when theſe drops fall on your cloaths, and grow dry upon them, they turn to white ſpots, and a white powder like chalk comes from it.

It is reported, that once, on the eve of St. Peter and Paul, twenty-five perſons bound themſelves by oath to each other to go into this cavern, and not to come out of it again till they had viewed all the curioſities therein, and found out the end; therefore they provided themſelves with a number of candles, a ladder, and ſtrings, and proviſion for ſeveral days.

When they were advanced about nine hundred fathoms, they found many curioſities, large places like palaces, all ſorts of figures formed by the *Drop-ſtone*; alſo ſome ſprings, running waters, quantities of human bones, ſome of a gigantic ſize. Then creeping again through other narrow paſſages, they came into ſpacious places, where twenty-five could walk a-breaſt. Thus they went on till they could go no farther: by following the thread which they had tied to the entry of the cavern, they found their way back again without difficulty; but by the coldneſs of the place, and many frights, they were become ſo pale, and their countenances ſo altered, that their friends hardly knew them again.

Here is alſo found the foſſile unicorn, but not near in ſuch quantity as formerly, becauſe the peaſants, who uſed to dig for it, and to ſell it to the apothecaries and druggiſts, have almoſt exhauſted the place. This foſſile is of different ſhapes; ſometimes 'tis formed like a ſtraight horn, a ſcull, a jaw-bone, a ſhoulder-blade, and a back-bone, a rib, a tooth, a thigh-bone, and all other ſorts of bones both of men and beaſts; and there is ſome found like an unſhapen lump or maſs of ſtone, having no reſemblance to any bone at all.

There have been great diſputes among the learned about this foſſile: ſome, conſidering that there are pieces ſo exactly like true bones, affirm, they muſt really have been part of ſome animal; and, that thoſe of an anomalous form are of the mineral kind. But others reply, that upon examination they cannot find that great likeneſs to bones as their adverſaries are pleaſed to fancy: in particular they ſay, that thoſe bones of the foſſile unicorn, which are called the jaw-bone, have ſuch apophyſes as are never to be met with in the natural way; and that ſome being like no bone at all, they ſcruple not to conclude the whole to be a *luſus naturæ*, or an accidental produce of nature. Moreover, they add, that granting ſome to be like true bones, it cannot be inferred from thence that they were really ſo; becauſe elſe it would follow, that the figures repreſented in ſome pieces of ſlate, and the *Cornua Ammonis*, were once real; which are now allowed on all hands to be ſtones of a particular kind.

Conringius, in his diſſertation *De antiquo Helmiadiſt ſtatu*, thinks the foſſile unicorn were petrifyed bones. And Otto de Querick, in his *Experimenta Magdeburgica*, maintains the ſame opinion. That there has been ſuch animals as unicorns, he pretends to corroborate by the following fact: he ſays, that anno 1663, in a lime-pit near Quedlinburg, there was found an entire ſkeleton of an unicorn, which had fixed to its forehead a long bone, or horn, as thick as a man's thigh-bone, and was preſented to the Abbeſs of Quedlinburg; and, that theſe bones had been conveyed to this place in the general flood, is proved ſufficiently by the various bones dug up in moſt parts of the world. The *Theatrum Europæum*, part V. mentions, that anno 1645 the Swedes dug up, near Crems in Auſtria, a giant's ſkeleton, whoſe head was as big as a middle-ſized table, and one tooth weighed five pounds and a half, and the bone of his arm as big as a man's middle. Eckſtormius alſo confirms it, with the author of the *Topographia of Brunſwick*, that one time there was found in the Baumans cave an human ſcull of a gigantic ſize.

But the bigneſs of ſome of theſe bones ſeem to argue that they could not be human; and therefore 'tis probable they either have increaſed under ground, or elſe are a *luſus naturæ:* for the talleſt man we know of, was Og of Baſan, whoſe bed is ſaid, in Deuteronomy, chap. iii. to have been eighteen feet long: now, allowing the bed to be but one foot longer than the man, he was ſeventeen feet high. But if the head and tooth found by the Swedes had belonged to a regularly-proportioned man, he muſt have exceeded Og by a vaſt deal; for the tooth is ſaid to have weighed five pounds and an half, and ſuppoſing that of a common man to weigh half an ounce, which is too much, then the giant muſt have had a height anſwerable to 176 times the bulk of a middle-ſized man.

Others cannot comprehend how theſe ſuppoſed bones ſhould have been brought together in ſuch quantities into theſe caverns; nor will they be ſatisfied with the reaſons ſome naturaliſts give for their manner of petrifaction; wherefore Sennertus, in his *Epitome Scientia naturalis*, lib. v. cap. 4. Schræder, in his *Pharmacopœia medica*, and Laurentius Bauſchius, in his *Schediamſa Curioſum de Unicornu foſſili*, and others, count it among the minerals.

Kircher, in his *Mundus ſubterraneus*, lib. viii. c. 8. makes this diſtinction betwixt bones of a mineral produce, and petrifyed ones: he ſays, the firſt are ſolid throughout, but the latter hollow. Which obſervation I have found not to be infal-

infallible, having ſeen ſome bones of the mineral kind that were concave, as if they had formerly contained marrow.

This has this controverſy been canvaſſed pro and con; but as I have had the opportunity of examining great quantities of this foſſile, particularly in my father's cabinet, who had various pieces of it, I have found moſt of that dug about the Hartz to be of a mineral kind.

This being taken for granted, we are next to conſider the matter it is compoſed of. Some think with Libavius, Part. 3. Singular, l. 18. c. 17. that it is a bituminous earth; and others ſay it is a kind of agate putrified: but to me it ſeems moſt probable that it is made of a clay, or fattiſh earth, called in Latin *Marga*, or *Marl*, which is very plentiful in this country, and ſerves to manure the ground, inſtead of dung. According to the figure this earth lies in underground, when the petrifying water comes to it, and cauſes it to grow hard, ſo it remains, and thus becomes ſometimes a well-ſhapen bone, and often a lump of matter of no diſtinct form at all. This formation is not perfected at once; for it is obſerved, that ſome pieces lying in a place where there is room for increaſe, will grow to a monſtrous ſize.

This foſſile hath ſeveral names, viz. *Unicornu minerale*, *Ebur foſſile*, *Oſteites*, *Monoceros vulgi*, *Lithomarga alba*, &c. The moſt common term it is known by, is *Unicornu foſſile*; but I can ſee no reaſon why it ſhould rather be called *Unicorn* than any other animal, ſince it is found of all ſorts of forms, and thoſe pieces reſembling the horn of an unicorn but very rarely to be met with.

It is moſt commonly of a light grey, black, or yellowiſh colour, and very ſeldom perfectly white: ſometimes it is as hard as a ſtone, and other times ſoft like clay, and grows harder the longer it is expoſed to the air. It has commonly neither ſmell nor taſte, yet ſometimes I have found it with a ſcent like that of quinces; which probably might proceed from a bituminous ſubſtance mixed with the petrifying water. It is introduced in the *Materia Medica*, and the whiteſt and melloweſt is reckoned the beſt for that purpoſe. The common people try it by putting it into cold water; and that which cauſes moſt bubbles to riſe, they count for the beſt ſort. The reaſon of the riſing of theſe bubbles is, becauſe as this foſſile is full of pores, wherein air is contained, the water getting into them, drives out the air, which being ſpecifically lighter than the water, riſes in the form of thoſe bubbles to the ſurface.

The common people looked formerly upon it as a medicine of extraordinary efficacy, thinking it to be the true unicorn; but ſince it is come to be common, it hath loſt much of its repute. It operates very like the Terra ſigillata, abſorbs, adſtringes, and promotes perſpiration, (Vide Franciſc. Joel. Pract. tom. 5.) and is one of the ingredients of the Bezoardic powder deſcribed by D. Ludovici in *Pharmaocpœia moderno ſæculo applicanda*, and produces a very good effect, unleſs a ſymptomatic coſtiveneſs forbid its uſe. Externally it ſerves in puſtulary eruptions and eroſions about the pudendum and fundament in children, and in eyewaters. Laſtly, D. Hoffman, in his *Clavis Schrœderiana*, admoniſhes nifhes people to try the foffile unicorn firft upon a dog, before it is made ufe of in medicine, becaufe he thinks it is fometimes of a poifonous nature; which however is never obferved in any found in or near Hartz foreft.

From Mr. Groffe's voyage to the Eaft Indies.

Account of a very remarkable Ifland near Bombay in the Eaft-Indies.

OVer-againft the caftle of Bombay, about the diftance of five miles, lies the very fmall, but famous, ifland of Elephanta. It can at moft be but about three miles in compafs, and confifts of almoft all hill: at the foot of which as you land, you fee, juft above the fhore, on your right, an elephant, coarfely cut out in ftone, of the natural bignefs, and at fome little diftance not impoffible to be taken for a real elephant, from the ftone being naturally of the colour of that beaft. It ftands on a platform of ftones of the fame colour. On the back of this elephant was placed ftanding, another young one, appearing to have been all of the fame ftone, but has been long broken down. Of the meaning, or hiftory of this image, there is no tradition old enough to give any account.

Returning then to the foot of the hill, you afcend to an eafy flant, which about half way up the hill brings you to the opening or portal of a large cavern hewn out of a folid rock, into a magnificent temple: for fuch furely it may be termed, confidering the immenfe workmanfhip of fuch an excavation; and feems to me a far more bold attempt, than that of the pyramids of Egypt. There is a fair entrance into this fubterraneous temple, which is an oblong fquare, in length about 80 or 90 feet, by 40 broad. The roof is nothing but the rock cut flat at top, and in which I could not difcern any thing that did not fhew it to be all of one piece. It is about ten feet high, and fupported towards the middle, at equi-diftance from the fides, and from one another, with two regular rows of pillars of a fingular order. They are very maffive, fhort in proportion to their thicknefs, and their capital bears fome refemblance to a round cufhion, preffed by the fuper-incumbent mountain, with which they are alfo of one piece. At the further end of this temple are three gigantic figures, the face of one of them is at leaft five feet in length, and of a proportionable breadth. But thefe reprefentations have no reference, or connection, either to any known hiftory, or the mythology of the Gentoos. They had continued in a tolerable ftate of prefervation and wholenefs, confidering the remotenefs of their antiquity, until the arrival of the Portuguefe, who made themfelves mafters of the place, and in the blind fury of their bigotry, not fuffering any idols but their own, they muft have been at even fome pains to maim and deface them, as they now remain, confidering the hardnefs of the ftone. It is faid they even brought field-pieces to the demolition of images, which fo greatly deferved to be fpared for the unequalled curiofity of them. Of this Queen Catherine of Portugal was, it feems, fo fenfible, that fhe could not conceive that any traveller would return from that fide of India, without visiting the wonders of this cavern; of which too the sight appeared to me to exceed all the descriptions I had heard of them. About two thirds of the way up this temple, on each side, and fronting each other, are two doors or outlets, into smaller grots er excavations, and freely open to the air. Near and about the door way, on the right hand, are also several mutilated images, single and in groupes. In one of the last, I remarked a kind of resemblance to the story of Solomon dividing the child, there standing a figure with a drawn sword, holding in one hand an infant with the head downwards, which it appears in act to cleave through the middle. The outlet of the other on the left hand, is into an area of about 20 feet in length, and 12 in breadth, at the upper end of which, as you turn to the right, presents itself a colonnade covered a-top, of 10 or 12 feet deep, and in length answering to the breadth of the area; this joins to an apartment of the most regular architecture, an oblong square, with a door in perfect symmetry; and the whole executed in quite a contrary taste and manner from any of the oldest or best Gentoo buildings any where extant. I took particular notice of some paintings round the cornices, not for any thing curious in the design, but for the beauty and freshness of the colouring, which must have lasted some thousands of years, on supposing it, as there is all reason to suppose it, cotemporary with the building itself. The floor of the apartment is generally full of water, its pavement or ground-work not permitting it to be drawn off, or to be soaked up. For it is to be observed, that even the cavern itself is not visitable after the rains, until the ground of it has had time to dry into a competent hardness.

The reader too will please to observe, that in the dimensions I have ventured to give, I am far from warranting the exactness, any further than to the best of my gross guess by the eye; and if any one shall hereafter, on a personal survey, or on a competent draught of it, think I have exaggerated its importance, I hope he will only pity my misapprehension, and acquit me of any design of imposing on him, by dealing in the marvellous, nothing being more certain than that I have said no more of it, than as it struck me at the sight of it, and still remains on my memory.

This place too being so near Bombay, affords the English inhabitants, not only an easy opportunity of gratifying their curiosity, in visiting so remarkable a spot, but occasionally a very agreeable party of pleasure. Sometimes, in the way thither, they dine at Butcher's Island, which is two miles nearer to Bombay, on account of the conveniency of the officer's house to receive them, an ensign's guard being kept there. Others again prefer carrying their provisions with them, and dine in the cave itself, than which in the very sultriest days of the heats, there cannot be imagined a cooler pleasanter retreat. For though the air be almost on fire round you, you are no sooner entered the cave, than you are refreshed with a sensible coolness; the three openings above-mentioned not only furnishing sufficient light, but a thorough draught of air, that does not so much convey freshness into the cave, as it receives it from constant temperature, preserved

ſerved to it by its impenetrability to the ſun, from the thickneſs of the mountainous maſs above it. And even the light that comes into it through the portals has loſt, by the way, all the force of thoſe fiery particles to which it gives ſo great an activity. For, it is obſerved in India, as well as in all hot countries, that the excluſion of light is in ſome meaſure an excluſion of heat, and that but darkening an apartment only, ſenſibly cools. This rule too admits of no exception. except in places where the ſoil and ſituation are of ſuch a nature, as to continue the heat even after the actual preſence of the ſun is withdrawn; as in Gambroon on the coaſt of Perſia, for example, where a high maſſive hill behind it, to which it is a kind of focal point, and the bituminous quality of the earth, are circumſtances that do not allow of the air's cooling between the ſun-ſet and ſun-riſe.

But, aſking pardon for this digreſſion, and reſuming my preſent ſubject, I am to obſerve that, for the reſt, this iſland contains nothing more that is worthy of notice. There are not above two or three huts upon it; which is not ſurprizing, conſidering the little land there is to cultivate, and that there is no water on it, but what is ſaved from the rains. The growth of the hill itſelf is only underwood, and graſs, which in the dry ſeaſon is often ſet on fire, and will continue burning for three or four days; which has this benefit, of fertilizing any cultivable ſpots on it, and of the ſalts being waſhed down by the rains into the lower grounds, a practice that is much followed in all thoſe countries; which they call burning the land.

An Eſſay on the Quantity or Meaſure of Engliſh Verſe. The Examples from Milton.

I. *The meaſure of Engliſh Heroics, and of the Iambic.*
II. *The ſyllaba hypercatalectica, or redundant ſyllable.*
III. *Of the Trochee.*
IV. *Of the Spondee.*
V. *Of the Pyrrhic.*
VI. *Of very ſhort Syllables.*
VII. *Of the Anapæſt.*
VIII. *Of the Dactyle.*
IX. *Of Aphæreſis.*
X. *Many like feet in the ſame verſe.*
XI. *Many different feet in the ſame verſe.*

I. *The meaſure of Engliſh Heroics, and of the Iambic.*

THE Engliſh Heroic verſe is an Iambic of five feet, ſometimes pure, as,

His ōnlў Sōn, ŏn eārth hĕ fīrſt bĕhēld
ăboūt hĭm āll thĕ sānctĭtīes ŏf hev'n,

> ĭn heāv'n ŏr eārth, ŏr ūndĕr eārth ĭn hēll
> Thĭs ōne, thĭs eāsy̆ chārge ŏf āll thĕ treēs, &c.

Sometimes nearly ſo, as

> Tŏ thēir defĕnce whŏ hōld ĭt, hēre pĕrhāps
> Preſcrīb'd, nŏ bārs ŏf hĕll, nŏr āll thĕ chaīns
> ămōng thĕ grōves, thĕ foūntains ănd thĕ flōwers
> Mȳ ōnly̆ Sōn, and ōn my̆ hōly̆ hīll
> Rĕ-ēntĕr heāv'n, ŏr elſĕ in ſomĕ mīld zōne
> Hĭs āngĕr, and pĕrhāps thus fār rĕmōv'd
> Thĕ dārk, unbŏttom'd īnfinīte ăby̆ſs.
> Outſhōne thĕ weālth ŏf ōrmŭs, ănd ŏf Īnd.

From theſe laſt inſtances, where the ſyllables not marked are by derivation, nature, or poſition, long, yet in the ſound and meaſure of the verſe are ſhort, I obſerve, that the quantity of Engliſh ſyllables is not meaſured by the rules of Latin and Greek Proſody, but by the tone of the voice, or accent, which generally riſes at every ſecond ſyllable, and therefore I call *long*; the intermediate ſyllables, over which we haſten to come at it, I call *ſhort*, whatever their quantity may be with reſpect to conſonants, vowels, diphthongs; thus,

> While ſmoōth ădōnis frōm his nātive rŏck,

is a very muſical Engliſh Iambic, though four out of the five ſhort ſyllables are naturally long; *while* and *tive* by the final *e*, and *nis* and *his* long by poſition. Indeed an Engliſh Iambic may be juſt meaſure, and yet have never a ſyllable in it ſhort, according to the rules of Proſody, as,

> Wĭth floōds ănd whīrlwĭnds ōf tĕmpēſtŭōus firē.

And the proſodeal ſhort ſyllables may become long in the Engliſh meaſure, as,

> Qŭiĕt thŏ sād B. 11.
> By̆ prāy'r th' ŏffĕndĕd dĕity̆ t'ăppeāſe 11.
> Lămĕnt nŏt ēve, bŭt pātiĕntly̆ rĕsīgn 11.
> Oŭr ſĕcŏnd ādăm īn thĕ wīldĕrnĕſs 11.

II. *Of the ſyllaba hypercatalectica, or redundant ſyllable.*

A redundant ſyllable is often added at the end of an Iambic with grace in blank verſe, as

> ŏf heāv'n rĕceīv'd ŭs fāllĭng, ănd thĕ thūnder.

In rhyme it grows offenſive, or burleſque, as it creates a double jingle.

Perhaps many Alexandrines may be beſt accounted from for ſuch redundant ſyllables. [See § VI. of very ſhort ſyllables.]

III. *Of the Trochee.*

The moſt common and muſical variation of this meaſure is by ſubſtituting a Trochee inſtead of an Iambic.

1mo loco Mȳſtĭcăl dānce, whĭch yōndĕr ſtārry̆ ſphēre 5.
> Ceāſe ĭ tŏ wāndĕr whēre thĕ mūsĕs hāunt 3.

Nor

Nor is this always accidental, but often by choice, as;

——— ———that God's own ear

Liſtens delighted——— ——— 5.

Wherever a foot ends at the pauſe, a Trochee will follow gracefully; as

2do loco Thus ſaid, Native of heav'n, for other place 5.
undeck'd, ſave with herſelf, more lovely fair 5.
His ſeed, when is not ſet, ſhall bruiſe my head 10.
3tio in myſtic dance, not without ſong, reſound 5.
Faireſt of ſtars, laſt in the train of night 5.
With the fixt ſtars, fixt in their orb that flies 5.
4to Theſe are thy glorious works, parent of good 5.
Each in their cryſtal ſluice; he ere they fell 5.
and choral ſymphonies, day without end 5.
Now on the polar winds, now with quick fan 5.
5to Spoil'd principalities and pow'rs, triumph'd 10.

A Trochee is not common in this place; in moſt caſes where a word, which in ordinary pronunciation is a Trochee, ends the verſe, Milton throws the accent on the laſt ſyllable, which makes it an Iambic; and indeed I believe it is ſo in this very verſe, for I remember elſewhere he accents triumph after the latin.

A Trochee is not ſo harmonious if no comma or pauſe precedes, as;

in their triple degrees, regions to which 5.
Law and edict on us, who without law 5.
and thou Moon in the vale of ajalon 2.
That when fair morning firſt ſmiles on the world 5.
Drew after him the third part of heav'n's hoſt. 5.

I meet with a line of Mr. Pope's in the eighth odyſſey, where perhaps it may be allowable, as exemplifying the ſpring he mentions,

None in the leap ſpring with ſo ſtrong a bound, v. 103.

but then we are forced to ſtop at *leap*, where there is no comma.

IV. *Of the Spondee.*

This foot is admitted into every one of the five places; as;

1mo Thus they in heav'n; above the ſtarry ſphere 3.
Smooth, eaſy, inoffenſive down to hell 10.
2do account me man, I for his ſake will leave
at ſuch bold words, vouch'd with a deed ſo bold 5.
Taſtes not well join'd inelegant, but bring 5.
and ye five other wand'ring fires that move 5.
3tio a cloudy ſpot, down thither prone in flight 5.
and faithful now prov'd falſe: but think not here 6.
Reſerv'd him to more wrath: for now the thought 6.
4to and reſt can never dwell, hope never comes 1.
While day ariſes, that ſweet hour of prime 5.
in curls on either cheek play'd, wings he wore 3.
Iſſuing from me; on your joint vigor now 10.

 Silence,

5to Silence, ye troubled waves; and thou, deep, peace 7.
Nor lawful to reveal; yet for thy good 5.
So scented the grim feature and up turn'd 10.

The Spondee is often produced by the emphasis falling on a syllable that should regularly be short, as,

account me man, I for his sake will leave
Tastes not well join'd inelegant——

Often, when the emphasis placed on a short syllable lengthens that foot into a Spondee, it shortens the preceding foot into a Pyrrhic, as,

Finds no acceptance nor can find; for how 5.
I offer, on me let thine anger fall 3.
His other half in the great zone of heav'n 5.

V. *Of the Pyrrhic.*

This foot also is found in every of the five places:

1mo in his own strength, this place may lie expos'd 2.
on the proud crest of Satan, that no sight 6.

Unmusical when not ballanced by a Spondee, as,

By the waters of life, where-e'er they sate 10.
2do Disperse it, as now light dispels the dark 5.
Happiness in his pow'r left free to will 5.
Springs lighter the green stalk, from thence the leaves
Eve easily may faith admit, that all 11.
3tio Converse with adam in what bow'r or shade 5.
Finds no acceptance nor can find; for how 5.
of easy thorowfare. Therefore, while I 10.
4to Forthwith behold the excellence, the pow'r 6.
By pray'r th' offended deity t' appease 11.
5to His danger, and from whom, what enemy 5.
Had to her center shook. What wonder, when
Millions — —— —
By Eve, tho all unweeting, seconded 10.

The Pyrrhic is generally ballanced by a Spondee, unless in the fifth place, or at the pause, where a Trochee follows; otherwise unmusical, perhaps it is false quantity, as in Paradise Regained,

With them from bliss to the bottomless deep.

Or perhaps, if any quick motion, or remarkable shortness was to be described, it might be introduced; but I can recollect no instances.

(Mr. Pope, when very young, wrote such a verse,
" So imperceptible was the motion.")

VI. *Of very short Syllables.*

The Spondee increased, and the Pyrrhic lessened, the quantity of the measure in the verse; but when mixt and ballanced in the same verse, it was reduced to true time. The Anapæst and Dactyle have each of them

an

an exceſs of a ſhort ſyllable, unleſs we meaſure them by muſical time, thus,

Iambic. Trochee. Spondee. Pyrrhic. Anapæſt. Dactyle.

Quinctilian mentions ſyllables that are *brevibus breviores*, and this I think is the caſe in the Engliſh Anapæſt and Dactyle, in which we are apt to cruſh the two ſhort ſyllables into one, which has produced the Syncope, ſo commonly marked in our verſe, for which, I think, juſt occaſion is not ſo frequent; the ſyllables might generally be pronounced diſtinct, though quick, and wrote full.

ănd flōw'rĭng ōdōrs, căſsĭă, nārd, ănd bālm. 5.

Why is flow'ring ſyncopated? if to avoid the redundant ſyllable that would make an Anapæſt, why is not caſſia ſyncopated into caſs'a? if the reaſon is, that *ſia* is pronounced as two *very ſhort* ſyllables, which will not hurt the quantity: for the ſame reaſon we may, and, I think, ought to read,

ănd flōwĕrĭng ōdōrs, căſsĭă, nārd, ănd bālm.

How would the following verſes look or ſound, if we were to crowd the two ſhort ſyllables into one?

Nŏ ĭngrātefŭl fōod, ănd fōod ălīke thōſe pūre
N' ĭngrātefŭl fōod, &c.
Twō onlȳ whŏ yĕt bȳ sōv'reĭgn gĭft pŏſsēſs
Twō ōnl', whŏ yĕt, &c,

If in theſe and many other caſes we muſt write and pronounce the ſyllables diſtinctly, why not in many others where we generally uſe the Syncope? thus,

ănd dĭctātĕs tō mĕ ſlūmb'rĭng, ŏr ĭnſpīres 9.
Hĕrōĭc deed, chīef māſt'rȳ tō diſſĕct 9.
ĭn bĭllōws, leāve ĭ'th'mĭdſt ă hŏrrĭd vāle. 1.

Why is not the Anapæſt admitted here as well as in the foregoing inſtances?

And dictates to mĕ ſlūmbĕrĭng, ŏr ĭnſpires
Heroic deed, chīef māſtĕrȳ tō dĭſsĕct
ĭn bĭllōws, leāve ĭn thĕ mĭdſt ă hŏrrĭd vāle

e in *ed* the participle, and the præter tenſe, may ſtill ſuffer Syncope, as we frequently leave it out in proſe and diſcourſe: but heaven, and ſpirits, and powers, &c. which are generally wrote in verſe, heav'n, and ſp'rits, and pow'rs, &c. are often two ſyllables, as,

ăs māy cŏmpōrt wĭth hēavĕn; ānd tŏ tāſte 5.
Spĭrĭts ōdōrous breāthes, &c.

and may generally be conſidered as ſuch, and wrote full in moſt inſtances, thus,

Bāne, ănd ĭn hēavĕn mŭch wōrſe wōuld bĕ mȳ ſtāte 9.
Sĭng, hēavĕnlȳ mūſe, thăt ōn thĕ sĕcrĕt tŏp 1.
ō mȳrĭăds ōf ĭmmōrtăl ſpĭrĭts, ō pōwĕrs!

To my ear this verse would have been truer had it been yĕ pōwĕrs; otherwise we must say that a redundant syllable must be left at the end of a pause, as well as of a verse: or else in this, as well as perhaps in the following and some like instances, spirit makes but one syllable.

Tŏ sprĭtŭăl nātūres; ōnlȳ thĭs ĭ knōw 5.
Mȳ lĭkenĭng sprĭtŭăl tŏ cŏrpŏrăl fōrms 5.

unless we admit feet of four syllables, which I think we must in the two following verses,

Cōmes thŭndĕrĭng băck wĭth dreadfŭl rĕvŏlūtiŏn. 10.
Fŏr Sŏlĭtūde sŏmetĭmes ĭs bĕst Sŏcĭĕtȳ.

Perhaps the two last syllables in these verses are *very short* ones, and amount to no more than the hypercatalectica or redundant one at the end of a verse, and must not be considered as Alexandrines.

VII. *Of the Anapæst.*

This foot is admitted into every one of the five places; and is the most musical after the Iambic and Trochee, but is least so in the first seat, as,

1mo ŏphĭūsă, bŭt stĭll greatĕst, hĕ thĕ mĭdst 10.
ĭs hĭs wrāth, ălsŏ? Bĕ ĭt, măn ĭs nŏt sŏ 10.
Tŏ ĕvăngĕlĭze thĕ nătĭŏns thĕn ŏn ăll 12.

The rest are more harmonious, as,

2do ŏf mănȳ ă cŏloŭr'd plūme, sprĭnklĕd wĭth gŏld 3.
Sŏ săyĭng ă nŏblĕ strŏke hĕ lĭftĕd hĭgh 6.
ŏf mĕrcȳ ănd jŭstĭcĕ ĭn thȳ fāce dĭscērn'd 3.
Alreadȳ ĭn pārt, thŏ hĭd ĭn glŏŏmĭĕst shāde 10.
Stoŏd tŏ ĕntĕrtaĭn hĭs guĕst frŏm hēavĕn, nŏ veil 5.
3tio, ĭn ĕmŭlātĭŏn ŏppŏsĭte tŏ hēavĕn 2.
ŏf bĭrds ŏn ĕvĕrȳ bŏŭgh; sŏ mŭch thĕ mōre 5.
Neăr thăt bĭtūmĭnŏus lăke whĕre Sŏdŏm flăm'd 10.
ănd scŏŭrg'd wĭth mănȳ ă strŏke thĕ ĭndĭgnănt waves 10.
ŏf ŭnŏrĭgĭnăl nĭght, ănd chăŏs wĭld 10.
4to Lămĕnt nŏt ēve, bŭt pătĭĕntlȳ rĕsign 10.
Thrŏws hĭs stĕep flĭght ĭn mănȳ ăn ăĕrȳ wheel 3.
Thĕ earth tŏ yĭeld ŭnsăvŏrȳ foŏd pĕrhăps 5.
5to Hȳpŏcrĭsȳ, thĕ ŏnlȳ ĕvĭl thăt wălks 3.
Bȳ dăy ă clŏŭd, bȳ nĭght ă pĭllăr ŏf fire 12.
Thĕ bĭrd ŏf Jŏve stŏŏp'd frŏm hĭs ăĕrȳ toŭr 11.
Hŭrl'd headlŏng flămĭng frŏm thĕ ĕthĕrĕăl skȳ. 1.

VIII. *Of the Dactyle.*

This is used, I think, only in the first four places.

1mo Mȳrĭăds thŏ brĭght: ĭf hĕ whŏm mūtŭăl league 1.
Mānȳ ă dărk league rĕdŭc'd ĭn cărefŭl wătch 10.
Shădŏwȳ sĕts ŏff thĕ făce ŏf thĭngs ĭn vāin 5.
Fŏllŏwĭng ăbŏve thĕ ŏlȳmpĭăn hĭll ĭ sŏar 7.
Tĭmelȳ ĭntĕrpŏsĕs, ănd hĕr mŏnthlȳ roŭnd 3.

With

2do With ĭmpĕtŭoŭs rĕcōil, ănd jărrĭng ſoūnd 2.
ănd Tīrĕsĭăs ănd Phīneŭs, prōphĕts ōld 3.
ānd cŏrpōrĕăl tŏ īncŏrpōrĕăl tūrn 5.
3tio Mōre jŭſtlȳ, ſēat wŏrthĭĕr ŏf gŏds ĭs būilt
4to ĭn sīght ŏf Gōd's hīgh thrōne glōrĭŏuſlȳ brīght 3.
Bĕfōre thȳ fĕllŏws, ămbītĭŏus tŏ wīn 6.
ămmōnĭăn Jōve ŏr Căpītŏlĭne wăs ſeen 9.
ōvĕr thĕ vĕxt ăbȳſs, fōllŏwĭng thĕ trăct 10.
Fŏr thăt coēlĕſtĭăl līght. Bē ĭt sŏ, sĭnce Hē 1.

In the fifth place I recollect no inſtance, but can conceive it in two caſes;

1. After three Iambics and a pauſe, then a Trochee and a Dactyle;
2. After four Iambics and a pauſe, then a Dactyle.

IX. *Aphæreſis.*

A word, which is an Iambic in ſound, muſt ſuffer Aphæreſis, rather than be ſhortened to make the two firſt ſyllables of an Anapæſt.

Bēaſt nōw wĭth bēaſt 'găn wār, ănd fōwl wĭth fōwl 10.

X. *Many like feet in the ſame verſe.*

A verſe will admit not only one, but ſometimes two, and ſometimes three Trochees; thus,

2 Troch. Miniſtring ſpīrīts, trāin'd ŭp in feaſt and ſong 6.
3 Troch. Shōots ĭnviſible vīrtuĕ, e'ēn tŏ the deep 3.
And likewiſe two or three Spondees;
2 Spond. ānd thĕ dīre kīſs renew'd, and the dīre fōrm 10.
3 Spond. Rōcks, cāves, lākes, fēns, bōgs, dēns, and ſhades of death
So alſo two or three Anapæſts;
2 Anap. Celeſtĭăl, whĕthĕr ămōng the thrones or named 11.
3 Anap. O'er manȳ ă frōzen manȳ ăn āerȳ ālp 2.

I believe never more than two Pyrrhics, becauſe they generally require to be mixt with Spondees, and would therefore leave no Iambic in the verſe.

Nor do I recollect more than two Dactyles,
Lĭttlĕ ĭnfĕrĭŏr by my adventure hard. 10.

XI. *Many different feet in the ſame verſe.*

This has already appeared in ſeveral of the foregoing inſtances, and ſometimes leave only two, ſometimes only one Iambic in a verſe: thus under obſervation X we had a Dactyle, and two Trochees; a Trochee, and two Spondees; and in the following, a Pyrrhic, a Spondee, a Trochee.

ănd cōuntrȳ whĕrcōf hēre nēeds nŏ ăccoūnt 4.

Sometimes only one Iambic is left; thus we had obſervation X three Trochees and a Dactyle; and in the following, one Trochee, one Spondee, two Anapæſts,

Thrōws hĭs ſteēp flīght ĭn măny̆ ăn āĕry̆ wheēl 3.
Two Spondees, one Pyrrhic, one Trochee,
Drēw āftĕr hĭm thĕ thīrd pārt ŏf hēav'n's hōſt 5.
Two Trochees, one Pyrrhic, one Spondee,
Prōſpĕroūs ŏr ādvĕrſe, ſō ſhālt thoū lēad 11.
And many other varieties needleſs to note.

From the Gentleman's Magazine.

Staffordſhire, Sept. 24, 1757.

THE Roman numerals, though found to be greatly inferior in point of utility to the Arabic characters, by which all operations in arithmetic are now uſually performed, are yet retained in uſe in ſome caſes; but I much queſtion, whether it be generally known, or at leaſt agreed upon, how they originally received their value.—The reaſon why M and C ſhould ſignify the one a hundred, and the other a thouſand, is very obvious, they being the initial letters of *Mille* and *Centum*. But why does D ſtand for five hundred, L for fifty, X for ten, and V for five? The ſolution of this difficulty, to me appears to be this; the old antique way of writing the letter M was thus,

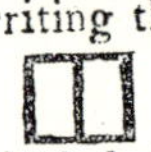 or rather thus, 

which being cut in two in the middle, by a perpendicular line, leaves two D's, each of which expreſſes juſt half the value of M. The like reaſoning will hold good in regard to the letter L, for if the C be horizontally diſſected, the lower part makes an L, two of which are equal to C.— As to the letter V, I think it may be accounted for thus; the words *quinque*, *quiſquis*, *quoniam*, and many others, beginning with q, were anciently written with C, as may be ſeen in the old copies of Plautus, and other authors; now as they had already made uſe of C to repreſent a hundred, it could not again be uſed here, therefore it is probable they took the next letter, which happens to be U, or V, as it was formerly written. This being admitted, the X may be eaſily made out, by joining the V's together, the poſition of the lower being only inverted. Theſe, Mr. Urban, are my conjectures upon this ſubject; if you think they have any degree of probability in them, or may excite others to give us a better rationale, you are at liberty to make uſe of them as you think proper.

PHILARITHMUS.

Mr. URBAN,

YOUR correſpondent, Philarithmus, has endeavoured to ſhew how the Roman numeral letters received their value; and tho' his hypotheſis is ingenious, yet I think I can ſhew that he is radically miſtaken, by proving, that there is great reaſon to believe the Romans never expreſſed any numbers by letters, except as the characters which they uſed to expreſs numbers, became letters by accident.

In the firſt place, however, I am ready to acknowledge, that the Greeks, and other eaſtern nations, did

did use their letters for numerical characters; but from the manner in which they used them, I draw my first arguments, to prove that letters were not thus used by the Romans. Every letter in the alphabet was used to denote some number by the Greeks and Orientals, and each letter denoted a less or greater number, as it was nearer or more remote from the first letter in their alphabetical order, and no letter, which in the order of the alphabet stands after another, ever denoted a number less than the letter that stands before it. Now, if the Romans, who derived their letters originally from the Greeks, had derived also their numeration by letters, it is in the highest degree probable, that these particulars would have been the same in both: but as not one third of the Roman letters are numerals, so neither is the numeral value of those that are so, more or less, according to their place in alphabetic order; for D and C, which are among the first letters of the alphabet, and M and L, which are in the middle, are of much greater numeral value than X and V, which are near the end.

But it has been supposed that the Romans used M to denote 1000, because it is the first letter of *Mille*, which is Latin for 1000; and C to denote 100, because it is the first letter of *Centum*, which is Latin for 100. Your correspondent also supposes, that D being formed by dividing the old M in the middle, was therefore appointed to stand for 500, that is, half as much as the M stood for when it was whole; and that L being half a C, was, for the same reason, used to denominate 50. But what reason is there to suppose, that 1000 and 100 were the numbers which letters were first used to express? And what reason can be assigned why D, the first letter in the Latin word *decem*, ten, should not rather have been chosen to stand for that number than for 500, because it had a rude resemblance to half an M? But if these questions could be satisfactorily answered, there are other numeral letters, which have never yet been accounted for at all. I think these considerations render it probable, that the Romans did not, in their original intention, use letters to express numbers at all; the most natural account of the matter seems to be this:

The Romans probably put down a single stroke I for one, as is still the practice of those who score on a slate, or with chalk; this stroke I they doubled, trebled, and quadrupled, to express 2, 3, and 4, thus, II. III. IIII. So far they could easily number the minums, or strokes, with a glance of the eye, but they presently found, that if more were added, it would soon be necessary to tell the strokes one by one: for this reason, when they came to 5, they expressed it by joining two strokes together in an acute angle, thus V, which will appear the more probable, if it be considered, that the progression of the Roman numbers is from 5 to 5, i. e. from the fingers on one hand to the fingers of the other.

Ovid has touched upon the original of this in his *Fastorum*, lib. iii. and Vitruv. lib. c. 1. has made the same remark.

After they had made this acute angle V for five, they added single strokes to it to the number of 4, thus, VI. VII. VIII. VIIII. and then as the minums could not be further multiplied without confusion,

ſion, they doubled their acute angle, by prolonging the two lines beyond their interſection thus X, to denote two fives, or ten. After they had doubled, trebled, and quadrupled this double acute angle thus, XX. XXX. XXXX. they then, for the ſame reaſon which induced them firſt to make a ſingle angle, and then to double it, joined two ſingle ſtrokes in another form, and, inſtead of an acute angle, made a right angle L, to denote fifty. When this 50 was doubled, they then doubled the right angle thus ⊏, to denote 100, and having numbered this double right angle four times, thus, ⊏⊏. ⊏⊏⊏. ⊏⊏⊏⊏; when they came to the fifth number, as before, they reverted it, and put a ſingle ſtroke before it thus, I⊐ to denote 500; and when this 500 was doubled, then they alſo doubled their double right angle, ſetting two double right angles oppoſite to each other, with a ſingle ſtroke between them, thus ⊏I⊐ to denote one thouſand: when this note for 1000 had been four times repeated, then they put down I⊐⊐ for 5,000, ⊏⊏I⊐⊐ for 10,000, and I⊐⊐⊐ for 50,000, ⊏⊏⊏I⊐⊐⊐ for 100,000, I⊐⊐⊐⊐ for 500,000, and ⊏⊏⊏⊏I⊐⊐⊐⊐ for one million.

That the Romans did not originally write M for 1,000, and C for 100, but ſquare characters, as they are written above, we are expreſsly informed by Paulus Manutius; but the corners of the angles being cut off by tranſcribers for diſpatch, theſe figures were gradually brought into what are now numeral letters. When the corners of ⊏I⊐ were made round, it ſtood thus CIↃ, which is ſo near the Gothic ↀ, that it ſoon deviated into that letter; ſo I⊐ having the corner made round ſtood thus IↃ and then eaſily deviated into D. ⊏ alſo became a plain C by the ſame means; the ſingle rectangle which denoted 50, was, without alteration, a capital L; the double acute angle was an X; the ſingle acute angle a V conſonant, and a plain ſingle ſtroke, the letter I. And thus theſe ſeven letters, M, D, C, L, X, V, I, became numerals.

And as a further proof of this hypotheſis, let it be conſidered, that CIↃ and IↃ are ſtill uſed for 1000 and 500, inſtead of M and D; and this mark ↀ, or this ω, denote 1,000, which may be eaſily derived from this figure ⊏I⊐, but cannot be deviations from, or corruptions of the Roman letter M.

I am, Mr. Urban, yours,
and Philarithmus's
very humble Servant,
A. B.

An account of ſeveral wonderful particularities diſcovered on opening a hive, that had a few days before received a young ſwarm.

From Dr. Swammerdam's Book of Nature, or Hiſtory of Inſects.

HAppening to be in the country on the 25th of July, I obſerved a great ſwarm of bees, which, on its hanging to an elm, I ordered to be received into a hive; but in a little time they all left this new habitation, and fled back to the elm, where they hung entangled by each others legs. The female bee had not dropt from the hive with the others: I was therefore obliged to have recourſe to another ſhaking; when having brought the female into the hive, all the reſt ſoon followed.

On

On the 26th of July the weather was tolerably good, with a bright funfhine; the 27th cloudy; the 28th and 29th rainy: on the 30th, on examining the hive, I found where it ftood, a piece of a honey-comb, which had fallen thither, either becaufe it had not been ftrongly enough faftened to the top of the hive, or becaufe too many bees had lighted upon it at one time. This piece of a comb contained 418 cells of the working bees, fome were building, and others were finifhed, and there was alfo ten eggs fticking to the wax by one of their ends. All the forenoon of the 31ft it was rainy, and about mid-day very cloudy and windy, with fome rain. In the evening I ordered the hive to be taken into my chamber, in order to examine what the bees had done in the fpace of thefe fix days.

But as I was afraid of being ftung in this enterprize, I refolved to have all the bees killed before I went to handle or infpect them; for this reafon I fumigated them with a bundle of lighted matches rolled up in linen rags, to fuch a thicknefs, that it would juft fit in the upper opening of the hive. All my endeavours to kill thefe bees this way were however to no purpofe; for after plying them with this fume, from eight o'clock to eleven, lighting the matches from time to time, as they went out, the bees continued alive; but they feemed grievoufly complaining of, and refented the injury offered them, with the moft horrid noife and loudeft buzzings.

The next morning all was quiet again, fo I removed the hive, at the bottom of which I found fome hundreds of bees lying dead upon the ground; but the greateft part of them were ftill alive, and fome of them were beginning to fly away. I therefore refolved to fumigate the hive a fecond time, and I gave its inhabitants liberty to efcape while it was doing. For fear of being ftung on this occafion, I took a half pint bottle, and having rolled fome foft paper about the neck of it, thruft it into the opening of the hive, taking care afterwards to ftop all gaps between the door and opening of the hive, and the neck of the bottle, with more paper of the fame kind. As foon as the fulphureous vapour began to fill the hive, the bees in the greateft hurry and confufion, and with the moft dreadful buzzing, rufhed to the number of 1898, in a manner all at once into the bottle, which I then removed to fubftitute another in its place; and by repeating the operation in this manner, I at laft fo thoroughly accomplifhed my purpofe, that not the leaft noife could be heard in the hive.

Having then turned the hive upfide down, I found the queen lying dead, in appearance, upon the ground, and fome of the others which had fallen upon the ground, killed downright and wet all over; whilft fome other bees that had remained in the upper part of the hive were quite dry, and when put into the bottles flew about as brifkly as if they had not received the leaft harm.

I next poured fome water upon the prifoners I had in the bottle; by this means they were all drowned in a very fhort time. I then made my examination, and found the fwarm confifted of 5669 bees, and was therefore a very good one, according to the judgment I had formed of it on its firft appearance.

ance. Neverthelefs, as the feafon was very far advanced, and the fpot the bees lighted upon very ill furnifhed with materials for making honey, I thought it worth while to facrifice them to the curiofity I had of knowing what work fuch a number could perform in fo fhort a time, and withal in fo unfavourable weather.

Among this great multitude, there was but one female bee. The greateft number of them were working bees, which are neither males nor females; and there were befides thefe and the female bee already mentioned, only 33 male bees, prepofteroufly called by the vulgar hatching bees; for the young bees are hatched by the mere heat of the fummer, and that which is caufed by the perpetual hurry and motion of the old bees flying about, or working in the hive. It is very remarkable that the bottle into which the firft 1898 bees, driven out of the hive, had been received, was thoroughly heated by the perpetual motion of thefe imprifoned creatures, and the warm vapours which exhaled from their bodies.

The number of waxen cells begun and finifhed, including thofe of the comb I had found on the ground on my firft examining the hive, amounted to 3392: they were all of the fame fize and form, and were intended only for nefts to hatch the working bees. In 236 of the cells fome honey had been ftored up, but it had been afterwards made ufe of, as very little could be then gathered abroad. It was no difficult matter to diftinguifh the cells thus made ufe of from the others, for they had received a yellow tincture from the honey depofited in them; whereas thofe which had not as yet been employed this way were of a fhining white.

There were alfo 62 of thefe cells, in which the bees had already begun to lay up their ordinary food or bread called erithace. This fubftance was of a changeable colour, between a yellow and a purplifh red; but perhaps this tinge might be owing to the fumigation; the whitenefs of the unemployed wax was in fome parts alfo impaired by the fame means; coloured and covered befides with black fpots.

In 35 cells I found as many eggs fixed in them at one end; fo that including the eggs found in the comb, which had fallen to the ground as already mentioned, there were 45 eggs in all. There were befides in 150 of the cells fo many new-hatched worms, but thefe lay almoft infenfible and motionlefs. They were of different fizes. All thefe worms were furrounded with that kind of food which the moft expert obfervers of bees think is honey thrown up by the old ones, out of their ftomachs. This kind of honey is white, like a folution of gum tragacanth, or ftarch diffolved in water, and is almoft infipid; it fhews nothing remarkable on being viewed with the microfcope. In the worms themfelves I could perceive pulmonary tubes of a filver whitenefs running moft beautifully on each fide through their little tranfparent bodies.

I examined attentively the wax cemented by way of foundation to the top of the hive, but I could find no difference between that and the other wax of which the cells confift. They appear both to have the fame nature and properties. I could not, however, but admire this

this ſtrong union or faſtening; this ſubſtance being juſt ſpread upon the hive like a cruſt, and conſequently faſtened to it by a very ſmall portion of its ſurface; whereas the reſt of the wax hung perpendicularly from this foundation, without any lateral or other ſupport whatſoever, as if a wooden bowl were fixed to a plain cieling by a ſmall part of its circumference.

This hive contained the rudiments of a great many more ſuch combs of wax, of an oval form, and full of cells on each ſide; the empty ſpaces left between the combs, for the bees to paſs and repaſs, did not exceed half an inch in breadth; ſo that it is plain the comb I found open upon the ground, and in which I reckoned 418 cells, had been torn from its foundation by its own weight, and that of the bees walking upon it. Hence it appears with what good reaſon thoſe who keep bees, place ſticks croſs-ways in their hives, that the combs may have the more ſupport; and accordingly we obſerve that in theſe hives, the bees themſelves on each ſide ſuſpend their combs to theſe ſticks.

Conſidering the great multitude of bees employed in building the waxen cells, which I have been juſt examining, there is no great reaſon to be ſurpriſed at their having done ſo much work that way, though the time they had to do it in was ſo ſhort, and the weather ſo unfavourable. But it is really more aſtoniſhing to think how a ſingle female could lay ſo many eggs in the ſame ſmall interval, and withal depoſit every egg in a ſeparate cell, and there firmly faſten it. We muſt alſo allow ſome time for laying the perpendicular foundations. It is, moreover, very ſurpriſing how theſe eggs ſhould ſo ſpeedily turn to worms, and how thoſe worms ſhould grow ſo very ſuddenly to their ſtate of change. But I muſt now conclude, and I ſhall do it with the following account of what the hive I have been deſcribing contained.

33 males.
1 female.
5635 working bees.
3392 wax cells, for the uſe of the working bees.
45 eggs.
150 worms.
62 cells containing bees bread.
236 cells in which honey had been laid up.

An account of an extraordinary ſhower of black duſt, that fell in the iſland of Zetland, Oct. 20, 1755. Being the extract of a letter from Sir Andrew Mitchell, of Weſtſhore, Bart. to John Pringle, M.D. F.R.S.

IN compliance with your deſire, I made particular enquiry, whether at or about the time the earthquake happened at Liſbon, Nov. 1. 1755, any uncommon phænomena were obſerved to appear in the iſlands of Orkney or Zetland, as ſuch had happened about that time in other parts of Scotland. From Orkney I was informed, that nothing particular had happened, only, that about the time mentioned, the tides were obſerved to be much higher than ordinary. I received from Zetland a letter, dated May 28, 1756, from Mr.

Mr. William Brown, master of the grammar-school at Scalloway in that country, a sensible and observing man; wherein he writes verbatim as follows: "Blessed be God, notwithstanding the great devastations that have been made in other parts of the world by earthquakes, we have been entirely free from any disaster of that nature: Nor has any thing extraordinary happened in this country since you left it, only on Monday, October 20th last, between the hours of three and four in the afternoon, the sky being very hazy, as it uses to be before a storm of thunder and lightening, there fell a black dust over all the country, though in greater quantities in some places than in others. It was very much like lamp-black, but smelled strongly of sulphur. People in the fields had their faces, hands, and linen, blackened by it. It was followed by rain.— Some people assign the cause of it to some extraordinary eruption of Hecla. But I shall trouble you no more about it, as no doubt some of your friends have written to you of it some time ago."—

In June, 1756, I returned to Zetland; and upon further enquiry, found what Mr. Brown had written me was attested by Mr. Mitchell, parson of the parish of Tengwall, and by several gentlemen of credit and reputation, who had seen and observed the same phænomenon in different parts of the country at the time above-mentioned.

Mr. Brown having omitted to mention how the wind did blow at the time the black dust was observed, I made particular enquiry about that circumstance, and found it was from the S. W. which does not seem to favour the opinion, that the dust proceeded from an eruption of mount Hecla, which lies about N. W. from Zetland, unless it may be supposed that a north wind happening just before, had carried this dust to the southward, and the south-west wind immediately following had brought it back to the northward. But in this case, would not this black dust have been observed in Zetland at its first travelling to the southward? Upon enquiry, I did not hear it was.

The method of cultivating madder in England, from many experiments, made in the course of thirty years on the culture of that useful plant. Extracted from a treatise lately published on that subject; by Philip Miller, F. R. S.

THIS piece is dedicated to Lord Folkestone, president of the society for the encouragement of arts, manufactures, and commerce. The author, in his preface, imputes the total neglect of cultivating madder in England, for a great number of years, to the many disputes occasioned about ascertaining the tithes upon it; a neglect the Dutch availed themselves of, by whom it is cultivated with the utmost diligence, and almost monopolized. This ingredient is so very essential in dying of cloth and staining of linen, that neither can be carried on without it, and the Dutch have received from us, for many years

years paſt, upon an average, more than 180,000l. per ann. for that commodity. In England there is ground better adapted to the growth of madder, than the beſt land they have in Holland, and it may be raiſed at leſs expence. The legiſlature have been ſo well convinced, therefore, of the national utility of raiſing madder, as to paſs two laws, in the laſt ſeſſion, to aſcertain the tithes for 14 years; and the ſociety for the encouragement of arts, &c. have offered a handſome premium to promote the planting thereof.

The root of the cultivated madder, (our author ſays) is compoſed of many long fibres larger than a gooſe quill; they are taper and much branched, of a brown colour on the outſide, but clear, tranſparent, and of an orange colour within, having a tough ſlender pith in the middle, of a bright yellow colour, of a ſweetiſh taſte, mixed with a little bitter; from theſe ariſe many four-cornered ſtalks, which grow from four to ſix or ſeven feet high, according to the goodneſs of the land; they are armed with ſhort herbaceous ſpines, and at each joint are garniſhed with five or ſix ſpear-ſhaped leaves, about three inches long, and almoſt one broad in the middle, drawing to a point at each end; their upper ſurfaces are ſmooth, but their mid-rib on the under ſide is armed with ſhort, crooked, herbaceous ſpines, which faſten to the clothes of thoſe who rub againſt them. The leaves are placed in whorls round the ſtalks, ſpreading out every way like the points of a ſtar. From the ſide of the ſtalk, at each joint, come out the foot ſtalks which ſupport the flowers; they are oppoſite on each ſide the ſtalk, and branch into ſeveral diviſions, having a few ſmall leaves at bottom, in ſhape like the other; there are ſometimes three of theſe at the ſame joint, and at others but two. The flowers are ſmall, of a bright yellow colour, and have but one petal or leaf, which is cut into four parts, which ſpread open. Theſe appear in July, and are ſometimes ſucceeded by ſmall, rough, burry ſeeds, growing by pairs, which never ripen in this country. The ſtalk or haulm of this plant decays in autumn, and new ſhoots ariſe in the ſpring; the roots ſend out many ſide fibres to a good diſtance, and theſe alſo put out ſhoots, whereby the plants propagate greatly.

The country where this plant grows naturally is ſuppoſed to be the Levant. I was informed by a gentleman, who brought over ſeveral ſpecimens of the plant to the late Sir Hans Sloane, that he gathered them between Scanderoon and Aleppo, where he ſaw the plants growing wild without culture.

Mr. Miller next gives a curious account of the culture, &c. of this plant, as practiſed by the Dutch, with drawings, viz. plan of the cold ſtove, ſection of the kiln-room and kiln, plan and ſection of the drying tower, and plan and ſection of the pounding-houſe. His method of cultivating it in England, take in his own words, as follows.

" The land upon which I have found madder thrive beſt, is a ſoft ſandy loam, and if it has been in tillage ſome years, it will be better than that which is freſh broken

5 up.

up. This ſhould have at leaſt a depth of two feet and a half, or three feet of good earth, that the roots may run down without obſtruction, and muſt be quite clear from couch, or the roots of any bad weeds; for as the roots of madder ſhould remain three years in the ground, ſo where there are any of thoſe weeds which ſpread and multiply at their roots, they will intermix with the madder roots, and in three years will have taken ſuch poſſeſſion of the ground as to greatly weaken the madder, and render it very troubleſome to ſeparate when the madder is taken up.

The ground ſhould be ploughed deep before winter, and laid in very high rough ridges to mellow; and if it is not too ſtrong, there will be no neceſſity for ploughing again, till juſt before the time of planting the madder, when the land ſhould be ploughed as deep as the beam of the plough will admit; and there ſhould be men following the plough in the furrows, who ſhould dig a full ſpit below the bottom of the furrow, and turn it up on the top. By preparing the ground of this depth, the roots of the madder will ſtrike down and be of greater length, in which the goodneſs of the crop chiefly conſiſts. The land being thus prepared and made level, will be fit to receive the plants. The beſt time for planting the madder, is about the middle or latter end of April, according as the ſeaſon is more or leſs forward, which muſt be determined by the young ſhoots; for when theſe are about an inch and a half, or two inches above ground, they are in the beſt ſtate for planting. When the ſhoots are longer, they are very apt to droop upon being moved, eſpecially if the ſeaſon ſhould prove warm and dry, and if their tops wither and decay the roots will be greatly weakened.

In the taking up of theſe ſhoots for planting, the ground ſhould be opened with a ſpade, that they may be ſeparated from the mother plants with as much root as poſſible; for if the roots are broken off, they will not ſucceed. Theſe plants ſhould be drawn up no faſter than they are planted, for if they lie long above ground, they will ſhrink, and their tops wither, and then they often miſcarry; therefore if they are brought from a diſtant place, the ſlips ſhould be taken off as ſoon as they begin to ſhoot, for the leſs top they have the better they will bear carriage; there ſhould be great care taken in the packing of them up for carriage; eſpecial regard ſhould be had not to pack them ſo cloſe, or in ſo great quantity, as to cauſe them to heat, for that will ſoon ſpoil them; but if they are a little withered by lying out of the ground, their roots ſhould be ſet upright in water for a few hours before they are planted, which will ſtiffen and recover them again.

In the planting of madder, there are ſome who make the rows but one foot aſunder, others one foot and a half, ſome two feet, and others who allow them three feet diſtance; I have made trial of the three laſt diſtances, and have found when the roots have been left three years in the ground, that three feet diſtance row from row is the beſt; but if they are taken up in two years, two feet aſunder

may

may do very well; and the diſtance in the rows, plant from plant, ſhould be one foot, if to ſtand two years, or a foot and a half if to ſtand three.

If there is no danger of the ground being too wet in winter, the plants may be planted on the level ground; but if, on the contrary, the ground ſhould be raiſed in ridges where each row of plants is to be ſet, that their roots may not reach the water in winter, for if they do, it will ſtop their downright growth; and this is the reaſon why the Dutch who plant madder in the Low Countries, between Helvoetſluys and the Brill, raiſe their ridges ſo high as two or three feet, but in Zealand, where the ground is drier, they do not raiſe the beds more than four or five inches above the intervals, that the wet may drain off from the beds where the madder is planted.

The method of planting the madder on level ground is as follows, viz. The ground being made ſmooth, a line is drawn croſs it to mark out the rows, that they may be ſtraight for the more convenient cleaning, and for the better digging or ploughing the ground between the rows; then with an iron-ſhod dibble, holes are made, at the diſtance which the plants are to ſtand from each other, The depth of the holes muſt be in proportion to the length of the roots of the plants, which muſt be planted the ſame depth in the ground which they had been while they were upon the mother plants, for if any part of the root is left above ground, the ſun and winds will dry it, which will retard the growth of the plants; and, ſhould any part of the green be buried in the ground it will not be ſo well, tho', of the two, the latter will be leſs prejudicial, eſpecially if there be not too much of the green buried. When the plants are put into the holes, the earth ſhould be preſſed cloſe to them to ſecure them from being drawn out of the ground, for crows and rooks frequently draw the young plants out of the ground, before they get new roots, where there is not this care taken; ſo that in two or three days, I have known half the plants, on a large piece of land, deſtroyed by theſe birds.

If there happens to be ſome ſhowers of rain fall in a day or two after the plants are planted, it will be of great ſervice to them, for they will preſently put out new roots, and become ſtrong, ſo that, if dry weather ſhould afterwards happen, they will not be in ſo much danger of ſuffering thereby, as thoſe which are later planted. There are ſome who, from a covetous temper of making moſt uſe of the ground, plant a row of dwarf peas, or kidney-beans, between each row of madder, and pretend that hereby the land is kept cleaner from weeds; but I am very certain the crop of madder is injured thereby much more than the value of thoſe things which grow between the rows, as I have experienced; therefore I adviſe thoſe perſons who plant madder, never to ſow or plant any thing between the rows, but to keep the madder quite clean from weeds, or any other kind of vegetable.

In order to keep the ground thus clean, it ſhould be ſcuffled over with a Dutch hoe, as ſoon as the young weeds appear in the ſpring, when a man can perform a great deal of this work in a day, and if it is done in dry weather, the weeds will die as faſt as they are cut down; whereas, when the weeds are left to grow ſo long as to get ſtrength, they are not ſo ſoon deſtroyed, and the expence of hoeing the ground then will be more than treble what it might be performed for early in the ſeaſon; beſides, there will be danger of cutting down ſome of the weaker plants with the weeds, if the perſons employed to perform this work are not very careful, therefore it is much cheaper as alſo better for the madder, to begin this work early in the ſpring, and to repeat it as often as the weeds render it neceſſary; for by keeping the ground thus conſtantly clean, the madder will thrive the better, and the expence in the whole year will be leſs, for when weeds are ſuffered to grow large, they are not eaſily ſubdued.

During the firſt ſummer, the only culture which the madder requires, is that of keeping it clean in the manner before directed, and, when the ſhoots or haulm of the plants decay in autumn, they ſhould be raked off the ground; then the intervals between the rows ſhould either be dug with a ſpade, or ploughed, with a hoeing plough, laying up the earth over the heads of the plants in a roundiſh ridge, which will be of great ſervice to the roots. The Dutch cover the haulm of their madder with earth, leaving it to rot upon the ground; this perhaps may be neceſſary in their country to keep the froſt out of the ground; but, as I have never found that the ſevereſt winters have ever injured the madder roots in England, ſo there is not the ſame neceſſity for that practice here.

The following ſpring, before the madder begins to ſhoot, the ground ſhould be raked over ſmooth, that the young ſhoots may have no obſtruction, and, if there ſhould be any young weeds appearing on the ground, it ſhould be firſt ſcuffled over to deſtroy the weeds, and then raked over ſmooth; after this the ſame care muſt be taken in the following ſummer, as in the former, to keep the ground clean from weeds, and, if it is performed by the hoe-plough, the earth of the intervals ſhould be thrown up againſt one ſide of the ridges, which will earth up the roots, and greatly increaſe their ſtrength; but, before the ground of one interval is ſo hoed, the haulm of the plants ſhould be turned over to the next adjoining interval, and, if they are permitted ſo to lie for a fortnight or three weeks, and then turned back again on thoſe intervals which were hoed, obſerving firſt to ſcuffle the ground to deſtroy any young weeds, which may have appeared ſince the ſtirring of the ground, then the alternate intervals ſhould be ploughed in like manner, turning the earth up againſt the oppoſite ſides of the roots; by this method the intervals will be alternately ploughed, and the plants earthed up, whereby the ground will be kept clean and ſtirred, which will greatly promote the growth of the roots, and by this method the ſuperficial ſhoots will be ſubdued, and the principal roots greatly ſtrengthened. The following autumn the ground ſhould be cleared of the haulm and weeds, and the earth raiſed in ridges over the roots, as in the foregoing year.

The

The third ſpring the roots will furniſh a great ſupply of young plants, but, before theſe appear, the ground ſhould be cleaned and raked ſmooth, that the ſhoots may have no obſtruction to their coming up; and, when the young plants are fit to take off, it ſhould be performed with great care, always taking off thoſe which are produced at the greateſt diſtance from the crown of the mother-plants, firſt, becauſe thoſe are what rob them moſt of their nouriſhment, and the wounds made by ſeparating them from the old roots are not near ſo hurtful as thoſe near the crown, for the ſtripping off too many of the ſhoots there, will retard the growth of the plants.

The culture of the madder in the third ſummer muſt be the ſame as the ſecond, but, as the roots will then be much ſtronger, the earth ſhould be laid up a little higher to them at the times when the ground is cleaned and ploughed, and, if all the diſtant ſuperficial ſhoots, which come up in the intervals, are hoed or ploughed off, it will be of ſervice to ſtrengthen the larger downright roots, and, as the haulm will now be very ſtrong and thick, the frequent turning it over, from one interval to another, will prevent its rotting, for if it lies long in the ſame poſition, the ſhoots, which are near the ground, where there will be always more or leſs damp, and being covered with the upper ſhoots, the air will be excluded from them, which will cauſe them to rot, for the ſhoots of madder are naturally diſpoſed to climb upon any neighbouring ſupport, and in places where they have been ſupported, I have ſeen them more than ten feet high, but the expence of ſtaking the plants to ſupport their ſhoots would be much too great to be practiſed in general, therefore the other method of turning the haulm over, from one interval to the other, will be found of great uſe; for hereby it is kept from decaying, and by ſo doing the ſun is alternately admitted to each ſide of the roots, which is of more conſequence to the growth of the madder than moſt people conceive; and from many repeated trials I have found, that where the haulm has decayed or rotted in ſummer, it has greatly retarded the growth of the roots. There have been ſome ignorant pretenders who have adviſed the cutting of the haulm in ſummer, in order to ſtrengthen the roots, but whoever practiſes this, will find, to their coſt, the abſurdity of this method, for I have fully tried this many years ago, and have always found that every other root, upon which this was practiſed, was at leaſt a third part ſmaller than the intermediate roots, whoſe haulm was left entire. The occaſion of firſt making this experiment was, becauſe the plants had been ſet too near each other, and the ſeaſon proving moiſt had increaſed the number and ſtrength of the ſhoots, ſo that they became ſo thick, as that many of them began to rot; to prevent which, I cut off the ſhoots of every other plant to give room for ſpreading the others thinner, but ſoon after this was done, the plants produced a greater number of ſhoots than before, but they were weaker, and the effect it had upon the roots was as before related, and ſince then I have frequently repeated the experiment on a few roots, and have always found the effect the same.

As soon as the haulm of the madder begins to decay in autumn, the roots may be taken up for use, because then the roots have done growing for that season, and will then be plumper, and less liable to shrink, than if they are dug up when the plants are growing; for I have always found that the roots of every kind of plant, which are taken out of the ground during the time of their growth, are very apt to shrink, and lose much of their weight in a short time.

When the season for digging up the madder roots is come, it should be done in the following manner, viz. A deep trench should be dug at one side of the ground next to the first row of madder, to make a sufficient opening to receive the earth, which must be laid therein in digging up the row of roots, so that it should be at least two feet broad, and two spits, and two shovelings deep, and should be as close as possible to the roots, without breaking or cutting them in doing it; then the row of roots must be carefully dug up, turning the earth into the trench before mentioned. In the doing of this there should be to every person who digs, two or three persons to take out the roots, that none may be lost, and as much of the earth should be shaken out of the roots as possible; and after the principal roots are taken up, there will be many of the long fibres remaining below, therefore, in order to get the roots as clean as possible, the whole spot of ground should be dug of the same depth as the first trench, and the pickers must follow the diggers to get them all out to the bottom. As the digging of the land to this depth is necessary, in order to take up the roots with as little loss as possible, it is a fine preparation for any succeeding crop; and I have always found that the ground, where madder has grown, produced better crops of all kinds than land of equal goodness, which had not the like culture.

After the roots are taken up, the sooner they are carried to the place of drying, the finer will be their colour, for if they lie in heaps, they are apt to heat, which will discolour them, or if rain should happen to wet them much, it will have the same effect, therefore no more roots should be taken up than can be carried under shelter the same day.

The first place, in which the roots should be laid dry, must be open to admit the air, but covered on the top to keep out the wet. If a building is to be erected new, such as the tanners have for drying their skins will be as proper as any, for these have weather-boards from top to bottom, at equal distances, to keep out the driving rain, but the spaces between being open, admit the air freely; and if instead of plank floors or stages above each other, they are laid with hurdles or basket work, upon which the roots are laid to dry, the air will have freer passage to the under side of the roots, which will dry them more equally.

In this place they may remain three or four days, but the roots should be turned over once or twice, that every part may dry equally, by which time the earth, which adhered to the roots, will be so dry as easily to rub off, which should

ſhould be done before the roots are removed to the cold ſtove; for the ſlower the roots are dried, the leſs they will ſhrink and, the better will be the colour of the madder; and the cleaner the roots are from earth, the better the commodity will be for the uſe when prepared.

Wherever there are any large barns or other buildings, whoſe ſides are open to admit the air, there will be no occaſion for erecting buildings for this purpoſe; becauſe theſe will anſwer full as well; but if there are different ſtages of hurdles erected in theſe buildings, at three or four feet above each other, to lay the roots upon them, the hurdles being open, will admit the air to the under ſide of the roots, whereby they will dry more equally than when they are ſpread on a cloſe floor, and hereby a much greater quantity of roots may be dried under the ſame roof. During the time they remain here, the doors and all other apertures of the building ſhould be kept conſtantly open, for the greater quantity of free air is admitted to the roots, the better they will dry; and the ſlower they dry at firſt, the leſs of their weight will be diminiſhed, and the colour will be the better; but they muſt be guarded from wet, which will be very prejudicial to the colour. When the roots have lain in this place ſo long as to dry their outſides ſufficiently to rub off the dirt which adhered to them, then they ſhould be carried to the kiln to be farther dried; and as there are in moſt parts of England kilns already built for drying of malt and hops, they may be uſed for drying of madder; but if there were ventilators fixed to theſe kilns, for blowing a ſufficient quantity of air through the rooms where the madder roots are drying, in the manner directed by the Reverend Dr. Hales for drying of malt and hops, it will be found a much better method than that which is practiſed by the Dutch, and will ſave a great expence of fuel.

When the outſide of the roots have been ſufficiently dried in this cold ſtove or kiln, they ſhould be removed to the threſhing floor, which may be the ſame as in a common barn where corn is threſhed. The floor of this ſhould be ſwept, and made as clean as poſſible; then the roots ſhould be threſhed to beat off their ſkins or outſide coverings; this is the part which is prepared ſeparately from the inner part of the root, and is called mull, which is ſeld at a very low price, being the warſt ſort of madder, ſo cannot be uſed where the permanency or beauty of the colours are regarded; theſe huſks are ſeparated from the roots, pounded by themſelves, and are afterwards packed up in ſeparate caſks, and ſold by the title of mull. If this is well prepared, and not mixed with dirt, it may be ſold for about fifteen ſhillings per hundred weight, at the price which madder now bears, and this, as is ſuppoſed, will defray the whole expence of drying the crop.

After the mull is ſeparated from the roots, they muſt then be removed to the kiln again, which muſt now have a greater heat than before, where they muſt be dried with care, for if the heat is too great, the roots will dry too faſt, whereby they will loſe much in weight, and the colour of the madder will not be near ſo bright: to avoid which, the roots ſhould be frequently turned, while they remain in this ſtove, and the fires muſt be properly regulated, and a ſufficient quanity of freſh air blown through the kiln, which will drive out the foul air occaſioned by the perſpiration of the roots, which will be found very uſeful in preſerving their colour. If ſome trials are made by fixing a good thermo meter in the room, the neceſſary heat may be better aſcertained than can be done any other way, but this will require to be greater at ſome times than at others, according as the roots are more or leſs ſucculent, or the weather more or leſs cold or damp, but it will always be better to have the heat rather leſs than over hot, for though the roots may require a longer time to dry with a ſlow heat, yet the colour will be better.

When the roots are properly dried in this ſtove, they muſt be carried to the pounding-houſe, where they muſt be reduced to powder; but whether it is neceſſary to ſeparate the kraps from the gemeens as is now practiſed by the Dutch, the conſumers of madder will be better judges than myſelf

The expence in erecting of the pounding-houſes in Holland is very great, ſo need not be built here, for any common building will ſerve for this purpoſe, where there is room to fix up the apparatus for pounding the roots; the block for this purpoſe ſhould be like thoſe uſed in Holland, as ſhould alſo be the ſtampers, which are bound round at bottom with thick iron bands, framed like the points of a ſtar; for if the ſurface of the ſtampers are ſmooth and even, the madder will adhere to them ſo cloſely, as to render it impoſſible to pulverize the roots properly. The ſtampers may be ſo contrived as to be worked by water, where there is conveniency, or perhaps by wind; but if it is done by horſes, as in Holland, there need not ſo great an apparatus, for no doubt many of our mechanicks, when they ſee the Dutch plans, can make great improvemeuts to them."

Mr. Miller, at the cloſe of his performance, anſwers ſuch objections as have been made againſt retrieving the cultivation of madder in England, and gives a ſhort abſtract of the two acts mentioned above, and we hope for the honour and intereſt of this country a ſpirit of emulation will be exerted to recover ſo valuable a branch of agriculture.

The ſtrange effects of ſome effervescent mixtures. In a letter from Dr. James Mounſey, Phyſician of the Ruſſian army, and F. R. S. to Mr. Henry Baker, F. R. S. Communicated by Mr. Baker.

From the Philoſophical Tranſactions.

Moſcow, Sept. 20. 1756.

MR. Butler, a paper ſtainer, trying to make ſome diſcoveries for the better fixing of colours, was put in great danger of his life by the following experiments.

Having put into one gallipot a quarter of an ounce of verdegris, and into another pot two leaves of falſe gold-leaf, to each he poured about a ſpoonful of aqua fortis. They began immediately to ferment, eſpecially the gold leaf. He was very aſſiduous in ſtirring them, to make the ſolution perfect. Having nothing elſe at hand, he did this

this with a pair of ſmall ſciſſars, at arms length, carefully turning away his face, to prevent the fumes from entering his lungs. He was called away, about other buſineſs, before he had quite ended his proceſs, and ſoon after waſhed and ſhifted himſelf: but he had ſcarce finiſhed, before he felt a burning pain in the ring finger of his right-hand, which he imputed to his having inadvertently touched the aqua-fortis. This increaſed every moment, and affected the whole hand with burning pain and ſwelling, which very ſoon ſubſided: but then it flew into the left hand, and a few minutes afterwards, into the inſides of his legs, as if ſcalding water had been thrown on them. His ſtockings being immediately pulled off, there appeared a great many red ſpots, as large as ſixpences, ſomething raiſed above the ſkin, and all covered with very ſmall bliſters.

In about two hours after the accident, I firſt ſaw him: he was very uneaſy, complaining of pain, and great anxiety, at the pit of the ſtomach, as if a burning hot iron was laid on it; ſo he expreſſed himſelf. His pulſe was regular, but ſlower and weaker than natural: he had a nauſea, and complained of a very coppery ſmell and taſte. I ordered him ſome alcaline volatile medicines, and to drink ſmall ſack-whey. He vomited once, and had four or five ſtools, and then his ſtomach grew eaſy. But the ſcene ſoon began again with lancing pains in the left eye. He continued the ſame medicines, drank plentifully of the whey, and was kept in a breathing ſweat, by which he found ſome eaſe at night: but whenever the ſweating leſſened, the burning pains returned in broad flakes, changing from one part of the body to the other; ſometimes with ſhootings in his eye, and ſometimes along the penis, but he had no heat of urine. His pulſe continued regular, but weak; and in ſeveral places of his body ſuch kind of ſpots ſtruck out as thoſe in his legs.

Monday, the third day in the morning after ſleeping well, his pulſe was ſomewhat raiſed, and he continued eaſy till about eleven o'clock, when the burning pains returned, ſhooting from place to place; but always ſo ſuperficial, that he could not diſtinguiſh whether it was in or under the ſkin. Rubbing the part affected with one's hand gave eaſe; but when the ſweating went off, and the burnings and ſhooting became inſufferable, I always put him into a bath of hot water, with ſome wood aſhes, kept ready in the room, which gave him great relief. This afternoon he felt violent burning pain in his great toes, and ſometimes in his left hand, with ſhootings up to the ſhoulder. Once he cried out, in great pain, that his ſhoulder was burſt; for he felt ſomething fly out with a ſort of exploſion: but, examining the part, I found nothing particular. He obſerved, when the flaky burnings began, they were as if they kindled from a point, and flaſhed like lightning, as he termed it. He was very often tormented with ſuch pains on the pit of the ſtomach; and this evening had ſhootings thro' the back, with a pain in the belly. He complained of a ſtrong ſulphurous ſmell, which, he ſaid, was like to ſuffocate him; though his breathing ſeemed eaſy, and his lungs no ways affected. In the night he was ſeized with great pain about the heart, and cried out violently, that his heart was on fire; but after taking a dose of nervous medicines, and being put into the bath, he was soon freed from this, and passed the rest of the night tolerably well. At the time of such violent attacks the pulse continued regular, but still slower and softer than usual.

Tuesday. He complained most of his toes, and now and then burning pain in the fore-head.

Wednesday. This whole day it continued most in the toes of the left foot; but in the evening the pain on the stomach returned, which lanced to the left side, with dartings inwardly. He became so uneasy and restless, that I was obliged to add some opium to the other medicines; which answered very well.

Thursday. The pains kept most in the toes of the left foot.

Friday. Nothing particular, except his feeling with sharp pain, a spark (as he called it) fly out of his right cheek, in the same way, he said, as that, which burst on his shoulder, but much less. He perceived no pain in that part before this; nor any thing after, besides a soreness, which lasted for some days. Hitherto he had been kept in a continual sweat; his appetite was greater than his allowance; his digestion good; and his rest indifferent. From this time he was not attacked with any violent symptoms, and could be quiet though he did not sweat.

On Sunday he began to get out of bed, but was often seized with glowing pains, suddenly affecting different part of the body, which seldom continued an hour in one part, but shifted from place to place: these he was troubled with in a less degree even long after he went abroad.

By care and watchfulness the violence of the symptoms were kept under; and by the use of antidotes for poisons, of the nature of what he received this from, the disease was overcome, and the patient recovered his perfect health and strength.

A remarkable case of the efficacy of the bark in a mortification. In a letter to William Watson, M. D. F. R. S. from Mr. Richard Grindall, Surgeon to the London Hospital. Read before the Royal Society, Dec. 8, 1757.

Austin Friars, Dec. 7, 1757.

SIR,

THE following case, being very singular, has induced me to lay it before the Royal Society. Although numerous instances are related in the records of medicine, of the great danger in interrupting nature in her operations, there is not one (so far as I know) in which more violent and extraordinary effects have been produced than in the following.

It may happen also, that this instance may be of service in ascertaining the virtue of the medicine in intermittents, when in the hands of men of judgment.

On the 28th of June, 1757, Mary Alexander, of the parish of Whitechapel, aged 31 years, was brought into the London hospital, having a mortification in both hands, which reached about an inch and an half above the wrists. All her toes, and about an inch of one foot beyond the last joint, were mortified; her nose was also intirely destroyed by a mortification; and all these happened at the same time. Upon inquiry into the cause of of this misfortune, I found, that on Monday the 30th of May ſhe was ſeized with a quotidian ague, which uſually began about three o'clock in the afternoon, and laſted near two hours, which was ſucceeded by a hot fit, and then a violent ſweat. And in this manner ſhe was afflicted for ſeven days, without any material alteration; when, being informed by a neighbour of a perſon who had an infallible remedy for the cure of an ague, ſhe applied to him. He brought her two phials, containing about an ounce and half each, of a pale yellowiſh liquor; one of which he directed her to take directly, promiſing, that ſhe ſhould have no return of the fit of conſequence; and that if ſhe had any ſmall return, the ſecond bottle ſhould cure her effectually. In conſequence of which ſhe took one doſe, which was at the time the cold fit had been on about a quarter of an hour: ſhe had no ſooner ſwallowed it, but, as ſhe ſays, her ſtomach was on fire, and felt as if ſhe had ſwallowed the ſtrongeſt dram poſſible. The cold fit left her inſtantly; but ſhe was immediately ſeized with ſo violent a fever, as to make her burn and be extremely thirſty all the following night; much more than ever ſhe had been before, till the next morning, when a ſweat a little relieved her from the violent heat. When ſhe roſe in the morning, ſhe was much troubled with a great itching in the hands, feet, and noſe; and, ſoon after, all thoſe parts began to feel numbed, or, as ſhe deſcribes it, as if her hands and feet were aſleep; which ſhe took but little notice of till the evening of that day, when ſhe found the nails of both hands and feet were turning black, and, at the ſame time, feeling great pain in both, as alſo in her noſe, and that they appeared of a darkiſh red colour, like the ſkin in cold weather. Upon which at nine o'clock that night, ſhe ſent for an apothecary, from whom, I have ſince been informed, the perſon before-mentioned had bought the medicine, which he gave her. The apothecary was not at home; his journeyman went, and finding the woman had a difficulty of breathing, ordered her a mixture with ſperma ceti and ammoniacum, to be taken occaſionally. The apothecary did not ſee her himſelf till the 16th of June, when, finding her in a very bad condition, that her hands and feet, and noſe, were entirely black, and had many veſicles or ſmall bladders upon them, filled with a blackiſh bloody water, he opened them, and let out the fluid, and dreſſed them with yellow baſilicon: and in this manner continued treating her till the 20th of the ſame month, when finding no material alteration for the better, he ordered her a browniſh mixture, of which ſhe was to take four ſpoonfuls every four hours, which, he informed me, was a decoction of the bark; and ſays, on taking this, ſhe was better, as the mortification ſeemed inclined to ſtop. But, as it was a bad caſe, he adviſed the woman to be carried to an hoſpital: and in this condition ſhe was brought in, when ſhe was immediately put into a courſe of the bark, taking a drachm of the powder every four hours; and in forty-eight hours taking it there was a perfect ſeparation of all the mortified parts. She was then ordered to take it only three times in twenty-four hours; and, purſuing this method for eight days, there

there was a very good digeſtion from the parts above the mortification.

The mortified parts became now ſo offenſive, that the poor woman preſſed me much to take off her hands, aſſuring me ſhe would go through the operations with good courage, being very deſirous to live, though in this miſerable condition.

On the 12th of July I took off both her hands; I had very little more to do than ſaw the bones, nature having ſtopped the bleeding when ſhe ſtopped the mortification. In a day or two after, I took off all the toes from both feet, and now diſcontinued the bark, the parts appearing in a healthy and healing condition; which went on ſo for five weeks, when on a ſudden, the parts began to look livid, her ſtomach failed her, and ſhe was feveriſh; but upon taking an ounce of the bark, in thirty-ſix hours her ſores began again to look well. She was not ſuffered to leave off the bark ſo ſoon this time, but continued taking it twice a day for a month. She is now almoſt well: that part of her face, from whence the noſe mortified, was healed in ſeven weeks; the ſtumps of both arms are entirely healed, and both feet are well, only waiting for one piece of bone ſcaling off, which I believe will be in a very ſhort time, and ſhe is now in good health.

The perſon who gave her this medicine is a barber and peruke-maker at Bow. I applied to him ſeveral times, to inform me what it was he had given her. The affair was talked of ſo much in his neighbourhood, and the man threatened by the woman's huſband, that for a long time I could not get him to tell me, till I told him I had been informed where he bought the medicines; and the time of the day that he had them correſponding with the time of his giving them to the woman, and that I knew it was tincture of myrrh, he at laſt told me, that he had frequently given the above quantity of an ounce and half of it in an ague, that it had never done any harm, and hardly ever failed to cure. Upon which information I carried ſome tincture of myrrh to the woman, who taſted it, and is well aſſured it is the ſame liquor the barber gave her in her ague-fit. I am, with reſpect,

Your obliged,
and obedient ſervant,
R. Grindall.

An account of the political eſtabliſhment of the Jeſuits in Paraguay.

From the Spaniſh of Don Jorge Juan, &c.

THE territories of the miſſions of Paraguay comprehended not only the province of that name, but alſo a great part of the provinces of Santa Cruz de la Sierra, Tucuman, and Buenos Ayres. The temperature of the air is good, though ſomewhat moiſt, and in ſome parts rather cold: the ſoil in many places is fertile, and produces in great abundance not only the fruits and vegetables peculiar to America, but alſo thoſe of Europe, which have been introduced there. The chief articles of their commerce are, cotton, tobacco, ſome ſugar, and the herb called Paraguay. Every town gathers annually more than 200 arrobas of of cotton, of a quarter of an hundred weight each, which the Indians manufacture into ſtuffs. There are alſo great quantities of tobacco produced: but the chief article is the herb Paraguay, for it grows only in the diſtricts of the miſſions, and there is a vaſt conſumption of this herb in all the provinces of Chili and Peru, eſpecially of that called Camini, which is the pure leaf, the infuſion of which is called mate, and is drank by the inhabitants of Lima twice a day in lieu of tea or chocolate: the mate, which is made by the infuſion of the ſtalk, is not ſo much eſteemed.

'Tis now about a century and a half ſince theſe miſſions were firſt ſet on foot by the Jeſuits: the bad management of the Portugueſe greatly favoured the views of theſe fathers. There was a ſtation of Indians called Guaranies, ſome whereof were ſettled upon the banks of the rivers Uruguay and Parana, and others an hundred leagues higher up in the country to the north weſt of Guayra: the Portugueſe frequently came upon them, and by force carried away as many as they thought proper to their plantations and made ſlaves of them: offended by ſuch treatment the Guaranies reſolved to quit their ſettlements in the neighbourhood of the Portugueſe, and to remove into the province of Paraguay. Accordingly a migration of 12000 perſons great and ſmall enſued. Theſe the Jeſuits ſoon converted, and, having had the like ſucceſs in converting about an equal number of the natives of Tape, a diſtrict in Paraguay, they united the two nations, and laid the foundation of their future dominion. Theſe fathers ſeem to have trod in the ſteps of the firſt Incas, and to have civilized nations, and converted ſouls in order to acquire ſubjects.

According to a very exact account taken in the year 1734, there were then 32 towns of the Guaranies, which were reckoned to contain above 30,000 families; and as the new converts were continually increaſing, they were then about laying the foundations of three new towns. There were alſo then ſeven very populous towns inhabited by the converted Chiquito Indians, and they were preparing to build others for the reception of the new converts of that nation which were daily made.

The miſſions of Paraguay are ſurrounded on all ſides with wild or uncovered Indians: ſome of whom live in friendſhip with the towns, but others harraſs them by frequent incurſions. The father miſſionaries frequently viſit theſe Indians and preach to them, and from theſe expeditions they ſeldom return without bringing along with them ſome new converts to incorporate with their civilized ſubjects. In the performance of this duty they ſometimes penetrate an hundred leagues into the wild uncultivated tracts where wild Indians range, and it is obſerved that they meet with the leaſt ſucceſs amongſt thoſe nations with whom any fugitive Meſtizos, or Spaniſh criminals have taken refuge. The diligence of theſe fathers is certainly worthy the imitation of the Proteſtant clergy.

Every town has its curate, who is aſſiſted by one, and very often by two prieſts of the ſame order, according to the largeneſs and extent of the town and its diſtrict. Theſe two or three prieſts, together

ther with six boys, who assist them in the service of the church, form a small college in every town, wherein the hours and other exercises are regulated with the same formality and exactness as in the large colleges in the cities of Peru and Chili. The most troublesome part of the duty of the assistant priests are the personal visitations, which they are obliged to make to the Indians to prevent their giving themselves up to idleness; for such is the slothfulness of the Guaranies, that if they are not very carefully looked after, the society would receive no benefit or advantage from them.—They also attend the public shambles, where the cattle necessary for the sustenance of the Indians are daily slaughtered, and distribute the flesh amongst all the families in the town, in proportion to the number of persons whereof each family consists; so that all may have what is necessary, none what is superfluous. They also visit the sick, and see that they are properly taken care of. They are generally employed the whole day in these affairs, so that they have seldom time to assist the curate in his spiritual functions. All the boys and girls in the parish go to church every day in the week (except on festivals and Sundays,) where they are instructed by the curate: on Sundays the whole parish goes to the church to be instructed. The curate is besides obliged to go to confess the sick, and to administer the viaticum to those who desire it, and also to perform all the other functions peculiar to his office.

In strictness the curates should be appointed in this manner. The society should nominate three persons o the governor of Buenos Ayres (in whose government the missions of Paraguay are included) as being vice-patron of the missions, that he may choose one of them for curate; and the curates should be instructed in the duties of their office by the bishop: but as the provincials of the order can best judge who are properly qualified for the office, the governor and bishop have ceded their rights to them, and by them the curates are always appointed.

The missions of the Guaranies, and the missions of the Chiquitos, into which the missions of Paraguay are divided, have each their distinct father-superior, by whom the coadjutors or assistant-curates of the several towns in their respective divisions are appointed. These superiors are continually visiting the towns to see that they be well governed, and to endeavour to improve and augment them: they likewise, from time to time, take care to send out some fathers of the order into the countries of the wild Indians to make new converts. The better to enable him to discharge these duties, the superior of the Guaranies is assisted by two vice-superiors, one of whom resides in Parana, the other upon the banks of the river Uruguay, and the superior himself resides in the town of Candelaria. The post of superior of the Chiquitos is not near so troublesome as that of the superior of the Guaranies; for the Chiquitos are not less numerous, but much more docile and industrious than the Guaranies, so that they need not be continually watched and attended in order to prevent their idleness.

The king allows an annual stipend

ſtipend of 300 pezos to each curate of the Guaranies, for the maintenance of himſelf and his aſſiſtants: the money is paid to the ſuperior, who iſſues out monthly to each curate as much as is neceſſary for his ſubſiſtence, and when they want any thing extraordinary their wants are ſupplied upon application to him. But the Chiquitos maintain their own curates. In every town there is a plantation ſet apart for the maintenance of the curate, which is cultivated by the joint labour of all the inhabitants. The produce of theſe plantations is generally more than ſufficient for the ſubſiſtence of the curates, and the ſurplus is ſold to buy ornaments for the churches.

Nor are the curates ſpiritual rectors of the towns only, they are alſo in effect the civil governors. It is true, there are in every town of the miſſions a governor, regidores, and alcades, as there are in the other towns and cities under the Spaniſh government. But though the governor is elected by the Indians, he muſt be approved by the curate before he enters upon his office, nor can he chaſtiſe or puniſh delinquents without the curate's permiſſion. The curate examines thoſe who are accuſed of offences, and, if he finds them guilty, delivers them to the governor to be puniſhed, according to the nature and quality of the offence committed. He ſometimes orders them to be impriſoned for a few days, ſometimes to faſt, and when the fault is conſiderable to be whipped, which is the ſevereſt puniſhment that is ever inflicted. For the regulations and inſtructions of the curates have been ſo efficacious, that murder, and ſuch like heinous crimes, are never here committed. And even before they undergo theſe gentle corrections, the curate diſcourſes the offenders in a mild friendly manner, and endeavours to excite in them a due ſenſe of their crime, and of the ill conſequences that might flow from it, and to convince them that they merit a much greater puniſhment than is inflicted. This mild treatment prevents tumults and inſurrections, and acquires the curates univerſal veneration and eſteem. The alcades are choſen annually by the regidores. The governor, regidores, and alcades are all Indians of the beſt capacities, and are, in effect, ſo many overſeers appointed by the curate, and dignified with theſe empty titles.

Every town has its armoury, or magazine, in which are lodged the fire arms and other weapons, wherewith the militia are armed when they take the field, to repel the irruptions of the Portugueſe and wild Indians. The militia are very dextrous and expert in the management of their arms, and are exerciſed on the eves of feſtivals in the ſquares or public places of the towns. The militia is compoſed of all thoſe who are able to bear arms; they are formed into companies, which have each a proper number of officers choſen from amongſt thoſe who are moſt diſtinguiſhed for judgment and conduct. The dreſs of the officers is rich, adorned with gold and ſilver, and the device of the town to which they belong: they always appear in their uniforms on feſtivals, and on the days of military exerciſes. The governor, alcades, and regidores, have alſo proper robes

robes and dreſſes ſuitable to their reſpective offices, in which they appear on public occaſions.

There are ſchools in every town in which the common people are taught reading and writing, and alſo muſic and dancing : in which arts they become very ſkilful. The Jeſuits are very careful in conſulting the natural bent and genius of their ſcholars, and in directing their ſtudies and application accordingly. The lads of the moſt promiſing genius are taught the Latin tongue with great ſucceſs. In one of the court yards of every curate's houſe are the various ſhops or workhouſes of painters, or carvers, gilders, ſilverſmiths, carpenters, weavers, and clockmakers, and of ſeveral other mechanics and artizans, who daily work for the public under the direction of the coadjutors, and at the ſame time teach the youth their reſpective arts, and occupations.

The churches are large, well built, finely decorated and enlightened, and not inferior to the richeſt in Peru. Each church has a choir of muſic, compoſed of inſtruments of all ſorts, and very good voices, ſo that divine ſervice is celebrated here with as much pomp and ſolemnity as in cathedrals : nor are the public proceſſions leſs ſplendid, eſpecially that of the hoſt, which, whenever it is carried abroad, is attended by the governor, alcades, and regidores, in their robes, and alſo by the militia in a body.

The houſes of the Indians are as well built and as well furniſhed as moſt of the Spaniſh houſes in Peru. The greateſt part indeed have mud walls, others are built with brick, and ſome with ſtone, but all are covered with tiles. In every town there is a houſe where gun-powder is made, that they may never want it when they are obliged to take arms, and always have it ready to make artificial fireworks on rejoicing days ; for all feſtivals are here obſerved with as great ceremony and exactneſs as in the greateſt cities. Upon the proclamation of a new king in Spain, the governors, alcades, regidores, and officers of the militia, appear dreſſed in new robes and uniforms of a different faſhion from thoſe they wore before.

There is a ſort of convent in every town, in one part whereof are confined women of an ill life, and the other part is deſtined for the reception of married women who have no family, and who retire thither when their huſbands are abſent : for the maintenance of this houſe, and for the ſupport of orphans, and of old and infirm people, all the inhabitants of the town work two days in every week, and the profits of their labour, which is called the labour of the community, are ſet apart for this purpoſe. If the produce of the labour be more than is neceſſary for their ſubſiſtence, the ſurplus is laid out to buy ornaments for the churches, and clothes for the orphans and aged, and infirm people : ſo that here are are no beggars, nor any who want the neceſſaries of life. In ſhort, by the wiſe policy and prudent regulations of the Jeſuits, the whole community enjoys peace and happineſs.

The Guaranies are ſo profuſe and negligent, that the curates are obliged to take into their hands all their goods and ſtuffs as as ſoon as they are manufactured and made ready for ſale, otherwiſe they would waſte and deſtroy them, and not be able to maintain themſelves. The Chiquitos on the contrary, are diligent and frugal, ſo that the curates have no other trouble with them than the aſſiſting them in the diſpoſal of their goods, and procuring returns for them. For this purpoſe, the ſociety keeps a factor or procurator at Santa Fie, and Buenos Ayres, to whom the merchandize of the miſſions is ſent to be diſpoſed of, and theſe factors return the value to the fathers, in ſuch ſorts of European commodities as are wanted. The goods of every town are kept ſeparate, and the royal taxes are taken out of them without any other diſcounts, or allowances, ſave the ſtipends of the curates of the Guaranies, and the penſions of the caciques The fathers chooſe to manage the commerce of their ſubjects themſelves, leſt they ſhould contract vices by their communication with other people. In this reſpect the fathers are ſo careful, that they will not ſuffer any of the people of Peru, whether they be Spaniards, Meſtizos, or Indians, to enter into the territories of the miſſions. They ſay that the Indians are but juſt recovered from a barbarous and diſſolute way of life, and that their manners are now pure and innocent; but that if ſtrangers are ſuffered to come among them, the Indians would ſoon become acquainted with people of looſe lives; and as the Guaranies eſpecially are very prone to vice and wickedneſs, diſorder and rebellion would ſoon be introduced, the ſociety would loſe all the ſouls they have converted, and their little republic would be utterly ſubverted. However there are ſome who ſuſpect that theſe are all ſpecious pretences, and that the ſociety's real motive for prohibiting all intercourſe with ſtrangers, is the fear of rivals in the beneficial commerce of Paraguay, which is now entirely in their hands.

From the Univerſal Weekly Chronicle.

—In vitium libertas excidit et vim
Dignam lege regi. HOR.

SIR,

I Am engaged in a viſit at a friend's houſe in the country, where I promiſed myſelf much ſatisfaction. I have however been greatly diſappointed in my expectations; for on my arrival here, I found a houſe full of children, who are *humoured* beyond meaſure, and indeed, abſolutely ſpoiled by the ridiculous indulgence of a fond mother. This unlucky circumſtance has ſubjected me to many inconveniencies; and as I am a man of a grave reſerved diſpoſition, has been a perpetual ſource of embarraſſment and perplexity. The ſecond day of my viſit, in the midſt of dinner, the eldeſt boy, who is eight years old, whipped off my periwig with great dexterity, and received the applauſe of the table for his humour and ſpirit. This lad, when he has reached his fourteenth year, and is big enough to lie without the maid, is to be ſent to a ſchool in the neighbourhood, which has no other merit than that of being but ſeven miles off. Six of the children are permitted to ſit at table, who entirely monopolize the wings of fowls, and the moſt delicate morſels of every diſh; becauſe the

the mother has discovered, that her children have not *strong* stomachs. In the morning, before my friend is up, I generally take a turn upon the gravel-walk, where I could wish to enjoy my own thoughts without interruption; but I am here instantly attended by my little tormentors, who follow me backwards and forwards, and play at what they call *Running after the Gentleman*. My whip, which was a present from an old friend, has been lashed to pieces by one of the boys who is fond of horses, and the handle is turned into a hobby horse. The main-spring of my repeating-watch has been broke in the nursery, which, at the mother's request, I had lent to the youngest boy, who was just breeched, and who cried to wear it. The mother's attention to the children entirely destroys all conversation: and once, as an amusement for the evenings, we attempted to begin reading *Tom Jones*, but were interrupted, in the second page, by little *Sammy*, who is suffered to whip his top in the parlour. I am known to be troubled with violent head-achs; notwithstanding which, another of the boys, without notice given, or any regard paid to the company, is permitted to break out into the braying of an ass, for which the strength of his lungs is commended; and a little miss, at breakfast, is allowed to drink up all the cream, and put her fingers into the sugar-dish, because she was once *sickly*. I am teazed with familiarities, which I can only repay with a frown; and pestered with the petulance of ludicrous prattle, in which I am unqualified to join. It is whispered in the family, that I am a mighty good sort of a man, but that I cannot *talk to children*. Nor am I the only person who suffers from this folly: a neighbouring clergyman, of great merit and modesty, and much acquainted in the family, has received hints to forbear coming to the house, because little *Sukey* always cries when she sees him, and has told her mamma, she can't bear that *ugly parson*.

Mrs. Qualm, my friend's wife, the mother of this hopeful offspring, is perpetually breeding; or rather her whole existence is spent in a series of great bellies, lyings-in, visitings, churchings, and christenings. Every transaction of her life is dated from her several pregnancies. The grandmother, and the man-midwife, a serious sensible man, constantly reside in the house, to be always ready on these solemn occasions. She boasts, that no family has ever sent out more numerous advertisements for nurses *with a fine breast of milk*. As her longings have of late been in the vegetable way, the garden is cultivated for this purpose alone, and totally filled with forward pease, and melon-glasses, in hopes that she may luckily long for what is at hand. She preserves, to the utmost, the prerogative of frequent pregnancy, and conscious of the dignity and importance of being often *big*, exerts an absolute authority over her husband. He was once a keen fox-hunter, but has long ago dropped his hounds: his wife having remonstrated, that his early rising disturbed the family unseasonably, and having dreamed, that he broke his leg in leaping a ditch.

I revere Mrs. Qualm as the mother, and only wish I could recommend her as the manager of children. I hope this letter may fall into her hands, to convince her how

how abſurd it is to ſuppoſe, that others can be as much intereſted in her own children as herſelf. I would teach her, that, what I complain of as matter of inconvenience, may, one day, prove to her a ſevere trial: and that, early licentiouſneſs will, at laſt, mock that paternal affection, from whoſe miſtaken indulgence it aroſe.

I am, yours,
X. Y. Z.

The IDLER.

CRedulity, or confidence of opinion too great for the evidence from which opinion is derived, we find to be a general weakneſs imputed by every ſect and party to all others, and, indeed, by every man to every other man.

Of all kinds of credulity, the moſt obſtinate and wonderful is that of political zealots; of men, who, being numbered, they know not how nor why, in any of the parties that divide a ſtate, reſign the uſe of their own eyes and ears, and reſolve to believe nothing that does not favour thoſe whom they profeſs to follow.

The bigot of philoſophy is ſeduced by authorities which he has not always opportunities to examine, is intangled in ſyſtems by which truth and falſhood are inextricably complicated, or undertakes to talk on ſubjects, which nature did not form him able to comprehend.

The Carteſian, who denies that his horſe feels the ſpur, or that the hare is afraid when the hounds approach her; the diſciple of Malbranche, who maintains that the man was not hurt by the bullet, which, according to vulgar apprehenſions, ſwept away his head; the follower of Berkley, who, while he ſits writing at his table, declares that he has neither table, paper, nor fingers; have all the honour at leaſt of being deceived by fallacies not eaſily detected, and may plead that they did not forſake truth, but for appearances which they were not able to diſtinguiſh from it.

But the man who engages in a party has ſeldom to do with any thing remote or abſtruſe. The preſent of ſtate of things is before his eyes; and, if he cannot be ſatisfied without retroſpection, yet he ſeldom extends his views beyond the hiſtorical events of the laſt century. All the knowledge that he can want is within his attainment, and moſt of the arguments which he can hear are within his capacity.

Yet ſo it is, that an *Idler* meets, every hour of his life, with men who have different opinions upon every thing paſt, preſent, and future; who deny the moſt notorious facts, contradict the moſt cogent truths, and perſiſt in aſſerting to-day what they aſſerted yeſterday, in defiance of evidence, and contempt of confutation.

Two of my companions, who are grown old in idleneſs, are *Tom Tempeſt* and *Jack Sneaker*. Both of them men who conſider themſelves as neglected by their parties, and therefore intitled to credit, as having no motive to favour ingratitude. They are both men of integrity where no factious intereſt is to be promoted, and both lovers of truth, when they are not heated with political debate.

Tom Tempest is a steady friend to the house of *Stuart*. He can recount the prodigies that have appeared in the sky, and the calamities that have afflicted the nation every year from the revolution, and is of opinion, that if the exiled family had conнued to reign, there would have neither been worms in our ships nor caterpillars in our trees. He wonders that the nation was not awaked by the hard frost to a revocation of the true king, and is hourly afraid that the whole island will be lost in the sea. He believes that King William burned Whitehall that he might steal the furniture, and that Tillotson died an atheist. Of Queen Anne he speaks with more tenderness, owns that she meant well, and can tell by whom and why she was poisoned. In the succeeding reigns all has been corruption, malice, and design. He believes that nothing ill has ever happened for these forty years by chance or error. He holds that the battle of Dettingen was won by mistake, and that of Fontenoy lost by contract; that the *Victory* was sunk by a private order; that *Cornhill* was burnt by emissaries from the council; and the arch of Westminster bridge was so contrived as to sink on purpose that the nation might be put to charge. He considers the new road to Islington as an encroachment on liberty, and often asserts that *broad wheels* will be the ruin of England.

Tom is generally vehement and noisy, but nevertheless has some secrets which he always communicates in a whisper. Many and many a time has *Tom* told me, in a corner, that our miseries were almost at an end, and that we should see, in a month, another monarch on the throne: the time elapses without a revolution; *Tom* meets me again with new intelligence, the whole scheme is now settled, and we shall see great events in another month.

Jack Sneaker is a hearty adherent to the present establishment; he has known those who saw the bed into which the pretender was conveyed in a warming pan. He often rejoices that the nation was not enslaved by the Irish. He believes that King William never lost a battle, and that if he had lived one year longer he would have conquered France. He holds that Charles the first was a papist. He allows there were some good men in the reign of Queen Anne, but the peace of Utrecht brought a blast upon the nation, and has been the cause of all the evil that we have suffered to the present hour. He believes that the scheme of the South Sea was well intended, but that it miscarried by the influence of France. He considers a standing army as the bulwark of liberty, thinks us secured from corruption by septennial parliaments, relates how we are enriched and strengthened by the electoral dominions, and declares that the public debt is a blessing to the nation.

Yet amidst all this prosperity, poor *Jack* is hourly disturbed by the dread of popery. He wonders that some stricter laws are not made against papists, and is sometimes afraid that they are busy with French gold among the bishops and judges.

He cannot believe that the nonjurors are so quiet for nothing, they must certainly be forming some plot for

for the eſtabliſhment of popery; he does not think the preſent oaths ſufficiently binding, and wiſhes that ſome better ſecurity could be found for the ſucceſſion of the houſe of Hanover. He is zealous for the naturalization of foreign proteſtants, and rejoiced at the admiſſion of the Jews to the Engliſh privileges, becauſe he thought a Jew would never a papiſt.

The IDLER.

MANY naturaliſts are of opinion, that the animals which we commonly conſider as mute, have the power of imparting their thoughts to one another. That they can expreſs general ſenſations is very certain; every being that can utter ſounds has a different voice for pleaſure and for pain. The hound informs his fellows when he ſcents his game; the hen calls her chickens to their food by her cluck, and drives them from danger by her ſcream.

Birds have the greateſt variety of notes; they have indeed a variety, which ſeems almoſt ſufficient to make a ſpeech adequate to the purpoſes of a life, which is regulated by inſtinct, and can admit little change or improvement. To the cries of birds, curioſity or ſuperſtition has been always attentive, many have ſtudied the language of the feathered tribes, and ſome have boaſted that they underſtood it.

The moſt ſkilful or moſt confident interpreters of the ſylvan dialogues have been commonly found among the philoſophers of the eaſt, in a country where the calmneſs of the air, and the mildneſs of the ſeaſons, allow the ſtudent to paſs a great part of the year in groves and bowers. But what may be done in one place by peculiar opportunities, may be performed in another by peculiar diligence. A ſhepherd of Bohemia has, by long abode in the foreſts, enabled himſelf to underſtand the voice of birds, at leaſt he relates with great confidence a ſtory of which the credibility may be conſidered by the learned.

As I was ſitting (ſaid he) within a hollow rock, and watching my ſheep that fed in the valley, I heard two vultures interchangeably crying on the ſummit of the cliff. Both voices were earneſt and deliberate. My curioſity prevailed over my care of the flock; I climbed ſlowly and ſilently from crag to crag, concealed among the ſhrubs, till I found a cavity where I might ſit and liſten without ſuffering, or giving diſturbance.

I ſoon perceived, that my labour would be well repaid; for an old vulture was ſitting on a naked prominence, with her young about her, whom ſhe was inſtructing in the arts of a vulture's life, and preparing, by the laſt lecture, for their final diſmiſſion to the mountains and the ſkies.

My children, ſaid the old vulture, you will leſs want my inſtructions, becauſe you have had my practice before your eyes; you have ſeen me ſnatch from the farm the houſhold fowl; you have ſeen me ſeize the leveret in the buſh, and the kid in the paſture; you know how to fix your talons, and how to balance your flight when you are laden with your prey. But you remember the taſte of more delicious food; I have often regaled you with the flesh of man. Tell us, said the young vultures, where man may be found, and how he may be known; his flesh, is surely the natural food of a vulture. Why have you never brought a man in your talons to the nest? He is too bulky, said the mother; when we find a man, we can only tear away his flesh and leave the bones upon the ground. Since man is so big, said the young ones, how do you kill him? You are afraid of the wolf and of the bear; by what power are vultures superior to man? Is man more defenceless than a sheep? We have not the strength of man, returned the mother, and I am sometimes in doubt whether we have the subtilty; aud the vultures would seldom feast upon his flesh, had not nature that devoted him to our uses, infused into him a strange ferocity, which I have never observed in any other being that feeds upon the earth. Two herds of men will often meet and shake the earth with noise, and fill the air with fire. When you hear noise and see fire with flashes along the ground, hasten to the place with your swiftest wing, for men are surely destroying one another; you will then find the ground smoaking with blood and covered with carcases, of which many are dismembered and mangled for the convenience of the vulture. But when men have killed their prey, says the pupil, why do they not eat it? When the wolf has killed a sheep, he suffers not the vulture to touch it till he has satisfied himself. Is not man another kind of wolf? Man, said the mother, is the only beast who kills that which he does not devour, and this quality makes him so much a benefactor to our species. If men kill our prey and lay it in our way, said the young one, what need shall we have of labouring for ourselves? Because man will sometimes, replied the mother, remain for a long time quiet in his den. The old vultures will tell you when you are to watch his motions. When you see men in great numbers moving close together, like a flight of storks, you may conclude that they are hunting, and that you will soon revel in human blood. But still, said the young one, I would gladly know the reason of this mutual slaughter; I could never kill what I could not eat. My child, said the mother, this is a question which I cannot answer, tho' I am reckoned the most subtle bird of the mountain. When I was young I used frequently to visit the ayry of an old vulture, who dwelt upon the Carpathian rocks; he had made many observations; he knew the places that afforded prey round his habitation, as far in every direction as the strongest wing can fly between the rising and setting of the summer sun; he had fed year after year on the entrails of men. His opinion was, that men had only the appearance of animal life, being really vegetables with a power of motion; and that as the boughs of an oak are dashed together by the storm, that swine may fatten upon the falling acorns, so men are by some unaccountable power driven one against another, till they lose their motion, that vultures may be fed. Others think they have observed something of contrivance and policy

licy among these mischievous beings; and those that hover more closely round them, pretend, that there is, in every herd, one that gives directions to the rest, and seems to be more eminently delighted with a wide carnage. What is it that intitles him to such preeminence we know not; he is seldom the biggest or the swiftest; but he shews by his eagerness and diligence that he is, more than any of the others, a friend to vultures.

The humble remonstrance of the mob of Great Britain, against the importation of French words, &c.

IT is with infinite concern that we behold an inundation of French words pouring in upon us, and this at a time too when there is some sort of merit in detesting every thing that is French. In regard to ourselves, we are daily insulted, by some of the finest lips in the world, with the opprobrious term of *Canaille:* we cannot resent the insult from them, as they are too sacred for our unhallowed hands; besides, they are sufficiently punished, by the mirth they afford to the *Mademoiselles*, when they attempt to pronounce the uncouth word; for *Canaille*, from English lips, sounds *Canal.* But as most things are pardonable to the pride of the creation, we should readily excuse *them*, if the infection had not spread among the officers of our army; and as we chiefly compose the numerous squadrons that are to guard the liberties of Britain, we cannot conceive that we ought to have any more to do with their language, than we have with their religion. All our business is to beat them, and that we can do in plain English: if our officers order us to form a line, we can do it; but if they call that line a *Cordon*, we must be obliged to apply to the chaplain for a *Denouement* of the mysterious word.— *Coup de main*, and *Manoeuvre*, might be excusable in Marshal Saxe, as he was in the service of France, and perfectly acquainted with both; but we cannot see what apology can be made for our officers lugging them in by head and shoulders, without the least necessity, as a sudden stroke, might have done for one, and a proper motion, for the other. ---*Reconnoitre* is another favourite word in the military way; and as we cannot find out that it is much more significant than *take a view*, we beg leave it may be sent home again. We should not have troubled the public with this address, if we had not received a fresh insult by the papers of Saturday last, in a supposed letter from Germany, where the ingenious author tells us, speaking of the intended operations of war, that the general's intention remains *perdu*; which, we are informed, signifies *lost*. In what sense we are to understand this gentleman, we cannot say; his meaning indeed seems *perdu*; he may perhaps, give us to understand, by printing the word in Italics, that the army and treasure sent to Germany, is all *perdu:* the word then wants a little *epaulement*, to support it, or rather a little *eclaircissement*; for, in the present application of it, it is dark and mysterious.

We muſt beg the gentlemen of the army pardon, if next to them we ſhould take the liberty of mentioning the barbers ; a ſet of gentlemen very uſeful in their ſtation, but under no abſolute neceſſity of hanging out falſe French upon their ſigns : it may indeed become a French *friſeur*, to acquaint the public that he makes a *tete de mouton*, or ſimply a *tete* ; but we are a little offended when an Engliſh tonſor under the ſign of a thing, which in ſome countries might be called a periwig, ſhall write ladies *taites*, or *tates*, or *taets* or *taites*, or *taites's* made here ; it looks as if they meant a reflection upon the ladies of Great Britain, by acquainting the public, that their heads were made in barbers ſhops, and to be had either in Middle-row or Rag-fair. Now their intended purpoſe of ſerving the community would certainly be better anſwered, if they would ſuffer their ſigns to ſpeak plain Engliſh, and inform the world that *ſheeps heads* (which we are told is the meaning of the three French words above) were ſold there, as by that means they would bid fair to ſerve gentlemen well as ladies, who were not already provided.

Je-ne-ſcai-quoy, though of French extraction, we ſhall not preſume to find fault with, becauſe it has been naturalized, and productive of infinite good in England ; it has helped many an unfortunate girl to an huſband ; it has indeed ſometimes parted man and wife, but has ſoon brought them together again ; ſeldom fails of healing up the breaches, it had made between friends ; has fitted out fleets and armies, and brought them home again ; has been a theme for orators in velvet and crape, and has furniſhed matter for many volumes.

Chicane, we dare not meddle with, as we are told the lawyers have taken it under their immediate protection ; but as quicks and tricks are as foreign to their profeſſion, as ambition and avarice to that of a more venerable order, we ſuppoſe the charge is without foundation.

Bagatelle, or *trifle*, we ſhall leave to the ſmarts, as it would be a pity to rob them of the chief object of their ſtudy.

Pet-en-l'air, may ſuit very well with French *effronterie* ; for if the ladies of that country make no ſcruple of watering their *ruelles* before the gentlemen who attend their *levees*, I ſee no reaſon why they ſhould be aſhamed of a f---t ; but as no ſuch offenſive wind is ever ſuppoſed to blow from fair Engliſh b---ms, we could wiſh they had found a name of a little more delicacy for this garment.

We therefore humbly pray, that French words, as well as French dreſs and French manners, may be laid aſide, at leaſt during the continuance of the preſent war ; for we are apprehenſive, ſhould their language and cuſtoms deſcend to us, we ſhould be taught by their example, on the day of battle to *f---te le camp*.

For theſe reaſons we pray as above : and ſhall, as in duty bound, hold them in everlaſting abhorrence,

LEGION.

To

To the K---'s most excellent M——y.

*The humble petition of P*** E. of C****, Knight of the most noble order of the Garter,*

Sheweth,

THAT your petitioner being rendered by deafness, as useless and inefficent, as most of his cotemporaries are by nature, hopes, in common with them, to share your majesty's royal favour and bounty, whereby he may be enabled to save or spend, as he may think proper, a great deal more than he possibly can at present.

That your petitioner having had the honour to serve your majesty in several very lucrative employments, seems thereby entitled to a lucrative retreat from business, and to enjoy *otium cum dignitate*, that is, leisure and a large pension.

Your petitioner humbly apprehends, that he has a justifiable claim to a considerable pension, as he neither wants, nor deserves, but only desires, and (pardon, dread Sir, an expression you are pretty much used to) insists upon it.

Your petitioner is little apt, and always unwilling, to speak advantageously of himself; but as some degree of justice is due to one's self, as well as to others, he begs leave to represent, that his loyalty to your majesty has always been unshaken, even in the worst of times: That particularly, in the late unnatural rebellion, when the young pretender had advanced as far as Derby, at the head of an army of at least three thousand men, composed of the flower of the Scotch nobility and gentry, who had virtue enough to avow, and courage enough to venture their lives in support of their real principles, your petitioner did not join him, as unquestionably he might have done, had he been so inclined; but, on the contrary, raised, at the public expence, sixteen companies, of one hundred men each, in defence of your majesty's undoubted right to the imperial crown of these realms; which service remains to this hour unrewarded.

Your petitioner is well aware, that your majesty's civil list must necessarily be in a very weak and languid condition, after the various and profuse evacuations it has undergone; but, at the same time, he humbly hopes, that an argument which does not seem to have been urged against any other person whatsoever, will not, in a singular manner, be urged against him, especially as he has some reasons to believe, that the deficiencies of the pension fund will by no means be the last to be made good by parliament.

Your petitioner begs leave to observe, that a small pension is disgraceful, as it intimates opprobrious indigence on the part of the receiver, and a degrading sort of dole or charity on the part of the giver; but that a great one implies dignity and affluence on the one side, on the other esteem and consideration; which doubtless your majesty must entertain in the highest degree for those great personages, whose reputable names glare in capitals upon your elemosynary list.

Your petitioner humbly flatters himself, that upon this principle, less than three thousand pounds a year will not be proposed to him, and if made gold the more agreeable.

Your petitioner persuades himself, that your majesty will not impute

pute this his humble application to any mean interested motive, of which he has always had the utmost abhorrence.

No, Sir! he confesses his weakness---*Honour* alone is his object, *honour* is his passion---that *honour*, which is sacred to him as a peer, and tender to him as a gentleman; that *honour*, in short, to which he has sacrificed all other considerations. It is upon this single principle, that your petitioner sollicits an *honour*, which at present in so extraordinary a manner adorns the British peerage, and which, in the most shining periods of ancient Greece, distinguished the greatest men, who were fed in the Prytaneum at the expence of the public.

Upon this *honour*, far dearer to your petitioner than his life, he begs leave in the most solemn manner, to assure your majesty, that in case you shall be pleased to grant this his most modest request, he will honourably support and promote, to the utmost of his abilities, the very worst measures, that the very worst ministers can suggest; but at the same time should he unfortunately, and, in a singular manner, be branded by a refusal, he thinks himself obliged in *honour* to declare, that he will, with the utmost acrimony, oppose the very best measures which your majesty yourself shall ever propose or promote.

And your petitioner, &c.

---

*To the R---t R------d the D---n and C------r of W****, the humble petition of POSTERITY,*

Sheweth,

THAT your petitioners humbly apprehend your reverences are no other than trustees for us your petitioners, in the same manner as your predecessors were trustees for the times succeeding them.

That your petitioners observe with great concern the late immoderate increase of funeral monuments within your abbey and the precincts thereof, to the great encouragement of family vanity, historical falshood, jobbing articles, and ignorant statuaries; as well as to the disgrace of national taste, and the destruction of various kinds of marble, which ought to have remained in the bowels of the earth for the use of your petitioners, who hope to employ the art of sculpture with more credit to their country.

That your petitioners observe with concern, the vast profusion of money which the present war requires, and apprehend that when it shall be their turn to serve their country, nothing will remain for their rewards but honorary monuments; and it is with the greatest regret they see the pavement and walls of your abbey already possest by names of Generals, never known but by their preferments; Poets never mentioned, but for their dulness; Patriots never heard of, but by their posts; and Orators never known to pronounce a significant word but the monosyllables, aye and no. Your petitioners, therefore, apprehensive that the revenue of fame may be as much anticipated within you abbey, as that of money is, in an adjoining chapel; and that therefore they may be reduced to the melancholy condition of neither being rewarded while living, nor remembered when dead; most humbly beg leave to represent to your reverences this their uncomfortable prospect.

Your

Your petitioners are the more emboldened to make this application, as they are fully ſenſible and aſhamed of the cowardice and miſmanagement of their preſent predeceſſors, and are reſolved to do all they can to efface the memory of their miſdeeds, by a ſincere attachment to the ſervice of their country; and therefore your petitioners muſt be the more ſenſible of the mortification and diſgrace to which they muſt be reduced, by their being obliged to mingle their duſt, or their names, or both, with ſuch company as are already in poſſeſſion of your walls and pavements; tho' your petitioners acknowledge, that many of them are ſuch as your petitioners propoſe as models for their own conduct.

That your petitioners obſerve, with great concern, many heathen deities have been introduced within your walls, to adorn the tombs of thoſe who were ſtrangers to all heathen virtues; and as your petitioners are not aſhamed of their reſolution to live and die Chriſtians, they hope your reverences will have ſome regard to the tenderneſs of their conſciences in this reſpect, eſpecially as there is a ſufficiency of Chriſtian attributes to ſerve, if ingeniouſly and properly applied, all the purpoſes of ſculpture, in embelliſhing the monuments of the Chriſtian dead.

Your petitioners beg leave farther to repreſent to your reverences, that the wiſeſt nations of antiquity looked upon the conferring monumental honours as a public concern, and the nobleſt incitement to virtuous deeds; and that as ſoon as they ceaſed to be frugal of thoſe honours, when they proſtituted them to flattery, or ſeld them for lucre, their public ſpirit fled; and tho' your petitioners have the higheſt opinion of the diſintereſtedneſs and judgment of your reverences, yet they think they cannot be too watchful in a matter that ſo highly concerns them, eſpecially (according to what your petitioners have hinted above) as this will probably be the only return our country will be able to give them for their ſervices.

And your petitioners ſhall ever pray, &c.

A remarkable dying ſpeech of Mr. Cuffe, Secretary to the Earl of Eſſex, who was executed in the reign of Queen Elizabeth, for the ſame offence which brought his maſter to the block.

I Am here adjudged to die for acting an act never plotted, for plotting a plot never acted. Juſtice will have her courſe; accuſers muſt be heard; greatneſs will have the victory: ſcholars and martialiſts (though learning and valour ſhould have the pre-eminence) in England muſt like like dogs, and be hanged. To miſlike this, were but folly: to diſpute it, but time loſt: to alter it, impoſſible: but to endure it, is manly; and to ſcorn it, magnanimity. The Queen is diſpleaſed, the lawyers injurious, and death terrible: but I crave pardon of the Queen; forgive the lawyers, and the world; deſire to be forgiven; and welcome death.

The following moſt excellent letter was wrote, in the reign of Queen Elizabeth, by the gallant and renowned Earl of Eſſex, to his boſom-friend the Earl of Southampton.

My

My Lord,

As neither nature nor cuſtom ever made me a man of compliment, ſo now I ſhall have leſs will than ever for to uſe ſuch ceremonies, when I have left with Martha to be *Sollicitus circa multa*, and believe with Mary *Unum ſufficit*. But it is no compliment or ceremony, but a real and neceſſary duty that one friend oweth to another in abſence, and eſpecially at their leave-taking, when in man's reaſon many accidents may keep them long divided, or perhaps bar them ever meeting till they meet in another world; for then ſhall I think that my friend, whoſe honour, whoſe perſon, and whoſe fortune is dear unto me, ſhall proſper and be happy, where-ever he goes, and whatever he takes in hand, when he is in the favour of that *God*, under whoſe protection there is *only* ſafety, and in whoſe ſervice there is *only true* happineſs to be found. What I think of your natural gifts or ability in this age, or in this ſtate, to give glory to *God*, and to win honour to yourſelf, if you employ the talents you have received to their beſt uſe, I will now tell you; it ſufficeth, that when I was fartheſt of all times from diſſembling, I ſpake truly, and have witneſs enough: but theſe things only I will put your Lordſhip in mind of.

Firſt, That you have *nothing* that you have not received.

Secondly, That you poſſeſs them not as *Lord* over them, but as an *Accomptant* for them.

Thirdly, If you employ them to ſerve this world, or your own worldly delights (which the prince of this world will ſeek to entertain you with) it is ingratitude, it is injuſtice, yea, it is perfidious treachery; for what would you think of ſuch a ſervant of yours, that ſhould convert your goods, committed to his charge, to the advantage or ſervice of your greateſt enemy; and what do you leſs than this with *God*, ſince you have *all* from him, and know that the world, and princes thereof, are at a continual enmity with him? And therefore, if ever the admonition of your trueſt friend ſhall be heard by you, or if your country, which you may ſerve in ſo great and many things, be dear unto you; if your *God*, whom you muſt (if you deal *truly* with yourſelf) acknowledge to be powerful over all, and juſt in all, be feared by you; yea, if you be dear unto yourſelf, and prefer an everlaſting happineſs before a pleaſant dream, which you muſt *ſhortly* awake out of, and then repent in the bitterneſs of your ſoul; if any of theſe things be regarded by you, then I ſay, call yourſelf to account for what is paſt, cancel all the leagues you have made without the warrant of a religious conſcience, make a reſolute covenant with your *God*, to ſerve him with all your natural and ſpiritual, inward and outward gifts and abilities, and then he that is faithful (and cannot lie) hath promiſed to honour them that honour him; he will give you that inward peace of ſoul, and true joy of heart, which till you have, you ſhall never reſt, and which, when you have, you ſhall never be ſhaken, and which you can never attain to *any other* way than this that I have ſhewed you.

I know your Lordſhip may ſay to yourſelf, and object to me, this is but a vapour of melancholy, and the ſti e of a priſoner, and that I was far enough from it, when I lived

lived in the world as you do now, and may be ſo again, when my fetters be taken from me. I anſwer, though your Lordſhip ſhould think ſo, yet cannot I diſtruſt the goodneſs of my *God*, that his mercy will fail me, or his grace forſake me; I have ſo deeply engaged myſelf, that I ſhould be one of the moſt miſerable apoſtates that ever was: I have ſo avowed my profeſſion, and called ſo many from time to time, to witneſs it, and to be watchmen over me, that I ſhould be the holloweſt hypocrite that ever was born: but though I ſhould periſh in my own ſin, and draw upon myſelf my own damnation, ſhould not you take hold of the grace and mercy in *God*, which is offered unto you, and make your profit of my fearful and wretched example? I was longer a ſlave and ſervant to the world, and the corruptions of it, than you have been, and therefore could hardly be drawn from it. I had many calls, and anſwered ſome of them ſlowly, thinking a ſoft pace faſt enough to come to Chriſt, and myſelf forward enough when I ſaw the end of my journey, though I arrived not at it; and therefore I have been, by *God*'s providence, violently pulled, hauled, and dragged to the marriage feaſt, as the world hath ſeen. It was juſt with *God* to afflict me in this world that he might give me joy in another. I had too much knowledge when I performed too little obedience, and was therefore to be beaten with double ſtripes: *God* grant your Lordſhip may feel the comfort I now enjoy in my unfeigned converſion, but that you may never feel the torments I have ſuffered for my too long delaying it. I had none but divines to call upon me, to whom I ſaid, if my ambition could have entered into their narrow hearts, they would not have been ſo humble; or if my delights had been taſted by them, they could not have been ſo preciſe: but your Lordſhip hath one to call upon you, that knows what it is you now enjoy, and what the greateſt fruit and end is of *all* the contentments that this world can afford. Think therefore, dear Earl, that I have ſtaked and buoyed all the ways of pleaſure to you, and left them as ſea marks for you to keep the channel of religious virtue; for ſhut your eyes never ſo long, they *muſt* be open at *laſt*; and then you muſt ſay with me, *there is no peace to the wicked.*

I will make a covenant with my ſoul, not to ſuffer my eyes to ſleep in the night, nor my thoughts to attend the firſt buſineſs of the day, till I have prayed to my *God*, that your Lordſhip may believe and make profit of this plain, but faithful admonition; and then I know your country and friends ſhall be happy in you, and yourſelf ſucceſsful in all you take in hand; which ſhall be an unſpeakable comfort to

Your Lordſhip's couſin,
and true friend,
whom no worldly cauſe
can divide from you,
ESSEX.

An extraordinary ſermon having appeared, entitled, Conjugal Love and Duty: *A Diſcourſe upon* Heb. xiii. 4. *Preached at St.* Ann's, *in* Dublin, Sept. 11, 1757. *By Dr.* Brett. *With a dedication to the Right Honourable Lady* Caroline Ruſſel, *aſſerting the prerogative of beauty, and vindicating the privileges of the fair ſex; an*

extract

extract or two from the dedication, and the sermon itself, we presume will not be disagreeable to our readers.

MADAM, there is an Italian proverb, which says, that *handsome girls are born married:* The meaning whereof is not what hath been vulgarly supposed, that *marriages are made in heaven:* But, that such is the power of beauty over the human heart, that when they *will*, they *may*. This being so, the intimation to your Ladyship, is to look out, and provide for a change of condition. To remain single, will not be long in your power, for beauty that strikes every eye, will necessarily charm many hearts: Nature ordained it universal sway, and the corruptions of nature, multiplied as they have been through a series of 5000 years, have even yet been able to give it but one rival. In the human heart (I speak it to their shame) temples have been erected to the god of wealth: Many fair victims have we seen bleeding at his altars; and, what is worse, the very hand now writing to your Ladyship, hath sometimes been the sacrificer. What therefore you have to learn, is only to chuse with discretion; to maintain with dignity the proffered sovereignty which contending suppliants will intreat you to accept.

All the great heroes, the most renowned in their generations, the scripture worthies in particular, have had their Dalilahs, to whose bewitching charms they one and all yielded; reluctantly some, and fondly others: *These* proving their wisdom, and *those* their folly, since *there is no inchantment against beauty*, nor any thing which it cannot inchant. He must be something more, or something worse, than a man—*i. e.* a god or a devil, who hath escaped, or who can resist its power: The gods of the heathens could not; Jupiter, Mars, Mercury, Apollo, their amours are as famous as their names: So, that that sturdiness in human nature, wherever it is found, which can resist, argues plainly how much of the devil is wrought up in the composition: If the native power were not so great as it is, so many arts, so many opportunities to sooth and to persuade, would make it impossible.

This prating old man! will he never have done? Not yet; for to you, madam, and of you I could prate for ever. Garrulity is indeed the vice of old age: The highest honorary tribute that youth pays to it, is patient attention: We grow fond of prating, when we are good for nothing else. Besides, Madam, it is, though I am sorry to remind you of it, a vice common in both sexes; old women can prate as well as old men; and the same allowance on your part, if ever you come to it, will be demanded: and, alas! young, gay, and blooming as you are, to this you will come at last: lovely as that form is, it will wrinkle and wither, that vermilion will be turned into paleness, those brilliant eyes grow dim and faint: in the gazing crowd, that now surrounds you, notwithstanding the blaze you make, the lustre with which you enamel and gild the spot you stand upon; though you reanimate, give life, sensation, appetite, a kind of rejuvenescence, a desire at least, a wish to live and be young again, to every thing you touch or look upon, the meanest of your

your admirers, even I, wizened and worn out by labour, age, nay worse by disappointments, in the course of a few suns and moons, will be as much respected, heeded, listened to. Pity indeed it is! but it must be so: what are you then to do? why briefly this, look as well into yourself, as at yourself, and thence learn how to preserve and improve the authority which beauty gives, to make it indefectible, and, as I maintain it may, interminable.

[*From the sermon itself.*]

The humour of ridiculing this rite [of marriage] was introduced, and become fashionable, under the example of a dissolute prince; which encouraged such licentiousness in the stage, as soon corrupted the general taste, to the degree, that hardly any thing entertained, or was received there with applause, that was not salted with some obscene raillery. In consequence of which, not only the thing, but even the persons who made it their choice were laughed at. They were objects of pity, the butts of sneer, whom necessity had forced into it. A humour so inconsistent with common sense, and every social dear regard, could not hold long. The pulpit, which, in that universal degeneracy of men and manners, was not silent, got, in this instance, the better of the stage, and, at last, happily reformed it. To the honour of the present age, the few patrons it hath are as despicable, as they are dissolute: but it may be observed, that the pains taken to correct it, had possiby met with quicker success, had not the fair sex, by a lewd and wanton behaviour, contributed to keep it up: without encouragement from them it could never have run to the extravagance it did; for how little soever some of them may suspect or believe it, they are the only sure guardians of men's virtue, and have more power to reform than either priest or magistrate can pretend to. If therefore the manners of the age should ever take the same disagreeable turn, though they may be the principal sufferers, they must bear the blame of it, and the infamy too; for this reason, that it was always in their power to support the honour and dignity due to the married state, from the influence, which, few of them want to be told, they have over the affections and inclinations of mankind. I will offer no apology therefore for telling them, that if their discretion was equal to their charms; if they were at equal pains to embellish their minds, as they are to adorn their bodies, they might go near to reverse the customs of the world, and the maxims of nature; might sway the scepters of kingdoms, and be the law-givers and governors both of states and families, without either wearing of arms, or changing apparel.----If modesty, good sense, and the general practice of virtue, met with proper distinction in female regard, men would certainly take more pains, than they usually do, to cultivate those graces; for where we court, we wish to be approved, and naturally pursue such courses, as we judge will best recommend us: But whilst women are so insensible, and blind to their own interest and happiness, as to encourage those most, who use this holy institute to base and dishonourable purposes; whilst they prefer empty and profligate rakes, to virtuous and honourable lovers, they may thank themselves for a great share of that misery to which they

are

are tied, and we ſhall in vain hope to ſee the evil of this caſe ever corrected.

The copy of the will of a Citizen in Bern, in Switzerland.

AT the city of Bern in Switzerland, a man of buſineſs, by ſucceſs in his way of trade, had acquired a conſiderable real and perſonal eſtate: being grown in years, and having no family, he made a will to the following effect, viz.

"Being anxious for my fellow citizens of Bern, (who have often ſuffered by dearth of corn and wine) my will is, that, by the permiſſion of Providence, they ſhall never for the future ſuffer again under the like calamity: to which end and purpoſe I give my eſtate, real and perſonal, to the Senate of Bern, in truſt for the people; that is to ſay, that they receive the produce of my eſtate, till it ſhall come to the ſum of [ſuppoſe two thouſand pounds;] that then they ſhall lay out this two thouſand pounds in building a town-houſe, according to a plan by me left: the lower ſtory whereof to conſiſt of large vaults or repoſitories for wine; the ſtory above I direct to be formed into a piazza, for ſuch perſons as ſhall come to market at Bern, for diſpoſing of their goods, free from the injuries of the weather; above that I direct a council-chamber to be erected, for the committee of the Senate to meet in from time to time, to adjuſt my accounts, and to direct ſuch things as may be neceſſary for the charity; and above the council-chamber as many floors or granaries as can be conveniently raiſed, to depoſit a quantity of corn for the uſe of the people, whenever they ſhall have occaſion for it. And when this building ſhall be erected, and the expence of it diſcharged, I direct the Senate of Bern to receive the produce of my eſtate, till the ſame ſhall amount to the ſum [ſuppoſe two thouſand pounds;] and when the price of corn ſhall be under the mean rate of the laſt ten years, one fourth part, they ſhall then lay out one thouſand pounds in corn, and ſtow it in my granaries; and the ſame in wine, when under one fourth of the mean rate of the laſt ten years: and my will is, that none of the ſaid corn or wine ſhall be ſold, until the price of corn or wine ſhall exceed, at the common market, one fourth of the mean rate for the laſt ten years; and then every citizen of Bern ſhall demand daily (or proportionably weekly) as many pounds weight of wheat, and as many pints of wine, as he hath mouths in his family to conſume, and no more; and that for the ſame he pay ready money, after the mean rate that it has been at for the laſt ten years paſt, a due proportion being allowed for waſte, and that to be ſettled by the Senate; and that each houſholder ſhall be ſo ſupplied, as long as the price of corn or wine ſhall continue above the rate of one fourth more than the mean rate; and whatſoever increaſe ſhall be made of the capital, it ſhall be laid out, under the ſame reſtrictions, in adding to the ſtock of corn and wine; which, under the bleſſing of God, will, I hope, in a certain time, reduce theſe two neceſſary articles of life to very near a fixed price, to the glory of God, and the benefit of the poor."

This

This legacy has fubfifted near two hundred years, and has had the defired effect at Bern.

An Englifh merchant returning from Aleppo, by Bern, took this hint, and fettled a fum of money, for the ufe the poor at Kingfton-on-Thames, for the purchafe of coals in the fame manner. The Right Honourable Arthur Onflow, Speaker of the Honourable Houfe of Commons, and Nicholas Hardinge, Efq; (lately deceafed) were two of the truftees, under whofe aufpices the poor were abundantly fupplied, and the fund greatly augmented.

About five years ago the hint was given, and fome gentlemen in Northampton collected a fum of money, for purchafing fuel at prime coft, and felling to the poor at the fame rate; which anfwered perfectly well.

Method of taking off paintings in oil, from the cloths or wood on which they were originally done; and transferring them entire, and without damage, to new pieces.

THE art of removing paintings in oil, from the cloth or wood on which they are originally done, and transferring them to new grounds of either kind of fubftance, is of very great ufe; as not only pictures may be preferved, where the canvas is fo decayed and damaged, that they would otherwife fall to pieces, but paintings on ceiling or wainfcot, which, when taken away from the places where they were originally placed, would have little value, may be conveyed to cloths; and by being thus brought to the ftate of pictures, become of equal worth with thofe painted originally on canvas. The manner in which this is done is by cementing the face of the picture to a new cloth, by means of fuch a fubftance as can afterwards be diffolved, and confequently taken off by water; deftroying the texture of the old cloth, by means of a proper corroding fluid; and then feparating the corroded parts of it entirely from the painting: after which, a new cloth being cemented to the reverfe of the painting in its place, the cloth cemented to the front in like manner to be corroded and feparated; and the cemented matter cleanfed away by diffolving it in water, and rubbing it off from the face of the picture. The particular method of doing this, with moft convenience, is as follows:

Let the decayed picture be cleanfed from all greafe that may be on its furface, which may be done by rubbing it very gently with crumb of ftale bread, and then wiping it with a very fine foft linen cloth. It muft then be laid, with the face downwards, on a fmooth table covered with fan-paper, or the India-paper; and the cloth on the reverfe muft be well foaked with boiling water, fpread upon it by means of a fponge, till it appear perfectly foft and pliable. The picture is then to be turned with the face upwards; and, being ftretched in the moft even and flat manner on the table, muft be pinned down to it in that ftate, by nails driven in through the edge, at proper diftances from each other. A quantity of glue fhould be then melted, and ftrained through a flannel cloth, to prevent any gravel, or other impurities from lurking in it; and when it is a little ftiffened a part of it ſhould be ſpread on a linen cloth, of the ſize of the painting, where it ſhould be ſuffered to ſet and dry; and then another coat put over it: when this is become ſtiff alſo, the glue ſhould be again heated; and while it remains of ſuch heat as to be eaſily ſpread, it ſhould be laid over the face of the picture, and a linen cloth immediately put over it in the moſt even manner, and nailed down to the picture and table at the edge likewiſe. The glue ſhould not be uſed boiling hot, as that would hazard ſome of the delicate colours of the painting; and the linen cloth ſhould be fine and half worn, that it may be the ſofter, and lie the flatter on the ſurface of the picture; in order to which it is proper to heat it till the glue be ſoft and pliable before it be laid on, and to compreſs each part gently with a ball formed of a linen rag tied round with thread. The table, with the picture, cloth, &c. nailed down to it in this ſtate, ſhould be then expoſed to the heat of the ſun, in a place where it may be ſecured from rain; and there continued till the glue be perfectly dry and hard; at which time the nails ſhould be drawn, and the picture and linen cloth taken off from the table. The picture muſt now be again turned with the face downwards, and ſtretched and nailed to the table as before; and a border of wax muſt be raiſed round the edge, in the ſame manner as is directed for the copper-plates, forming as it were a ſhallow trough with the ſurface of the picture; into which trough ſhould be poured a proper corroding fluid, to eat and deſtroy the thread of the original canvas or cloth of the picture. The corroding fluid uſed for this purpoſe, may be either oil of vitriol, aqua fortis, or ſpirit of ſalt: but the laſt is preferable, as it will more effectually deſtroy the thread, when it is ſo weakened by the admixture of water as not to have any effect on the oil of the painting: which ever is uſed, it is neceſſary they ſhould be properly diluted with water; to find the due proportion of which, it is expedient to make ſome previous trials; and when they are found to be of ſuch ſtrength, as to deſtroy the texture of thread, without diſcolouring it, they are in the due ſtate. When the corroding fluid has done its office, a paſſage muſt be made through the border of wax at one end of it; and the fluid muſt be poured off, by inclining the table in the requiſite manner; and the remaining part muſt be waſhed away, by putting repeated quantities of freſh water upon the cloth. The threads of the cloth muſt then be carefully picked out till the whole be taken away: but if any part be found to adhere, all kind of violence, even in the leaſt degree, muſt be avoided in removing them: inſtead of which, they ſhould be again touched, by means of a pencil, with the corroſive fluid leſs diluted than before, till they will readily come off from the paint. The reverſe ſurface of the painting being thus wholly freed from the old cloth, muſt be then waſhed with water, by means of a ſponge, till the corroding fluid employed be thoroughly cleanſed away: when being wiped with a ſoft ſponge till all the moiſture that may be collected by that means be taken off, it muſt be left till it be perfectly dry. In the mean time a new

new piece of canvas muſt be cut of the ſize of the painting, which now remains cemented to the linen cloth put on the face of it; and the reverſe of the painting being dry, and ſpread over by ſome hot glew, purified as before, and melted with a little brandy, or ſpirit of wine, the new canvas muſt be laid on it, in the moſt even manner, while the glew yet remains hot, and ſettled to it by compreſſion: which may be performed by thick plates of lead, or flat pieces of poliſhed marble. Great care ſhould however be taken in the laying them on to prevent the edge from cutting or bruiſing the paint; as alſo during the ſetting of the glew to take them off; and wipe them at proper intervals, to prevent their adhering to the cloth by means of the glue, which may be preſſed through it. The lead or marble, by which the compreſſure is made, being removed when the glew is ſet, the cloth muſt be kept in the ſame ſtate, till the glue be perfectly dry and hard. Then the whole muſt be again turned with the other ſide upwards, and the border of wax being replaced, the linen cloth on the face of the painting muſt be deſtroyed by means of the corroding fluid, in the ſame manner as the canvas was before: but greater care muſt be taken with reſpect to the ſtrength of the corroding matter, and in the picking out the threads of the cloth; becauſe the face of the painting is defended only by the coat of glue which cemented the linen cloth to it. The painting muſt then be freed from the glue, by waſhing it with hot water, ſpread and rubbed on the ſurface by a ſponge; which ſhould be cleanſed frequently during the operation, by dipping and ſqueezing it in clean water. The painting may afterwards be varniſhed as a new picture: and if the operation be well conducted, it will be transferred to the new cloth in a perfect ſtate.

When the painting is originally on wood, it muſt be firſt detached from the ceiling or wainſcot where it was fixed; and the ſurface of it covered with a linen cloth, cemented to it by means of glue, in the manner before directed for the paintings on canvas. A proper table being then provided, and overſpread with a blanket, or thinner woollen cloth, if laid ſeveral doubles, the painting muſt be laid upon it with the face downwards, and fixed ſteady; and the boards or wood on which it was done muſt be planed away, till the ſhell remain as thin as it can be made, without damaging the paint under it. The proceedings muſt afterwards be the ſame as was before practiſed in the caſe of the paintings on canvas, till that on the wood be in like manner transferred to a cloth or canvas.

The whole of the above operation muſt be managed with the greateſt care, otherwiſe the painting will receive ſome damage; and ſo much nicety is required in the corroſion, and taking off the threads of the cloth, that it can ſcarcely be performed rightly, but by ſuch as have had ſome experience in the matter. It is proper, therefore, for any perſon who would practiſe it in the caſe of of valuable paintings, to try it firſt with ſome old pictures of little value, till they find they have the right method of proceeding : and even then in ſome inſtances, where the coats of paint lie very thin on the cloth, it is ſcarcely practicable without miſcarriage. But as in the caſe of pictures greatly decayed, or paintings on wood taken from buildings that do not admit of being commodiouſly replaced elſewhere, there can be no great loſs if a failure ſhould happen ; and a conſiderable advantage may accrue, if the experiment ſucceed ; for which there is good chance if the operation be properly conducted, and the ſubject favourable ; and it is very well worth while to make the trial.

POETRY.

WE have the advantage of beginning our collection in a year which has produced so many elegant pieces of poetry, that we are not under a necessity, in order to make this article full, of inserting any mean performance.

MELPOMENE: *or the regions of Terror and Pity. An Ode.*
By R. DODSLEY.

I.

QUEEN of the human heart! at whose command
The swelling tides of mighty passion rise;
MELPOMENE, support my vent'rous hand,
And aid thy suppliant in his bold emprise.
From the gay scenes of pride
Do thou his footsteps guide
To Nature's aweful courts, where nurst of yore,
Young SHAKESPEAR, Fancy's child, was taught his various lore.

II.

So may his favour'd eye explore the source,
To few reveal'd, whence human sorrows charm:
So may his numbers, with pathetic force,
Bid *Terror* shake us, or *Compassion* warm,
As different strains controul
The movements of the soul,
Adjust its passions, harmonize its tone,
To feel for others' woe, or nobly bear its own.

III.

Deep in the covert of a shadowy grove,
Mid broken rocks where dashing currents play;
Dear to the pensive Pleasures, dear to Love,
And *Damon*'s Muse, that breathes her melting lay,
This ardent prayer was made.
When lo! the secret shade,
As conscious of some heavenly presence, shook——
Strength, firmness, reason, all——my astonish'd soul forsook.

IV.

Ah! whither Goddefs! whither am I borne?
To what wild region's necromantic fhore?
Thefe pannics whence? and why my bofom torne
With fudden terrors never felt before?
Darknefs inwraps me round,
While from the vaft profound
Emerging fpectres dreadful fhapes affume,
And, gleaming on my fight, add horror to the gloom.

V.

Ha! what is He whofe fierce indignant eye,
Denouncing vengeance, kindles into flame?
Whofe boifterous fury blows a ftorm fo high,
As with its thunder fhakes his labouring frame.
What can fuch Rage provoke?
His words their paffage choak:
His eager fteps nor time nor truce allow,
And dreadful dangers wait the menace of his brow.

VI.

Protect me Goddefs! whence that fearful fhriek
Of confternation? as grim death had laid
His icy fingers on fome guilty cheek,
And all the powers of manhood fhrunk difmay'd;
Ah fee! befmear'd with gore,
Revenge ftands threatening o'er
A pale delinquent, whofe retorted eyes
In vain for pity call——the wretched victim dies.

VII.

Nor long the fpace———abandon'd to Defpair,
With eyes aghaft, or hopelefs fixt on earth,
This flave of paffion rends his fcatter'd hair,
Beats his fad breaft, and execrates his birth:
While torn within, he feels
The pangs of whips and wheels;
And fees, or fancies, all the fiends below,
Beckoning his frightful foul to realms of endlefs woe.

VIII.

Before my wondering fenfe new phantoms dance,
And ftamp their horrid fhapes upon my brain——
A wretch with jealous brow, and eyes afkance,
Feeds all in fecret on his bofom pain.
Fond love, fierce hate, affail;
Alternate they prevail:
While confcious pride and fhame with rage confpire,
And urge the latent fparks to flames of torturing fire.

IX. The

IX.

The ftorm proceeds——his changeful vifage trace:
From rage to madnefs every feature breaks.
A growing phrenzy grins upon his face,
And in his frightful ftare Diftraction fpeaks:
His ftraw-invefted head
Proclaims all reafon fled;
And not a tear bedews thofe vacant eyes——
But fongs and fhouts fucceed, and laughter-mingled fighs.

X.

Yet, yet again!——a Murderer's hand appears
Grafping a pointed dagger ftain'd with blood!
His look malignant chills with boding fears,
That check the current of life's ebbing flood.
In midnight's darkeft clouds
The dreary mifcreant fhrowds
His felon ftep——as 'twere to darknefs given
To dim the watchful eye of all-pervading Heaven.

XI.

And hark! ah Mercy! whence that hollow found?
Why with ftrange horror ftarts my briftling hair?
Earth opens wide, and from unhallow'd ground
A pallid Ghoft flow-rifing fteals on air.
To where a mangled corfe
Expos'd without remorfe
Lies fhroudlefs, unentomb'd, he points the way——
Points to the prowling wolf exultant o'er his prey.

XII.

" Was it for this, he cries, with kindly fhower
" Of daily gifts the traytor I carefs'd?
" For this, array'd him in the robe of power,
" And lodg'd my royal fecrets in his breaft?
" O kindnefs ill repay'd!
" To bare the murdering blade
" Againft my life!——may Heav'n his guilt explore,
" And to my fuffering race their fplendid rights reftore."

XIII.

He faid, and ftalk'd away.——Ah! Goddefs, ceafe,
Thus with terrific forms to rack my brain;
Thefe horrid phantoms fhake the throne of Peace,
And Reafon calls her boafted powers in vain:
Then change thy magic wand,
Thy dreadful troops disband,'
And gentler fhapes, and fofter fcenes difclofe,
To melt the feeling heart, yet footh its tendereft woes.

XIV.

The fervent prayer was heard —— With hideous ſound
Her ebon gates of darkneſs open flew ;
A dawning twilight chears the dread profound,
The train of terror vaniſhes from view.
More mild enchantments riſe ;
New ſcenes ſalute my eyes,
Groves, fountains, bowers, and temples grace the plain,
And turtles cooe around, and nightingales complain.

XV.

And every myrtle bower and cypreſs grove,
And every ſolemn temple teems with life ;
Here glows the ſcene with fond but hapleſs love,
There with the deeper woes of human ſtrife.
In groups around the lawn,
By freſh diſaſters drawn,
The ſad ſpectators ſeem transfix'd in woe,
And pitying ſighs are heard, and heart-felt ſorrows flow.

XVI.

Behold that beauteous maid ! her languid head,
Bends like a drooping lily charg'd with rain ;
With floods of tears ſhe bathes a Lover dead,
In brave aſſertion of her honour ſlain.
Her boſom heaves with ſighs,
To Heaven ſhe lifts her eyes,
With grief beyond the power of words oppreſt,
Sinks on the lifeleſs corſe, and dies upon his breaſt.

XVII.

How ſtrong the bands of Friendſhip ! yet, alas !
Behind yon mouldering tower with ivy crown'd,
Of two, the foremoſt in her ſacred claſs,
One from his friend receives the fatal wound !
What could ſuch fury move ?
Ah, what but ill-ſtar'd love !
The ſame fair object each fond heart enthralls,
And he, the favour'd youth, her hapleſs victim falls.

XVIII.

Can aught ſo deeply ſway the generous mind
To mutual truth, as female truſt in love ?
Then what relief ſhall yon fair mourner find,
Scorn'd by the man who ſhould her plaints remove ?
By fair, but falſe pretence,
She loſt her innocence ;
And that ſweet babe, the fruit of treacherous art,
Claſpt in her arms expires, and breaks the parent's heart.

XIX. Ah !

XIX.

Ah! who to pomp or grandeur would aſpire?
Kings are not rais'd above Misfortune's frown.
That form ſo graceful even in mean attire,
Sway'd once a ſcepter, once ſuſtain'd a crown.
From Filial rage and ſtrife,
To ſcreen his cloſing life,
He quits his throne, a father's ſorrow feels,
And in the lap of Want his patient head conceals.

XX.

More yet remain'd —— but lo! the PENSIVE QUEEN
Appears confeſt before my dazzled ſight;
Grace in her ſteps, and ſoftneſs in her mien,
The face of ſorrow mingled with delight.
Not ſuch her noble frame,
When kindling into flame,
And bold in Virtue's cauſe, her zeal aſpires
To waken guilty pangs, or breathe heroic fires.

XXI.

Aw'd into ſilence, my rapt ſoul attends ——
The POWER, with eyes complacent, ſaw my fear;
And, as with grace ineffable ſhe bends,
Theſe accents vibrate on my liſtening ear.
" Aſpiring ſon of art,
" Know, tho' thy feeling heart
" Glow with theſe wonders to thy fancy ſhewn,
" Still may the Delian God thy powerleſs toils diſown.

XXII.

" A thouſand tender ſcenes of ſoft diſtreſs
" May ſwell thy breaſt with ſympathetic woes;
" A thouſand ſuch dread forms on fancy preſs,
" As from my dreary realms of darkneſs roſe,
" Whence SHAKESPEAR's chilling fears,
" Whence OTWAY's melting tears ——
" That aweful gloom, this melancholy plain,
" The *types* of every *theme* that ſuits the TRAGIC STRAIN.

XXIII.

" But doſt thou worſhip Nature night and morn,
" And all due honour to her precepts pay?
" Can'ſt thou the lure of Affectation ſcorn,
" Pleas'd in the ſimpler paths of Truth to ſtray?
" Haſt thou the Graces fair
" Invok'd with ardent prayer?
" 'Tis they attire, as Nature muſt impart,
" The ſentiment ſublime, the language of the heart.

XXIV.

" Then if creative Genius pour his ray,
" Warm with inſpiring influence on thy breaſt;
" Taſte, judgment, fancy, if thou can'ſt diſplay,
" And the deep ſource of Paſſion ſtand confeſt;
" Then may the liſtening train,
" Affected, feel thy ſtrain;
" Feel Grief, or Terror, Rage or Pity move:
" Change with thy varying ſcenes, and every ſcene approve."

XXV.

Humbled before her ſight, and bending low,
I kiſs'd the borders of her crimſon veſt;
Eager to ſpeak, I felt my boſom glow,
But fear upon my lip her ſeal impreſt,
While awe-ſtruck thus I ſtood,
The bowers, the lawn, the wood,
The FORM CELESTIAL, fading on my ſight,
Diſſolv'd in liquid air, and fleeting gleams of light.

Ode for his Majeſty's Birth-Day, Nov. 10, 1758.

Written by WILLIAM WHITEHEAD, Eſq; Poet-Laureat, and ſet to muſick by Dr. Boyce, Maſter of the King's Band. The vocal parts by Meſſ. Beard, Savage, Waſs, Cowper, Barrow, and the reſt of the gentlemen and children of the chapel royal; the inſtrumental by his Majeſty's band, &c.

ARGUMENT.

About the year 963, *Ottoberto, of the family of Eſte, paſſed from Italy into Germany, with the Emperor Otho the Great. Azo, his deſcendant, in the next century, by a marriage with the daughter of Welfus Count Altdorf, inherited the dominions of that family in Suabia. Welfus, a ſon of that marriage, in the year* 1061, *received the Dukedom of Bavaria from the Emperor Henry the* IVth. *The deſcendants of Welfus became afterwards poſſeſſed of thoſe Dutchies which lie between the Elbe and the Weſer (Brunſwick, Wolfenbuttle, Lunenburg, Zell, Hanover, &c.) and in the year* 1714 *George the firſt, Duke and Elector of Hanover, ſucceeded to the throne of Great Britain.*

I.

WHEN Othbert left th' Italian plain,
And ſoft Ateſtè's green domain,
Attendant on Imperial ſway
Where Fame and Otho led the way,

The

The Genius of the Julian hills
(Whose piny summits nod with snow,
Whose Naiads pour their thousand rills
To swell th' exulting Po)
An eager look prophetic cast,
And hail'd the Hero as he pass'd.
Hail, all hail, the woods reply'd,
And Echo on her airy tide
Roll'd the long murmurs down the mountain's side.

II.

The voice resum'd again. " *Proceed*,
Nor cast one lingering look behind;
By those who toil for virtue's meed
By every softer thought resign'd;
Nor social home, nor genial air,
Nor glowing suns are worth thy care;
New realms await thee in a harsher sky,
Thee, and thy chosen race from Azo's nuptial tie.

III.

'Tis Glory wakes; her active flame
Nor time shall quench, nor danger tame.
Nor * Boia's amplest range confine,
Tho' Guelpho reigns, the Guelphic line.
Yon Northern Star, which dimly gleams
Athwart the twilight veil of eve,
Must point their path to distant streams,
And many a wreath shall Vict'ry weave,
And many a palm shall Fame display
To grace the warriors on their way,
Till regions bow to their commands
Where Albis widens thro' the lands,
And vast Visurgis spreads his golden sands.

IV.

Nor rest they there. Yon guiding fire
Still shines aloft, and gilds the main!
Not Lion † Henry's soft desire
To grasp th' Italian realms again,

Nor

* Bavaria.

† Henry the Lion, Duke of Bavaria, Saxony, &c. was one of the greatest heroes of the XIIth century. He united in his own person the hereditary dominions of five families. His claims upon Italy hindered him from joining with the Emperor Frederic I. in his third attack upon the Pope, tho' he had assisted him in the two former. For which he was stripped of his dominions by that Emperor, and died in 1195, possessed only of those dutchies which lie between the Elbe and the Weser.

From this Henry, and a sister or daughter of Henry II. of England, his present Majesty is lineally descended.

Nor warring winds, nor wintry ſeas
Shall ſtop the progreſs Fate decrees:
For lo! Britannia calls, to happier coaſts
And vales more verdant far than ſoft Ateſtè boaſts!

V.

Behold, with Euphraſy I clear
Thy viſual nerve, and fix it there,
Where, crown'd with rocks groteſque and ſteep,
The White Iſle riſes o'er the deep!
There Glory reſts. For there arrive
Thy choſen ſons; and there attain
To the firſt title fate can give,
The father Kings of free-born men!
Proceed. Rejoice. Deſcend the vale,
And bid the future monarchs hail!
Hail, all hail, the Hero cry'd,
And Echo on her airy tide
Purſu'd him murmuring down the mountain's ſide.

VI.

'Twas thus, O King, to heroes old
The mountains breath'd the ſtrain divine,
'Ere yet her volumes Fame unroll'd
To trace the wonders of thy line;
'Ere Freedom yet on Ocean's breaſt
Had northward fix'd her halcyon neſt;
Or Albion's oaks deſcending to the main,
Had roll'd her thunders wide, and claim'd the watry reign.

VII.

But now each Briton's glowing tongue,
Proclaims the truths the Genius ſung;
On Brunſwick's name with rapture dwells,
And hark, the generous Chorus ſwells!
" May years and happy years roll o'er,
'Till glory cloſe the ſhining page,
And our ill-fated ſons deplore
The ſhortneſs of a Neſtor's age!
Hail, all hail, on Albion's plains
The friend of man and freedom reigns!
Echo waft the triumph round,
'Till Gallia's utmoſt ſhores rebound,
And all her bulwarks tremble at the ſound."

Ode

Ode for the New Year 1759.

Written by WILLIAM WHITEHEAD, *Esq; Poet Laureat, and set by Dr. Boyce, Master of his Majesty's band of music.*

The vocal parts by Mess. Beard, Savage, Baildon, Wass, Barrow, Ladd, Denham, Cowper, and the other gentlemen and children of the chapel royal. The instrumental by Dr. Nares, the King's band, &c.

Strophe.

YE guardian Powers, to whose command,
At Nature's birth, th' Almighty Mind,
The delegated task assign'd
To watch o'er Albion's favour'd land,
What time your hosts with choral lay,
Emerging from its kindred deep,
Applausive hail'd each verdant steep,
And white rock, glitt'ring to the new-born day!
Angelic hands, where'er ye rove,
Whilst lock'd in sleep creation lies,
Whether to genial dews above
You melt the congregated skies,
Or teach the torrent streams below
To wake the verdure of the vale,
Or guide the varying winds that blow
To speed the coming or the parting sail,
Where'er ye bend your roving flight,
Whilst now the radiant Lord of light
Winds to the North his sliding sphere,
Avert each ill, each bliss improve,
And teach the minutes as they move
To bless the op'ning year.

Antistrophe.

Already Albion's lifted spear
And rolling thunders of the main,
Which Justice' sacred laws maintain,
Have taught the haughty Gaul to fear.
On other earths, in other skies
Beyond old Ocean's western bound,
Tho' bleeds afresh th' eternal wound,
Again Britannia's cross triumphant flies.
To British George, the King of Isles,
The tribes that rove th' Acadian snows,
Redeem'd from Gallia's polish'd wiles,
Shall breathe their voluntary vows:

Where

Where Nature guards her laſt retreat,
And pleas'd Aſtræa lingers ſtill,
While Faith yet triumphs o'er Deceit,
And Virtue reigns, from ignorance of ill.
Yet Angel-powers, tho' Gallia bend,
Tho' Fame, with all her wreaths, attend
On bleeding War's tremendous ſway,
The ſons of Leiſure ſtill complain,
And muſing Science ſighs in vain,
For Peace is ſtill away.

Epode.

Go, then, ye faithful guides
Of her returning ſteps, angelic band,
Explore the ſacred ſeats where Peace reſides,
And waves her olive wand.
Bid her the waſtes of War repair.
——O ſouthward ſeek the flying Fair,
For not on poor Germania's harraſs'd plain,
Nor where the Viſtula's proud current ſwells,
Nor on the borders of the frighted Seine,
Nor in the depths of Ruſſia's ſnows ſhe dwells,
Yet O, where'er, deſerting Freedom's iſle,
She gilds the ſlave's deluſive toil,
Whether on Ebro's bank ſhe ſtrays,
Or ſighing traces Taio's winding ways,
Or ſoft Auſonia's ſhores her feet detain,
O bring the wanderer back, with Glory in her train.

Verſes to the People of England 1758. *By* WIL. WHITEHEAD, *Eſq*; *Poet Laureat*.

- - - - - *Mures animos in martia bella*
Verſibus exacuit. - - - - - Hor.

BRITONS, rouſe to deeds of death!
Waſte not zeal in idle breath,
Nor loſe the harveſt of your ſwords
In a civil-war of words!
Wherefore teems the ſhameleſs preſs
With labour'd births of emptineſs?
Reas'nings, which no facts produce,
Eloquence, that murders uſe;
Ill-tim'd *Humour*, that beguiles
Weeping ideots of their ſmiles;
Wit, that knows but to defame,
And *Satire*, that profanes the name.
Let th' undaunted *Grecian* teach
The uſe and dignity of ſpeech,
At whoſe thunders nobly thrown
Shrunk the MAN of MACEDON.

If

If the ſtorm of words *muſt* riſe,
Let it blaſt our enemies.
Sure and nervous be it hurl'd
On the PHILIPS of the world.
Learn not vainly to deſpiſe
(Proud of EDWARD's victories !)
Warriors wedg'd in firm array,
And navies powerful to diſplay
Their woven wings to every wind,
And leave the panting foe behind.
Give to *France* the honours due,
France has chiefs and ſtateſmen too ;
Breaſts which patriot-paſſions feel,
Lovers of the common-weal.
And when ſuch the foes we brave,
Whether on the land or wave,
Greater is the pride of war,
And the conqueſt nobler far.
Agincourt and *Creſſy* long
Have flouriſh'd in immortal ſong;
And liſping babes aſpire to praiſe
The wonders of ELIZA's days.
And what elſe of late renown
Has added wreaths to *Britain*'s crown ;
Whether on th' impetuous *Rhine*
She bad her harneſs'd warriors ſhine,
Or ſnatch'd the dangerous palm of praiſe
Where the *Sambre* meets the *Maeſe* ;
Or *Danube* rolls his watry train ;
Or the yellow-treſſed *Mayne*
Thro' *Dettingen*'s immortal vale.——
Even *Fontenoy* could tell a tale,
Might modeſt Worth ingenuous ſpeak,
To raiſe a bluſh on Victory's cheek ;
And bid the vanquiſh'd wreaths diſplay
Great as on *Culloden*'s day.
But glory which aſpires to laſt
Leans not meanly on the paſt.
'Tis the preſent Now demands
Britiſh hearts, and *Britiſh* hands.
Curſt be he, the willing ſlave,
Who doubts, who lingers to be brave.
Curſt be the coward tongue that dare
Breathe one accent of deſpair,
Cold as Winter's icy hand
To chill the Genius of the land.

Chiefly

Chiefly you, who ride the deep,
And bid our thunders wake or ſleep,
As Pity pleads, or Glory calls——
Monarchs of our wooden walls!
Midſt your mingling ſeas and ſkies
Riſe ye BLAKES, ye RALEIGHS riſe!
Let the ſordid luſt of gain
Be baniſh'd from the liberal main.
He who ſtrikes the generous blow
Aims it at the public foe.
Let glory be the guiding ſtar,
Wealth and honours follow her.
See! ſhe ſpreads her luſtre wide
O'er the vaſt *Atlantic* tide!
Conſtant as the ſolar ray
Points the path, and leads the way!
Other worlds demand your care,
Other worlds to *Britain* dear;
Where the foe inſidious roves
O'er headlong ſtreams, and pathleſs groves;
And Juſtice' ſimple laws confounds
With imaginary bounds.
If protected Commerce keep
Her tenor o'er yon heaving deep,
What have we from War to fear?
Commerce ſteels the nerves of War;
Heals the havoc Rapine makes,
And new ſtrength from conqueſt takes.
Nor leſs at home O deign to ſmile,
Goddeſs of *Britannia*'s iſle!
Thou, that from her rocks ſurvey'ſt
Her boundleſs realms the watry waſte;
Thou, that rov'ſt the hill and mead
Where her flocks, and heifers feed;
Thou, that chear'ſt the induſtrious ſwain
While he ſtrows the pregnant grain;
Thou, that hear'ſt his caroll'd vows
When th' expanded barn o'erflows;
Thou, the bulwark of our cauſe,
Thou, the guardian of our laws,
Sweet Liberty!——O deign to ſmile,
Goddeſs of *Britannia*'s iſle!
If to us indulgent Heaven
Nobler ſeeds of ſtrength has given,
Nobler ſhould the produce be;
Brave, yet gen'rous, are the free.
Come then, all thy powers diffuſe,
Goddeſs of extended views!

Every

Every breast which feels *thy* flame
Shall kindle into martial fame,
'Till shame shall make the coward bold,
And *Indolence* her arms unfold;
Ev'n *Avarice* shall protect his hoard,
And the plough-share gleam a sword.
Goddess, all thy powers diffuse!
And thou, genuine BRITISH MUSE,
Nurs'd amidst the *Druids* old
Where *Deva*'s wizard waters roll'd,
Thou, that bear'st the golden key
To unlock Eternity,
Summon thy poetic guard——
Britain still has many a bard,
Whom, when Time and Death shall join
T' expand the ore, and stamp the coin,
Late posterity shall own
Lineal to the Muse's throne——
Bid them leave th' inglorious theme
Of fabled shade, or haunted stream.
In the daisy-painted mead
'Tis to *Peace* we tune the reed;
But when *War*'s tremendous roar
Shakes the isle from shore to shore,
Every bard of purer fire
Tyrtæus-like should grasp the lyre;
Wake with verse the hardy deed,
Or in the generous strife like * SYDNEY bleed.

* Sir Philip Sidney, mortally wounded in an action near Zutphen, in Gelderland.

Ode

Ode a S. M. le Roi de PRUSSE.
Par M. DE VOLTAIRE.

PRINCE vaillant & magnanime,
Affailli d'ennemis cruels
Dont tu fais arracher leftime
Heros digne de leurs autels:
Je fens une fureur divine
Qui me preffe, qui me domine,
Je cede a fa brulante ardeur.
Recois mon homage fincere:
Grand *Frederic!* il doit de plaire,
C'eft le pur homage du cœur.

Deja la politique affreufe,
Monftre affame de grands forfaits.
Dans fa caverne tenebreufe
A concu le plus noirs projets.
L'Ambition a l'œil perfide,
La Jaloufie au teint livide,
Ont prefide dans fon confeil.
Bellone, fombre & menacante,
D'une guerre injufte & fanglante
Prepare l'horrible appareil.

De trois puiffances redoutable
Je vois s'unir les etendarts;
Du foldat les cris effroyables
Retentiffent de toute part:
Plein d'une courage mercenaire,
Il arme fon bras fanguinaire.
Ah! mon cœur eft faifi d'effroi—
Prince! l'ennemi t'environne.—
Il va t'enlever la couronne.
Qui la merite mieux que toi?

Dans une tranquille retraite
Goutaut les douceurs de la paix,
Sa grande ame ne s'inquiete
Que du bonheur de fes fujets.
La foudre gronde fur fa tete,
La plus effrayante tempete
Souleve contre lui les flots:
Il perce enfin l'epais nuage,
Son œil etonne voit l'orage,
Mais il le contemple en heros.

O vous dont l'ardeur temeraire
Va femer le trouble & l'horreur,
Un roi qui font peuple revere,
Un roi qu'il porte dans fon cœur,
Tombera-t-il votre victime?
Et fera-t-il dit que le crime
S'immole toutes les vertus?

Non:

Ode to the King of PRUSSIA.
By M. DE VOLTAIRE.

O Thou! whofe mighty mind difdains
Of life the frauds, and fears, and pains;
Thou, whom thy foes, in fpite of hate,
Revere at heart, and call the Great!
I feel the facred phrenzy ftrong,
Which rules me and compels the fong;
Accept the ftrains that flow fincere,
Such ftrains thy virtues ought to hear.

Deep in her gloomy cell retir'd,
With luft of dreadful mifchiefs fir'd,
Fell Cunning plots to curfe mankind,
With half the powers of hell combin'd.
Ambition with her double view,
And Jealoufy of pallid hue;
The project form'd, *Bellona* rears
Her horrid front diffufing fears,
For war prepares, injurious War,
And frowning mounts her iron car.

Three mighty pow'rs their ftandards bring,
The foldiers fhout, the valleys ring;
The ruthlefs hand which fights for hire,
Is ftretch'd to fet the world on fire:
Fear chills my heart and dims my eyes;
O Prince, thy foes furround thee! rife!
They come to fnatch thy crown! beware!
For who *thy* crown deferves to wear?

Reclin'd in foft ferene repofe,
And bleft with all that Peace beftows;
The Prince no anxious cares diftreft,
By bleffing wifhful to be bleft,
When o'er his head the thunder roars,
The founding billows lafh the fhores,
The clouds difpart, the ftorm appears,
He fees furpriz'd, furpriz'd he hears;
Yet with calm wonder weighs the fcene,
As heroes ufe, fedate! ferene!

Ye hoftile bands, who rafhly dare
To fcatter wide the plagues of war,
Can *Frederic* fall by your decrees,
Who lives in ev'ry heart he fees?
For Vice fhall every Virtue die,
To pile her impious altars high?

No,

Non: *Frederic* a vu les trames
Ourdies au fond de vos ames:
Tous vos projets ſont confondus.

No, *Frederic* ſees the latent ſnare,
And all your projects mix with air.

Soldats, un ennemi parjure,
Dont l'ambition eſt la loi,
Vous fait la plus ſanglante injure,
Il oſe attaquer votre Roi.
Il vient ſe montrer a vos portes:
Deja ſes nombreuſes cohortes
Repandent partout la terreur;
Soutenez la plus juſte cauſe,
Sur vous *Frederic* ſe repoſe;
Si vous l'aimez il eſt vainqueur.

Soldiers, ſaid he, a lawleſs pow'r
With war profanes the peaceful hour;
Your King aſſails, invades his gates,
And ſhakes with terror all his ſtates.
Support my cauſe, my cauſe is juſt;
In you your *Frederic* puts his truſt:
Of all his wiſh, your love, poſſeſt,
Of conqueſt ſure, your King is bleſt.

Il dit. Son courage intrepide
Paſſe dans l'ame des ſoldats:
Et chacun d'eux, nouvel Alcide,
Brule de volar aux combats.
Autrichien vain & farouche,
Oui, l'inſolence eſt dans ta bouche,
Mais l'epouvante eſt dans ton cœur:
Francois ta valeur ſi vantee
Devant le Pruſſien eſt glacee:
Tout diſparoit juſqu'a l'honneur.

He ſaid, and ſoon the ſacred fire
That warms his breaſt, his troops acquire.
A new Alcides now in might,
Each burns impatient for the fight.
Proud *Auſtria* ſtill in threats is brave,
And ſinks at heart; to fear a ſlave;
Of France the boaſted valour's fled,
The *Pruſſian* comes, ſhe's chill'd with dread
Ev'n Honour frighted quits her breaſt,
Her lov'd, her long familiar gueſt.

Jadis les enfans de la terre,
Les tyrans fiers audacieux,
Oſerent declarer la guerre
Au ſouverain maitre des dieux:
Deja leur fureur arrogante
Levoit une main triomphante.
Jupiter tonne, ils ſont vaincus.
Toi, *Frederic*, en ta colere
Tu jettes un regarde ſevere,
Tes ennemis ſont eperdus.

When erſt ſons of Earth aroſe,
Of mighty *Jove* th' audacious foes,
The God ſerene, in aweful ſtate,
Launc'd the red bolt, their inſtant fate:
So when with headlong fury fir'd,
To *Frederic*'s crown his foes aſpir'd,
The hero frown'd with martial grace,
And ſwift they vaniſh'd from the place.

Aux plaintes de la Germanie
L'orgueil Francois eſt ecraſe;
Frederic vole en Sileſie,
L'Autrichien eſt terraſſe:
Ses ſoldats lancent ils la foudre?
Ils paroiſſent, tout eſt en poudre.
La victoire eſt devant leurs pas,
Non, il n'eſt rien la qui m'etonne.
Il faut que le ſucces couronne
Des heros que ſoutient ſon bras.

Germania ſighs, her voice is heard,
And *France* chaſtis'd no more is fear'd;
To aid *Sileſia*, *Frederic* flies,
And low on earth proud *Auſtria* lies.
Does *Jove* his troops with thunder truſt?
They march—and foes and tow'rs are duſt
Before them Vict'ry wings her way,
And ſtays where'er the heroes ſtay.
What ſecret cauſe theſe wonders breeds?
No wonders theſe — for *Frederic* leads.

Et toi, feroce Moſcovite,
Tu crains d'affronter ſa valeur:
Une prompte & heureuſe fuite
Te ſouſtrait a ſon bras vangeur.
Va raconter dans les provinces
Que le plus auguſte des princes
A pour ſoldats des demi dieux:

Fierce *Ruſſia* fear'd his piercing ſight
And ſaved her troops by timely flight.
Ye fugitives, proclaim around
What demi gods combin'd ye found;

Que ſon nom ſeul en ſon abſence,
Produit l'effet de ſa preſence,
Et que ſon ame vit en eux.

That *Frederic*'s name his place ſupplies
And wither's nations as they riſe ;
That all his ſoul diffus'd inſpires
Each breaſt with more then mortal fires.

Ces evenemens memorables
Que celebra l'antiquite
Ne ſeront plus d'illuſtres fables
Aux yeux de la poſterite.
Hommes courages invincibles,
Tous vos faits incomprehenſibles
Etonneroient-ils nos eſprits
Quand nous voyons de votre gloire
Les rayons, epars dans l'hiſtoire,
En *Frederic* ſeul reunis.

What raptur'd bards, in times of old,
Of demi-gods and heroes told,
No more ſhall paſs for ſplendid dreams,
Inſpir'd by rich *Pierean* ſtreams.
Ye mighty dead, we doubt no more
The feats your arms atchiev'd of yore ;
Your envy'd glory's ſcatter'd rays,
Combin'd in *Pruſſia's* monarch, blaze.

Mets fin a tes travaux ſans nombre,
Termine tes exploits guerriers,
Et viens te repoſer a l'ombre,
Frederic, de tant de lauriers,
Donne a l'Europe deſolee
Une paix qui ſoit aſſuree,
Qu'elle la tienne du vainqueur.
Le triumphe les plus illuſtre
N'aquiert-il pas ſon dernier luſtre
Quand il ramene le bonheur ?

O *Frederic*, ſpeed the bliſsful hour,
When all thy foes ſhall own thy pow'r ;
When yet once more at eaſe reclin'd,
Thy tranquil ſmiles ſhall bleſs mankind.
Her peace from thee let *Europe* claim,
Peace gives the victor's utmoſt fame ;
That fame which conqueſts ne'er beſtow,
Won but to waſte the world below.

De tout un peuple qui t'adore
Lorſque les vœux ſont exauces,
Voudrois tu qu'il fremit encore
En voyant tes jours expoſes ?
Acheve la plus belle vie,
En eclairant par ton genie
Des ſujects ſauves par ton bras.
Remonte la lyre d'Horace,
Sois Apollon ſur le Parnaſſe
Comme tu fus Mars aux combats.

O ! why, belov'd, admir'd, ador'd,
Thy life with endleſs pray'rs implor'd ?
Why ſhould whole realms with panting breath,
Still watch thee thro' the fields of death ?
O let thy days in peace decline,
Thy life and death alike divine ;
Whom valour ſav'd, let genius cheer,
Reſume the lyre we joy to hear :
And beam around thy lov'd domain
The rays of mental light again,
The world's great *Phœbus*, known from far
Its *Mars* before ſupreme in war.

The

The following Copy of Verses of the King of Prussia were presented by him to Mr. Professor Gottsched at Leipsic, the 18th day of October, 1757.

LE Ciel, en dispensant ses dons
  Ne les prodigue point d'un main liberale,
Il nous refuse plus que nous ne le recevons :
  Pour tout peuple à peu près sa faveur est ègale.

Les Francois sont legres, les Anglois sont profonds ;
  Et s'il denie à l'un ce qu'il accorde à l'autre ;
L'amour propre, en changeant, en roses ses chardons
  Au talent du voisin fait prefere le nôtre.

Sparte possedoit la valeur,
  Mars se plut d'ye former de fameux Capitaines,
Tandis que la molle douceur
  Des arts & des talens respiroit dans Athenes.

De Sparte nos vaillans Germains
  Out recueilli l' antique gloire:
Combien des grands exploits ont place en leur histoire!

  Mais s'ils on trouvé les chemins,
A travers les perils, au temple de Mémoire,
  Les fleurs se fânent dans leurs mains
Dont ills couronnent la victoire.

C'est à toi, le Cygne Saxon
  D'arracher ce talent à la nature avare,
  D'adoucir, par tes soins, d'une langue barbare
La dure âpreté de ses tons ;
  Ajoute par les chants que ta Muse prepare,
  Aux lauriers des vainqueurs, dont le Germain se pare
Les plus beaux lueriers d' Apollon.

Parodie sur les Vers precedens.

LE Ciel en dispensant ses dons,
Fut prodigue pour vous, Monarque incomparable!
Par les talens de Mars, et par ceux d'Apollon
Aux siecles à venir il vous rend respectable.
Si d'un Francois leger, d'un Anglois de très profond,
Le caractère outré leure attire du blâme;
Le vôtre en équilibre, & toujours sans passion
Ne nous trace partout que sens & grandeur d'âme.
C'est sous vos étendarts, Monarque valeureux,
Que Mars forme à present de fameux Capitaines:
Vos Germains, animès par vos fait glorieux,
Ternissent tout l'éclat de la grandeur Romaine.
Les arts & le savoir dans Athènes nourris,
Vont chercher au milieu ne vos braves cohortes
Un asile assuré, et fiers de cette escorte
Suivent tranquillement leur protecteur cheri.
C'est ainsi, Prince unique en vos travaux guerriers,
Qu' avec un livre en main vous cueilles des lauriers,
Laissant à ces temoins d'une immortelle gloire,
Le soin de mediter la plus parfait histoire.
Usez de ces talens! mais que bientot vos faits
Ceignent se front sacré de l' olive de paix!
Donnez-nous la, Grand Roi; surmontes tout obstacle,
Et laissez-nous le soin de crier au miracle.

Translation of the King of Prussia's Verses to Professor Gottsched.

WITH bounteous yet with frugal hand,
Its mental gifts judicious Heav'n
Deals near alike to every land,
Tho' different kinds to each are giv'n.

The *French* of airy genius prove,
Britannia's sons profound are known:
Charm'd by the magic of self-love,
Each prizes, each prefers his own.

In

In *Sparta*, once for arms renown'd,
  Mars train'd his noblest sons of fame;
Politest arts and manners crown'd,
  With *Attic* sweets, th' *Athenian* name.

From *Lacedæmon*'s hardy race
  Our *Germans*, fir'd with martial rage,
Dauntless to fame, thro' danger, press,
  Ennobled in th' historic page.

But soon their flow'ry garlands fade,
  And wither from the public view;
No tuneful bard's reforming aid,
  Their harsh neglected language knew.

This task, *Saxonian Swan!* be thine;
  Thy native tongue, with pow'rful art
In niggard nature's spite, refine,
  And sweetly-melting sounds impart.

In *Heliconian* strains assume,
  And swell our *German* Hero's praise:
Immortal shall then laurels bloom,
  Entwin'd with thy *Parnassian* bays.

The Professor's Answer.

HEav'n that distinguishes but few,
Was lavish, matchless Prince! to you;
It grac'd you with the mingled charms
Of wisdom, poetry, and arms,
And bade you, thus adorn'd, engage
The wonder of each future age:
It form'd you in that happy mean
Those blameable extremes between,
Of *British* genius, too profound,
And *French*, for levity renown'd.
Hence, nicely poiz'd, and well refin'd,
True grandeur dignifies your mind;
No clouds of passion ever roll,
T' obscure the brightness of your soul.
  Mars now, where e'er your standards fly,
Submits to your corrective eye,
And forms, as in his noblest schools,
His heroes by your better rules;

And hence your *Germans* riſe in fame
Superior to the *Roman* name.
Long exil'd from their native home
Th' *Athenian Muſes* forc'd to roam
In ſearch of ſome belov'd retreat,
Amidſt your cohorts fix their ſeat,
Tranſported, your beheſts obey,
And follow where you lead the way.
Fame's greeneſt laureat-wreath you ſeize,
And pluck, ſerene in learned eaſe,
Leaving th' hiſtorians of your age,
T' inſcribe you on th' immortal page.
Theſe godlike talents uſe——and ſoon
May ſmiling *Peace*, (celeſtial boon!)
Her blooming olives all divine
Around your ſacred temples twine.
This bleſſing, mighty Prince! beſtow,
And every obſtacle o'erthrow,
While, with poetic raptures warm'd,
I ſing the wonders you've perform'd.

Rotterdam, Jan. 24, 1758. B. S——n.

Ode, in the ſecond Act of Agis, a Tragedy, as it was performed at the Theatre-Royal in Drury-lane.

Mrs. Pritchard.

WOES approach, till now unknown;
Diſcord ſhakes the Spartan throne,
Heav'n avert the ills we fear!
Jove, from high Olympus, hear!

CHORUS.

Ever may his mighty arm
Save the Spartan ſtate from harm!
Ne'er may proud invaders boaſt
Glory from our glory loſt.
Light, O Jove, that ſacred fire
Which did Sparta's ſons inſpire,
When the Prince and people ſtrove,
Burning with their country's love,
Xerxes, lord of great alarms,
Xerxes rouz'd the world to arms.

Prieſt of Jupiter, *Mr. Champneſs.*

The earth was troubled at his hoſt,
The ſprings were dry'd, the rivers loſt;

But

But Spartan valour check'd his pride,
A ſlender band his hoſt defy'd:
Thermopylæ, (immortal name!)
Beheld the Perſian tyrant's ſhame.

Chorus of all.

There the brave three hundred dy'd,
Faithful, by their Prince's ſide,
There they conquer'd tho' they dy'd.

Prieſt of Hercules, *Mr. Beard.*

On earth below, in heav'n above,
Rever'd, victorious, ſon of Jove!
Hear, Alcides, hear our pray'r,
Thy godlike offspring claims thy care.

CHORUS.

Agis of thy race divine,
Try'd in labours like to thine.
Undaunted, like thee, with monſters he ſtrives;
The fierceſt of Hydras in faction revives.
If he falls a ſacrifice,
Never more ſhall Sparta riſe!

Ode in the fifth Act.

Mr. Garrick.

MOURN, ye ſons of Sparta mourn,
Pour the ſad lamenting ſtrain,
Wretched people! land forlorn!
Mourn the beſt of Princes ſlain.

Prieſt of Jupiter, *Mr. Champneſs.*

He fell not as the warrior falls,
Whoſe breaſt defends the native walls;
To treaſon Agis bow'd his head,
And by his guilty ſubjects bled:
Betray'd by thoſe his mercy ſpar'd;
Ingratitude was his reward.

Prieſt of Hercules, *Mr. Beard.*

Yet Agis triumph'd in his fall;
For Virtue triumphs over all:
Great, ſuperior to his fate,
He only griev'd for Sparta's ſtate:
When Jove decrees a nation's doom,
He calls their heroes to the tomb.
Fearleſs they fall, immortal riſe,
And claim the freedom of the ſkies.

CHORUS.

Agis triumph'd in his fall,
Virtue triumphs over all!
Such a King ſhall ne'er return,
Our country and ourſelves we mourn.

Chorus of all.

Now in peace our Hero lies,
Ceas'd his toil, his race is run;
Freedom is the glorious prize
Agis for his people won.

An Epitaph upon Johnny Armſtrong.

HERE lies the mortal part of poor Johnny Armſtrong,
Who from his ſetting out in life
Gave an early promiſe of what he afterwards perform'd.
He enter'd upon the ſervice of the field
With incredible intrepidity,
And run for a few years
Almoſt an uninterrupted courſe of victories.
He got the ſtart of every thing that oppos'd him,
Was more expeditious than Cæſar,
And was never known to inſult thoſe he had conquered;
Or detract from thoſe, who were ſuperior to himſelf.
His temper was always equal,
Never too much elated with ſucceſs,
Or dejected in diſtreſs:
His numerous conteſts teſtify the former,
And the ſcarcity of his defeats is ſufficient to certify the latter.
He wanted no other ſpur,
Than his own ambition and thirſt of glory:
If they at any time ever hurry'd him on too raſhly,
He could patiently bear the curb of him,
Who was ſet over him.
To ſum up his public character in a few words;
If any body ever was,
He certainly was cut out by Nature for the field,
In which ſervice he preſerv'd to his dying day,
A credit to his maſter, and an honour to his country.

Reader, however you may admire his public character, his private life will much more charm you. All his good qualities were intirely the gift of Nature; and like a true *Houyhnhmn*, he never ſpoke the thing which was not. Want of humanity was never objected to him by ſuch as properly conſidered the rank of life he fill'd. He was moderate, neither coſtly, nor mean in his diet; ſober even to abſtinence, for he was never known to drink a glaſs of wine in his life; or eat of more than one, or two things at moſt at a meal; ſo virtuous that he never knew woman. He was rather tall in his perſon, of excellent parts, well proportioned, and of a beautiful complexion. If he had any religion, it was the religion of nature; but the whole tenor of his life ſhews he was no atheiſt. And if he did not live in the obſervance of all the commandments, it is but juſtice to his aſhes to ſay, he never broke one of them to his dying day.

Windſor.

Tranſlation

Translation of a French Ode in Lloyd's Evening Post.

SOUBISE and Lorrain in dispute
 Concerning their hapless mischance;
To the gen'ral of Austria, thus said
 The doughty commander of France.

'That you always are vanquish'd, dear Charles,
 'Surprizes me not, by my troth:
'For Frederic you know, *entre nous*,
 'Is more than a match for us both.

'But at Breslau how came you to leave
 'So many brave men in disgrace?
'*Mai foi!* I'd have led them all off,
 'If I had been there in your place.'

"True, answer'd Lorrain, I agree,
 "This you, with your Frenchmen, had done:
"And mine too had got clear away
 "If they, like the French, could have *run*."

Ode on Death. Translated from the French of the King of Prussia, by Dr. HAWKESWORTH.

YET a few years, or days perhaps,
Or moments pass in silent lapse,
 And time to me shall be no more;
No more the sun these eyes shall view;
Earth o'er these limbs her dust shall strew,
 And life's fantastic dream be o'er.

Alas! I touch the dreadful brink,
From Nature's verge impell'd I sink,
 And endless darkness wraps me round!
Yes, Death is ever at my hand,
Fast by my bed he takes his stand,
 And constant at my board is found.

Earth, air, and fire and water join
Against this fleeting life of mine,
 And where for succour can I fly?
If Art with flattering wiles pretend
To shield me like a guardian friend,
 By Art, ere Nature bids, I die.

I see this tyrant of the mind,
This idol flesh, to dust consign'd,
 Once call'd from dust by Pow'r divine;
Its features change, 'tis pale, 'tis cold——
Hence, dreadful spectre! to behold
 Thy aspect, is to make it mine.

And

And can I then with guilty pride,
Which fear nor ſhame can quell nor hide,
  This fleſh ſtill pamper and adorn!
Thus viewing what I ſoon *ſhall be*,
Can what I *am* demand the knee,
  Or look on aught around with ſcorn?

But then this ſpark that warms, that guides,
That lives, that thinks, what fate betides?
  Can this be duſt, a kneaded clod!
This yield to death! the ſoul, the mind,
That meaſures heav'n, and mounts the wind,
  That knows at once itſelf and God?

Great Cauſe of all, above, below,
Who knows Thee muſt for ever know,
  Immortal or divine!
Thy image on my ſoul impreſt,
Of endleſs being is the teſt,
  And bids Eternity be mine!

Tranſporting thought!—but am I ſure
That endleſs life will joy ſecure?
  Joys only to the juſt decreed!
The guilty wretch, expiring, goes
Where vengeance endleſs life beſtows,
  That endleſs miſery may ſucceed.

Great God! how aweful is the ſcene!
A breath, a tranſient breath between;
  And can I jeſt, and laugh, and play!
To earth, alas! too firmly bound,
Trees deeply rooted in the ground,
  Are ſhiver'd when they're torn away.

Vain joys, which envy'd greatneſs gains,
How do ye bind with ſilken chains,
  Which aſk Herculean ſtrength to break!
How with new terrors have ye arm'd
The power whoſe ſlighteſt glance alarm'd!
  How many deaths of one ye make

Yet, dumb with wonder I behold
Man's thoughtleſs race, in error bold,
  Forget or ſcorn the *laws* of Death;
With *theſe* no projects coincide,
Nor vows, nor toils, nor hopes, *they* guide,
  Each thinks he draws immortal breath.

Each, blind to fate's approaching hour,
Intrigues, or fights, for wealth or power,

And

And ſlumb'ring dangers dare provoke;
And he, who tott'ring ſcarce ſuſtains
A cent'ry's age, plans future gains,
And feels an unexpected ſtroke.

Go on, unbridled deſp'rate band,
Scorn rocks, gulphs, winds, ſearch ſea and land,
And ſpoil new worlds wherever found.
Seize, haſte to ſeize, the glitt'ring prize,
And ſighs and tears, and pray'rs deſpiſe,
Nor ſpare the temple's holy ground.

They go, ſucceed, but look again,
The deſp'rate band you ſeek in vain,
Now trod in duſt the peaſant's ſcorn.
But who that ſaw their treaſures ſwell,
That heard the inſatiate vow rebel,
Would e'er have thought them mortal born?

See the world's Victor mounts his car,
Blood marks his progreſs wide and far,
Sure he ſhall reign while ages fly;
No, vaniſh'd like a morning cloud,
The Hero was but juſt allow'd
To fight, to conquer, and to die.

And is it true, I aſk with dread,
That nations heap'd on nations bled
Beneath his chariot's fervid wheel,
With trophies to adorn the ſpot
Where his pale corſe was left to rot,
And doom'd the hungry reptile's meal!

Yes, Fortune, weary'd with her play,
Her toy, this Hero, caſts away,
And ſcarce the form of Man is ſeen:
Awe chills my breaſt, my eyes o'erflow,
Around my brows no roſes glow,
The cypreſs mine, funereal green!

Yet in this hour of grief and fears,
When aweful Truth unveil'd appears,
Some power unknown uſurps my breaſt;
Back to the world my thoughts are led!
My feet in Folly's lab'rinth tread,
And fancy dreams that life is bleſt.

How weak an Empreſs is the Mind,
Whom Pleaſure's flow'ry wreaths can bind,
And captive to her altars lead!
Weak Reaſon yields to Phrenzy's rage,
And all the world is Folly's ſtage,
And all that act are fools indeed.

And yet this ſtrange, this ſudden flight,
From gloomy cares to gay delight,
This fickleneſs, ſo light and vain,
In life's deluſive tranſient dream
When men nor things are what they ſeem,
Is all the real good we gain.

Epiſtle from the King of PRUSSIA *to Monſieur* VOLTAIRE. *Tranſlated by* J. G. COOPER, *Eſq*;

VOLTAIRE, believe me, were I now
In private life's calm ſtation plac'd,
Let Heav'n for Nature's wants allow,
With cold indiff'rence would I view
Departing Fortune's winged haſte,
And at the Goddeſs laugh like you.
Th' inſipid farce of tedious ſtate,
Imperial duty's real weight,
The faithleſs courtier's ſupple bow,
The fickle multitude's careſs,
And flatt'rer's wordy emptineſs,
By long experience well I know;
And, tho' a Prince and Poet born,
Vain blandiſhments of glory ſcorn.
For when the ruthleſs ſheers of fate
Have cut my life's precarious thread,
And rank me with th' unconſcious dead,
What will't avail that I was great,
Or that th' uncertain tongue of fame
In Mem'ry's temple chants my name?
One bliſsful moment whilſt we live
Weighs more than ages of renown;
What then do Potentates receive
Of good peculiarly their own?
Sweet eaſe, and unaffected joy,
Domeſtic peace and ſportive pleaſure,
The regal throne and palace fly,
And, born for liberty, prefer
Soft ſilent ſcenes of lovely leiſure
To, what we Monarchs buy ſo dear,
The thorny pomp of ſcepter'd care.
My pain or bliſs ſhall ne'er depend
On fickle Fortune's caſual flight,
For, whether ſhe's my foe or friend,
In calm repoſe I'll paſs the night:
And ne'er by watchful homage own
I court her ſmile, or fear her frown.
But from our ſtations we derive
Unerring precepts how to live,

And

And certain deeds each rank calls forth,
By which is measur'd human worth.
Voltaire, within his private cell,
In realms where ancient honesty
Is patrimonial property,
And sacred Freedom loves to dwell,
May give up all his peaceful mind,
Guided by Plato's deathless page,
In silent solitude resign'd
To the mild virtues of a sage;
But I, 'gainst whom wild wirlwinds wage
Fierce war with wreck denouncing wing,
Must be, to face the tempest's rage,
In thought, in life, and death a King.

WINTER, *a Poem, being a translation of Mr.* WILLIAM THOMPSON's ODE BRUMALIS.

By the Reverend Mr. TATTERSAL, *late Fellow of Trinity College, Cambridge.*

ALas! no longer now appear
The softer seasons of the year.
Of sports and loves what Muse now sings?
Away my lyre;—boy, break the strings.

Old joyless Winter, who disdains
Your sprightly, flow'ry, Attic strains,
Wrapt into sable, calls for airs,
Rough, gloomy, as the rug he wears.

Pleasure, for ever on the wing,
Wild, wanton, restless, flutt'ring thing,
Airy springs by with sudden speed,
Swifter than Maro's flying steed.

Ah! where is hid the sylvan scene,
The leafy shade, the vernal green?
In Flora's meads the sweets that grew,
Colours which Nature's pencil drew,
Chaplets, the bust of Pope might wear,
Worthy to bloom around Ianthe's hair?

Gay-mantled Spring away is flown,
The silver-tressed Summer's gone,
And golden Autumn; nought remains
But Winter with his iron chains.

The feather-footed hours that fly,
Say, "Human life thus passes by."

What

What ſhall the wiſe, the prudent? they
Will ſeize the bounty of to day,
And proſtrate to the Gods their grateful homage pay.

The man, whom Iſis' ſtream inſpires,
Whom Pallas owns, and Phœbus fires,
Whom Suada, ſmiling goddeſs, deigns
To guide in ſweet Hyblæan plains,
He winter's ſtorms, undaunted ſtill, ſuſtains

Black low'ring ſkies ne'er hurt the breaſt
By white-rob'd Innocence poſſeſt.
Roar as ye liſt, ye winds,——begin,——
Virtue proclaims fair Peace within;
Ethereal pow'r! 'tis you that bring
The balmy Zephyrs, and reſtore the Spring.

The Pleaſures of the Mind.

KIND Nature with a mother's joys
Her every art to charm employs,
For man the golden King of day
Pours light, health, beauty, in his ray.
The Morn in ſilver treſſes bright,
With milder charms ſalutes his ſight,
And Night her ſhadowy curtain draws,
Indulging ſleep's refreſhing pauſe:
For man the purple-finger'd Hours
Dreſs beauteous Spring in new-born flow'rs,
Teach her to breathe a rich perfume,
And ſmile with eye-inchanting bloom.
Then ripe in beauty's glowing pride,
Blithe Summer, *Sol*'s refulgent bride,
Bids Plenty revel o'er the plains,
And carol heart-enlivening ſtrains.
Next Autumn calls the ſylvan pow'rs,
To lay him ſoft in ſhady bow'rs,
Where grape and nectarine, plumb and peach,
May tempting hang within his reach!
Laſt, Winter comes to rule the year,
In ſweet viciſſitude ſevere;
See him on *Zembla*'s mountains ſtand,
He ſtretches out his palſied hand,
And all his magazines unfold
Their copious hoards of ice and cold:
The hail in vollies rattles round,
The ſnow deſcending, ſhrouds the ground:
Deep-bellowing burſts of thunder roll,
And pleaſing horror ſwells the ſoul.

With

With ſtill improv'd delight, the Mind
Beholds her powers unconfin'd,
She roves with Nature, and explains
What virtues live in ſecret veins
Of herbs; bids *Flora*'s children riſe
In naked beauty to her eyes,
To the ſoft ſerenade of gales
Thro' Ocean's liquid realms ſhe ſails,
Thro' pearly worlds, thro' coral groves,
Where every ſcaly wonder roves:
With *Phœbus*, in his chariot driv'n,
She journeys thro' th' expanſe of heaven:
Now rolling round on *Saturn*'s ring,
Now roving on the comet's wing,
And urging ſtill her airy flight,
She gains thoſe ſmiling realms of light,
Where ſons of bliſs, immortals dwell,
In golden groves of Aſphodel.
Now conſcious of celeſtial ſkill,
Her forming pow'r ſhe tries at will,
Her pencil weds aſſenting dies,
And ſee a new-born world ariſe.
Here charms the eye the bloſſom'd grove,
Where, looking bliſs, young lovers rove;
There ſerpentine the river glides,
And nibbling flocks adorn its ſides.
Soft'ning to fleſh the marble lives,
And takes each attitude ſhe gives:
Here nerv'd to ſtrength the hero ſtands,
There orators extend their hands;
The patriot here, by Freedom's ſide,
Smiling pours out the vital tide;
Here Beauty charms the gazing eye,
The Loves and Graces waiting by:
Is it the breeze that wakes the ſpring?
Or ſay, does *Philomela* ſing,
And bid the liſt'ning ear rejoice?
'Tis Muſic tunes her heav'nly voice,
Her voice of ſweeteſt ſkill to raiſe
The drooping heart ten thouſand ways.
Now heav'n-caught fury fires the ſoul,
And ſpurning oft earth's dull controul,
Vent'rous ſhe wings her full-plum'd flight,
Detects new regions of delight;
Led by enchantreſs Fancy roves
The Muſes gay ideal groves,
Where countleſs beings ſtrike her eye,
Confus'd in glitt'ring novelty:

But what the varied year's delight,
Or what the mental ken fo bright,
Or what the kind infpiring Mufes,
To blefs that genuine love transfufes!
The parent's fond impaffion'd flow,
The filial, duteous, grateful glow,
Congenial friendfhip, heav'nly true,
And pity preffing balmy dew;
The feaft of Converfe, that difpenfes
Blifs to the heart, and all the fenfes,
Where Reafon, Mirth, Good-humour fit,
And beauty fparkles into wit.
Here too, as in the natural fcene,
Triumphs the Mind, creative queen,
Here Fancy, with allufion kind
Indulges ev'ry longing mind,
Brings to the lover in defpair
His mutually-impaffion'd fair,
Adorns the meaneft female face
With beauties cull'd from ev'ry grace;
Inftructs Ambition's flave to nod,
And bids the reptile foar a God,
Applauds the bard's profaic fongs,
Gives eloquence to ftamm'ring tongues,
Lets Ocean's fons their haven gain,
Unbinds the captive's galling chain;
On Poverty each joy beftows,
From rich humanity that flows,
Gives her at once herfelf to blefs,
And charm the Virtues in diftrefs,
Yet ftill referves the fapient mind,
Her darling free-born joy behind,
When with fond eyes fhe loves to trace
The beauties of her moral race,
And with blithe confidence can fay
She liv'd with Virtue ev'ry day,
That ftill fhe urg'd life's great defign,
To fit herfelf with blifs divine.
Then Confcience lends the plaufive note
Thro' ev'ry fenfe of joy to float,
Strikes mufic from each vital ftring
That envies not when angels fing,
Diffolv'd in extacy fhe lies,
And fweetly pre-enjoys the fkies.

To PEACE.

COME lovely gentle Peace of mind
With all thy fmiling nymphs around,
Content and Innocence combin'd,
With wreaths of facred olive crown'd.

Come

Come thou, that lov'ſt the walk at eve,
The banks of murm'ring ſtreams along,
That loves the crowded court to leave,
And hear the milk-maid's ſimple ſong;

That lov'ſt with Contemplation's eye
The headlong cataract to view,
That foams and thunders from on high,
While echoes oft the ſound renew;

That lov'ſt the dark ſequeſter'd wood,
Where Silence ſpreads her brooding wings,
Nor leſs the lake's tranſlucent flood,
The moſſy grotts and bubbling ſprings.

With thee the lamp of Wiſdom burns,
The guiding light to realms above;
With thee the raptur'd mortal learns
The wonders of celeſtial love.

With thee, the poor have endleſs wealth,
And ſacred freedom glads the ſlave,
With thee! the ſick rejoice in health,
The weak are ſtrong, the fearful brave.

O lovely gentle Peace of mind!
Be thou on earth my conſtant gueſt,
With thee, whate'er on earth I find,
The pledge of heaven ſhall make me bleſt.

To a Kinſman, on his intended marriage.

1.

SEE! the wild herds of nymphs and ſwains!
A deſpicable throng:
See! how they ſtrive in Hymen's chains,
And drag their plagues along.

2.

Keen Anguiſh, Hate, or waſting Care
On every footſtep treads,
While pining Want, and black Deſpair
Hang hov'ring o'er their heads.

3.

Yet fools, in crowds are following ſtill
Through the ſame thoughtleſs road,
Which leads far wide from Wiſdom's hill,
To Sorrow's dark abode.

4.

See! how they ruſh before the prieſt,
And bid his altars ſmoke:
He deems them juſt above the beaſt,
The fitter for the yoke.

5.
Fondly they view the golden gate,
And haſte to enter in,
Where Mirth diſplays its guileful bait,
And veils the ſnare within.

6.
Blind Cupid helps the dire deceit,
As folly guides his hand,
And laughing Momus hides the cheat,
Till Fancy ties the band.

7.
Then for a while in giddy noiſe
The revels ſhake the plain:
One hour is ſpent in empty joys,
And All beyond is pain.

8.
The dawn appears! the ſhades retire!
And the gay viſion flies:
Loſt are the dreams of fond deſire:
But ſolid woes ariſe.

9.
In ſtrong tumultuous paſſions toſt,
Their comforts ſoon are dead:
Fair Peace and Happineſs are loſt,
And Hope for ever fled.

10.
Juſt is their doom. 'Tis luſt; 'tis gold;
'Tis Sex alone can pleaſe;
While mercenary Love is ſold,
And pairs ſuch minds as theſe.

11.
The village ſwain thus views his flock,
And governs abſolute:
Whilſt he attentive rears his ſtock,
And couples every brute.

12.
Such common things may well be bound
With any of their kind:
But who, young kinſman, ſhall be found
To match thy nobler mind?

13.
The brighteſt nymphs who crowd our ſcenes,
And bid the world admire,
Are but ſome finer clay machines,
Void of celeſtial fire.

14.
Thus China's vaſes give delight;
Trim, gaudy, ſmooth, and gay;
Whilſt gazing females bleſs the ſight
And wiſh their hearts away.

15. So

15.

So ſhine themſelves in Beauty's dreſs :
As clear their poliſh'd ſkin ;
But elſe 'tis all vaſt emptineſs,
Or duſt and filth within.

16.

Uſeleſs alike the painted jar,
And ſhowy tinſel maid :
Both charm the ſenſes, viewed afar,
And pall when near diſplay'd.

17.

Bluſhes and Virtue hence are fled,
In theſe degen'rate days :
This huge rotundity we tread
And loſt mankind decays.

18.

Few heavenly forms adorn the ſtage,
Since Nature waxes old :
One is the labour of an age
Wrought in a perfect mould.

19.

Could I but find that ſingle She,
Incomparable Boy!
Stamp'd by the hand which faſhion'd Thee,
And pure without alloy,

20.

Then ſhould my Muſe to Hymen bend,
And ſhout his wheels along,
With eager joy his ſteps attend,
And tune the grateful ſong.

21.

And lo! propitious to my vows,
Behold the God appears,
Smiling he leads thy deſtin'd ſpouſe,
And chaſes all my fears.

22.

Fair Virgin, hail! hail, blooming Fair!
Thrice hail! exalted Maid!
High as my warmeſt wiſhes were,
They nobly here are paid.

23.

Bleſt are mine eyes which view the ſight:
But doubly bleſt is He
Who gives thy gentle thoughts delight,
And reſts his ſoul on Thee.

24.

With conſcious Innocence ſhe moves
Where Honour points the way ;
Sage Pallas all her ſteps approves,
And glads the nuptial day.

Here praise is weak; here words are vain;
Let Fancy reign supreme;
Since Pope in his sublimest strain,
Must sink beneath the theme.

The latter part of Chap. VI. *of St. Matthew, Paraphrased.*

By the late celebrated Mr. THOMSON, *Author of the* SEASONS.

WHEN my breast labours with oppressive care,
And o'er my cheek descends the falling tear,
While all my warring passions are at strife,
Oh, let me listen to the word of life!
Raptures deep-felt his doctrine did impart,
And thus he rais'd from earth the drooping heart.
Think not, when all your scanty stores afford
Is spread at once upon the sparing board;
Think not, when worn the homely robe appears,
While on the roof the howling tempest bears;
What farther shall this feeble life sustain,
And what shall cloath these shivering limbs again.
Says, does not life its nourishment exceed?
And the fair body its investing weed?
Behold! and look away your low despair——
See the light tenants of the barren air:
To them, nor stores, nor granaries belong,
Nought but the woodland, and the pleasing song;
Yet, your kind heavenly Father bends his eye
On the least wing that flits along the sky.
To him they sing, when Spring renews the plain,
To him they cry in Winter's pinching reign;
Nor is their music, nor their plaint in vain:
He hears the gay, and the distressful call,
And with unsparing bounty fills them all.
Observe the rising lilly's snowy grace,
Observe the various vegetable race;
They neither toil nor spin, but careless grow,
Yet see how warm they blush! how bright they glow
What regal vestments can with them compare!
What King so shining! or what Queen so fair!
If, careless thus the fowls of heav'n he feeds,
If, o'er the fields such lucid robes he spreads;
Will he not care for you, ye faithless say!
Is he unwise, or are you less than they?

On

On reading HUTCHINSON *on the Paſſions.*

THOU who thro' Nature's various faults canſt rove,
And ſhew what ſprings our eager paſſions move,
Teach us to combat anger, grief and fear,
Recall the ſigh, and drop the falling tear.
Oh! be thy ſoft philoſophy addreſt
To the untroubled ear and tranquil breaſt!
To theſe be all thy peaceful maxims taught,
Who idly roam amidſt a calm of thought;
Whoſe ſouls were ne'er by love or hate poſſeſt,
Who ne'er were wretched, and who ne'er were bleſt;
Whoſe fainter wiſhes, pleaſures, fears, remain,
Dreams but of bliſs, and ſhadows but of pain.
Serenely ſtupid——" So ſome ſhallow ſtream,
" Flows gently thro' the valley, ſtill the ſame;
" Whom no rude winds can ever diſcompoſe,
" Who fears no winter rains, nor falling ſnows,
" But ſlowly down its flow'ry border creeps,
" While the ſoft zephyr on its boſom ſleeps."
Oh! could'ſt thou teach the tortur'd ſoul to know,
With patience, each extreme of human woe;
To bear with ills, and unrepining prove
The frowns of fortune, and the racks of love;
Still ſhould my breaſt ſome pious moment ſhare,
Still riſe ſuperior to each threatening care,
Nor fear approaching ills, or diſtant woes,
But in Philemon's abſence find repoſe.

EPHELINDA.

To FEAR.

O Thou, dread foe to honour, wealth and fame,
Whoſe tongue can quell the ſtrong, the fierce can tame,
Relentleſs Fear! ah! why did fate ordain
My trembling heart to own thy iron reign?
There are, thrice happy! who diſdain thy ſway,
The merchant wand'ring o'er the wat'ry way;
The chief ſerene before th' aſſaulted wall;
The climbing ſtateſman thoughtleſs of his fall;
All whom the love of wealth or pow'r inſpires,
And all who burn with proud Ambition's fires;
But peaceful bards thy conſtant preſence know,
O thou of ev'ry glorious deed the foe!
Of thee the ſilent ſtudious race complains,
And Learning groans a captive in thy chains
The ſecret wiſh when ſome fair object moves,
And cautious Reaſon what we wiſh approves,

Thy gorgon front forbids to grasp the prize,
And seas are spread betwixt and mountains rise.
Thy magic arts a thousand phantoms raise,
And fancy'd deaths and dangers fill our ways;
With smiling Hope you wage eternal strife,
And envious snatch the cup of joy from life.
O leave, tremendous pow'r! the blameless breast,
Of guilt alone the tyrant, and the guest;
Go, and thy train of sable horrors spread
Where Murder meditates the future deed,
Where Rapine watches for the gloom of night,
And lawless Passion pants for others' right;
Go to the bad, but from the good recede,
No more the foe of ev'ry glorious deed.

The LOVER CURED.

Imitated from the Italian of METASTASIO.

THE indulgent gods unveiling thy deceit,
  Nice, at length have pity'd the distrest:
The wretch so late a captive in thy net,
  Is now with freedom, real freedom blest.

No more to hide my love, despair and shame,
  My brow dissembled airs of scorn displays;
No more my colour changes at thy name,
  Nor beats my heart tumultuous when I gaze.

Dream I? no more in dreams thy form I see:
  No more thy charms my earliest thought employ:
Thou'rt absent, I perceive no wish for thee;
  Thou'rt present, and I feel nor pain, nor joy.

Calm I can meet, and calm can pass thee by;
  Unhumbled can reflect I fail'd to please;
Can talk about thy lip or radiant eye;
  Nay, talk with rivals, and yet talk with ease.

Frown'st thou disdainful? know thy frowns are vain!
  Smil'st thou? thy smiles no extacies impart:
Those lips no more their wonted power retain;
  Nor find those eyes a passage to my heart.

If now of gay or gloomy mood I be:
  Nor thou the bliss creat'st, nor thou the care:
Hills, woods, and meads can please tho' far from thee
  Nor lours the desart less when thou art there.

Still, when I view thee, I confess thee fair;
  Yet equal charms in other nymphs allow:
And (may thy ear the rude expression bear!)
  That face, once faultless, is not faultless now.

When from my tortur'd heart the ſhaft I drew,
Sighs, ſtruggling after ſighs, convulſive ſtole:
For oh! 'twas hard thy empire to ſubdue;
'Twas hard th' impetuous paſſion to controul.

The linnet, flutt'ring on the bird-lime ſprays,
Thus leaves his captiv'd feathers, and is free;
But ſoon his little wings new plum'd diſplays,
And flies with caution by the fatal tree.

So much of freedom and of eaſe I boaſt;
Miſtaken Nicè thinks I ſtill adore:
But do not thoſe declaim on hardſhips moſt,
Who moſt have felt them, and who feel no more?

The warrior thus deſcribes th' embattled plain;
Thus bares his ſcars, thus fights his perils o'er:
Thus the freed ſlave o'erjoy'd points out the chain,
Which late he dragg'd on Afric's hoſtile ſhore.

I ſpeak of freedom, 'tis the theme I love,
Nor care if Nicè credit what I ſay;
I ſpeak, nor curious aſk, if ſhe approve,
Or, when ſhe names me, if ſhe's grave or gay.

Thus parts a fickle fair, and lover true;
Let thoſe, who loſe the moſt, the moſt regret!
A heart ſo faithful thou can'ſt ne'er ſubdue;
It is not hard to find a new coquet.

The INDIAN PHILOSOPHER.

1.

WHY ſhould our joys transform to pain?
Why gentle Hymen's ſilken chain
A plague of iron prove?
Good Gods! 'tis ſtrange the chain that binds
Millions of hands, ſhould leave their minds
At ſuch a looſe from love!

2.

In vain I ſought the wond'rous cauſe,
Search'd the wide fields of nature's laws,
And urg'd the ſchools in vain;
'Till deep in thought, within my breaſt
My ſoul retir'd, and Slumber dreſt
A bright inſtructive ſcene,

3.

O'er the wide land, and croſs the tide,
On Fancy's airy wing I ride;
Sweet rapture of the mind!
'Till on the banks of Ganges' flood,
In a tall ancient grove I ſtood,
For ſacred uſe deſign'd.

4.

Hard by a venerable prieſt,
Riſ'n with his God, the Sun, from reſt,
Began his morning ſong:
Thrice he conjur'd the murm'ring ſtream,
The birth of ſouls was all his theme,
And half divine his tongue.

5.

He ſang th' eternal rolling flame,
That vital maſs that's ſtill the ſame,
Does all our minds compoſe;
Whence ſhap'd in twice ten thouſand frames,
Whence differing ſouls of different names
And different paſſions roſe.

6.

The mighty Pow'r that form'd the mind,
One mould for ev'ry two deſign'd;
Then bleſt the new-born pair:
This be a match for this, he ſaid;
Then down he ſent the ſouls he made,
To ſeek them bodies here.

7.

But parting from their warm abodes,
They loſt their fellows on the roads,
And never join'd their hands:
O cruel chance, aud croſſing Fates!
Our Eaſtern ſouls have loſt their mates
On Europe's barbarous lands.

8.

Thus ſung the wond'rous Indian bard;
My liſt'ning ear attentive hear'd;
Whilſt Ganges ceas'd to flow;
Sure then, ſaid I, cou'd I but ſee
The gentle Nymph that twin'd with me,
I might be happy too.

9.

Some courteous angel tell me where,
What diſtant lands the unknown fair,
Or diſtant ſeas detain;
Swift as the wheel of nature rolls;
I'd fly too meet and mingle ſouls,
And wear the joyful chain.

To the NYMPH *of* P*** WATERS.

——καλιϛον ὑδωρ ϛπι γαιαν ιησιν. Hom.

I.

O Green-ſtol'd Nymph, whoſe fount reſtor'd my fair,
  When ſickneſs crop'd the beauties of her face;
Ne'er may the rainy South thy pow'rs impair,
  May never reptile foul thy ſtream diſgrace.

II.

While on the T—— deep-harrowing Winter reigns,
  Not the leaſt wrinkle may thy ſurface know;
And while the north binds E— in icy chains,
  In lapſe unfetter'd may thy waters flow.

III.

May Spring's firſt cowſlips on thy borders bloom;
  Thy banks firſt echo to the cuckoo's lay;
Firſt round thee, Fragrance fling each rich perfume;
  Thy thickets firſt exclude the noon-tide ray.

IV.

What time blythe Auguſt on thy margin plays,
  To thee, ſweet-featur'd Nymph (ſo Jove ordains)
Each year bland Health a ſolemn viſit pays,
  And, while thy groves are green, with thee remains.

V.

O may no wayward hags, of aſpect foul,
  Brew their dire potions near thy willowed ſpring;
Nor melt the waxen ſemblance, as they howl
  Dread orgies to their grimly-ſmiling king.

VI.

But oft when Night has hung with black the ſky,
  And only Heſper ſheds his ſilent ray,
May dapper Fays around their revels ply,
  Till Chanticleer awake the dawn of day.

VII.

Oft may their muſic lonely trav'lers cheer,
  And ſwains belated oft their lights perceive;
Thy rills ſhall ſtop their dimly courſe to hear,
  And love-lorn Philomel forget to grieve.

VIII.

May gay-dreſt Pleaſure wanton on thy plains,
  May vaſt increaſe thy ploughman's toil repay;
May never clarion fright thy peaceful ſwains,
  Nor battle tear them from their wives away.

IX. Thy

IX.

Thy healing powers the Youth ſhall yearly ſing,
  And Age, recruited, wreaths on thee beſtow;
For, truſt the preſcient Muſe, O virtuous Spring!
  While murmurs Helicon, thy fount ſhall flow.

X.

Not mine, be told the truth, not mine the lays,
  Unheard, the favour of the Nine I ſue;
Love cull'd this chaplet of immortal praiſe,
  And grateful ſprinkled with Caſtalian dew.

An Epiſode. From AVON; *a Poem in three parts.*

IN ages paſt, as holy bards record,
  Locrine of fair Loegria's fields was lord;
From Brutus he; who ſpread at Heaven's command
His fated ſails for Albion's happy land:
His ſails the valiant Corinæus bore
His bold aſſociate to the chalky ſhore.
Tho' much the chief for arduous deeds might claim,
His daughter's beauty match'd his arms in fame.
Yet lovely as ſhe ſhone, ſhe ſhone in vain
To Locrine's eyes, and met with cold diſdain:
Tho' to give firmneſs to the tott'ring throne,
And make her *father*'s dreaded pow'r his own,
The Prince with pray'rs and policy comply'd,
And made the ſlighted Gueldolen his bride.
Peace took her flight, for Love had never ſpread
His joyous pinions o'er the nuptial bed.
But ſoon th' ill-fated chief was doom'd to prove
The power of charms and tyranny of love.
When fled the Hun before his conqu'ring hoſt,
And left his name to boiſt'rous Humber's coaſt,
A *Nymph* as Summer warm, and ſweet as Spring,
Enrich'd the ſpoils of fair Loegria's King.
The victor's eye the lovely captive ſeiz'd,
At once ſhe pain'd him, and at once ſhe pleas'd.
Diſtreſs had ſoften'd ev'ry tender grace,
And pour'd reſiſtleſs languor o'er her face.
Love made th' aſſault, and ſoon at large poſſeſs'd,
With all a conqu'ror's pomp, his yielding breaſt;
While her great father's aweful pow'r alone
Secur'd the ſlighted Gueldolen the throne:
With her awhile the glitt'ring pride remain'd,
But bright Eſtrildis only charm'd and reign'd.
The fair, not conſcious of the ſacred claim,
Approv'd his paſſion, as ſhe ſhar'd his flame.
But Locrine ſought the ſylvan ſhade among,
Studious of peace, and mindful of the wrong.

Some

Some ſtill retreat; remov'd from curious eyes
Of the fierce rival, or aſſiduous ſpies.
As flies the parent bird on wings of fear,
And anguiſh'd ſees the watchful ſhepherd near,
Now ſtops, and looks, and heaves the downy breaſt,
Then trembling hurries to the ſecret neſt:
So the fond *Prince* his cautious viſits paid:
So fear'd obſervance, and ſo watch'd the ſhade.
Their paſſion here the lovely Sabra crown'd,
In life as blameleſs, as in death renown'd;
Behold the ſweet but unexpanded roſe,
Behold in bright effulgence when it glows:
The *Virgin* thus gave hints of ev'ry grace
That time had open'd in her parent face.
Harmonious health of mind and body bleſs'd
Her days with pleaſure, and her nights with reſt;
No care had love for her, no torments hate,
No charms ambition, or allurements ſtate.
Sweet were thy days ere Locrine's reſtleſs mind
Diſdain'd the grant of even a bliſs confin'd.
But tho' *life's* giddy cup we wiſely blend,
Folly's light froth will yet at laſt aſcend.
Thus when the *Queen* enough diſtreſs'd to prove
The ſharp reflection of rejected love,
Wept her great *ſire*, who full of years and praiſe
Had ſeal'd the glorious records of his days;
He gave the ſcepter to the fav'rite *fair*,
That one the kingdom, and the King might ſhare.
The ſacred vows of holy love abus'd,
Her glory darken'd, and her crown refus'd,
Her charms deteſted, and a rival bleſs'd,
Were wrongs the *Queen* in tented fields redreſs'd;
There ſtern *Revenge* dug Locrine's early grave,
And ſunk the *fair* beneath th' avenging wave.
Enough is given to *love*, enough to *pride*,
Eſtrildis wrong'd *thee*, and Eſtrildis died.
Inſatiate *fury* what has Sabra done?
Or wherefore expiates errors not her own?
See Death's dread agents hide their reeking hands,
And ſtart with horror at thy dire commands.
O feel her tears! O read her ſuaſive eyes!
But what can ruthleſs jealouſy ſuffice?
For trembling as it flow'd, the ſedgy ſtream
Receiv'd the virgin, and retain'd her name.

Verses written at the gardens of WILLIAM SHENSTONE, *Esq; near Birmingham*, 1756.

Ille terrarum mihi præter omnes
Angulus ridet. HOR.

WOULD you these lov'd recesses trace,
And view fair Nature's modest face?
See her in every field-flow'r bloom?
O'er every thicket shed perfume?
By verdant groves, and vocal hills,
By mossy grots near purling rills,
Where'er you turn your wondering eyes,
Behold her win without disguise!
What tho' no pageant trifles *here*,
As in the glare of courts, appear;
Tho' rarely *here* be heard the *name*
Of rank, of title, pow'r, or fame;
Yet, if ingenuous be your mind,
A bliss more pure and unconfin'd
Your step attends--Draw freely nigh,
And meet the bard's benignant eye:
On *him* no pendant forms await:
No proud reserve shuts up his gate;
No spleen, no party-views controul
That warm benevolence of soul,
Which prompts the candid friendly part;
Regardless of each gainful art;
Regardless of the world's acclaim;
And courteous with no selfish aim.
Draw freely nigh, and welcome find,
If not the costly, yet the kind:
O! he will lead you to the cells
Where every *Muse* and *Virtue* dwells;
Where the green *Dryads* guard his woods.
Where the blue *Naiads* guide his floods;
Where all the sister *Graces*, gay,
That shap'd his walk's meand'ring way,
Stark naked, or but wreath'd with flow'rs,
Lie slumbering soft beneath his bow'rs.
Wak'd by the stock-dove's melting strain
Behold *them* rise! and with the train
Of nymphs that haunt the stream or grove,
Or o'er the flow'ry champain rove,
Join hand in hand, attentive gaze ——
And mark the *Dance's* mystic *maze*.
"Such is the *waving line*, they cry,
"For ever dear to Fancy's eye!
"Yon stream that wanders down the dale,
"The spiral wood, the winding vale,

"The

" The path, which wrought with hidden ſkil,
" Slow twining ſcales yon diſtant hill
" With fir inveſted——all combine
" To recommend the *waving line*.
" The wreathing rod of Bacchus fair,
" The ringlets of Apollo's hair,
" The wand by Maia's offspring born,
" The ſmooth volutes of Ammon's horn
" The ſtructure of the Cyprian dame,
" And *each* fair female's beauteous frame,
" Shew, to the pupils of deſign,
" The triumphs of the *waving line*."
Then gaze, and mark that union ſweet,
Where fair Convex and Concave meet:
And while, quick-ſhifting as you ſtray,
The vivid ſcenes on fancy play,
The lawn of aſpect ſmooth and mild;
The foreſt ground groteſque and wild;
The ſhrub that ſcents the mountain gale;
The ſtream rough-daſhing down the dale,
From rock to rock, in eddies toſt;
The diſtant lake, in which 'tis loſt;
Blue hills, gay beaming thro' the glade;
Lone urns that ſolemnize the ſhade;
Sweet interchange of all that charms
In groves, meads, dingles, riv'lets, farms!
If aught the fair confuſion *pleaſe*,
With laſting *health*, and laſting *eaſe*,
To *him* who form'd the bliſsful bow'r,
And gave thy life one tranquil hour;
With *peace* and *freedom*—theſe poſſeſt,
His temperate mind ſecures the reſt.
But if the ſoul ſuch *bliſs* deſpiſe,
Avert thy dull incurious eyes;
Go fix them *there*, where gems and gold,
Improv'd by art, their pow'r unfold;
Go try in courtly ſcenes to trace
A fairer form of Nature's face;
Go ſcorn *Simplicity!* but know,
That all our heart-felt joys below,
That all our virtue loves to name,
Which Art conſigns to *laſting* fame,
Which *fixes* Wit, or Beauty's throne,
Derives its ſource from *her alone*.

ARCADIO.

To the Rev. Dr. Warburton, Dean of Bristol, on reading his Dissertation on the Sixth Book of Virgil.

By Richard B—r—ng—r, Esq;

IN Learning's maze low critics stray,
And blindly bold mistake their way;
Supplying want of taste and sense
With confidence and false pretence;
Still darker each dark passage make,
Then consecrate their own mistake;
Till by their notes with learning fraught
O'erlaid expires the hapless thought.
Thus med'cine quacks presume to give,
And murder those they mean to live.
Such, Virgil, such, for many an age
Have mangled thy celestial page;
Thy nobler meaning left unknown,
And, harder still, impos'd their own:
Sure in that * hell, which you design'd
For miscreants vile of ev'ry kind,
Bad critics well deserve a place,
Nor mercy e'er should find, nor grace.
Translators too those realms should hold,
Who put off dross instead of gold:
Chief those who thy bright Muse disgrace,
And hide with stains her beauteous face.
There creeping † Lauderdale should be,
Cold † Trapp, and murd'ring † Ogilby,
But see! again the heav'n-born maid
With joy triumphant lifts her head!
For to confute, expose, chastise,
Behold! her great avenger rise!
Behold! great bard, thy fame to clear,
Behold! thy Warburton appear!
And worthy he in those blest plains §
To share the bliss which Virtue gains,
With those who toil'd to bless mankind,
And form to Wisdom's lore the mind,
Where Tully, Plato, range the glade
With Thine and ‡ Pitt's attendant shade.
As the fam'd †† chief could ne'er have seen,
The regions sway'd by Pluto's Queen,
Without that wond'rous |||| branch whose rind
Radiant with gold immortal shin'd:

* Vide Sixth Book. † Translators of Virgil. § Vide Sixth Book. ‡ A most excellent Translator of Virgil's Æneid. †† Æneas. |||| Vide Sixth Book.

A bough

A bough of power not lefs divine,
O much-learn'd Warburton! is thine:
Which thou from that fair † tree didft pull,
Whofe heav'nly fruit thou lov'ft to cull:
Hence hell's thick gloom thou couldft pervade
Without the Sybil's potent aid,
Each myftic fcene there comprehend,
And trace their latent caufe and end!
And hence, while wanting this fure guide,
Others in darknefs wander'd wide.
And truth from error could not fee,
But all was doubt and myftery,
To thy enlighten'd mind alone,
The myfteries themfelves || were none.

The following Verfes, dropt in Mr. GARRICK'*s Temple of Shakefpear, at Hampton, are faid to have been written by a Gentleman, whofe poetical productions have been very defervedly admired.*

WHILE here to SHAKESPEAR *Garrick* pays
His tributary thanks and praife,
Invokes the animated ftone,
To make the poet's mind his own;
That he each character may trace
With humour, dignity, and grace,
And mark, unerring mark, to men,
The rich creation of his pen.
Prefer'd the prayer—the marble god,
Methinks I fee affenting nod;
And pointing to his laurel'd brow.
Cry—" Half this wreath to you I owe.
Loft to the ftage, and loft to fame,
Murder'd my fcenes, fcarce known my name,
Sunk in oblivion and difgrace
Among the common fcribbling race,
Unnotic'd long thy Shakefpear lay,
To Dulnefs and to Time a prey;
But lo! I rife, I breathe, I live
In you, my reprefentative!
Again the hero's breaft I fire,
Again the tender figh infpire,
Each fide, again, with laughter fhake,
And teach the villain's heart to quake;
All this, my fon, again I do,
I,——no, my fon——'tis I and You."
Whilft thus the grateful ftatue fpeaks,
A blufh o'erfpreads the fuppliant's cheeks:

† Of Knowledge, alluded to above. || Vide Differtation.

" What

" What, half thy wreath? Wit's mighty chief!
O grant! (he cries) one ſingle leaf!
That far o'erpays his humble merit,
Who's but the organ of thy ſpirit."
Phœbus the gen'rous conteſt heard,
When thus the God addreſs'd the bard:
" Here! take this laurel from my brow;
On him your mortal wreath beſtow;
Each matchleſs, each the palm ſhall bear;
In heav'n, the bard; on earth, the play'r."

Prologue to the Tragedy of AGIS. *Written by a Friend. Spoken by* Mr. GARRICK.

IF in theſe days of luxury and eaſe,
A tale from Sparta's rigid ſtate can pleaſe;
If patriot plans a Britiſh breaſt can warm;
If Kings aſſerting liberty can charm;
If virtue ſtill a graceful aſpect wear;
Check not at Agis' fall the gen'rous tear.
He view'd his ſubjects with a parent's love;
With zeal to ſave a ſinking people ſtrove;
Strove their chang'd hearts with glory to inflame;
To mend their morals; and reſtore their name;
'Till Faction roſe with Murder at her ſide;
Then mourn'd his country; perſever'd; and died.
That country once, for virtue was rever'd;
Admir'd by Greece; by haughty Aſia fear'd.
Then citizens and ſoldiers were the ſame;
And ſoldiers heroes; for their wealth was fame.
Then for the brave the fair reſerv'd her charms;
And ſcorn'd to claſp a coward in her arms.
The trumpet call'd; ſhe ſeiz'd the ſword and ſhield;
Array'd in haſte her huſband for the field;
And ſighing whiſper'd in a fond embrace,
" Remember! death is better than diſgrace."
The widow'd mother ſhew'd her parting ſon
The race of glory which his ſire had run.
" My ſon, thy flight alone I ſhall deplore.
" Return victorious! or return no more!"
While beauty thus with patriot zeal combin'd,
And round the laurel'd head her myrtle twin'd;
While all confeſt the Virtuous were the Great;
Fame, valour, conqueſt, grac'd the Spartan ſtate.
Her pow'r congenial with her virtue grew,
And Freedom's banner o'er her phalanx flew;
But ſoon as Virtue dropt her ſick'ning head,
Fame, valour, conqueſt, pow'r and freedom fled.

May

May this ſad ſcene improve each Briton's heart
Rouſe him with warmth to act a Briton's part!
Prompt him with Sparta's nobleſt ſons to vie;
To live in glory, and in freedom die!

Epilogue to AGIS. *Spoken by Mrs.* PRITCHARD.

A King in bloom of youth for freedom die!——
Our bard, tho' bold durſt not have ſoar'd ſo high.
This is no credulous admiring age;
But ſacred ſure the faith of Plutarch's page.
In ſimple ſtyle that ancient ſage relates
The tale of Sparta, chief of Grecian ſtates:
Eight hundred years it flouriſh'd, great in arms,
On dangers roſe, and grew amidſt alarms.
Of Sparta's triumph you have heard the cauſe,
More ſtrong, more noble, than Lycurgus' laws:
How Spartan dames, by Glory's charms inſpir'd,
The ſon, the lover, and the huſband fir'd.
Ye fair of Britain's iſle, which juſtly claims
The Grecian title, land of lovely dames,
In Britain's cauſe exert your matchleſs charms,
And rouſe your lovers to the love of arms.
Hid, not extinct, the ſpark of valour lies;
Your breath ſhall raiſe it flaming to the ſkies.
Now Mars his bloody banner hangs in air,
And bids Britannia's ſons for war prepare:
Let each lov'd maid, each mother bring the ſhield,
And arm their country's champions for the field.
Arm'd and inflam'd each Britiſh breaſt ſhall burn,
No youth unlaurel'd ſhall to you return.
Then ſhall we ceaſe t'exult at trophies won,
In Glory's field, by heroes——not our own.
France then ſhall tremble at the Britiſh ſword,
And dread the vengeance of her ancient Lord.

Prologue to the Tragedy of CLEONE, *by* WILLIAM MELMOTH, *Eſq; ſpoken by Mr.* ROSS.

'TWAS once the mode inglorious war to wage
With each bold bard that durſt attempt the ſtage,
And prologues were but preludes to engage.
Then mourn'd the Muſe, not ſtory'd woes alone,
Condemn'd, with tears, unfeign'd, to weep her own.
Paſt are thoſe hoſtile days: and wits no more
One undiſtinguiſh'd fate with fools deplore.
No more the Muſe laments her long-felt wrongs,
From the rude licence of tumultuous tongues:

In peace each bard prefers his doubtful claim,
And as he merits, meets, or miſſes, fame.
'Twas thus in Greece (when Greece fair Science bleſt,
And heav'n-born Arts their choſen land poſſeſt)
Th' aſſembled People ſat with decent pride,
Patient to hear, and ſkilful to decide;
Leſs forward far to cenſure than to praiſe,
Unwillingly refus'd the rival bays.
Yes; they whom candor and true taſte inſpire
Blame not with half the paſſion they admire:
Each little blemiſh with regret deſcry,
But mark the beauties with a raptur'd eye.
Yet modeſt fears invade our Author's breaſt,
With Attic lore, or Latian, all unbleſt;
Deny'd by fate thro' claſſic fields to ſtray,
Where bloom thoſe wreaths, which never know decay;
Where arts from kindred arts new force acquire,
And Poets catch from Poets genial fire:
Not thus he boaſts the breaſt humane to prove,
And touch thoſe ſprings which generous paſſions move,
To melt the ſoul by ſcenes of fabled woe,
And bid the tear for fancy'd ſorrows flow;
Far humbler paths he treads in queſt of fame,
And truſts to Nature what from Nature came.

Epilogue to CLEONE. *As originally written by* WILLIAM SHENSTONE, *Eſq*; *ſpoken by Mrs.* BELLAMY.

WELL, ladies——ſo much for the tragic ſtile——
And now, the cuſtom is——to make you ſmile.
" To make us ſmile, I hear *Flippanta* ſay,
" Yes——we have *ſmil'd* indeed—thro' half the play:
" We *always* laugh; when bards, demure and ſly,
" Beſtow ſuch mighty pains——to make us *cry*.
" And truly to bring ſorrow to a criſis,
" Mad-folks, and murder'd babes are *ſhrewd* devices.
" The Captain gone three years——and *then* to blame
" The veſtal conduct of his virtuous dame!——
" What *French*, what *Engliſh* bride would think it treaſon,
" When thus accus'd——to give the brute ſome reaſon?
" Out of my houſe——this night, forſooth——depart!
" A *modern* wife had ſaid——With all my heart:
" But think not, haughty Sir, I'll go *alone*!
" Order your coach——conduct me ſafe to town——
" Give me my jewels—wardrobe—and my maid——
" And pray take care, my pin-money be paid.
" Elſe know, I wield a pen——and, for its glory,
" My dear's domeſtic feats——may ſhine in ſtory!

" Then

" Then for the Child—the tale was truly sad——
" But who for such a bantling would run mad?
" What wife, at midnight hour inclin'd to roam,
" Would fondly drag her little chit from *home*?
" What has a mother with her child to do?——
" Dear brats—the *Nursery*'s the place for you!"
Such are the strains of many a modish Fair!
Yet memoires—not of *modern* growth—declare
The time *has been*, when modesty and truth
Were deem'd additions to the charms of youth;
Ere, in the dice-box, Ladies found delight;
Or swoon'd, for lack of cards, on Sunday-night;
When women hid their necks and veil'd their faces,
Not romp'd, nor rak'd, nor star'd, at public places:
Nor took the airs of Amazons——for *graces*!
When plain domestic virtues were the *mode*;
And wives ne'er dreamt of happiness abroad,
But cheer'd their offspring, shun'd fantastic airs;
And, with the *Joys* of wedlock, mixt the *Cares*.
Such modes are past—— yet sure they merit praise;
For marriage *triumph'd* in those wassel days:
No virgin sigh'd in vain; no fears arose,
Lest hostile wars should cause a dearth of beaux;
By chaste decorum, Each, affection gain'd;
By faith and fondness, what she won, maintain'd.
'Tis yours, ye Fair! to mend a thoughtless age,
That scorns the press, the pulpit, and the stage!
To yield frail Husbands no *pretence* to stray:
(Men will be rakes, if women lead the way)
To sooth—— But truce with these preceptive lays;
The Muse, who, dazzled with your ancient praise,
On present Worth, and modern Beauty tramples,
Must own, she ne'er could boast more bright *examples*.*

* Addressing the boxes.

A Familiar Epistle *from a Clergyman to a young gentleman of the Law.*

IN great Augustus' golden days,
When Horace held the seal of bays,
And sagely made reports of cases,
To serve all future times and places;
'Twas found that * not a human wight,
(If I conceive his meaning right)
Liv'd easy in his own estate,
But always prais'd his neighbour's fate.

* Vide Sat. I. Lib. 1.

Succeeding times with ſacred awe
Have the preſcription held as law ;
And to this day you cannot find
One creature that with patient mind,
Endures for better and for worſe,
His proper life's determin'd courſe.
Thus the fond country damſel prays
For balls, and maſquerades, and plays ;
Whilſt your town-ladies wiſh to rove
Thro' the green glade and ſhady grove :
Thus damns the Captain, blood and fire,
And longs to reſt an eaſy 'Squire ;
Whilſt the fierce 'Squire impatient glows
To meet in arms his country's foes :
And thus to cut the matter ſhort,
(For why in long exampling ſport
When one home caſe the truth will ſhew ?)
You like the church, and I the law.
But ſince no pow'r propitious hears
The peeviſh tenor of our pray'rs,
And, ſpite of all our noiſe and din,
You muſt read briefs, I rail at ſin ;
Let us, my friend, with nicer eye,
The nature of our ſtations try ;
See if the maſs we ſo deplore
Contain not ſome intrinſic ore ;
Some latent principle of good,
Sure to be priz'd when underſtood.
And firſt, t' obſerve an order due,
'Tis proper my own caſe to view ;
As children of diſtinguiſh'd taſte,
Still eat the daintieſt bits the laſt.
'Tis true, from crape ſome torment ſprings ;
Lean curacies are hateful things ;
Diſtreſſing cramps to gen'rous ſpirit,
You ſcarce can treat a friend of merit :
And then your ruſty wig and gown
Excite the laugh of ev'ry clown.
But when ſome years have roll'd away,
Some patron of benignant clay
(Time move thy lazy pinions quicker ;)
May ſet me down a thankful vicar.
Now ſee the proſpect brighten round ;
Unnumber'd comforts ſtrait abound ;
A fair three hundred pounds a year,
Good books, neat houſe, and dainty cheer,
A mettled nag, perhaps a chair,
To ride abroad and take the air ;

" In

"In ſummer, ſhade; in winter, fire,"
And Sunday, dinners with the 'Squire.
Mean while, my ev'ry bliſs t' improve.
With life's beſt cordial, gen'rous love,
Some fair Selinda, lovely name,
May gradual catch the tender flame,
And yield the treaſure of her charms
With ſweet reluctance to my arms.
If then my friend ſhould ſteal from town,
And all the anger of the gown,
And ſee his parſon in good caſe,
Bleſt with th' eſteem of all the place;
See the dear partner of my heart,
All ſoftneſs act the kindeſt part;
See young Selindas, good and fair,
Climb up my knee the kiſs to ſhare:
Pray how could Fortune more preſent?
What room for pining diſcontent?
  Proceed we now to place the next
(Like good dividers of a text)
In which the Muſe ſhall make appear
You've much to hope, and nought to fear.
Where Garrick holds his mimic reign
Mere mortals call it *Drury-lane)*
You've ſeen, the firſt or ſecond night,
A new-born piece produc'd to light.
Scene firſt, a friend o'th' hero ſays
Something that puts you in amaze,
Of great events impending near,
And dangers threaten'd to his dear;
But for your life you can't divine
Where tends this ſtrange involv'd deſign;
The plot proceeds: you've got a clue
That guides the whole performance thro';
And plain as noſe upon your face
You ev'ry turn and winding trace.
Hear, gentle friend, th' inſtructive lay;
Your law reſembles juſt the play.
At *writ*, *ejectment*, *certiorari*,
Trover, and *ſcirefacias* ſtare ye?
Have patience; mark with eye profound;
And ſoon you'll tread on clearer ground.
What viſion's that? In court you ſtand,
With nervous tongue and waving hand,
Pleading the injur'd orphan's cauſe.
  hilſt ſtill Attention ſpeaks applauſe.
And now Britannia's patriots join
To bid you in the ſenate ſhine:

With all a Pitt's undaunted force,
You ſtem Corruption's head-long courſe;
Break the vile chain by Slav'ry worn,
And bleſs the ages yet unborn.
O may I live to ſee the day,
When crowds ſhall hail you on your way,
For ſelfiſh ſchemes of feigning good,
Of frontleſs Rapine juſt ſubdu'd;
The Muſe ſhall pour her ſtrongeſt lays,
And grow immortal by your praiſe.
Thus ev'ry ſtate, at diſtance due,
If we the piece attentive view,
Shews tints in ſweet aſſemblage laid,
Nor all is light, nor all is ſhade.
Then let us, to our lot reſign'd,
All-patient ply with ſteady mind
The preſent oar, howe'er it teize us;——
The reſt when heav'n-born Fortune pleaſes.

The following Fable was written by the ingenious Mr. CHRISTOPHER SMART, *late of Pembroke Hall, Cambridge, when his Grace the Duke of Devonſhire (then Lord Hartington) was appointed Lord Lieutenant of Ireland.*

The Engliſh Bull Dog, Dutch Maſtif, and Quail. A FABLE.

ARE we not all of race divine,
Alike of an immortal line,
Shall man to man afford deriſion,
But for ſome caſual diviſion,
To malice and to miſchief prone,
From climate, canton, or from zone?
Are all to idle diſcord bent
Theſe Kentiſh men, *thoſe* men of Kent,
And parties and diſtinction make
For parties and diſtinction ſake?
Souls ſprung from an ætherial flame,
However clad, are ſtill the ſame;
Nor ſhould we judge the heart or head,
By air we breathe, or earth we tread.
Dame Nature, who, all meritorious,
In a true Engliſhman is glorious,
Is lively, honeſt, brave, and bonny,
In Monſieur, Taffy, Teague, and Sawny.
Give prejudices to the wind,
And let's be patriots to mankind.
Bigots, avaunt! Senſe can't endure ye,
But Fabuliſts ſhould try to cure ye.

A ſnub-

A ſnub-nos'd dog to fat inclin'd,
Of the true hogan-mogan kind,
The fav'rite of an Engliſh dame,
Mynheer Van Trumpo was his name,
One morning as he chanc'd to range,
Met honeſt Towzer on the change,
And who have we got here I beg?
Quoth he,—and lifted up his leg;
An Engliſh dog can't take an airing
But foreign ſcoundrels muſt be ſtaring.
I'd have your French, and all your Spaniſh,
And all the Dutch, and all the Daniſh,
By which our ſpecies is confounded,
Be hang'd, be poiſon'd, or be drowned.
Well, of all dogs it is confeſs'd,
Your Engliſh bull-dogs are the beſt.
I ſay it, and will ſet my hand to't,
Camden records it, and I'll ſtand to't.
'Tis true, we have too much urbanity,
Are overcharg'd with ſoft humanity,
The beſt things muſt find food for railing,
And ev'ry creature has its failing.
And who are you, reply'd Van Trump,
(Curling his tail upon his rump)
Vaunting the regions of diſtraction,
The land of party and of faction?
In all fair Europe who but we
For national œconomy,
For wealth and peace, that have more charms
Than learned arts, or noiſy arms?
You envy us our dancing bogs,
With all the muſic of the frogs,
Join'd to the Tretchſcutz's bonny loon,
Who on the cymbal grinds the tune;
For poets, and the muſes nine,
Beyond compariſon we ſhine;
Oh! how we warble in our gizzards,
With XX's, HH's, and with ZZ's.
For fighting—now you think I'm joking,
We love it better far than ſmoaking,
Aſk but our troops from man to boy,
Who all ſurviv'd at Fontenoy;
'Tis true as friends, and as allies,
We're ever ready to deviſe
Our love, or any kind aſſiſtance
That may be granted at a diſtance;
And if you go to brag, good bye to'ye,
Nor dare to brave the high and mighty.

 Wrong

Wrong are you both, rejoins a Quail,
Confin'd within its wiery jail;
Frequent from realm to realm I've rang'd,
And with the seasons, climates chang'd.
Mankind is not so void of grace,
But good I've found in ev'ry place.
I've seen sincerity in France,
Among the Germans complaisance;
In foggy Holland wit may reign,
I've known humility in Spain:
Freed was I by a turban'd Turk,
Whose life was one entire good work;
And in this land, fair Freedom's boast,
Behold my liberty is lost.
Despis'd Hibernia have I seen,
Dejected like a widow'd queen,
Her robe, with dignity long worn,
And cap of liberty were torn,
Her broken fife and harp unstrung,
On the uncultur'd ground were flung,
Down lay her spear, defil'd with rust,
And book of learning in the dust.
Her loyalty still blameless found,
And hospitality renown'd,
No more the voice of Fame engross'd,
In discontent and clamour lost.
Ah! dire Corruption, art thou spread
Where never viper rear'd its head?
And did'st thy baleful influence sow
Where hemlock nor the night-shade grow?
Hapless, disconsolate, and brave,
Hibernia, who'll Hibernia save?
Who shall assist thee in thy woe?
Who ward from thee the fatal blow?
'Tis done, the glorious work is done,
All thanks to Heav'n and HARTINGTON.

On the first FIT *of the* GOUT.

O Thou! to man the earnest of fourscore,
Guest of the rich, unenvy'd by the *poor*,
Thou that great Esculapius dost deride,
And o'er his galley-pots in triumph ride;
Thou that was wont to hover near the throne,
And underprop the head that wears the *crown*;
Thou that dost oft in privy councils wait,
And guard from sleep the drowsy eyes of *state*;
Thou that upon the bench art mounted high,
And warn'st the *judges* when they tread awry;

The

Thou that dost oft from pamper'd *prelates* toe,
Emphatically urge the pains below;
Thou that art always half the *city*'s grace,
And add'st to solemn *noddle* solemn pace;
Thou that art us'd to sit on *lady*'s knee,
To feed on jellies, and to drink cold *tea*;
Thou whose luxurious sense can scarcely bear
The velvet slipper and the feather'd chair;
Whence does thy mighty condescension flow,
To visit my poor tabernacle?——Oh!
Her knee indulgent here no lady lends,
To watch thy looks no liv'ry'd train attends,
No costly jellies, and no chairs of down,
Invite soft slumbers, or the banquet crown.
Yet what I have for solace or for state,
I give, and envy for thy sake the great.
Jove, who vouchsaf'd in ancient times, 'tis said,
At poor Philemon's cot to take a bed;
Pleas'd with the mean, but hospitable feast,
First bad him ask, and granted his request——
O! then (for thou art of the race divine,
Begot on Venus by the God of wine)
Since, not incognito thy visit paid,
I meet thee conscious of my wants dismay'd,
Do thou to entertain thee give me *store*,
Or with thy presence honour me no more.

A Sea Chaplain's Petition to the Lieutenants in the ward-room, for the use of the Quarter Gallery.

In the manner of SWIFT.

YOU that can grant or can refuse the pow'r,
Low from the stern to drop the golden show'r,
When Nature prompts, ——— O patient deign to hear,
If not a parson's ——— yet a poet's pray'r!
E'er taught the diff'rence, to commissions due,
Presumptuous I aspir'd to mess with you:
But since the diff'rence known 'twixt sea and shore,
That mighty happiness I urge no more,
An humble boon and of a diff'rent kind,
(Grant heav'n a diff'rent answer it may find)
Attends you now——excuse the rhyme I write,
And tho' I mess not with you——let me sh—te.
When in old bards, Arion tunes his song,
The ravish'd dolphins round the vessel throng,
Verse sooth'd of old the monsters of the sea,
Let then what sav'd Arion, plead for me:

And,

And, if my Muſe can aught of truth divine,
The boon the Muſe petitions ſhall be mine:
For ſure this anſwer would be monſt'rous odd,
Sh—te with the common tars, thou man of God!
Of thoſe more vulgar tubes that downward peep,
Near where the lion awes the raging deep,
The waggiſh youths, I tell what I am told,
Oft ſmear the ſides with excremental gold;
Say then, when peaſe within the belly pent,
Roar at the port and ſtruggle for a vent,
Say—ſhall I plunge on dung remiſsly down,
And with unſeemly ordure ſtain the gown?
Or ſhall I (terrible to think) diſplode,
Againſt th' unbutton'd pluſh the ſmoaky load?
The laugh of ſwabbers——heav'n avert the jeſt!
And from th' impending ſtorm preſerve your prieſt!
But grant that Cloacina, gracious queen!
Should keep her od'rous ſhrine for ever clean,
Yet frequent muſt I feel the offenſive ſpray,
When the toſs'd veſſel ploughs the ſwelling ſea;
And, as I ſit, inceſſant muſt I hear,
The language of the nauſeous galley * near,
Where blockheads by the liſt'ning prieſt unaw'd,
Tho' uncommiſſion'd, dare blaſpheme their God!
Happy the man † admitted oft to ride
Within the ward-room, where his tools abide,
The man of leather———he, when Nature calls,
Can for the needful ſpace repoſe his awls,
And, while I ſqueeze o'er ſome ignoble ſeat,
Can diſembogue his vile burgoo in ſtate;
While peeping Nereids ſmoke the Chriſtian jeſt,
The honour'd cobler and neglected prieſt,
And ſwear by Styx, and all the pow'rs below,
In good old heathen days 'twas never ſo.
Ah! what avails it, that in days of yore,
Th' inſtructive laſhes of the birch I bore!
For four long years with logic ſtuff'd my head,
And feeding thought went ſupperleſs to bed,
Since you with whom my lot afloat is thrown,
(O! elegance of taſte to land unknown)
Superior rev'rence to the man refuſe,
Who mends your morals, than who mends your ſhoes.——
But Criſpin ſaves your purſe, you anſwer—True,
Nor does your prieſt without his offerings ſue:
Whene'er compell'd to uſe the fragrant hole,
In ſome bye nook I'll leave a moral ſcroll:

* A place near the cook-room always throng'd with the ſhip's people.
† A cobler who uſed to mend the lieutenants ſhoes in the quarter gallery.

The

The moral ſcroll who next ſucceeds may reach,
And to his brains apply it, or his br——h,
Thus ſhall your fingers find a juſt excuſe,
And one ſea chaplain boaſt his works of uſe.
And as yourſelves from time to time repair,
To drop the reliques of digeſtion there,
Still may your pork an eaſy exit gain,
Nor make you form one ugly face in vain,
Still may your flip, refin'd to amber flow,
In ſtreams ſalubrious, to the brine below;
Nor ever in too hot a current hiſs,
But may all holes prove innocent like this;
Thus grant my ſuit, (as grant unhurt you may)
Your chaplain then without your *groats* will pray.*

An epitaph out of a church-yard in Dorſetſhire, anſwered by a gentleman on the Widower's marrying again in a fortnight.

Epitaph.

For me deceas'd weep not, my dear,
I am not dead, but ſleepeth here:
Your time will come, prepare to die;
Wait but awhile, you'll follow I.

Anſwer.

I am not griev'd, my deareſt life;
Sleep on—I've got another wife:
And therefore cannot come to thee,
For I muſt go to bed to ſhe.

A Gentleman has cauſed a marble to be erected in St. Anne's church-yard, Weſtminſter, for the late King Theodore, Baron Neuhoff, with the following inſcription.

Near this place is interred
THEODORE, King of Corſica,
Who died in this pariſh Dec. 11, 1756,
Immediately after leaving
The King's Bench priſon,
By the benefit of the late act of Inſolvency:
In conſequence of which
He regiſtered his kingdom of Corſica
For the uſe of his creditors.

The grave, great teacher, to a level brings
Heroes and beggars, galley ſlaves and kings;
That Theodore this moral learn'd, ere dead
Fate pour'd its leſſons on his living head,
Beſtow'd a kingdom, and deny'd him bread.

* Every common ſeaman pays a groat a month out of his pay to the chaplain, but the lieutenants pay nothing.

An Account of Books publiſhed in 1758.

An Eſtimate of the Manners and Principles of the Times, by the Author of Eſſays on the Characteriſtics. Davis *and* Reymers.

FEW books have met with a warmer reception or ſeverer cenſure than the work before us. Its great ſucceſs aroſe partly from the circumſtances of the time when it appeared, partly from its own merit. It appeared at a time when our ill ſucceſs in the war had infuſed ſo general a diſcontent into the minds of all people, that even a ſevere national ſatire was not then diſagreeable to the public diſpoſition. And as to the work itſelf, though the obſervations it contains were many of them not abſolutely new; yet they were ſo methodized, the connection and relation of the ſeveral reigning vices and follies were ſo well marked, and their neceſſary influence on the proſperity of the ſtate were ſo well diſplayed, that it had an appearance of being both new and uſeful.

The diſadvantageous picture given of modern times in this work, revived a topic which has often been diſcuſſed with far more zeal and curioſity than real advantage; the diſpute concerning the preference of antient and modern times. *Vetera admirari, præſentia ſequi,* has ever been the diſpoſition of mankind. Always diſcontented with the preſent ſtate of things, to which however we always conform ourſelves, we naturally lament thoſe periods of our lives which we have paſſed, and the ages that have paſſed before us. We are apt to take our examples of what we ought to ſhun from preſent, and therefore more odious vice; and our examples of what we ought to follow from departed, and therefore leſs envied and more venerable virtue. Theſe diſpoſitions have led ſeveral to throw virtue as far backward as poſſible, and very extravagantly to maintain that the world is continually degenerating.

Another ſort of philoſophers have however lately appeared, who take a very different courſe; they aſſert that they can diſcover no ſuperiorities that any former age has over the preſent. That the degeneracy of the times has been the complaint even of the times which we admire. *Ætates parentium pejor avis tulit, &c.* is one of the oldeſt complaints in the world. That if we were to ſuppoſe mankind proceeded in an uniform progreſs in degeneracy and corruption, it is inconceivable how human ſociety could have ſubſiſted to this time. On the whole, they conclude that the race of men has been much the ſame in all ages.

This opinion, full as extravagant as the former, is much more pernicious; it has been found one of the moſt uſeful topics for ſpreading vice and corruption, and in its beſt conſequence can only induce a dull acquieſcence in our preſent condition. An uniform progreſſion in vice is an opinion ſupported by no reaſon: and can only be conſidered as a poetical exaggeration: but, on the other hand, a man muſt ſhut his eyes in good earneſt, not to perceive that nations at at one period ſtrongly marked with all the characters of vice and barbariſm, by ſome happy conjuncture emerge to light at another; and diſtinguiſh themſelves by virtue, by patriotiſm, by thoſe arts that improve and adorn life; theſe nations fall again into corruption, vice, and ignorance. Shall it be ſaid that the Romans were the ſame kind of people in the flouriſhing times of their commonwealth that they were under Nero, or even under Trajan or Antoninus? or the ſame that we find them at this day? However, this degeneracy is by no means in an even courſe, ſome commonwealths having been moſt glorious in their beginnings; others after they had long continued.

The work before us no otherwiſe inclines to the former party, than by a tendency to ſhew the picture of the preſent times in the moſt diſadvantageous point of light. It is indeed throughout a moſt ſevere invective againſt the manners and principles of the times in our country. The work diſcovers reading and reflection; the characters are ſtrongly marked, the ſtile is elegant, pointed and lively. But the author ſeems ſometimes too minute in his paintings, ſometimes overcharges them; and ſeveral have obſerved that a certain air of arrogance and ſuperiority prevails through the whole work. Theſe were the blemiſhes which took ſomething from the reputation which this piece had at firſt generally and juſtly acquired, on account of theſe beauties which we have mentioned.

The firſt volume of this work was printed the year before our deſign; but as the ſecond cannot be well underſtood without ſome knowledge of that to which it chiefly refers, we thought it not amiſs to give ſome account of it.

Our author lays it down as the corner ſtone of his ſtructure, that a vain, luxurious, and ſelfiſh effeminacy is the character of the preſent times; and the deſign is to ſhew how far the preſent ruling manners and principles of the nation may tend to its continuance or deſtruction.

The more fully to delineate the reigning manners, he takes the modern man even in his cradle, where he finds the firſt ſeeds of his effeminacy ſown, and follows him through his education, his travels and his appearance in town, and finds every thing in all calculated to form him to folly, effeminacy, and diſſipation. Here he conſiders the frivolous vein of common converſation, the trifling amuſements in faſhion, and the predominant luſt of gaming. From the amuſements he paſſes to the learning of the times.

" A knowledge of books, ſays he, a taſte in arts, a proficiency in ſcience, was formerly regarded as a proper qualification in a man of faſhion. The annals of our country have tranſmitted to us the name and memory of men, as eminent in learning and taſte, as in rank and fortune. It will not, I preſume, be regarded as any kind of ſatire on the preſent age, to ſay, that, among the higher ranks, this literary ſpirit is generally vaniſhed. *Reading* is now ſunk at beſt into a morning's *amuſement*; till the important hour of dreſs comes on. Books are no longer regarded as the repoſitories of taſte and knowledge; but are rather

rather laid hold of as a gentle relaxation from the tedious round of pleasure."

He then proceeds to examine the prevailing taste in music, painting, and theatrical entertainments.

" No wonder, if these leading characters of false delicacy influence our other entertainments, and be attended with a low and unmanly taste in *music*. That divine art, capable of inspiring every thing that is great or excellent, of rouzing every nobler passion of the soul, is at length dwindled into a woman's or an eunuch's effeminate trill. The chaste and solemn airs of Corelli, of Geminiani, and their best disciples; the divine and lofty flights of Caldara and Marcello; the elegant simplicity of Bononcini; the manly, the pathetic, the astonishing strains of Handel, are neglected and despised: while instead of these, our concerts and operas are disgraced with the lowest insipidity of composition, and unmeaning *sing-song*. The question now concerns not the expression, the grace, the energy, or dignity of the music; we go not to admire the *composition*, but the *tricks* of the *performer*, who is then surest of our ignorant applause, when he runs thro' the compass of the *throat*, or traverses the *finger-board* with the *swiftest dexterity*.

While *music* is thus debased into effeminacy, her sister-art of *painting* cannot hope a better fate: for the same dignity of manners must *support*; the same indignity *depress* them. Connoisseurs there are, indeed, who have either *taste* or *vanity*: yet even by these, the art is considered as a matter of *curiosity*, not of *influence*; a circumstance which proves their taste to be spurious, undirected, or superficial. But with regard to the public eye; this is generally depraved. Neither the comic pencil, nor the serious pen of our ingenious countryman †, have been able to keep alive the taste of nature, or of beauty. The fantastic and grotesque have banished *both*. Every house of fashion is now crowded with porcelain trees and birds, porcelain men and beasts, cross-legged Mandarins and Bramins, perpendicular lines and stiff right angles: every gaudy Chinese crudity, either in colour, form, attitude, or grouping, is adopted into fashionable use, and become the standard of taste and elegance.

Let us then search the theatre for the remains of manly taste: and *here*, apparently at least, it must be acknowledged we shall find it. A great genius hath arisen to dignify the stage; who, when it was sinking into the lowest insipidity, restored it to the fulness of its ancient splendor, and, with a variety of powers beyond example, established *Nature, Shakespear*, and *Himself*.

But as the attractions of the theatre arise from a complication of causes, beyond those of any other entertainment; so while the judicious critic admires his original excellencies, it may be well questioned whether the crowd be not drawn by certain secondary circumstances, rather than by a discernment of his real powers. Need we any other proofs of this than the conduct of his fashionable hearers? who sit with the same face of admiration at Lear, an Opera or a Pantomime.

These

† Mr. Hogarth's treatise on the principles of beauty.

These seem to be the main and leading articles of our unmanly winter-delicacies. And as to our summer-amusements, they are much of the same *make*, only *lighter*, and, if possible, more *trifling*. As soon as the season is grown so mild, as that the man of fashion can stir abroad, he is seen lolling in his *post-chariot*, about the purlieus of the town. The manly exercise of *riding* is generally disused, as too coarse and indelicate for the fine gentleman. The metropolis growing thin as the spring advances, the same rage of pleasure, dress, equipage, and dissipation, which in winter had chained him to the town, now drives him to the country. For as a vain and empty mind can never give entertainment to itself; so to avoid the tædium of solitude and self-converse, *parties* of pleasure are again formed; the same effeminacies, under new appearances, are acted over again, and become the *business* of the season. There is hardly a corner of the kingdom, where a *summer scene* of public *dissipation* is not now established: Here the parties meet till the winter sets in, and the separate societies are once more met in London.

Thus we have attempted a simple delineation of the ruling manners of the times: if any thing like ridicule appears to mix itself with this review, it ariseth not from the *aggravation*, but the natural *display* of *folly*.

It may probably be asked, why the ruling manners of our women have not been particularly delineated? The reason is, because they are essentially the same with those of the men, and are therefore included in this Estimate. The sexes have now little other apparent distinction, beyond that of person and dress: their peculiar and characteristic manners are confounded and lost; the one sex having at once advanced into *boldness*, as the other sunk into *effeminacy*."

After the manners, he examines the principles of the times, which he shews must be greatly influenced by them. The principles he considers, are those which tend to counterwork the selfish passions; the principles of religion, honour, and public spirit. As in his first part our author endeavours to establish the general predominance of selfish manners, it follows that the principles which are to counterwork them must be weak. He finds little religion or honour in the nation, and no public spirit.

In his second part he discourses on the public effect of these manners and principles, as they operate on the national capacity; the national spirit of defence; and the national spirit of union; all which he endeavours to shew, they have weakened and destroyed. On the spirit of union his remarks are just and fine.

"When the spirit of union is checked, and divisions arise, from the variety and freedom of opinion only; or from the contested rights and privileges of the different ranks or orders of a state, not from the detached and selfish views of individuals; a republic is then in its strength, and gathers warmth and fire from these collisions. Such was the state of ancient Rome, in the simpler and more disinterested periods of that republic.

But when principle is weakened and manners lost, and factions run high from selfish ambition, revenge, or avarice, a republic is then on the very

very eve of its deſtruction: and ſuch was the ſtate of Rome, in the times of Marius and Sylla, Pompey and Cæſar, Anthony and Auguſtus.

Therefore, before we can determine whether the factions that divide a free country be ſalutary or dangerous, it is neceſſary to know what is their foundation and their object. If they ariſe from freedom of opinion, and aim at the public welfare, they are ſalutary: if their ſource be ſelfiſh intereſt, of what kind ſoever; they are then dangerous and deſtructive."

He concludes with the following very juſt remark.

"That when factions ariſe from the exceſs of military ſpirit and ambition of dominion, they increaſe the national capacity and ſpirit of defence: on the contrary, where factions ariſe from ſelfiſh effeminacy, the national capacity and ſpirit of defence will certainly be weakened or deſtroyed."

In his fourth part are conſidered the ſources of theſe manners and principles, which be chiefly derived from exorbitant trade and wealth; which naturally, in a country conſtituted like ours, produces luxury, avarice and effeminacy in manners; and a deficiency if not a profligacy in principles. He ſums up the whole in the concluſion.

"From theſe accumulated proofs, ſays the author, then, it ſeems evident, that our preſent effeminate manners and defect of principle have ariſen from our exhorbitant trade and wealth, left without check, to their natural operations and uncontrouled influence. And that theſe manners, and this defect of principle, by weakening or deſtroying the national capacity, ſpirit of defence, and union, have produced ſuch a general debility as naturally leads to deſtruction.

We might now proceed to confirm theſe reaſonings, by examples drawn from hiſtory. For there is hardly an ancient or modern ſtate of any note recorded in ſtory, which would not, in one reſpect or other, confirm the leading principles on which this argument is built.

In theſe, throughout their ſeveral periods, we ſhould ſee trade and wealth, or (what is in this reſpect equivalent) conqueſt and opulence, taking their progreſs: at one period poliſhing and ſtrengthening; at another, refining, corrupting, weakening, deſtroying, the ſtate that gave them entrance: working indeed in different ways, and under a variety of appearances; by avarice, by faction, by effeminacy, by profligacy; by mixture and combination of all theſe evils; ſometimes dividing a nation againſt itſelf; at others, quelling its ſpirit, and leaving it an eaſy prey to the firſt invader: ſometimes checked by a riſing patriot, or oounterworked by national misfortunes: in one country corrupting manners; in another, principles; in a third, both manners and principles: rendering one people blind, another cowardly, another treacherous to itſelf: ſtealing ſecretly and inſenſibly on one nation; overwhelming another in certain deſtruction.

But to enlarge on theſe ſubjects in that vague and undiſtinguiſhing manner, which moſt writers have purſued in treating them, though it might carry the *appearance* of reaſoning, would in truth be no more than *Declamation* in diſguiſe. And to to develope and unravel the particularity of causes and effects, thro' all their variety of combination and mutual influence, as it would extend this Estimate beyond its designed limits, must be left to make a part of some future enquiry."

Notwithstanding this striking picture of a degenerate age, the author allows us some virtues; and admits that we still possess the spirit of liberty, the spirit of humanity, and public justice in an high degree.

The second volume of this work contains retractions of such mistakes as the author thinks he has committed in his first volume; proofs of his assertions; illustrations of what had not been fully explained; replies to objections; and such further consequences as may be deduced from his principles. He concludes this volume with two pictures; one of a great minister, the other of a true political writer, for the original of either the reader cannot possibly be at a loss: of the minister he says:

"He will not only have honest intentions of mind, but wisdom to plan, and courage to execute.

He will regard the interests of the prince and people, as inseparably and invariably united.

He will, to the utmost of his power, abolish ministerial influence on parliaments, and discourage parliamentary influence among the great.

He will endeavour to destroy party distinctions; and to unite all men, in the support of the common and national welfare.

In consequence of this, he will be hated by the corrupt part of the kingdom, high and low, because *their* expectations of advantage, can only arise from those distinctions and that influence which he labours to abolish.

The honest and unprejudiced part of the nation will adore him, for the contrary reason.

He will be remarkable rather for his knowledge in the great principles of wisdom and virtue, than in the oblique ways and mysteries of selfish cunning.

He may be displaced once, or more than once, by the power of faction: but the united voice of an uncorrupt people will restore him to the favour of the Sovereign; especially in a time of danger. And the oftener he is cut down by corrupt power, the deeper root he will take in the affections of the prince and people, and rise and flourish with renewed vigour.

His private life will be consistent with his public conduct: he will not adopt, but scorn the degenerate manners of the times. Above luxury and parade he will be modest and temperate; and his contempt of wealth will be as signal as his contempt of luxury.

He will be distinguished by his regard to religion, honour, and his country.

He will not despise, but honour the people, and listen to their united voice.

If his measures are not always clear to the people in their *Means*, they will always be so in their *Ends*. In this he will imitate a great Queen, or her great minister, 'whose policy was deep, and the means she employed were often very secret; but the ends to which this policy and these means were directed, *were never equivalent*.'

As a neutral and happy consequence of this conduct, should he happen either to err in a *design*,

ſign, or fail in its *execution,* an uncorrupt people will ſtill *confide* in him. They will continue to repoſe on his general wiſdom and integrity; will regard him as a kind and watchful father; yet, tho' *wiſe,* not *infallible.*

He will look *forward,* rather than to what is *paſt*; and be more zealous to ſelect and reward thoſe who may do well, than to proſecute thoſe whom, in his own opinion, he may think delinquents.

His principles and conduct, as they will be *hated* by *vile,* ſo they will be *derided* by *narrow* minds, which cannot enlarge their conceptions beyond the beaten track of preſent practice. Prince Maurice was *ridiculed* in his *firſt attempts,* for thoſe very expedients by which he drove the Spaniards out of his country.

If his little or no influence in parliament be objected to him, he will anſwer as Henry the Great did with regard to Rochelle, 'I 'do all I deſire to do there, 'in doing nothing but what I 'ought.'

He will practiſe 'that double 'oeconomy, which is ſo rarely 'found, or even underſtood. I 'mean not only that inferior 'oeconomy, which conſiſts in the 'management of the receipts and 'iſſues of the public revenue; 'but that ſuperior oeconomy, 'which conſiſts in contriving the 'great ſchemes of negotiation and 'action.'

The laws he frames, will be generous and comprehenſive; that is, in Lord Verulam's nervous expreſſion, 'deep, not vulgar; not made 'upon the ſpur of a particular oc'caſion for the preſent, but out of 'providence of the future; to 'make the eſtate of the people ſtill 'more and more happy, after the 'manner of the legiſlators in an'cient and heroical times.'

Above all, he will ſtudy to reſtore and ſecure upright *manners* and *principles*; knowing *theſe* to be the very *ſtrength* and *vitals* of *every ſtate.*

As by all theſe means he will put the natural and internal ſprings of government into action; ſo he will keep up that action in its full vigour, by employing ability and merit: and hence, men of genius, capacity, and virtue, will of courſe fill the moſt important and public ſtations, in every department.

To fulfil this great purpoſe, he will ſearch for men, capable of ſerving the public, with regard to wealth, family, parliamentary intereſt, or connection.

He will deſpiſe thoſe idle claims, of *priority* of rank, or *ſeniority* in ſtation, when they are *unſupported* by *ſervices* performed in that rank and ſtation: he will ſearch for thoſe, wherever they are to be found, whoſe active ſpirits and ſuperior capacity promiſe advantage to the public.

He will not abuſe this power indulged to him, of ſuperſeding ſuperior rank, by preferring his own favourites. If he finds the appearance of ability and worth among the friends or dependents of his enemies, he will truſt them with the execution of his moſt important deſigns, on the ſucceſs of which, even his own character may depend.

Having no motive, but the welfare of his country; if he cannot accompliſh *that,* by ſuch meaſures as his heart approves, he will

will not ſtruggle for a continuance in power, but bravely and peaceably *reſign.*

Whether ſuch a character as is here delineated, may ever ariſe, is a queſtion which it were ſuperfluous for the writer to determine; if ever ſuch a miniſter appears, he will beſt be ſeen by his own luſtre.

There is another character, belonging indeed to a much lower walk in life, which might be no leſs ſtrange than that which is here delineated. I mean the character of a political writer, not only *intentionally*, but *in fact* impartial.

This is a character which hath never yet exiſted; nor, probably, will ever appear, in our own country. However, let us attempt a ſketch of this ideal pourtrait, for the uſe of thoſe who may aſpire to impartiality; and conſider, by 'what characteriſtics he would 'be diſtinguiſhed.'

He would chuſe an untrodden path of politics, where no party-man ever dared to enter.

He would be diſliked by party-bigots of every denomination: who, while they applauded one page of his work, would execrate the next.

The undiſguiſed freedom and boldneſs of his manner, would pleaſe the brave, aſtoniſh the weak, diſguſt and confound the guilty.

Every rank, party, and profeſſion, would acknowledge he had done tolerable juſtice to every rank, party, and profeſſion, their own only excepted.

He would be called *arrogant* by thoſe who call every thing *arrogance* that is not *ſervility.*

If he writ in a period, when his country was declining; while he pointed out the means from whence alone honeſt *hope* could ariſe, he would be charged by ſcribbling ſycophants with plunging a nation in *deſpair.*

While he pointed out the abuſes of freedom, and their fatal effects, he would be blackened by deſigning whiſpers, as the enemy of freedom itſelf.

The worthleſs of every profeſſion would be his ſworn enemies; but moſt of all, the worthleſs of his own profeſſion.

As he would be reviled and defamed by the *diſſolute* great, without cauſe; ſo he would be applauded by an *honeſt* people, beyond his deſervings.

Tho' his abilities were ſmall, yet the integrity of his intention would make amends for the mediocrity of his talents.

As ſuch a writer could have little pretenſions to literary fame, ſo he would not be intoxicated with the fumes of literary vanity: But would think, with Sheffield, that

> One moral, or a mere well-natur'd deed,
> Does all deſert in ſciences exceed.

Yet, tho' he ſcorned the gildings of falſe ambition, and riches acquired by adulation; he might not, poſſibly, be unconſcious of that unſought dignity, that envy'd ſuperiority to wealth and titles, which even the love of wiſdom and virtue give.

Should any of the great, therefore, affect to diſdain him, on account of his private ſtation, he might perhaps reply with Perdita,

I was not much afraid; for once or twice
I was about to ſpeak, and tell him plainly,
The ſelf-ſame ſun that ſhines upon his palace,
Hides not his heav'nly viſage from my cottage,
But looks on both alike.

His free and unconquered ſpirit would look down with contempt on views of intereſt, when they came in competition with views of duty.

Nay, were he called to ſo ſevere a trial, he would even dare to make the greateſt and the rareſt of all honeſt ſacrifices, that of friendſhip itſelf, to truth and virtue.

Should the ſenſe of his duty to his country determine him to a farther proſecution of his labours, he would ſay,

If ſuch his fate, do thou, fair Truth, deſcend,
And watchful, guard him in an honeſt end:
Kindly ſevere, inſtruct his equal line,
To court no friend, nor own a foe, but thine.
But if his giddy eye ſhould vainly quit
Thy ſacred paths, to run the maze of wit;
If his apoſtate heart ſhould e'er incline
To offer incenſe at corruption's ſhrine,
Urge, urge thy power; the black attempt confound;
Oh, daſh the ſmoaking cenſer to the ground:
Thus aw'd to fear, inſtructed man may ſee
That guilt is doomed to ſink in infamy.

A diſcourſe on the Study of the Law, read in the public ſchools at Oxford, Oct. 24, 1758. Octavo.

WE cannot help congratulating the public on the fair proſpect we now have, that one learned foundation at leaſt will fully anſwer the intention of the founder. The diſcourſe before us is a ſolid, judicious and elegant oration, containing at once, an hiſtory of our law, a juſt panegyric on it, arguments for putting the ſtudy of it under proper regulations, and a ſpirited perſuaſive to make that ſtudy ſo regulated, a conſiderable part of academical education, eſpecially for perſons of rank. After ſtrongly urging this to gentlemen in general, he particularly applies to the nobility.

"What is ſaid of our gentlemen in general, and the propriety of their application to the ſtudy of the laws of their country, will hold equally ſtrong or ſtill ſtronger with regard to the nobility of this realm, except only in the article of ſerving upon juries. But, inſtead of this, they have ſeveral peculiar provinces, of far greater conſequence and concern; being not only by birth hereditary counſellors of the crown, and judges upon their honour of the lives of their brother peers, but alſo arbiters of the property of all their fellow ſubjects, and that in the laſt reſort. In this their judicial capacity they are bound to decide the niceſt and moſt critical points of law; to examine and correct ſuch errors as have eſcaped the moſt experienced ſages of the profeſſion, the lord keeper and the judges of the courts at Weſtminſter. Their ſentence is final, deciſive, irrevocable: no appeal, no correction, not even a review can be had: and to their determination, whatever it be, the inferior courts of juſtice muſt conform; otherwiſe the rule of property would no longer be uniform and ſteady.

Should

Should a judge in the moſt ſubordinate juriſdiction be deficient in the knowledge of the law, it would reflect infinite contempt upon himſelf, and diſgrace upon thoſe who employ him. And yet the conſequence of his ignorance is comparatively very trifling and ſmall: his judgment may be examined, and his errors rectified by other courts. But how much more ſerious and affecting is the caſe of a ſuperior judge, if without any ſkill in the laws he will boldly venture to decide a queſtion, upon which the welfare and ſubſiſtence of whoſe families may depend! where the chance of his judging right, or wrong, is barely equal; and where, if he chances to judge wrong, he does an injury of the moſt alarming nature, an injury without poſſibility of redreſs!

Yet, vaſt as this truſt is, it can no where be ſo properly repoſed as in the noble hands where our excellent conſtitution has placed it: and therefore placed it, becauſe, from the independence of their fortune, and the dignity of their ſtation, they are preſumed to employ that leiſure which is the conſequence of both, in attaining a more extenſive knowledge of the laws than perſons of an inferior rank; and becauſe the founders of our policy relied upon that delicacy of ſentiment, ſo peculiar to noble birth; which, as on the one hand it will prevent either intereſt or affection from interfering in queſtions of right, ſo on the other it will bind a peer in honour, an obligation which the law eſteems equal to another's oath, to be maſter of thoſe points upon which it is his birthright to decide.

The Roman pandects will furniſh us with a piece of hiſtory not unapplicable to our preſent purpoſe. Servius Sulpicius, a gentleman of the patrician order, and a celebrated orator, had occaſion to take the opinion of Quintus Mutius Scaevola, the oracle of the Roman law; but for want of being converſant in that ſcience, could not ſo much as underſtand even the technical terms, which his counſel was obliged to make uſe of. Upon which Mutius Scaevola could not forbear to upbraid him with this memorable reproof, 'that it was 'a ſhame for a partrician, a noble-'man, and an orator, to be igno-'rant of the law under which he 'lived.' Which reproof made ſo deep an impreſſion on Sulpicius, that he immediately applied himſelf to the ſtudy of the law; wherein he arrived to that proficiency, that he left behind him about a hundred and fourſcore volumes of his own compiling upon the ſubject; and became in the opinion of Cicero, a much more compleat lawyer than even Mutius Scaevola himſelf."

The cauſe of the neglect of the ſtudy of the common law in our univerſities, he delivers thus:

"That ancient collection of unwritten maxims and cuſtoms, which is called the common law, however compounded, or from whatever fountains derived, had ſubſiſted immemorially in this kingdom; and, though ſomewhat altered and impaired by the violence of the times, had in great meaſure weathered the rude ſhock of the Norman conqueſt. This had endeared it to the people in general, as well becauſe its deciſions were univerſally known, as becauſe it was found to be excellently adapted to the genius of the Englifh nation. In the knowledge of this law confifted great part of the learning of thofe dark ages; it was then taught, fays Mr. Selden, in the monafteries, *in the univerfities*, and in the families of the principal nobility. The clergy in particular, as they then engroffed almoft every other branch of learning, fo, like their predeceffors the Britifh druids, they were peculiarly remarkable for their proficiency in the ftudy of the law. *Nullus clericus nifi caufidicus*, is the character given of them foon after the conqueft by William of Malmfbury. The judges therefore were ufually created out of the facred order, as was likewife the cafe among the Normans; and all the inferior offices were fupplied by the lower clergy, which has occafioned their fucceffors to be denominated *clerks* to this day.

But the common law of England, being not committed to writing, but only handed down by tradition, ufe, and experience, was not fo heartily relifhed by the foreign clergy; who came over hither in fhoals during the reign of the Conqueror and his two fons, and were utter ftrangers to our conftitution as well as our language. And an accident, which foon after happened, had nearly compleated its ruin. A copy of Juftinian's pandects, being newly difcovered at Amalfi, foon brought the civil law into vogue all over the weft of Europe, where before it was quite laid afide and in a manner forgotten; though fome traces of its authority remained in Italy and the eaftern provinces of the empire. This now became in a particular manner the favourite of the popifh clergy, who borrowed the method and many of the maxims of their canon law from this original. The ftudy of it was introduced into feveral univerfities abroad, particularly that of Bologna; where exercifes were performed, lectures read, and degrees conferred in this faculty, as in other branches of fcience: and many nations on the continent, juft then beginning to recover from the convulfions confequent upon the overthrow of the Roman empire, and fettling by degrees into peaceable forms of government, adopted the civil law, (being the beft written fyftem then extant) as the bafis of their feveral conftitutions; blending and interweaving it among their own feodal cuftoms, in fome places with a more extenfive, in others a more confined authority.

Nor was it long before the prevailing mode of the times reached England. For Theobald, a Norman abbot, being elected to the fee of Canterbury, and extremely addicted to this new ftudy, brought over with him in his retinue many learned proficients therein; and among the reft Roger firnamed Vacarius, whom he placed in the univerfity of Oxford, to teach it to the people of this country. But it did not meet with the fame eafy reception in England, where a mild and rational fyftem of laws had long been eftablifhed, as it did upon the continent; and, though the monkifh clergy (devoted to the will of a foreign primate) received it with eagernefs and zeal, yet the laity who were more interefted to preferve the old conftitution, and had

already

already ſeverely felt the effect of many Norman innovations, continued wedded to the uſe of the common law. King Stephen immediately publiſhed a proclamation, forbidding the ſtudy of the laws, then newly imported from Italy; which was treated by the monks as a piece of impiety, and though it might prevent the introduction of the civil law proceſs into our courts of juſtice, yet did not hinder the clergy from reading and teaching it in their own ſchools and monaſteries.

From this time the nation ſeems to have been divided into two parties; the biſhops and clergy, many of them foreigners, who applied themſelves wholly to the ſtudy of the civil and canon laws, which now came to be inſeparably interwoven with each other; and the nobility and laity, who adhered with equal pertinacity to the old common law; both of them reciprocally jealous of what they were unacquainted with, and neither of them perhaps allowing the oppoſite ſyſtem that real merit which is abundantly to be found in each. This appears on the one hand from the ſpleen with which the monaſtic writers ſpeak of our municipal laws upon all occaſions; and, on the other, from the firm temper which the nobility ſhewed at the famous parliament of Merton; when the prelates endeavoured to procure an act, to declare all baſtards legitimate in caſe the parents intermarried at any time afterwards; alledging this only reaſon, becauſe holy church (that is, the canon law) declared ſuch children legitimate: but, 'all the earls and 'barons (ſays the parliament roll) 'with one voice anſwered, that 'they would not change the laws 'of England, which have hitherto 'been uſed and approved.' And we find the ſame jealouſy prevaling above a century afterwards, when the nobility declared with a kind of prophetic ſpirit, 'that the 'realm of England hath never 'been unto this hour, neither by 'the conſent of our lord the king 'and the lords of parliament ſhall 'it ever be, ruled or governed 'by the civil law.' And of this temper between the clergy and laity many more inſtances might be given.

While things were in this ſituation, the clergy finding it impoſſible to root out the municipal law, began to withdraw themſelves by degrees from the temporal courts; and to that end, very early in the reign of King Henry the third, epiſcopal conſtitutions were publiſhed, forbidding all eccleſiaſtics to appear as advocates *in foro ſeculari*; nor did they long continue to act as judges there, not caring to take the oath of office which was then found neceſſary to be adminiſtered, that they ſhould in all things determine according to the law and cuſtom of this realm: though they ſtill kept poſſeſſion of the high office of chancellor, an office then of little juridical power; and afterwards, as its buſineſs increaſed by degrees, they modelled the proceſs of the court at their own diſcretion.

But wherever they retired, and wherever their authority extended, they carried with them the ſame zeal to introduce the rules of the civil, in excluſion of the municipal law. This appears in a particular manner from the

ſpiritual

ſpiritual courts of all denominations, from the chancellor's courts in both our univerſities, and from the high court of chancery before mentioned; in all of which the proceedings are to this day in a courſe much conformed to the civil law: for which no tolerable reaſon can be aſſigned, unleſs that theſe courts were all under the immediate direction of the popiſh eccleſiaſtics, among whom it was a point of religion to exclude the municipal law; Pope Innocent the fourth having forbidden the very reading of it by the clergy, becauſe its deciſions were not founded on the imperial conſtitutions, but merely on the cuſtoms of the laity. And if it be conſidered, that our univerſities began about that period to receive their preſent form of ſcholaſtic diſcipline; that they were then, and continued to be till the time of the reformation, entirely under the influence of the popiſh clergy; (Sir John Maſon the firſt Proteſtant, being alſo the firſt lay, chancellor of Oxford) this will lend us to perceive the reaſon, why the ſtudy of the Roman laws was in thoſe days of bigotry purſued with ſuch alacrity in theſe ſeats of learning: and why the common law was entirely deſpiſed, and eſteemed little better than heretical.

And, ſince the reformation, many cauſes have conſpired to prevent its becoming a part of academical education. As, firſt, long uſage and eſtabliſhed cuſtom; which, as in every thing elſe, ſo eſpeciall in the forms of ſcholaſtic exerciſe, have juſtly great weight and authority. Secondly, the real intrinſic merit of the civil law, conſidered upon the footing of reaſon and not of obligation, which was well known to the inſtructors of our youth; and their total ignorance of the merit of the common law, though equal at leaſt, and perhaps an improvement on the other. But the principal reaſon of all, that has hindered the introduction of that branch of learning, is, that the ſtudy of the common law, being baniſhed from hence in the times of popery, has fallen into a quite different channel, and has hitherto been wholly cultivated in another place. But as this long uſage and eſtabliſhed cuſtom, of ignorance of the laws of the land, begin now to be thought reaſonable; and has by this means the merit of thoſe laws will probably be more generally known; we may hope that the method of ſtudying them will ſoon revert to its ancient courſe, and the foundations at leaſt of that ſcience will be laid in the two univerſities; without being excluſively confined to the channel which it fell into at the times I have been juſt deſcribing.

For, being then entirely abandoned by the clergy, a few ſtragglers excepted, the ſtudy and practice of it devolved of courſe into the hands of laymen; who entertained upon their parts a moſt hearty averſion to the civil law, and made no ſcruple to profeſs their contempt, nay even their ignorance of it, in the moſt public manner. But ſtill as the balance of learning was greatly on the ſide of the clergy, and as the common law was no longer *taught*, as formerly, in any part of the kingdom, it muſt have been ſubjected to many inconveniencies, and perhaps would have been gradually

gradually loſt and overrun by the civil, (a ſuſpicion well juſtified from the frequent tranſcripts of Juſtinian to be met with in Bracton and Fleta) had it not been for a peculiar incident, which happened at a very critical time, and contributed greatly to its ſupport.

The incident I mean was the fixing the court of common pleas, the grand tribunal for diſputes of property, to be held in one certain ſpot; that the ſeat of ordinary juſtice might be permanent and notorious to all the nation. Formerly that, in conjunction with all the other ſuperior courts, was held before the king's capital juſticiary of England, in the *aula regis*, or ſuch of his palaces wherein his royal perſon reſided, and removed with his houſhold from one end of the kingdom to the other. This was found to occaſion great inconvenience to the ſuitors; to remedy which it was made an article of the great charter of liberties, both that of King John and King Henry the third, that 'common pleas ſhould no longer 'follow the king's court, but be 'held in ſome certain place:' in conſequence of which they have ever ſince been held (a few neceſſary removals in times of the plague excepted) in the palace of Weſtminſter only. This brought together the profeſſors of the municipal law, who before were diſperſed about the kingdom, and formed them into an aggregate body; whereby a ſociety was eſtabliſhed of perſons, who (as Spelman obſerves) addicting themſelves wholly to the ſtudy of the laws of the land, and no longer conſidering it as a mere ſubordinate ſcience for the amuſement of leiſure hours, ſoon raiſed thoſe laws to that pitch of perfection, which they ſuddenly attained under the auſpices of our Engliſh Juſtinian, King Edward the firſt.

In conſequence of this lucky aſſemblage, they naturally fell into a kind of collegiate order; and being excluded from Oxford and Cambridge, found it neceſſary to eſtabliſh a new univerſity of their own. This they did by purchaſing at various times certain houſes (now called the inns of court and of chancery) between the city of Weſtminſter, the place of holding the king's courts, and the city of London; for advantage of ready acceſs to the one, and plenty of proviſions in the other. Here exerciſes were performed, lectures read, and degrees were at length conferred in the common laws, as at other univerſities in the canon and civil. The degrees were thoſe of barriſters (firſt ſtiled apprentices from *apprendre*, to learn) who anſwered to our batchelors; as the ſtate and degree of a ſerjeant, *ſervientis ad legem*, did to that of doctor."

The author has alſo the following moſt uſeful remarks on certain illiberal notions and practices with regard to a legal education.

"The evident want of ſome aſſiſtance in the rudiments of legal knowledge, has given birth to a practice, which, if ever it had grown to be general, muſt have proved of extremely pernicious conſequence: I mean the cuſtom, by ſome very warmly recommended, to drop all liberal education, as of no uſe to lawyers; and to place them, in its ſtead, at the deſk

desk of some skilful attorney; in order to initiate them early in all the depths of practice, and render them more dextrous in the mechanical part of business. A few instances of particular persons, (men of excellent learning, and unblemished integrity) who, in spight of this method of education, have shone in the foremost ranks of the bar, have afforded some kind of sanction to this illiberal path to the profession, and biassed many parents of short-sighted judgment, in its favour: not considering, that there are some geniuses, formed to overcome all disadvantages, and that from such particular instances no general rules can be formed; nor observing, that those very persons have frequently recommended by the most forcible of all examples, the disposal of their own offspring, a very different foundation of legal studies, a regular academical education. Perhaps too, in return, I could now direct their eyes to our principal seats of justice, and suggest a few hints, in favour of universal learning:—— but in these all who hear me, I know, have already prevented me.

Making therefore all due allowance for one or two shining exceptions, experience may teach us to foretell, that a lawyer thus educated to the bar, in subservience to attorneys and solicitors, will find he has begun at the wrong end. If practice be the whole he is taught, practice must also be the whole he will ever know: if he be uninstructed in the elements and first principles upon which the rule of practice is founded, the least variation from established precedents will totally distract and bewilder him: *ita lex scripta est* is the utmost his knowledge will arrive at; he must never aspire to form, and seldom expect to comprehend, any arguments drawn *a priori*, from the spirit of the laws and the natural foundation of justice.

Nor is this all; for (as few persons of birth, or fortune, or even of scholastic education, will submit to the drudgery of servitude and the manual labour of copying the trash of an office) should this infatuation prevail to any cosiderable degree, we must rarely expect to see a gentleman of distinction or learning at the bar. And what the consequence may be, to have the interpretation and enforcement of the laws (which include the entire disposal of our properties, liberties and lives) fall wholly into the hands of obscure or illiterate men, is a matter of very public concern.

The History of the Life and Reign of Philip King of Macedon, the father of Alexander. By Tho. Leland, D. D. Fellow of Trinity-College, Dublin. Johnston, *Paul's Church-yard. Two vols Quarto.*

THE translation of the orations of Demosthenes by Dr. Leland was so well executed, that the public expected to see the life of Philip, the illustrious antagonist of that great orator, handled with equal ability; and the actions of the one as well delivered as the eloquence of the other. Nor were the expectations of the public disappointed. From scattered passages in orators and historians, by the united efforts of great labour

and

and great judgment, we have a well-connected, clear, and ſpirited hiſtory of one of the moſt extraordinary men whom Greece, or perhaps any other country, has ever produced; as well for the greatneſs of his talents, as the ſtrength both of his virtues and his vices. The author has thoroughly ſtudied the conſtitution of ancient Greece, with an account of which he very judiciouſly begins his work. We ſhall give it as a ſpecimen of his ſtyle and manner of writing.

" Ancient Greece was inhabited by people, whoſe origin and language were the ſame; but their manners, cuſtoms, inſtitutions, aud forms of government, in many reſpects totally different. Yet, amidſt this diverſity, their general principles were alſo the ſame, an ardor for liberty, and a ſtrict regard to the public good. . . .

" A number of neighbouring ſocieties, thus formed and modelled, becauſe gradually to be conſidered as one body or nation, compoſed of ſo many diſtinct members, all united and connected together by intereſt and affection. As the good of each individual was ſubſervient to that of his community ſo the good of each community was conſidered as ſubordinate to that of the whole nation. Hence aroſe a familiar ſpecies of *civility*, if it may be ſo called, which each ſociety owes to the general aſſemblage. Even amidſt thoſe conteſts and diſorders which unruly paſſions, or the accidental claſhing of intereſts, might produce, war had its laws and imitations; the univerſal intereſt of Greece was profeſſedly at leaſt the firſt and greateſt object of attention; the attempt of any ſtate to extend its power beyond the juſt and equitable bounds, was conſidered as an injury to Greece in general: juſtice, moderation, equality, were ever ſtrenuouſly enforced, and all military conteſts carried among the Greeks in a manner ſomewhat ſimilar to judicial controverſies in private ſocieties: and, while it was allowed thus to ſeek redreſs of particular injuries, the general rights of the contending parties were ſecured by national laws, and demanded a juſt and ſcrupulous attention, even amidſt all the confuſion and violence of arms. Thus the great Athenian orator deſcribes the principles and ſentiments of the Greeks, ſpeaking of the ancient wars of Athens and Sparta. Οὕτω δ'αρχαιως εἶχον, μαλλον δε ΠΘΛΛΙΤΙΚΩΣ, ὥστε ὐδε χρηματων ὠνεισθαι παρ ὐδενος ουδεν· αλλ' ειναι NOMIMON τινα ϰ̀ προφανη τον πολεμον. *Such was their ſimplicity, or rather their* civility, (that is, their deference to the general laws of Greece, and their attention to the common good of that nation) *that corruption was never made the inſtrument of their ſucceſs; but they carried on a* legal *and open war*.

While theſe principles preſerved their due vigour and influence, Greece continued a really united body, happy in itſelf, and formidable to its enemies. Many circumſtances contributed to form this union: and many inſtitutions were ſuggeſted, by the ſagacity of ſtateſmen and legiſlators, to ſecure and confirm it. Of theſe, the famous *council of Amphictyons* deſerves particular regard; whoſe origin and conſtitution are here to be explained, that the reader may come duly prepared to underſtand the hiſtory now preſented to him, in which this auguſt body

body makes ſo conſiderable a figure.

The council of Amphictyons, like other inſtitutions of the ſame kind, was at firſt but inconſiderable; nor did it arrive to its full ſtrength and luſtre but by gradual advances, and in a long ſeries of years. Its firſt original we are to aſcribe to Amphictyon, the ſon of Deucalion, an ancient king of Theſſaly, as the authority of the Arundelian Marbles warrants us to determine . . . .

The intention of Amphictyon, in inſtituting this aſſembly, was, that the children of Deucalion, who, at his deceaſe, divided the kingdon between them, ſhould have a common tribunal, to which they might appeal in all private conteſts; and a council, in which they might concert all meaſures neceſſary for their defence againſt their foreign enemies. And for theſe purpoſes, beſides thoſe laws by which each particular city was governed, he enacted others of general force and obligation to all, which were called Amphictyonic laws. By means of theſe, ſaith Dionyſius, the people thus united, continued in ſtrict and mutual amity; regarded each other as real brethren and countrymen; and were inabled to annoy and ſtrike terror into their barbarous enemies. Thermopylae was the limit which divided the territories of Amphictyon and Hellen, the two brothers; here, therefore, they built a temple to Ceres at the common charge, near the mouth of the river AEſopus, in which the members of the Amphictyonic council aſſembled, to offer their ſacrifices, and to conſult about their common intereſt, twice in every year, in ſpring and autumn; and hence the names Πυλαια ἐαρινη ϗ μετοπωρινη, the vernal and autumnal convention.

The aſſembly, thus formed, was at firſt but ſmall, being wholly compoſed of thoſe people whom Deucalion had commanded, and who from his ſon Hellen, were called ῾ΕΛΛΗΝΕΣ. The Dorians and Ionians, who were deſcended from the poſterity of this Hellen, as yet had no being; nor were any of the Peleponneſians now accounted Hellenes, but were called Pelaſgi; nor were they diſpoſed to unite with the ſons of Deucalion, by whom they had been deprived of Theſſaly, and all that part of Greece which lay beyond the iſthmus. As Greece improved, and the Hellenes increaſed in number, new regulations became neceſſary: and accordingly we find, that, in ſome time after the original inſtitution, Acriſius, king of Argos, when, through fear of Perſeus, (who, as the oracle declared, was to kill him) he retired into Theſſaly, obſerved the defects of the Amphictyonic council, and undertook to new-model and regulate it; extended its privileges; augmented the number of its members; enacted new laws, by which the collective body was to be governed; and aſſigned to each ſtate one ſingle deputy, and one ſingle voice, to be enjoyed by ſome, in their own ſole right; by others, in conjunction with one or more inferior ſtates: and thus came to be conſidered as the founder of this famous repreſentative of the Hellenic body.

From the time of Acriſius, the Amphictyons ſtill continued to hold one of their annual councils at Thermopylae, that of autumn. But it was now made a part of their function

function (and, in time of peace, became the most considerable part of it) to guard and protect the national religion. The vernal assembly therefore was held at Delphi, the great seat of the Grecian religion; the object of universal veneration; whither all people, Greeks and Barbarians, resorted, to seek the advice and direction of the famous Pythian oracle. The immense quanity of wealth, the number of rich votive offerings, which the superstition of so many ages and nations had lavished on the temple, demanded the exactest care and most vigorous protection. The prodigious concourse which attended there, at particular seasons, naturally produced many contests, and required a well regulated polity, and the frequent interposition of a respectable and powerful jurisdiction. The Delphians themselves were intrusted with the possession and general guardianship of the temple: they attended intirely on the service of the god, and were solely employed in the ceremonials of his religion: they were accounted in some sort sacred; the priests, the attendants, and as it were the family of Apollo. So they are called by Lucian (in Phalarid. I.) ἱεροὶ τε καὶ παρεδροι τε Πυθιε, καὶ μονους συνοικοι καὶ ὁμοροφιοι. But although they enjoyed certain powers and privileges with respect to the temple, and could even grant some honours and favours to particular persons, such as that of the Προμαντεια, or right of precedence in consulting the oracle, as appears from an imperfect inscription preserved by Spon and Wheeler, and quoted by Van Dale: yet still were they subject to the inspection and jurisdiction of the Amphictyons, who were the great conservators and protectors of the shrine; and who, besides their general care, appointed certain of their members, either by lot or rotation, to preside over the temple; an honour which according to Van Dale, was also called by the name Προμαντεια. . . .

The whole nation of Greece was divided into twelve districts or provinces: each of these contained a certain number of Amphictyonic states, or cities, each of which enjoyed an equal right of voting and determining in all affairs relative to the general interest. Other inferior cities were dependent on some of these, and as members of their community, were also represented by the same deputies: and thus the assembly of the Amphictyons became really and properly the representative of the whole Hellenic body. . . .

Each of these cities, which had a right to assist in the Amphictyonic council, was obliged to send its deputies to every meeting; and the number of these deputies was usually and regularly two; the one entitled hieromnemon, to whom was particularly entrusted the care of religion and its rites. His office was annual, as appears from several decrees, in which his name is joined with that of the Athenian archon επωνυμος; and he was appointed by lot. The other deputy was called by the general name pylagoras, and was chosen by election each particular meeting. Each of these deputies however differing in their functions, enjoyed an equal power of determining all affairs relative to the general interest. And thus the cities which they represented,

ſented, without any diſtinction or ſubordination, each gave two voices in the council of the Amphictyons, a privilege known by the name of the *double ſuffrage*; which term, ſo frequent in the ancient writings, is thus fully explained, without any refinement or difficulty. . . .

When the deputies, thus appointed, appeared to execute their commiſſion, they in the firſt place offered up their ſolemn ſacrifices to the gods; to Ceres, when they aſſembled at Thermopylae; when at Delphi, to Apollo, Diana, Latona, and Minerva: and, before they entered on their function, each deputy was obliged to take an oath, which AEſchines hath preſerved, or at leaſt ſome part of it; and which was conceived in theſe terms:

'I ſwear that I will never ſubvert any Amphictyonic city; I will never ſtop the courſes of their waters, either in war or peace. If any ſuch outrages ſhould be attempted, I will oppoſe them by force of arms, and deſtroy thoſe cities who may be guilty of ſuch attempts. If any devaſtations ſhall be committed in the territory of the god; if any ſhall be privy to ſuch offence, or entertain any deſign againſt the temple; I will make uſe of my feet, my hands, my whole force, to bring the offending party to condign puniſhment.'

To render this oath ſtill more ſolemn, the following aweful imprecations were ſubjoined:

'If any one ſhall violate any part of this ſolemn engagement, whether city, private perſon, or country, may ſuch violators be obnoxious to the vengeance of Apollo, Diana, Latona, and Minerva the provident. May their lands never produce their fruits: may their women never bring forth children of the ſame nature of their parents, but offsprings of an unnatural and monſtrous kind: may they be for ever defeated in war, in judicial controverſies, and in all civil tranſactions; and may they, their families, and their whole race, be utterly deſtroyed: may they never offer up an acceptable ſacrifice to Apollo, Diana, Latona, and Minerva the provident; but may all their ſacred rights be for ever rejected.'

Such was the conſtitution of this famous Grecian council. As to the diſputes of particular perſons, it was accounted beneath the dignity of the Amphictyons to take the cognizance of them. Nor do we hear of any private man ſummoned to appear, or condemned in this aſſembly, except Ephialtes, who, when the Spartans poſſeſſed themſelves of Thermopylae, under the command of Leonidas, conducted the Perſians over the Getean mountains into Greece. But all offences againſt religion, all inſtances of impiety and profanation, all conteſts between the Grecian ſtates and cities, came under the particular cognizance of the Amphictyons, who had a right to determine, to impoſe fines, and even to levy forces, and to make war on thoſe who preſumed to rebel againſt their ſovereign authority.

The

The Life of Erasmus. By Dr. Jortin. Whiston *and* White, *Fleet-street.* 1758. *Quarto.*

THE life of no author is better calculated to interest our curiosity than that of Erasmus. He lived at the first dawn of literature, and was himself one of the principal lights which dispelled that gloom of ignorance and barbarism, which had overspread the world for so many ages. There is also some variety in the events of his life, which was more diversified than is common with the lives of literary men. And there is the same variety in his character, that is found in his fortune: a genius, as well as a profound scholar; and a man of wit and humour, as well as an able divine. The work before us is the joint produce of two very learned men, Le Clerc and Dr. Jortin. The latter of these writers has followed, but he has improved and enlarged, the plan of the former. It is therefore not to be wondered, that this work is executed with uncommon diligence, skill, and accuracy. It not only contains an account of the life of Erasmus, but of all the eminent men, in whatever branch of literature, who adorned that period. Dr. Jortin has followed Le Clerc, in disposing his facts and observations by the years of the author's age, whose life they write. This, with deference to the learned author's judgment, we do not think the happiest method. Great affairs may be digested into the form of annals, because they engage by their own importance, and the time in which they happened is necessary to be known: but in biography, especially of this kind, such an arrangement renders the narration broken and tedious. In short, as the work now stands, it may rather be considered as an excellent collection of materials for the life of Erasmus, than the history of his life. Such a history would prove a much more agreeable entertainment to the generality of readers, though it may not perhaps afford quite so much matter to the inquisitive and learned.

It were to be wished, that the learned author had been a little more attentive to his style, particularly that he had purged it of certain low familiar words and modes of expression, such as, 'The author of the paraphrase so *bedashed* by Gardner.' 'Like the candle's end burning in a socket. soon cease both to blaze and stink.' 'There was a *brace* of monks.' 'Seriously it is a disagreeable thing to be in the condition of Gil Blas, and connected with one who will take it in *dudgeon*, if you do not *smoke* him with as much incense as would satisfy three *or thrice three* goddesses.'

As a specimen of the author's general manner of writing we give the following passage; especially as it serves to illustrate the character and way of life of Erasmus, which was by no means so happy and independent, as his great parts and virtues deserved.

"Collet had told him, that he would give him a small matter, if if he would beg with humility, and ask with modesty; had advised him to imitate Diogenes; and had hinted to him, that he was too querulous and greedy. It seems, they

they bantered him, becaufe he was frequently importuning his friends. Erafmus in his anfwer tells him, that in the opinion of Seneca, favours were dearly purchafed, which were extorted by begging. Socrates, talking once with fome friends, faid, I would have bought me a coat to-day, if I had had money. They, fays Seneca, who gave him what he wanted, after he had made this fpeech, fhewed their liberality too late. Another feeing a friend, who was poor and fick, and too modeft to make his wants known, put fome money under his pillow, whilft he was afleep.

When I ufed to read this in the days of my youth, fays Erafmus, I was extremely ftruck with the modefty of the one, and the generofity of the other. But, fince you talk of begging without fhame, who, I befeech you, can be more fubmiffive and more fhamelefs than myfelf, who live in England upon the foot of a public beggar? I have received fo much from the archbifhop, that it would be fcandalous to take any more of him, though he were to offer it. I afked N. with fufficient effrontery. And he refufed me with ftill greater impudence. Even our good friend Linacer thinks me too bold, who knowing my poor ftate of health, and that I was going from London with hardly fix angels in my pocket, and that the winter was coming on, yet exhorted me moft preffingly to fpare the archbifhop and Lord Montjoy, and advifed me to retrench, and learn to bear poverty with patience. A moft friendly counfel! For this reafon above all, I hate my hard fortune, becaufe fhe will not fuffer me to be modeft. Whilft I had health and ftrength, I ufed to deffemble my poverty: now I cannot, unlefs I would rifque my life. But I am not fuch a beggar neither, as to afk all things from all perfons. To fome I fay nothing, becaufe I would not be refufed; and I have no pretence to folicit you, who do not fuperabound in wealth. But, fince you feem to approve impudence, I will end my letter in the moft impudent manner I can. I have not affurance enough to afk you for anything; and yet I am not fo proud, as to reject a prefent, if a friend like you fhould offer it to one in my circumftances. Ep. 150.

One, who could talk at this rate, muft be reduced to hard neceffity. Unlefs he were a bad manager, it is fcarcely to be conceived, how a fingle man, and a learned man, could have found it fo difficult to maintain himfelf *at that time* in England, partly by his pupils, and partly by the prefents which were made to him. However that be, there feems to be fome reafon to fufpect that Erafmus underftood not the important art of paying his court to the Great; and that there was fomething in his manner, which difgufted fome of thofe to whom he made his applications; fo that he was more agreeable to them in his writings, than in his perfon: and this might fpoil his fortunes. Perhaps alfo he talked too freely, as he confeffes in the character which he hath given of himfelf, in the *Compendium* of his life.

Yet Erafmus, though open and facetious, was good tempered; and good temper is a natural politenefs, which to reafonable perfons is more acceptable, than that which is artificial; as, on the contrary,

trary, the politeneſs of an ill-natured man is ſhocking, for it is hypocriſy ſuperadded to malignity.

As, by being converſant with antiquity, he knew many things, which others knew not, and was diſpoſed to jeſting, he could hardly refrain from ridiculing, at one time or other, the follies of the age, and of a certain ſet of people. It is well known, that this temper fails not to give offence, eſpecially to thoſe, who expect that their weakneſſes or vices ſhould be ſpared on account of their ſtation and character; elſe the king, the courtiers, and the biſhops, who often beſtowed preferments upon drones, void of all capacity and merit, and ſometimes loaded them with pluralities, might eaſily have given him ſomething in the church, without cure of ſouls, which would have afforded him leiſure to ſtudy, and means to live. But perhaps he, who hated confinement on any account, did not care to be connected with monks and chapters of canons. As the people were exceſſively envious, they would have teized him with their chicaneries upon every occaſion. He had long perceived, and declared to the world, that the religion of theſe eccleſiaſtics conſiſted entirely in minute obſervations and formal grimaces, with which the wicked can comply, as well as the good. He, on the contrary, made religion to conſiſt in ſuch things, as none, except worthy perſons, ever obſerve; in the exerciſe of thoſe chriſtian virtues, which are formed in the mind, from a knowledge of our duty, and a perſuaſion of its importance. A man fixed in theſe ſentiments, and continually occupied in learned ſtudies, would have found it very difficult to practiſe the rites and ceremonies with which religion was overrun and choked up in thoſe days. This neglect in England, as as in all other places, was accounted a far more heinous crime than the vileſt immorality and debauchery. The monks, above all others, were inexorable upon this article, and doubtleſs oppoſed and harraſſed openly and ſecretly all who were not in their way of thinking and acting. So that, to ſet Eraſmus thoroughly at eaſe, Henry VIII. ought to have beſtowed a handſome penſion upon him, which would have exempted him from worldly cares and avocations, and furniſhed him with books, and leiſure, and the conveniencies of life. But this the king would not do; and if he afterwards invited Eraſmus again to his dominions, it was at a time when that learned man was not able to undertake the journey."

Towards the end of the work are ſome curious particulars concerning the character of Eraſmus, and a very good defence of ſome parts of learning which he particularly cultivated.

"Bayle hath obſerved of Eraſmus, that he had rather too much ſenſibility, when he was attacked by malicious and inconſiderable adverſaries, made too many complaints of them, and was too ready to anſwer them. It is true. He wanted ſome friend to overrule him, and to ſay to him, LET *thoſe men alone: they cannot live in their own writings; and why ſhould they live in yours?* Yet thus much may be obſerved, by way of excuſe, that he was fighting for his honour, and for his life, being often accuſed of nothing leſs than heterodoxy, impiety, and blaſphemy, by men whoſe forehead was a rock, and whoſe tongue was a razor. To be miſrepreſented, as a pedant and a dunce, this is no great matter; for time and truth put folly to flight: to be accuſed of hereſy by bigots, hypocrites, politicians, and infidels, this is a ſerious affair; as they know too well, who have had the misfortune to feel the effects of it.

The celebrated Peter Ramus never replied to the invectives of his numerous adverſaries: and the writer of his life mentions it as an inſtance of his uncommon patience and prudence. . . . . .

The ſtyle of Eraſmus is that of a man, who had a ſtrong memory, a natural eloquence, a lively fancy, and a ready invention, who compoſed with great facility and rapadity, and who did not care for the trouble of reviſing and correcting; who had ſpent all his days in reading, writing, and talking Latin; for he ſeems to have had no turn for modern languages, and perhaps he had almoſt forgotten his mother-tongue. His ſtyle therefore is always unaffected, eaſy, copious, fluent, and clear; but not always perfectly pure, and ſtrictly claſſical. He hath been cenſured, as a dealer in barbariſms, by perſons, who not only had not half of his abilities and erudition, but who did not even write Latin half ſo well as he.

His verſes are plainly the compoſitions of one, who had much learning and good ſenſe, and who underſtood proſody, or the technicale art of poetry; but who had not an equal elegance of taſte, and an ear for poetical numbers. So that upon the whole he is rather a verſifier than a poet, and is not to beranked amongſt the Italian poets of thoſe days, Sannazarius, Fracaſtorius, Vida, &c. many of whom write better than any of the ancients, except Lucretius, Virgil, Horace, and a few more.

Eraſmus uſed to dine late, that he might have a long morning to ſtudy in. After dinner he would converſe chearfully with his friends about all ſorts of ſubjects, and deliver his opinions very freely upon men and things. So ſays Milichius, who was a ſtudent at Friburg, and there had the pleaſure of being well acquainted with Eraſmus.

Eraſmus, in the earlier part of his life, carefully ſtudied the Greek and Latin grammar, read lectures upon them, and tranſlated Greek books into Latin. This was laying a right foundation for criticiſm and philology; and it is much to be wiſhed, that our young ſtudents of promiſing abilities would, in ſome meaſure, follow his example. Be you ever ſo ingenious and induſtrious, yet if you neglect to cultivate and to preſerve this humble part of knowledge, you will be perpetually ſtumbling, when you tread on claſſic ground, when you attempt to explain, to tranſlate, or to correct ancient authors, or to diſcuſs any learned ſubject, or to compoſe a few pages in Latin in proſe, or in verſe. Then beware of blunders; and think not to make amends for them by inſulting and ridiculing grammarians, ſcholiaſts, commentators, lexicographers, verbal critics, word-catchers, ſyllable-mongers and poachers in Stobæus and Suidas.

'It is a wonder that no bookſeller could be found, who would 'venture to print the commentary 'of Meziriac upon Apollodorus.

'The

'The taste for this kind of erudition is entirely extinct; and if 'Meziriac were to return to life 'in these days, he might stay long 'enough at Bresse, before he would 'receive an invitation to be a member of the French academy. The 'same qualifications, which formerly procured him that honour, would now suffice to exclude him. It was not the politeness of his style, or the 'beauty of his verses, which 'made him accounted worthy 'of being an academician, for 'in this respect he was inferior to 'most of the fraternity; but it 'was his reputation for learning, 'and the proofs which he had 'given of a vast erudition. Times 'are altered: no regard is paid to 'an author who perfectly understands mythology, Greek poets 'and scholiasts, and by this knowledge can clear up difficulties in 'chronology, geography, grammar, &c. Not only compositions 'without the least tincture of literature are preferred to the 'works of such an author, but he 'is treated as a mere pedant: 'and this is the sure way to discourage all young men, who 'have talents for the study of 'humanities. There is something odious and contemptible 'in the very name of pedantry; 'and who would take pains to 'acquire nothing besides scorn and 'infamy by becoming very learned 'and appearing to be well versed 'in the works of the ancients? 'Nothing hath more contributed 'to bring literature into contempt, 'than the custom which the wits 'and the fine geniuses, real or 'pretended, have taken up to 'condemn, as school-learning and 'pedantry, citations from Latin 'and Greek authors, and philological remarks. They have 'been so unjust, as to deride 'even these scholars, who had, 'besides erudition, a politeness 'and a knowledge of the world; 'Costar for example. Had they 'been contented to ridicule those, 'who, to make a parade of their 'reading, cite a Plato, a Varro, 'and an Aristotle, either to prove 'nothing at all, or to confirm 'something which no man ever 'denied, and which every man 'knows, they had not done amiss: 'but with disdainful airs and insolent scoffs they have banished 'from the polite world all those 'who dared to shew that they had 'made collections from the ancients; they have laughed at 'the Costars, and even at those 'letters of Voiture which are 'sprinkled with Latin. These 'censures have had the more effect, because there is something 'plausible in them; and it is 'certainly true, that men should 'be more careful to polish their 'mind, and to form their judgment, than to load their memory 'with the remarks and sayings of 'other people. The more truth 'there is in this maxim, the more 'it charms and seduces the conceited, the superficial, and the 'lazy, and incites them to turn 'to ridicule every thing that is called erudition. Perhaps at the bottom, the principal motive is to 'depreciate the goods of their 'neighbours, with a view to enhance the value of their own: 'for if one was to say to them, 'You condemn such and such authors for citing Latin and Greek; 'lay your hands upon your heart, 'and tell me whether you would 'not do the same if you were 'able; we ſhould put their ſincerity to hard trial.——— Now 'things are come to ſuch a paſs (that is, A. 1700) 'that, as we 'are informed, the Bookſeller at 'Paris, who deſigns to print madam Dacier's tranſlation of Homer, dares not join the original 'to it, leſt the very ſight of Greek 'ſhould diſcourage and diſguſt his 'cuſtomers. —— Judge by this of 'the reigning taſte, and conclude 'that the commentary upon Apollodorus would be hiſſed off the 'ſtage at Paris. It contains too 'much erudition." *Bayle Meziriac, not. c.*

In Eraſmus we behold a man, who in the days of his youth, lying under no ſmall diſadvantages of birth and education, depreſſed by poverty, friendleſs and unſupported, or very ſlenderly ſupported, made his way through all theſe obſtacles, and, by the help of bright parts and conſtant application, became one of the moſt conſiderable ſcholars of the age, and acquired the favour and the protection of princes, nobles, and prelates, of the greateſt names in church and ſtate.

Every man of letters muſt not indulge the vain hope, though he ſhould be as learned, as ingenious, and as induſtrious as Eraſmus, to be as much favoured and encouraged as he was.——But this is not a ſufficient a cauſe to deter any perſon from a ſtudious life. Learning is in many reſpects its own reward; learning applied to uſeful purpoſes, and adorned with good manners. Without theſe, though it may be of ſome ſervice to the public, it will be of ſmall comfort to the profeſſor.

'After perſonal merit, (ſays Bruyere) 'it muſt be confeſſed that 'high ſtations and pompous titles 'are the principal and the moſt 'ſplendid marks of diſtinction: 'and he who cannot be an 'Eraſmus, muſt think of being a 'biſhop.'

Memoirs of the Life of Sir Thomas More, with his hiſtory of Utopia, tranſlated into Engliſh by Ferdinando Warner, L. L. D. London printed for Davis *and* Reymers. *Octavo.*

THERE are no ſort of books more uſeful towards forming the mind and manners, than the lives of good and eminent men. The book before us, is one of thoſe. The ſubject of it, Sir Thomas More, though a man addicted much to contemplative piety, lived much in the world, and filled with great credit for abilities and integrity the higheſt offices in the ſtate; he reſigned them too with a dignity no ways inferior to that in which he held them, and at length gave up his life as he had his employments, rather than ſubject his conſcience to the will of an arbitrary prince. We are obliged to Dr. Warner for a well-digeſted and ſatisfactory account of this great man. Nothing of the kind had been executed before. The learned hiſtorian before us is intereſting in his narrative, makes a good choice, and apt diſtribution of his facts, and interſperſes them with ſeveral pertinent and uſeful reflections. It were to be wiſhed indeed, that he had intirely foreborn all thoſe that might be conſidered as perſonal invectives; and that he had confined his thoughts to the times of which he wrote.

Sir

Sir T. More gave in the course of his studies, and at his entrance both into domestic and public life, strong marks of the character which distinguished him to the last.

" At the time of his residing at Lincoln's-Inn as a student, he read a public lecture in St. Austin *de civitate Dei*; to which almost all the learned men of the city of London resorted. The reputation which he acquired by these public lectures, procured him the place of reader at Furnival's-Inn; in which he continued with the same reputation for some time: And then giving himself up to devotion in the Charter-house, he lived there as a religious about four years, though without any vow, abstracted entirely from the world, and from all science. — It is wonderful how a man of his turn of mind, of such prodigious lively parts, and so much activity and facetiousness, could seclude himself so long from business and affairs to be shut up in a cloister. But in order to take off this surprize, we must recollect the piety that was then in fashion; to which he had likewise notwithstanding his pleasantry —— supposed absurdly by the world to be incompatible —— a strong and natural inclination. He was sated however at last, with this inactive useless way of life; and having been often pressed by Mr. Colt of New-Hall in Essex, who delighted much in his company, to live with him, our author left the Charter-house, and went to make him a visit. His friend had three daughters, who were all accomplished, handsome, and well behaved young ladies; and giving him his choice of these for a wife, the consequence of this visit was, that he married the eldest, merely for being such, that it might be no vexation or disgrace to her to be passed by; but his fancy led him to prefer the second. Upon his marriage with this lady, who lived with him about seven years, he took a house in Buckler's-bury, and prosecuted his study and practice of the law at Lincoln's-Inn.

Whilst he was thus employed in fitting himself for his profession, he was elected a burgess, before he was two and twenty years of age, in the reign of Henry VII. The design of the king in calling this parliament, was to demand a subsidy and three fifteenths, for the marriage of his eldest daughter to the King of Scotland: And when it was moved in the house of commons, though the majority were against the demand, yet many of the members being afraid of the king's displeasure, and others having reasons not more justifiable nor important, they made no opposition to it. Here was therefore a fair occasion for Mr. More, to shew his courage and integrity in defence of liberty and his country; and this occasion he took. He argued with such strength and clearness against this unjust and arbitrary imposition, though he was then so very young, that his majesty's demand was in the end rejected. Upon this, Mr. Tyler, one of the king's privy council, who was present in the house of commons when this speech was made, went immediately to the king, and told him, ' that a beardless boy had disappointed all his purpose.'

This was giving his country a very early pledge indeed of that patriotiſm and probity, from which nothing could ever ſeduce him whilſt he lived. He had too much intrepidity to be deterred by power, and too great a contempt for the things of the world to be allured by the proſpect of wealth or honour. But a prince ſo tyrannical and avaricious as Henry VII. could not fail to be much incenſed at this vigorous oppoſition to a demand of money——the favourite meaſure of his reign—in ſo young a man: and we are not to wonder that he ſhould be determined to be revenged on him in ſome ſhape or other, that ſo the courage of this riſing lawyer might give him no more diſturbance. As our patriot, however, having nothing, could loſe nothing, the king was obliged to pretend a quarrel without any cauſe, againſt Sir John More his father; whom his majeſty ordered to be impriſoned in the Tower, till he had paid a fine of an hundred pounds.....

Soon after this offence had been given the king in the houſe of commons, Mr. More having ſome buſineſs with Fox, Biſhop of Wincheſter——the favourite miniſter of Henry VII,—— his Lordſhip took him aſide; and pretending great kindneſs to him, aſſured him that if he would be ruled and take his advice, he would remove the king's reſentment, and reſtore him to his majeſty's favour: Intending, as it was conjectured—— in a way not unuſual with this prelate — to get him to confeſs ſome perſonal enmity to the king, that a puniſhment might be inflicted upon him not without ſome ſhew of reaſon. But he was not caught in the biſhop's ſnare; and deſired ſome time to conſider what he ſhould do. When he had taken his leave with this anſwer, he went to his Lordſhip's chaplain, who was his intimate friend, and aſked his advice upon the propoſal that had been made him. The chaplain, being a much honeſter and a much better man than his lordſhip, diſſuaded him with great earneſtneſs from following the biſhop's counſel: 'For my lord my maſter,' ſays he, 'to ſerve his majeſty's turn, 'will not ſtick to conſent to his 'own father's death.' Upon this, we may be ſure, he returned no more to this righteous biſhop: And he was once on the point of going abroad, as thinking it would not be ſafe for him to live in England, thus expoſed to the indignation of an arbitrary revengeful king. For during this time, he was obliged to lay aſide his practice, and to live in a retired manner at home; where he diverted himſelf with muſic, arithmetic, geometry, aſtronomy, and ſtudying French; and in this retirement he made himſelf a perfect maſter of hiſtory."

Of his reſolute and prudent behaviour when Speaker of the houſe of commons, beſides others he gives the following remarkable inſtances.

"It happened however, that a great ſubſidy having been demanded by the king, which Wolſey apprehended would meet with great oppoſition in the lower houſe, he was determined to be preſent when the motion ſhould be made, in order to prevent its being rejected. The houſe being apprized of his reſolution, it was a great while under debate, whether it was beſt to receive him, with a few of his Lords only, or with his whole train.

The

The majority of the house inclined to the first; upon which the speaker got up, and said, '——Gentlemen; forasmuch as my lord cardinal hath not long since, as you all know, laid to our charge the lightness of our tongues for things spoken out of this house, it shall not in my judgment be amiss to receive him with all his pomp; with his maces, his pillars, his poll-axes, his crosses, his hat, and his great seal too; that so if he blames us hereafter, we may be the bolder to excuse ourselves, and lay it upon those his grace shall bring hither with him.' The house being pleased with the humour, as well as the propriety, of the speaker's motion, the cardinal was received accordingly: And having shewn in a solemn speech, how necessary it was for the king's affairs that the subsidies moved for should be granted, and that a less sum would not answer his majesty's purpose at that time; but finding that no member made any answer, nor shewed the least inclination to comply with what he asked, he said, with some emotion, 'Gentlemen; you have many wise and learned men amongst you; and since I am sent hither immediately from the king, for the preservation of yourselves and all the realm, I think it meet that you give me a reasonable answer to my demand.' But every body being still silent, he addressed himself particularly to Mr. Murray; who making no answer, he put the same question to several other members, that were esteemed the greatest men in the house; and none of these making any answer neither——it being before agreed, as the custom was, to give him an answer by their speaker——the cardinal lost his temper at this contemptuous treatment, and with great indignation said to them further: 'Gentlemen; unless it be the manner of your house, as perchance it may, to express your minds in such cases by your speaker only, whom you have chosen for trusty and wise, as indeed he is, here is without doubt, a surprizing obstinate silence.' He then required the speaker to give him an answer to the demand which he had made in the king's name, of the house. The speaker having first, with great reverence on his knees, excused their silence, as being abashed at the presence of so noble and extraordinary a personage, proceeded then to shew him by many arguments, that it was not expedient or agreeable to the ancient liberty of the house, to make an answer to his majesty's message, by any other person, how great soever, than some of their own members: And in conclusion he told his eminence, 'that though they had trusted him with their voices, yet except every one of them could put their several judgments into his head, he alone in so weighty a matter was not able to make a sufficient answer to his grace.' The cardinal taking offence at the speaker for this evasive answer, and for not promoting the subsidy, rose up on a sudden, and departed in great displeasure with the whole house.

It is very certain that Sir Thomas More had seconded the motion for complying with the king's demand, when it was first moved in the house, and thought it absolutely necessary for carrying on the war. But he had a mind absolutely to distinguish, between the reasonable demands of the king, and the insolence of his minister; and therefore played off this farce against him in the house of commons, Not was this done perhaps with a view of mortifying the cardinal, but it might be also probably to let his majesty see, by this contumelious usage, that the person of his minister was not acceptable to the parliament. But be this as it might. The speaker, in a few days after, being in Wolsey's gallery at Whitehall, his eminence complained to him of this ill treatment with great vehemence; and reproaching him for his ingratitude, said, 'Would to God you had 'been at Rome Mr. More when 'I made you speaker.' To this Sir Thomas replied, 'Your grace 'not offended, so would I too, 'my lord.' And then to divert him from his ill-humour, which would probably have vented itself in some indecent language, he began to commend the cardinal's gallery; and said that he liked it better than his other gallery at Hampton court,"

There are several instances of his disinterested conduct, and of the serenity and good humour with which he resigned the greatest employments.

" About the time of his resignation, died in extreme old age his father Sir John More; whom he often visited and comforted in his illness, and to whom he expressed the utmost tenderness and affection of filial piety in his expiring moments. This was an event however, which brought him a very inconsiderable increase of fortune; because the greatest part of his father's estate, with his seat at Gubbins in Hertfordshire, were settled upon his second wife, who outlived Sir Thomas many years; and therefore he enjoyed but little inheritance from his father. When he had delivered up the seal, he wrote an apology for himself; in which he declares to the public, 'that all the revenues and pen'sions which he had, by his father, 'by his wife, or by his own pur'chase, except the manors given 'him by the king of his mere li'berality'---which from a king to such a servant are not worth the naming---' did not amount to the 'value of fifty pounds a year.'—— Strange indeed it will appear in this age, that a privy counsellor, who had gone through so many great offices, as we have seen, for above twenty years, and who had been all his life an abstemious man, should not have been able to purchase an hundred pounds a year. But such was his great charity, and such his greater contempt of money!

The day after he had resigned the seal, which his own family knew nothing of, he went as usual, it being an holy-day, to Chelsea church with his wife and daughters: and after mass was over — it being customary for one of the gentlemen to go to his lady to tell her the chancellor was gone out of church----he went himself to the pew-doors; and making her a low bow, said, 'Madam, my lord is 'gone.' But she knowing his pleasantry, and apprehending this to be some joke, took little notice of it. However, as they were walking home, he assured her very seriously, that what he had said, was true; having resigned his office of lord chancellor to the king the day before. When she found that he was in earnest, and as she was a worldly-minded woman, being much chagrined at it, it, ſhe replied in her accuſtomed manner, ‘ Tilly Vally, what will ‘ you do Mr. More? Will you ſit ‘ and make goſlings in the aſhes? ‘ What, it is not better to rule ‘ than to be ruled?” But to divert the ill-humour which he ſaw ſhe was in, he began to find fault with her dreſs; which ſhe chiding her daughters for not ſeeing, and they affirming that there was no fault to be found, he replied with great mirth, ‘ Don't you perceive ‘ your mother's noſe is ſomewhat ‘ awry?’ Upon which ſhe went from him in a paſſion. It muſt be confeſſed that this is a trifling ſtory to relate in the life of ſo great a man: But the reader muſt obſerve, that the characters of men are learnt beſt from trifles. It is related here however to ſhew, that his facetious humour was natural to him without any affectation; and that powers, honours and great revenues, had no charms for him, who could part with them ſo freely, and with ſuch a mirthful temper of mind. It will likewiſe ſhew, it was his opinion, that in his conduct as a ſtateſman, his lady had no right to be conſulted, or to intermeddle.

The firſt thing that he ſet about after the ſurrender of his office, was to provide places for all his gentlemen and ſervants among the nobility and the biſhops; that they might not ſuffer by any act of his. This being done to his ſatisfaction, he next called all his children and their huſbands round him; and telling them that he could not now, as he was wont and ſtill gladly would, bear all their expence himſelf, aſked their advice what they ſhould do that they might continue to live together, as he much deſired:— And finding them all ſilent, he told them, that though he had been brought up from the loweſt degree to the higheſt, yet he had now in yearly revenues left him but a very little above an hundred pounds a year; ſo that hereafter if they lived together, they muſt be contented to become contributors. Notwithſtanding the king had taken him from his profeſſion, and employed him in the moſt important ſervices to himſelf and the kingdom, during the beſt part of his life, yet he made ſo little advantage of his majeſty's ſervice, or that of the public, that all the land which ever he purchaſed, —— and he purchaſed it all before he was Lord Chancellor —— was not above the value of twenty marks a year: And after all his debts were paid when he reſigned that office, he had not left in gold and ſilver, his chain excepted, the worth of one hundred pounds.”

The ſcene between him and his daughter after his ſentence, is extremely pathetic and well painted.

“ Having taken his leave of the court in this ſolemn manner, he was conducted from the bar to the Tower, with the axe carried before him in the uſual manner after condemnation: And when he came to the Tower wharfe, his ſavourite daughter Mrs. Roper, thinking this would be the laſt opportunity ſhe ſhould ever have, was waiting there to ſee him. As ſoon as he appeared in ſight, ſhe burſt through the throng and guard that ſurrounded him; and having received his bleſſing upon her knees, ſhe embraced him eagerly before them all; and amidſt a flood of tears and a thouſand kiſſes of tenderneſs and affection, her

her heart being ready to break with grief, the only words that ſhe could utter were, 'My father, oh 'my father!' If any thing could have ſhaken his fortitude it muſt be this. But he only took her up in his arms, and told her, 'that 'whatſoever he ſhould ſuffer, 'though he was innocent, yet it 'was not without the will of 'God, to whoſe bleſſed pleaſure 'ſhe ſhould conform her own will; 'that ſhe knew well enough all 'the ſecret ſteps of his heart, 'and that ſhe muſt be patient for 'her loſs.' Upon this ſhe parted from him; but ſcarce was ſhe turned aſide, before her paſſion of grief and love became irreſiſtible: and ſhe again ſuddenly burſt through the croud, ran eagerly upon him a ſecond time, took him round the neck, and hung upon him with her embraces, ready to die with ſorrow. This was rather too much for a man to bear: And though he did not ſpeak a word, yet the tears flowed down his cheeks in great abundance; till ſhe took her laſt kiſs and left him. In this tender moment his heart may be ſaid to fail him; and it was a ſcene which did him honour. Here was a favourite daughter of very extraordinary accompliſhments, and by nature and education modeſt; who without care of her perſon, or any conſideration of her ſex, moved by the deepeſt ſorrow and the moſt tender affection for him, ſurmounted every obſtacle of fear, of danger, and of difficulty to ſee him; who when ſhe had ſeen him, and taken her leave of him in the moſt paſſionate and heart-diſtracting ſituation, ſhook off all the regards of modeſty and peril a ſecond time, and pouring out her ſoul into his boſom could not be ſeparated from him without force. It was impoſſible for humanity to be more unmoved at ſuch a ſcene than only to ſhed ſilent tears: The ſenſations of his heart muſt have been exquiſite, how much ſoever his fortitude enabled him to ſuppreſs them, when he heard himſelf addreſſed with that pathetic eloquence which deſcribed all her agony at once, 'My father, 'oh my father!' If a few ſilent tears in this diſtreſsful ſcene, oweing to the tenderneſs of nature in a parent's breaſt, were all the ſigns of dejection or diſpiritedneſs which Sir Thomas More ſhewed at a fate which was ſo deplorable, and yet ſo unmerited —— and it is uncertain that theſe were all, from the time of his commitment to the laſt minute of his life —— then he inſtructed the world as well by this circumſtance of his leaving it, as by the whole courſe of his living in it. This great example will teach us a leſſon of fortitude, under ſufferings for conſcience ſake; of contempt of a life of fleſh which is in itſelf ſhort and tranſitory; and of reſignation to the will of heaven under the moſt trying afflictions of mortality."

It were uſeleſs to ſay any thing of the celebrated Utopia, which is annexed to his life. The tranſlation was made by Biſhop Burnet, and corrected by Doctor Warner, and is executed, as it might be expected, in a very maſterly manner.

A Catalogue of the Royal and Noble Authors of England, with Lists of their Works. In 2 vols. Duodecimo. Dodsley.

THERE never was a time in which anecdotes, especially literary anecdotes, were read with greater eagerness than they are now. Such reading suits extremely well with the spirit of indolent curiosity and learned loitering, which is so much the character of these times. The present work is certainly one of the best of that kind. By confining himself to these noble and royal personages who have applied their leisure to literature, he has certainly not given us the account of those authors whose works are the most valuable. But the large share which many of them have had in the transactions of public life, affords a greater variety of materials for agreeable biography, than could be expected from the lives of far better authors of lower rank. Very few writers, however, could have had the happy secret of making out of so dry a matter so agreeable an entertainment; and of uniting so much laborious industry in the compiling, with so much wit and spirit in the execution. It were to be wished that the author had indulged himself less in points and turns.

Some of the most remarkable lives which may serve to mark the most striking æras in literature, are

ANTONY WIDVILLE Earl Rivers.

"Though Caxton knew 'none like to the Erle of Worcester,' and though the author last quoted thinks that all learning in the nobility perished with Tiptoft, yet there flourished at the same period a noble gentleman, by no means inferior to him in learning and politeness, in birth his equal, by alliance his superior, greater in feats of arms, and in pilgrimages more abundant: this was Antony Widville earl Rivers, lord Scales, and Newsells, lord of the Isle of Wight, 'defenseur and directeur of the causes Apostolique for our holy fader the Pope in his royame of Englond, and uncle and governour to my Lord Prince of Wales,'

He was son of Sir Richard Widville by Jaqueline of Luxemburgh duchess dowager of Bedford, and brother of the fair lady Gray, who captivated that monarch of pleasure Edward the fourth. When about seventeen years of age he was taken by force from Sandwich with his father, and carried to Calais by some of the opposite faction. The credit of his sister, the countenance and example of his prince, the boisterousness of the times, nothing softened, nothing roughened the mind of this amiable lord, who was as gallant as his luxurious brother-in-law, without his weaknesses; as brave as the heroes of either rose, without their savageness; studious in the intervals of business, and devout after the manner of those whimsical times, when men challenged others whom they never saw, and went barefooted to visit shrines in countries of which they had scarce a map. In short, Lord Antony was, as Sir Thomas More says, 'Vir haud facile discernas, manuve aut consilio promptior.

He distinguished himself both as a warrior and a statesman: The Lancastrians making an insurſurrection in Northumberland, he attended the king into thoſe parts, and was a chief commander at the ſiege of Alnwick-caſtle; ſoon after which he was elected into the order of the garter. In the tenth of the ſame reign he defeated the Dukes of Clarence and Warwick in a ſkirmiſh near Southampton, and prevented their ſeizing a great ſhip called the Trinity belonging to the latter. He attended the king into Holland on the change of the ſcene, returned with him, and had a great ſhare in his victories, and was conſtituted governor of Calais, and captain-general of all the king's forces by ſea and land. He had before been ſent embaſſador to negotiate a marriage between the king's ſiſter and the Duke of Burgundy; and in the ſame character concluded a treaty between King Edward and the Duke of Bretagne. On Prince Edward being created Prince of Wales, he was appointed his governor, and had a grant of the office of chief butler of England; and was even on the point of attaining the high honour of eſpouſing the Scottiſh princeſs, ſiſter of King James the Third; the biſhop of Rocheſter, lord privy-ſeal, and Sir Edward Widville, being diſpatched into Scotland to perfect that marriage.*

A remarkable event of this earl's life was a perſonal victory he gained in a tournament over Antony Count de la Roche, called the Baſtard of Burgundy, natural ſon of Duke Philip the Good. This illuſtrious encounter was performed in a ſolemn and magnificent tilt held for that purpoſe in Smithfield: Our earl was the challenger: and from the date of the year and affinity of the perſon challenged, this ceremony was probably in honour of the afore-mentioned marriage of the lady Margaret, the king's ſiſter, with Charles the Hardy, laſt Duke of Burgundy. Nothing could be better adapted to the humour of the age, and to the union of that hero and virago, than a ſingle combat between two of their near relations. In the Biographia Britannica is a long account extracted from a curious manuſcript of this tournament, for which letters of ſafe conduct were granted by the king, as appears from Rymer's Fœdera; the title of which are, 'Pro baſtardo Burgundiæ ſuper 'punctis armorum perficiendis.' At theſe juſts the Earl of Worceſter (before mentioned) preſided as lord high conſtable, and atteſted the queen's giving *The flower of Souvenance* to the Lord Scales, as a charge to undertake the enterprize, and his delivery of it to Cheſter-herald, that he might carry it over to be touched by the Baſtard, in token of his accepting the challenge. This prize was a collar of gold with the rich flower of Souvenance enamelled, and was faſtened above the earl's knee by ſome of the queen's ladies on the Wedneſday after the feaſt of the Reſurrection. The Baſtard, attended by four hundred lords, knights, ſquires and heralds, landed at Graveſend; and

* The queen had before projected to marry him to that great heireſs Mary of Burgundy, who at the ſame time was ſought by Clarence; a circumſtance that muſt have heightened that prince's averſion to the queen and her family.

at

at Blackwall he was met by the lord high conſtable with ſeven barges and a galley full of attendants, richly covered with cloth of gold and arras. The king proceeded to London; in Fleet-ſtreet the champions ſolemnly met in his preſence; and the palaces of the Biſhops of Saliſbury and Ely were appointed to lodge theſe brave ſons of holy church; as St. Paul's cathedral was for holding a chapter for the ſolution of certain doubts upon the articles of combat. The timber and workmanſhip of the liſts coſt above 200 marks. The pavilions, trappings, &c. were ſumptuous in proportion. Yet, however weighty the expence, the queen could not but think it well diſpoſed, when ſhe had the ſatisfaction of beholding her brother victorious in ſo ſturdy an encounter; the ſpike in the front of the Lord Scales's horſe having run into the noſtril of the Baſtard's horſe, ſo that he reared an end and threw his rider to the ground. The generous conqueror diſdained the advantage, and would have renewed the combat, but the Baſtard refuſed to fight any more on horſe-back. The next day they fought on foot, when Widville again prevailing, and the ſport waxing warm, the King gave the ſignal to part them.

Earl Rivers had his ſhare of his ſiſter's afflictions as well as of her triumphs; but making a right uſe of adverſity, and underſtanding that there was to be a jubilee and pardon at St. James's in Spain in 1473, he ſailed from Southampton, and for ſome time was 'full 'vertuouſly occupied in going of 'pilgrimages to St. James in Galice, 'to Rome, and to Seint Nicholas 'de Bar in Puyle, and other diverſe holy places. Alſo he procured and got of our holy father the Pope a greet and large 'indulgence and grace unto the 'chapel of our lady of the 'Piewe by St. Stephen's at Weſt-'menſtre.'

The diſmal cataſtrophe of this accompliſhed Lord, in the forty-ſixth year of his age, is well known.

' ——Rivers, Vaughan and Gray *,
' Ere this lie ſhorter by the heads at
' Poufret.'

The works of this gallant and learned perſon were;

I. 'The dictes and ſayinges of 'the philoſophers; tranſlated out 'of Latyn into Frenſhe by a 'worſhipful man called Meſſire 'Jehan de Teonville, Provoſt of 'Paris;' and from thence rendered into Engliſh by our Lord Rivers, who ſailing to the Spaniſh Jubilee, 'and lackyng ſyght of 'all londes, the wynde being good

* Queen Elizabeth Gray is deſervedly pitied for loſing her two ſons, but the royalty of their birth has ſo engroſſed the attention of hiſtorians, that they never reckon into the number of her misfortunes the murder of this her ſecond ſon Sir Richard Gray. It is as remarkable how ſlightly the death of our Earl Rivers is always mentioned, though a man inveſted with ſuch high offices of truſt and dignity; and how much we dwell on the execution of the lord chamberlain Haſtings, a man in every light his inferior. In truth the generality draw their ideas of Engliſh ſtory from the tragic rather than the hiſtoric authors.

and

'and the weder fayr, thenne for 'a recreacyon and paſſyng of time, 'had delyte and axed to rede ſome 'good hiſtorye. A worſhipfull 'gentylman called Lowys de Bre- 'taylles,' lent him the abovementioned treatiſe, which when he had 'hieded and looked upon, as he 'had tyme and ſpace, he gaaf 'thereto a veray affection; and 'in ſpecial by cauſe of the holſom 'and ſwete ſanges of the Pay- 'nems, which is a glorious fair 'myrrour to all good Chriſten 'people to behold and under- 'ſtonde.' And afterwards being appointed governor to the prince, he undertook this tranſlation for the uſe and inſtruction of his royal pupil. The book is ſuppoſed to be the ſecond ever printed in England by Caxton; at leaſt the firſt which he printed at Weſtminſter, being dated November 18, 1477. A fair manuſcript of this tranſlation, with an illumination repreſenting the earl introducing Caxton to Edward the fourth, his queen and the prince, is preſerved in the archbiſhop's library at Lambeth.

The moſt remarkable circumſtance attending this book is the gallantry of the earl, who omitted to tranſlate part of it, becauſe it contained ſarcaſms of Socrates againſt the fair ſex: And it is no leſs remarkable that his printer ventured to tranſlate the ſatire, and added it to his lordſhip's performance; yet with an apology for his preſumption.

II. 'The moral proverbs of 'Chriſtina of Pyſe;' another tranſlation. The authoreſs Chriſtina was daughter of Thomas of Piſa, otherwiſe called of Boulogne, whither her father removed; and though ſhe ſtiled herſelf a woman Ytalien, yet ſhe wrote in French, and flouriſhed about the year 1400, In this tranſlation the earl diſcovered new talents, turning the work into a poem of two hundred and three lines, the greateſt part of which he contrived to make conclude with the letter *E*: an inſtance at once of his lordſhip's application, and of the bad taſte of an age, which had witticiſms and whims to ſtruggle with as well as ignorance. It concludes with two ſtanzas of ſeven lines each, beginning thus;

'The grete vertus of our elders notable
'Ofte to remembre is thing profitable;
'An happy hous is, where dwelleth prudence,
'For where ſhe is, reaſon is in preſence, &c.

EXPLICIT.

'Of theſe ſayynges Criſtyne was the 'aucturesse,
'Which in makyn had ſuch intelli- 'gence,
'That therefore ſhe was mireur and 'maiſtreſſe;
'Her werkes teſtifie the experience;
'In Frensſh language was written this 'ſentence:
'And thus engliſhed doth hit reherſe
'Antoin Widevylle therle Ryvers.'

Caxton, inſpir'd by his patron's muſe, concludes the work thus;

'Go thou litil quayer and recommaund 'me
'Unto the good grace of my ſpecial 'Lorde
'Therle Ryveris, for I have emprinted 'the
'At his commandement, following 'evry worde
'His copye, as his ſecretary can re- corde;

'At

'At Weſtmenſtre, of Feverer the xx
' day,
'And of King Edward the xvii yere
' vraye.

'Emprinted by CAXTON.

'In Feverer the colde ſeaſon.'

III. The book named 'Cordial, 'or Memorare noviſſima;' a third tranſlation from the French; the original author not named: begun to be printed by Caxton 'the 'morn after the purification of 'our bliſſid Lady in the yere '1478, which was the daye of 'Seint Baſe, biſhop and martir: 'and finiſhed on the even of 'thannunciation of our ſaid bliſſid 'Lady in the xix yere of Kyng 'Edward the fourth, 1480.' By which it ſeems that Caxton was above two years in printing this book. It does not appear that he publiſhed any other work in that period: yet he was generally more expeditious; but the new art did not, or could not multiply its productions, as it does now in its maturity.

Theſe are all the remains of this illuſtrious Lord, though, as Caxton ſays, 'notwithſtonding the 'greet labours and charges he 'had in the ſervice of the King 'and of my ſaid Lord Prince, 'which hath be to him no little 'thought and biſineſs, yet over 'that, tenrich his vertuous diſ'poſition, he put him in devoyr 'at all tymes, when he might 'have a leyſer, which was but 'ſtarte mete, to tranſlate diverſe 'bookes out of Frenſh into Eng'liſh.' He then mentions thoſe I have recited, and adds,

'IV. Over that hath made di'vers balade ayenſt the ſeven dede'ly ſynnes.'

It is obſervable with what timidity and lowlineſs young Learning ventured to unfold her recent pinions, how little ſhe dared to raiſe herſelf above the ground. We have ſeen that Earl Tiptoft and Earl Rivers, the reſtorers and patrons of ſcience in this country, contented themſelves with tranſlating the works of others; the latter condeſcending even to tranſlate a tranſlation. But we muſt remember how ſcarce books were; how few of the claſſic ſtandards were known, and how much leſs underſtood. Whoever conſiders the account which Caxton gives of his meeting 'with the lytyle 'book in Frenſhe, tranſlated out 'of Latyn by that noble Poete 'and grete Clerke Virgyle,' will not wonder that invention did not exert itſelf. Whatever was tranſlated, was new, and a real preſent to the age. Invention operates only where there is no pattern, or where all patterns are exhauſted. He, who in the dawn of ſcience made a verſion of Chriſtina of Piſa, in its vigorous maturity would tranſlate Monteſquieu — and, I truſt, not in metre!

I have dwelled the longer on the articles of theſe two lords, as they are very ſlightly known, and as I think their country in a great meaſure indebted to them for the reſtoration of learning. The countenance, the example of men in their ſituation, muſt have operated more ſtrongly than the attempts of an hundred profeſſors, benedictines, and commentators. The ſimilitude of their ſtudies was terminated by too fatal a reſemblance in their cataſtrophe!

HENRY HOWARD Earl of SURRY.

"We now emerge from the twilight of learning to an almost classic author, that ornament of a boisterous, yet not unpolished court, the Earl of Surry, celebrated by Drayton, Dryden, Fenton and Pope, illustrated by his own muse, and lamented for his unhappy and unmerited death: 'a man,' as Sir Walter Raleigh says, 'no less valiant than learned, and of excellent hopes.'

We was son and grandson of two lord treasurers, dukes of Norfolk, and seemed to have promise of fortune as illustrious, by being the friend, and at length the brother-in-law of the Duke of Richmond, Henry's natural son. ——— —But the cement of that union proved the bane of her brother! He shone in all the accomplishments of that martial age; his name is renowned in its tournaments and in his father's battles: In an expedition of his own he was unfortunate, being defeated endeavouring to cut off a convoy to Boulogne; a disgrace he soon repaired, though he never recovered the king's favour, in whose eyes a moment would cancel an age of services!

The unwieldy king growing distempered and froward, and apprehensive for the tranquility of his boy-successor, easily conceived or admitted jealousies infused into him by the Earl of Hertford and the Protestant party, though one of the last acts of his fickle life, was to found a convent! Rapin says, he apprehended if the popish party should prevail, that his marriage with Catharine of Arragon would be declared good, and by consequence his son Edward bastardized.———A most inaccurate conclusion! It would have affected the legitimacy of Elizabeth, whose mother was married during the life of Catharine, but the latter was dead before the king married Jane Seymour: An odd circumstance is recorded, that Boleyn wore yellow for mourning for her predecessor.

It seems that the family of Howard were greatly at variance; the duke and his son had been but lately reconciled; the duchess was frantic with jealousy, had been parted four years from her husband, and now turned his accuser; as her daughter the Duchess of Richmond, who inclined to the Protestants, and hated her brother, deposed against him. The duke's mistress too, one Mrs. Holland, took care to provide for her own safety, by telling all she knew. That was little, yet equal to the charge, and coincided with it. The chief accusation against the earl was his quartering the arms of Edward the Confessor: The duke had forborn them, but left a blank quarter. Mrs. Holland deposed, that the duke disapproved his son's bearing them, and forbad her to work them on the furniture of his house. The Duchess of Richmond's testimony was so trifling, that she deposed her brother's giving a coronet *, which

* This shews that at that time there was no established rule for coronets. I cannot find when those of Dukes, Marquisses and Earls were settled: Sir Robert Cecil Earl of Salisbury, when Viscount Cranborn, was the first of that degree that bore a coronet. Barons received theirs from Charles the Second.

to

to her judgment seemed a close crown, and a cypher which she took to be the king's: and that he dissuaded her from going too far in reading the scripture. Some swore that he loved to converse with foreigners; and as if ridiculous charges, when multiplied, would amount to one real crime, Sir Richard Southwell affirmed, without specifying what, that he knew certain things, which touched the earl's fidelity to the king. The brave young lord vehemently affirmed himself a true man, and offered to fight his accuser in his shirt; and with great spirit and ready wit, defended himself against all the witnesses——to little purpose! When such accusations could be alledged, they were sure of being thought to be proved. Lord Herbert insinuates, that the earl would not have been condemned, if he had not been a commoner and tried by a jury. On what could he ground this favourable opinion of the peers? What twelve tradesmen could be found more servile than almost every court of Peers during that reign? Was the Duke of Buckingham, was Anne Boleyn condemned by a jury, or by great Lords. †

The duke, better acquainted with the humour of his master, or fonder of life as it grew nearer the dregs, signed a most abject confession, in which however the greatest crime he avowed was having concealed the manner in which his son bore his coat-armour—— an offence by the way to which the king himself and all the court must long have been privy. As this is intended as *a treatise of curiosity*, it may not be amiss to mention, that the duke presented another petition to the Lords, desiring to have some books from Lambeth, without which he had not been able to recompose himself to sleep for a dozen of years. He desired leave too to buy St.

† The parliaments of that reign were not less obsequious than the peers distinctively: 'The Countess of Salisbury, says Stowe in his annals, p. 581. 'was condemned in parliament, though she was never arraigned nor tried be- 'fore. Catherine Howard was attainted by parliament and suffered without trial. 'Cromwell Earl of Essex, though a lord of parliament, was attainted without 'being heard.' The power granted to the king of regulating the succession by his will was an unheard of abuse. If we pass from the peers to the house of commons, and from thence to the convocation, we shall find that juries by no means deserved to be stigmatiz'd for peculiar servility. The commons besought the king to let his marriage with Anne Cleves be inquired into. The dissolution of that marriage for such absurd reasons as his majesty vouchsafed to give, *as her being no virgin*, which it seems he discovered by a peculiar secret of his own, without using the common method of knowing ⁑; and his whimsical inability, which he pretended to have in vain attempted to remove by taking physic the more to enable him; that dissolution, I say, was an instance of the grossest compliance; as Cranmer's having before pronounced the divorce from Anne Boleyn was an effect of the most wretched timidity.

⁑ *In the case of his next wife it proved how bad a judge he was of those matters*; *nay, so humble did he grow on that head, and consequently so uncertain did his conforming parliament immediately think that disquisition, that an act was passed to oblige any woman before she should espouse a king*, To declare whether she was a virgin or not.

Austin, Josephus and Sabellicus *; and he begged for some sheets. ——So hardly was treated a man, who had married a daughter † of Edward the fourth, who had enjoyed such dignities, and what was still more, had gained such victories for his master!

The noble earl perished; the father escaped by the death of the tyrant.

We have a small volume of elegant and tender sonnets composed by Surry; and with them || some others of that age, particularly of Sir Thomas Wyat the elder, a very accomplished gentleman, father of him who fell in a rebellion against Queen Mary. Francis the first had given a new air to literature, which he encouraged by mixing gallantry with it, and producing the ladies at his court along with the learned. Henry, who had at least as much taste for women as letters, and was fond of splendor and feats of arms, contributed to give a romantic turn to composition; and Petrarch, the poet of the fair, was naturally a pattern to a court of that complexion. In imitation of Laura, our earl had his Geraldine. Who she was, we are not told directly: himself mentions several particulars relating to her, but not her name. The author of the last edition of his poems, says, in some short notes on his life, that she was the greatest beauty of her time, and maid of honour to Queen Catharine; to which of the three queens of that name he does not specify. I think I have very nearly discovered who this fair person was; here is the earl's description:

'From Tuscane came my ladies worthy
'race,
'Fair Florence was sometyme *her*
'auncient seate;
'The western yle whose pleasant shore
'doth face
'Wild Camber's cliffs, did geve her
'lyvely heate:
'Fostered she was with milke of Irishe
'brest:
'Her sire, an earl; her dame, of princes
'blood;
'From tender yeres in Britaine she doth
'rest
'With kinges childe, where she tasteth
'costly foode.
'Honsdon did first present her to myne
'yien:
'Bright is her hewe, and Geraldine
'she hight,
'Hampton me taught to wish her first
'for mine,
'And Windsor alas! doth chase me
'from her sight.
'Her beauty of kinde, her vertue from
'above,
'Happy is he, that can obtain her
'love.'

I am inclined to think that her poetical appellation was her real name, as every one of the circumstances tally. Gerald Fitz-

* The artful duke, though a strong papist, pretended to ask for Sabellicus as the most vehement detector of the usurpations of the bishop of Rome.

† His first wife was the Lady Anne, who left no issue. His second was daughter of the Duke of Buckingham.

|| The earl was intimate too with Sir Thomas More and Erasmus; and built a magnificent house, called Mount-Surry, on Lennard's Hill, near Norwich.

‡ *I would read* their.

gerald

gerald Earl of Kildare, in the reign of Henry the Eighth, married to his second wife Margaret, daughter of Thomas Gray Marquis of Dorset; by whom he had three daughters. Lady Margaret, who was born deaf and dumb, (probably not the fair Geraldine) Elizabeth third wife of Edward Clinton Earl of Lincoln, and the Lady Cicely.

Our genealogists say, that the family of Fitzgerald descended from the Dukes of Tuscany, who in the reign of King Alfred settled in England, and from thence transplanted themselves into Ireland Thus

'From Tuscane came his Lady's noble
'race.'

Her sire an earl, and her being fostered with milk of Irish breast, followed of course. Her dame being of prince's blood is as exact; Thomas Marquis of Dorset being son of Queen Elizabeth Gray, daughter of the Duchess of Bedford, of the princely house of Luxembourg. The only question is, whether the Lady Elizabeth Fitzgerald, or her sister Lady Cicely was the fair Geraldine: I should think the former, as it is evident that she was settled in England.

The circumstance of his first seeing her at Hunsdon, indifferent as it seems, leads to a strong confirmation of this conjecture: Sir Henry Chauncy says, that Hunsdon-house in Hertfordshire was built by Henry the Eighth, and destined to the education of his children. The Lady Elizabeth Fitzgerald was second cousin to the Princesses Mary and Elizabeth, and it was very natural for her to be educated with them, as the sonnet expressly says the fair Geraldine was. The Earl of Surry was in like manner brought up with the Duke of Richmond at Windsor †; here the two circumstances clearly correspond to the earl's account of his first seeing his mistress at Hunsdon ||, and being deprived of her by Windsor; when he attended the young Duke to visit the Princesses, he got sight of their companion; when he followed him to Windsor, he lost that opportunity. If this assumption wanted any corroborating incidents, here is a strong one; the Lord Leonard Gray, uncle of the Fitzgeralds, was deputy of Ireland for the Duke of Richmond, and that connection alone would easily account for the earl's acquaintance with a young lady bred up with the royal family.

† One of the most beautiful of Lord Surry's compositions is a very tender elegy written by him when a prisoner at Windsor, lamenting the happier days be formerly passed there. His punishment was for eating flesh in Lent.

|| Strype has preserved a curious letter, relating to the maintenance of the Lady Elizabeth after the death of her mother. It is written from Hunsdon by Margaret Lady Bryan, governess to the Princess, and who, as she says herself, had been made a baroness on her former preferment to the same post about the Lady Mary; a creation which seems to have escaped all our writers on the peerage. The letter mentions *the untowardly and gentle conditions of her grace.* Vol. 1. No. lxx. In the same collection are letters of Prince Edward from Hunsdon.

ROBERT DEVEREUX Earl of ESSEX.

To enter into all the particulars of this remarkable person's life, would be writing a hiſtory of the ſixteen or eighteen laſt years of the reign of Queen Elizabeth: yet I ſhall touch many paſſages of his ſtory, and enter into a larger diſcuſſion of ſome circumſtances relating to him, than may be agreeable to perſons who are not curious about ſuch minute facts as do not compoſe the hiſtory of illuſtrious men, though they in a great meaſure compoſe their character. It is eſſential to the plan of this work to examine many particulars of this lord's ſtory, becauſe it was not choice or private amuſement, but the caſt of his public life that converted him into an author. Having conſulted a great variety of writers, who deſcribe or mention him, I may perhaps be able to unfold ſome of the darker parts of his hiſtory: at leaſt, ſome anecdotes, though of a trifling ſort, will appear in a ſtronger light than I think they have hitherto done. Theſe ſheets are calculated for the cloſets of the *idle* and *inquiſitive:* they do not look up to the ſhelves of what Voltaire ſo happily calls, 'La bibliotheque du 'monde.'

'The elegant perſpicuity,' the conciſeneſs, the quick ſtrong reaſonings, and the engaging good breeding of his letters, carry great marks of genius-- Yet his youth gave no promiſe of parts: his father died with a mean opinion of him. The malicious ſubtleties of an able court were an over-match for his impetuous ſpirit: yet he was far from wanting art; but was ſo confident of the queen's partiality, that he did not bend to her as his enemies did, who had not the ſame hold on her tender paſſions: he truſted to being always able to maſter her by abſenting himſelf: his enemies embraced thoſe moments to ruin him. I am aware that it is become a mode to treat the queen's paſſion for him as a romance. Voltaire laughs at it, and obſerves, that when her ſtruggle about him muſt have been the greateſt (the time of his death) ſhe was ſixty-eight——had *he* been ſixty-eight, it is probable ſhe would *not* have been in love with him. As a great deal turns upon this point, and as there are the ſtrongeſt preſumptions of the reality of her majeſty's inclination for him, I ſhall take leave to enter into the diſcuſſion.

I do not date this paſſion from her firſt ſight of him, nor impute his immediate riſe to it, as ſome have done, who did not obſerve how nearly he was related to the queen, as appears by the following ſhort table;

THOMAS

THOMAS BOLEYN Earl of WILTSHIRE.

ANNE,
HENRY VIII.
Q. ELIZABETH.

Mary,
Wm Ld. Hunſdon.
Katherine,
Sir Francis Knolles.
Lettice,
Walter Earl of Eſſex.
Robert Earl of Leiceſter.
Robert Earl of Eſſex.

His mother being couſin to the queen, and wife of her great favourite, Leiceſter, eaſily accounted for young Eſſex's ſudden promotion: it went on rapidly without thoſe ſupports. At twenty he was made maſter of the horſe; the next year general of the horſe at the camp at Tilbury, and knight of the garter. On theſe dignities were afterwards heaped the great poſts of maſter of the ordnance, earl marſhal, chancellor of Cambridge, and lord lieutenant of Ireland. —— Lofty diſtinctions from a princeſs ſo ſparing of her favours. —— Of what ſhe was ſtill more ſparing, he obtained to the value of 300,000 l. In one of her letters ſhe reproached him with her great favours beſtowed without his deſert: in every inſtance but in his and Leiceſter's, ſhe was not wont to overpay ſervices.

His early marriage with the widow of Sir Philip Sidney did not look as if he himſelf had any idea of her majeſty's inclination for him: perhaps he had learned from the example of his father-in-law, that her majeſty's paſſions never extended to matrimony. Yet before this he had inſulted Sir Charles Blount, on a † jealouſy of the queen's partiality. Inſtead of ſentimental ſoftneſs, the ſpirit of her father broke out on that occaſion, ſhe ſwore a round oath, 'That unleſs ſome one or other 'took him down, there would be no 'ruling him.'

Lord Clarendon in his ſenſible anſwer to Sir Harry Wotton's parallel of the Earl of Eſſex and the Duke of Buckingham, obſerves, that the former endeavoured rather to maſter the queen's affection than to win it: if he was croſſed in a ſuit, he abſented himſelf from court, and made her purchaſe his return. A fond woman may be

† Sir Charles Blonnt, afterwards Earl of Devonſhire, a very comely young man, having diſtinguiſhed himſelf at a tilt, her majeſty ſent him a cheſs-queen of gold enamelled, which he tied upon his arm with a crimſon ribbon. Eſſex perceiving it, ſaid with affected ſcorn, 'Now I perceive every fool muſt have a fa-'vour!' On this Sir Charles challenged, fought him in Marybone park, diſarmed and wounded him in the thigh.'

moulded thus; it is not the method practised on princes by mere favourites. When Charles the first on some jealousy restrained the Earl of Holland to his house, the queen would not cohabit with the king till the restraint was taken off. Whenever Essex acted a fit of sickness, not a day passed without the queen's sending often to see him; and once went so far as to sit long by him, *and order his broths and things.* It is recorded by a diligent observer of that court, that in one of his sick moods he took the liberty of going up to the queen in his night-gown. In the height of these fret fooleries, there was a mask at Black-friers on the marriage of Lord Herbert and Mrs. Russel. Eight lady-maskers chose eight more to dance the measures. Mr. Fitton, who led them, went to the queen and wooed her to dance. Her majesty asked what she was? ——— *Affection* ——— she said. *Affection!* ——— said the queen; ——— *Affection is false.* ——————— Were these not the murmurs of a heart ill at ease? ——— Yet her majesty rose and *dawnced.* —— She was then sixty-eight ——— Sure it was as natural for her to be in love!

That her court and cotemporaries had an uniform opinion of her passion, is evident from many passages. Sir Francis Bacon, in a letter of most sensible advice to the earl, in which he dissuades him from popular courses, which the queen could not brook in her greatest favourites, says to him, 'Win the queen: I will not now 'speak of favour or affection, 'but of other correspondence and 'agreeableness.' ——————— That is, do not be content with her possession in your favour, but humour and make yourself agreeable to her. 'How dangerous, adds he, 'to have her think you a man 'not to be ruled, that has her 'affection and knows it; that 'seeks a popular reputation and 'a military dependence.' He advises the earl not to play or stratagem with too long journeys from her: and bids him consult her taste in his very apparel and gestures. He concludes remarkably with advising the earl even to give way to any other inclination she may have, 'for whosover shall 'tell me that you may not have 'singular use of a favourite at your 'devotion, I will say he under-'standeth not the queen's affec-'tion, nor your lordship's condi-'tion.' The queen herself Sir Francis advised, as knowing her inclination, to keep the earl about her for *Society.* Osborne ascribes Essex's presumption to the fond opinion which he entertained, that the queen would not rob her eyes of the dear delight she took in his person. But the most marked expression is one of Henry the fourth of France to the queen's embassador Sir Antony Mildmay, 'Que sa majesté ne laisseroit ja-'mais son cousin d'Essex s'esloigner 'de son cotillon.' Sir Antony reporting this to the queen, she wrote four lines with her own hand to the king, which one may well believe were sharp enough, for he was near striking Sir Antony, and drove him out of his chamber.

When the earl had offended the queen so much by his abrupt return from Ireland, he was treated with a whimsical fond mixture of tenderness and severity. Though he he burst into her bed-chamber as she was rising, she talked to him long with coolness and kindness: when her other counsellors had represented his boldness, she resented it too. She suspended him from all his offices but the mastership of the horse; she gave him a keeper, but who was soon withdrawn. On hearing Essex was ill, she sent him word with tears in her eyes, 'That 'if she might with her honour, 'she would visit him.'—These are more than symptoms of favour: royal favour is not romantic; it is extravagant, not galant.

If these instances are problematic, are the following so? In one of the curious letters of Rowland White, he says, 'the Queen hath of late 'used the *fair Mrs. Bridges* with 'words and blows of anger,' In a subsequent letter he says, 'the 'earl is again fallen in love with 'his *fairest B.* it cannot chuse but 'come to the queen's ears, and 'then he is undone. The coun-'tess hears of it, or rather suspects 'it, and is greatly unquiet.' I think there can be doubt but that the *fairest B.* and the *fair Mrs. Bridges* were the same: If so, it is evident why she felt the weight of her majesty's displeasure.

It is indeed a very trifling matter for what reason a prince chases a favourite; nor is it meant as a reproach to this great woman, that she could not divest herself of all *sensibility*: Her *feeling* and *mastering* her passion adds to her character. The favourites of other princes never fail to infuse into them their own prejudices against their enemies: that was not the case with Elizabeth; she was more jealous of the greatness she bestowed, than her subjects could be. How did she mortify Leicester, when the States heaped unusual honours on him! For Essex, it is evident from multiplied instances that his very solicitation was prejudicial. Bacon says to his brother Antony, 'against 'me she is never peremptory, but 'to my Lord of Essex.' Amongst the papers of the Bacons is a most extraordinary letter from Lord Treasurer Burleigh to Lord Essex, recounting unmeasured abuse that he had received from the queen, on her suspecting Burleigh of favouring the earl.——So quick was her nature to apprehend union where she loved to disunite, and with what refinement did old Cecil colour his invetarcy †. Her majesty was wont to accuse the earl of *opiniastreté*, and *that he would not be ruled, but she would bridle and stay him.* On another occasion she said, 'she observed such as follow-'ed *Her*; and those which accom-'panied such as were in her dis-'pleasure, and that they should 'know as much before it were 'long.' No wonder the earl complained, 'that he was as much 'distasted with the glorious great-'ness of a favourite, as he was be-'fore with the supposed happiness 'of a courtier.' No wonder his mind was tost with so contradictory passions, when her soul, on whom he depended, was a composition of tenderness and haughtiness!—nay, when even œconomy combated her affection! He professes, 'that her

† It may be worth while to direct the reader to another curious letter, in which that wise man forgot himself most indecently, speaking of Henry the fourth to his embassador in the most illiberal terms, and with the greatest contempt for the person of the embassador himself. *Bacon-papers*, vol. I. p. 328.

'fond parting with him, when he 'set out for Ireland, pierced his 'very soul.' In a few weeks she quarrelled with him for demanding a poor supply of one thousand foot and three hundred horse *.

Having pretty clearly ascertained the existence of the sentiment, it seems that the earl's ruin was in great measure owing to the little homage he paid to a sovereign, jealous of his person and of her own, and not accustomed to pardon the want of a proper degree of awe and adoration! Before his voyage to Ireland, she had treated him as she did the fair Mrs. Bridges —— in short, had given him a box on the ear for turning his back on her in contempt. What must she have felt on hearing he had said, 'That she grew old and cankered, 'and that her mind was become as 'crooked as her carcase!' What provocation to a woman so disposed to believe all the flattery of her court! How did she torture Melville to make him prefer her beauty to his charming queen's! Elizabeth's foible about her person was so well known, that when she was sixty-seven, Veriken the Dutch embassador told her at his audience, 'That he had longed to undertake 'that voyage to see her majesty, 'who for *beauty* and wisdom ex'celled all other princes of the 'world.' The next year Lord Essex's sister, Lady Rich, interceding for him, tells her majesty, 'Early did I hope this morning to 'have had mine eyes blessed with 'your majesty's *beauty*. —— That 'her brother's life, his love, his 'services to her *beauties* did not de'serve so hard a punishment. —— 'That he would be disabled from 'ever serving again his sacred God'dess! whose excellent *beauties* 'and perfections ought to feel more 'compassion.' Whenever the weather would permit, she gave audience in the garden; her lines were strong, and in open day-light the shades had less force. Vertue the engraver had a pocket-book of Isaac Oliver, in which the latter had made a memorandum that the queen would not let him give any shade to her features, telling him, 'That shade 'was an accident, and not natu'rally existing in a face.' Her portraits are generally without any shadow. I have in my possession another strongly presumptive proof of this weakness: It is a fragment of one of her last broad pieces, representing her horridly old and deformed; An entire coin with this image is not known: It is universally † supposed that the die was broken by her command, and that some workman of the mint cut out this morsel, which contains barely the face. As it has never been engraved, so singular a curiosity may have its merit, in a work which has no other kind of merit ‡.

On whatever her favour was founded, it was by no means placed undeservedly: The earl's courage was impetuous and heroic: To this was added, great talents for the state, great affection for

* She even mortified him so bitterly, as to oblige him to dispossess his dear friend the Earl of Southampton of the generalship of the horse, which the earl had conferred on him.

† This piece was purchased from the cabinet of the late Earl of Oxford.

‡ This engraving is in vol. 1, p. 142, of the catalogue of Royal and Noble Authors.

litera-

literature and protection of learned men, and the greatest zeal for the service and safety of his mistress. At nineteen he distinguished himself at the battle of Zutphen, where Sir Philip Sidney fell. At twenty-two he undertook as a volunteer to promote the restoration of Don Antonio to the throne of Portugal, usurped by the queen's black enemy, Philip; and challenged the governor of Corunna by sound of trumpet, or any of equal quality to single combat. He treated Villars *, the governor of Rouen, in the same style. In the expedition to Cadiz he threw his hat into the sea for joy, that the Lord Admiral consented to attack the Spanish fleet. Few royal favourites are so prodigal of life! His indignation against Philip rose to the dignity of a personal aversion: In his letters he used to say, 'I will teach that 'proud king to know.' As much reason as she had to hate Philip, the queen could not endure the earl's assuming such arrogance against a crowned head. So formidable an enemy he was, that when the greatest offers could not bribe him from his duty, the court of Spain attempted to have him poisoned;——luckily they addressed their poison to the arms of his great chair, which no more than the pummel † of a saddle are a mortal part. And as he supported the enemies of the Spaniard, he endeavoured to dispossess the Pope of the dutchy of Ferrara, sending the famous Sir Antony Shirly thither, to promote the interests of a Bastard of the house of Este. There was as much policy and activity of enterprize in this, as in his Holiness sending a plume of Phœnix-feathers to Tir Oen. While the one island flourished with Cecils, Walsinghams, Bacons, the other was so buried in barbarism, that Rome ventured to reward its martyrs with the spoils of an imaginary fowl! The earl's intelligences, his spies, his pensioners in foreign courts, were as numerous as the boasted informations of Walsingham. His munificence was unbounded.——What sums did the perjured house of Bacon obtain or extort from him! He buried Spenser; and which was more remarkable, was heir to Sir Roger Williams ‡, a brave soldier, whom he

* In his letter to Villars the earl said, " si vous volez combattre vous meme " à cheval ou à pied, je maintiendrai que la querelle du Roi (Henry iv.) est " plus juste que celle de la ligue; que le suis meilleur que vous; & que ma " *Maitresse* est plus belle que la votre, &c. *Essais histor. sur Paris, par Saint-foix, vol.* 2. *p.* 82.

† Walpole, a Jesuit, was hanged for attempting to poison the queen's saddle.

‡ He had been one of the standing Council of Nine, appointed to provide for defence of the realm against the Spanish Armada. *Biograph. vol.* 4. *p.* 2287. He wrote a valuable history of the wars in the Low Countries, in which he had served with great reputation, and where he was one of the introducers of a new military discipline. *Camb. Epist. p.* 350. A Spanish captain having challenged the general Sir John Norris, Sir Roger fought him; afterwards assaulted the Prince of Parma's camp near Venlo, and penetrated to his very tent; and made a brave defence of Sluys. *Fuller in Monmouth, p.* 52. James the First lamented his death so much, that he wished rather to have lost five thousand of his own subjects; and intended to write his epitaph. *Bacon-papers, vol.* 1. *pages* 296, 355.

brought

brought to a religious and penitent death. But what deserved most, and must have drawn the queen's affection to him, was his extreme attention to the security of her person: each year he promoted some acts of parliament for the defence of it; and alone persisted in unravelling the mysterious treasons of her physician Lopez, who was screened and protected by the Cecils — not merely by the son, whose base nature was capable of any ingratitude.——It is melancholy that faction could make even Burleigh careless of the safety of his queen, when detection of the treason would reflect honour on the prosecutor? Yet this zealous Essex did she suffer her council to keep kneeling for eleven hours at his examination; for this man's liberty did she accept presents from his mother and sister, yet without vouchsafing to see them, or grant their suit.——Indeed she did permit him to celebrate St. George's day alone: one should like to know how he played at this ceremony by himself. In short, this gallant, though rash man, she delivered over to the executioner, because his bitterest enemies had told her he had declared, That his life was inconsistent with her safety.——A tale so ridiculous, that it is amazing how most of our historians can give credit to it!——How was he dangerous, or could he be?—His wild attempt on the city had demonstrated his impotence. So far from this declaration, on receiving sentence he besought the lords, 'not to tell the 'queen that he neglected or 'slighted her mercy.' He died with devotion, yet undaunted. Marshal Biron derided his death, and died himself like a frantic coward. Raleigh imitated his death more worthily than he beheld it! *

The queen at first carried her resentment so far, as to have a sermon preached at St. Paul's cross to blacken his memory. Besides the ridicule thrown on her person, many passages in his behaviour had shocked her haughtiness, and combated her affection. His pretending to be head of the puritans, and to dislike monarchy, in order to flatter the Dutch; his speaking of the King of Spain in terms too familiar; his presuming to create knights in some of his Spanish expeditions; his blaming the queen's parsimony in the affairs of Ireland, which she had once near lost for the trifling sum of two thousand pounds; his treating with Tir † Oen

* Sir Walter Raleigh was known to bear personal enmity to the earl, and endeavoured to excuse his appearing at the execution, by pretending it was to clear himself if the earl should tax him with any indirect dealings. One of their first quarrels was the earl's braving Sir Walter at a tilt, and appearing there in defiance of him with two thousand orange tawney feathers; an affront not very intelligible at present. *Vide Lord Clarendon's disparity, p.* 190. However, it is certain that Sir Walter bore great malice to the earl, and fell sick on the apprehension of his being restored to the queen's favour. *Bacon-papers, vol.* 2. *p.* 438; *and Sidney-papers, vol.* 2. *p.* 139.

† The earl's treaty with Tir Oen is a great blemish on his memory. Though the Irish general had an army of five thousand foot and five hundred horse, and Essex

2

Oen to abridge his own ſtay in that iſland; his threatening that he would make the earth tremble under him; his boaſting of one hundred and twenty lords devoted to him; his popularity; his importunity for his friends; and his paying court to her ſucceſſor, probably exaggerated to her by Sir Robert Cecil, who was ten times more guilty in that reſpect; all this had alienated her tenderneſs, and imprinted an aſperity, which it ſeems even his death could not ſoften.

On a review of his character, it appears, that if the queen's partiality had not inflated him, he would have made one of the braveſt generals, one of the moſt active ſtateſmen, and the brighteſt * Mæcenas of that accompliſhed age. With the zeal, though without the diſcretion of Burleigh, he had nothing of the dark ſoul of Leiceſter. Raleigh excelled him in abilities, but came not near him in generoſity. It was no ſmall merit to have inſiſted on giving Bacon to that orb, from which one of Bacon's firſt employments was to contribute to expell his benefactor. The earl had a ſolemn tincture of religion, of which his enemies availed themſelves to work him to the greateſt blemiſh of his life, the diſcovery of the abettors of his laſt raſh deſign. He had ſcarce a fault beſides which did not flow from the nobleneſs of his nature. Sir Henry Wotton ſays he was delicate in his baths; it was a ſlight luxury, and proceeded ſo little from any effeminacy in his perſon, that he read letters and attended to ſuitors the whole time he was dreſſing. Brutality of manners is not eſſentially neceſſary to courage: Leodatus, one of Alexander's generals, no unmanly ſchool, in all the marches of the army was followed by camels loaded with ſand, which he got from Egypt, to rub his body for his gymnaſtic exerciſes. Eſſex was gallant, romantic and oſtentatious; his ſhooting-machines in the eye of the city gained him great popularity; the ladies and the people never ceaſed to adore him. His genius for ſhows, and thoſe pleaſures that carry an image of war, was as re-

Eſſex but two thouſand five hundred foot and three hundred horſe, yet Tir Oen had diſcovered evident marks of dreading the Engliſh; and as the earl had received ſuch unuſual powers in his commiſſion, it behoved him to do a little more than patch up a treaty with the Iriſh. There even appeared on his trial ſome ſymptoms of too ambitious deſigns in his union with Tir Oen. Sir Chriſtopher Blount, father-in-law of Eſſex, confeſſed that there had been ſome mention of tranſporting part of the Iriſh army into England, that they meditated no hurt to the queen, yet rather than miſcarry, they would have drawn blood even from herſelf. *Bacon-papers, vol. 2. p.* 493. I fear, no practices of his enemies could juſtify Eſſex in ſuch views! If it is true that Sir Robert Cecil, to draw him into an unwarrantable and haſty journey to England, ſtopped all veſſels but one, which was to ſpread a falſe report of the queen's death, Cecil's art was equal to his iniquity. The paltry account he gives of Eſſex's inſurrection in a letter to Sir G. Carew, is by no means of a piece with ſuch capacity. *ib. p.* 468.

* As an inſtance of his affection for learning, he gave to the univerſity of Oxford his ſhare of the library of the celebrated Biſhop Oſorius, which his lordſhip got at the plunder of Faro. *Bacon-papers, vol.* 2. *p.* 58.

markable

markable as his ſpirit in the profeſſion itſelf. His † impreſſes and inventions of entertainment were much admired. One of his maſks is deſcribed by a § cotemporary; I ſhall give a little extract of it, to preſent the idea of the amuſements of that age, and as it coincides with what I have already remarked of the queen's paſſion.

My Lord of Eſſex's device, ſays Rowland White, is much commended in theſe late triumphs. Some pretty while before he came in himſelf to the tilt, he ſent his page with ſome ſpeech to the queen, who returned with her majeſty's glove. And when he came himſelf, he was met by an old hermit, a ſecretary of ſtate, a brave ſoldier, and an eſquire. The firſt preſented him with a book of meditations; the ſecond with political diſcourſes; the third with orations of brave fought battles; the fourth was but his own follower, to whom the other three imparted much of their purpoſe before the earl's entry. In ſhort, each of them endeavoured to win him over to their profeſſion, and to perſuade him to leave his vain following of love, and to betake him to heavenly meditation. But the eſquire anſwered them all, and told them plainly, 'That this 'knight would never forſake his 'Miſtreſs's love, whoſe virtue made 'all his thoughts divine, whoſe 'wiſdom taught him all true po'licy, whoſe * *beauty* and worth 'were at all times able to make 'him fit to command armies.' He pointed out all the defects of their ſeveral purſuits, and therefore thought his own courſe of life to be beſt in ſerving his miſtreſs.——The queen ſaid, 'That if ſhe had 'thought there would have been 'ſo much ſaid of *her*, ſhe would 'not have been there that night.' The part of the eſquire was played by Sir Toby Matthews, who lived to be an admired wit in the court of Charles the Firſt, and wrote an affected panegyric on that affected beauty the Counteſs of Carliſle.

The works of this Lord were,

'A memorial drawn up on the 'apprehenſion of an invaſion from 'Spain.'

'A narrative of the expedition 'to Cadiz.'

'To Mr. Antony Bacon, an apo'logy of the Earl of Eſſex, a'gainſt thoſe which falſely and 'maliciouſly take him to be the 'only hindrance of the peace and 'quiet of his country.' Reprinted in 1729, under the title of, 'The 'Earl of Eſſex's vindication of the 'war with Spain.' Both theſe pieces were juſtifications of himſelf from the aſperſions of his enemies. A very good judge commends both pieces much, and ſays of the latter particularly, 'that the earl reſolv'ed to deliver his own arguments 'with all the advantages that his 'own pathetic eloquence could 'give them, and which ſtill re'mains a memorial of his great 'virtues and admirable abilities.'

'Advice to the Earl of Rutland 'for his travels;' publiſhed at London in 1633, 8vo. in a book intituled,

† Sir H. Wotton, p. 174. His device was a diamond with this motto, DUM FORMAS MINUIS. *Camden's remains.*

§ Rowland White, in the Sidney-papers, vol. 1. p. 362.

* The queen was then ſixty-three.

tituled, ‘ Profitable instructions, de-
‘ scribing what special observations
‘ are to be taken by travellers in all
‘ nations.’

‘ Verses in his trouble,’ likewise ‘ Meditations,’ both preserved in the King's library.

‘ A letter of great energy, with ‘ a sonnet to the Queen.’

‘ Another sonnet,’ sung before the Queen by one Hales, in whose voice she took some pleasure. It was occasioned by a discovery that Sir Fulke Greville, his seeming friend, had projected to plant the Lord Southampton in the Queen's favour in Essex's room, during one of his eclipses. ‘ This sonnet, methinks,’ says Sir Harry Wotton, ‘ had as much of the Hermit as of ‘ the Poet;’ It concluded thus,

And if thou shouldst by her be now forsaken,
She made thy heart too strong for to be shaken.

The same author mentions another of the earl's compositions, but unfortunately does not give any account what it was; he calls it

‘ His Darling piece of Love and Self-love.

‘ A pretious and most divine letter, from that famous and ever ‘ to be renowned Earl of Essex ‘ [father to the now Lord General ‘ his Excellence] to the Earl of ‘ Southampton, in the latter end of ‘ Queen Elizabeth's reign.’ Printed in 1643. Reprinted in Cogan's Collection of Tracts from Lord Somers's library, vol. 4. p. 132.

‘ A letter to the lord Chamber‑ ‘ lain.’

Some of his letters in beautiful Latin to the celebrated Antonio Perez are published among the Bacon-papers. But of all his compositions the most excellent, and in many respects equal to the performances of the greatest genius's, is a long letter to the Queen from Ireland †, stating the situation of that country in a most masterly manner, both as a general and statesman, and concluding with strains of the tenderest eloquence on finding himself so unhappily exposed to the artifices of his enemies during his absence. It cannot fail to excite admiration, that a man ravished from all improvement and reflection at the age of seventeen, to be nursed, perverted, fondled, dazled in a court, should notwithstanding have snatched such opportunities of cultivating his mind and understanding! In another letter from Ireland he says movingly, ‘ I provided for this ‘ service a breast-plate, but not a ‘ cuirass; that is, I am armed on ‘ the breast, but not on the back.’ Dr. Birch has a volume of letters manuscript, containing some from the earl, and others addressed to him. Besides these, we have great variety in the Cabala and among Bacon's papers of the earl's occasional letters *, written in a style as nervous as the best compositions of

† It should be mentioned here, that formerly his dispatches were attributed to Bacon; of late, to his Secretary Cuffe. The latter might have some hand in collecting the materials relative to business, but there runs through all the Earl's letters a peculiarity of style, so adapted to his situation and feelings, as could not have been felt for him, or dictated by any body else. See the letter mentioned in the text in the Bacon-papers, vol. 2. p. 415.

* Two little notes of his are in the introduction to the Sidney-papers, vol. 1. p. 115.

that

that age, and as easy and flowing as those of the present. The vehement friend, the bold injured enemy, the statesman and the fine gentleman, are conspicuous in them. ——He ceased to be all these by the age of thirty four. *

EDWARD Lord HERBERT of Cherbury.

One of the greatest ornaments of the learned peerage, was a man of a martial spirit and a profound understanding. He was made Knight of the Bath when Prince Henry was installed for the Garter; and being sent embassador to France to interpose in behalf of the Protestants of that kingdom, he returned the insolence of the great constable Luynes with the spirit of a gentleman, without committing his dignity of embassador. It occasioned a coolness between the courts, but the blame fell wholly on the constable. In 1625 Sir Edward was made a Baron of Ireland, 1631 of England, but in the cause of his country, sided with its representatives †. He died in 1648, having written

'De Veritate, prout distinguitur 'à Revelatione, à verisimili, à 'possibili, à falso. Cui operi ad'diti sunt duo alii tractatus; pri'mus, de causis errorum; aliter, 'de religione Laici. Unà cum 'appendice ad Sacerdotes de reli'gione Laici; & quibusdam poe'matibus.' It was translated into French, and printed at Paris in quarto, in 1639. In this book the author asserts the doctrine of innate ideas, Mr. Locke, who has taken notice of this work, allows his Lordship to be *a Man of great parts*. Gassendi answered it at the request of Pieresc and Diodati, but the answer was not published till after Gassendi's death. Baxter made remarks on the treatise De Veritate, in his 'More reasons for the 'Christian religion;' and one Kortholt, a foolish German zealot, took such offence at it, that he wrote a treatise intituled, 'De tribus Im'postoribus magnis, Edvardo Her'bert, Thomâ Hobbes, and Bene'dicto Spinosa, liber.'||

'De

* I shall not dwell on the now almost authenticated story of Lady Nottingham, though That too long passed for part of the romantic history of this Lord. I mention it but to observe that the earl *had* given provocation to her husband—though no provocation is an excuse for murder. How much to be lamented that so black an act was committed by one of our greatest heroes, to whom Britain has signal obligations. This was Charles Howard, Earl of Nottingham, the lord high admiral, and destroyer of the Spanish Armada. It seems, Essex had highly resented its being expressed in the Earl of Nottingham's patent, that the latter had equal share in the taking of Cadiz. He was so unreasonable as to propose to have the patent cancelled, or offered to fight Nottingham or any of his sons. *Bacon-papers, p.* 365. Alas! that revenge, interest, and ingratitude should have stained such services and abilities as those of Nottingham, Raleigh and Bacon.

† In the Parliamentary History it is said, that Lord Herbert offended the House of Lords by a speech in behalf of the King, and that he attended his majesty at York. Yet the very next year, on a closer insight into the spirit of that party, he quitted them, and was a great sufferer in his fortune from their vengeance. *V. Parl. Hist. vol.* xi. *p.* 3. 87.

|| Gen. Dict. vol. 6. p. 122. Wood, vol. 2. p. 118. In Leland's view of Deistical writers, vol. 1, p. 24. it is said that there exists a manuscript life of this Lord,

'De religione gentilium, eorum 'que apud eos causis.' The first part was printed at London 1645, 8vo. and the whole in 1663, quarto, and reprinted in 1700 octavo. It was translated into English by Mr. W. Lewis, 1705, octavo.

'Expeditio Buckinghami Ducis 'in Ream insulam.' Published by Tim. Baldwin, L. L. D. 1656, Lond. octavo.

'Life and reign of Henry the 'Eighth.' Lond. 1659, 1672, and 1682. Reprinted in Kennett's compleat History of England. The original manuscript was deposited by the author in 1643, in the archives of the Bodleian library. It was undertaken by the command of King James the First, and is much esteemed: Yet one cannot help regretting, that a man who found it necessary to take up arms against Charles the First, should have palliated the enormities of Henry the Eighth, in comparison of whom King Charles was an excellent prince. It is strange that writing a man's life should generally make the biographer become enamoured of his subject; whereas one should think that the nicer disquisition one makes into the life of any man, the less reason one should find to love or admire him.

'Occasional poems.' Lond. 1665, octavo. Published by H. Herbert, his younger Son, and by him dedicated to Edward Lord Herbert, grandson of the author.

Others of his poems are dispersed among the works of other authors, particularly in Joshua Sylvester's 'Lacrymæ lacrymarum, or 'the spirit of tears distilled for the 'untimely death of Prince Henry.' Lond. 1613. quarto.

In the library of Jesus College, Oxford, are preserved his Lordship's historical collections.

He is buried in St. Giles's in the Fields, but had erected an allegoric monument for himself in the church of Montgomery, a description of which is given by Loyd. His Lordship had been indemnified by the Parliament for his castle of Montgomery, which they thought proper to demolish.

Lord, *drawn up from memorials penned by himself,* in which is a most extraordinary account of his Lordship putting up a solemn prayer for a sign to direct him whether he should publish his treatise De Veritate or not; and that he interpreted a sudden noise as an imprimatur. There is no stronger characteristic of human nature than its being open to the grossest contradictions: One of Lord Herbert's chief arguments against revealed religion, is, the improbability that Heaven should reveal its will to only a portion of the earth, which he terms *particular religion.* How could a man (supposing the anecdote genuine) who doubted of *partial,* believe *individual revelation?* What vanity to think his Book of such importance to the cause of truth, that it could extort a declaration of the Divine Will, when the interests of half mankind could not?

THE

CONTENTS.

History of the present War.

CHAP. I.

CHAP. II.

CHAP. III.

CHAP. IV.

CHAP. V.

CHAP. VI.

CHAP. VII.

CHAP. VIII.

CHAP. IX.

CHAP.

CONTENTS.

CHAP. X.

CHAP. XI.

CHAP. XII.

CHAP. XIII.

The CHRONICLE.

STATE PAPERS. 78

CONTENTS.

CHARACTERS.

The

CONTENTS.

EXTRAORDINARY ADVENTURES.

Literary and Miscellaneous Essays.

Petition

CONTENTS.

POETRY.

Epilogue

CONTENTS.

An Account of remarkable Books published in 1758.

The END.